LES

ŒUVRES

COMPLETES

DE

VOLTAIRE

8

THE VOLTAIRE FOUNDATION
TAYLOR INSTITUTION
OXFORD

1988

THE
COMPLETE
WORKS
OF
VOLTAIRE

8

THE VOLTAIRE FOUNDATION

TAYLOR INSTITUTION

OXFORD

1988

ISBN 0 7294 0359 9

PRINTED IN ENGLAND
AT THE ALDEN PRESS
OXFORD

under the sponsorship of
sous le haut patronage de

L'ACADÉMIE FRANÇAISE

L'ACADÉMIE ROYALE DE LANGUE ET DE
LITTÉRATURE FRANÇAISES DE BELGIQUE

THE AMERICAN COUNCIL OF LEARNED SOCIETIES

THE BRITISH ACADEMY

L'UNION ACADÉMIQUE INTERNATIONALE

prepared with the kind co-operation of
réalisée avec le concours gracieux de

THE SALTYKOV-SHCHEDRIN
STATE PUBLIC LIBRARY
OF LENINGRAD

this volume prepared for the press by
ce volume préparé pour la presse par

ULLA KÖLVING
ANDREW BROWN

1731 – 1732

TABLE OF CONTENTS

TABLE OF CONTENTS

x

TABLE OF CONTENTS

LIST OF ILLUSTRATIONS

LIST OF ABBREVIATIONS

Arsenal   Bibliothèque de l'Arsenal, Paris
Barbier   *Chronique de la régence*, 1867
Bengesco   *Voltaire: bibliographie de ses œuvres*, 1882-1890
Best   *Voltaire's correspondence*, 1953-1965
Beuchot   *Œuvres de Voltaire*, 1829-1840
Bh   Bibliothèque historique de la ville de Paris
BL   British Library, London
Bn   Bibliothèque nationale, Paris
BnC   *Catalogue général des livres imprimés de la Bibliothèque
nationale: auteurs*, tome 214, Voltaire, 1978
Bn F   Bn, Manuscrits français
Bn N   Bn, Nouvelles acquisitions françaises
Bodleian   Bodleian Library, Oxford
Bpu   Bibliothèque publique et universitaire, Geneva
Br   Bibliothèque royale, Brussels
BV   *Bibliothèque de Voltaire: catalogue des livres*, 1961
Cideville   Papiers Cideville, Fonds de l'Académie de Rouen,
Bibliothèque municipale, Rouen
D   Voltaire, *Correspondence and related documents*, Voltaire 85-
135, 1968-1977
Desnoiresterres   *Voltaire et la société française*, 1867-1876
Essai   Voltaire, *Essai sur les mœurs*, 1963
Graffigny   *Correspondance*, 1985-
ImV   Institut et musée Voltaire, Geneva
Kehl   *Œuvres complètes de Voltaire*, 1784-1789
Leningrad   Saltykov-Shchedrin State Public Library, Leningrad
M   *Œuvres complètes de Voltaire*, 1877-1885
MF   *Le Mercure de France*
Mln   *Modern language notes*
Mlr   *Modern language review*
PMla   *Publications of the Modern language association*

Registres   H. C. Lancaster, *The Comédie française, 1701-1774*, 1951

Rhl   *Revue d'histoire littéraire de la France*

Stockholm   Kungliga Biblioteket, Stockholm

Studies   *Studies on Voltaire and the eighteenth century*

Taylor   Taylor Institution, Oxford

Uppsala   Universitetsbiblioteket, Uppsala

Voltaire   *Œuvres complètes de Voltaire / Complete works of Voltaire*, 1968- [the present edition]

KEY TO THE CRITICAL APPARATUS

The critical apparatus, printed at the foot of the page, gives variant readings from those manuscripts and ediiitions listed on pages 58, 337-38 and 491 below. Each variant consists of some or all of the following elements:

- The number of the text line or lines to which the variant relates; headings, character names and stage directions bear the number of the preceding text line, plus a, b, c, etc.
- The sigla of the sources of the variant, as given on p.32-57, 296-335 and 487-91. Simple numbers, or numbers followed by letters, generally stand for separate editions of the work in question; letters followed by numbers are normally collections of one sort or another, w being reserved for collected editions of Voltaire's works and T for collected editions of his theatre; an asterisk after the siglum indicates a specific copy of the edition, usually containing manuscript corrections.
- Editorial explanation or comment.
- A colon, indicating the start of the variant; any editorial remarks after the colon are enclosed within square brackets.
- The text of the variant itself, preceded and followed, if appropriate, by one or more words from the base text, to indicate its position.

Several signs and typographic conventions are employed:

- Angle brackets ⟨ ⟩ encompass deleted matter.
- Beta β stands for the base text.
- The paragraph sign ¶ indicates the start of a new paragraph.
- The forward arrow → means 'followed by', in the case of manuscript corrections subsequently adopted in print.
- Up ↑ and down ↓ arrows precede text added above or below the line, with + to terminate the addition, where necessary .

– A superior ^V precedes text in Voltaire's hand, ^W indicating that of Wagnière.

– A pair of slashes // indicates the end of a paragraph or other section of text.

Thus, 'il ⟨allait⟩ $^{W\uparrow}$⟨courait⟩$^+$ donc $^{V\downarrow}\beta$' indicates that 'allait' was deleted, that Wagnière added 'courait' over the line, that 'courait' was deleted and that Voltaire inserted the reading of the base text below the line. The notation 'w75G* (→κ)' indicates that a manuscript correction to the *encadrée* edition was followed in the Kehl editions.

PREFACE

During 1731 and 1732, only certain of Voltaire's closest friends were allowed to know that he was preoccupied with the composition of *La Mort de César*, *Zaïre*, and *Le Temple du Goût*, the major works to be found in this volume and its successor. Other writings kept him very much in the public eye. At the Comédie-Française, *Brutus*, first staged in December 1730, received seven further performances in January 1731, and ran to several editions in that year, as well as provoking controversy in the literary journals, in which Voltaire himself participated vigorously (D412, 415, 416). 1732 saw the first performance of *Eriphyle* in March and it remained in the repertoire until May, to be followed in August by the resoundingly successful first production of *Zaïre*. A further edition of *Hérode et Mariamne* appeared in Amsterdam in 1731, and the play was briefly revived in 1732, both in Paris and before royalty at Fontainebleau, where the performance involved Voltaire in a typical *tracasserie de cour* (D532). Similarly, *L'Indiscret* was revived (though once only) in that year, and was also re-published in Amsterdam.

Outside the theatre, and outside as well as within France, Voltaire remained in the public eye through new editions of known works: his English *Essay upon the civil wars of France* reached a fourth edition in London in 1731, and *La Henriade* was reprinted in both Amsterdam and Geneva in 1732. The major publishing event of these two years was however the appearance, after much difficulty with the authorities, of the *Histoire de Charles XII*, which ran to four editions in 1731 and another six in the following year, presenting in many ways a new Voltaire, and a new approach to the writing of history, to the reading public. Finally, we must note the publication in Amsterdam in 1732 of a two-volume collection of *Œuvres de M. de Voltaire*, which though merely an assembly of separately printed and paginated editions of his individual works was at least more comprehensive than a similar compilation produced at The Hague in 1728; this seems not merely to testify to Voltaire's enhanced standing in the eyes of commercially-minded pirate publishers in Holland, but also to have alerted Voltaire himself to the desirability of himself planning and supervising an authentic collected edition (D504, D525, D553). This 1732 edition, moreover, contained one *inédit* of some significance, the poem *La Mort de Mlle Lecouvreur*, of 1730: an expression not merely of personal grief at the early death of a talented and beloved actress, but of bitter indignation against a church which had denied her Christian burial because of her profession, and his most outspoken public anti-clerical attack to date.

Beneath this surface, creative work was afoot on a number of further projects. In 1731, Voltaire prepared a French version of his *Essay upon the epic poetry*, for inclusion in the edition of *La Henriade* which was to appear in 1733 (D421, D435): he apparently revised, and offered to show to Thiriot (D417) the scandalously deistic *Epître à Uranie*, which did not get into print before 1738: and active revision of *Eriphyle* not only preceded its first performance, but also continued afterwards into 1732, to the point where in September (D526) a comment that he intends to *refondre* his play suggests the foreshadowing of *Sémiramis*. In 1732, Voltaire takes up again the project that is to become the *Lettres philosophiques* (D488, D526) and in particular engages Maupertuis in an extended correspondence to acquire a better understanding of Newtonian physics (D533 etc.). And finally, in that year we find the first references in the correspondence to a new and ambitious historical enterprise, *Le Siècle de Louis XIV* (D488, D526), to be pursued steadily over the years until its publication in 1751.

These were years of relatively tranquil literary activity for Voltaire, in spite of official harassments over *Charles XII*, some transient fears that manuscript copies of *La Mort de Mlle Lecouvreur* had strayed into the wrong hands (D414), quarrels with Desfontaines, and perennial ill-health. They saw the consolidation of his fame as a dramatist with the success of *Zaïre*; they saw the first germination of a new conception of historiography with *Le Siècle de Louis XIV*, and a first attempt to achieve an intellectual grasp of Newtonian science which was eventually to allow him to emerge as a successful popularizer of scientific knowledge with the *Eléments de la philosophie de Newton* of 1738; but the *Lettres philosophiques* themselves, for which this scientific preparation was being undertaken, were to transform in 1734 not only Voltaire's public image, but the whole pattern of his personal life. On might say that, little as he knew it, by the end of 1732 Voltaire's feet were already set upon the path to Cirey, Berlin and Ferney.

W. H. B.

La Mort de César

critical edition

by

D. J. Fletcher

FOR MARY

ACKNOWLEDGEMENTS

It is a pleasure for me to acknowledge my indebtedness to so many institutions and individuals without whose help this edition would never have materialised. I am deeply grateful to the Leverhulme Research Awards Advisory Committee for granting me the fellowship which enabled me to embark upon the project. The enlightened generosity of the University College of Wales, Aberystwyth and the University of Durham allowed me to travel extensively to further my researches and accumulate important debts to the helpful members of staff of many libraries. I have benefited from the rewarding experience of working in Paris in the Bibliothèque nationale, Bibliothèque de l'Arsenal, Bibliothèque de la Comédie-Française, and the Bibliothèque historique de la Ville de Paris; in Britain, in the British Library and the National Library of Wales; in Geneva, in the Institut et musée Voltaire and the Bibliothèque publique et universitaire; in Brussels, in the Bibliothèque royale. I am very grateful also to all those librarians in Europe and the U.S.A., in establishments great and small, who were kind enough to answer my inquiries.

In the final stages of the preparation of this edition the expertise of the team at the Voltaire Foundation was generously put at my disposal.

INTRODUCTION

1. *Genesis*

The image of Voltaire as the supreme representative of some mythical and monolithic age of reason no longer has the authority it once had. It has, happily, been superseded by the more faithful picture of a rationalist who was typical of his age in being also a man of feeling.[1] This is certainly how he is painted by his secretary Wagnière in an amusing account of his behaviour as a playgoer:

Il était un peu désagréable de se trouver à côté de lui aux représentations, parce qu'il ne pouvait se contenir quand il était vivement ému. Tranquille d'abord, il s'animait insensiblement; sa voix, ses pieds, sa canne, se faisaient entendre plus ou moins. Il se soulevait à demi de son fauteuil, se rasseyait; tout à coup il se trouvait droit, paraissait plus haut de six pouces qu'il ne l'était réellement. C'était alors qu'il faisait le plus de bruit. Les acteurs de profession redoutaient même, à cause de cela, de jouer devant lui.[2]

The liberal endowment of sympathetic imagination so evident in this portrait was not fully exploited by Voltaire the dramatist, so that his characters can hardly ever be credited with a truly autonomous existence. He persisted however in drawing upon his personal experience as a theatre-goer: this is nowhere perhaps more apparent than in the case of *La Mort de César*, a play which owes its existence if not its final form and content to the impact made upon its author's sensibilities by the unforgettable representation of Caesar's death and its sequel on a London stage.

---

[1] Maurice Cranston's review of Theodore Besterman's biography of Voltaire (*The Listener* 83, 23 April 1970, p.541-42) was entitled 'Voltaire: man of feeling'. Many of the contributions to the first and second international congresses on the Enlightenment, held in 1963 and 1967, presented him as 'une âme sensible'.

[2] Longchamp et Wagnière, *Mémoires sur Voltaire et sur ses ouvrages* (Paris 1826), i.51-52. For a comprehensive account of the subject, see R. S. Ridgway, *Voltaire and sensibility* (Montreal and London 1973).

Voltaire had more than one opportunity of seeing Shake-speare's *Julius Caesar* performed during his stay in England. The frequency with which he refers to the play in his works suggests that he may well have seen it more than once. It was put on three times in 1727 (5 April, 31 May, 3 October) and once in 1728 (1 April) at Drury Lane, once in 1726 (11 November) and once in 1728 (20 November) at Lincoln's Inn Fields. In addition to these performances, there was another of a less conventional nature which Voltaire may have seen at the New Haymarket Theatre on Friday, 16 February 1728, when 'young Noblemen of the Westminster School' took all the roles including, in good Eliza-bethan fashion, the female ones.[3] The tempting conjecture that Voltaire's sponsoring of the first semi-public performance of his own *Mort de César* by the pupils of the Collège d'Harcourt may have been influenced by the efforts of these English schoolboys is decidedly slim. It is highly probable however that he received the initial impulse to write *La Mort de César* as an occupant of a seat in the stalls at Drury Lane, where one of his English contacts, Colley Cibber, was associate-director. W. R. Chetwood, the author of the *General history of the stage* which appeared in 1749, describes himself on the title page as 'Twenty Years Prompter to His Majesty's Company of Comedians at the Theatre royal in Drury Lane, London'. In his work there is an informative footnote (p.46-47), the first part of which is worth quoting in this context:

This noted author, about twenty years past, resided in London. His acquaintance with the Laureate brought him frequently to the Theatre, where (he confessed) he improved in the English orthography more in a week, than he should otherwise have done by laboured study in a month. I furnished him every evening with the play of the night, which he took with him into the orchestre (his accustomed seat): in four or five months, he not only conversed in elegant English, but he wrote it with exact propriety.

---

[3] *The London stage 1660-1800*: ii, *1700-1729*, ed. Emmet L. Avery (Carbondale 1960), p.959. Details of other performances of *Julius Caesar* mentioned have been taken from the same source.

6

The copy provided by Chetwood enabled Voltaire to follow the action more easily; for more detailed examination he would have obtained his own copy: his library at Ferney included the sixth volume of Rowe's 1714 edition of Shakespeare's works (BV, no.3160), in which *Julius Caesar* is to be found together with *Romeo and Juliet, Timon of Athens, Macbeth* and *Hamlet*. A study of sources and influences relating to Voltaire's play will show that Shakespeare, with his *Julius Caesar*, cannot be regarded as its only begetter. Nor was the process of parturition a simple one; the enthusiasm initially generated was later tempered by a variety of artistic intentions and critical reservations. In the beginning however, of most importance was Voltaire's first, fine careless rapture – not too strong a word to describe his feelings as he watched the unfamiliar spectacle of an impressionable mob being swayed this way and that by the oratory of Brutus and Antony.

Towards the end of 1722, Voltaire had already discussed English literature with the exiled Bolingbroke at La Source (D135). In the *Discours sur la tragédie*, printed with *Brutus* in 1731 and dedicated to Bolingbroke, the latter's disparaging opinion is quoted with respect in the section headed 'Caractère du théâtre anglais':

J'ai entendu de votre bouche que vous n'aviez pas une bonne tragédie; mais en récompense, dans ces pièces si monstrueuses, vous avez des scènes admirables. (M.ii.314)

In the course of this same short section, however, Voltaire very noticeably shifts the emphasis away from the defects of the English theatre to its excitingly rewarding merits. In the 'Examen du Jules-César de Shakespeare' he recalls the powerful impression made upon him by the stage presentation of the second scene of act 3, which he never ceased to regard as one of the greatest of the 'admirable scenes' to be found in English dramatic literature. Here again Voltaire puts up only a token measure of critical resistance; the dominant note is one of enthusiastic advocacy:

Avec quel plaisir n'ai-je point vu à Londres votre tragédie de *Jules-César* qui, depuis cent cinquante ans, fait les délices de votre nation! Je ne prétends pas assurément approuver les irrégularités barbares dont elle est remplie; il est seulement étonnant qu'il ne s'en trouve pas davantage dans un ouvrage composé dans un siècle d'ignorance, par un homme qui même ne savait pas le latin, et qui n'eut de maître que son génie. Mais, au milieu de tant de fautes grossières, avec quel ravissement je voyais Brutus, tenant encore un poignard teint du sang de César, assembler le peuple romain, et lui parler ainsi du haut de la tribune aux harangues.[4]

At this point Voltaire offers his readers a translation of Brutus's funeral oration and concludes his *examen* with an expression of warm approval of what appeared to him as the strikingly novel feature of this scene: Antony's rabble-rousing, so powerfully aided by the exhibition of Caesar's corpse.

In the immediate aftermath of his stay in England, Voltaire was increasingly concerned to winnow out and publicise what he felt to be the best of Shakespeare. In the eighteenth of the *Letters concerning the English nation* (1733), he deplores the fact that so much has been said about the worst of Shakespeare and 'that no one has translated any of those strong, forcible Passages which atone for all his Faults'. He attempts forthwith to remedy the situation to some extent by offering his translation of the famous 'To be or not to be' soliloquy from *Hamlet*. Another step in the same direction was clearly called for: the translation of Antony's speech in *Julius Caesar* (iii.ii), a natural pendant to his rendering of Brutus's funeral oration in the *Discours sur la tragédie*.

The circumstances in which the translation of Antony's oration was undertaken in 1728 are described in the opening paragraph of the 'Avertissement' published with the first authorised edition of *La Mort de César* in 1736.[5] The 'Avertissement' was written by

---

[4] M.ii.316-17. In the later 'Observations sur le *Jules César* de Shakespeare' (1764), Voltaire's enthusiasm is muted, but he still stresses the powerful impact of the play. He describes how, as a spectator, his interest was caught from the very first scene and held throughout, stifling criticism: 'malgré tant de disparates ridicules, je sentis que la pièce m'attachait' (Voltaire 54, p.230).

[5] See below, appendix 1. The same details are given in *MF* (October 1743), p.2265, in an introduction to extracts from the play.

La Marre from notes provided by Voltaire, who had promised (13 October 1735; D928) to send his protégé 'un petit modèle' for this purpose, and therefore it constitutes a reliable guide to at least a part of the story of the genesis of *La Mort de César*. We learn that Voltaire for the benefit and instruction of some of his friends made a verse-translation of Antony's speech – 'un des morceaux les plus frappants et les plus pathétiques qu'on ait jamais mis sur aucun théâtre'. Though earnestly entreated to translate the whole of *Julius Caesar*, he declined on the grounds that Shakespeare had produced an artistic monstrosity which offended so much against good taste and broke so many of the rules observed in neoclassical drama that any attempt at translating the whole play was out of the question. Later on, Voltaire was to resolve to some extent the problem of reconciling his continued attachment to the play with his regard for the unities (which Shakespeare had so blatantly disregarded) by translating as much of *Julius Caesar* as he considered compatible with an artistically satisfying form.[6] At this earlier stage of his literary career, however, he adopted a different method of achieving his objective of introducing the best features of English dramatic practice in general and of Shakespeare's plays in particular to a cultured French public. We learn from the 'Avertissement': 'Il se détermina pour satisfaire ses amis à faire un Jules César, qui sans ressembler à celui de Shakespeare fût pourtant tout entier dans le goût anglais'. The result of this compromise solution was *La Mort de César*, which assumed embryonic form during Voltaire's stay in England. According to La Marre, the translation of Antony's speech had been made 'about eight years' before his 'Avertissement'. This would mean that Voltaire's first rough draft of *La Mort de César* may well have been written (as A.-M. Rousseau

---

[6] The translation of the first three acts of the play, together with a preface and tailpiece, form part of Voltaire's *Commentaires sur Corneille*. Voltaire's aim was to provide his readers with a basis for comparing Shakespeare's treatment of the conspiracy against Caesar with Corneille's handling of the conspiracy against Augustus in *Cinna* (Voltaire 54, p.172-237).

suggests)[7] shortly after he escaped from the whirl of activity created by the publication of *La Henriade* to the calm of Wandsworth in April 1728.

In his preface to the Amsterdam Ledet edition of *La Mort de César* (36A; see below, appendix II), Voltaire is at pains to emphasise the imprint which his experience of England, the land of liberty, has left upon his play (lines 28-31):

Il est aisé d'apercevoir dans la tragédie de la Mort de César le génie et le caractère des écrivains anglais, aussi bien que celui du peuple romain. On y voit cet amour dominant de la liberté, et ces hardiesses que les auteurs français ont rarement.

The foundations of his much cherished reputation as a populariser of English letters and thought had already been laid with the publication of the *Lettres philosophiques* (1734). 'Le génie poétique des Anglais' is introduced in letter 18 where the real strength of the English dramatic tradition is attributed to the liberated creative spirit of a dying breed of dramatists. The latter are being superseded, Voltaire believes, by others 'plus corrects et moins hardis', only capable of turning out plays 'fort sages mais froides' in the neoclassical mould. The 'hardiesses' to which Voltaire's preface refers provide him with the model for the innovations 'dans le goût anglais' in his *Mort de César*. A similar admiration for English impatience with constraints upon personal freedom prompts him to focus the attention of the readers of his preface upon the parallel between the public servants of the Roman republic and the collective mentality of the citizens of contemporary England. The affinity of the English, passionately attached to civil and political liberty, with the freedom-loving inhabitants of ancient Rome is taken for granted by Frederick when he writes from Prussia (8 August 1736; D1126) to congratulate Voltaire on *La Mort de César*: 'Cesar nous fait voir des caractères soutenus; les

[7] See *Lettres philosophiques*, ed. G. Lanson and A.-M. Rousseau (Paris 1964), ii.310, n.2.

sentiments y sont tous grands et magnifiques, et l'on sent que Brutus est ou Romain ou Anglais'. In England this affinity had become a commonplace[8] and it had been the subject of some gently ironic references in the *Lettres philosophiques*, where the English merchant's habit of comparing himself to a Roman citizen (letter 10) echoes an earlier allusion in the eighth letter to the members of the English parliament, who liken their role as frequently as possible to that of the politicians of ancient Rome. The eighth *Lettre philosophique*, in fact, centres upon the contrast between the absolute government of the ancien régime and the limited monarchy of England. Regicide takes on a favourable complexion in the picture of Charles 1 'vaincu en bataille rangée, prisonnier, jugé, condamné dans Westminster' and his execution may be regarded as part of the operation of the rule of law. The relevance of this view to the tyrannicide upon which the plot of *La Mort de César* hinges and to Voltaire's intentions in his composition of the play is obviously important. His admiration of the way things were ordered across the Channel was not totally indiscriminate, however, and the wary reader will not swallow whole the influential judgement of Voltaire's disciple, La Harpe, who set the tone for a great deal of later comment upon the play by placing it in the category of *pièces républicaines*: 'Cet ouvrage était encore un des fruits [...] du goût qu'il y [à Londres] avait pris pour les beautés fortes et les idées républicaines'.[9]

Voltaire's interest in English politics was whetted during his

---

[8] A character in Mrs Centlivre's *The Wonder* (1714) expresses this sentiment which occurs in so many other forms and places in early eighteenth-century England: 'My Lord, the English are by nature, what the ancient Romans were by discipline – courageous, bold, hardy, and in love with liberty' (I.i).

[9] *Lycée, ou cours de littérature ancienne et moderne* (Paris 1799-1805), ix.317-18. Voltaire, in his *Idées républicaines*, gives us some idea of how the term *républicain* was most frequently used by his compatriots. For them, England was a 'pays monarchique, mais où les hommes sont plus libres qu'ailleurs, parce qu'ils sont plus éclairés' (M.xxiv.418). See Montesquieu, *De l'esprit des lois*, book v, ch. 19, where England is described as 'une nation où la république se cache sous la forme de la monarchie'.

stay in London by the polemical battle between the government and opposition factions which was being waged fiercely on all fronts, with the periodical press in the vanguard. The issues in this war of words are germane to the political discussion on the art of government which constitutes the 'Cornelian' aspect of *La Mort de César*. As an avid reader of the ephemeral essays which appeared in support of the government in a weekly newspaper like *The London journal* or against it in *The Craftsman* (or *The Country journal*), edited very largely and written to a great extent by the director of the Opposition, his friend and patron, Bolingbroke, Voltaire would have had the analogy between England and Rome thrust upon him time and time again.[10] The waning of the 'spirit of liberty' under the baneful influence of 'corruption, luxury and libertinism' in ancient Rome, with the consequent collapse of free institutions, is pointed out in the fourth issue of *The Craftsman* (16 December 1726),[11] and from that time onwards, corruption of the civic integrity of the British people, taking multifarious forms from open bribery to more insidious methods of manipulation, was 'a never failing topic' for the journal, as an opponent pointed out in *The Gentleman's magazine*.[12] Voltaire in the eighth of his *Lettres philosophiques* singled out pecuniary corruption as the only feature which the English and Roman systems of government had in common. He would have been aware of the position of the writers in the government interest who were frequently castigated in the pages of *The Craftsman* and elsewhere for an approach to politics so flexibly pragmatic as to admit the possibility of vindicating corruption as an administrative expedient as long as the result was efficient government. This is precisely the view which appears in Voltaire's play as far more reasonable as

[10] Voltaire was still a reader of *The Craftsman* in 1732 thanks to Thiriot (D488).

[11] No.221 (all references are to the reprint edition of 1731, in 14 vols.).

[12] 1731, p.346. Cited by Lanson in his edition of the *Lettres philosophiques* (i.93, n.4). The references to this subject in *The Craftsman* which he cites 'entre autres' could be augmented considerably. No.56 (not cited by him) is particularly interesting for its use of the Roman analogy on this subject.

expressed by his mild and moderate dictator than the doctrinaire attitude of the idealistic Brutus. Strangely enough, in *A letter on the spirit of patriotism* which he wrote in 1736, Bolingbroke, in censuring Brutus's mentor, comes close to supporting the view of the grand master of corruption himself, his arch-enemy Walpole:

That Cato erred in his conduct, by giving way too much to the natural roughness of his temper, and by allowing too little for that of the Romans, among whom luxury had long prevailed, and corruption was openly practised, is most true. He was incapable of employing those seeming compliances, that are reconcilable to the greatest steadiness; and treated unskilfully a crazy constitution'.[13]

The high valuation which César puts upon political stability in his final discussion with Brutus (III.iv.181-190) underlines the origins of Voltaire's play in Walpole's England.

Voltaire's firm intention of writing his tragedy is mentioned briefly but emphatically by Formont in a letter written from Paris to his friend Cideville at Rouen on 8 January 1731 (D393): 'Il va faire La mort de Caesar'. Shortly afterwards, Cideville heard more news from Formont on the same subject:

Voltairre s'en va en Angleterre. Il poura bien y faire La mort de Caesar. Je ne croy pas qu'il Réusisse mieux qu'à Brutus. Il disoit L'autre jour qu'il n'avoit qu'un demy génie pour le dramatique. Je Luy dis que c'étoit un génie et demy mais je le Crus cependant, son talent est de peindre et non d'inventer. (D398)

Formont, though unreliable as an informant on Voltaire's movements, can be trusted as a critic, if we are to judge by the comparative merit of *Ériphyle* and *Charles XII*. These two works took up most of Voltaire's attention in a period of feverish creative activity spent not in England but at or near Rouen, where he went in mid-March to begin a three months' stay (initially with the publisher Jore) before going to ground nearby in the village

---

[13] *Works* (London 1809), iv.204-205.

of Canteleu, which he playfully anglicised in his correspondence as 'Fakener, près de Canterbury'. The idea that he was devoting most of his energy to putting the finishing touches to *La Mort de César* was a red herring provided by Voltaire for Thiriot to divert the inquisitive from his more important activities (1 May 1731; D407). On 30 June however Voltaire was able, despite the manic-depressive illness which had confined him to his bed for a month, to announce again to his friend in Paris:

J'ay fait toutte la tragédie de Cesar depuis qu'Eriphile est dans son cadre. J'ay cru que c'étoit un sûr moyen pour dépayser les curieux sur Eriphile, car le moyen de croire que j'aye fait Cesar et Eriphile, et achevé Charles douze en trois mois! Je n'aurois pas fait pareille besogne à Paris en trois ans. (D417)

It is clear from his correspondence for the next few months that Voltaire had every intention of introducing his *Mort de César*, which had been praised by his friends in Rouen, to a wider circle of readers and, it was to be hoped, spectators. The idea of a performance of some sort is suggested by the terms of a letter which he wrote to Formont on his return to Paris, probably towards the end of July:

Je regarde mon voyage de Rouen comme un des plus heureux événements de ma vie. Quand nos éditions se noieraient en chemin, quand Eriphyle et Jules César seraient sifflés, j'aurais bien de quoi me dédommager puisque je vous ai connu. (D419)

As a means of testing the reaction of a group of potential admirers of his work and at the same time providing his tragedy with an official and respectable seal of approval, Voltaire conceived the idea of assembling before the *garde des sceaux*, Chauvelin, a select company of reverend fathers, including Tournemine, Brumoy and Porée together with some of his fellow alumni of the Collège Louis-le-Grand, and delivering himself the alexandrines which he considered among the best he had yet wrought. A letter written to Tournemine on 9 August (D423) suggests that since this scheme did not come to fruition he is sending him a copy of his play instead and he envisages a reading arranged by the Jesuit father for his professional colleagues which will provide highly-valued advice and criticism. The very real esteem in which his Jesuit teachers, and le père Porée especially, were held by Voltaire is indicated by his proposal to dedicate his play to the most revered of his masters. Porée out of modesty declined Voltaire's invitation (D421, D423). By 19 August Voltaire was able to announce the verdict of his former mentors to Cideville: 'On a lu Jules Cesar devant dix jesuittes, ils en pensent comme vous' (D426). This was a favourable verdict even if one takes with a large grain of salt Cideville's own hyperbolic judgement: 'depuis Corneille et Racine c'est La pièce du plus grand et du meilleur ton qui ait parû' (D420). Voltaire had no illusions however about the probable reaction of the play-going public to a work purged, to accord with Jesuit taste, of all *galanterie*. To the informal tribunal's judgement he adds immediately his own wry but realistic appraisal: 'Mais nos jeunes gens de la cour, ne goûtent en aucune façon ces mœurs stoiques et dures' (D426). In view of this assessment, it is not altogether surprising to find Formont writing to Cideville on 23 November: 'Tiriot m'a marqué que La mort de Caesar étoit jettée au feu et que tout Bien examiné ce sujet ne pouvoit se soutenir' (D440).

The death sentence pronounced by Thiriot proved to be premature. The special attachment which Voltaire felt for a work different in so many ways from his other creations must, after some consideration, have restrained him from consigning it to the flames. Thiriot was to learn that the idea of showing off this cherished product of his imagination was still very much alive in Voltaire's mind. He is told in a letter of 14 April 1732 to keep the copy of the play which he has in his possession away from curious eyes; its author has 'many alterations' to make before any public exhibition can take place (D478). These corrections would appear to have been completed within a month; on 13 May (D488) Voltaire sent to Thiriot, who was in England at the time, another letter in English which contained the request: 'Tell me what way j mai send you the tragedy of Julius Cesar, for you have not the right copy'. It could well be that the possibility of the publication in England of an edition of the play – a possibility to be realised later – had already been mooted at this time. Be that as it may, it was in fact the fate of *La Mort de César* to be performed before it was published, and to be published without its author's consent before appearing in an authorised version.

2. *Sources and influences*

In any consideration of French influences upon the conception of *La Mort de César*, Voltaire's initiation into the world of drama at the Collège Louis-le-Grand must rank as of the first importance. The value which the Jesuits attached to the theatre in the moral education of the young was evident in the life of the college: in the study of dramatic literature as part of the curriculum, in the obligatory writing of plays (in Latin) by the teachers of rhetoric, in the exercises in original composition by the pupils and in the performance on prize-giving days and holidays of a variety of forms of stage-entertainment, including comedy and ballet as well as tragedy. During his school days at Louis-le-Grand it was possible for Voltaire to have seen four dramas, eight ballets or *pastorales*, and fifteen tragedies.[14] There can be little doubt that this experience as a spectator formed an important part of his apprenticeship as a dramatist. E. Boysse, in his study of Jesuit theatre, raises the interesting possibility that Voltaire may have been introduced well before his visit to England to forms of drama which had freed themselves from the neoclassical strait-jacket: the Jesuit fathers 'ont pris avec les règles les plus grandes libertés, et certains de leurs ouvrages, sous le rapport de la contexture, ont une allure qui les rapproche beaucoup plus de Shakespeare que de Sophocle ou de Sénèque'.[15] However, the tone of enthusiastic discovery with which Voltaire described his first contact with the

[14] René Pomeau, 'Voltaire au collège', *Rhl* 52 (1952), p.6.
[15] *Le Théâtre des jésuites* (Paris 1880), p.25.

audacities of the living English theatre suggests that Louis-le-Grand cannot be considered the real source of his own later attempts at innovation in the French theatre. Nevertheless, the Jesuit departure from conventional theatrical practice may have influenced the author of *La Mort de César* in several significant ways.

One of the conspicuously novel features of Voltaire's tragedy was its division into three acts. It is interesting to note that the quite lengthy discussion of this aspect of the work which is contained in Algarotti's prefatory letter echoes in a number of respects a preface which le père Lejay (with le père Porée, one of the two *régents* who were in charge of the *classe de rhétorique* of 1709-10 of which Arouet was a member) wrote for his play, *Joseph vendu par ses frères*. (This work was one of the minor tragedies, traditionally in three acts as distinct from the five-act plays reserved for more important occasions, performed during the holiday of Mardi gras). Lejay favours three-act plays and makes a point which is insisted upon by Algarotti and reiterated frequently by Voltaire himself later: 'Cette brièveté a cet avantage de supprimer les épisodes et les narrations pris en dehors du sujet, et auxquels il faut quelquefois avoir recours, au grand ennui des spectateurs pour remplir les cinq actes'.[16]

In one particular respect Voltaire surpassed his Jesuit mentors in their concern for the purity of the young minds of their audience. In le père Jouvancy's *Ratio docendi et discendi* (1685) this concern is expressed in a practical precaution: 'Que l'on s'abstienne donc de tout amour profane, même chaste, et de tout personnage de femme, de quelque costume qu'on le revête. On ne peut toucher sans danger au feu, même sous la cendre, et les tisons, même éteints, ne laissent pas que de salir'.[17] The precaution

---

[16] Quoted by Boysse, p.29. Voltaire discusses the question of 'remplissage' frequently in his *Commentaires sur Corneille* (see 'Remarques sur Œdipe', III.iii, v.vii; Voltaire 55, p.811, 820, and 'Remarques sur Sertorius', IV.i, v.i; Voltaire 55, p.877, 883).

[17] Quoted by Boysse, p.27.

was not always observed, however, and a certain degree of temporary transvestism was sometimes judged permissible in the cause of art and morality. Voltaire's reaction against the *galanterie* which had vitiated French tragedy (and had even, according to his teachers, contaminated some of Racine's works)[18] led him, in *La Mort de César*, to take le père Jouvancy's advice to the letter and to banish 'les émotions et les plaintes frivoles des amants, que la Grèce ancienne n'a jamais admises sur la scène et qui repousse la majesté de la tragédie'.[19] Voltaire was simply following Jesuit practice in replacing heterosexual love by friendship and paternal love.[20] In his letter to le père Tournemine (D423) Voltaire says of his play: 'Vous ne verrez dans cette tragédie ny femmes ny la moindre mention de la galanterie qui infecte le théâtre françois. *Crimen amoris abest.* Je vous avoue même que je l'ay composée sur ce plan afin de la dédier au père Porée'.

In a letter written shortly after the performance of *La Mort de César* at the Collège d'Harcourt, Voltaire describes the play as follows: 'Elle est d'une espèce nouvelle: il n'y a point de femmes, et il y a des espèces de chœurs' (D905). The Jesuits were keenly aware of the dramatic value of a chorus used to sing passages of verse between each act as in the drama of classical antiquity. Voltaire readily admitted its powerful effect in Greek tragedy,[21] and never abandoned his attachment to this feature of Jesuit drama. He provided passages for chorus between each act of his first tragedy *Œdipe* (1718) but he had to bow before the opposition of the *comédiens français* who would not perform his play unless

---

[18] See A. Schimberg, *L'Education morale dans les collèges de la compagnie de Jésus en France sous l'ancien régime* (Paris 1913), p.410: 'Les Pères conviennent [...] que Racine a fait à l'amour une place trop envahissante'.

[19] Preface to Lejay's *Bibliothèque des rhéteurs*, quoted by Boysse, p.94.

[20] See Schimberg, p.378.

[21] 'On sait les effets prodigieux que faisaient ces chœurs, accompagnés de musique et de danse: à en juger par ces effets, la musique devait merveilleusement seconder et augmenter le terrible et le pathétique des vers' (addition made in 1757 to the *Dissertation sur les principales tragédies d'Electre*; M.v.182).

they were removed.[22] He had earlier endorsed Dacier's view that the chorus 'est indispensablement nécessaire à la tragédie' (25 September 1714; D26), but by 1730 he was writing to Porée to suggest that the traditional function of the chorus needed to be adapted to contemporary taste. At one stage in the composition of *Eriphyle*, a chorus was envisaged (1733; D608), but it never materialised. The form which the 'espèces de chœurs' takes in *La Mort de César* is related to the experience which Voltaire gained from his début as a tragedian. In the sixth of the *Lettres sur Œdipe* he declares that the chorus 'ne peut convenir qu'à des pièces où il s'agit du salut de tout un peuple' (M.ii.43). While the existence of the Roman republic is certainly in danger, the events which will decide its fate merely form the background to *La Mort de César* and the foreground of the drama is taken up with personal relationships. Nevertheless, *les Romains* listed among the *dramatis personae* evidently make up the chorus to which Voltaire refers, just as in his translation of Brutus's funeral oration in the *Discours sur la tragédie* he attributes interjections to a 'Chœur des Romains'. Voltaire's use of the crowd as a chorus, then, can hardly be pronounced a success and Th. Besterman's criticism of the 'impossibly literary or flat exclamations' which members of Antoine's audience are made to utter can be readily endorsed.[23]

In any consideration of the possible sources of *La Mort de César*, the question of the literary preferences of Voltaire's mentors assumes an obvious importance. It seems very likely that Voltaire was influenced by his revered master, Porée, some of whose tragedies may have left a decisive imprint upon his memory. Porée seems to have excelled particularly in rendering the strength of the bonds of family love. Thus, we are told by a notable historian of Jesuit education under the ancien régime that Porée in his tragedy *Agapit* presented a situation not unlike that of Voltaire's Brutus, son of César (on which concept see further

[22] See J.-J. Olivier, *Voltaire et les comédiens interprètes de son théâtre* (Paris 1900), p.8-9.

[23] *Voltaire* (Oxford 1976), p.151.

below, p.23-24, 37): 'un fils aimant qui pleure à la pensée des dangers qu'il fait courir à son père et dont l'affection fait mollir un instant la fermeté'.[24] The first of Porée's tragedies to be staged at Louis-le-Grand and the one which was most likely to have had some influence upon Voltaire was *Brutus*, which was performed on 1 August 1708. Comparing Porée's play with Voltaire's on the same subject, Saint-Marc Girardin rates the teacher's work more highly than the pupil's and suggests that perhaps Voltaire took a leaf from his mentor's book between the composition of his first and second plays on Roman subjects: 'Dans son *Brutus*, Porée a fait un admirable usage de l'amour fraternel. Dans Voltaire, c'est l'amour que Titus a pour la fille de Tarquin, amour qui paraît gauche et mal à l'aise au milieu de l'austérité républicaine du sujet, qui pousse Titus à trahir sa patrie. Dans Porée, c'est pour sauver son frère que Titus consent à devenir coupable, et c'est de là que naît le pathétique du drame'.[25] The principal character of Porée's play suffers the same sort of excruciating inner struggle as Brutus in *La Mort de César*: 'D'un côté la patrie exhorte le consul; de l'autre, l'amour paternel retient le père; la patrie réclame une main vengeresse; la nature arrête cette main vengeresse. Nature, patrie; laquelle de vous triomphera?'[26]

The tragedian of classical antiquity with whom Voltaire would have become most familiar at Louis-le-Grand was Seneca. There was first of all the direct contact with his plays or choruses from them used as material for classwork, and then there was the direct influence exerted by the Roman dramatist through the conscious imitations of his style in the work of the teacher-playwrights of the college: 'La langue des pièces est habituellement vive et concise; le vers iambique, dont elle se sert, à l'exemple de Sénèque, se prête heureusement au dialogue'.[27] There is evidence to suggest

[24] Schimberg, p.377-78.
[25] Quoted by Schimberg, p.378, and by Boysse, p.239-40.
[26] Quoted by Boysse, p.241.
[27] G. Dupont-Ferrier, *Du Collège de Clermont au Lycée Louis-le-Grand* (Paris 1921), i.291. Though ostensibly a play *dans le goût anglais*, *La Mort de César* shows no sign of any indirect influence of Seneca via Shakespeare. On the

that Voltaire put to some use certain stylistic features of Seneca's work which he would naturally have encountered in his early studies. The dialogue in act 1 scene 4 recalls the familiar Senecan thrust and counter-thrust of discussion (especially in lines 297 ff) without adhering too rigidly to the pattern of stichomythia found in the works of the Roman dramatist. The material of the exchanges in Seneca is made up of opposing views of the correct approach to government, authoritarian versus liberal and humane rule. Voltaire introduces a variation upon the Senecan theme, however, insofar as he reverses the roles of the parties to the debate. Whereas in Seneca it is usually the tyrant who urges use of the mailed fist and his minister who attempts to persuade him of the value of the velvet glove (see *Thyestes*, 204 ff, *Œdipus*, 509 and 699 ff, and especially – even though it is not always admitted into the Senecan canon – *Octavia*, 440 ff),[28] César (in accord with historical fact) is the spokesman for clemency and Antoine the counsellor who advocates government by fear.

At Louis-le-Grand Voltaire came under the influence of Jesuit history as well as Jesuit theatre.[29] The Roman republic tended to obtrude itself frequently in the teaching of Porée, for example, who was wont to seize upon a convenient allusion in a Latin or Greek text to demonstrate the superiority of the absolute government of Louis xiv.[30] The *Histoire romaine* (1725-1737), for which one of the staff of Louis-le-Grand, François Catrou, was mainly responsible, offers a favourable portrayal of Caesar bringing to Rome the inestimable gift of peace which was to be wrenched away by the ill-considered action of a group of malcontents under the leadership of the treacherous Brutus and Cassius. Among the ancient sources of the Caesar-story (especially in its

---

contrary, Voltaire eschews the flamboyant profusion of similes, metaphors and images which he recognises as a characteristically English stylistic feature.

[28] See Seneca, *Four tragedies and Octavia*, ed. E. F. Watling (London 1966).

[29] See O. R. Taylor, 'Voltaire's apprenticeship as a historian: *La Henriade*', *The Age of Enlightenment: studies presented to Theodore Besterman* (Edinburgh and London 1967), p.1-14.

[30] See Taylor, p.3 (based on Schimberg, p.133-34).

later phases) Plutarch and Velleius Paterculus might well have provided Voltaire with substantial information even during his schooldays. Velleius lauds Caesar's generosity and clemency in his two-volume *Compendium of Roman history* and makes a comparison (ii.lxii.1-2) between his views on government and those of Antony which will be recalled in the discussion between César and Antoine on the issue of clemency versus rigour.

Among the historians of classical antiquity Voltaire's most important source was Plutarch. It is from the Greek historian that Shakespeare (by way of Sir Thomas North's rendering of Amyot's translation of the Greek original) derived the basis of his *Julius Caesar*, but besides Voltaire's indirect indebtedness to Shakespeare's source in those parts of his tragedy modelled upon the English play, he owes to Plutarch some subject matter which he treats in a different way from Shakespeare. In addition, he draws directly from the *Lives*[31] material which Shakespeare does not use in his play. The most important difference between Voltaire and Shakespeare in their use of Plutarch lies in the presentation of the two chief characters of the assassination drama, and especially in the portrayal of Caesar. Shakespeare's Caesar is portrayed unsympathetically enough for a scholar like J. Dover Wilson to see in him a Führer-figure;[32] his humanity is less in evidence than his human frailty and he appears as pitiable, and almost as ridiculous as a Chaplinesque Great Dictator, as he tries to shield the infirmity of his person behind an imposing public *persona*. Voltaire's Caesar is closer to Plutarch's: magnanimous, astute, restlessly ambitious and thirsty for the glory of fresh conquests in Asia. Shakespeare's Brutus, on the other hand, is not far

---

[31] In Voltaire's private library there were two French translations (Amyot, 1535; Dacier, 1734) and one English (R. Steele, 1713) (BV, no.2773, 2774, 2772). In *Jules César* (1764), a translation of the bulk of the first three acts of Shakespeare's play, Voltaire notes (i.ii) that Shakespeare had obviously read Plutarch but nevertheless had debased the ideas of Roman majesty which he found in his source just to please the crude taste of his audience.

[32] *Julius Caesar*, ed. J. Dover Wilson (Cambridge 1949), p.xxxiii.

removed from Plutarch's; he is essentially noble of character and his motives are of the purest. Yet Shakespeare diverges widely from his source by amplifying what Plutarch offers as rumour, namely that Cassius was 'rather a hater of Caesar on his own private account, than a hater of tyranny on public grounds'[33] (*Brutus*, VIII). Plutarch rejects the rumour flatly in the next paragraph with the statement that always 'there was in the nature of Cassius great hostility and bitterness towards the whole race of tyrants' (*Brutus*, IX). The personal grudge which Cassius works off by describing to Brutus Caesar's physical weaknesses and his lack of courage (*Julius Caesar*, I.ii) is ignored by Voltaire. He follows Plutarch more faithfully by depicting Cassius as a rabid tyrant-hater and Brutus as being moved to the point of resolution *before* the dialogue with Cassius (II.iii) which parallels roughly that in *Julius Caesar*. Brutus's monologue in *La Mort de César* (II.ii) has the same general shape as the soliloquy in *Julius Caesar* (II.i.46-58) but there are significant differences of detail. Voltaire adheres to Plutarch's account more strictly than Shakespeare. His Brutus is stirred to action by letters found near Pompey's statue (in Plutarch, near the statue of his ancestor Lucius Junius Brutus), letters which reproach him with his quiescent attitude in a situation where Romans are merely slaves; but the source of these letters is not specified. In Shakespeare it is Cassius, the instigator of the conspiracy, who has Cinna put letters on the Praetor's chair used by Brutus in office, at the foot of Brutus's ancestor's statue, and in at his very window. In Voltaire Cassius merely tells Brutus (II.iv.135) that he has received similar letters. Brutus is represented by Voltaire as being keenly aware of the example of his forebear Lucius Junius Brutus and he is moved to indignation before the letters spell out his duty for him. In *Julius Caesar*, however, it is the letter thrown in at his window which goads him into emulating his ancestor (II.i.53-54).

The idea of making his plot hinge upon Brutus's discovery that

---

[33] Quotations from Plutarch's *Lives* are from the Loeb Classical Library translations, edited by Bernadotte Perrin.

23

he is César's son may have been suggested to Voltaire by Plutarch. The consequence of building his play around this relationship was that Brutus was necessarily eliminated from the action of the play after his fruitless attempt to dissuade César from attending the Senate – a divergence from the historical account given by Plutarch. There is a slight hint in Plutarch which may be adduced as support for the speech made by Cassius after the assassination in *La Mort de César*, insofar as all the conspirators, we are told, 'their hands smeared with blood, and displaying their naked daggers [...] exhorted the citizens to assert their liberty' (*Brutus*, XVIII). There is an even clearer hint of this initiative taken by Cassius in *Julius Caesar* (III.ii), where he is shown leading off some of the crowd into another street to deliver a speech about which we learn nothing more. Voltaire, having decided to make Brutus only hover on the brink of parricide and to appear as only '*presque fanatique*', needed no such hints in any case to follow the logical implications of this decision. Voltaire drew from Plutarch the emphasis upon Caesar's capture of Brutus and the favoured position he accorded him after Pharsalus, and also the idea that Brutus was deemed by Caesar to be the only suitable inheritor of his great power (*Brutus*, VIII).

Caesar's opinion of Brutus as the only possible successor to him is given in an answer to a warning that Brutus might constitute a dangerous threat to his supremacy in Rome. Immediately before in this same section of the *Life of Brutus* occurs the mention (as it does in *Caesar*, LXII and *Antonius*, XI) of Caesar's preference for 'fat and long-haired fellows' (more specifically Antony and Dolabella) as less likely to be conspirators than 'pale and lean ones' (meaning Brutus and Cassius). It is interesting to see the different uses made of this reference by Shakespeare and Voltaire. Shakespeare's Caesar is made to concentrate his dislike upon the 'lean and hungry' Cassius who 'thinks too much', 'loves no plays' and 'hears no music' – in contrast to Brutus in this respect (*Julius Caesar*, I.ii.192-195, 198-210). Voltaire, on the other hand, without taking up the points about physical appearance, tends to devote more attention to presenting Brutus as austere

24

and unbending in his principles to the point of lacking urbanity and even humanity, until he is revealed under pressure to be not as impervious to emotion as had been suggested earlier, particularly by Antoine. Plutarch's pairing of Antony's name with that of Dolabella (neglected by Shakespeare) is taken up by Voltaire, who assigns to the latter a privileged position as César's friend though not on the same intimate terms with the dictator as Antoine. It is to Dolabella that the final words of the play are spoken by Antoine: a suggestion that they jointly avenge César's death and succeed him in power. In fact, Dolabella proclaimed himself consul after Caesar's death and Antony did not oppose the move; Plutarch does not mention this fact, but he does describe (*Antonius*, XI.iii) Caesar's earlier move to allow Dolabella to take his own place and become joint consul with Antony, which was violently (and successfully) opposed by the latter. Voltaire makes Dolabella figure prominently in a crucial phase of the sequence of events leading to César's assassination. The scene in which the dictator decides to attend the fatal meeting of the Senate despite the efforts to dissuade him (III.v) parallels Shakespeare's (II.ii), but the participants in this minor drama which precedes the assassination are different. Shakespeare follows Plutarch (*Caesar*, LXIII, LXIV) in his description of the supernatural portents, the unfavourable augury, Calphurnia's dream and her frantic anxiety to communicate her sense of impending disaster to Caesar, her temporary success in this aim, and finally Decimus Brutus's decisive intervention and Caesar's resolution to attend the Senate, mainly because of the latter's assurance that the Senate had decided to confer the title of king upon him. Voltaire, in his version, discards Decimus Brutus's role in the affair and simplifies the Plutarchian account by making Dolabella stress the inadvisability of flouting omens and augurers, and having him voice Calpurnia's concern about César's safety. Besides Shakespeare's Caesar with his blustering vacillation, Voltaire's dictator cuts a more impressive figure, quietly and bravely resigned to his fate whatever it may be, modestly disclaiming (in typically Voltairean fashion) the idea that the inexorable processes of the natural

25

universe could be interpreted as bearing some particular dispensation for himself, yet bent on achieving his ambition of regal status.

The particular signs of favour which Caesar showed Antony are mentioned by Plutarch (*Antonius*, XI), and used by Shakespeare and Voltaire to present the relations of the two men as those of close friendship. Shakespeare, in the first glimpse he offers of the two in his *Julius Caesar* (1.ii), suggests the relationship between a reverent, almost obsequious courtier and an oriental monarch; only later through Antony's manifestly genuine grief after Caesar's death does he convey a different impression. Voltaire, from the opening scene of his play, however, establishes the atmosphere of intimacy and warmth in which César expresses his innermost hopes, aspirations and misgivings, unburdens himself of the secret of the clandestine marriage with Servilia and its consequence, and places upon Antoine the heavy responsibility of acting for him after his death *in loco parentis*. In this scene Voltaire follows Plutarch (*Caesar*, LVIII) in showing César driven by a compulsive desire to surpass himself in the achievement of fresh feats of glory by undertaking a punitive expedition against the Parthians (1.i.16 ff). The plan of extending his conquests is amplified by César in the audience which he gives to the senators, and in the same scene (1.iii) Voltaire follows Plutarch (*Caesar*, LX) in making César's overt aspiration after royal power (his coveting 'l'éclat du diadème' mentioned by Antoine; 1.iv.270) a source of friction between himself and the Senate. He modified the Greek historian's account of Caesar's followers spreading abroad the story that according to the Sibylline books only a king could defeat the Parthians. Voltaire's dictator merely mentions this 'bruit trop confirmé' (1.iii.189) to the senators as a reason for assuming the title of king. The simple stage-direction 'César, assis' at the beginning of the scene takes on greater significance in the light of Plutarch's long account of a similar incident and its unfortunate wounding of senatorial pride. Finally, in the last scene of the first act of *La Mort de César*, César shares the point of view of Plutarch's Caesar that it was wise 'to surround himself with men's goodwill as the fairest and at the same time the securest protection' (*Caesar*, LVII). Plutarch's own opinion of the appropriateness of the temple of clemency set up to honour Caesar (*Caesar*, LVIII) is echoed by the dictator in Voltaire's play (I.iv.301).

In *La Mort de César*, Brutus, as has already been remarked, resolves (before his discussion with Cassius) to become the instrument of a public vengeance which will bring the punishment of death to César for his tyranny. During the discussion (II.iii), the cries of the 'vil peuple' (to use the phrase of Brutus, who expresses his distaste somewhat less pungently than Shakespeare's Casca) are heard as they react to the spectacle of Antoine attempting to crown César. The next scene follows *Julius Caesar* inasmuch as these attempts are described to the conspirators by an eye-witness; in this case, however, it is Cimber who is the narrator not Casca as in Shakespeare. Casca's account contains elements from the two closely similar versions in Plutarch (*Caesar*, LXI and *Antonius*, XII). Cimber's account differs from Casca's and Voltaire seems to have followed a version of Plutarch's different from that utilised by Shakespeare or else he has supplied details of his own invention. Whereas Shakespeare's Antony simply offers Caesar a diadem ('yet 'twas not a crown neither, 'twas one of those coronets', in Casca's words), as in the version Plutarch gives in *Caesar*, LXI,[34] Voltaire describes how Antoine enters 'la couronne et le sceptre à la main' and deliberately places the crown upon César's head (II.iv.82-84). The sceptre would seem to be an anachronistic accessory which emerged from Voltaire's imagination and provides a spectacular gesture when, with the crown, it is later dashed underfoot by the dictator, but the actual crowning of César follows *Antonius*, XI. The precision introduced by Casca

---

[34] Voltaire adds to his translation of this part of Casca's speech, in his *Jules César*, the note: 'Les coronnets sont de petites couronnes que les pairesses d'Angleterre portent sur la tête au sacre des rois et des reines, et dont les pairs ornent leurs armoiries' (Voltaire 54, p.188). He goes on to deplore Shakespeare's pandering to popular taste by rendering comic 'un récit dont le fond est si noble et si intéressant'.

into his description of the regal head-dress is based on the use of the term 'diadem', naturally employed by Plutarch since it was associated with Hellenistic monarchy. Voltaire uses this same term elsewhere in his play. Both Shakespeare and Voltaire follow Plutarch in presenting the incident as part of a preconceived plan which misfired when the people, instead of acclaiming Caesar as king, showed their dislike of the very idea of kingship. César's reaction in this situation (II.iv.99-100) follows Plutarch: 'Caesar with affected modesty declined the diadem' (*Antonius*, XII). It is entirely in keeping with the unfavourable Shakespearean portrayal of a physically infirm dictator that he is represented, on the basis of an earlier incident recounted by Plutarch in *Caesar*, LX, as swooning during these proceedings. Voltaire, more moderately, and more flatteringly as far as César's image is concerned, adheres to Plutarch's account of the Caesar-Antony charade and only allows his César some blushing and frowning (II.iv.97-104).

In the remainder of this scene (II.iv) Voltaire shows Brutus asserting the moral authority which made him the effective leader in both Plutarch's account of the conspiracy and Shakespeare's. Whether Voltaire is drawing upon these sources or diverging from them, his objective is clearly to present Brutus as forceful and resolute, so as to increase the poignancy of his dilemma when it arises later. Thus, the position in Plutarch (*Brutus*, x) where Brutus tells Cassius he is ready to die in the cause of liberty (only to be told that no Roman would consent to the useless death of a leader capable of directing the enterprise of abolishing tyranny) is reversed in *La Mort de César*. Cassius's suicidal despair and invocation of Cato's example of *felo de se* (II.iv.114-122) is met with a stirring call to action from Brutus who condemns Cato's death by his own hand as a futile gesture. Voltaire diverges from Plutarch and Shakespeare in the conspirators' discussion of the question as to whether Cicero should be included in the plot. He follows Shakespeare in giving Brutus the decisive voice but there is hardly any discussion as there is in *Julius Caesar*; he follows Plutarch in giving Cicero's cowardice (and not his independence of mind, as Shakespeare's Brutus is made to suggest) as the main cause of his exclusion from the conspiracy but differs from him in attributing this argument to Brutus alone, and not presenting it as the result of a vague general consensus of opinion. Brutus's dominating role in the conspiracy is emphasised by both Voltaire and Shakespeare; whereas Shakespeare follows Plutarch, however, Voltaire takes a diametrically opposite approach. The Greek historian states specifically (*Brutus*, xii) that the conspirators 'exchanged neither oaths nor secret pledges' and Shakespeare gives Brutus a long speech (ii.i.114-140) in which he denounces oaths: 'Swear priests and cowards and men cautelous'. Voltaire, however, ends the conspiracy scene with a long passage (ii.iv.191-213) in which Brutus initiates an oath-taking ceremony and the conspirators, following his moral (and vocal) leadership, swear by the blood of Pompey and Cato, whose statues on either flank provide an effective décor, to kill César. Cassius's introduction of the further vow to slay any tyrant, be he brother, son or father, adds a touch of dramatic irony.

For the last three scenes of his play which deal with César's murder and the ensuing events, Voltaire follows Shakespeare fairly closely. The ultimate source is Plutarch, upon whom Shakespeare had relied for this section of his play, but there are differences to be noted between all these accounts. Both Shakespeare and Voltaire make the Capitol the scene of the assassination but Plutarch states, correctly, that the Senate met on that fateful Ides of March in Pompey's theatre. The sequence of events described by Plutarch (*Caesar*, lxvi; *Brutus*, xvii) is enacted in *Julius Caesar* and made the basis for the visually exciting spectacle of a savage killing, later graphically evoked for his own purposes by Antony in his funeral-speech. Voltaire, through his acceptance of the conventions of neoclassical drama, has to forego both the climax of Caesar's death and the build-up to it which we find in Shakespeare, and contents himself with recalling the assassination in Antoine's oration. Shakespeare has effectively rendered the Plutarchian representation of a Caesar darting to and fro like a trapped beast as he tries to avoid the flailing daggers of his killers. In Voltaire, there is a vague clamour offstage and the conspirators are heard to shout the single line 'Meurs, expire, tyran. Courage, Cassius' (III.vi.267); this exhortation to Cassius emphasises the preponderant role he has played in the murder and the part he will continue to play subsequently in Brutus's absence. Immediately after the murder, Plutarch recounts how Brutus and his associates 'their hands smeared with blood, and displaying their naked daggers' (*Brutus*, XVIII; see *Caesar*, LXVII for an almost identical description) left the scene of their crime and urged the citizens to assert their liberty. Voltaire and Shakespeare differ in their treatment of this phase of the story. In *La Mort de César* Cassius appears 'un poignard à la main' and there is a personal confrontation between him and Dolabella with each of them making a cursory attempt to sway the crowd before Cassius delivers the speech, the first part of which is an imitation of Brutus's much-admired funeral-oration in *Julius Caesar* (already translated and praised by Voltaire in his *Discours sur la tragédie*). In *Julius Caesar*, the assassins, at the suggestion of Brutus (who has been eliminated from the proceedings by this time in *La Mort de César*), bathe their hands and arms up to the elbows in Caesar's blood and go to the market-place waving their 'red weapons' above their heads. Cassius's words as he and his fellow-murderers stoop to the blood-bath – 'How many ages hence / Shall this our lofty scene be acted over / In states unborn and accents yet unknown!' – were not to prove prophetic as far as Voltaire's treatment of the subject was concerned. Indeed, the same neo-classical regard for decorum in eighteenth-century England ensured that in most productions of Shakespeare's play, Roman senators were not allowed to indulge in an action deemed to be incompatible with their dignity. The welter of gore relished by the groundlings at the Globe in Shakespeare's day would have been reduced to minuscule proportions in the performance of the play which Voltaire saw in England, but how blood-stained was the dagger brandished by Brutus and retained by the author of *La Mort de César* for Cassius's use, one can only surmise.

In the speech which Cassius makes in *La Mort de César* after the assassination, he represents himself to the crowd as generously observing Antoine's right to make his voice heard (III.vii.291-292). In *Julius Caesar*, however, Cassius always views with misgiving the formidable influence of Antony (III.i.96, 145-147, 212, 232-236, 244) and tries to dissuade Brutus from allowing him to speak at Caesar's funeral; Brutus, however, prefers to let it be known that Antony is speaking with the permission of the tyrant-slayers. There is never any question of what is legal or customary, only of what is expedient. According to Plutarch (*Brutus*, xx), the decision to allow Antony to speak at Caesar's funeral emanated from a discussion in the Senate held two days after the murder and in this discussion Brutus spoke for the motion, Cassius against. Plutarch certainly furnishes no hint for Voltaire's presentation of Cassius as a defender of the rule of law. Closer to Plutarch (and to Shakespeare) is the way in which Cassius, in the penultimate scene of *La Mort de César* (III.vii.305) warns the crowd not to be taken in by the oratorical blandishments of Antoine.

Antoine's entrance follows closely upon César's murder and Cassius's speech. It may well be that Voltaire, besides feeling the necessity of compression in a three-act play, preferred to aim at pathos more directly by presenting César's friend grief-stricken and tearful, and so ignored Shakespeare's presentation of his tactical parleying with the assassins (not in Plutarch) before his inflammatory address to the mob. Plutarch does not go into great detail over the content of Antony's speech; Shakespeare's genius is nowhere more manifest than in the way in which he has created a minor masterpiece from the slight materials available.

Voltaire did not imitate Shakespeare's amplifications slavishly, however, and there are a number of significant divergences. Plutarch gives three separate and slightly different accounts of Caesar's funeral: (a) *Antonius*, xIV, (b) *Brutus*, xx, (c) *Caesar*, LXVIII. In accounts (a) and (b), Antony's manipulation of the mob is represented as the result of a decision to adapt his approach to the mood of sympathy for Caesar which he senses in his audience. In the third account the fury of the crowd is attributed not to Antony's oratory but to hearing the generous terms of Caesar's will, mentioned in (b) but not in (a), and seeing his mutilated body. The first two accounts mention only Caesar's blood-stained robe, and both agree in stressing the use Antony makes of it to bring his audience's emotions to boiling point. Voltaire clearly follows Shakespeare in rejecting Plutarch's idea of Antony acting on the spur of the moment. Antoine subjects his audience to a premeditated battery, drawing upon an armoury of rhetorical weapons which includes the will, César's corpse and his torn and bloody toga. Antony's speech had already been described by Voltaire, in the *Discours sur la tragédie*, as 'un discours artificieux', and 'l'artifice' is exactly what Cassius tells the crowd to expect from it (III.vii.305). Shakespeare presents Antony achieving a skilful gradation of rhetorical effects to produce the final destructive rage in the mob. In Voltaire's avowed imitation of Shakespeare the same props – will, corpse, toga – are used, but Antony's essential flair for showmanship is absent. An element present in Shakespeare, but not touched upon by Plutarch, is the very real grief which Antony feels and which has such a telling effect upon his audience. The spontaneous natural upsurge of his emotion stifles speech, and it is this, rather than his conscious rhetoric or his pretence of being 'a plain, blunt man' (III.ii.219), which makes most impression and may well have greatly influenced Voltaire despite his awareness of the wiles of the mob-orator.

There is, all the same, noticeably more guile in Antony's handling of the crowd (III.ii.74-108) than in Antoine's address to them. Voltaire's imitation of Antony's oration reveals differences of approach which spring from a basically different attitude to the subject. Lachrymosity sets in early, with Antoine weeping and sighing before he even begins his speech. He opens on a note of tenderness and continues in the same vein, shedding 'des pleurs à l'amitié' (III.viii.320) and stressing not the hard-hearted murderers but the mild, gentle and forgiving nature of their victim. Antony, with his calculated catch in the throat and his well-timed pause for tears, is transformed into a reeling, staggering Antoine, apparently so dazed by the enormity of Brutus's crime that he can only offer half-formulated thoughts to his audience (III.350-352). His grief, unlike Antony's, proves immediately infectious and he is led to remark upon the tearful appearance of his audience (III.354). Voltaire chooses to diverge from both Plutarch and Shakespeare in not allowing César's corpse to appear before Antoine begins his oration. Indeed, he introduces it in spectacular fashion, with the back-stage opening in the middle of the funeral-speech to allow lictors to bring on the body covered with a blood-stained robe. After the revelation that parricide had been committed, Antoine mentions the will – but only very briefly, informing his fellow-citizens that they are legatees but saying nothing about his friend's bequests. César's paternal aspect, just revealed in his relationship to Brutus, is then further emphasised in his role as 'le père de l'Etat' (III.367) and Voltaire prepares for the spectacular entry of the lictors bearing César's body by an appeal to the crowd to allow their paternal benefactor the honours of a funeral pyre. This appeal seems to be based on the plea made by Antony in the Senate on the day after the Ides of March which is mentioned by Plutarch in *Brutus* (xx). Plutarch's account of how the crowd erected a pyre for Caesar's body and used burning brands from it to set fire to the houses of his slayers (*Brutus*, xx) is treated in different ways by Shakespeare and Voltaire. The crowd in *Julius Caesar* thinks spontaneously of this method of revenge; in *La Mort de César* Antoine is made to propose vengeance to the crowd and to suggest that it could take this form.

Voltaire does not make it clear whether César's body remains 'couvert d'une robe sanglante', whereas Shakespeare follows the accounts given by Plutarch in *Brutus* and *Antonius* and fully exploits the dramatic possibilities offered by Antony's removal of the toga from the body. Voltaire follows Shakespeare and Plutarch (*Brutus*, xx) in presenting Antoine as attributing the rents in the garment to individual assassins by name, but certain lines (III.381-393) suggest a closer adherence to the account in Plutarch's *Caesar*, LXVIII, which stresses the effect upon the crowd of seeing (and even touching) Caesar's wounds. The account of Caesar's last moments and especially of his confrontation with Brutus is given as much attention by Voltaire's Antoine as by Shakespeare's Antony and the dead body is present in each case to reinforce the

33

impact of the orator's art. Though Shakespeare follows quite closely the accounts of the murder given by Plutarch (*Brutus*, XVII; *Caesar*, LXVII) both in the enacting of the deed on stage and in Antony's evocation of it in his funeral speech, Voltaire modifies certain details from these sources in such a way as to make Antoine conjure up a quite different picture of what took place. In *Julius Caesar* (III.ii.177-190) Caesar dies heart-broken at the thought of Brutus's ingratitude, 'in his mantle muffling up his face' (as in Plutarch) to hide his utter despair from the friend who has forsaken him. Voltaire's César on the other hand looks at his son 'd'un œil tranquille et doux'. His last words are interpreted by Antoine as a shining example of forgiveness – one of the dominant themes of the play and one of Voltaire's own personal preoccupations.

Whatever else it is, *La Mort de César* is an important document in the history of literary cosmopolitanism. It dates from a phase in Voltaire's career when he was moving towards a position of aesthetic relativism and exemplifies his willingness to promote cross-fertilisation between cultures. He takes Desfontaines to task for not having recognised this fact in his review of the play:

Je suis persuadé que vous auriez rendu un service aux belles lettres si, au lieu de parler en peu de mots de cette tragédie comme d'une pièce ordinaire, vous aviez saisi l'occasion d'examiner le théâtre anglais et même le théâtre d'Italie, dont elle peut donner quelque idée. (D940)

Voltaire's claim to have put his *Mort de César* in an international context which raised it above the ordinary run of contemporary plays is supported later in his letter by reference to Antonio Conti's *Il Cesare* (1726). He yokes Conti's play (representing 'le théâtre d'Italie') with another dramatic treatment of Caesar's assassination (exemplifying 'le théâtre anglais') from the pen of John Sheffield, Duke of Buckingham. All three plays (Buckingham's, Conti's and Voltaire's) illustrate the process of interaction between the literatures of different countries. More specifically, they share in varying degrees a debt to Shakespeare's *Julius Caesar*.

The multilingual competence and catholicity of taste which made the exiled Lord Bolingbroke an exemplar of cosmopolitan spirit in Voltaire's eyes[35] characterised many of the friends who frequented his salon at La Source in the early 1720s.[36] Among these none was more prominent than the abbé Conti. Conti had visited England in 1715 and again in 1717-18 and acquired a certain notoriety as mediator in the controversy between Newton and Leibniz. His subsequent role as a populariser of Newtonian ideas, and in particular as a skilled exponent of 'il newtonianismo per le dame', chimed in with Bolingbroke's intellectual and social preoccupations.[37] English literature had as prominent a place as English science in the discussions which took place at La Source. We find the comtesse de Caylus, whose husband had introduced Conti to the Bolingbroke circle, producing a French prose translation of Pope's *Rape of the lock* in 1721 from a newly-minted Italian verse translation by Conti. Earlier, in the course of his stay in England, Conti's literary tastes were much in evidence. The Duchess of Buckingham quickened his interest in her husband's *Essay on poetry* so effectively that he rendered it into Italian verse. This led to a closer relationship between Conti and Buckingham who took it upon himself to act as a guide to English poetry and, especially, tragedy. Such guidance as Conti received only strengthened his neoclassical preferences. In terms recalling those used later by Voltaire (*Lettres philosophiques*, XXII, 'Sur M. Pope et quelques autres poètes fameux'), he describes Addison's *Cato* as 'la prima tragedia regolare degl'Inglesi'.[38] Shakespeare (whom he calls 'Sasper') is given a clearly subordinate place in the literary

[35] See D135 (December 1722) on Bolingbroke: 'il aime la poésie angloise, la françoise, et l'italienne mais il les aime différemment, parce qu'il discerne parfaittement leurs différens génies'.

[36] See D. J. Fletcher, 'The fortunes of Bolingbroke in France in the eighteenth century', *Studies* 47 (1966), p.207-32.

[37] See D. J. Fletcher, 'Bolingbroke and the diffusion of Newtonianism in France', *Studies* 53 (1967), p.29-46.

[38] *Risposta del signor abate Conti al signore Jacopo Martelli* (which prefaces the 1726 edition of *Il Cesare*), p.55.

hierarchy. Buckingham was nevertheless insistent in bringing the Bard to Conti's attention. He had composed two tragedies by bisecting and adapting Shakespeare's *Julius Caesar* and he offered them to his friend to peruse.[39] Conti, impressed by Buckingham's ardent vindication of Caesar's character, lost no time in setting to work on a play on the same subject in hendecasyllabic verse. Shortly after he returned to France in 1718, fortified by his reading of Suetonius, Dio Cassius and Plutarch in the library of Lord Pembroke, he completed his *Il Cesare*. It was published in 1726 under the imprint of Gioseffantonio Archi, Faenza. This was the volume (BV, no.854) which was possessed by Voltaire. Buckingham's reworking of *Julius Caesar* in two parts (which Pope presented to the public) was based, it would appear from the evidence assembled by Mielck,[40] on the text in Nicholas Rowe's 1709 edition of Shakespeare's work.[41] Buckingham made additions to Shakespeare's text, however, both of his own invention and from his reading of Plutarch. As we have seen, Voltaire, like his predecessors Shakespeare, Conti and Buckingham, put the writings of the Greek historian directly to account.

It must be said that, on the whole, Voltaire owes more to Plutarch and Shakespeare for the material of *La Mort de César* than he does to either Buckingham or Conti. The numerous verbal echoes of *Julius Caesar* which are indicated in the textual footnotes show how

[39] *The Tragedy of Julius Caesar, altered* (dated 1722), and *The Tragedy of Marcus Brutus* (dated 1722), *The Works* (London 1723), p.209 and 329 ff.

[40] Otto Mielck, 'John Sheffield Duke of Buckingham's Zweitheilung und Bearbeitung des Shakespeare'schen *Julius Caesar*', *Shakespeare Jahrbuch* 25 (1889), p.29-70.

[41] The adaptation of Shakespeare's *Julius Caesar* credited by oral tradition to Dryden and Davenant and published in 1719 was the text used for performances by the Drury Lane Company. The Theatre Royal's prompter, R. Chetwood, was responsible for its publication, so it is very probable that his friend Voltaire was acquainted with this text which shows a considerable number of cuts in the original. Some of Shakespeare's lines which etched themselves into Voltaire's memory (e.g. III.i.269-273, the passage including Antony's 'Cry havoc and let slip the dogs of war') are omitted from this acting version (cf. D7727).

closely Voltaire followed Shakespeare. In his characterisation, however, he shows a greater affinity with Buckingham and Conti. This is true not only of the minor characters (reduced in number to achieve dramatic economy and enhanced impact) but also of the major ones.[42] Caesar's image, tarnished by Shakespeare, is refurbished by Buckingham and Voltaire; he is no longer the arrogant despot, superstitious and distrustful, but rather a man conscious of his own worth and justifiably proud of his achievements. Significantly, Voltaire is at one with Buckingham in rejecting the Shakespearian prelude to the assassination: Caesar's insistence on justice rather than mercy in the case of Cimber's banished brother. Conti, likewise, presents his Cesare as a dictator and political realist, but one whose dominant instinct of forgiveness prompts him to speak the language of Auguste in Corneille's *Cinna*: 'è mio costume, / E'l sarà finch'io viva, il perdonare / A'miei nemici, e lor mostrar ch'io sono / Di me stesso Signor, come del Mondo' (III.ii).[43] In the preceding scene of this act, we find a close parallel between Conti and Voltaire. Cesare, in a dialogue with Antonio, puts forward arguments for efficient and beneficent autocracy to take the place of an obsolete republicanism – arguments which will find an echo in the homily which César delivers to his son in *La Mort de César* (III.181 ff). Even closer to Voltaire's treatment of Caesar's political attitude is the way Conti contrasts Cesare's mildness with Antonio's advocacy of punitive measures and fear as a principle of government. Calfurnia's belligerent appeal later for a show of force from her husband will merely elicit the gentle retort: 'Il mio regno è di pace, e di clemenza, / Non d'ira, e di vendetta' (IV.i).

Voltaire may to some extent have been influenced by the

---

[42] For a more detailed discussion see D. J. Fletcher, 'Three authors in search of a character: Julius Caesar as seen by Buckingham, Conti and Voltaire', *Mélanges à la mémoire de Franco Simone: France et Italie dans la culture européenne* (Genève 1981), ii.440-53.

[43] *Cinna*, v.iii.1696-1697: 'Je suis maître de moi comme de l'univers; / Je le suis, je veux l'être'.

Caesar-tragedies of Conti, Buckingham and Shakespeare in one particularly important respect. For the most controversial feature of his play, the central relationship between César and Brutus, he may have expanded hints which can be found, in one form or another, in all three works. 'L'amour paternel intéresse toujours' (D991) was one of Voltaire's most frequent recipes for success as a dramatist. It is not surprising therefore that the particular aspect of the Caesar story which he chose to exploit was one which stemmed from baseless rumour rather than well-attested fact: namely, the suggestion that the relationship between Caesar and Marcus Brutus was that of father and son.[44] Voltaire could have found precedents in French literature for perpetuating the rumour of Caesar's paternity: Montaigne (*Essais*, I, xxxiii) and La Rochefoucauld (*Réflexions diverses*, 14) both retail it. To be fair to him, however, it must be said that he did not simply take up the tale of the illegitimate birth of Brutus; he made a decent woman of his mother Servilia by joining her in a first marriage to Caesar 'par un hymen secret' (i.i.86). Furthermore, he supported his presentation of a Brutus faced with the horrifying prospect of parricide by whatever arguments he could muster rather than by flimsy or apocryphal evidence. He cites in telescoped form, as Theodore Besterman points out in his commentary on D989, a statement from one of Brutus's letters: 'Pro republica occidissem patrem', and makes this hint the basis for his semi-fictional account of the events preceding the assassination. In the critical letter he wrote to La Marre after the publication of his play, he mentions Brutus's letter again: 'Je vous avais dit, à la vérité, qu'il y avait parmi les lettres de Cicéron une lettre de Brutus, par

---

[44] Cf. Plutarch, *Lives, Brutus*, v. Suetonius, in his account of the dictator's murder (*Lives of the Caesars*, 1.82) attributed to him the words addressed to Brutus: 'καὶ σὺ τέκνον' ('You, too, my son?') rendered by Shakespeare as 'Et tu, Brute' (iii.i.77) and by Voltaire as 'O mon fils' (iii.viii.391). See, however, J. Carcopino, *Jules César* (1968), p.564, n.4: 'Le mot τέκνον était couramment employé comme un terme d'affection envers plus jeune que soi: "Mon petit". Il n'y a donc pas lieu de tirer de l'exclamation de César le moindre indice que Brutus ait été son fils'.

laquelle on peut inférer qu'il aurait tué son père pour la cause de la liberté' (D1034). Earlier in the letter he had declared that it was quite probable that Brutus knew he was Caesar's son. In the preface which he wrote to replace La Marre's 'Avertissement' this suggestion has hardened into the statement: 'On sait que César était son père'.

Conti had presented the relationship between the assassin and his victim in a way strongly suggestive of this closest tie of kinship without, however, making the blood-bond explicit. Cesare thinks of 'Bruto mio figlio' and remembers his tender embraces when he surrendered to him after the battle of Pharsalia; he finds the thought of his treachery barely conceivable: 'Tradirebbe il suo amico, anzi il suo padre?' (III.ii). After his part in releasing the tribunes has been revealed, he pardons him with loving words: 'Come figlio t'amai, come mio figlio / Innocente t'abbraccio, e reo t'assolvo' and, in the presence of and in preference to Cassio, awards him the urban praetorship, explaining to the rival candidate 'a favore di Bruto il padre impetra' (III.iii). To pluck up enough courage to kill Cesare, Bruto seeks strength from Rome's heroic past: 'L'invitta forza dell'antico Bruto, / Che in tua difesa i propri figli uccise' (III.iv).

Buckingham's Brutus is not surrounded by the same ambiguity; the final line of *The Tragedy of Marcus Brutus* passes a clear judgement on the assassin: 'He lov'd his country, but he killed his friend', and Brutus is, in fact, presented throughout the earlier *Julius Caesar altered* as doomed 'to kill the kindest of his friends' (chorus after act 4). Some lines spoken by Cassius (I.iv) would have given Voltaire a hint for his *Mort de César*. Lucius Junius Brutus, ancestor of Marcus Brutus, is portrayed from an interesting angle:

> There was a Brutus once who kill'd his sons
> And would have slain his dearest friend, nay father,
> Rather than suffer Rome to be enslav'd.[45]

[45] Voltaire's idea of introducing filial love so as to temper Brutus's fanatical patriotism in the *Mort de César* is paralleled by the advice he received from

39

The bond of affection between Caesar and Brutus is nowhere better illustrated than in Shakespeare's *Julius Caesar*. Brutus from the outset shows Cassius that his recruitment into the ranks of the conspirators is going to be achieved only by putting a great strain upon this bond when he says of Caesar 'I love him well' (I.ii.82). The love which existed between the murderer and his victim is the insistent, almost obsessive, theme of Brutus's funeral oration, which ends with the confession 'I slew my best lover for the good of Rome' (III.ii.45) and an offer of suicide, eventually to be realised with a feeling of relief: 'Caesar now be still: / I killed not thee with half so good a will'. Antony's funeral oration, for all its artifice, merely exploited a relationship accurately conveyed in the lines: 'For Brutus as you know, was Caesar's angel: / Judge, O you Gods, how dearly Caesar loved him!' (III.ii.182-183). It is more likely that the central relationship of *La Mort de César* arose from a transposition of this love on to the paternal and filial planes, than that Voltaire should have used (if he were even acquainted with it) a hint from another of Shakespeare's works (*2 Henry VI*, IV.i.137-138): 'Brutus's bastard hand / Stabb'd Julius Caesar'. It is certainly true that Voltaire did not share Dr Johnson's view of *Julius Caesar* as being 'somewhat cold and unaffecting'; on the contrary, he responded to what Wilson Knight's essays have revealed as 'its soft, warm and emotional side'.[46] There is every reason to suppose that he was influenced by the way in which Shakespeare made his play one in which the claims of love and friendship emerge as more important than those of abstract political idealism, and public virtue appears as less exemplary than personal devotion. The more barbaric aspects of the play would have offended his neoclassical taste; he would have agreed with Wilson Knight's view that 'the blood-imagery of *Julius Caesar*

Bolingbroke and his friends on his earlier *Brutus*: 'Ils m'encourageaient à tempérer l'austérité de Brutus par l'amour paternel, afin qu'on admirât et qu'on plaignît l'effort qu'il se fait en condamnant son fils' (*Discours sur la tragédie*; M.ii.321, n.2).
[46] See Shakespeare, *Julius Caesar: a casebook*, ed. P. Ure (London 1968), p.20.

is flagrant and excessive'.[47] Yet, in a deeper sense, it may well have been Shakespeare's mastery in evoking the sheer physical horror of the assassination that moved Voltaire to place the emphasis even more heavily on man's inhumanity to man by making the victim the principal conspirator's own flesh and blood.

Gustave Lanson, in his edition of the *Lettres philosophiques*, illustrates abundantly (ii.88 ff) in relation to Shakespeare his remark that 'les réserves du goût français de Voltaire ne sont souvent que l'écho des réserves de la bonne compagnie anglaise du premier tiers du xviiie siècle'. Though he also takes into account Voltaire's avowed preference for the primitive force of the Elizabethan dramatist when compared with the dullness and frigidity of most of the Augustan tragedians, he does not explore this preference sufficiently to convey an adequate idea of the deep impact which Shakespeare's tragedies made upon Voltaire's feelings. It is interesting however that one of the few authors he does quote in this connection is Buckingham (to whom he refers here and elsewhere as Lord Mulgrave); the lines from the *Essay on poetry* which he cites (ii.101, n.36) sum up the nature of a great part of Shakespeare's influence upon Voltaire (the 'they' refers to Shakespeare and Fletcher):

> For 'tho in many things they grossly fail,
> Over our passions still they so prevail,
> That our own grief by theirs is rock'd asleep,
> The dull are forced to feel, the wise to weep.

The same aspect of Shakespeare's genius is evoked by Pope, whose judgement (in the preface to his 1725 edition of the dramatist's work) is all the more noteworthy when one remembers that Voltaire, as a student of English literature, regarded him (together with Shakespeare, Dryden and Addison) as one of his first masters (letter to Martin Ffolkes; D2890). He was still referring to him as a pundit in Shakespearian criticism many years later (letter to George Keate of 1760; D8858) at a time when he

---

[47] *The Wheel of fire*, revised edition (London 1954), p.132.

was more critical of the crudeness and irregularity of the plays then being presented to the French public as superlative examples of the dramatic art of Shakespeare. The following passage from Pope's preface reflects the view of many of his contemporaries:

The power over our passions was never possessed in a more eminent degree, or displayed in so different instances. Yet all along, there is seen no labour, no pains to raise them, no preparation to guide our guess to the effect, or be perceived to lead toward it. But the heart swells and the tears burst out just at the proper place. We are surprised the moment we weep, and yet upon reflection find the passion so just that we should be surprised if we had not wept at that very moment.[48]

Voltaire, for his part, was in no doubt about the supreme importance of 'la pitié et la crainte, les deux pivots de la tragédie'.[49] Whilst impatient with the Aristotelian concept of catharsis, he was fully aware that his job as a tragedian was to touch the springs of pity and terror in the hearts and minds of his audience: 'Sans cette crainte et cette pitié tout languit au théâtre. Si on ne remue pas l'âme, on l'affadit. Point de milieu entre s'attendrir et s'ennuyer' (Voltaire 55, p.1031). The last sentence here hints at the primacy which Voltaire attached to pity; elsewhere he says even more explicitly 'le pathétique [qui] doit être l'âme de la tragédie' (p.817); 'les applaudissements les plus vrais, ce sont les larmes' (p.939). At about the same period as *La Mort de César* was being performed privately, one finds in the prologue to Voltaire's comedy *Le Comte de Boursoufle* (1734?) the prescriptive 'La pitié, non l'horreur, doit régner sur la scène' (M.iii.254). His tragedy might well have been written to that prescription.

The views expressed by Voltaire on the way in which the dramatist should play upon the emotions of his audience suggest that he would have admired the attack as well as the artifice of Antony's speech. 'If you have tears prepare to shed them now' says Caesar's friend at a crucial point (III.ii.170) in his funeral

---

[48] *Eighteenth-century critical essays*, ed. Scott Elledge (Ithaca 1961), i.279.
[49] *Commentaires sur Corneille* (Voltaire 55, p.807).

speech, and the assault he proceeds to make upon the feelings of his audience is calculated to reduce them to the state he is in himself, 'his eyes [...] red as fire with weeping' (III.ii.116). Voltaire adopts Antony's approach: 'Préparez quand vous voulez toucher. N'interrompez jamais les assauts que vous livrez au cœur' (Voltaire 55, p.1022). For him, 'le grand art de la tragédie est que le cœur soit toujours frappé des mêmes coups' (Voltaire 54, p.518), otherwise the audience gets away: 'Si vous ne frappez le cœur du spectateur par des coups toujours redoublés au même endroit, ce cœur vous échappe' (Voltaire 55, p.817). In the case of *La Mort de César* he inevitably retains for its pathos the scene of the funeral orations, 'scène [...] qui a été comme la cause occasionnelle de sa tragédie'.[50] He uses the Brutus-César relationship to build up the same affective tonality through the pathetic situation in which César craves for filial affection which is denied to him by a son who is his political opponent and Brutus is placed in the excruciating predicament, by the sudden revelation of his parentage, of contemplating what would no longer be simply an act of glorious tyrannicide but a murder most foul and unnatural.

In the context of a discussion of Shakespeare's *Julius Caesar*, Lion remarks of Voltaire: 'ce qu'il admire dans le théâtre anglais, c'est le terrible' (p.56). For many eighteenth-century English critics, this indeed was Shakespeare's forte. His master-passion was terror, as John Dennis puts it.[51] In *La Mort de César*, Voltaire, far from neglecting this passion, claims that he made it the main source of the play's appeal. He derides, in a letter to La Marre, the idea of a straightforward representation of a conspiracy and an assassination. He says of Brutus: 'Il est assez vraisemblable qu'il [Brutus] savait que César était son père, et que cette considération ne le retint pas. C'est même cette circonstance terrible, et ce combat singulier entre la tendresse et la fureur de la liberté, qui seul pouvait rendre la pièce intéressante' (D1034). The play

[50] H. Lion, *Les Tragédies et les théories dramatiques de Voltaire* (Paris 1895), p.60.

[51] *Essay on the genius and writings of Shakespear* (1712), *Critical works*, ed. Hooker (Baltimore 1943), ii.4.

does, in fact, strive to create its most telling effects from the conflict between Brutus's head and his heart. This conflict is maintained up to the end of the play and it is a distraught son sickened by the monstrous deed of parricide to whom Antoine refers, as he points to the dead César's bloody toga (III.viii.385-386): 'Là, Brutus éperdu, Brutus l'âme égarée, / A souillé dans ses flancs sa main dénaturée.' In the version written for performance at the Collège d'Harcourt however, Brutus refuses to kill his father (see 35H variants for III.117-124, 292-301 and 381-392). Thiriot points out in his letter to the *Observations sur les écrits modernes*: 'Si César fut dans la suite assassiné par les conjurés, Brutus ne paraît point tremper dans ce meurtre. L'auteur s'est bien gardé de le rendre coupable de parricide'. Voltaire explains in a letter to Asselin: 'Il est très vrai que l'assassinat d'un homme aussi généreux que César, par son fils, et l'homicide tourné en parricide, peut révolter beaucoup de Français: c'est dans cette vue que j'avais retranché dans la pièce que je vous donnai les vers qui indiquent un parricide dans Brutus; mais j'ai laissé ces mêmes vers pour ceux qui ne veulent pas que les choses soient à demi tragiques, qui aiment l'horreur portée au comble' (D989; 15 [?January 1736]). The horrifying prospect raised by his father's revelation had led Brutus to crave a solidarity with his fellow-conspirators which would not preclude non-involvement in the actual assassination. His half-hearted declaration of intent echoes the explicit profession of non-violence which Voltaire had ascribed to him in the earlier version for the *collégiens* (see 35H variant for III.117-124 and footnote). By making Cassius assume the principal role in the assassination, Voltaire is able to present Brutus as a reluctant and anguished assassin and to avoid at least one divergence from Antony's funeral oration in *Julius Caesar*. In giving the speech of Shakespeare's Brutus to Cassius, however, he invites trouble: the poignancy of 'I slew my best lover for the good of Rome', for example, is reduced to the bland implausibility of 'J'ai tué mon ami, pour le salut de Rome'.[52]

[52] See below, III.274 and note 19.

44

In the *Discours sur la tragédie* (1730), Voltaire shows that he is aware of the difficulty of finding the dividing-line between terror and horror; he feels that 'les Anglais surtout ont donné des spectacles effroyables, voulant en donner de terribles'. His realisation of the value of action and visual appeal as means of enhancing emotional impact is clear in this same preface. His imitation of *Julius Caesar* is foreshadowed in both his account of Antony's speech over Caesar's bleeding corpse and his enthusiastic description of the emotive appeal of the scene in Addison's *Cato* where the eponymous hero's patriotic sentiments are voiced over the dead body of his son, Marcus. The scene (v.i, much admired by Voltaire) in *La Mort de Pompée* where Cornélie laments her dead husband, resembles the scene in which Shakespeare's Antony mourns his dead friend, especially in the touching use made in each case of the proper name of Pompey/Caesar. In *La Mort de César* the author attempts to go beyond the French tradition (which had at least permitted Cornélie to clutch with pathetic effect the urn containing her husband's ashes) and to make a more spectacular appeal to the eye as his stage-direction indicates: 'Le fond du théâtre s'ouvre: des licteurs apportent le corps de César, couvert d'une robe sanglante; Antoine descend de la tribune, et se jette à genoux auprès du corps'. He drew the line here however; the shock of witnessing the furious hacking blows of Caesar's assassins was denied French audiences, whilst the spectacle of the dictator dying on stage was reduced to the sound of a scuffle in the wings. In the *Discours*, Voltaire transforms the angry mob who tear the poet Cinna limb from limb in Shakespeare's play into 'un chœur composé d'artisans et de plébéiens romans' (M.ii.317), whose role appears restricted to even more sedate and less moving functions than those normally accorded a chorus. Conscious that English dramatists (like the Greeks before them) had overstepped the mark in their essays in horror, he believed that he could imitate what he saw was valuable in their attempts: 'un vrai pathétique' (M.ii.318).

Voltaire locates the real interest of his play in Brutus's inner conflict. In Shakespeare's play there is the same emphasis on

45

Brutus 'with himself at war' (I.ii.46).[53] The poignancy surrounding
Brutus's relations with his wife Portia in *Julius Caesar* has no exact
equivalent in *La Mort de César*. Love of the romantic or even
tenderly conjugal kind is banished from Voltaire's play. In its
place, however, there is love in fuller measure, in its paternal
and filial forms. Besides the bare bones of action and incident,
Voltaire's play may owe something to Shakespeare for its soft
centre, the *substantifique moelle* which is at the emotional core of
the relations between a father and his son. The author of *La Mort
de César* does not neglect high affairs of state but a personal
dilemma lies at the heart of his play, which is essentially a
psychological drama[54] tautened by a framework of three, rather
than the usual five, acts. Its dimensions are consciously reduced
compared with those of Shakespeare's *Julius Caesar*, the last two
acts of which present the historic clash of great political forces as
Caesar's spirit ranges for revenge far from the scene of his death.
Some of Voltaire's editors, some of his friends, and even Voltaire
himself, have tended, in this connection, to give readers a false
impression of the real nature of his play. Condorcet, for example,
in the Kehl 'Avertissement' to *Rome sauvée*, classes the later play
with *La Mort de César* and goes on: 'Dans ces pièces, ce n'est ni
à un seul personnage, ni à une famille qu'on s'intéresse, c'est
à un grand événement historique' (M.v.202). Algarotti, in his
prefatory letter, applauds Voltaire for having excluded female
characters from *La Mort de César* and goes to the extreme of
describing the play as 'una tragedia dove no entran donne, tutta
sentimenti di libertà e patriche di politica', and 'che non è intorno
à un matrimonio o à un amoretto, ma che è intorno à un fatto
atrocissimo e alla più gran rivoluzione che sia avvenuta nel più
grande imperio del mondo'. There is certainly no trace of *galanterie*
in Voltaire's play, but Algarotti omits to mention that for the

---

[53] Voltaire quotes as one of the highlights of Shakespeare's play Brutus's
lines about the 'insurrection' in his mind (II.i.63-69) in the article 'Art dramatique'
which appears in the *Questions sur l'Encyclopédie* (1770).

[54] See Lion, p.61: 'tout le drame se resserre dans une âme'.

amorous sigh of the lover has been substituted the strangled sob of the tormented son on the rack of his own emotions. Voltaire too can be charged with misleading his correspondents by emphasising only one aspect of his play when he writes: 'Il n'y a point de femme dans cette pièce, il n'est question que de l'amour de la patrie' (D910) and 'Il y a de la férocité romaine. Nos jeunes femmes trouveroient cela horrible. On ne reconoitroit pas l'auteur de la tendre Zaïre' (D906). It would be foolhardy to deny the presence in the play of the elements he mentions, but the warm-hearted vindication of the values of love, friendship and forgiveness may be said to point to the sensibility of the author of *Zaïre*. The adherence to political ideals like liberty and patriotism obviously cannot be regarded as uncharacteristic of Voltaire, but when these ideals come into conflict with those of humanity, mercy and personal loyalty, the question of *La Mort de César*'s 'message' becomes more complicated and the play cannot be considered simply 'comme une résultante de l'enthousiasme de Voltaire pour le message de liberté des dramaturges anglais et de l'ivresse qui le saisit en respirant l'atmosphère de liberté d'outre-Manche'.[55]

The important innovations in French dramatic practice due to English influence, and particularly to Shakespeare, which Voltaire was proudly conscious of incorporating in *La Mort de César* should not, however, be underestimated. They have been profitably discussed by Fenger (p.202, 209), David Williams[56] and Theodore Besterman.[57] Briefly (apart from the visual effects of act 3, scenes 7 and 8: the brandishing of Cassius's dagger and the impressive funeral cortège), Voltaire has attempted to implement a more dynamic conception of stage presentation. The traditional récit-technique of imparting information is used alongside other techniques which involve the informant in the dramatic action and prompt his hearers to make lively interjections. Thus, César

---

[55] H. Fenger, *Voltaire et le théâtre anglais* (Copenhague 1949), p.213.
[56] *Voltaire: literary critic*, Studies 48 (1966), p.297-341.
[57] *Voltaire* (Oxford 1976), p.131-58.

imparts his views to a large group of interestingly recalcitrant senators (i.iii); the conspiracy is hatched on the spot and reflected in multi-lateral discussion (ii.iv); Brutus breaks the shattering news of his discovery that César is his father to fellow-conspirators who are invited to advise him and respond with animation; and lastly, the funeral speech of Antoine (which in certain details – like the description of César's dying – conforms, in the Senecan tradition taken up by Shakespeare, to the time-honoured pattern of the *nuntius* informing the chorus) is enlivened to some extent at least by the albeit over-formal observations of various *Romains*.

La Mort de César could justly be described in the terms used by Allardyce Nicoll to describe the typical Augustan drama: 'a mixture of heterogeneous elements, inharmoniously fused together', 'a peculiar amalgam of diverse forces',[58] which included the omnipresent influence of Shakespeare. Nicoll indicates what could be considered as one of the more significant aspects of *La Mort de César* when he says that Voltaire 'pointed the way towards the *drame* of later years both in France and England' (ii.73). In the preface to *Mariamne* there is an interesting passage in which Voltaire divides tragedy into two kinds: one chiefly concerned with 'les intérêts de toute une nation' and the other which deals with 'les intérêts particuliers de quelques princes' and in which 'tout l'intérêt est renfermé dans la famille du héros de la pièce; tout roule sur des passions que des bourgeois ressentent comme les princes' (M.ii.167). *La Mort de César* recalls the 'conglomerate' type of Augustan tragedy in having affinities with both these kinds of drama. Its author aspires to treat 'les intérêts de toute une nation' whilst remaining attached to the lowlier personal problems and feelings of average humanity. Voltaire's admiration for the author of *Mithridate* in his discussion of the second kind of drama ('Racine [...] a attendri, a effrayé, a fait verser des larmes') underlines the common ground between his own tragedies and the later *drame bourgeois*.

---

[58] *A history of English drama*, 3rd edition (Cambridge 1955), ii.115, 61.

Even if homogeneity is not one of the striking features of *La Mort de César*, Voltaire's concern with the question of unity – of time, place and action – is evident enough. The reviewer of the play in the November issue of *The Literary magazine* remarks that 'unity of place, and unity of time, are exactly observed' (p.440).[59] Shakespeare's *Julius Caesar* stood out for Voltaire as a play in which the unities were not observed. La Marre in his 'Avertissement' to *La Mort de César* says of Shakespeare: 'Ses pièces sont des monstres dans lesquelles il y a des parties qui sont des chefs d'œuvre de la nature. Sa tragédie intitulée *La Mort de César* [Voltaire frequently refers to Shakespeare's play in the same way and is followed in this by the editors of the Kehl edition amongst others] commence par son triomphe au Capitole, et finit par la mort de Brutus et Cassius à la bataille de Phillipes'. Much later, Voltaire uses the same example in his *Commentaires sur Corneille* when, speaking of the double action which for him constitutes an imperfection in *Horace*, he remarks 'Il est vrai qu'en Espagne, en Angleterre, on joint quelquefois plusieurs actions sur le théâtre; on représente dans la même pièce la mort de César, et la bataille de Phillipes. *Nos musas colimus severiores*' (Voltaire 54, p.276). Conti, enlarging in the *Risposta al sig. Martelli* on Shakespeare's irregularities, notes how Caesar's death occurs in the third act and the rest of his play is taken up with Antony's speech to the people, the ensuing civil war and the deaths of Brutus and Cassius (p.54). It was the violation of the unity of action in *Julius Caesar* which would appear to have offended Voltaire most. The point that Shakespeare's play as it appears in the folio of 1623 is a combination of two plays, a 'Fall of Caesar' and a 'Revenge of Caesar', has often been made.[60] It was this lack of unity which offended Buckingham's neoclassical taste and prompted him to divide Shakespeare's play

[59] P. G. Adams, 'Poe, critic of Voltaire', *Mln* 57 (1942), p.273-75, vindicates Voltaire against Poe's charge of violation of the unity of place in the play.

[60] For a fuller discussion, see H. M. Ayres, 'Shakespeare's *Julius Caesar* in the light of some other versions', *PMla* 18 (1910), ii.183-227.

into two parts. He was not the first (nor the last)[61] to bisect the story of *Julius Caesar* as told by Shakespeare. Georges de Scudéry's *La Mort de César* (1636) had a swift sequel – *La Mort de Brute et de Porcie ou la vengeance de la mort de César*, written by Guérin de Bouscal and published in 1637. Voltaire in retaining, like Buckingham, the scene of the funeral-orations exposed himself to the same charge of damaging the unity of action which he had made against Shakespeare. La Harpe commented that if one considered the structure of the play, Antony's speech was really a 'hors d'œuvre'.[62] Voltaire was doubtless aware of this, and although on the theoretical level he deplores (as strongly as Aristotle) 'les épisodes détachés',[63] he is willing to concede a structural defect if it gives rise to a source of beauty and power. This is evident in his comment on *La Mort de Pompée* (III.iii): 'D'ailleurs, après la mort de Pompée, la tragédie ne roule plus que sur un rendez-vous de César avec Cléopâtre, sur une bonne fortune; tout devient hors d'œuvre; il n'y a ni nœud, ni intrigue. Cornélie n'arrive que pour déplorer la mort de son mari; mais telle est la beauté de son rôle, qu'elle soutient presque seule la dignité de la pièce' (Voltaire 54, p.429). Voltaire is as consistent in his criticism of Shakespeare's inability as a dramatist to create what he considered a satisfyingly unified aesthetic whole, as he is in his praise and admiration for the many admirable *scènes/morceaux/endroits* in his monstrous *œuvre*.

In the account of English tragedy which he gives in the eighteenth of his *Lettres philosophiques*, Voltaire unequivocally puts

---

[61] In the 'Liste complète de tragédies et drames publiés ou représentés pour la première fois en France pendant la Révolution (1789-1799)', contained in J.-A. Rivoire, *Le Patriotisme dans le théâtre sérieux de la Révolution* (Paris 1950), one finds the entry: Buffardin, (S): *Brutus et Cassius, ou la bataille de Phillipes*, suite de la 'Mort de César', tragédie en vers et en 2 actes, imitée de l'anglais de Shakespear (Paris, l'auteur, an IV, in-8, 30 p: Bn 8° Yth 2376).

[62] *Lycée*, ix.350.

[63] Witness his comment on Corneille's *Premier discours*: 'Un épisode inutile à la pièce est toujours mauvais; et en aucun genre ce qui est hors d'œuvre ne peut plaire ni aux yeux, ni aux oreilles ni à l'esprit' (Voltaire 55, p.1039).

the rude force of genius before the sophistication of good taste: 'Les monstres brillants de Shakespeare plaisent mille fois plus que la sagesse moderne'. 'Le sage Addison' is admired for his elegance and correctness but does not arouse noticeable enthusiasm in Voltaire, who will later comment in the *Questions sur l'Encyclopédie* (1770) upon the decline in popularity of Addison's *Cato*: 'On revint bientôt aux irrégularités grossières mais attachantes de Shakespeare' (M.xvii.405). The influence *Cato* had upon *La Mort de César* was, for the most part, of a cautionary nature – Voltaire's decision to write a play devoid of female characters was prompted by his determination that no-one should say of his own play on a Roman subject what he had said about *Cato* in the letter 'Sur la tragédie': 'cet ouvrage si bien écrit est défiguré par une intrigue froide d'amour, qui répand sur la pièce une langueur qui la tue'. He could not fail, however, to be impressed by the 'pensées fortes et vraies' which Addison formulated, or to be moved by the powerful speech of Cato inspired by the sight of his dead son.[64] These features also characterised Shakespeare's play. In Voltaire's mind the Augustan was linked to the Elizabethan playwright as an exemplar of something he deemed typically English: 'cette force et cette énergie qu'inspire la noble liberté de penser'.

It is tempting, in any consideration of the possible sources of Voltaire's plays, to dismiss sixteenth-century French drama since his own references to it are invariably contemptuous. In the first section of 'Art dramatique' (*Questions sur l'Encyclopédie*), he says tersely: 'Les Français n'eurent que de misérables farces, comme on sait, pendant tout le xve et xvie siècle' (M.xvii.394). He is more specific in the second section, 'Du théâtre espagnol', the last

---

[64] In one of Voltaire's earlier notebooks is the following entry: 'Differences between the Englh and French stage. One kills him self here; why shant he kill another? One is carried dead out of the scene, why not brought dead? Hippolitus appears wonded, in Euripides. Cato's son is brought in murdered' (Voltaire 81, p.107).

sentence of which reads: 'Hardy et Garnier n'écrivirent que des platitudes d'un style insupportable; et ces platitudes furent jouées sur des tréteaux au lieu de théâtre' (p.397). Despite such disparaging remarks, the work of certain sixteenth-century exponents of the Senecan tradition in France deserves some attention. As far as *La Mort de César* is concerned, it would be unwise to assume from Voltaire's blanket condemnation of sixteenth-century French drama that he totally neglected the Latin *Julius Caesar* of Marc-Antoine Muret (which was published in his *Juvenilia* in 1553 and composed towards the middle of the previous decade), the *César* of Jacques Grévin (1558) closely based on Muret's play, and three plays of Garnier dealing with the period of the civil wars in Rome: *Porcie* (1568), *Cornélie* (1574) and *Marc-Antoine* (1578). All these plays belong to the tradition to which Voltaire had been introduced at school.

Voltaire's acquaintance with the work of Garnier is evident from his *Commentaires sur Corneille*. He finds some lines in *La Mort de Pompée* (one of the plays which he suggests he has taken as a model for his *La Mort de César*) reminiscent of a *réplique* in the sixteenth-century dramatist's *Cornélie* (Voltaire 54, p.446). Some possible echoes of Garnier in his own tragedy, muffled by the periphrastic, image-laden style of the earlier dramatist, are too elusive to allow definite influence to be posited. The crisp stichomythic passages in Garnier, on the other hand, suggest a more plausible source. Most of these passages are in the Senecan tradition and concern the stock debate upon the advantages to a ruler of benevolence compared with those of severity. Gillian Jondorf gives a great deal of profitable attention to this *clémence/rigueur* debate, as she calls it.[65] Among the dialogues which suggest themselves as possible sources for the conversation between César and Antoine in *La Mort de César* (i.iv) are the ones between Arée and Octave in *Porcie* (III. p.47-48), between César (i.e. Octavius) and Agrippe in *Marc-Antoine* (IV. p.220-22) – where the

---

[65] See her *Robert Garnier and the themes of political tragedy in the sixteenth century* (Cambridge 1969), especially p.105-13.

great-nephew of Julius Caesar in each case speaks out against the clemency for which his kinsman had been famous – and, most plausibly of all, the discussion between Marc-Antoine and César (i.e. Julius Caesar) in *Cornélie* (IV. p.145-46), where Caesar trusts in the loyalty inspired by his own magnanimity against the advice of his friend who takes a more realistic view.

There are affinities between Garnier's approach to the treatment of political problems in his plays and Voltaire's presentation of the central political issue in *La Mort de César*. The rallying-calls of liberty, republicanism and public virtue resound throughout Garnier's work but do not obscure his personal conviction of the value of monarchical government. Basically, Voltaire's attitude is similar: an academic admiration for the civic spirit of the republicans of ancient Rome coupled with a realistic appraisal of the need for a firm monarch standing above sectional interests in his own country. In *La Mort de César*, César's ideas on dealing with the political situation in Rome in 44 BC (III.iv.181-194) reflect the author's own point of view on the best form of government for a state. Voltaire shares with Garnier an intellectual distaste for tyranny counterbalanced by a realisation of the fanaticism engendered by excessive regard for liberty. His remarks to La Marre make this clear: 'Vous auriez donc pu dire, que César est un grand homme, ambitieux, jusqu'à la tyrannie, et Brutus un héros d'un autre genre, qui poussa l'amour de la liberté jusqu'à la fureur. Vous pourriez remarquer qu'ils sont représentés tous deux condamnables mais à plaindre, et que c'est en quoi consiste l'artifice de cette pièce' (D1034).

Grévin, like Voltaire, glorifies the idealism of the genuine adherents of republicanism whilst stressing the historical necessity of monarchy for Rome, which had become too corrupt to be governed successfully by an aristocratic oligarchy (see Grévin 1.73 ff and Voltaire III.186-199). Shakespeare, it should not be forgotten, vindicates monarchic principles in *Julius Caesar*, as he does consistently elsewhere.[66]

[66] See J. E. Phillips, *The State in Shakespeare's Greek and Roman plays* (New

Voltaire's dismissive references to French Renaissance drama are matched by his scathing comments on tragedy in early seventeenth-century France. His remarks according to one critic invariably spring from 'the scorn of ignorance'.[67] This observation would seem to be borne out by Voltaire's low opinion of Georges de Scudéry's *La Mort de César* (1636), based it would seem on prejudice rather than detailed knowledge of the work. The available evidence suggests that Voltaire did not make use of the play but there is the possibility of an indirect debt if we accept that Scudéry's *Mort de César* was a direct source of certain scenes in Corneille which in turn influenced Voltaire in the composition of his play. A case in point would be the opening scene of act 2 of *Cinna* which, it has been suggested,[68] derived from the first scene of act 3 of Scudéry's play. What is even more to the point perhaps is the existence of a strong tradition of discussion of *l'art de régner* in seventeenth-century French tragedy,[69] and the recurrence of the *clémence/rigueur* motif in this discussion. Voltaire was likely to have been more closely acquainted with the earlier manifestations of this tradition in classical antiquity (e.g. Seneca's *De clementia*, 1.9) than with the cognate discussions to be found in the works of Hardy and Guérin de Bouscal.

Apart from Shakespeare, Corneille is the only dramatist to whom the author of *La Mort de César* directly acknowledges a

York 1940). Johann Petkovic (*Voltaires Tragödie 'La Mort de César' verglichen mit Shakespeares 'Julius Cäsar'*, Wien 1909, p.11) points out that many of the parallels between Voltaire and Grévin adduced by G. A. O. Collischonn (*Jacques Grévins Tragödie 'César' in ihrem Verhältniss zu Muret, Voltaire und Shakespere*, Ausgaben und Abhandlungen aus dem Gebiete der romanischen Philologie 52, Marburg 1886, p.37 ff) are tenuous and inconclusive and shows that more convincing ones could be made between Voltaire and Shakespeare.

[67] Robert Lowenstein, *Voltaire as an historian of seventeenth-century French drama* (Baltimore and London 1935), p.187.

[68] L. M. Riddle, *The Genesis and sources of Pierre Corneille's tragedies from 'Médée' to 'Pertharite'* (Baltimore and Paris 1926).

[69] Many examples of the struggle between the human impulses of monarchs and the claims of *Realpolitik* are given in M. Baudin, 'L'art de régner in seventeenth-century French tragedy', *Mln* 50 (1935), 417-26.

debt. In the letter (D869) in which he offers the play to Asselin for performance at the Collège d'Harcourt, Voltaire says: 'Je m'y suis proposé pour modèle votre illustre compatriote, et j'ai fait ce que j'ai pu pour imiter de loin

> La main qui crayonna
> L'âme du grand Pompée et l'esprit de Cinna.

Il est vrai que c'est un peu la grenouille qui s'enfle pour être aussi grosse que le bœuf, mais enfin, je vous offre ce que j'ai'. The reference to La Fontaine's fable is not just a piece of mock modesty on his part. It reflects a consistently high regard for Corneille which remained unimpaired by a growing awareness of his imperfections. Voltaire's attitude to Corneille is paralleled by his attitude to Shakespeare with whom he often associates him:[70] 'Shakespear, le Corneille de Londre, grand fou, d'ailleurs et ressemblant plus souvent à Gilles qu'à Corneille' (to Cideville, 3 November 1735; D934). Shakespeare is, nevertheless, recognised by Voltaire as a genius and in the works of this genius he found in abundance passages which could be described as sublime. Casting the same anthologist's eye on Corneille's œuvre, he saw a collection of plays not each in itself worthy of imitation but most of which contained scenes and passages which were models of their kind. He recognised Corneille as a master of the art of presenting political discussion on stage and put him on a par with Shakespeare in his capacity for producing memorable 'conférences entre de grands hommes'. This judgement is supported by his bracketing in his 'Remarques sur Sertorius' (III.i; Voltaire 55, p.862) the quarrel scene in Julius Caesar (IV.iii.18-24), (part of which he translated freely in the article 'Art dramatique'), with a conversation between Sertorius and Pompée. In the 'Remarques sur Pompée' (v.5), this play, which has the strongest claim after Cinna to be considered as having some influence upon the conception of La Mort de César, is described in terms which underline the affinity which Voltaire discerns between Corneille and Shake-

[70] See Lanson's edition of the Lettres philosophiques, ii.90, n.4.

speare: 'Mais *Pompée* n'est point une véritable tragédie, c'est une tentative que fit Corneille, pour mettre sur la scène des morceaux excellents, qui ne faisaient point un tout; c'est un ouvrage d'un genre unique, qu'il ne faudrait pas imiter, et que son génie, animé par la grandeur romaine, pouvait seul faire réussir. Telle est la force de ce génie, que cette pièce l'emporte encore sur mille pièces régulières, que leur froideur a fait oublier' (Voltaire 54, p.454).

Among the 'morceaux excellents' in *Pompée* which Voltaire might have regarded as worthy of imitation, the opening scene stands out. After making many minor criticisms, Voltaire goes on: 'Ces défauts dans le détail n'empêchent pas que le fond de cette première scène ne soit une des plus belles expositions qu'on ait vues sur aucun théâtre; les anciens n'ont rien qui en approche; elle est auguste, intéressante, importante; elle entre tout d'un coup en action; les autres expositions ne font qu'instruire du sujet de la pièce, celle-ci en est le nœud; placez-la dans quelque acte que vous vouliez, elle sera toujours attachante. C'est la seule qui soit dans ce goût' (Voltaire 54, p.400-401). The first scene of *La Mort de César* also begins, strikingly, in *medias res* with Antoine's 'César, tu vas régner' summing up the dictator's desire to replace outmoded republican institutions by an effective monarchy, an ambition which provoked the conspiracy which was to culminate in his death. The subject-matter of the opening scene of *Pompée* is the ubiquitous *clémence/rigueur* debate. Ptolomée is advised to assassinate Pompée by Photin who takes the same line as that adopted by Antoine in *La Mort de César* (1.107-110):

> Le droit des rois consiste à ne rien épargner.
> La timide équité détruit l'art de régner.
> Quand on craint d'être injuste on a toujours à craindre,
> Et qui veut tout pouvoir doit oser tout enfreindre.

He is supported by Septime who adds another trait to Corneille's unfavourable portrait of César when he refers to his 'fausse clémence' (1.176). Achillas stresses the argument of expediency in speaking (in vain) against 'une extrême rigueur' (1.123).

In Voltaire's judgement the construction of *Pompée* was, according to the strictest standards of regularity, defective; it should have ended with the death of Ptolomée. 'Tout le reste', he says, 'n'est qu'une *superstructure* inutile à l'édifice' (Voltaire 54, p.448). Nevertheless, Voltaire is prepared to waive his critical requirements for 'cette scène de Cornélie, qui est un chef d'œuvre de génie' (p.447). Commenting on the scene, he says: 'Ce qui dans les règles sévères de la tragédie est un véritable défaut, devient ici une beauté frappante par les détails, par les beaux vers' (p.444). It is not unlikely that Voltaire had in mind the powerful appeal of the scene when he imitated Corneille's example by not ending his play with Caesar's death. Splendid though inessential superstructure that it was, his imitation of the masterpiece which Shakespeare had created in Antony's funeral oration had obviously been regarded from the outset as a fitting finale.

Voltaire was manifestly unhappy with the portrayal of Julius Caesar in *Pompée*. In his remarks on the play, he censures Corneille for having followed the contemporary fashion for *galanterie*; as he put it: 'César, qui trace des soupirs d'un style plaintif, n'est point César' (p.409). On the whole, the portrait of Caesar which emerges from his own play is a very favourable one. An important factor in Voltaire's decision to present his character in this light was a desire to redress the balance which had been unfairly weighted by Corneille in his over-flattering picture of Augustus in *Cinna*.[71] It is the ideal of balance which Voltaire is attempting to realise when he presents Brutus and César as both pitiable and reprehensible and when he tries to sustain in his audience a mixture of compassion and repugnance. He is critical of Corneille in his 'Remarques sur *Cinna*' because Cinna appears as the wholly admirable hero in the first act, only to be progressively revealed as a cowardly hypocrite who alienates the sympathies of the audience and directs them towards Auguste (Voltaire 54, p.135). Voltaire would seem to have had in mind this defect when he

---

[71] Voltaire will adopt a more direct approach to this task in *Le Triumvirat* (1763) and in the accompanying historical notes which systematically blacken Augustus's character.

portrays a César who does not deny the practical utility of clemency (1.287-296) but, at the same time, makes it clear to Antoine that it is not in his nature to be vindictive (1.312). In his treatment of the conspirators he tries to elicit the desired response of mingled sympathy and antipathy which, in his view, Corneille had failed to evoke. The correlation between the conspiracy against Auguste and that against his great-uncle Julius is brought out frequently in *Cinna*. Cinna excuses his pangs of conscience to Maxime by suggesting that Brutus had been plagued by scruples before committing the act of assassination (III.829-832). In the *Lettre de Balzac à Corneille*, used by Corneille in 1648 as a preface for the play, Emilie is presented as 'la rivale de Caton et de Brutus dans la passion de la liberté'. She recalls to her lover the glorious example set by Caesar's assassins (1.265-272). Both Cinna and Emilie resemble Voltaire's Brutus in being the victims of a struggle between *la voix du sang* and the claims of gratitude. Emilie's desire to avenge her father, Toranius, a victim of the proscriptions at the time of the Triumvirate, however, seems to Voltaire to constitute an illegitimate and wholly unrealistic recourse on Corneille's part to the call of the blood, since she has never seen her father and Auguste, her adoptive father, has treated her generously for thirty years. The contemporary view of Emilie as a model of nobility (expressed by Balzac in his letter) is rejected firmly by Voltaire: 'Alors cette furie n'est point du tout adorable; elle est réellement parricide' (Voltaire 54, p.135). His own Brutus will be placed in a more heart-rending (and plausible) dilemma by the sudden revelation of his relationship to César. He is told that filial feeling is not all by Cassius who sharply reminds him of the fact that he is the adoptive son of Caton and disciple of Pompée, but who is unable for all that to bring him to make the final thrust (III.80). Cinna's upbringing is similar to that of Brutus – he is the son of that same Cinna who had taken part in Caesar's murder and was, as he reminds himself, 'du sang de Pompée' (v.1546). Voltaire is scathing on the tardiness of Cinna's scruples about the projected murder of his benefactor (p.143). His Brutus, undaunted by distracting thoughts of gratitude, has been steadfast to his vow of tyrannicide right up to the moment that César is revealed as his father. Moreover, he addresses the dictator throughout the play with a dignity and forthrightness in direct contrast with the disingenuous praise of Augustus, which debases the character of Cinna in Voltaire's eyes. It would seem that Emilie represented a more congenial model for Brutus than did Cinna. The vigorous Cornelian verse in which she utters her sentiments of vengeance and hate must have impressed Voltaire. Whilst feeling that he did not want any women in his play (not even the gentle Portias or fearful Calpurnias of other Caesar plays, much less the formidable Emilie), he saw the analogy between her spirited vindication of republicanism and 'les sentiments d'un Brutus, d'un Cassius'. Nevertheless, he made his Brutus more tender-hearted than this Cornelian example of 'ces femmes qui font des leçons d'héroïsme aux hommes' (p.147). The parallel between Auguste and Emilie on the one hand and César and Brutus on the other is underlined by Auguste echoing the words of the dying Caesar when his adopted daughter is presented to him as one of the conspirators (v.1564): 'Et toi, ma fille, aussi!'

Just as Shakespeare's Brutus provided Voltaire with the speech which he gives to Cassius (*Mort de César*, III.275 ff), so the same process can be seen at work in the way Voltaire uses *Cinna*. The parallelism between Cinna and Brutus can be traced in the second scene of Voltaire's third act: Cinna's predicament – 'Des deux côtés j'offense et ma gloire et les Dieux: / Je deviens sacrilège, ou je suis parricide' (III.816-817) – is that of Brutus who feels bound to 'L'affreux serment' (III.101), that oath which he had felt, like Cinna, to be a source of honour and glory at the time it was made (see *Mort de César*, II.123-126, and *Cinna*, I.241-244). Cinna's soul-searching in the presence of Maxime is distinctly similar to Brutus's agonies of mind which Cassius makes strenuous efforts to dispel. His admiration for Auguste, however implausible in the light of his earlier fierce denunciations of his cruelty, is matched by Brutus's expression of a genuinely high regard for the man revealed as his father (III.iv). Besides this parallelism, however, one can sometimes detect echoes of Cinna's words in the lines which Voltaire gives to his César. I the opening scene of act 2 for example, Cinna argues the case for firm monarchical rule in terms which recall those used by César to impress upon his son the necessity of an authoritarian régime in a situation which was developing into anarchy (see *Cinna*, II.500-552, 570-590, and *La Mort de César*, III.181-190). Finally, Auguste's situation, occasioning the uneasiness expressed in his long monologue (IV.ii) and his rejection of Livie's advice (IV.iii), is paralleled in the opening scene of *La Mort de César*. The similarity between Auguste's state of mind and César's is underlined by Antoine's reference to his friend's 'longs soupirs' (I.11) and by his incredulous question 'César peut-il gémir, ou César peut-il craindre?' (I.14). The resolution of Auguste's doubts by the rejection (not definitive in the event) of Livie's counsels is neatly reversed by Voltaire in the conversation between César and Antoine (I.iv) in which the dictator, like Livie, opts for mild measures and rejects the stringency urged by his friend.

For all his mastery of the art of presenting political discussion on stage, Corneille, too often in Voltaire's view, allowed the emotional temperature to drop dangerously low. Even in the case of *Cinna*, which exemplified Corneille's gift of political dialogue at its best, Voltaire voiced reservations: 'je crois que les combats du cœur sont toujours plus intéressants que des raisonnements politiques, et ces contestations qui au fond sont souvent un jeu d'esprit assez froid. C'est au cœur qu'il faut parler dans une tragédie' (Voltaire 54, p.134). The 'chapitre des arts' of the *Essai sur les mœurs*[72] makes clear the effect that the competing influence of Racine had on his earlier work: mere emulation of Corneille is discarded ('qui ne ferait que bien imiter Corneille serait peu de chose', p.856) and heroic tragedy makes way for *tragédie larmoyante*: 'Il manquait à la perfection du théâtre un art au-dessus du sublime, celui de faire verser des larmes. Racine vint dans la décadence de Corneille et atteignit quelquefois à ce but de l'art' (p.855).

---

[72] *Essai*, ii.818-56.

'Admiration' had been the dramatic emotion *par excellence* up to the end of the first decade of the eighteenth century in England with Corneille's disciple, Dryden, leading the way. Thereafter it lost favour. The author of *Cato examin'd* (1713) was expressing the generally-held view when he judged it 'too cold a passion for tragical effects' (p.8). Voltaire discussing Homer in his *Essay on epick poetry* (which dates from roughly the same period as the genesis of *La Mort de César*), underlines the emotional inadequacy of admiration in the epic genre with arguments equally applicable to tragedy.[73] It was on such grounds that he frequently criticised Cornelian tragedy in his later life.[74] It had much to offer him for *La Mort de César* but little as far as pity and terror were concerned. For these essential elements of tragedy he would naturally have turned for inspiration to Racine, the practitioner of 'un art au-dessus du sublime'.

In the preface which he wrote to replace La Marre's 'Avertisse-ment', Voltaire refers confusingly to a play called *Jules César*, which he says had been written about thirty-five years earlier by 'un des plus beaux génies de France' in collaboration with a certain Mlle Barbier (see below, appendix II). It is damned for having represented Caesar and Brutus as 'amoureux et jaloux'. The unnamed author to whom Voltaire attributes the lion's share

---

[73] Florence D. White, *Voltaire's Essay on epic poetry, a study and an edition* (New York 1915): 'Thus the Reader's Imagination is often fill'd with great and noble Ideas, while the Affections of the Soul stagnate; and if in any long Work whatever, the Motions of the Heart do not keep pace with the Pleasures of the Fancy, 'tis no Wonder if we may at once admire and be tir'd' (p.92). T. W. Russell in his *Voltaire, Dryden and heroic tragedy* (New York 1946) tends to exaggerate the influence of Corneille and Dryden as well as the extent of Voltaire's attachment to admiration.

[74] 'Quand l'admiration se joint à la pitié et à la terreur, l'art est poussé alors au plus haut point où l'esprit puisse atteindre. L'admiration seule passe trop vite' (Voltaire 54, p.440). 'Quiconque ne veut qu'exciter l'admiration peut faire dire, "voilà qui est beau!"; mais il ne fera point verser des larmes' ('Art dramatique', *Questions sur l'Encyclopédie*). 'Il a élevé l'âme quelquefois, il a excité l'admiration; il a presque toujours négligé les deux grands pivots du tragique, la terreur et la pitié' (Voltaire 54, p.474).

of the work in the composition of the tragedy is Fontenelle, Beuchot suggests, but the play (included in Fontenelle's collected works) is *Brutus*, first performed in 1699 though written a decade earlier. The putative co-author is Mlle Bernard and the eponymous hero is the Lucius Junius Brutus of Voltaire's earlier play, not the Marcus Brutus of his *Mort de César*. The work entitled *La Mort de César* which was published in 1710 under the name of Mlle Barbier[75] would seem to have no connection with Fontenelle. Part of the confusion surrounding the play and its authorship may stem from the fact that Fontenelle's involvement with the play is indicated in the official *approbation* which appears under his signature at the end. Despite Voltaire's slighting and inaccurate reference to it, the most recent of French dramatic treatments of Caesar's death to appear before his own play might have given him food for thought.

Although in her dedication to d'Argenson, Mlle Barbier says she is sharing his sympathies in representing the greatness of Caesar and the base treachery of Brutus, she tries to defend herself in her preface to the play against the charge that she has made the assassin a figure of greater stature than his victim. On the face of it, Voltaire would have been repelled by her portrayal of a hag-ridden indecisive husband, bemoaning his fate; a man consumed by ambition, yet trying to gain his ends by the ludicrous expedient of turning himself into a one-man matrimonial agency to pair Brutus with Octavie and Porcie with Antoine. Yet, if we ignore these traits which make the characterisation often border on caricature, some of the basic situations of the play are not dissimilar to those presented by Voltaire. His opening scene, with Antoine's excited anticipation of his friend's elevation to kingship and César's response muted by his consuming preoccupation with his personal relationship to Brutus, can be matched by the third scene of Mlle Barbier's first act. The paternalistic standpoint of Voltaire's César in his dialogue with Antoine on the art of

[75] The copy consulted is Bn Yf. 8162.

government (I.iv) is that of Mlle Barbier's benevolent despot in his confrontation with Brutus (III.v, p.34):

> Je n'aspire, Brutus qu'à régner sur les cœurs, [...]
> Prévenez le sénat, et faites-lui connaître
> Que César en ces lieux est plus père que maître.

The central relationship upon which the plot of Voltaire's play hinges, that of Brutus and his father, is also in Mlle Barbier's play the crucial factor in the hesitations of Brutus over the projected act of tyrannicide after he has been honoured (in his own eyes) with 'le tendre nom de fils', through Caesar's plan to thrust Octavia upon him as a spouse. Mlle Barbier makes the most of this new status as can be seen in Brutus's self-questioning (v.i, p.58):

> Du nom de fils sa bouche a daigné m'appeler;
> Et je pourrais encore, inhumain et perfide,
> Sous ce beau nom de fils cacher un parricide!
> Ah! que plutôt cent fois ma main, ma propre main,
> Si Rome veut du sang, en cherche dans mon sein.

Voltaire would certainly have found this aspect of her play suggestive and, at the same time, inadequate. A marriage-bond by his criterion made parricide a prospect only *à demi terrible*. An altogether more awesome transgression of natural morality faced Voltaire's Brutus.

'Il n'y a peut-être jamais eu de réputation plus usurpée que celle de Saint-Evremond'. The occasion for Voltaire's unfavourable judgement was Saint-Evremond's misplaced admiration for some bad verses of Corneille, and, what was far more heinous, the faintness of his praise for the glorious Racine (Voltaire 55, p.901). Voltaire's *protégé*, Linant, echoes his master's adverse comments: 'Tout le monde convient que Saint-Evremond n'est pas poète, que ses comédies sont indignes même d'un homme médiocre, que sa prose est pleine de longueurs et d'affectations' (D656). In the preface to *La Mort de César*, one of Saint-Evremond's comedies is singled out for special attention: *Sir Politick Would-be*, 'comédie à la manière des Anglais', is dismissed as 'ni dans le goût des Anglais, ni dans celui d'aucune autre nation'. Voltaire's strictures are coloured by his awareness of the threat posed by Saint-Evremond to his own claim to primacy as an intermediary of English ideas in France. To be set against them is the modicum of praise which he was prepared, when in more indulgent mood, to bestow upon Saint-Evremond who was denied genius but credited with 'beaucoup d'esprit et de goût' (M.xxiv.218). His various judgements would in any case seem to be based on a close enough acquaintance with Saint-Evremond's works to justify comparison between certain aspects of *La Mort de César* and some of the ideas expressed in works which appeared in the same collection as the maligned *Sir Politick Would-be*.[76]

Saint-Evremond's view of Roman history is as urbane and tolerant as his general view of life. The hedonistic attitude of the seventeenth-century *libertin* anticipated the enlightened epicurean-ism of the *sociétaire du Temple*; it is not surprising therefore to find a parallelism between Saint-Evremond's presentation of certain aspects of the life and thought of classical Rome and Voltaire's treatment of these same aspects in *La Mort de César*. Saint-Evremond's analysis of the evolution of the Roman republic in his *Réflexions sur les divers génies du peuple romain dans les divers temps de la République* is essentially Voltairean in spirit. It seeks to dispel the myth of a golden age of Rome which had been largely created by the ancestor-worship of posterity and consistently upholds the values of progress and civilisation, of refinement and sophistica-tion in opposition to the nostalgic attachment to the heroic barbarities of a more primitive era. This view is forcibly expressed in the final paragraph of the second chapter:

cette aspreté de naturel qui ne se rendoit jamais aux difficultez, établissoit Rome plus fortement que n'auroient fait des humeurs douces avec plus de lumiere et de raison. Neantmoins à dire vray, cette qualité considerée

---

[76] Besides a later (1740) edition of Saint-Evremond's works (BV, no.3061), Voltaire possessed the 1689 edition of the *Œuvres meslées* (BV, no.3062).

en elle-mesme, estoit bien sauvage, et ne merite de respect que pour avoir donné commencement à la plus grande puissance de l'Univers.[77]

Saint-Evremond traces the development of this primitive mentality with little sympathy: 'Dans les commencemens de la Republique, le Peuple Romain avoit quelque chose de farouche; cette humeur farouche se tourna depuis en austerité; et de cette austerité, il se fit ensuite une vertue severe, éloignée de la politesse et de l'agrément, mais ennemie de la moindre apparence de corruption' (p.249-50). Clearly, he has little time for 'la vertu héroïque', the passion for justice, the self-abnegation and utter devotion to the common weal and to the ideal of liberty, when these qualities resulted in the dehumanisation of the heroes who manifested them: 'Dans les premiers temps de la Republique, on estoit furieux de liberté, si on le peut dire, et de bien public; l'amour de la patrie nc laissoit rien aux mouvemens de la nature. Le zele du citoyen déroboit l'homme à luy mesme' (p.231). Lucius Junius Brutus, the revered ancestor of the leader of the conspiracy against Caesar, may, suggests Saint-Evremond, have been driven to kill his sons 'par la dureté d'une humeur farouche et dénaturée' under the guise of 'une vertu heroïque' (p.228). Whereas his action could to some extent be condoned, or at least understood, in the context of a society still in a fairly rudimentary state of evolution, that of his descendant was less easily excusable since it ran counter to 'le génie du temps'. In Saint-Evremond's eyes Caesar's assassin is an ignoble anachronism, whilst the illustrious leader he kills is in tune with his time: 'on peut dire veritablement que les bons Citoyens estoient chez les vieux Romains, et chez les derniers les bons Capitaines' (p.238). In his historical analysis of the Roman state, Saint-Evremond traces the decline of public spirit and the growth of 'l'esprit particulier', the emergence of the ideal of personal loyalty with the concomitant erosion of civic consciousness. In the light of this evolution Brutus appears as a criminal

[77] Saint-Evremond, *Œuvres en prose*, ed. R. Ternois (Paris 1962-1969), ii.234 (hereafter Ternois).

in terms of human decency and elementary personal obligation but a hero in the eyes of those for whom political liberty is the *summum bonum*. Caesar's assassination can be seen from two angles: 'Crime horrible à l'égard des reconnaissans; vertu admirable à l'égard des partisans de la liberté' (*Sur les ingrats*, Ternois, iv.94).

Caesar's greatness is never in question in Saint-Evremond's discussion of his place in Roman history. He is categorical on the point: 'par la beauté d'un génie universel, Cesar fut le premier des Romains en toutes choses [...] l'on n'a gueres veu dans personne tant d'égalité dans la vie, tant de modération dans la fortune, tant de clémence dans les injures' (*Sur Alexandre et César*, Ternois, i.224, 226). It is clear that Saint-Evremond saw in Caesar a kindred spirit. He makes much of the fact that he was an epicurean, and adds important and revelatory qualifications to this philosophical tag, pointing out that the Roman leader was no academic recluse; he belonged not to the group of esoteric epicurean philosophers, but rather to the more worldly group of epicureans 'qui ne pouvans approuver l'austérité des Philosophes trop rigoureux, se laissoient aller seulement à des opinions plus naturelles'. He goes on: 'De ces derniers ont été la pluspart des honnêtes gens de ce temps-là, qui sçavoient separer la personne du Magistrat, et donner leurs soings à la Republique en telle sorte, qu'il leur en restoit et pour leurs amis et pour eux mêmes' (*Jugement sur les sciences où peut s'appliquer un honneste homme*, Ternois, ii.14). Epicureanism accorded well with Caesar's temperamental fatalism vis-à-vis the human condition and his own personal lot. Above all, however, in opting for Epicurus he was choosing the party of humanity: 'Dans la Philosophie d'Epicure, qu'il prefera à toutes les autres, il s'attacha principalement à ce qui regarde l'homme' (*Sur Alexandre et César*, Ternois, i.205).

As a stoic, Cato the Younger insisted upon the necessity of inflexible probity. Caesar, in contrast, as a political realist, accepted the fact of human corruptibility and decided to turn it to account for the good of all including himself. A passage in Saint-Evremond's *Les Sentiments d'un honnête et habile courtisan sur cette vertu rigide et ce sale intérêt* condemns Cato's approach: 'Une probité moins entiere, qui se fust accommodée aux vices de quelques particuliers, eut empesché l'oppression generale; il faloit souffrir la puissance, pour éviter la tyrannie, et par là on eust conservé la Republique, à la vérité corrompuë, mais toujours Republique'.

The polarity which one can discern in Saint-Evremond's reflections on the Roman republic: the contrast between an inhuman stoicism personified in Brutus's mentor Cato and a more humane and accommodating epicureanism of which Caesar is the paragon; the opposition of *Realpolitik* to the politics of nostalgia, of human relations to civic duty, of nature to culture, of the call of one's country to *la voix du sang* is also present in *La Mort de César* and will be discussed later.

The balance is weighted heavily in favour of Caesar and against Brutus by Saint-Evremond. A corrective can be found in the view of Saint-Evremond's contemporary, Pierre Bayle, whose article on Brutus in his *Dictionnaire* clearly reveals an admiration for Caesar's assassin, which is tempered only slightly by the admission that his action in assassinating his benefactor was not only morally reprehensible but also quixotic in its faulty appraisal of political realities. Voltaire's high regard for Bayle (seen in the multiform imprint of the seventeenth-century scholar's work upon his own)[78] would have led him to pay close attention to his treatment of Caesar's assassination. Superficially, Voltaire's presentation of a Caesar tragically flawed by ambition accords with Bayle's, but the tone of censure which Bayle adopts in speaking of Caesar, and the complete absence of compassion in the reference he makes to his death ('Celui qu'il [Brutus] fit mourir, je l'avoue, méritait la mort: cent mille vies, s'il les avait eues, n'auraient pas suffi à l'expiation de son crime', note E) shows that his attitude is far removed from that of Voltaire. His view of Brutus is also very different from Voltaire's in *La Mort de César*. For Bayle, he is 'le plus grand Républicain que l'on vit jamais'.

---

[78] See H. T. Mason, *Pierre Bayle and Voltaire* (Oxford 1963).

'Il était coiffé', we are told, 'de ces grandes et nobles idées de liberté, et d'amour de la patrie, que les auteurs grecs et romains ont décrites si pompeusement'. His disinterestedness in leading the conspiracy was put beyond question even by his enemies; Bayle follows Plutarch (as does Shakespeare, *Julius Caesar*, v.v.68-75) in citing Antony who singles out Brutus from all those who had taken part in the assassination as 'le seul des conjurés qui eût été dirigé par la beauté apparente de cette action' (note M). Voltaire recognises the loftiness of Brutus's ideals in his play, but also presents him as 'presque fanatique' (D1034), a note which he certainly did not find in Bayle. The qualifying adverb is justified in *La Mort de César* by qualities which establish an affinity between Brutus and the man he had vowed to kill, not the qualities which make him the staunchest of patriots and earn him Bayle's admiration. Bayle only mentions Brutus's philosophical views as an indication of his general culture: 'Il suivit la secte des Stoïciens: il aimait les livres et en faisait'. There is no hint from him of the pejorative associations which surround Brutus's stoicism in both Saint-Evremond's works and Voltaire's play. In *La Mort de César* it is Antoine who is most outspoken in criticism of the stoic position and who exemplifies the values of personal loyalty and friendship which are shown to be inconsonant with that position. He is shown as having some unpleasant traits of character, but one would never guess from this play that Voltaire actually subscribed largely to Bayle's view of Antony as 'le plus scélérat de tous les hommes' (note D). Voltaire is quite clearly in accord with Bayle, however, in his view of the tragic folly of the assassination, which by eliminating the dictator simply initiated a struggle for power which would inevitably result in the emergence of some other form of autocracy. Bayle stresses that Rome had for a long time before Caesar's death been a republic in name only and that the expansion of a city state into an empire of colossal proportions had made the possibility of a real republican regime an idle and dangerous dream. Voltaire's César puts this same view forcibly to Brutus in his final interview with him (III.iv.181-190).

Voltaire's low opinion of contemporary English historians is based on the polemical character of what he had read of their writings: 'en Angleterre on a des factums et point d'histoire' (*Lettres philosophiques*, XXII). He would doubtless have found their treatment of Roman history as flawed as their approach to the history of their own country in this respect. Among the works of English historians, Laurence Echard's *Roman history* (1695) certainly attracted his attention. This work is to be found in his library in the six-volume translation of 1728 by Larroque and Desfontaines alongside the new, corrected edition which appeared in 1737 (BV, no.1200, 1201). Echard's favourable presentation of Julius Caesar ('a man of the greatest soul, the most magnanimous spirit, and of the most wonderful accomplishments and abilities that Rome, or perhaps the world, ever saw', 1695 edition, iii.361) accords with that of Voltaire. The author of *La Mort de César*, however, manifestly refrains from going as far as Echard in one aspect of Caesar's characterisation, that of 'setting aside his ambition, which was the fault of the times as well as his temper'.

An even more ardent contributor to the rehabilitation of Caesar's reputation, and one with whose opinions Voltaire would very probably have been acquainted, was a protégé of Buckingham's, John Dennis. As a literary critic, Dennis would have appealed to Voltaire since his enthusiasm for Shakespeare was tempered with a due regard for neoclassical canons of taste. In his *Essay on the genius and writings of Shakespear* (1712), he deplores that in *Julius Caesar* the audience should have been offered a Caesar who is 'a Fourth-rate Actor in his own Tragedy' and resents the one-sided dialogue between Brutus and Cassius (I.ii), in which the latter is allowed to blacken Caesar's character. He proceeds, in no uncertain fashion, to redress the balance and weighs in heavily with a sustained eulogy of his hero:

For when Cassius tells Brutus that Caesar was but a Man like them, and had the same natural Imperfections which they had, how natural had it been for Brutus to reply, that Caesar indeed had their Imperfections of Nature, but neither he nor Cassius had by any means the great Qualities of Caesar: neither his Military Virtue, nor Science, nor his

69

matchless Renown, nor his unparallell'd Victories, his unwearied Bounty to his Friends, nor his Godlike Clemency to his Foes, his Beneficence, his Munificence nor his Easiness of Access to the meanest Roman, his indefatigable Labours, his incredible Celerity, the Plausibleness if not Justness of his Ambition, that knowing himself to be the greatest of Men, he only sought occasion to make the World confess him such.[79]

Voltaire's own contribution to enhancing the posthumous reputation of Julius Caesar, solid though it is, is clearly not characterised by the same degree of personal involvement and strenuous advocacy as is suggested here and in Dennis's later pamphlet *Julius Caesar acquitted*. Of the other works of John Dennis, his *Remarks upon Cato* (1713) and *Letters upon the sentiments of the two first acts of Cato* (1721) deserve some consideration as having a certain relevance to *La Mort de César*, and, possibly, as providing some hints for Voltaire when he wrote his play. In *La Mort de César* Brutus continually invokes the authority and inspiration of Cato the Younger, an inflexible stoic, stubborn patriot and ardent republican right up to his self-inflicted death. Dennis in the *Letters* debunks Cato, his philosophy, his political views and his conduct in a way echoed in Voltaire's play in both Brutus's attachment to the stance of rigid traditionalism and his condemnation of the obstinate pride which led to Cato's useless gesture of suicide (II.127-132). He dismisses as 'a wretched affectation and a miserable inconsistency' in his *Remarks*, Cato's dry-eyed reaction to the news of his son's death and his weeping for the calamities of his country. In the remarks which follow (Hooker, ii.67), he stands up for 'Nature and Instinct' against 'Reason and Duty', and criticises stoicism for its suppression of the passions natural to all mankind. Voltaire shared Dennis's doubts about the suitability of an utterly dedicated stoic as a hero for a tragedy. He showed that he approved his contention that 'Nature requires a Flood of Tears and the most moving Tenderness' when he decided to mitigate Brutus's stoicism by making him succumb to 'nature and instinct' in his agonising attempts to save his father.

[79] John Dennis, *The Critical works*, ed. E. N. Hooker (Baltimore 1943), ii.10.

3. Themes

In *La Mort de César* certain themes are clearly articulated through the use of the conventional dramatic apparatus of plot, character and situation. These themes appear as binary oppositions – nature / culture, mercy / justice, moderation / extremism, pragmatism / doctrinairism – and underline the central element of conflict in the play. When judged by Voltaire's own prime criterion of emotional impact, the second of his 'Roman' plays marks an advance upon his first, in so far as the conflict between Lucius Junius Brutus's duty to the republic and his fatherly feelings is minimal compared with the tragic dilemma of the later Brutus torn between filial feelings and his strong sense of civic responsibility. Brutus, son of César, responding instinctively to his father's love and affection, is repelled by the prospect of parricide but remains attached to the tenets of his father-in-law and philosophical mentor, Cato, which justify tyrannicide. His decision to abandon his earlier resolve to strike the first blow and his quasi-symbolic participation in his father's murder[80] reflect Voltaire's increasing attachment to the value of compassion and his aprioristic belief in the instinctual basis of all morality:

la nature seule nous inspire des idées utiles qui précèdent toutes nos réflexions. Il en est de même dans la morale. Nous avons tous deux sentiments qui sont le fondement de la société, la commisération et la justice. (Voltaire 59, p.113-14)

These two fundamental elements of mankind's affective nature figure prominently in *La Mort de César*. They tend to contradict rather than complement each other, however, and more often than not the dramatically fruitful contrast between justice and mercy is exploited. Voltaire was aware of the advantage in purely

---

[80] Cassius's statement to the crowd after the murder (III.298*v*): 'Brutus vous a vengés' appears in 36P. It was eliminated in later editions and Brutus was saved from appearing as a monster.

dramatic terms of a *dénouement à l'anglaise* which would strike terror into the hearts of an audience. In making Brutus less ferocious after César's revelation of their blood relationship, however, he shows his concern, evident in other works of the period, to present the milder aspects of human nature in a favourable light and to 'prendre le parti de l'humanité'.

Although Cato the Younger does not figure among the *dramatis personae*, he represents one of the animating forces of the drama through the inspiration he gives the conspirators. What Cato stood for pre-eminently was justice. As Lucan (*Civil war*, II.389) saw him he was 'Iustitiae cultor, rigidi servator honesti'; Virgil represented him as the stern but noble law-giver in the lower world; Voltaire was to refer to him later (in *Le Philosophe ignorant*, ch.45) as 'l'éternel honneur de Rome' and, in a long note at the beginning of the first scene of act 3 of *Le Triumvirat*, he is at pains to eulogise this 'héros de Rome' whose rigorous execution of justice was but a facet of the intransigence which manifested itself in his stubborn defence of 'la cause divine de la liberté'. In *La Mort de César* the emphasis is quite different: Cato's inflexibility of character is presented as less than admirable and even more baleful in the form in which it has been transmitted to Brutus. Compared with his son-in-law, Cato was 'moins altier, moins dur, et moins à craindre' (I.141), Antoine suggests. The truth of this judgement is borne out by the determined example set the conspirators by their leader (II.171-174):

> Dans une heure au sénat le tyran doit se rendre:
> Là, je le punirai; là, je le veux surprendre;
> Là, je veux que ce fer, enfoncé dans son sein,
> Venge Caton, Pompée, et le peuple romain.

For Brutus and his colleagues justice means vengeance. However, it is not private revenge (what Bacon in the fourth of his *Essays* called 'a kind of wild justice') but public retribution which is in question. The conspirators see themselves as a band of avengers of public wrongs, selfless instruments of the principle of justice – as enshrined in the laws of the Roman state – which requires that a dictator who has violated this principle should be slain. This conception of vengeance is never far from their minds, and the words to express it are ever on their lips. Brutus addresses them as 'vengeurs de la patrie' (II.195), and 'venger la patrie' (II.160) is understood by him to be the main aim of their enterprise. The same thought is expressed in the same form by Cimber (II.153), by Cassius (III.6) and again by Brutus (II.166) when urging that Cicero should be excluded from the conspiracy. The patriotism of the conspirators is not just an emotional attachment to the physical realities of the Rome which they had known and loved from birth. It is, rather, a strong sense of public virtue, the virtue which Montesquieu believed to be the principle (or animating spirit) of a republic and which he defined as 'l'amour des lois et de la patrie'. It is Cassius who most often urges that César be punished for his crime of trampling underfoot the legal structure of the Roman republic. Bemoaning 'les débris des lois' (II.50) and the debasement of political life he sees around him, he represents himself as a servant of the laws (III.292), an upholder of the rights of the people (III.295) and a restorer of justice and the traditional way of life of the republic (III.300). The intimate connection between politics and religion in ancient Rome is reflected in Cassius's determination to bring back 'les dieux exilés' (III.300; see also III.135-136).[81] When Brutus tries to avert César's impending death by appealing to him to respect the laws of the republic 'au nom des dieux dans ton cœur oubliés' (III.212), he is appealing as he had earlier (II.226) to the vestigial attachment of the self-confessed 'citoyen manqué' to a way of life that characterised an earlier phase of the republic. In the eyes of the conspirators, the spirit of the laws was the spirit of liberty and whoever sinned against it deserved to die (II.64, 67; III.272).

---

[81] Montesquieu in his *Dissertation sur la politique des Romains dans la religion* (1716 but not published until 1799) presents the idea of religion as a mere support for the political structure of the state. The final paragraph refers to 'Les Romains, qui n'avaient proprement d'autre divinité que le génie de la république'.

The ideals – *patrie, liberté, lois, dieux, honneur, devoir* – upon which the conspirators base their claim to exact public retribution are later invoked by Antoine to serve the end of private revenge. Vengeance is the clarion-call which sounds throughout his funeral-oration (III.393, 404, 408). This punitive ardour recalls the orator's earlier dialogue with César in which he urged the efficacy of harshness in matters of government. In this confrontation of attitudes, César had argued in favour of a more compassionate style of ruling: this opposition between vengefulness and forgiveness, between justice and mercy can be seen throughout the play. César has his own conception of justice. Far from being abstract and doctrinaire, it is, as is appropriate to a man of feeling, based on his sense of the natural obligations which arise from human relations. It is seigneurial in character, centred upon the personal bond which should exist between a lord and those who owe their lives to him. He says of the senators: 'Ils sont nés mes égaux; mes armes les vainquirent' (I.278). He addresses them as: 'Vous qui m'appartenez par le droit de l'épée' (I.229). The yoke which he imposes is so gentle as barely to deserve the name, yet Brutus and his colleagues chafe under it. César's son reproaches his father with the insidious appeal of his system of repressive tolerance: 'Ton pouvoir, tes vertus, qui font tes injustices, / [...] Ta funeste bonté, qui fait aimer tes fers' (II.231, 233). Voltaire, one feels, sympathises with Brutus's love of liberty, but nevertheless presents César's paternalism as a practical system of government which was the more commendable since it stemmed from the real goodness and compassion in his character.[82] César is aware that he is a despot but justifies himself on the grounds that he is a benevolent one. The persuasive lines in which he compares his enlightened rule with that of Pompey and Sulla (II.237-241; I.116-118; I.282-286) do not convince the recalcitrant senators. These lines should, however, have hinted to those contemporaries of Voltaire who criticised his play as seditious that he was not wholly

---

[82] See the balanced view of G. Defaux, 'L'idéal politique de Voltaire dans *La Mort de César*', *Revue de l'Université d'Ottawa* 40 (1970), p.418-40.

sympathetic to the misplaced idealism of the conspirators and
their rigid conception of retributive justice. His César does not
exclude vengeance entirely from his plans; but he appears, above
all, as the 'vengeur des Romains' and 'vainqueur de la terre' (II.76)
in relation to those outside the walls of Rome. Within them, 'ce
dieu vengeur', as Antoine describes him (III.375), speaks only the
language of peace (I.312-314):[83]

> Je sais combattre, vaincre, et ne sais point punir.
> Allons, et n'écoutant ni soupçon ni vengeance,
> Sur l'univers soumis régnons sans violence.

A tender-hearted César, craving for affection ('Je veux me faire
aimer de Rome et de mon fils'; I.148), is contrasted with opponents
whose attachment to duty is barbaric in its denial of natural
feelings. César's good nature and the actions which reveal it are
emphasised heavily throughout the play. The words *bonté* (or
bontés)[84] and *clémence*[85] recur frequently. There is no lack of more
general terms to indicate the emotional side of César's nature, his
humanity and capacity for love and friendship.[86] The coldly
cerebral approach of those struggling to save a legal constitution
from ruin stands out in sharp contrast with César's admission
that, though he has lost the right to claim the title of 'citoyen',
he is still proud to own those of 'homme et père' (I.107). He
longs to hear Brutus address him by the 'tendre nom de père'
(II.271) and to feel his love reciprocated. Brutus, when suddenly
confronted by the realisation that he is the son of César, shows
himself as much a man of feeling as his father. In their final
meeting it is he who, overcome by frantic concern for his father's

[83] See I.236; III.346.

[84] See I.61, 207, 235, 264, 268, 272, 300; II.3; III.151, 201.

[85] See I.149, 205, 233, 289, 301; III.345. The same idea is expressed often in
other words: see I.312; III.176, 341, 344.

[86] See I.59; III.141 *et passim*. R. D. Cottrell comments upon César's use of 'the
traditional language of erotic affection' ('Ulcerated hearts: love in Voltaire's
Mort de César', *Literature and history in the age of ideas*, ed. C. Williams, Columbus
1975, p.171).

safety, shows his deeply emotional attachment to César. The
bond between father and son thus demonstrated in action carries
more weight than Cassius's scornful reference to it as an illusion
'Qu'un préjugé vulgaire impute à la nature' (III.70).

In his funeral oration over César's body Antoine refers to the
dead dictator as 'Ce père, cet ami, qui vous était si cher' (III.372).
There is some justification for the reference to 'ce père' insofar
as the plebs looked upon Caesar as a *pater patriae* and would not
have been offended as much as the patrician senators by his
paternalistic style of government. The use of the word 'ami'
however is inevitably tainted by association with Antoine's de-
magogy and is less appropriate. Elsewhere in his oration Antoine
emphasises the real bond of love and friendship which united him
with César and he surrounds the severing of this bond with an
aura of pathos born of true feeling. Yet his love for César, he
realises, is a card which he can play to his own advantage. As
soon as he appears, one of the crowd says: 'Il aimait trop César';
Antoine follows this remark with: 'Oui, je l'aimais, Romains'
(III.311) and proceeds to make this the key-note of his speech.
Amitié was the first word that César had uttered in the opening
dialogue between Antoine and himself (I.16); by the end of the
play it has become a leitmotiv.[87]

Antoine's role in the play is ambivalent. On the one hand he
openly advocates the rule of fear (like the conspirators he is a
self-appointed instrument of public vengeance), on the other he
stands for certain values to which Voltaire is obviously attached.
It is he who charges the conspirators with allowing their lofty
dedication to public virtue to blind them to the normal, natural
feelings of humanity. The contradiction between his transparently
honest profession of friendship and warmth of feeling ('Je suis
ami, Brutus, et porte un cœur humain'; II.14) and his commitment

---

[87] *Amicitia*, it should be noted, was a political catchword which connoted
(besides 'friendship') the relationship, based upon mutual interest and services,
between the members of a political faction – a system with which Voltaire as a
visitor to England under the Walpole regime would have been familiar.

to objectives like political repression and civil war is blatant and remains unresolved. Yet in the confrontation between Brutus and Antoine in the first scene of the second act, there is no doubt as to which way Voltaire weights the balance in his presentation of their irreconcilable attitudes. The fanaticism of Brutus is unalloyed before he receives the crucial revelation of the circumstances of his birth; in portraying him as son-in-law and disciple of Cato (rather than as son of César), Voltaire uses the darkest colours. However good-hearted he is by nature, his upbringing is shown to have made him wrong-headed in his approach to life. He suffers from a serious deficiency of what Voltaire called in the 'Discours préliminaire' to *Alzire* (a play roughly contemporaneous with *La Mort de César*) 'cette humanité qui doit être le premier caractère d'un être pensant'. More than once in his *Julius Caesar* Shakespeare used the image of a stag being torn to pieces by a pack of hounds to suggest the level of animality to which the assassins descended in killing Caesar. Voltaire, without attempting to imitate Shakespeare's image-laden style, manages to suggest that the concept of rough-handed justice to which Brutus and his fellow-conspirators subscribe make them akin to the brute creation. 'Farouche' is the word which recurs most frequently to describe Brutus (1.76, 129; 11.220, 251; 111.147); others like 'sauvage' (1.154), 'cruel' (1.304; 11.277; 111.117), 'barbare' (11.16; 11.275) and 'férocité' (11.2) are redolent of a primitive stage of social evolution – the 'nature red in tooth and claw' that César himself suggests when he refers to his son as 'un tigre' (11.275).

The obsessive concern with 'vertu', with the duty which subordinates the claim of 'l'homme' to those of 'le citoyen', is summed up by Brutus when he says (111.131-132):

> Toujours indépendant, et toujours citoyen,
> Mon devoir me suffit, tout le reste n'est rien.

Brutus's inhuman devotion to duty raises the question of his philosophy. Voltaire presents him unambiguously as a stoic and voices his own criticism of stoicism through Antoine and César. Although these two characters are never overtly presented as

77

epicureans, their attitude towards stoicism and their profession of ideals at variance with those of Brutus and Cassius provide a counterweight to the body of ideas to which the conspirators subscribe. Antoine castigates (I.131-133):

> Cette secte intraitable, et qui fait vanité
> D'endurcir les esprits contre l'humanité,
> Qui dompte et foule aux pieds la nature irritée.

He and César, he claims, are men of feeling and as such are repelled by the stoics, 'ces cœurs de bronze' (I.136), whose exaggeratedly high sense of duty puts them beyond the reach of the emotions of average humanity. The equation between the more rebarbative aspects of stoicism and religious fanaticism is at all times implicit in Voltaire's play.[88]

Throughout the period of his residence at Cirey with Mme Du Châtelet, Voltaire's view of the world is predominantly optimistic. There is a noticeable epicurean strain in his thinking. As he wrote to Frederick of Prussia on 20 May 1738 (D1506): 'Je souffre très patiemment; et quoique les douleurs soient quelquefois longues et aiguës, je suis très éloigné de me croire malheureux. Ce n'est pas que je sois stoïcien, au contraire, c'est parce que je suis très épicurien, parce que je crois la douleur un mal et le plaisir un bien, et que, tout bien compté et bien pesé, je trouve infiniment plus de douceurs que d'amertumes dans cette vie.'[89] The sort of

---

[88] See Stephen Werner, 'Voltaire and Seneca', *Studies* 67 (1969), p.42. Voltaire 'associated early Stoicism (that of Zeno for example) with Jansenism and the extravagant rigours a *philosophe* would despise'.

[89] The more rigorous forms of stoicism come under attack in the *Discours en vers sur l'homme* (1738). See the fifth *Discours* ('Sur la nature du plaisir'), 87-90:

> Voilà votre portrait, stoïques abusés,
> Vous voulez changer l'homme, et vous le détruisez.
> Usez, n'abusez point; le sage ainsi l'ordonne.
> Je fuis également Epictète et Pétrone.

Later, in the seventh *Discours* ('Sur la vraie vertu'), 11-15, Brutus's profession of disillusionment with virtue as a moral ideal is immediately followed by criticism of Zeno's equation of virtue and insensibility. See the article 'Vertu', *Questions sur l'Encyclopédie* (1770): 'Tu avais raison, Brutus, si tu mettais la vertu à être chef de parti et l'assassin de ton bienfaiteur, de ton père Jules César: mais

genial eclecticism espoused by Voltaire ('je n'adopte des stoïques que les principes qui laissent l'âme sensible aux douceurs de l'amitié, et qui avouent que la douleur est un mal'; D6522) is reminiscent of Cicero's philosophical position. In Voltaire's later 'Roman' plays Cicero is treated with respect and admiration. In *Rome sauvée* (1750) he is praised for his virtue and emerges from a comparison with Caesar as a worthy, if not a great man. His eloquence and skill as an orator earn him high praise in *Le Triumvirat* (1764; III.ii.note). Brutus's unflattering portrait of him in *La Mort de César* (II.163-168) is nevertheless endorsed to some extent by Voltaire's own description of him as an 'illustre bavard' (D1006). Listening to Mme Du Châtelet reading aloud from Cicero however (see D1012) was a great consolation to the invalid when confined to his sick-bed. Intellectual affinity of this sort is the dominant element in the stoic conception of friendship. The friendship of 'la divine Emilie' inspired in Voltaire something more: a warmth of feeling clearly more akin to epicureanism which taught that 'of all things that contribute to happiness, the greatest is Affection'.[90] The epicureans' more humane outlook colours the important theme of friendship in *La Mort de César*. Unlike Shakespeare's Caesar who, according to one critic, is portrayed 'as a kind of god-like block, a marble monster', 'the incarnation of Stoic man',[91] Voltaire's appears as an all too human mixture of good and bad ('à la fois la gloire et le fléau de Rome'; III.158) attracted to the more indulgent epicurean view of man's nature. His creator's sympathies are made clear in his judgement on the historical Caesar: 'Je l'admire plus que Caton, / Car il est tendre et magnanime' (to Frederick of Prussia, 15 June 1743; D2771).

In this particular context, Henri IV and several of the lesser

---

si tu avais fait consister la vertu à ne rien faire que du bien à ceux qui dépendaient de toi, tu ne l'aurais pas appelé fantôme, et tu ne te serais pas tué de désespoir' (M.xx.571-72).

[90] See G. Murray, *Five stages of Greek religion* (London 1946), p.104.

[91] John Anson, 'Caesar's stoic pride', in *Julius Caesar: a casebook*, ed. Ure, p.218.

characters of the *Henriade* may be seen as prefigurations of later tragic heroes used by Voltaire as vehicles for his continuing inquiry into the nature of human greatness and his search for an ideal of humanity.[92] Henri himself, 'ce héros magnanime' (IV.280), foreshadows César in his forgiving nature: he belongs, like him, to the noble breed of 'âmes sensibles'. It is in his compassion, rather than in his justice, that Henri is presented as the image of God on earth (X.382). His capacity for tearful manifestations of pity is frequently in evidence.[93] When he is told by Saint Louis that he is going to be rewarded for his clemency, he falls to his knees, sobbing and sighing (VI.348), in much the same way as Brutus does before César in their last meeting, except that Henri's tears are tears of joy, whilst Brutus's spring from anguish. Indeed, Henri is *sensible* to a fault, and Voltaire may well be offering an ideal balance between the affective and rational sides of human nature when he places besides his lachrymose hero a more phlegmatic figure, merely an 'être de raison', as Frederick of Prussia calls him in the 'Avant-propos' to Voltaire's poem which he composed in 1739. 'Ce fidèle et stoïque ami' (in Frederick's words), 'Mornay, toujours sévère et toujours inflexible' (IX.361), bears a distinct resemblance to Brutus, as he appears (up to act 2, scene 5) in *La Mort de César*. He serves as a foil to Henri in the same way as César's son in the stoic outlook which he owes to Cato, appears as a counterweight to his father in the ideally balanced figure which would constitute for Voltaire the truly great man. Jacques Clément is painted in the same colours as the leader of the conspiracy against Caesar. Like Brutus, he has been the victim of an upbringing which has produced the same sort of rigorism: 'Clément dans la retraite avait, dès son jeune âge / Porté les noirs accès d'une vertu sauvage' (V.53-54). His situation is comparable with that of César's son and is described in much the

[92] See R. Pomeau, 'Voltaire et le héros', *Revue des sciences humaines* 16 (1951), p.345-51 and C. Mazouer, 'Les tragédies romaines de Voltaire', *Dix-huitième siècle* 18 (1986), p.367-68.
[93] See I.279-280, III.224 *et passim*.

same terms: 'Son front de la vertu porte l'empreinte austère; / Et son fer parricide est caché sous sa haire' (v.181-182).

Frederick, in his 'Avant-propos', highlights the affinity between Voltaire's epic poem and his later *tragédies larmoyantes*: 'M. de Voltaire s'applique à décrire d'une manière touchante les sujets pathétiques; il sait le grand art de toucher le cœur' (Voltaire 2, p.356). His remarks on Henri's character are of great interest in the light of further discussion of the subject of *le grand homme* in his correspondence with Voltaire. They have a special interest here since they emanate from a monarch to whom Voltaire was often to liken Caesar, and for whom *La Mort de César* represented the acme of Voltaire's dramatic output. 'La valeur prudente de Henri IV, jointe à sa générosité et à son humanité', says Frederick (p.357-58), 'devraient servir d'exemple à tous les rois et à tous les héros qui se piquent quelquefois mal à propos de dureté et de brutalité envers ceux que le destin des Etats ou le sort de la guerre a soumis sous leur puissance; qu'il leur soit dit, en passant, que ce n'était point dans l'inflexibilité ni dans la tyrannie que consiste la vraie grandeur, mais bien dans ces sentiments que l'auteur exprime avec tant de noblesse:

> Amitié, don du ciel, plaisir des grandes âmes,
> Amitié, que les rois, ces illustres ingrats,
> Sont assez malheureux pour ne connaître pas!'

Henri's conduct is characterised by that same clemency for which Caesar had become famous. The clemency/rigour debate which is conducted between César and Antoine in Voltaire's play finds a parallel in his poem in the opposition between Henri and Mayenne. The latter is presented by Henri as ruthless, not scrupling to invoke 'la nécessité, l'excuse des Tyrans' (x.344) for the suffering which he is causing Henri's subjects. Referring to these subjects, Henri adopts a paternalistic attitude which contrasts with Mayenne's contempt for them: 'Il en est l'ennemi, j'en dois être le père' (x.346; see below, III.363-364). César, comparing his own mildness with Sulla's terrorising of Rome, declares: 'Il en

81

était l'effroi, j'en serai les délices' (1.286). The similarity between Mayenne and Antoine is not only that of their common political stance; their situations are also comparable. Mayenne after the death of Guise works the crowd up to a high pitch of vengeful fury (III.309-318) in a way recalled by Antoine's oration after César's death, and he, too, succeeds to the vacant position of leadership. In the celestial company of 'les vrais héros' (VII.246) whom Henri is allowed to contemplate in rapture, one stands out for his spiritual kinship with Voltaire's César: 'Le sage Louis douze' (VII.251), of whose compassion Voltaire says (VII.255-256; see *La Mort de César*, 1.314; III.338, 344):

> Il pardonna souvent, il régna sur les cœurs,
> Et des yeux de son peuple il essuya les pleurs.

The attitude of Coligny –'ce héros' (II.224), 'ce grand homme' (II.219) – to his death is one of calm resignation. It will be that of Voltaire's César too, and the way in which this heroic figure forgives the assassins who surround him will be recalled in Antoine's description of the dying dictator in Voltaire's play.

In *Alzire*, first performed about a month before the publication of the final authorised version of *La Mort de César*, Gusman in his death-throes pardons his assassin Zamore. Voltaire declares in the 'Epître à Mme Du Châtelet' which precedes *Alzire*: 'J'ai essayé de peindre ce sentiment généreux, cette humanité, cette grandeur d'âme qui fait le bien et qui pardonne le mal' (M.iii.377). To press home the point, he culls an epigraph from Du Resnel's translation of Pope's *Essay on man*, which could be said to set the tone of both plays: 'Errer est d'un mortel, pardonner est divin'. The idea of a forgiving God, the direct opposite of the vengeful Old Testament Jehovah, was very much in Voltaire's mind during and after the period of the composition of *La Henriade*.[94]

Clemency and forgiveness are themes which clearly relate

---

[94] The conception of a God whose justice was tempered with mercy to the extent of offering salvation to all, including virtuous heathens, is enlarged upon by Henri (VII.101-112); cf. *Poème sur la loi naturelle* (1751), IVe partie.

Voltaire's *Mort de César* to many of his previous and subsequent works. What these works have in common is that they are all permeated by their author's obsessive concern with a father figure in various guises. This obsession would seem to be rooted in Voltaire's childhood and adolescent experience; his difficult relationship with Arouet *père* was complicated by sibling rivalry between his only brother and himself. Both the idealised image of a benevolent father and the converse hostile paternal imago lurking in Voltaire's unconscious came to the surface from time to time in his works. The Œdipus complex manifested later in his life in his incestuous relationship with his niece, Mme Denis, clearly had much to do with the choice of subject of his first (huge) success in the theatre. *Œdipe* (1718) exploits the contemporary popularity of the dramatic use of both parricide and incest. J.-M. Moureaux in his study of the play[95] comments on Voltaire's conviction that he was the son of his mother's lover, Rochebrune: 'Rien de plus utile au fond que de se croire un bâtard pour accaparer la mère sans plus compter avec le père détesté [...] On se venge du père réel, regardé comme un tyran, en le destituant de sa paternité qu'on attribue à un père idéal investi des qualités dont on reproche au père réel d'être dépourvu'. René Pomeau eschews the psychoanalytical approach, but points to a possible allusion to Voltaire's bastardy in Cassius's hints (malevolent and self-interested) that Brutus was conceived out of wedlock.[96] *La Mort de César*, devoid of female characters[97] and restricted to parricide, nevertheless exhibits other features of the Œdipal situation. There is a distinct parallel between the characters of Brutus and the Philoctète of *Œdipe*: both are self-made men who proclaim the priority of personal merit and achievement over high birth,

[95] *L'Œdipe de Voltaire: introduction à une psycholecture*, Archives de lettres modernes 146 (Paris 1973), p.50.

[96] 'Voltaire et Shakespeare: du père justicier au père assassiné', *Littératures* 9-10 (1984), p.105.

[97] See, however, the role of 'l'image anthropomorphe de Rome' in G.-L. Bérubé, 'Voltaire et *La Mort de César*', *L'Homme et la nature: actes de la Société canadienne d'étude du dix-huitième siècle* 1 (1982), p.15-20.

both laud the benign attitude of a congenial mentor and father-figure (Alcide in Philoctète's case, Caton in Brutus's). Like Voltaire who threw off the yoke imposed by Arouet *père* and created a new name for himself to go with his new life, they both exemplify the triumph of culture over nature by rejecting blind obedience to paternal authority. Brutus's participation in his father's assassination (paralleled by the murder of Laüs by his son Œdipe) may be taken to indicate Voltaire's strong reaction to the hostile paternal imago, whereas the benevolent imago would seem to assert itself in the depiction of Antoine's quasi-filial relationship with César which is as effective an advertisement for friendship as Philoctète's more strenuous glorification of Alcide's companionship.[98]

In *La Mort de César*, Cassius and Brutus share a sense of brotherhood which they believe to be stronger than ties of blood. As Cassius reminds his brother-in-arms, culture should transcend nature:

> Caton forma tes mœurs, Caton seul est ton père. (III.86)

> Un vrai républicain n'a pour père et pour fils,
> Que la vertu, les dieux, les lois et son pays. (II.201-202)

Fraternal camaraderie eclipses filial piety and the death of Brutus's father suggests in more drastic form Voltaire's action to free himself from the trammels of paternal authority. The loosening of the natural bond between father and son is commonly accompanied (and not infrequently caused) by the parent's seeming favouritism in his relationship with his children. Voltaire was certainly aggrieved by the favour which he felt that his elder

---

[98] Other Voltairean heroes cast in the same mould as Philoctète and Brutus who put personal merit before pedigree are Alcméon in *Eriphyle* (1731) who declares 'Les mortels sont égaux: ce n'est point la naissance, / C'est la seule vertu qui fait leur différence' (II.i; M.ii.471), and Arzace in *Sémiramis*, to whom an admirer says 'Vous êtes devenu l'ouvrage de vos mains' (I.i; M.iv.511).

brother, Armand, enjoyed in his father's eyes. The real-life rift between brothers is mirrored in several of his plays.[99]

The eponymous hero of Voltaire's earlier play, Lucius Junius Brutus, at odds with his son, Titus, is as ardent a patriot as the son of César. His passionate attachment to 'l'inflexible équité' ensures the judicial murder of his son who expects nothing less for his treason ('Je sais ce qu'est un père, et ses droits absolus', III.v). Clemency is renounced in *Brutus* and the father orders the execution of his son in the name of patriotism; in *La Mort de César* the son in the service of the same cause rejects leniency and 'toujours indépendant et toujours citoyen' commits his father to a violent death. The hostile paternal image in Voltaire's psyche which is apparently at work here is also indicated in the relation between the adamantine father and the vengeful gods: Brutus, resolved that his son Titus should die, begs the gods ('vengeurs de nos lois, vengeurs de mon pays', v.iv) to avenge the disgrace which has been brought upon Rome.[100]

César, in contrast, enjoys a reputation for clemency; he rarely mentions the gods, a fact which is underlined in their final conversation by his son's plea 'au nom des Dieux, dans ton cœur oubliés' (III.iv). The idea of an enlightened monarchy persuasively put to Titus by Messala in *Brutus* (III.vii):

> Ce pouvoir souverain [...]

---

[99] Nemours and Vendôme, the 'frères ennemis' of *Adélaïde Du Guesclin* (1734) are not the first such couple to appear in Voltaire's work. In *Brutus* (1731) the exploits of Titus arouse the poisonous jealousy of his brother Tibérinus, and even earlier, the schoolboy's first attempt at a tragedy, *Amulius et Numitor*, might well have provided an outlet for his resentment towards his elder brother Armand. Philoctète, it has been suggested by J.-M. Moureaux, fills the same role vis-à-vis Œdipe; his friendship with Hercule is paralleled in *Adélaïde* by Vendôme's relationship with the admirable Coucy whom he regards as 'un second frère' (II.vii.330; Voltaire 10, p.249).

[100] The dead fathers in *Œdipe* and *Eriphyle* cry out from beyond the grave for revenge. The wrathful Laüs seeks the satisfaction of having his son Œdipe punished by the gods. The implacable Amphiaraüs is indebted to 'la vengeance inhumaine' of the gods for their contriving to have his wife Eriphyle killed by the son she has borne him.

Est des gouvernements le meilleur ou le pire;
Affreux sous un tyran, divin sous un bon roi.

is comparable to the case for benevolent despotism which César makes to Brutus and falls on equally deaf ears. César's reputation for benevolence, sedulously fostered by Antoine, continues to be cultivated by Voltaire in his later works. In a note to *Le Triumvirat* or *La Clémence d'Auguste* (M.vi.198-99) the false magnanimity of Caesar Augustus, Julius Caesar's adoptive nephew, is exposed and his 'clemency' (as presented by Corneille in *Cinna*) is reduced to base expediency and self-interest in such a way as to show up his uncle's genuinely merciful acts. The quality of mercy which tempers justice in Voltaire's characterisation of César is exemplified in the emperor Trajan as he appears in the preface to *Le Temple de la Gloire*, an opera-ballet performed at Versailles in 1745: 'Plus connu encore par ses bienfaits que par ses victoires, il était humain, accessible; son cœur était tendre, et cette tendresse était en lui une vertu; elle répandait un charme inexprimable sur ces grandes qualités qui prennent souvent un caractère de dureté dans une âme qui n'est que juste' (M.iv.350).

If the benign imago is uppermost in the description of Trajan's style of earthly government, the hostile paternal imago on the other hand can be seen to be active at the higher level of theodicy in Voltaire's libretto for *Pandore* (1740). The pagan gods and particularly the father of the gods, Jupiter, revel in persecution. Prométhée (whose name provides the opera's alternative title) joins with Pandore to resist this oppression: 'Le ciel en vain sur nous rassemble / Les maux, la crainte, et l'horreur de mourir, / Nous souffrirons ensemble, / Et ce n'est point souffrir' (M.iii.600). Such solidarity may be viewed in the context of Voltaire's attitude towards religion and towards Christianity in particular. The pagan myth of Pandora is transposed into Christianity as the doctrine of the Fall: Voltaire's playful suggestion of an alternative title for *Pandore* was *Le péché originel*. The rigour of Jansenist theology with its unmerciful God who denied his grace to all but a few of his many children had been rejected in the 'anti-Pascal' of 1734.

The increasing difficulty Voltaire experienced in reconciling the existence of evil in the world with a loving God reached a critical stage in 1755. Before this point was reached, several of the works he produced in the 1730s suggest – in the importance which they attach to the gentler and more noble side of human nature – the need for consolation felt by a son bereft of parents and reluctant to admit that his God was no less cruel and uncaring than the heavenly father worshipped by Christians. Among these works, one may certainly count *La Mort de César* with its emphasis upon the father-son relationship and the clemency/rigour debate.

4. *Publication, performance and reception*

La Mort de César received its first performance in the privacy of the hôtel de Sassenage in 1733.[101] Voltaire was present at this performance, and seems to have been satisfied enough with the reception of his work by the limited audience to repeat the experiment a couple of years later on a slightly more ambitious scale by offering his work to the *proviseur* of the Collège d'Harcourt, the abbé Asselin, so that it might be staged by the pupils on the occasion of the annual prize distribution on 11 August 1735. The *Mercure de France* for October 1735 introduces an analysis of the play by giving its readers the following account of this performance (p.2259):

Il y eut à cette représentation un grand concours de personnes de la première distinction, attirées par la nouveauté de la pièce, et plus encore par la réputation de son auteur. On peut dire que l'assemblée fut également satisfaite et de la beauté de cet ouvrage, et de la manière dont les acteurs s'acquittèrent de leurs personnages.

After analysing the play, the reviewer raises the possibility of introducing the work to a wider audience: 'C'est ainsi que finit

---

[101] See D908, D910 and *MF* (octobre 1735), p.2271.

cette pièce digne des applaudissements qu'elle a eus sur le théâtre, et qu'elle aura dans le public' (p.2271).

Voltaire for his part took pains to present the play as the work of a 'poète de collège' indulging an urge to experiment. In a letter in the *Observations sur les écrits modernes* of 16 September 1735, the author characterises his play in this way and states emphatically: 'En un mot elle n'est point faite pour le public' (D910), but he undoubtedly realised from the beginning that his ambition to mould public taste would necessitate a professional production of the play. However, there is no reason to doubt that Voltaire did not wish to see his play published before it had been sent, as usual, to those of his friends whose powers of critical scrutiny he appreciated, and, possibly, before it had been given a few more trial performances.

When Voltaire wrote to Asselin in May 1735 to thank him for agreeing to put on his play, he expressed some apprehension about the possible hazard of a copy of the text being used for a pirated edition (D873). This apprehension turned out to be well founded. Whilst Voltaire busied himself after the performance correcting and revising the play (D899, D904), a corrupt 'précepteur du collège des jésuites' was preparing a mangled version for the press from one of the acting copies distributed amongst the cast (D997). The news of its swift publication before the month of August was out was received with dismay by Voltaire. In a letter written from Cirey to Thiriot on 1 September, he professed himself 'très affligé de cette misérable édition' (D908) and urged his friend to arrange for a disclaimer to appear on his behalf in the Parisian weekly press. He himself wrote to Desfontaines, the editor of the *Observations sur les écrits modernes*, on 7 September (D910), requesting him to inform his readers that he had had no part in the publication of the edition, the text of which did not correspond to what he had written. What satisfaction Voltaire may have had from seeing his letter published in the 16 September number of the *Observations* was soured by the fact that Desfontaines merely used it, preceded by a snide one-sentence introduction, as a tail-piece for a long and unfavourable review of the play based on the defective text. When the 'wretched edition' actually arrived at Cirey, Voltaire was able to judge how badly his work had been mauled. He wrote to Formont on 22 September:

J'ai lu, mon cher Formont, depuis peu un tas de sottises nouvelles. J'ai été bien surpris de rencontrer, dans cet amas de brochures impertinentes qu'on m'a envoyées de Paris, la tragédie de la Mort de César, imprimée dieu sait comment. César n'a jamais été plus massacré par Brutus et par Cassius que par l'abominable éditeur qui m'a joué ce tour. Les entrailles paternelles s'émeuvent à la vue de mes enfants ainsi mutilés. Cela est déplorable. (D916)

If this is not genuine indignation, it is certainly well feigned. Voltaire (who was not above such tricks) knew that there would be those who would suspect him of having arranged for his play to be published surreptitiously and who would regard his outcry as a familiar means of attracting attention to the work.[102] Injured professional pride, however, seems to motivate the repeated attempts (D911, D918, D924) on his part to move the dilatory Thiriot to denounce the defects of the unauthorised edition of *La Mort de César*.

The fruits of Voltaire's perseverance can be seen in the letter (D929) which Thiriot wrote to Desfontaines in October and which was published in the *Observations* on 5 November. An editorial statement which appeared with it acknowledged the force of the arguments deployed by Thiriot against the initial attack upon the play and exonerated Voltaire from taking any part in the publication of the patently defective edition. Desfontaines states that he had been allowed by Asselin (whom Voltaire had taken care to predispose in his favour; see D922, D931) to consult the original and had recognised that the unauthorised edition diverged substantially from it. A copy of Thiriot's letter sent to l'abbé Prévost reached him the same week as it appeared

---

[102] This possibility is suggested by Dubuisson (see editorial commentary on D925). More recently, Fenger (*Voltaire et le théâtre anglais*, p.208) does not discount the possibility.

in the *Observations*; having no desire to be reduced to the indignity of becoming a mere echo of Desfontaines, he felt justified in refusing to print it in his *Le Pour et contre* (see D933). Counterbalancing this refusal was the article which had appeared in the *Mercure* for October with its favourable account of the Harcourt performance and of the play itself. The article also contained Voltaire's own denunciation of the clandestine edition which was marred by faults galore and contained lines clearly not of his authorship since they did not even scan properly. In addition, Voltaire had the satisfaction of seeing in print his answers to the specific criticisms made by Desfontaines in his review of 16 September.

However badly maimed Voltaire's brain-child had appeared at birth, there was never any question of its being abandoned. 'Il est bien dur de voir ainsi ses enfants estropiés' (D1004) was the constant wail of the fond father who was all the while engaged in the practical task of remedial surgery. Much of this effort was directed towards correcting a deformity for which he had been in part responsible. The last scene of the play, directly inspired by Shakespeare, had obviously been envisaged as one of its principal attractions but it was considered unsuitable in its original form for a school performance. Voltaire told Asselin that he would have to adapt it if his tragedy were to be staged at the Collège d'Harcourt (D869). The shortened version which he produced was further truncated in the pirated edition and it was the disfigurement of this feature of his work in particular which moved Voltaire to send his friends the last scene before presenting it to a wider public as part of an approved edition.[103] In the accompanying letters, Voltaire acknowledges unreservedly his debt to Shakespeare. The scene is described by him, inaccurately, as 'une traduction assez fidèle de la dernière du Jules César de Shakespeare' (D937) or else it is referred to succinctly as 'la scène de Shakespeare' (D934, D937). The fact that his borrowing was not

---

[103] For this episode in the pre-publication phase of the history of the first authorised editions, see D928, D931, D934, D937, D942, D945, D950.

confined to act 3, scene 2 of Shakespeare's play is also admitted in a letter to Desfontaines (D940) which mentions 'La dernière scène et quelques morceaux traduits mot pour mot de Shakespeare'. What emerges, albeit obliquely, is a case for the claims which Voltaire made for primacy in the popularisation of Shakespeare's work in France. The obscurity shrouding the English dramatist's work at this period is eloquently indicated by the invariable use of explanatory phrases like 'ancien auteur anglais', 'un vieil auteur anglais', 'un auteur anglais qui vivoit il y a cent cinquante ans' (D931, D1004 and D934 respectively), which sound quaint to modern English ears attuned to the familiar strains of Bardolatry.

Voltaire's first attempt to organise the publication of his play by remote control from Cirey took the form of entrusting the prime responsibility for the enterprise to his friend Thiriot in Paris. The arrangements are set out in the letter he wrote to him on 13 October:

Je croi qu'il est nécessaire de faire une édition correcte de l'ouvrage. Voicy quel est mon projet. Faites faire cette édition. Que le libraire donne un peu d'argent, et quelques livres à votre choix. L'argent sera pour vous, les livres p^r moy. Seulement je voudrais que le pauvre abbé de la Mare pût avoir de cette affaire une légère gratification que vous réglerez. Il est dans un triste état. Je l'aide autant que je peux, mais je ne suis pas en état de faire baucoup. En faisant faire une jolie édition de cette tragédie il faudroit une petite préface où vous parleriez en votre nom. Je vous en enverray un petit modèle, que vous arrangerez selon la disposition que vous verrez dans les esprits. Je vous feray tenir la pièce avec tous les changements. (D928)

No sign of implementation of these proposals had appeared from Thiriot by 3 November and on that date Voltaire notified him that he was arranging for *La Mort de César* to be printed in Holland: 'Je vous avertis qu'on va imprimer le Jules César à Amsterdam. J'y enverray le manuscrit correct. Après cela il faudra bien qu'il paraisse en France' (D935). In Desfontaines' editorial reply to Thiriot's letter which appeared in the *Observations* for 5 November there is mention of 'l'édition annoncée par le sieur le

Det Libraire de Hollande' (iii.88), and Voltaire, writing to Asselin on 4 November (D937), suggests that the project is already under way. Although the idea of an Amsterdam edition appears to have priority in Voltaire's mind at this time, he had not forsaken the idea of a new, revised and corrected Paris edition. The need for such an edition was stressed by Voltaire in a letter which he wrote to Thiriot on 30 November. Another pirated edition had just appeared[104] and one feels a sense of urgency in Voltaire's realistic approach to Thiriot's inveterate inertia: 'Il est donc absolument nécessaire de donner ce petit ouvrage tel qu'il est, puisqu'on l'a comme il n'est pas. L'abbé de la Mare se chargera de L'édition, et le peu de profit qu'on poura en tirer sera pour luy' (D951). The impecunious La Marre must have been delighted with this response to the letter which he had addressed to his 'tendre et précieux bienfaiteur' at the beginning of the month.

La Marre's benefactor, however, was to become keenly disappointed with his young *protégé* who failed to justify the faith which had been placed in him. Bad reports reached Cirey from Thiriot, who may have been irked by La Marre's obvious disinclination to regard him, on Voltaire's advice, as a mentor. The absence of a personal *rapport* between those responsible for organising the publication of *La Mort de César* in Paris and the resultant lack of liaison made it inevitable that Voltaire should have been dissatisfied with the new edition. His dissatisfaction is expressed in a letter to Asselin written on 3 March 1736 (D1028) wherein he attempts to repair a possible sin of omission on La Marre's part by notifying the *proviseur* that he was arranging for him to receive a copy of the edition which had just appeared. While Voltaire does not describe in detail the numerous editorial shortcomings of La Marre, he is critical not only of his treatment of the actual text of the play but also of his handling of the material used to introduce it. This included the 'Avertissement' written by La Marre from Voltaire's notes; a French version of a letter about

[104] Perhaps 36HA or 36HP, but see note 6 of the editorial commentary on D951.

Voltaire's play written in Italian by Francesco Algarotti during the period when he was the guest of Mme Du Châtelet at Cirey for six weeks in October/November 1735; and an anonymous letter which is concerned with the allegedly subversive character of the work.[105] In the letter (15 March; D1034) in which he takes La Marre to task over the faults of the edition which he has seen through the press, Voltaire is exclusively concerned with the 'Avertissement' and the letter based upon Algarotti's original. La Marre is censured for having discredited Algarotti by falsely attributing to him a disparaging reference to pedantic Sorbonne professors which was eagerly seized upon by Desfontaines to defame the character of the Italian marquis in the *Observations sur les écrits modernes* of 10 March.

Voltaire's letter to Asselin of 3 March singles out one feature of the edition in particular: 'Une des plus grandes fautes de La Mare dans cette édition a été d'omettre ce que je lui avais dicté expressément touchant l'assassinat de César par Brutus, son fils, et sur la manière dont on peut retrancher si l'on veut cet endroit' (D1028). Given the trouble he took to send the original full-blooded version of act 3, scene 8 of his play not only to a large number of his friends and to Asselin himself but also to the *Mercure de France* (where it appeared in November 1735, p.2378-86), Voltaire would appear to be particularly churlish here in insisting upon La Marre's error in not having mentioned that an optional, emasculated last scene had been written for a special occasion. Another letter to Asselin, tentatively dated 15 [?January 1736] by Th. Besterman, emphasises the point that the lines which brand Brutus as a parricide were excised from the acting version offered to him for his *écoliers* (see above, p.44). Voltaire adds: 'mais j'ai laissé ces mêmes vers pour ceux qui ne veulent pas que les choses soient à demi tragiques, qui aiment l'horreur portée au comble, et qui se souviennent que Brutus, dans ses lettres, dit

---

[105] The items mentioned here, together with a preface which Voltaire substituted for the 'Avertissement' in later editions of the play, are presented below (p.243-67).

expressément: *Pro republica occidissem patrem*' (D989). These words are echoed in the preface which Voltaire substituted for the offending La Marre 'Avertissement' in later editions of the play. Not all of Voltaire's strictures on La Marre, then, can be regarded as just. In the first flush of solicitude for his play, he showered rebukes, most of them deserved, upon his *protégé*, but his final word is one of kindness and encouragement (see D1034). His attitude was not to remain benevolently paternal. Disparaging references begin to multiply in his correspondence (D1077, D1084, D1142). By September 1736, the editor of the first author-ised edition of *La Mort de César* is referred to as 'le petit la Mare, grand fureteur, grand étourdi, grand indiscret, et *super haec omnia ingratissimus*' (D1146). It is a token of Voltaire's final disenchant-ment with him that in a letter to Thiriot (D1158) he resigns himself to envisaging La Marre as the ally of J.-B. Rousseau and Desfontaines in the 'sotte guerre' which he felt forced to wage, often with evident self-disgust, against these enemies.

During the period of the play's gestation Voltaire, as has been seen, was busy with other works in various stages of completion. What he has to say of one of these, *Eriphyle*, applies equally to *La Mort de César* and indeed to his general approach towards creative writing: 'J'ai tout corrigé, mais je veux l'oublier, pour la revoir ensuite avec des yeux frais. Il ne faut pas se souvenir de son ouvrage quand on veut le bien juger' (D494). Thus, he decided in the autumn of 1731 that the version of *La Mort de César* completed at the end of June that year was not for burning and he put it aside to take a fresh look at it later. This was presumably the version for which Thiriot was promised a corrected replace-ment in the spring of 1732 (see above, p.15). By the time that Voltaire told his friend, on 13 October 1735, that he would send him 'la pièce avec tous les changements', the performance at the hôtel de Sassenage had taken place and in all probability Voltaire had made some changes in the light of his experience as a member of the audience on that occasion. No letters survive which might give us more information about the production or Voltaire's reactions. There is a very brief mention of the play in a letter to

Formont of 14 February 1734 (D710), in which Voltaire promises to send it to him with some other material. At this stage, the text would probably, apart from the last scene, have reached the state in which Voltaire sent it later in 1735 to Asselin for performance at the Collège d'Harcourt. 'La pièce avec tous les changements' which La Marre used as a basis for his edition was that which incorporated all the alterations which Voltaire had made to the text of the pirated edition of 1735. This revised version of the play may not have been identical with 'le manuscrit correct' which Voltaire told Thiriot on 3 November 1735 that he was going to send to Amsterdam. In the first place, Voltaire may have looked at his manuscript with a fresh eye in the period between 13 October and 3 November, and 'correct' may be synonymous here with 'corrigé'. Alternatively, he may have deferred sending a manuscript to Amsterdam or else sent corrections some considerable time after despatching the manuscript mentioned in the letter of 3 November. The latter possibility seems the most likely. There is fragmentary evidence to suggest that in the immediate aftermath of the publication of the disappointing La Marre edition, Voltaire decided to have yet another look at *La Mort de César*. In a letter sent by Voltaire and Mme Du Châtelet to Thiriot on 10 March 1736, part of which has been destroyed, the first words of the tantalisingly incomplete text read: 'retoucher dans Jule Caesar. Je les corigerais, car je ne plains jamais le travaille de la lime et c'est m'obliger de me dire, travaille' (D1033). In all probability the text which emerged from the polishing process referred to here is that of those editions, besides La Marre's, which appeared in 1736 (see below, p.122-23). The circumstances in which these editions were published must remain a matter of conjecture. Since there is internal evidence in a number of cases which offers scope for profitable speculation, the question of their publication may conveniently be left for discussion later.

Voltaire left Cirey towards the end of April 1736 to see to various business matters in Paris and did not return until early in July. It cannot be determined whether the publication of *La Mort de César* figured among the items of business which Voltaire had on his programme for this visit. It seems not unlikely that it did; a letter he wrote to Bonaventure Moussinot just before his departure for the capital (D1066) shows that he was considering the possibility of using another *protégé* in place of La Marre for minor editorial tasks in the future. Moussinot is asked to transmit the manuscript of the *Epître sur la calomnie* to a certain 'écolier externe au collège d'Harcour', Baculard d'Arnaud by name, who was later to achieve a greater literary reputation than 'le petit La Marre'. The ultimate destination of the manuscript was Amsterdam, since Voltaire's poem appeared immediately after the text of his play in the second issue of the edition of *La Mort de César* published there by Ledet and Desbordes in 1736 (36A). That it was published some time before 22 May is evident from the date of a letter sent by Jean-Baptiste Rousseau to the *Bibliothèque française* (D1078) in which the wounded victim of Voltaire's barbs mentions both the epistle and the preface to the play where he had been similarly maltreated. It may well be that Voltaire was also busy at this time with the arrangements for the publication of his collected works which were entrusted to the firm of this same Ledet whose hospitality Voltaire enjoyed during his stay in Holland in the period December 1736 – February 1737; 'le libraire Ledet qui a gagné quelque chose à débiter mes faibles ouvrages, et qui en fait actuellement une magnifique édition' (D1262). The 'magnificent edition' (w38) duly appeared under the imprint of Ledet or his partner Desbordes in four volumes in the course of 1738-39. The presence of *La Mort de César* in the third volume of this edition marks the only significant episode in the history of the play's fortunes between its first publication and its first professional performance by the Comédie-Française in 1743.

As far as the censorship authorities were concerned, *La Mort de César* had not, from the outset, been viewed too favourably. It had not been granted the *privilège du roi* and Voltaire had been forced to content himself with a *permission tacite* (D999). The 'Lettre de monsieur L… à monsieur D…', which appeared with some of the 1736 editions of the play (see below, p.264-67), clearly represents an attempt on Voltaire's part to counter the allegation that his work could have a dangerous influence, subversive of monarchical government. A short letter sent by a certain Claude Le Pelletier to the *garde des sceaux*, Chauvelin, dated 1 September 1735, is worth quoting in full since it puts forward the allegation in its most extreme form:

Je viens de lire une tragédie intitulée: *la Mort de César*, par Voltaire, et qui a été représentée depuis peu, au collège d'Harcourt, imprimée à Amsterdam. C'est l'ouvrage le plus séditieux, le plus opposé au gouvernement monarchique, et qui autorise tous les sujets à assassiner les rois et les princes souverains. Votre zèle pour l'autorité suprême du Roi souffrira-t-il qu'on répande dans le public, qu'on inculque des sentiments si barbares dans la jeunesse et parmi les cœurs français? Rien n'est plus contagieux ni plus pernicieux. Faites brûler cet ouvrage de ténèbres propre à former des Jacques Clément et des Ravaillac. Vous vous procurerez une gloire immortelle, et en protégeant celui qui s'est consacré à l'empire et à la religion de nos pères. (D909)

This letter could not have made much impression upon Chauvelin's subordinate, Hérault, the *lieutenant de police* for Paris, to whom it was transmitted, but it probably found its way to the censor, Rouillé. Whether he was influenced by it or was simply guided by his own cautious instincts, no *privilège* was forthcoming for 'cet ouvrage de ténèbres'.[106]

In the 'Lettre de monsieur L... à monsieur D...' (see below, p.266-67) the writer uses a double-edged argument in favour of the unrestricted publication of *La Mort de César*. He admits that stage-plays powerfully aided by the actors' skills can provoke resentment against the established form of monarchical govern-

---

[106] The only relevant items in the manuscript registers of *privilèges* in the Bibliothèque nationale would seem to be a collective *privilège* granted to the Parisian bookseller Duchesne for all Voltaire's dramatic works for three years from 7 March 1763 (Bn F22199, art. 966), and for ten years from 9 October 1763 (Bn F22000, art. 27). The separate editions of *La Mort de César* published by Duchesne in 1763 and 1772 were both 'avec approbation et privilège'. The *privilèges* on the title-pages of 36HP and the first state of 36L (see below p.120, 123) appear to be spurious.

ment, but points out that Voltaire's work was clearly addressed to a small circle of enlightened readers: 'On sent bien par la constitution de ce poème que l'auteur ne l'a pas composé pour le donner au Théâtre Français'. Whatever Voltaire's original intentions were, he would have found this argument embarrassing later in 1743 when, after the *comédiens français* had ensured the success of his *Mérope* (a play similarly devoid of conventional love interest), he felt encouraged to offer *La Mort de César* for their approval. Unfortunately, the censor's approval was not as easily won as that of the Comédie-Française and Voltaire was furious to learn, early in June, that Crébillon this time had rejected his play for public performance in Paris in the form in which it had been published. His reactions, expressed in the predictable round of letters to his friends, ranged from wounded pride and fear of ridicule (D2768) to scorn for the unenlightened readers in the service of French officialdom who had not the perception to approve what was praised and admired abroad. Voltaire is relieved that he is going to leave these barbarians, Visigoths and Ostrogoths, the whole horde of them (D2776, D2785), for the sweetness and light of the Prussian court, where Frederick, a truly enlightened monarch, had given yet another proof of his good taste by acting together with some of his courtiers in a private performance of what was his favourite amongst Voltaire's works. Voltaire's subsequent visit to Berlin was ostensibly a response to Frederick's repeated invitations and a reaction to official treatment of *La Mort de César*, virtually the last straw after the disappointment of his failure to enter the Académie française; in reality it was the occasion for him to undertake secret diplomatic activity on behalf of the French court. An element of elaborate charade was necessary to conceal this aspect of his visit from his friends in France and Prussia and even from permanent members of the French diplomatic service (see commentary on D2766 and D2778). However, it is doubtful whether Crébillon's unfavourable attitude to *La Mort de César* formed part of a tangled web of deceit which Voltaire helped to weave. His own letters and those of Mme Du Châtelet over this period suggest rather that the censorship authorities (dealing with domestic matters) acted like the left hand of a bureaucracy which did not know what the right hand (concerned with foreign affairs) was doing.

The censoring of stage plays by Crébillon was subject to the general guidance of his hierarchical superiors: Marville, the *lieutenant de police*, exercised his functions in Paris and his operations were in turn supervised from Versailles by the comte de Maurepas. Marville, it seems, was the weak link in this chain of command and the efforts of Voltaire's allies in the struggle to arrange a performance of an acceptable version of *La Mort de César* were concentrated on him. The dramatist's principal allies were Mme Du Châtelet and the star of the Comédie-Française production of *Mérope*, Mlle Dumesnil. The letter which Voltaire wrote to the actress from The Hague on 4 July (D2783) deals with Crébillon's objections to the performance of *La Mort de César* and counters them with arguments which Voltaire suggests could be used by Mlle Dumesnil to persuade Marville, or anybody else in a suitable position, to exercise the appropriate influence. Voltaire stresses the dubious attitude of Crébillon whose opposition might be construed by many as an attempt to stifle a play bearing upon much the same subject as his own unfinished *Catilina*. Furthermore, Crébillon's *Atrée et Thyeste* and *Sémiramis* had earlier surmounted the hurdle of censorship despite the fact that they contained elements more morally repugnant than Caesar's murder, which was represented in his play as being condemned by the Roman people. Voltaire suggests in this letter that Crébillon is determined to refuse a performance of *La Mort de César* under any circumstances, but Crébillon's first recorded proposal (D2786) was that he himself should undertake certain corrections in the text of the play. Maurepas found this procedure unacceptable, but asked Crébillon on 12 July to send him the manuscript of the play 'avec vos remarques séparées sur les endroits que vous ne croyez pas qui puissent se passer, tant en conséquence des règles de la censure, que même par rapport aux décences que le temps présent peut exiger' (D2789). Mme Du Châtelet, who had been exerting her influence on Voltaire's behalf

(D2778, D2781), sent him an indication of the offending lines in the pious hope that he would correct them so as to allow the play to be performed (D2797). When this hope remained unfulfilled, Maurepas wrote to Crébillon on 21 August (D2816) instructing him to undertake the job of correcting the lines which had originally met with his disapproval. In addition, he was asked to write into the role of either César or Antoine a passage in favour of monarchy which would reflect Caesar's benevolent intentions and counterbalance what was felt to be the excessively republican tone of the play. The extent of the corrections is summarised by Maurepas as 'huit ou dix vers à changer'. A more circumstantial account contained in an earlier letter from d'Argental to Cideville (8 August; D2804) corroborates Maurepas's suggestion of an addition and cites three lines which were the only ones which had been judged offensive enough to submit to Voltaire for correction. D'Argental misjudged Voltaire as much as Mme Du Châtelet had done, it would seem, in expecting him to acquiesce. As a result of the author's silence (and Maurepas's desire not to disappoint the *comédiens*), the play, after receiving an official mauling at the hands of Crébillon, was performed on 29 August 1743.

The reviewer of the *Mercure*, though well-disposed, was forced to admit that the play had only been moderately well received:

Quoique cette tragédie n'ait pas eu tout le succès que les Comédiens s'en étaient promis, on ne saurait disconvenir, sans injustice, qu'elle n'ait de grandes beautés. Plusieurs circonstances ont contribué à lui faire perdre de son prix, mais la principale c'est d'avoir été donnée sur le Théâtre Français, qui est nullement susceptible d'un sujet dénué d'amour, et par conséquent d'actrices. (October 1743, p.2264-65)

In fact, the play was only staged eight times in the course of the year, seven times in the period August-September and once on 21 November (*Registres*, p.742). Despite the *Mercure*'s suggestion that *La Mort de César* was really a piece for connoisseurs, it may be that some of the reasons for the play's not finding favour with the audiences of the Comédie-Française are more straightforward.

One of the main factors in the relative failure of the play may have been the generally poor casting. To make matters worse, the comparatively well-cast Legrand, playing Antoine, was deprived by Maurepas and his underlings of one excellent opportunity to show his talent to the full: from the summary of the performance in the *Mercure* (p.2277-78) it would appear that a considerable section of the final scene of the play was omitted.

Twenty years were to elapse before the next performance of *La Mort de César* at the Théâtre-Français. In the interval, the play was performed by amateurs in a variety of less prestigious establishments. The Bibliothèque nationale has an interesting set of programmes (Rés. Yf 2745-8, Yth 2883) relating to school productions, which show that in the period between 1743 and 1763, there were performances at the Collège Mazarin in 1748 and 1755 and others during this same period at Versailles (1749) and Nanterre (1753).[107] All these programmes take the same form and include, besides a cast list for *La Mort de César* and for the *petite pièce* (a farce which inevitably accompanied the tragedy on such prize-days), a brief statement of the subject followed by a synopsis of the main play. The historical facts upon which Voltaire based his play are mentioned very briefly by way of introducing the subject and invariably Caesar's ambition is singled out as the cause of his downfall, though there are differences of emphasis which reflect the division of opinion which has persisted throughout the centuries about the character of the assassins and their victim.

Voltaire's passion for the stage was manifested in the private theatre which he had constructed in his residence in the rue Traversière. *La Mort de César* was put on there in 1750 by Mandron's troupe which he had taken over. On this occasion, Lekain played César under the direction (in Voltaire's absence) of his niece, Mme Denis. Normally, Voltaire would supervise performances of his own plays as well as choosing a role for

---

[107] The earliest of these programmes (Rés. Yf 2745) was produced for a performance at Valognes on 13 August 1736.

himself – usually one which allowed him to play on the heart-strings of his audience. During his stay in Prussia, Voltaire chose to play Brutus in a performance of *La Mort de César* at court. Frederick, who had expressed distaste for what he considered to be Lekain's over-emphatic style of acting, would not, one imagines, have taken kindly to his friend's brand of barn-storming.

The second production of *La Mort de César* at the Théâtre-Français took place in 1763. This time the omens were distinctly more favourable. The *comédiens* were contributing to the festivities following the Seven Years War by performing to appreciative audiences Favart's *comédie-vaudeville, L'Anglais à Bordeaux*. Largely upon the initiative of Lekain, by now one of the established stars of the troupe, it was decided to revive *La Mort de César* as a curtain-raiser. Lekain, as Brutus, was eminently suited to display the more arresting features of 'le goût anglais' in the theatre. His ability to express violent emotions was unrivalled and his realisation of the value of visual accessories such as sensational stage-effects and realistic make-up ensured a production of *La Mort de César* which reflected its Shakespearean origin. Voltaire expressed his gratitude to him for having realised his own intention of giving French audiences a taste of what playgoers in other countries were offered, but it is tinged with a certain disquiet:

Vous venez de faire un miracle, vous avez fait suporter à la nation une Tragédie sans femme. Vous avez aussi fait paraitre un corps mort.[108] Vous parviendrez à changer l'ancienne monotonie de nôtre spectacle, qu'on nous a tant reprochée. Il faut avouer que jusques icy la scène n'a pas été assez agissante. Mais, aussi, gare les actions forcées et mal amenées: gare le fracas puéril de collège. Tout a ses inconvénients, et le chemin du bon est bien étroit. Vous avez trouvé ce chemin, mon grand acteur. ([c. 27 July 1763]; D11325)

The success of the production was only relative: there were just

---

[108] J. J. Olivier, *Henri-Louis Le Kain de la Comédie-Française* (Paris 1907), p.103, note 3: 'Le corps de César, qui mourait en scène et non "derrière le théâtre"'. Olivier is surely misinterpreting Voltaire's letter which more probably refers to the final funeral orations at this point.

five performances (*Registres*, p.808). The *Mercure* for August 1763 noted with satisfaction that the play had made more of an impact than on its first appearance at the Théâtre-Français and that the presence of a love interest and the strong appeal of the plot were no longer considered by the audience as indispensable to tragedy since the play had been heartily applauded. Thiriot corroborates this account but not without some reservations:

Je n'ai pas été content de Marc Antoine Dubois ny de la représentation de cette fin si belle qui n'a jamais eu à Paris le succès que j'ai veu à Londres dans cette belle situation que vous avés si bien rendüe. Nos acteurs françois sont des polissons qui rendent languissam^t de si beaux tableaux. (30 July [1763]; D11333)

Brizard who played César would hardly have met with Voltaire's approval if he ran to form as described in a letter to d'Argental of 11 March 1764: 'Mais votre Brisart est un prêtre à la glace, il n'attendrira personne; je n'ai jamais conçu comment l'on peut être froid; cela me passe; quiconque n'est pas animé est indigne de vivre. Je le compte au rang des morts' (D11761).

The production of *La Mort de César* by the Comédie-Française in 1783 ran for six performances and inaugurated a period of comparative popularity for the play. On the eve of the Revolution, the play was included in the repertoire of the Comédie each year from 1783 to 1788 and there were twenty-two performances in all.[109] This was but a prelude to the real hey-day of its success in the revolutionary period when, between 1790 and 1796, it was staged no less than forty-eight times. This is the figure arrived at by Phyllis S. Robinove based on a detailed study of announcements of Voltaire's plays in the Parisian press.[110] As one might expect, if one bears in mind the proliferation of new theatres and the great burst of dramatic activity which followed the suppression by the Assemblée nationale (on 13 January 1791) of the Comédie-

[109] A. Joannidès, *La Comédie-Française de 1680 à 1900* (Paris 1901).
[110] P. S. Robinove, 'Voltaire's theater on the Parisian stage, 1789-1799', *French review* 32 (1959), p.534-38.

Française's official monopoly of theatrical performances, her analysis shows that Joannidès's listings for the Comédie-Française constitute an unreliable gauge of the immense popularity of Voltaire's plays during the Revolution. *La Mort de César* shared in this popularity to a far greater extent than its meagre score of five performances at the Théâtre-Français would suggest.

The history of the play during the Revolution is not by any means, however, a straightforward success-story. The conflicting political view-points presented by Voltaire in *La Mort de César* made it inevitable that this work should be taken up for its extrinsic value in lending support to opposing factions. The first indications of the play as a political barometer can be seen quite early during the revolutionary period. The Comédie-Française was regarded as a bastion of reactionary and aristocratic elements, a vestige of the ancien régime; fervent patriots tried various means of intimidation to make the *comédiens* follow the lead of their colleague, the ardent revolutionary, Talma, and manifest their solidarity with the new revolutionary ideals. Without much enthusiasm, Voltaire's *Brutus* was staged on 17 November 1790 as an assurance of the patriotic intentions of the troupe. Violent demonstrations took place and, in the performances which followed, the auditorium soon rivalled the stage in its presentation of passionate conflict. Predictably, when *La Mort de César* was put on as the *comédiens*' next peace-offering, it was made the pretext for the same manifestations of partisan feeling. Larive, in the role of Brutus, would doubtless have realised from the nature of the applause which greeted the many sternly republican sentiments which he had to utter that his histrionic talent was not the only factor in the audience's appreciation. This impression would have been reinforced by the noisily unfavourable reception accorded to Antoine, the advocate of absolutism. The whole question of the monarchical régime had become a burning political issue. On 22 September 1792 the monarchy was abolished. While the question of the trial of Louis XVI (which took place in December) was being discussed, fuel was added to the flames of controversy by repeated presentations of both *Brutus* and *La Mort de César*.

The form of censorship of stage plays which had operated under the ancien régime had been abolished in 1791 but the propagandist zeal of those in authority ensured a form of censorship more stringent than the increasingly lax system of pre-revolutionary days. The logical culmination was the decree of the newly established *Commission de l'instruction publique* issued on 14 May 1794 which insisted upon theatres submitting all plays in their repertory for the closest scrutiny. Henceforth, the aim was clearly to spare no pains in making the most drastic cuts (or additions) so as to '*sans-culottiser*' each play before awarding it the *certificat de civisme* necessary for its performance.[111] There had been straws in the wind before this: the Convention had decreed on 2 August 1793 that any theatre staging plays deemed to be of an anti-revolutionary character would be closed, while unexceptionably republican plays should be offered free to the public once a week at state expense. The only plays of Voltaire to be performed in Paris from August to the end of 1793 were, as one might have expected, *Brutus* and *La Mort de César*. Less predictable, however, in the light of the original misgivings of the pre-revolutionary censors about the allegedly anti-royalist bias of *La Mort de César*, was the phenomenon of the play being mutilated (yet again) by a government official who considered it insufficiently republican in tenor and who, without the spur of any directive from above, indulged in an act of spontaneous desecration.

It is understandable, from the political if not from the artistic point of view, that the main object of this self-appointed censor's iconoclastic zeal should have been the justly admired dénouement which Voltaire had borrowed from Shakespeare. This was now replaced by a freshly composed and impeccably republican finale. It can be seen in the Réserve of the Bibliothèque nationale in a manuscript bound into the edition of the play at Z. Beuchot 582: 'La Mort de César, Tragédie en Trois Actes, de Voltaire, avec les changements fait [*sic*] par le Citoyen Gohier, Ministre de la Justice;

---

[111] See Etienne et Martainville, *Histoire du théâtre français* (Paris 1802), iii.141-44.

Représentée au Théâtre de la République, à Paris. A Commune-Affranchie, chez L. Cutty, Imprimeur, Place et Maison de la Charité, l'an second de la République.' Beuchot includes the changes made by Gohier together with the whole of the new dénouement in the list of variants appended to his edition of *La Mort de César* (see M.iii.361-66).

In Gohier's dénouement some attempt is made (by Dolabella) to present a case against Caesar's assassins which implies a general indictment of political assassination. It is not surprising, however, that Cassius is a more effective mouthpiece for the official line of anti-royalist sentiment and glorification of popular sovereignty. The voice of citizen Gohier, minister of justice of the Terror, can be heard in the lines (in scene 6) in which Caesar's assassin offers to Dolabella an apologia for assassination:

> C'est le fer à la main que l'on juge les rois.
> Qui nous asservit, meurt; telle est la loi suprême
> D'un peuple qui, né fier, se respecte lui-même.
> La justice éternelle a, de ses doigts sanglants,
> Gravé l'arrêt de mort sur le front des tyrans.

The warning which Cassius gives the people about the imminent alliance of 'le trône et l'autel' bent on avenging Caesar's death has more topical significance than historical accuracy.[112] In Gohier's version Dolabella and Antoine are arrested and the latter leaves the stage with the ironical exclamation, delivered 'd'une voix étouffée': 'La liberté triomphe!' Instead of Caesar's corpse and his friend's moving oration, we have the back-stage opening to reveal the statue of Liberty, the 'divinité chérie' to which Brutus, here explicitly involved in his father's death ('Que la main de

---

[112] It is interesting to note that some of Gohier's anti-clerical sentiments judged to be too tepid were changed without his consent. His 'Sachons apprécier le règne heureux des lois. / Prouvons que les Romains n'ont pas besoin de rois' became 'Affermissons le règne heureux des lois / Et ne portons le joug des prêtres ni des rois'; and 'Assez et trop longtemps des tyrans odieux / Ont osé se jouer des hommes et des dieux' became 'Assez et trop longtemps des tyrans odieux / Ont caché leur faiblesse en s'entourant des dieux'.

Brutus saintement parricide, / Porte à tous les tyrans et la mort et l'effroi!'), addresses a final invocation. Gohier's Dolabella had presented the people as 'inconstant dans ses goûts, ingrat, léger, frivole'; Voltaire's César had offered the same opinion: 'Je sais quel est le peuple: on le change en un jour; / Il prodigue aisément sa haine et son amour' (1.287-288). Proof of the changeability of public opinion, never hard to find throughout the revolutionary period, was provided after the fall of Robespierre and the consequent intensification of activity on the part of the opponents of the Terror.

The Comédie-Française (which had become the Théâtre de la Nation in 1789) was closed in 1793 and its actors arrested. They were allowed to return to their theatre which had been structurally *sans-culottisé* (no boxes, busts of revolutionary leaders everywhere) during the Terror and renamed the Théâtre de l'Egalité. The Terror had also decimated the affluent population of the Saint-Germain quarter where the theatre was located, and the Nation actors seeking a more favourable home found one towards the end of 1794 in the Palais-Royal area: the Théâtre Feydeau, where they were allowed to alternate performances with the resident company. The play with which the victims of Jacobin persecution chose to launch the new venture, on 27 January 1795, was Voltaire's *La Mort de César* – in its original form, not Gohier's version. Antoine's great speech in the last act was greeted with wild enthusiasm and Brutus and his fellow conspirators were hissed furiously. This was only one incident in a long series of manifestations of royalist feeling during the Directory in which the Feydeau headed the list of trouble spots and even suffered closure for a month in the spring of 1796. The closing years of the century were characterised by rigorous government censorship and an official insistence upon thorough republicanisation of all forms of entertainment which was reminiscent of the Terror. One might have thought that the republican aspect of *La Mort de César* which had earlier earned it the approval of the authorities would have ensured it more performances at this time, yet according to Robinove the play was not performed in Paris during the years 1797 to 1799. Welschinger,[113] however, presents a series of letters concerning the little Théâtre de l'Estrapade, situated in the unfashionable twelfth *arrondissement*, which reveals that *La Mort de César* had not been forgotten in that part of the capital at least. The theatre's director, Cardinaux, in an effort to win financial support, wrote to the *ministre de la police* on 21 May 1798: 'Des républicains, tous pères de famille, se sont dévoués à instruire le peuple par la représentation de pièces patriotiques, telles que *Brutus, La Mort de César* et autres' (p.86). The staging of these plays by Voltaire was authorised by a government official, but Cardinaux did not receive funds in time to prevent the Estrapade closing its doors and denying the public the opportunity of seeing further performances of *La Mort de César*, or any other 'pièce patriotique'.

While still first consul, Napoleon actively promoted the restoration of the pre-revolutionary primacy of the Comédie-Française; after its vicissitudes of fortune through the previous decade, it was officially placed under the protection of the government and guaranteed a theatre on 11 August 1800. Napoleon paid eight visits to the Comédie-Française in 1801 and one may assume that it was his attendance at the only performance of *La Mort de César* in that year which prompted him to dismiss it as a 'mauvaise pièce'.[114] This judgement may have had something to do with the play's not being put on at the state theatre again until 1806 when it was given a single performance, its last before the advent of the Third Republic towards the end of the century.

The ambiguity of the play's political content continued to be a factor in its stage history. The official censors in 1816, Lémontey and d'Avrigni, evidently saw nothing in Voltaire's play which could be deemed dangerous to the régime introduced by the Restoration and recommended its authorisation. Ministerial ap-

---

[113] H. Welschinger, *Le Théâtre de la Révolution, 1789-1799* (Paris 1880), p.85-93.

[114] Ronald S. Ridgway, *La Propagande philosophique dans les tragédies de Voltaire*, Studies 15 (1961), p.85, n.35.

proval was denied, however, as the manuscript comment in the margin of the censors' report indicates without throwing much light on the reasons for the minister's refusal: 'Si la pièce était au répertoire, je ne l'en ôterais pas, mais il n'est pas convenable de la remettre en ce moment' (Bengesco, i.25). Up to 1855 Voltaire's plays were regularly represented in the repertory of the Comédie-Française, but *La Mort de César* was never favoured. One might have expected a performance of the play during the Second Empire, given Napoleon III's keen interest in the figure of Caesar which actually bore fruit in a two-volume *Histoire de Jules César* published in 1865-1866. (The emperor's work might even be set in the wider context of a contemporary renewal of interest which produced in 1867 another *Mort de César* by a certain Lemestroff.) For its next performance at the Comédie-Française, however, Voltaire's play had to await a time when republicanism, though it had become the prevailing political orthodoxy, had sunk to a level of corruption (revealed by the Panama scandal in 1892) which was to encourage the development of an authoritarian cult of 'césarisme' in French political life. In the context of growing discontent with parliamentary democracy at this time it may be considered no accident that the 'republicanised' dénouement of Gohier was included in *La Mort de César* on 22 September 1892 for a run of three performances and then for a single (and, to date, final) performance the following year.

Voltaire's misgivings about the reception of *La Mort de César* (reflected in Algarotti's prefatory letter) turned out to be perfectly justified. The play's innovatory aspects, important as they are in the history of French drama, failed to make the desired impact and the conventional elements which he hoped would be well received by the public did nothing to mitigate the failure. His experience of the first production of the play by the Comédie-Française convinced him that the gamble he had taken in banishing *galanterie* and excluding female roles was ill-advised: 'César sans femmes ne peut être joué que chez des jesuittes' (May/June 1760; D8951). Moreover, the lofty ideal of majestic austerity ('Elevons nos esprits à la hauteur suprême/Des fiers enfants de Romulus', D4619) had been undermined from the outset by his own self-indulgence in yielding to the prevalent taste for tearful episodes, a taste which he shared with his audiences whilst professing the contrary: 'J'aime mieux, à la vérité une scène de César et de Catalina, que tout Zaïre; mais cette Zaïre fait pleurer les saintes âmes et les âmes tendres. Il y en a beaucoup, et à Paris il y a bien peu de Romains' (17 November 1750; D4269). Voltaire doubtless believed that the theme of tyrannicide, with its repercussion upon state and society, would raise the dramatic action above the merely domestic plane and surround it with an aura of grandeur – the 'sublime' of heroic tragedy. The introduction of the pathetic confrontation between father and son, however, allowed him to drop his sights and aim at pleasing 'les âmes tendres'. In this respect, his play anticipates the domestic clashes and crises of *le drame bourgeois*.

The opposing principles vindicated by the protagonists in the struggle leading up to the fall of the Roman republic offered Voltaire the basis for a straightforward political play. Though he rejected this option in favour of an amalgam of domestic and public tragedy, it is the political element in the play that constitutes its main appeal today. Republican ideals are vigorously and eloquently defended by Brutus and his fellow-conspirators in *La Mort de César* and it is easy to see how charges of harbouring seditious and anti-monarchical opinions were made against Voltaire when the play first appeared. The point of view of Caesar's opponents is still regarded by some critics as the play's main political message. Norman Hampson, for example, credits Voltaire with sponsoring 'a new cult of republican *vertu*' and speaks of the Romans appearing on stage 'in a new role, as both the embodiments of civic duty and the patrons of revolt'.[115] Other critics[116]

[115] *The Enlightenment*, The Pelican history of European thought (London 1968), iv.148.

[116] R. S. Ridgway in his succinct analysis of the play, p.81 ff; A.-M. Rousseau in the introduction to his edition (Paris 1964), p.23-28, '*La Mort de César*, tragédie politique'.

interpret the play as an expression of Voltaire's rejection of fanaticism, his pragmatic approach to politics and his attachment to the ideal of a firm, but just and humane, monarch at the head of a well-ordered state. These critics, however, are well aware that there is a certain amount of ambivalence in Voltaire's treatment of the ideological debate: César, with his 'Si je n'étais César, j'aurais été Brutus' (I.120) avoids the charge of zealotry whilst paying lip-service to the principles of liberty, justice and the rule of law which Voltaire himself championed in his constant struggle against arbitrary government.

In his presentation of César and Brutus, Voltaire aims, as Algarotti suggests, to preserve a balance between the 'deux forces égales et opposées' that they represent. The same balanced view is evident in Voltaire's characterisation of each of the protagonists. His César is neither the monster of Lucan's *Pharsalia* nor Theodor Mommsen's superman: he is 'à la fois la gloire et le fléau de Rome' (III.158). The first critical reactions to *La Mort de César* show a mixture of favourable and unfavourable judgements. Desfontaines criticised Voltaire in the *Observations sur les écrits modernes* (16 September 1735, p.271) for portraying César as 'un peu faible'. This comment elicited the rejoinder from the *Mercure* in its November issue (p.2385): 'il est cependant tendre, magnanime et ambitieux; c'était là son caractère'. In the *Mercure* of April 1736 (p.706) Baculard d'Arnaud, Voltaire's *protégé*, comments:

> César est bienfaisant, vertueux, magnanime,
> Et s'il n'était tyran, César serait sans crime.

Brutus, who had been treated by Dante as a vile parricide and consigned to the lowest reaches of the *Inferno* (canto xxxiv.616-669) and by Swift (*Gulliver's travels*, ch.8) as 'one of the most illustrious destroyers of tyrants and usurpers, and the restorer of liberty to oppressed nations', is dealt with more temperately by Voltaire. Desfontaines complained in the *Observations* of 16 September 1735 that Brutus was made to utter 'des sentiments plus monstrueux qu'héroïques'. Voltaire replied in the *Mercure* the following month that his portrayal was in accord with the historical character of Brutus. He believed that the morally monstrous elements in Brutus's attitude (before they were eroded by César's revelation of the secret of his birth) could be attributed to the primitive ethos prevailing in ancient Rome. Baculard d'Arnaud put this view succinctly in the *Mercure* of April 1736:

> Brutus semble aux Français un traître, un inhumain,
> Mais Rome dans Brutus reconnaît un Romain.

As far as his plays were concerned, Voltaire was in no doubt that the ephemeral glory of performance counted for little besides the perennial monument of publication. Performers could burnish or tarnish a playwright's reputation during his lifetime but posterity's judgement was what mattered most. Voltaire clearly employed a double criterion for his dramatic works; they were aimed first of all at moving an audience which reacted spontaneously to what was taking place on stage: 'le public assemblé, qui sent plus qu'il ne raisonne', but there was also the class of educated readers to be taken into account: 'les critiques éclairés qui jugent dans le cabinet'.[117] These readers looked to Voltaire for 'des tragédies qui ont assurément un autre mérite que celui de la représentation'.[118]

The editor of the most recent edition[119] of *La Mort de César*, André-Michel Rousseau, rightly emphasises that the play is 'pour l'histoire du théâtre, un document de premier ordre' (p.22). Though the intrinsic worth of Voltaire's play is summarily dismissed by him, it is redeemed 'comme document de l'histoire des idées, comme aveu oblique d'un tempérament et d'une philosophie de la vie' (p.23). This unexceptionable judgement is the culmination of a trend (which goes back to the earliest critical reactions to the work) towards minimising the importance of the play, *qua* play, and stressing its extrinsic interest. The unfavoura-

---

[117] *Commentaires sur Corneille* (Voltaire 54, p.557). See the final paragraph of D517: 'Quelle distance immense entre un ouvrage souffert au théâtre et un bon ouvrage'; and the 'Avertissement' of w68.

[118] This description of Voltaire's tragedies is used by Linant in a letter to l'abbé Prévost (D656).

[119] Voltaire, *La Mort de César*, ed. A.-M. Rousseau (Paris 1964).

ble appraisals of Villemain,[120] Deschanel,[121] Lion[122] and Lounsbury[123] add but little to the preponderantly adverse criticism of *La Mort de César* which one finds in J.-M.-B. Clément's searching study of 1784.[124] Clément's charge-sheet against Voltaire includes faulty construction (act 1 contributes nothing to the dramatic action and the final scene of act 3 is superfluous; ii.23-26), improbability of plot (i.16-17), no suspense generated (unforgivable in the short compass of three acts; i.141), *coups de théâtre* crudely contrived (i.189) and awkwardly managed dialogue (ii.284, 309-10). Clément is primarily concerned with the reader's enjoyment of the play in his study and he abjures 'le spectacle, les décorations, la pantomime, qui amusent la foule des spectateurs, dont tout l'esprit est dans les yeux' (i.17).

Despite his innovations, Voltaire was no revolutionary in aesthetic matters. He continued to worship Racine and emulate Corneille in the faint hope of sometimes coming near them in the art of composition and, especially, versification. Judged by this rigorous criterion, *La Mort de César* is moderately successful. Voltaire had worked hard and to good effect: 'c'est de tous mes ouvrages celui dont j'ai le plus travaillé la versification' (D869). La Harpe may be thought to be going too far when he declares: 'Nous n'avons point de plus beaux vers dans la langue française',[125] but his admiration does point to what may be considered one of the few sources of lasting appeal in Voltaire's dramatic works and one which will continue to delight the reader who derives pleasure as much from the mind's ear as the mind's eye.

---

[120] A. F. Villemain, *Tableau de la littérature française au 18e siècle* (Paris 1873).

[121] E. Deschanel, *Le Théâtre de Voltaire* (Paris 1883).

[122] H. Lion, *Les Tragédies et les théories dramatiques de Voltaire* (Paris 1895).

[123] T. R. Lounsbury, *Shakespeare and Voltaire* (London 1902).

[124] J.-M.-B. Clément, *De la tragédie, pour servir de suite aux Lettres à Voltaire* (Amsterdam 1784).

[125] *Commentaires sur le théâtre de Voltaire* (Paris 1814), p.138.

5. *The letter from Algarotti to Franchini*

Francesco Algarotti (1712-1764), a welcome recruit to the band of 'Emiliens', as Mme Du Châtelet liked to call those who shared her varied intellectual interests and her hospitability, stayed at Cirey for six weeks in the autumn of 1735 (see D978). La Marre's presentation of the youthful Italian prodigy in his 'Avertissement' as 'un bon poète, un bon philosophe, et un savant' is confirmed by Voltaire and by Mme Du Châtelet, who strengthens Algarotti's claim to be ranked among 'Les gens de génie' by representing him as being 22 years old (two years younger than in La Marre's reference to him). Besides giving proof of his scientific knowledge by putting the finishing touches to his *Il Neutonianismo per le dame* ('miei Dialoghi') at Cirey, Algarotti was able to demonstrate his powers of literary appreciation. During his stay, Voltaire was preoccupied with *La Mort de César*. A pirated edition of the work had been published a month or so before Algarotti's visit and had goaded its author into making preparations for offering a correct version to the public. These preparations were complete by 12 October: the corrected text accompanied Algarotti's letter to the Tuscan envoy in Paris. The following day (13 October), Voltaire was promising to send 'la pièce avec tous les changements' to Thiriot (D928).[126] The play itself obviously provided one of the many subjects of discussion at Cirey, and the letter which Algarotti sent to Franchini is important not only in its indication of the contribution of the writer to such discussion but also in its reflection of Voltaire's own view of his work, as it is relayed by Algarotti to his compatriot. It would appear that Algarotti, with the full approval of the author of *La Mort de César*, intended that the letter should be used to preface the play. Voltaire makes it quite clear that his intention was that his Italian friend should not be snubbed and that the letter should be published. Unfortunately,

[126] For a fuller discussion see above, p.88-91.

good intentions were not enough. Voltaire had written to Thiriot on 13 January 1736 (D987) asking him to impress upon d'Argental (who apparently had the document in his possession) the importance which he attached to the publication of the letter. D'Argental himself received a reminder of Voltaire's concern about this matter on 22 January (D993). In neither communication does Voltaire say that Algarotti's letter should be translated into French; the absence of any directive in this sense might be taken to suggest that he expected the letter to appear in the original Italian. Yet, Voltaire's criticisms of the French version of the letter[127] which appeared in 36P (see D1028, D1034) bear upon its subject-matter, and not upon the fact of Algarotti's letter not appearing in its original form.

One can still share Voltaire's immediate reaction to the so-called French translation of Algarotti's letter, which was one of bewilderment. Did Algarotti himself translate his own letter? The question which Voltaire put to Thiriot (16 March; D1035) must remain unanswered, and one has to fall back upon the vague 'celui qui a traduit la lettre italienne', the phrase which Voltaire employed in his letter to La Marre of 15 March (D1034). Nothing in any surviving correspondence between Voltaire and d'Argental, the third man in the mystery of the preparation of the prefatory material for 36P, sheds any light on the problem.

Voltaire refers to the occasion when Algarotti's letter was read out to him by its author, but what he says about it only makes confusion worse confounded: 'Je me souviens que quand M. Algarotti me lut sa lettre en italien, il y désignait un précepteur, qui ayant volé cet ouvrage le fit imprimer' (D1034). The French text which prefaced 36P bears only slight resemblances (which we have indicated) to either the Italian letter which first appeared in w56 (reproduced below, p.169-73, from w75G) or the letter which Th. Besterman reproduces from the 1794 edition of Algarotti's works (see appendix IV, with variants from the letter printed

---

[127] See below, p.253-58, appendix III: 'Lettre de M. N... à M. N...'.

in the 1783 edition of Algarotti's works). Voltaire, obviously having to rely on a vague memory, singled out only the reference to *doctores umbratici* as not having formed part of the original, but does not seem to have recognised that the French version was, in fact, a very free adaptation of either of the two Italian versions, composed by someone who would appear to have had access to the Italian original or to have received some account of its subject-matter, which he then used as a basis for his own 'translation'. Unless Voltaire's memory was playing him tricks, his reference to Algarotti's mention of a thieving tutor responsible for 35H merely heightens the mystery, for the text first published in w56 only refers to the pirated edition as 'alterato' and 'manco', and that of D927 as 'alterato' and 'guasto'.

Voltaire could not have been unduly concerned about the use of the French version, rather than the original Italian letter, in 36P, since it prefaced subsequent editions of *La Mort de César*, including 36A, 36L, w38, w48D and T64P. It was Mme Du Châtelet who expressed greatest concern about the absence of Algarotti's letter from 36P. Writing to Algarotti on 8 March 1736 (D1032), she explained that Voltaire was ill, and, on his behalf, poured forth excuses for the sin of omission, and made a definite promise (not to be fulfilled) that the letter would appear in its pristine integrity in the edition of the play to be published in Holland. Fears that Algarotti had taken umbrage seemed to be confirmed by the 'éternel silence' which followed this letter. These fears were unfounded, however: Algarotti's reply, written in mid-March, had merely been delayed, and good relations were maintained (see D1065). Algarotti's interest in the drama of Caesar's death remained undiminished; he must have recalled his own letter to Franchini, and the circumstances which produced it, when he wrote from England in the summer of 1736 to Mme Du Châtelet to tell her that he had been to see the play which had (in a sense) started the whole business: Shakespeare's *Julius Caesar*.

Despite the differences in presentation between the three versions the basic aim of underlining the significance of Voltaire's play and explaining the intentions of its author is achieved in each in such a way as to constitute a valuable complement to the material contained in the 'Avertissement' (appendix I) and the 'Préface des éditeurs' (appendix II). The novelty of *La Mort de César* evident in the attempt to impart a new note of high seriousness to tragedy is stressed. Voltaire's role as a pioneer is only made to emerge, however, against a background of contemporary taste which, it is pessimistically envisaged, will be offended as much by the absence of female characters and the usual love-interest as by the unprecedented division of a tragedy into three acts. The well-founded doubts about the open-mindedness of the French theatre-going public echo Voltaire's own statements about the play in his correspondence, where he appears less as the audacious trail-blazer than as a tentative experimenter, cherishing the never more than tepid hope that a moderately favourable reception accorded to his work by a restricted audience might be a straw in the wind of change which could ultimately transform the taste of a nation. The advocacy of a sort of cultural common market in Europe takes on something of a visionary aspect, but the vision is rendered less dazzling by the cautious approach to literary imitation which is adumbrated; Voltaire is praised for his catholicity of taste, but at the same time congratulated on the discrimination with which he has borrowed from Shakespeare, winnowing the wheat from the chaff, so that his play-going compatriots would not find the resulting *pabulum* so very different from what they had become used to. Similarly, the reference to the play's stylistic attractions – 'la force de la poésie, pleine d'images et de sentiments' – seems to point to a specific feature of 'le goût anglais': the predilection for richly-textured verse, replete with imagery ('Quelle profusion d'images chez les Anglais et chez les Italiens', exclaimed Voltaire in a letter to Louis Racine of 14 May 1736; D1074). Compared with the feast of metaphor and simile served by English, and especially Elizabethan, dramatists, however, Voltaire's *La Mort de César* appears as distinctly plain fare.

6. *Manuscripts and editions*

No manuscripts of the play itself have survived, apart from an old handwritten copy of one of the earlier collected editions (ImV, MS V5, p.173-234). The Comédie-Française holds a copy by Lekain of the role of Brutus: p.[*1*] 'Année 1763. / Troisiéme Rosle. Brutus. / Dans la Mort de César Tragédie De Monsieur de Voltaire'; [2] 'Personnages' (with a list of the actors); 1-10 'Rosle de Brutus dans la Mort de César' (p.10, 'Fin du rosle de Brutus de 318 vers').

From the information provided by Voltaire's correspondence and from the collation of the texts, the early editions of *La Mort de César* can be seen to fall into three groups:

a) those deriving from the text prepared for the Collège d'Harcourt performance (35H, 36HA, 36HP).

b) those based upon the edition (36P) for which La Marre assumed prime responsibility (36R and most subsequent separate editions).

c) those following, directly or indirectly, the manuscript which Voltaire said he was sending to Amsterdam (36A, 36L).

These editions, and collective publications containing the play, up to 1800, are described below. The state of the text of the later editions is commented upon only where Voltaire is thought to have taken some responsibility for their preparation: few include changes of any significance, after the revisions made for w38.

35H

LA / MORT / DE / CESAR, / *TRAGÉDIE* / De M. DE VOLTAIRE. / *Repre-fentée pour la premiere fois au College* / *d'Harcourt, le* 11 *Aouft* 1735. / PREMIERE E'DITION. / [*woodcut, flowers and vase, 22 x 20 mm*] / A AMSTERDAM. / [*rule, broken, 73 mm*] / M. DCC. XXXV. /

8°. sig. A-F⁴ G1; pag. 50; $3 signed, roman (– A1); sheet catchwords.

[1] title; [2] Acteurs; 3-50 La Mort de César, tragédie.

This is the surreptitious edition – Parisian, to judge by its appearance – which prompted Voltaire to organise the publication of the authorised edition of 1736 (36P). The many variations from the text of the subsequent editions are recorded in the critical apparatus.

As pointed out in BnC, sig. G exists in two states: 1) with a woodcut on p.50, measuring 37 x 34 mm (also found on p.16 and 30); and 2) with the woodcut from the title repeated on p.50. Page 49 is, in both cases, manifestly printed from the same setting of type, but the six lines on p.50 were reset.

Scenes 7 and 8 of act 3 are misnumbered 8 and 9.

The *Bibliothèque dramatique de monsieur de Soleinne* (Paris 1843-1845), ii.1680, records a 1735 Amsterdam edition in 72 pages: Bengesco plausibly suggests that 72 was an error for 50.

Bn: 8° Yth 12295 (state 1); – 8° Yth 12296 (state 1); – 8° Yth 12297 (state 2); Arsenal: 8° NF 5516 (state 1); ImV: BE 2 (8) (state 1).

MF35

In the course of a review of the Collège d'Harcourt performance of 11 August, the *Mercure de France* (Paris, octobre 1735), p.2259-2272, presented 14 extracts from the play: I.i.99-100, 101-120, 129-142, I.iii.217-224, II.i.8-13, II.v.229-234, 255-257, 291-292, III.ii.77-90, 109-112, III.iv.206-216, III.v.240-247, III.viii.374-380 and 405-408. Variations from the text of 35H are recorded in the critical apparatus to the present edition.

MF35A

A revised version of the last scene appeared in the *Mercure* for November 1735, p.2378-2386, prefaced by the following note: 'Voici la dernière scène de ce poème, que M. de Voltaire nous a fait l'honneur de nous envoyer lui-même.' This text, which corresponds to III.viii.309-408, is close to that of the base text: variations are recorded in the critical apparatus.

36HA

LA / MORT / DE / CESAR, / *TRAGEDIE* / De M. DE VOLTAIRE. / *Repre-sentée pour la Premiere fois au College* / *d'Harcourt, le 11 Aouſt 1735.* /

PREMIERE E'DITION. / [*woodcut, 44 x 31 mm*] / A AMSTERDAM. / [*rule, 80 mm*] / M. DCC. XXXVI. /

8°. sig. A-E⁴; pag. 40 (p.9 numbered '6'); $1 signed (+ Aij; – A1); the only catchword is on C4*v* 'ACTE III.'.

[1] title; [2] Acteurs; [3]-40 La Mort de César, tragédie.

An edition based upon 35H. The critical apparatus of the present edition records variations from the text of 35H, at II.216 and 289.

Bn: Rés. Z Bengesco 37; Arsenal: Rf 14258.

36HP

LA / MORT / DE / CESAR, / *TRAGÉDIE* / De M. DE VOLTAIRE. / *Repre-sentée pour la premiere fois au College* / *d'Harcourt, le* 11 *Aoust* 1735. / [*woodcut, flowers and foliage, 38 x 26 mm*] / A PARIS, / Chez JEAN-BAPTISTE BAUCHE, à la descente du / Pont-neuf, proche les Augustins, à Saint Jean- / Baptiste dans le Désert. / [*rule, 70 mm*] / M. DCC. XXXVI. / *AVEC PRIVILEGE DU ROY.* /

8°. sig. A-F⁴ G² (G2 blank); pag. 50; $3 signed, roman (– A1, G2); sheet catchwords.

[1] title; [2] Acteurs; [3]-50 La Mort de César, tragédie.

Another edition based upon 35H.

Arsenal: 8° NF 5517; Taylor: V3 M7 1736 (3); Pierpont Morgan Library, New York.

36P

LA MORT / DE CESAR, / *TRAGEDIE* / DE M. DE VOLTAIRE. / *NOUVELLE EDITION*, / *Revuë, corrigée & augmentée par l'Auteur.* / Avec un Avertissement & une Lettre à ce sujet. / [*intaglio engraving, the death of Caesar, signed in reverse* 'J. B. Scotin', *plate size 82 x 63 mm*] / Imprimée A LONDRES chez INNIS / *Et se vend*, A PARIS, / Chez JEAN-BAPTISTE-CLAUDE BAUCHE, / à la descente du Pont-neuf, près les Augus- / tins, à S. Jean dans le Désert. / [*rule, 77 mm*] / M. DCC. XXXVI. /

8°. sig. ã⁸ (– ã1) ẽ⁴ (ẽ3 + χ²) A-D⁸ E⁴ (± A1, C8, D4); pag. [2] [v]-xxj [7] 72; $4 signed, roman (– ã1-2, ẽ3-4, D4 cancel, E3-4; ã3 signed 'ãij', ã4 'aiij', ã5 'aiiij'); sheet catchwords.

[1] title; [2] blank; [v]-x Avertissement; [xi]-xxj Lettre de Mr N... à Mr

N... sur la tragédie de Jules-César, par M. de Voltaire; [xxii] blank; [xxiii-xxvi] Lettre de Mr L... à Mr D....; [xxvii] 'LA MORT / DE CESAR, / *TRAGEDIE* / DE M. DE VOLTAIRE.'; [xxviii] Personnages; [1]-72 La Mort de César, tragédie.

This is the first authorised edition of the play, and both the external evidence (see above, p.91-94) and the typographic style indicate its Parisian origins. The title-page is reproduced below, p.165.

The 'Lettre de Mr N...' occupies the inserted gathering, χ², and is not found in all copies. It differs in appearance from the rest of the volume.

The three cancels affect I.14, III.69-70 and III.193-194: see the critical apparatus.

Bn: 8° Yth 12299 (ẽ4 bound before title; χ² absent; no cancels; no inscription on title engraving); – 8° Yth 12300 (ẽ4 bound before title; χ² absent; no cancels; inscription on title engraving 'ROMAINS O SPECTACLE FUNESTE'); – 8° Yth 12301 (ẽ4 bound before title, but offset onto p.[xxii]; cancels A1 and C8 bound in at end, D4 cancelled in text; no inscription on title engraving); Taylor: V3 M7 1736 (6) (cancelled text; no inscription); – V3 M7 1736 (7)/2 (χ² absent; no cancels; no inscription); Arsenal: 8° GD 21318 (χ² absent; cancelled text; has inscription); – 8° NF 5517 (cancelled text, no inscription); ImV: D Mort 2/1736/1 (no cancels; no inscription; 'Caesar peut-il gémir, ou Caesar peut-il craindre?' added by hand on p.2); Br: FS 13.

36R

LA MORT / DE CESAR, / *TRAGEDIE* / DE M. DE VOLTAIRE. / *NOUVELLE EDITION*, / *Revûë, corrigée & augmentée par l'Auteur*. / Avec un Avertiſſement & une Lettre à ce ſujet. /

12°. sig. A-C¹²; pag. 72 (p.19 numbered '9'); $6 signed, arabic (– A1, A6); sheet catchwords.

[1] title; [2] blank; 3-6 Avertissement; 7-13 Lettre de Mr N... à Mr N... sur la tragédie de Jules-César, par M. de Voltaire; 14-16 Lettre de Mr L... à Mr D....; [17] A9r 'LA MORT / DE CESAR, / *TRAGEDIE*.'; [18] Personnages; '9'[=19]-72 La Mort de César, tragédie.

A Rouen edition, according to BnC, following the cancelled text of 36P. The date of publication is unknown: it is tentatively ascribed to 1736.

Bn: Rés. Z Beuchot 581.

36A

LA / MORT / DE / CESAR, / *TRAGE'DIE* / DE / M. DE VOLTAIRE, / SECONDE EDITION / *Revue, corrigée & augmentée par l'Auteur.* / [*intaglio engraving*] / *A AMSTERDAM,* / Chez JACQUES DESBORDES. [*or* Chez ETIENNE LEDET, & COMPAGNIE.] / M. DCC. XXXVI. / [*lines 2, 4, 7 and 11 in red*]

8°. sig. *⁸ A⁸ (– A1), B-D⁸ (D8 blank) E⁴; pag. XV [xvi] 3-70; $5 signed, arabic (– *1, A5, E4); page catchwords.

[i] title; [ii] blank; III-VII Préface des éditeurs; VIII-XV Lettre de Mr Algaroti à Mr l'abbé Franquini; [xvi] Acteurs; 3-61 La Mort de César, tragédie; [62] blank; 63-70 Epître sur la calomnie.

This Dutch edition was presumably based upon the manuscript sent by Voltaire to Amsterdam: differences from the text of 36P are recorded in the critical apparatus.

Apart from the variation in imprint (with a corresponding change in the title engraving), it is found in two states:

1) the first issue was in 61 pages, A-D⁸, without the 'Préface', the 'Lettre' or the 'Epître'. In this issue, sig. A1 consists of a title similar to that transcribed above (except that line 11 reads 'Chez JAQUES DESBORDES.' and line 7 ends with a full point), with 'Acteurs' on the verso);

2) sig. A1 was removed and replaced by *⁸ and E⁴ was added at the end, to give the result described above.

State 1 (all Desbordes). Bn: Rés. Z Bengesco 39; Arsenal: 8° BL 13640; Taylor: V3 M7 1736 (4); ImV: D Mort 2/1736/2; Br: FS 14; BL: 11736 ccc 3 (1); Stockholm: Litt. fr dram. pjes.

State 2 (Ledet unless otherwise stated). Bn: Rés. Z Bengesco 38; ImV: BE 15 (2); Taylor: V3 M7 1736 (5)/1 (Desbordes); – V3 A2 1764 (16); Stockholm: Litt. fr. dram. pjes. (Desbordes).

Arsenal Rf 14260 occupies an intermediate position, in that it has the Ledet title and sig. E⁴, but no prelims.

36L

LA MORT / DE CESAR, / *TRAGEDIE* / DE / M. DE VOLTAIRE. / *NOUVELLE EDITION,* / *Revüe, corrigée & augmentée par l'Auteur.* / Avec un Avertiſſement & deux Lettres à ce ſujet. / [*woodcut, basket of fruit, 35 x 25 mm*] / Imprimée A LONDRES chez INNIS. / *Et ſe vend*, A PARIS, / Chez JEAN-BAPTISTE-CLAUDE BAUCHE, / à la deſcente du Pont-neuf, près les Au- / guſtins, à S. Jean dans le Déſert. / [*rule, 78 mm*] / M. DCC. XXXVI. /

8°. sig. a⁴ πB⁴ πC⁴ A⁸ (– A1) B-D⁸ (D8 blank); pag. xxij 61 (p.12 numbered '10', 43 '45'); \$4 signed, arabic (– a1, a4, πB3-4, πC3-4); page catchwords (sheet catchwords on sigs a, πB, πC).

[i] title; [ii] blank; [iii]-vij Avertissement; [viii]-xviij Lettre de Mr N... à Mr N... sur la tragédie de Jules-Cesar, par M. de Voltaire; [xix]-xxij Lettre de Mr L... à Mr D...; [1] πC4r 'LA MORT / DE CESAR, / *TRAGEDIE* / DE M. DE VOLTAIRE.'; [2] Personnages; [3]-61 La Mort de César, tragédie.

An English edition, with press figures ('3' on A7v, B6r, B7r, C6v, C7v, D2v, D4r). K. I. D. Maslen attributes the printing, in part, to Woodfall; the 'Innis' of the title-page may be William Innys, the bookseller. The text is close to that of 36A: minor variants are to be found at ii.283 and 287.

Like 36A, this edition is found in two states:

1) the first issue was in 61 pages, without the three preliminary texts. Sig. A1 consisted of a different title (with 'Acteurs' on the verso): 'LA / MORT / DE / CESAR, / *TRAGE'DIE* / PAR / M. DE VOLTAIRE. / Le prix eſt de vingt quatre Sols. / [*woodcut, fruit bowl within scroll design, 37 x 24 mm*] / A PARIS, RUE S. JACQUES, / Chez JE. FR. JOSSE, Libr. Impr. ordinaire de / S. M. C. la Reine d'Eſpagne IIᵉ Douairiere / à la Fleur de Lys d'Or. / [*rule, 76 mm*] / M. DCC. XXXVI. / *AVEC APPROBATION ET PRIVILEGE DU ROY.*'.

2) sig. A1 was removed and replaced by a⁴, πB⁴ and πC⁴, to give the result described above.

The ornament on the earlier (Josse) title is also found on p.xviij.

State 1. Taylor: V3 M7 1736 (1) (D8 absent); – V3 M7 1736 (2)/1 (D8 absent); Bodleian: G Pamph 4 (5).

State 2. BL: 640 e 20 (1).

37N

[*first title*] LA / MORT / DE / CESAR, / TRAGEDIE / *DE* / MONSIEUR / DE / VOLTAIRE, / REVUE ET CORRIGEE / SUIVANT LA COPIE / D'AMSTERDAM. / [*two rules, 88 and 76 mm*] / SE VEND A NUREM- BERG CHEZ LES HE- / RITIERS DE FEU ADAM JONATHAN, / FELSECKER. 1737. /

[*second title*] Der / Tod / des / Cæsars, / Traüer-Spiel / des Herrn / von *VOLTAIRE*, / Aus dem Französischen in eben so viel teutsche / Verse übersetzet, / und / nebst einer Vorrede, / worinnen man dieses Werck nach den Reguln / der Tragödie untersucht, / wie auch / einem Poetischen Send-Schreiben über / die beygelegte Probe von einer Poeti- / schen Uberfetzung der Henriade, / ans Licht gesteller / von / M. J. F. Scharffen- stein, L. Occ. Pr. / [*rule, 94 mm*] / Nürnberg, verlegts Adam Jonathan Felßeckers / Erben. an 1737. /

8°. sig. π^2)(^{4})()(^{8} A-I^8; pag. [*28*] 119; $5 signed, arabic (–)(4, H5, I5); page catchwords.

Parallel French and German texts, the former following the tradition of 36A.

Taylor: V3 M7 G 1737.

W37

OEUVRES / DE MONSIEUR / DE / VOLTAIRE. / SUIVANT LA / NOUVELLE EDITION / D'AMSTERDAM de 1733. / *Revuë, corrigée & augmentée par l'Auteur.* / TOME TROISIEME. / [*woodcut, 65 x 45 mm*] / A BASLE. / [*rule, 86 mm*] / Chez Jean Brandmuller & Fils. / M. DCC. XXXVII. / [*lines 1, 4, 9 and 11 in red*]

8°. sig. π1 A-Y^8 Z^6; pag. [2] 364; $5 signed, arabic (– A1, O1, V5; E4 signed 'B4'); direction line '*Tome III.*' (– A, O); page catchwords.

[*1*] title; [2] blank; [1]-122 Zayre, tragédie; [123] H6*r* 'LA / MORT / DE / CESAR, / *TRAGEDIE*. / DE MONSIEUR / DE / VOLTAIRE. / *Revue, corrigée & augmentée par l'Auteur.* / [*woodcut, 37 x 28 mm*] / A BASLE. / [*rule, 86 mm*] / M. DCC. XXXVII.'; [124] blank; [125]-128 Préface des éditeurs d'Hollande; 129-135 Lettre de Mr Algaroti, à Mr l'abbé Franquini, envoyé de Florence. Sur la tragédie de Jules-César, par M. de Voltaire; 136 Acteurs; [137]-199 La Mort de Cesar, tragédie; 200-208 Epître sur la calomnie; [209]-364 other texts.

Stockholm: Litt. fransk.; Arsenal: GD 8° 23609; – Rf 14181 (both Arsenal copies consist of p.[123]-208 only).

w38

OEUVRES / DE / M. DE VOLTAIRE. / Nouvelle Edition, / *Revue, corrigée & confidérablement augmentée,* / *avec des Figures en Taille-douce.* / *TOME TROISIÈME.* / [*intaglio engraving*] / A AMSTERDAM, / Chez JAQUES DESBORDES. [*or* Chez ETIENNE LEDET & Compagnie.] / M. DCC. XXXVIII. [*or* M. DCC. XXXIX.] / [*lines 1, 3, 7 and 9 in red*]

8°. sig. *² A-Aa⁸ Bb⁸ (– Bb2.7 = D3, D2 of volume 2; – Bb3.6 = F1, F2); pag. [*4*] XIX [xx] 372 (p.335 numbered '333' in some copies); $5 signed, arabic (– *1, Bb4); no volume indication in direction line; page catchwords (p.[*4*] 'AVER-').

[*1*] title; [*2*] blank; [*3-4*] Pièces contenues dans le tome III; [i]-[xx], [1]-228 other texts; [229] Q5*r* 'LA / MORT / DE / CÉSAR, / *TRAGÉDIE.* / Q5'; [230] blank; 231-233 Préface des éditeurs; 234-241 Lettre de Mr Algaroti, à Mr l'abbé Franquini, envoyé de Florence, sur la tragédie de Jules-César, par Mr de Voltaire; [242] Acteurs; [243]-309 La Mort de César, tragédie; [310] blank; [311]-372 other texts.

The text of *La Mort de César* was revised by Voltaire for this edition: it differs from 36A at I.72, 140, 143, 313, II.64, 110, 121a, 283, III.268a and 306. Few further changes are to be found in later editions, and none of any substance: see below, w48D, w51, w56, w68 and w75G.

Bn: Ye 9213 (Ledet, 1738); Taylor: V1.1739 (Desbordes, 1739).

w39

OEUVRES / DE / M. VOLTAIRE, / *CONTENANT* / ALZIRE, LA MORT DE CESAR, / et Lettres Angloises. / *Nouvelle Edition, revûe, corrigée, & enrichie de* / *Figures en Taille-douce.* / [*intaglio engraving, motto* 'NON MORUNT HAEC MONUMENTA MORI'] / A AMSTERDAM, / *AUX DE'-PENS DE LA COMPAGNIE.* / M. DCC. XXXIX. / [*lines 1, 3, 5, 9 and 11 in red*]

8°. sig. π1 A-I⁸ K⁴; pag. [2] 152 (p.139 numbered '339'); $4 signed, arabic (– A1, K3-4); sheet catchwords.

[*1*] title; [*2*] blank; [1]-88 other texts; [89] F5*r* 'LA MORT / DE CESAR, / *TRAGEDIE.*'; [90] blank; 91-93 Avertissement; 94-100 Lettre de Mr

N... à Mr N... sur la tragédie de Jules-César, par M. de Voltaire; 101-103 Lettre de Mr L... à Mr D....; 104 Personnages; 105-152 La Mort de César, tragédie.

Bn: Rés. Z Bengesco 470 (3); – Rés. Z Beuchot 5 (3).

W40

OEUVRES / DE / M^R. DE VOLTAIRE. / NOUVELLE EDITION, / *Revuë, corrigée & confidérablement augmentée* / *avec des Figures en Taille-douce.* / TOME TROISIE'ME. / [*intaglio engraving*] / A AMSTERDAM, / Aux Dépens de la Compagnie. / M. DCC. XL. / [*lines 1, 3, 7 and 9 in red*]

12°. sig. π1 A-P¹² Q²; pag. 'XVIII'[=xix] [xx] 343 (p.xix numbered 'XVIII', 88 '86', 237 '137'); $6 signed, arabic (– I5, Q2; O3 signed 'N3', O5 'N5'); direction line '*Tome III.*' (sig. C '*Tome II.*'); sheet catchwords.

[*1*] title; [2] blank; [i-ii] Pièces contenues dans le tome III; [iii]-[xx], [1]-216 other texts; [217] K11r 'LA / MORT / DE / CÉSAR, / *TRAGÉDIE.*'; [218] blank; 219-221 Préface des éditeurs; 222-229 Lettre de Mr Algaroti, à Mr l'abbé Franquini, envoyé de Florence, sur la tragédie de Jules César, par Mr de Voltaire; 230 Acteurs; 231-290 La Mort de Cesar, tragédie; [291]-343 other texts.

The engraving on the title imitates that of volume 3 of w39.

Bn: Rés. Z Bengesco 5*bis* (3); Arsenal: 8° BL 34045 (3).

W41C

ŒUVRES / DE / M. DE VOLTAIRE. / NOUVELLE EDITION, / *Revûe, corrigée & confidérablement* / *augmentée, avec des Figures en* / *Taille-douce.* / TOME TROISIEME. / [*typographic ornament*] / A AMSTERDAM, / Aux dépens de la Compagnie. / MDCCXLII. /

[*half-title*] ŒUVRES / DE / M. DE VOLTAIRE. / TOME TROISIE'-ME. /

12°. sig. π² A-O¹²; pag. [*4*] 314 22; $6 signed, arabic (O2 signed '*', O3 '*2', O4 '*3', O5 '*4', O6 '*5'); direction line '*Tome III.*' (sig. E '*ome III.*'); sheet catchwords.

[*1*] half-title; [2] blank; [*3*] title; [*4*] blank; 1 Pièces contenues dans le tome III; 2-202 other texts; [203] I6r 'LA / MORT / DE / CÉSAR, / *TRAGÉDIE.* / I6'; [204] blank; 205-207 Préface des éditeurs; 208-213

Lettre de Mr Algaroti, à Mr l'abbé Franquini, envoyé de Florence, sur la tragédie de Jules César, par Mr de Voltaire; [214] Acteurs; 215-268 La Mort de César, tragédie; [269]-314 other texts; [1]-22 Pièces fugitives.

This edition, suppressed at Voltaire's request, was reissued (with his approval) in 1742: see below, w42.

Bn: Rés. Z Bengesco 471 (3).

W41R

OEUVRES / DE / M^R. DE VOLTAIRE. / NOUVELLE EDITION, / *Revuë, corrigée & confidérablement augmentée,* / *avec des Figures en Taille-douce.* / *TOME TROISIE'ME.* / [*intaglio engraving*] / A AMSTERDAM, / Aux Dépens de la Compagnie. / M. DCC. XLI. / [*lines 1, 3, 7 and 9 in red*]

12°. sig. π1 A-P¹² Q²; pag. [2] XX 344 (p.54 numbered '4', 265 '165', 297 '197'); $6 signed, arabic (– Q2); direction line '*Tome III.*'; page catchwords.

[1] title; [2] blank; I-II Pièces contenues dans le tome III; III-XX, 1-216 other texts; [217] K11r 'LA MORT / DE CÉSAR, / *TRAGE'DIE.*'; [218] blank; 219-221 Préface des éditeurs; 222-229 Lettre de Mr Algaroti, à Mr l'abbé Franquini, envoyé de Florence, sur la tragédie de Jules-César, par Mr de Voltaire; 230 Acteurs; 231-290 La Mort de César, tragédie; [291]-344 other texts.

Bn: Rés. Z Beuchot 6 (2,1).

W42

[*engraved title*] ŒUVRES / *MÉLÉES DE M^R.* / DE VOLTAIRE / NOUVELLE EDITION / *Revûe* / *sur toutes les précedentes* / *et Confidérablement* / *Augmentée.* / TOME III. / *A GENEVE* / *Chez Bousquet* / 1742. /

12°. sig. π1 A-N¹² O² (± A1, F9, H6); pag. [2] 314 [315-316] (p.295 numbered '195'); $6 signed, arabic (– O2; A1 signed 'A*', F9 '*Tome III.* *', H6 '*Tome III.* M6*'); direction line '*Tome III.*'; sheet catchwords.

[1] title; [2] blank; 1 Pièces contenues dans le tome III; 2-202 other texts; [203] I6r 'LA / MORT / DE / CÉSAR, / *TRAGÉDIE.* / I6'; [204] blank; 205-207 Préface des éditeurs; 208-213 Lettre de Mr Algaroti, à Mr l'abbé Franquini, envoyé de Florence, sur la tragédie de Jules-César, par Mr de Voltaire; [214] Acteurs; 215-268 La Mort de César, tragédie; [269]-314 other texts; [315-316] Errata du troisième volume.

A reissue, with cancels, of the sheets of w41c: the text of *La Mort de César* did not change.

Bn: Rés. Z Beuchot 51; – Z 24569.

MF43

The performance at the Comédie-Française on 29 August 1743 gave rise to another review in the *Mercure de France* (Paris, octobre 1743), p.2264-2279, under the title 'Extrait de la tragédie de la Mort de César, en trois actes, représentée au Théâtre Français, le 29 août dernier, annoncée dans le Mercure du même mois'. It included 38 extracts: I.i.1-4, 16-20, 29-30, 43-48, 65-72, 94-99, 116-120, 121-128, I.iii.162-166, 181-182, 197-200, 209-210, 217-220, 244-250, 257-260, I.iv.311-314, II.i.9-13, II.ii.37, 41 (or 43), II.iii.55-56, 64, II.iv.142, 147-148, 202-212, II.v.217-219, 229-234, 275-278, 288-292, 293-294, III.i.13-16, III.ii.38-43, 124-125, 134-136, 137-142, III.iv.225-226, III.v.251-252, III.vi.267 and III.viii.405-408. These extracts fall into the textual tradition set by 36P, except for variants at I.44, 218 and II.290.

w43

OEUVRES / DE / M^R. DE VOLTAIRE. / Nouvelle Edition, / *Revue, corrigée & confidérablement augmentée, / avec des Figures en Tailles-douces.* / *TOME TROISIEME.* / [*woodcut*] / A AMSTERDAM et A LEIPZIG, / *Chez ARKSTÉE et MERKUS.* / MDCCXLIII. / [*in red and black*]

8°. sig. *² A-Aa⁸ Bb⁸ (– Bb2.7 = D3, D2 of volume 2; – Bb3.6 = F1, F2); pag. [*4*] XIX [xx] 372; $5 signed, arabic (– *1); page catchwords.

[*1*] title; [*2*] blank; [*3-4*] Pièces contenues dans le tome III.

A reissue of the sheets of w38.

Universitäts- und Stadt-Bibliothek, Köln: 1955 G 1260.

w46

OEUVRES / DIVERSES / DE MONSIEUR / DE VOLTAIRE. / *NOU-VELLE EDITION,* / Recueillie avec foin, enrichie de Piéces / Curieufes, & la feule qui contienne / fes véritables Ouvrages. / *Avec Figures en Taille-*

Douce. / TOME TROISIÉME. / [*woodcut, armillary sphere, 28 x 34 mm*] / A LONDRES, / Chez JEAN NOURSE. / M. DCC. XLVI. / [*lines 1, 4, 10 and* 'JEAN NOURSE.' *in red*]

[*half-title*] OEUVRES / DIVERSES / DE MONSIEUR / DE VOLTAIRE. / [*treble rule, 70 mm*] / *TOME TROISIEME.* /

12°. sig. π^2 $*^{12}$ $**^6$ B-X^{12} Y^6 (Y6 blank); pag. [*4*] XXXI [xxxii] 492 [493-494] (p.334 numbered '335', 363 '263'); $6 signed, arabic (– $**$4; $**$3 signed '$**$5', $**$5 'Tome III. A', $**$6 'A2'); direction line '*Tome III.*' (+ M6; sig. F 'Tome III.'); page catchwords.

[*1*] half-title; [*2*] blank; [*3*] title; [*4*] blank; [i]-[xxxii], [*1*]-312 other texts; [313] O11*r* 'LA / MORT / DE / CESAR. / *TRAGEDIE.*'; [314] blank; [315]-317 Préface des éditeurs; [318]-325 Lettre de Mr Algaroti, à Mr l'abbé Franquini envoyé de Florence, sur la tragédie de Jules-César, par Mr de Voltaire; [326] Acteurs; [327]-380 La Mort de César, tragédie; 381-492 other texts; [493-494] Fautes à corriger.

Bn: Rés. Z Beuchot 8 (3).

w48D

OEUVRES / DE / M^r. DE VOLTAIRE / *NOUVELLE EDITION* / REVUE, CORRIGÉE / ET CONSIDERABLEMENT AUGMENTÉE / PAR L'AUTEUR / ENRICHIE DE FIGURES EN TAILLE-DOUCE. / *TOME CINQUIEME.* / [*engraving, plate size 81 x 72 mm*] / *A DRESDE 1748.* / CHEZ GEORGE CONRAD WALTHER / LIBRAIRE DU ROI. / *AVEC PRIVILEGE.* / [*lines 1, 3, 5, 7, 9, 11 and 13 in red*]

8°. sig. π^2 A-Gg^8 Hh^4 (± V5); pag. [*4*] 488 (p.289 numbered '189'); $5 signed, arabic (– Hh4); direction line 'VOLT. Tom. V.'; page catchwords.

[*1*] title; [*2*] blank; [*3*] Table des pièces contenues dans le tome V; [*4*] blank; [1]-316 other texts; [317] V7*r* 'LA / MORT / DE / CESAR. / *TRAGEDIE.*'; [318] blank; 319-320 Préface des éditeurs de l'édition de 1738; 321-325 Lettre de monsieur Algaroti, à Mr l'abbé Franquini envoyé de Florence; sur la tragédie de Jules-César, par Mr de Voltaire; [326] Acteurs; [327]-380 La Mort de César, tragédie; [381]-488 Mérope; 488 Fautes à corriger.

Produced with Voltaire's participation, this edition reproduces the w38 text of *La Mort de César*.

Bn: Rés. Z Beuchot 12 (5); Taylor: V1 1748 (5).

W48R

[COLLECTION / *COMPLETE* / DES ŒUVRES / *de Monsieur* / DE VOLTAIRE, / NOUVELLE ÉDITION, / *Augmentée de fes dernieres Pieces de Théâtre,* / *& enrichie de 61 Figures en taille-douce.* / TOME TROISIEME. / PREMIERE PARTIE. / [*typographic ornament*] / *A AMSTERDAM*, / AUX DÉPENS DE LA COMPAGNIE. / [*thick-thin rule, 48 mm*] / M. DCC. LXIV.]

12°. sig. π1 A-T¹² V² (– A10; A9 + *A⁶; O11 + *O²); pag. [2] XXX 312 [313-314] *315 315* *315 315* 315-440 (p.110 numbered '101'); $6 signed, arabic (– V2; *A1 signed '*Tome III.   *A7', *A2 '*A8', *A3 '*A9', *O1 '*Tome III.   *O7'); direction line '*Tome III.*'; page catchwords.

[*1*] title; [2] blank; [i]-XXX, [1]-230 other texts; [231] L6*r* 'LA / MORT / DE / CÉSAR, / *TRAGÉDIE.* / L6   PRE'-'; [232] blank; 233-235 Préface des éditeurs; 236-243 Lettre de Mr Algaroti, à Mr l'abbé Franquini, envoyé de Florence, sur la tragédie de Jules-César, par M. de Voltaire; 244 Acteurs; [245]-312 La Mort de César, tragédie; [313]-440 La Mérope.

This edition was printed in Rouen by Machuel in or before 1748 and was suppressed at Voltaire's request. Of this volume, only the title leaf dates from 1764; no copies with a 1748 title are known.

Gesamthochschulbibliothek, Kassel: 1948 C 266 (4).

50A

LA MORT / DE CÉSAR, / *TRAGEDIE* / PAR M. VOLTAIRE. / DE L'ACADEMIE FRANÇOISE. / Nouvelle Edition. / [*woodcut, basket of flowers within cartouche, 50 x 43 mm*] / A AMSTERDAM, / Aux dépens de la Compagnie. / [*thick-thin rule, 56 mm*] / M. DCC. L. /

8°. sig. π⁴ B-E⁴ F²; pag. 43 (p.15, 27 not numbered); $2 signed, roman; sheet catchwords.

[1] title; [2] Acteurs; [3]-43 La Mort de César, tragédie.

Folger Shakespeare Library, Washington: PQ 2077 M7 1750 Cage.

W50 (1751)

LA / HENRIADE / ET AUTRES / OUVRAGES / *DU MÊME AU-TEUR.* / NOUVELLE EDITION, / Revuë, corrigée, avec des augmentations confiderables, / particuliéres & incorporées dans tout ce Recueil, / *Enrichi de 56. Figures.* / TOME CINQUIE'ME. / [*woodcut, face in framed sun-burst, 43 x 30 mm*] / A LONDRES, / *AUX DE'PENS DE LA SOCIETE'.* / M. DCC. LI. / [*lines 2, 4, 6, 10, 11 and 13 in red*]

[*half-title*] OEUVRES / DE / MONSIEUR / DE VOLTAIRE. / *TOME CINQUIE'ME.* /

12°. sig. π^2 $*^2$ A-L^{12} $^1\pi^2$ M-V^{12} X^4 $^2\pi$1; pag. [*8*] XXXIV 230 [*4*] [231-232] 233-453 [*454-455*] (p.134 numbered '234', 152 '252', 293 '193', 351 '451'); $6 signed, arabic (– *2, X3-4; K3 signed 'K'); direction line 'Volt. *Tome V.*'; page catchwords.

[*1*] half-title; [*2*] blank; [*3*] title; [*4*] blank; [*5-8*] Table des pièces et titres contenus au tome cinquième; [i]-XXXIV, [1]-230 other texts; [*1*] $^1\pi$1r 'OEUVRES / DE / MONSIEUR / DE VOLTAIRE. / *SUITE DU TOME V.*'; [2] blank; [*3*] $^1\pi$2r 'LA / HENRIADE / ET AUTRES / OUVRAGES / *DU MÊME AUTEUR.* / NOUVELLE EDITION, / Revuë, corrigée, avec des augmentations confiderables, / particuliéres & incorporées dans tout ce Recueil, / *Enrichi de 56. Figures.* / SUITE DU TOME CINQUIE'ME. / [*woodcut, formal design, 46 x 30 mm*] / A LONDRES, / *AUX DE'PENS DE LA SOCIETE'.* / M. DCC. LI.' (*lines 2, 4, 6, 10, 11 and 13 in red*); [*4*] blank; [231] M1r 'LA / MORT / DE / CÉSAR, / *TRAGÉDIE.* / Volt. *Tome V.*   M   PRE'-'; [232] blank; 233-235 Préface des éditeurs de l'édition de 1738; 236-243 Lettre de Mr Algaroti, à Mr l'abbé Franquini, envoyé de Florence, sur la tragédie de Jules-César, par M. de Voltaire; 244 Acteurs; [245]-312 La Mort de Cesar, tragédie; [313]-453 other texts; [454] blank; [455] Errata du tome V.

ImV: A 1751/1 (5); Bibliothèque municipale, Grenoble.

W51

ŒUVRES / DE / M. DE VOLTAIRE. / NOUVELLE EDITION, / Confidérablement augmentée, / *Enrichie de Figures en taille-douce.* / TOME V. / [*typographic ornament*] / [*thick-thin rule, 57 mm*] / M. DCC. LI. / [*thin-thick rule, 57 mm*] / [*lines 1, 3, 5, 7 and 8 in red*]

[*half-title*] ŒUVRES / DE / M. DE VOLTAIRE. /

12°. sig. π^2 A-Ll^{8,4}; pag. [*4*] 408 (p.232 numbered '32'); $4,2 signed, roman; direction line '*Tome V.*' (sig. V '*Tome V*'); sheet catchwords.

[1]-224 other texts; [225] T5r 'LA / MORT / DE / CÉSAR, / *TRAGÉDIE*, / Repréfentée pour la premiére fois / le Jeudi 29 Août 1743.'; [226]

blank; [227]-230 Préface des éditeurs de l'édition de 1738; [231]-241 Lettre de M. Algaroti, à M. l'abbé Franquini. Envoyé de Florence, sur la tragédie de Jules-César, par Mr de Voltaire; [242] Acteurs; [243]-296 La Mort de César, tragédie; [297]-408 L'Enfant prodigue.

The text of this Lambert edition varies from that of w48D at I.224, 227, II.8 and 77.

Taylor: V1 1751 (5).

w52

OEUVRES / DE / M^{r.} DE VOLTAIRE / *NOUVELLE EDITION* / REVUE, CORRIGE'E / ET CONSIDERABLEMENT AUGMEN- TE'E / PAR L'AUTEUR / ENRICHIE DE FIGURES EN TAILLE- DOUCE. / *TOME SECOND.* / [*intaglio engraving*] / *A DRESDE 1752.* / CHEZ GEORGE CONRAD WALTHER / LIBRAIRE DU ROI. / *AVEC PRIVILEGE.* / [*lines 1, 3, 5, 7, 9, 11 and 13 in red*]

12°. sig. π² A-Oo⁸,⁴ Pp⁶ (± A2, E6, N4-5, O2, Q2-3, S3, Ff2, Pp6); pag. [4] 460; $5,3 signed, arabic (– Pp5); direction line 'VOLT. Tom. II.' (+ A2, E6, N4, O2, Q2, S3, Ff2, Pp6); page catchwords.

[*1*] title; [2] blank; [*3-4*] Table des pièces contenues dans le tome II (affected by A2 cancel); [1]-406 other texts; [407] Ll4r 'LA / MORT / DE / CESAR, / TRAGEDIE. / Ll4   *LET-*'; [408] blank; 409-413 Lettera del signor conte Algarotti al signor abate Franchini inviato del gran duca di Toscana a Parigi; [414] Acteurs; [415]-460 La Mort de César, tragédie; 460 Fautes à corriger.

This edition reprints the text of w48D. It is most likely that the cancel of Pp6 affected only the 'Fautes'.

Bn: Rés. Z Beuchot 14 (2); Österreichische Nationalbibliothek, Vienna: *38 L 1.

[T53]

Le Théâtre de M. de Voltaire. Nouvelle édition qui contient un recueil complet de toutes les pièces de théâtre que l'auteur a données jusqu'ici. Amsterdam, chez François-Canut Richoff, près le comptoir de Cologne, 1753.

Only volume 4 of this edition is known, containing *Samson, Pandore, La Prude, Rome sauvée* and *Le Duc de Foix*.

Bn: Yf 12337.

w56

OUVRAGES / DRAMATIQUES / AVEC / *LES PIECES RELA-TIVES A CHACUN.* / TOME PREMIER. / [*woodcut, theatrical emblems and manacles, 80 x 49 mm*] / [*thick-thin rule, 59 mm*] / *MDCCLVI.* / [*lines 2, 4 and rule in red*]

[*half-title*] COLLECTION / COMPLETTE / DES / ŒUVRES / *de Mr. de VOLTAIRE,* / PREMIERE EDITION. / *TOME SEPTIEME.* /

8°. sig. π^2 A-Ee^8 (Ee8 blank); pag. [*4*] 446 (p.177 numbered '187', 227 '22'); $4 signed, arabic; direction line '*Théatre* Tom. I' (sig. A '*Théatre* Tom. I.'; Aa, Bb '*Théâtre* Tom. I'); page catchwords.

[*1*] half-title; [*2*] blank; [*3*] title; [*4*] blank; [1]-292 other texts; [293] T3*r* 'LA / MORT / DE CESAR, / *TRAGEDIE.* / T3'; [294] blank; 295-301 Lettera del signor conte Algarotti al signore abate Franchini inviato del gran duca di Toscana a Parigi; [302] Acteurs; [303]-358 La Mort de Cesar, tragédie; [359]-445 other texts; 446 Ouvrages dramatiques contenus en ce volume avec les pièces qui sont relatives à chacun.

This first printing of the Cramer *Collection complette*, produced under Voltaire's supervision, makes changes to *La Mort de César* at I.213, 223, 280, II.205 and 241.

Bn: Z 24582.

w57G1

OUVRAGES / DRAMATIQUES / AVEC / *LES PIECES RELA-TIVES A CHACUN.* / TOME PREMIER. / [*woodcut, emblems of astronomy, 82 x 73 mm*] / [*thick-thin rule, 58 mm*] / *MDCCLVII.* / [*lines 2, 4 and rule in red*]

[*half-title*] COLLECTION / COMPLETTE / DES / ŒUVRES / *de Mr. de VOLTAIRE,* / PREMIERE EDITION. / *TOME SEPPTIEME.* [*sic*] /

8°. sig. π^2 A-Ee^8 (Ee8 blank); pag. [*4*] 446 (p.47 numbered '45'); $4 signed, arabic; direction line '*Théatre* Tom. I.' (sigs C, E, G, I-N, R, S, V, Aa, Bb, Dd '*Théâtre* Tom. I.'); page catchwords.

[*1*] half-title; [*2*] blank; [*3*] title; [*4*] blank; [1]-292 other texts; [293] T3*r* 'LA / MORT / DE CESAR, / *TRAGÉDIE.* / T3 *LET-*'; [294] blank; 295-301 Lettera del signor conte Algarotti al signore abate Franchini inviato del gran duca di Toscana a Parigi; [302] Acteurs; [303]-358 La

Mort de César, tragédie; [359]-445 other texts; 446 Ouvrages dramatiques contenus en ce volume: avec les pièces qui sont rélatives à chacun.

A revised edition of w56 in which *La Mort de César* appears unchanged. This printing may be distinguished from that next below by the presence, on p.111, of a woodcut of military emblems, measuring 53 x 35 mm.

Leningrad: 11-80 (from the library of Henri Rieu); Taylor: V1 1757 (7).

w57G2

OUVRAGES / DRAMATIQUES / AVEC / *LES PIECES RELA-TIVES A CHACUN.* / TOME PREMIER. / [*woodcut, emblems of astronomy, 82 x 73 mm*] / [*thick-thin rule, 62 mm*] / *MDCCLVII.* / [*lines 2, 4 and rule in red*]

[*half-title*] COLLECTION / COMPLETTE / DES / ŒUVRES / de Mr. de *VOLTAIRE*, / PREMIERE EDITION. / *TOME SEPTIEME.* /

8°. sig. π^2 A-Ee^8 (Ee8 blank); pag. [4] 446; $4 signed, arabic; direction line '*Théatre* Tom. I.' (sigs A, Aa '*Théâtre* Tom. I.'); page catchwords.

[*1*] half-title; [*2*] blank; [*3*] title; [*4*] blank; [1]-292 other texts; [293] T3*r* 'LA / MORT / DE CESAR, / *TRAGÈDIE.* / T3   *LET-*'; [294] blank; 295-301 Lettera del signor conte Algarotti al signore abate Franchini inviato del gran duca di Toscana a Parigi; [302] Acteurs; [303]-358 La Mort de César, tragédie; [359]-445 other texts; 446 Ouvrages dramatiques contenus en ce volume: avec les pièces qui sont rélatives à chacun.

Another Cramer printing, the date of which is open to question. It is unlikely that Cramer would have produced three editions in 1756-1757 and none from 1758 to 1763, and the typographic style is closer to that of w64G than to that of w57G1.

The woodcut on p.111, measuring 40 x 32 mm, features an animal skin draped over a club.

Leningrad: 11-74; Bn: Rés. Z Beuchot 21 (7); Taylor: V1 1757 (7A).

w57P

ŒUVRES / DE / M. DE VOLTAIRE, / SECONDE ÉDITION / Confidérablement augmentée, / *Enrichie de Figures en taille-douce.* / TOME IV. / Contenant fes Piéces de Théâtre. / [*typographic ornament*] / [*thick-thin rule, 57 mm*] / M. DCC. LVII. / [*thin-thick rule, 57 mm*] / [*lines 1, 3, 5, 7 and 9 in red*]

[*half-title*] ŒUVRES / DE / M. DE VOLTAIRE. /

12°. sig. π² A-Ii⁸,⁴ Kk⁴; pag. [*4*] 392 (p.64 numbered '94', 144 '148', 176 '276'); $4,2 signed, roman; direction line '*Tome IV.*'; sheet catchwords.

[*1*] half-title; [*2*] blank; [*3*] title; [*4*] Piéces contenues dans ce volume; [1] A1*r* 'LA MORT / DE CESAR / *TRAGEDIE,* / Repréfentée pour la première fois le 29 / Août 1743. / *Tome IV.*   A'; [2] blank; 3-6 Préface des éditeurs de l'édition de 1738; 7-13 Lettera del signor conte Algarotti, al signore abate Franchini inviato del gran duca di Toscana a Parigi; 14-21 Lettre de M. Algarotti, à M. l'abbé Franquini, envoyé de Florence, sur la tragédie de Jules-César, par Mr de Voltaire; 22 Acteurs; [23]-71 La Mort de César, tragédie; [72] blank; [73]-392 other texts.

The second Lambert edition of Voltaire's works, based upon w51.

Bn: Z 24645.

60A

LA / MORT / DE / CESAR, / *TRAGÉDIE.* / De Mr. DE VOLTAIRE. / *Nouvelle Edition.* / [*woodcut, sun in cartouche, motto* 'INDESINENTER', *56 x 45 mm*] / A AMSTERDAM. / [*thin-thick-thin rule, 59 mm*] / M. DCC. LX.

8°. sig. A-E⁴; pag. 40 (p.32 numbered '30'); $1 signed (– A1; + A2, signed 'Aij'); sheet catchwords.

[1] title; [2] Acteurs; [3]-40 La Mort de Cesar, tragédie.

Staats- und Universitäts-Bibliothek, Bern: Litt. XXXIV 67 (13).

T62

[*within ornamented border*] LE / THÉATRE / DE / M. DE VOLTAIRE. / *NOUVELLE ÉDITION,* / Qui contient un Recuëil complet de toutes / les Pièces de Théâtre que l'Auteur a / données jufqu'ici. / TOME PRE-MIER. / [*woodcut, bunch of flowers, 40 x 34 mm*] / *A AMSTERDAM,* / Chez FRANÇOIS-CANUT RICHOFF, / près le Comptoir de Cologne. / [*thick-thin rule, 54 mm*] / M. DCC. LXII. /

12°. sig. ã⁴ A-Bb⁸ Cc⁶; pag. [*8*] 412; $4 signed, arabic (– ã1; ã2 signed 'aij'); direction line '*Théâtre. Tome I.*' (sigs H, P, S, Aa '*Théâtre. Tom. I.*'; sig O '*Théâtre. Tome I.*'); sheet catchwords.

[*1*] title; [*2*] blank; [*3*] Table des ouvrages dramatiques contenus en ce volume: avec les pièces qui sont rélatives à chacun; [*4*] blank; [*5-8*] Préface; [1]-287 other texts; [288] blank, but for catchword 'LA MORT'; [289] T1*r* 'LA MORT / DE CESAR, / *TRAGEDIE.* / *Théâtre. Tome I.* T'; [290] blank; 291-297 Lettera del signor conte Algarotti al signore abate Franchini inviato del gran duca di Toscana à Parigi; 298 Acteurs; 299-342 La Mort de César, tragédie; [343]-412 other texts.

This edition follows the text of w56.

Bn: Rés. Z Bengesco 123 (1).

<h2 style="text-align:center">63P</h2>

LA MORT / DE CÉSAR, / *TRAGÉDIE* / EN TROIS ACTES: / PAR M. DE VOLTAIRE; / *Repréſentée pour la première fois par les* / *Comédiens Français ordinaires du Roi,* / *le 29 Août* 1743. / [*rule, 42 mm*] / Le prix eſt de 30 ſols. / [*rule, 42 mm*] / [*typographic ornament*] / *A PARIS*, / Chez DUCHESNE, / Libraire, rue Saint Jacques, / au-deſſous de la Fontaine Saint Benoit, / au Temple du Goût. / [*thick-thin rule, 46 mm*] / M. DCC. LXIII. / *AVEC APPROBATION ET PRIVILÉGE.* /

12°. sig. A-C¹²; pag. 72; $6 signed, arabic (– A1); sheet catchwords.

[1] title; [2] blank; 3-6 Préface des éditeurs de l'édition de 1738; 7-13 Lettera del signor conte Algarotti, al signore abate Franchini, inviato del gran duca di Toscana a Parigi; 14-21 Lettre de M. Algaroti, à M. l'abbé Franquini, envoyé de Florence, sur la tragédie de Jules-César, par M. de Voltaire; 22 Acteurs; [23]-72 La Mort de César, tragédie.

This is an 'offprint', reimposed, from T64P (which was printed in 1763).

Bn: Rés. Z Bengesco 40 (uncut); ImV: D Mort 2/1763/1.

<h2 style="text-align:center">T64A</h2>

[*within ornamented border*] / LE / THEATRE / DE / M. DE VOLTAIRE. / *NOUVELLE EDITION.*/ Qui contient un Recuëil complet de toutes / les Piéces de Théâtre que l'Auteur a / données juſqu'ici. / TOME PRE-MIER. / [*woodcut, basket of fruit and foliage, 38 x 35 mm*] / *A AMSTER-DAM*, / Chez FRANÇOIS-CANUT RICHOFF, / près le comptoir de Cologne. / [*thick-thin rule, 44 mm*] / M. DCC. LXIV. /

12°. sig. a⁴ A-Mm⁸,⁴; pag. [*8*] 416 (p.361 numbered 36, 364 '643'); $4,2 signed, arabic (– a1, a3-4; a2 signed 'aij'); direction line '*Théâtre. Tome I.*' (sigs Z, Ff, Mm '*Théâtre. Tome. I.*'); sheet catchwords.

[*1*] title; [*2*] blank; [*3*] Table des ouvrages dramatiques contenus en ce volume: avec les pièces qui sont rélatives à chacun; [*4*] blank; [*5-7*] Préface; [*8*] blank; [1]-291 other texts; [292] blank; [293] Bb3*r* 'LA MORT / DE CESAR, / *TRAGEDIE.* / Bb3'; [294] blank; 295-300 Lettera del signor conte Algarotti al signore abate Franchini inviato del gran duca di Toscana a Parigi; [301] blank; 302 Acteurs; 303-347 La Mort de César, tragédie; [348] blank; [349]-416 other texts.

ImV: BC 1764/1 (1); BL: 11735 aa 1 (1).

T64G

LE / THÉATRE / DE MONSIEUR / *DE VOLTAIRE.* / NOUVELLE ÉDITION. / *Qui contient un Récueil complet de tou-* / *tes les Pièces que l'Auteur a données* / *jufqu'à ce jour.* / TOME TROISIEME. / [*woodcut, two flowers, 22 x 25 mm*] / *A GÉNÉVE,* / Chez les Freres Cramer, Libraires. / [*thick-thin rule, composed of 3 elements, 46 mm*] / M. DCC. LXIV. /

12°. sig. π1 A-Ee⁶ Ff²; pag. [2] 338 ij; $3 signed, roman (– R3, X3, Y2-3, Aa3, Ff2; N3 signed 'Nij'); direction line '*Tome III.*'; sheet catchwords.

[*1*] title; [*2*] blank; [1]-100 other texts; [101] I3*r* 'LA / MORT / DE / CÉSAR, / *TRAGEDIE.* / *Représentée pour la premiere fois le Jeudi* / *29. Août* 1743. / I iij'; [102] blank; 103-104 Préface des éditeurs de l'édition de 1738; 105-109 Lettre de M. Algaroti, à M. l'abbé Franquini, envoyé de Florence. Sur la tragédie de Jules-Cesar, par Mr de Voltaire; [110] Acteurs; 111-158 La Mort de César, tragédie; [159]-338 other texts; [i]-ij Table des pièces contenues dans le III volume.

Arsenal: Rf 14092 (3).

T64P

ŒUVRES / *DE* / THÉATRE / *DE* / M. DE VOLTAIRE, / *De l'Académie Françaife, de celle de Berlin,* / *& de la Société Royale de Londres, &c.* / TOME TROISIEME. / [*woodcut, 39 x 25 mm*] / A PARIS, / Chez Duchesne, Libraire, rue Saint Jacques, / au-deffous de la Fontaine Saint Benoît, / au Temple du Goût. / [*thick-thin rule, 47 mm*] / M. DCC. LXIV. / *Avec Approbation & Privilége du Roi.* / [*lines 1, 3, 5, 8, 9 and 13 in red*]

[*half-title*] THÉATRE / *DE* / M. DE VOLTAIRE. / *TOME III.* /

12°. sig. π^3 A-L^{12} M^6 N-R^{12}; pag. [6] 396 (p.175 numbered '173'); $6 signed, arabic (– M4-6); direction line '*Tome III.*'; sheet catchwords.

[1] half-title; [2] blank; [3] title; [4] blank; [5] Table des pièces contenues dans ce troisième volume; [6] blank, but for catchword 'LA MORT'; [1] A1r 'LA MORT / DE CÉSAR, / *TRAGÉDIE* / EN TROIS ACTES, / *Repréſentée pour la première fois par les / Comédiens Français ordinaires du Roi, / le 29 Août* 1743. / *Tome III.* A'; [2] blank; 3-6 Préface des éditeurs de l'édition de 1738; 7-13 Lettera del signor conte Algarotti, al signore abate Franchini, inviato del gran duca di Toscana a Parigi; 14-21 Lettre de M. Algaroti, à M. l'abbé Franquini, envoyé de Florence, sur la tragédie de Jules-César, par M. de Voltaire; 22 Acteurs; [23]-72 La Mort de César, tragédie; [73]-396 other texts.

Most of the plays in this Duchesne edition, based on w57P, were also printed separately, from the same setting of type: see above, 63P. The sheets were reissued in 1767: see T67.

Leningrad: 11-100; Zentralbibliothek, Luzern: B 2172 (3); Bibliothèque municipale, Amiens: BL 2062 A (p.[1]-72 only, *La Mort de César*, with some alterations for a performance, and with the names of the actors added to p.22, including 'M. le P^{ce} de Sobre', 'M. de Montigny', 'M. le D. d'Havré', 'M. de Rheims', 'Georgia' and 'Castrop'; the roles of Decimus, Cinna and Casca have been rendered 'muets' by reassigning their lines to other characters).

W64G

OUVRAGES / DRAMATIQUES, / *AVEC* / LES PIÉCES RELA-TIVES / A CHACUN. / *TOME PREMIER.* / [*woodcut, theatrical emblems and manacles, 80 x 49 mm*] / [*thick-thin rule, 73 mm*] / M. DCC. LXIV. /

[*half-title*] COLLECTION / COMPLETTE / DES / ŒUVRES / DE / M^R. de *VOLTAIRE.* / DERNIERE EDITION. / *TOME SEPTIEME.* /

8°. sig. A-Bb^8 Cc^4 (Cc4 blank); pag. 405 (p.34, 62 not numbered; p.105 numbered '205', 366, '66'; p.214, the 2 inverted); $4 signed, arabic (– A1-2, C3-4); direction line '*Théatre.* Tom. I.' (sig. B '*Théatre* Tom. I.'; sig. P '*Théâtre. Tom. I.*'; sig. Q '*Théâtre.* Tom. I.'; sig. Bb '*Theatre.* Tom. I.'); page catchwords.

[1] half-title; [2] blank; [3] title; [4] blank; [5]-344 other texts; [345] Y5r 'LA MORT / DE / CÉSAR, / *TRAGÉDIE.*'; [346] blank; 347-353 Lettera

del signor conte Algarotti al signore abate Franchini inviato del gran duca di Toscana a Parigi; [354] Acteurs; [355]-403 La Mort de Cesar, tragédie; 404-405 Table des pièces contenues dans ce volume.

A new printing by Cramer, based upon w57G.

Merton College, Oxford: 36 f 9.

[w64R]

The relevant volume of this edition was printed and first published in 1748: see above, w48R.

[T66]

Le Théâtre de M. de Voltaire. Nouvelle édition, qui contient un recueil complet de toutes les pièces de théâtre que l'auteur a données jusqu'ici. Tome premier. Amsterdam: François-Canut Richoff, 1766.

12°. sig. π1 A-P¹² Q⁶; pag. [2] 372 (158 numbered '138'); signed $6 arabic (– Q4-6; C2 signed 'C'); direction line '*Théâtre. Tome I.*' (with variations); sheet catchwords.

[*1*] title; [2] blank; [1]-247 other texts; [248] blank; [249] L5r 'LA / MORT / DE CESAR, / *TRAGÉDIE.* / L5'; [250] blank; 251-257 Lettera del signor conte Algarotti al signore abate Franchini inviato del gran duca di Toscana a Parigi; [258] Acteurs; 259-302 La Mort de César, tragédie; [303]-371 other texts; 372 Table des pièces contenues dans ce premier volume.

No copy of this volume has been traced. The title is extrapolated from those of the other volumes in the edition; the remaining details are those of T68, which, in the case of volumes 2-6, is a reissue of the sheets of T66 under a new title-page.

67G

LA MORT / DE CESAR, / TRAGEDIE, / *Par M.* DE *VOLTAIRE.* / NOUVELLE ÉDITION. / [*woodcut, 49 x 31 mm*] / *A GENEVE,* / Chez les Freres CRAMER, Imprimeurs-Libraires. / [*thick-thin rule, 64 mm*] / M. DCC. LXVII. /

8°. sig. A-E⁴; pag. 39; $2 signed, roman (– A1); sheet catchwords.

[1] title; [2] Acteurs; [3]-39 La Mort de Cesar, tragédie.

The imprint is false.

Arsenal: Rf 14261.

[67P]

J.-M. Quérard, *La France littéraire* (Paris 1827-1864), x.312, cites an unknown edition, 'Paris, 1767, in-8.'

T67

ŒUVRES / *DE THEATRE* / DE / M. DE VOLTAIRE, / Gentilhomme Ordinaire du Roi, de / l'Académie Françaife, / &c. &c. / *NOUVELLE ÉDITION*, / *Revûe & corrigée exactement fur l'Édition* / *de Genève in-4°.* / TOME TROISIÈME. / [*woodcut, two cherubs in a cloud, 37 x 13 mm*] / *A PARIS*, / Chez la Veuve DUCHESNE, Libraire, rue Saint- / Jacques, au-deffous de la Fontaine Saint- / Benoît, au Temple du Goût. / [*thick-thin rule, 51 mm*] / M. DCC. LXVII. /

12°. sig. π^2 A-L^{12} M^6 N-R^{12} ($\pm$ K10, K11, M5); pag. [4] 396 (p.175 numbered '173'); \$6 signed, arabic (– M4-6); direction line '*Tome III.*' (K1*or* signed '*Tome III.* *', K11*r* '*', M5*r* '*Tome III.* *'); sheet catchwords.

[1] title; [2] blank; [3] Table des pièces contenues dans ce troisième volume; [4] Errata de ce troisième volume; [1]-396 see the entry for T64P, above.

A re-issue of the sheets of T64P, with new prelims (sig. π^2) and three cancels. The latter affect only *Oreste* (p.235-238, 273-274).

Bn: Rés. Yf 3389; BL: C 69 b 10 (3).

T68

LE / THÉATRE / *DE* / M. DE VOLTAIRE. / *NOUVELLE ÉDITION.* / Qui contient un Recueil complet de toutes / les Pieces de Théâtre que l'Auteur a / données jufqu'ici. / *TOME PREMIER.* / [*woodcut, basket of fruit and foliage suspended from a bracket, 29 x 24 mm*] / *A AMSTERDAM*, / Chez FRANÇOIS CANUT RICHOFF, / près le Comptoir de Cologne. / [*ornamented rule, 38 mm*] / M. DCC. LXVIII. /

A reissue of T66 (see above), using the same sheets under a new title page.

Bn: Yf 4257.

w68

THEATRE / Complet / DE / M^R. *DE VOLTAIRE*. / [*rule, 128 mm*] / TOME PREMIER. / [*rule, 127 mm*] / *CONTENANT* / OEDIPE, MARIAMNE, BRUTUS, LA MORT / DE CESAR, ZAYRE, ALZIRE, avec toutes / les piéces rélatives à ces Drames. / [*rule, 119 mm*] / *GENEVE*. / [*thin-thick rule, 119 mm*] / M. DCC. LXVIII. /

[*half-title*] COLLECTION / Complette / DES / *ŒUVRES* / DE / M^R. DE VOLTAIRE. / [*thick-thin rule, 119 mm*] / *TOME SECOND*. [or '*TOME TROISIÉME*.'] / [*thin-thick rule, 119 mm*] /

4°. sig. π^2 A-Yyy⁴ Zzz1; pag. 546 (p.219 numbered '223', 314 '14'); \$3 signed, roman; direction line '*Tom*. III. & *du Théâtre le premier*.' (sigs Cc-Ee, Zzz 'Tom. *III*. & du Théâtre le premier.'); sheet catchwords.

[*1*] half-title; [*2*] blank; [*3*] title; [*4*] blank; [1]-306 other texts; [307] Qq2*r* 'LA MORT / DE / CÉSAR, / *TRAGÉDIE*. / Qq ij'; 308-311 Lettera del signor conte Algarotti al signore abate Franchini inviato del gran duca di Toscana a Parigi; [312] Acteurs; 313-360 La Mort de César, tragédie; [361]-544 other texts; 545-546 Table des piéces contenues dans ce troisième volume.

This, the first volume of the theatre in the Cramer quarto edition, was volume 2 or 3 of the *Collection complette* depending upon the position of the *Histoire de Charles XII*, bound either as volume 2 or 7.

This edition generally follows w56. The only textual change in *La Mort de César* has the effect of eliding two speeches at III.322a-324.

Taylor: VF.

T70

LE / THEATRE / *DE* / M. DE VOLTAIRE, / *NOUVELLE EDITION*. / Qui contient un recueil complet de toutes / les Pieces de Théâtre que l'Auteur a don- / nées juſqu'ici. / *TOME PREMIER*. / [*woodcut, crossed branches, 48 x 34 mm*] / *A AMSTERDAM*, / Chez FRANÇOIS CANUT RICHOEF, [*sic*] / près le Comptoir de Cologne. / [*thick-thin rule, 55 mm*] / M. DCC. LXX. /

12°. sig. π1 A-P¹² Q⁶; pag. [2] 372 (p.311 numbered '211', 358 '835', 359 '459'); $6 signed, arabic (– Q4-6); direction line '*Théatre. Tome I.*' (sigs L, P '*Théatre. Tom. I.*'; sig. G '*héatre. Tome I.*'; sig. M '*Théatre. Tome. I.*'; sig. Q '*Theatre Tome I.*'); sheet catchwords.

[*1*] title; [2] blank; [1]-247 other texts; [248] blank; [249] L5*r* 'LA / MORT / DE CÉSAR, / *TRAGÉDIE.* / L5'; [250] blank; 251-257 Lettera del signor conte Algarotti al signore abate Franchini inviato del gran duca di Toscana. A Parigi; [258] Acteurs; 259-302 La Mort de César, tragédie; [303]-371 other texts; 372 Table des pièces contenues dans ce premier volume.

Bn: Yf 4263.

W70G

OUVRAGES / DRAMATIQUES, / *AVEC* / LES PIÉCES RELA-TIVES / A CHACUN. / *TOME PREMIER.* / [*woodcut, theatrical emblems and manacles, 80 x 49 mm*] / [*thick-thin rule, 70 mm*] / M. DCC. LXX. /

[*half-title*] COLLECTION / COMPLETTE / DES / ŒUVRES / DE / M*R*. de *VOLTAIRE.* / DERNIERE EDITION. / *TOME SEPTIEME.* /

8°. sig. A-Bb⁸ Cc⁴ (Cc4 blank); pag. 405; $4 signed, arabic (– A1-2, Cc3-4); direction line '*Théatre.* Tom. I.' (sigs K, R '*Théâtre.* Tom. I.'; sig. P '*Théâtre. Tom. I.*'); page catchwords.

[1] half-title; [2] blank; [3] title; [4] blank; [5]-344 other texts; [345] Y5*r* 'LA MORT / DE / CÉSAR, / *TRAGÉDIE.*'; [346] blank; 347-353 Lettera del signor conte Algarotti al signore abate Franchini inviato del gran duca di Toscana a Parigi; [354] Acteurs; [355]-403 La Mort de Cesar, tragédie; 404-405 Table des pièces contenues dans ce volume.

Another printing of the Cramer collection, based upon w64G.

Taylor: V1 1770G/1 (7).

71C

LA MORT / *DE* / CÉSAR, / *TRAGÉDIE,* / EN TROIS ACTES. / Par Mr. DE VOLTAIRE. / [*woodcut, sunrise, 41 x 36 mm*] / [*thick-thin rule, 83 mm*] / *A COPENHAGUE,* / Chez CL. PHILIBERT, / Imprimeur-Libraire. / [*rule, 82 mm*] / MDCCLXXI. / *Avec Permiſſion du Roi.* /

8°. sig. A-C⁸ D⁴; pag. 56; $5 signed, arabic (– A1, D4); page catchwords.

[1] title; [2] blank; [3]-7 Lettera del signor conte Algarotti al signore abate Franchini inviato del gran duca di Toscana a Parigi; [8] Acteurs; [9]-56 La Mort de Cesar, tragédie.

One of a series of Voltaire plays published by Philibert in the 1760s and 1770s.

Arsenal: Rf 14262.

w71

THEATRE / *COMPLET* / DE / *M^R. DE VOLTAIRE,* / [*rule, 73 mm*] / TOME PREMIER. / [*rule, 73 mm*] / *CONTENANT* / ŒDIPE, MARIAMNE, BRUTUS, LA MORT / DE CESAR, ZAYRE, ALZIRE, avec toutes / les piéces rélatives à ces Drames. / [*woodcut, beached ship, 36 x 27 mm*] / *GENEVE,* / [*ornamented rule, 36 mm*] / M. DCC. LXXI. /

[*half-title*] COLLECTION / *COMPLETTE* / DES / *ŒUVRES* / DE / M^R. DE VOLTAIRE. / [*ornamented rule, 74 mm*] / *TOME SECOND.* / [*ornamented rule, 74 mm*] /

12°. sig. π² A-T¹² V⁴; pag. [4] 464; $6 signed, arabic (– L2, V3-4); direction line 'Tome III. & du Théâtre le premier.' (sigs A, E, F 'Tome III. & du Théâtre le premier.'); sheet catchwords.

[*1*] half-title; [2] blank; [*3*] title; [*4*] blank; [1]-264 other texts; [265] M1r 'LA MORT / DE / CÉSAR, / *TRAGEDIE.* / Tome III. & du Théâtre le premier. M'; 266-270 Lettera del signor conte Algarotti al signore abate Franchini inviato del gran duca di Toscana a Parigi; [271] Acteurs; 272-308 La Mort de Cesar, tragédie; [309]-462 other texts; 463-464 Table des pièces contenues dans ce troisième volume.

Published by Plomteux at Liège, this edition reprints the text of w68.

Uppsala: Litt. fr.

72G

LA MORT / DE CÉSAR, / *TRAGÉDIE,* / Par M. DE VOLTAIRE. / *NOUVELLE ÉDITION.* / [*typographic ornament*] / *A GENEVE,* / Chez les Freres CRAMER, Imprimeurs-Libraires. / [*ornamented rule, 70 mm*] / M. DCC. LXXII. /

8°. sig. A-D⁴; pag. 32; $2 signed, roman (– A1; C2 signed four lines up from the foot of the page); sheet catchwords.

Scenes 5-8 of the last act are set in smaller type.

Collection of Robert L. Dawson, Texas; Yale University Library: Hfd 3 67d (title-page defective).

72P

LA MORT / DE CESAR, / *TRAGÉDIE*. / Par Mr. de Voltaire. / *Conforme à l'édition in-4° donnée par l'Auteur.* / [*woodcut, buildings within cartouche, 60 x 43 mm*] / A PARIS, / Chez la Veuve DUCHESNE, Libraire, rue Saint / Jacques, au-deſſous de la Fontaine Saint- / Benoît, au Temple du Goût. / [*thick-thin rule, 46 mm*] / M. DCC. LXXII. / *Avec Approbation & Privilége du Roi.* /

8°. sig. A-D⁴ E²; pag. 35; $2 signed, roman (– A1, B2, D2); sheet catchwords.

[1] title; [2] Acteurs; [3]-35 La Mort de Cesar, tragédie.

Folger Shakespeare Library, Washington: PQ 2077 M7 1772 Cage; Bibliothèque municipale, Nantes.

72X

[*ornamented border*] *LA MORT* / DE CÉSAR, / *TRAGÉDIE*. / Par M. DE VOLTAIRE. / [*woodcut, crossed branches, 47 x 33 mm*] / [*ornamented rule, 41 mm*] / M. DCC. LXXII. /

8°. sig. A-C⁸ D²; pag. 52; $4 signed, roman (– A1, D2); sheet catchwords.

[1] title; [2] Acteurs; [3]-52 La Mort de César, tragédie.

Arsenal: Rf 14263.

W70L (1772)

THÉATRE / COMPLET / *DE* / Mᴿ. DE VOLTAIRE. / LE TOUT REVU ET CORRIGÉ PAR / L'AUTEUR MEME. / TOME PREMIER, / *CONTENANT* / ŒDIPE, MARIAMNE, / BRUTUS, / LA MORT DE CÉSAR. / [*woodcut, theatrical emblems, 45 x 35 mm*] / *A LAUSANNE,* / Chez FRANÇ. GRASSET ᴇᴛ Comp. / [*thick-thin rule, 79 mm*] / M. DCC. LXXII. /

[*half-title*] *COLLECTION* / COMPLETTE / *DES* / ŒUVRES / *DE* / Mᴿ. DE VOLTAIRE. / [*ornamented rule, 80 mm*] / *TOME QUATOR-ZIEME.* / [*ornamented rule, 80 mm*] /

8°. sig. a-b⁸ c⁴ A-Aa⁸; pag. XXXIX [xl] 383 (no errors); $5 signed, arabic (– a1-2, c4; – c1 in some copies); direction line '*Théâtre*. Tom. I.' (sigs b, c, F, M, P-R, V, Y '*Théâtre*. Tome I.'; sig. G '*Thèâtre*. Tome I.'); sheet catchwords.

[i] half-title; [ii] blank; [iii] title; [iv] blank; V-VI Table des pièces contenues dans ce volume; VII-XII Avertissement ('Nous donnons ici toutes les pièces de théâtre de monsieur de Voltaire [...]'); XIII Avertissement des éditeurs de cette nouvelle édition; XIV-[xl], [1]-320 other texts; [321] X1*r* 'LA MORT / DE / CÉSAR, / *TRAGEDIE*. / *Théâtre*. Tom. I.   X'; [322] Avertissement; 323-326 Préface de l'année 1723 [*sic*]; 327-333 Lettre de Mr Algarotti, citoyen de Venise, à Mr l'abbé Franquini sur la tragédie de Jules-César, par monsieur de Voltaire; [334] Acteurs; 335-383 La Mort de César, tragédie.

Also issued with a cancel half-title: 'THÉATRE / COMPLET / DE / MᴿR. DE VOLTAIRE. / [*ornamented rule, 80 mm*] / *TOME PREMIER*. / [*ornamented rule, 80 mm*]'.

The theatre section of Grasset's edition was indeed 'revue et corrigée par l'auteur' but the text of *La Mort de César* appears not to have been affected. The 'Avertissement' on p.[322] reads: 'Nous restituons ici la préface et la lettre de monsieur Algaroti qui ont été oubliées dans l'édition in-4°.' The so-called 'Préface de l'année 1723' which follows is the La Marre 'Avertissement' of 1735.

Taylor: V1 1770L (14).

w72x

OUVRAGES / DRAMATIQUES, / *AVEC* / LES PIECES RELA-TIVES / A CHACUN. / *TOME PREMIER*. / [*typographic ornament*] / [*ornamented rule, 63 mm*] / M. DCC. LXXII. /

[*half-title*] COLLECTION / COMPLETTE / DES / ŒUVRES / DE / *Mᴿ. DE VOLTAIRE*. / DERNIERE ÉDITION. / *TOME SEP-TIEME*. /

8°. sig. A-Aa⁸ Bb⁴ (Bb4 blank); pag. 390 (p.158 numbered '58'); $4 signed, arabic (– A1-2, Bb3-4; I3 signed 'J3', O3 'G3'); direction line '*Théâtre*. Tome I.' (sig. B, D, F, I, L, Q, Aa '*Théatre*. Tome I.'; sig. K, O '*Théâtre*. Tom. I.'); sheet catchwords.

[1] half-title; [2] blank; [3] title; [4] blank; [5]-332 other texts; [333] X7*r*

'LA MORT / DE / CÉSAR, / *TRAGÉDIE*.'; [334] blank; 335-341 Lettera del signor conte Algarotti al signore abate Franchini inviato del gran duca di Toscana. A Parlgi [*sic*]; [342] Acteurs; [343]-388 La Mort de Cesar, tragédie; 389-390 Table des pièces contenues dans ce volume.

The last edition of the Cramer *Collection complette*, probably published (but not printed) by him.

Stockholm: Litt. fr.

73A

LA MORT / DE CÉSAR, / *TRAGÉDIE*. / EN VERS ET EN TROIS ACTES, / *Par Monfieur*, DE VOLTAIRE. / [*ornamented rule, 65 mm*] / *NOUVELLE ÉDITION*. / [*ornamented rule, 65 mm*] / [*woodcut, basket of flowers, 56 x 50 mm*] / A AVIGNON, / Chez *Louis Chambeau*, Imprimeur-Libraire, / près le Collège. / [*ornamented rule, 52 mm*] / M. DCC. LXXIII. /

8°. sig. A-D⁴; pag. 32; $2 signed, arabic (– A1); sheet catchwords.

[1] title; [2] Acteurs; [3]-32 La Mort de César, tragédie.

ImV: D Mort 2/1773/1.

73M

LA MORT / DE CESAR / *TRAGÉDIE* / DE M. DE VOLTAIRE / *Repréfentée* / AU COLLEGE DES NOBLES / DE MILAN / Pendant le Carnaval de l'an 1773. / [*woodcut*] / A MILAN, / [*rule*] / Chez Joseph Mazzucchelli / a l'Imprimerie de Malatesta. / *Avec approbation des Supérieurs.* /

8°. sig. A-C⁸; pag. 47; $4 signed, arabic (– A1, A4); page catchwords.

Biblioteca nazionale Braidense, Milan: Racc. dramm. 6137/6.

w72P (1773)

ŒUVRES / *DE M. DE VOLTAIRE*. / [*thick-thin rule, 75 mm*] / THÉA-TRE. / TOME PREMIER, / *Contenant* / *ŒDIPE, MARIAMNE, BRU-TUS*, / *LA MORT DE CÉSAR*. / [*woodcut, includes six putti, signed 'Papilon 1746', 44 x 28 mm*] / *A NEUFCHATEL*. / [*ornamented rule, 55 mm*] / M. DCC. LXXIII. /

12°. sig. π^2 A-T^{12} V^6 (V6 blank); pag. [2] ij 466; $6 signed, roman (– V4-6); direction line 'Th. *Tome I.*'; sheet catchwords.

[*1*] title; [2] blank; j-ij Avertissement des libraires associés; ij Distribution des ouvrages de M. de Voltaire, édition de Neufchatel; [1]-404 other texts; [405] R1 1*r* 'LA MORT / DE / CÉSAR, / *TRAGÉDIE.*'; [406] blank; 407-413 Lettera del signor conte Algarotti al signor abate Franchini, inviato del gran duca di Toscana a Parigi; [414] Personnages; [415]-466 La Mort de César, tragédie.

A reprint of the text of w68, usually attributed to Panckoucke.

Arsenal: Rf 14095 (1).

T73

THÉATRE / COMPLET / *DE* / M^R. DE VOLTAIRE. / LE TOUT REVU ET CORRIGÉ / PAR L'AUTEUR MÊME. / TOME SECOND. / *Contenant* / LA MORT DE CÉSAR, ZAYRE, / ET ALZIRE. / [*typographical ornament*] / *A AMSTERDAM,* / Chez les Libraires associés. / [*ornamented rule, 66 mm*] / M. DCC. LXXIII. /

12°. sig. π1 A-L^{12} M^4; pag. [2] 271 (the '1' of p.137 misplaced); $6 signed, arabic (– M3-4); direction line '*Tome II.*' (sig. B '*Tome I.*'); sheet catchwords.

[*1*] title; [2] blank; [1] A1*r* 'LA MORT / DE / CÉSAR, / *TRAGÉDIE.* / *Tome II.*   A'; [2] Avertissement; 3-6 Préface de l'année 1723 [*sic*]; 7-13 Lettre de Mr Algarotti, citoyen de Venise. A Mr l'abbé Franquini, sur la tragédie de Jules-César, par monsieur de Voltaire; [14] Acteurs; [15]-65 La Mort de César, tragédie; [66] blank; [67]-270 other texts; 271 Table des pièces contenues dans ce second volume.

An edition based upon w70L.

Zentralbibliothek, Solothurn: Qb 2566 (2).

T74

COLLECTION / *DE* / TRAGÉDIES, COMÉDIES, / ET DRAMES / *CHOISIS* / DES PLUS CÉLEBRES AUTEURS MODERNES. / [*ornamented rule, 59 mm*] / *TOME HUITIEME.* / [*ornamented rule, 58 mm*] / [*woodcut, including vase of flowers, 47 x 43 mm*] / *A LIVOURNE* 1774. / [*ornamented rule, 80 mm*] / Chez Thomas Masi et Compagnie, / Editeurs & Imprimeurs-Libraires. / *Avec Approbation.* /

8°. sig. A-Aa⁸ Bb⁶; pag. 394 [395]; $4 signed, arabic (– A1, E4, G4, H4, P3, Q4, R2, S2, T4, Y4; C4 signed 'C3'); direction line '*Tom. VIII.*' (– A); sheet catchwords.

[1] title; [2] blank; [3]-71 text by another author; [72] blank; [73] E5r '*LA MORT* / DE CESAR, / *TRAGÉDIE* / Par Monſieur DE VOLTAIRE.'; [74] Acteurs; [75]-122 La Mort de Cesar, tragédie; [123]-394 texts by other authors; [395] Table des pièces contenues dans ce huitième volume.

Arsenal: Rondel Rec. 45 VIII.

W75G

[*within ornamented border*] OUVRAGES / *DRAMATIQUES,* / PRÉCÉDÉS ET SUIVIS / DE TOUTES LES PIÉCES QUI LEUR / SONT RELATIFS. [*sic*] / [*rule, 75 mm*] / TOME PREMIER. / [*rule, 75 mm*] / *M. DCC. LXXV.* /

[*half-title, within ornamented border*] TOME SECOND. /

8°. sig. π² A-Bb⁸ Cc⁴ (Cc4 blank); pag. [4] 405; $4 signed, roman (– Cc3-4; Cc1 signed 'X'); direction line '*Théatre.* Tom. I.'; sheet catchwords.

[*1*] half-title; [2] blank; [*3*] title; [*4*] blank; [1]-6 Avertissement; [7]-346 other texts; [347] Y6r 'LA MORT / DE CÉSAR, / *TRAGÉDIE.*'; 348-353 Lettera del signor conte Algarotti al signore abate Franchini inviato del gran duca di Toscana a Parigi; [354] Acteurs; 355-403 La Mort de Cesar, tragédie; 404-405 Table des pièces contenues dans ce volume.

This, the last printing of *La Mort de César* produced under Voltaire's control, introduced errors at I.193, III.118, 204, 376 and 393.

Also issued by the publisher of w75x (see next below), with a new title in place of π²: '[*within ornamented border*] THÉATRE / COMPLET / *DE* / *M. DE VOLTAIRE.* / Divisé en 9 Volumes. / [*rule, 78 mm*] / *TOME PREMIER* / [*rule, 78 mm*] / [*woodcut, flowers and trumpet, 57 x 33 mm*] / *A GENEVE.* / [*thick-thin rule, 74 mm*] / 1776.' (Westfield College, London).

Taylor: VF.

W75G*

The copy of w75G marked up by Voltaire for the proposed Panckoucke edition contains four corrections to *La Mort de César*, at I.193, 270, 301 and II.16 (see S. S. B. Taylor, 'The definitive text of Voltaire's works: the Leningrad *encadrée*', *Studies* 124 (1974), p.45). It has been taken as the base text for the present edition.

Leningrad: 11-11.

W75X

[*within ornamented border*] OUVRAGES / *DRAMATIQUES*, / Précédés et suivis / *DE TOUTES LES PIÉCES QUI LEUR* / *SONT RELA-TIVES.* / [*rule, 73 mm*] / TOME PREMIER. / [*rule, 72 mm*] / [*typographic ornament*] / [*ornamented rule, 80 mm*] / *M. DCC. LXXV.* /

[*half-title, within ornamented border*] ŒUVRES / DE / M^R. *DE VOL-TAIRE.* / [*rule, 77 mm*] / TOME SECOND. / [*rule, 75 mm*] /

8°. sig. π^2 A-Bb^8 Cc^4 (Cc4 blank; ± G4); pag. [4] 405 (p.71 numbered '63', 216 '116' (in some copies), 219 '119', 221 '121', 362 '162'); $4 signed, roman (– Cc3-4; Bb3 signed 'Bbii'; G4 cancel signed '*Théatre*, Tom. I. Giiij 1'); direction line '*Théatre*. Tom. I.' (sigs T, Aa '*Théatre*. Tome I.'); sheet catchwords.

[*1*] half-title; [*2*] blank but for border; [*3*] title; [*4*] blank but for border; 1-6 Avertissement; [7]-346 other texts; [347] Y6r '*LA MORT* / DE CÉSAR, / *TRAGÉDIE.*'; 348-353 Lettera del signor conte Algarotti al signore abate Franchini, inviato del gran duca di Toscana a Parigi; [354] Acteurs; 355-403 La Mort de Cesar, tragédie; 404-405 Table des pièces contenues dans ce volume.

A parallel edition of Cramer's *encadrée*, probably printed in Lyons for the French market. The theatre volumes simply copy w75g.

Bn: Z 24811.

T76X

THÉATRE / COMPLET / DE MONSIEUR / DE VOLTAIRE. / TOME PREMIER. / *Contenant* Œdipe, Mariamne, / Brutus, la Mort de César, / Zayre, *avec toutes les Pièces* / *relatives à ces Drames.* / [*woodcut, cock with two books and hour-glass, signed* 'Caron', *55 x 38 mm*] / [*ornamented rule, 51 mm*] / M. DCC. LXXVI. / [*lines 1, 3, 5 and date in red*]

[*half-title*] THÉATRE / *COMPLET* / DE MONSIEUR / *DE VOL-TAIRE,* / TOME PREMIER, / *Contenant* Œdipe, Mariamne, / Brutus, la Mort de César, / Zayre, *avec toutes les Pièces relatives* / *à ces Drames.* /

8°. sig. π^2 A-Kk^8 Ll^6; pag. [4] 540; $4 signed, roman (– Y2, Ll4); direction line 'Théatre. Tom. I.' (sigs H, K 'Théatre. Tome I.'); sheet catchwords.

[1] half-title; [2] blank; [3] title; [4] blank; [1]-7 Avertissement; [8]-358 other texts; [359] Z4r 'LA MORT / DE / CÉSAR, / TRAGÉDIE. / Z iv'; 360-365 Lettera del signor conte Algarotti al signore abate Franchini inviato del gran duca di Toscana a Parigi; [366] Acteurs; [367]-416 La Mort de César, tragédie; [417]-538 Zayre; [539]-540 Table des pièces contenues dans ce premier volume.

Arsenal: Rf 14096 (1) (the half-title is bound after the title).

77A

LA MORT / DE / CESAR, / *TRAGÉDIE* / DE Mr. DE VOLTAIRE, / *Repréſentée, pour la premiere fois, au College / d'Harcourt, le 11 Août 1735.* / NOUVELLE ÉDITION. / [*woodcut, spray of flowers, 61 x 53 mm*] / A AMSTERDAM / [*double rule, 48 mm*] / M DCC LXXVII. /

8°. sig. A-E^4; pag. 39; $1 signed (– A1); sheet catchwords.

[1] title; [2] Acteurs; 3-39 La Mort de César, tragédie.

Bn: Yth 12303.

T77

THÉÂTRE / *COMPLET* / DE M. DE VOLTAIRE; / *NOUVELLE ÉDITION,* / *Revue & corrigée par l'*AUTEUR. / TOME SECOND. / CONTE-NANT / LA MORT DE CÉSAR, ZAÏRE, ALZIRE / *ou* LES AMER-ICAINS. / [*woodcut, flowers and foliage, 33 x 15 mm*] / *A AMSTERDAM,* / Chez les LIBRAIRES ASSOCIÉS. / [*thick-thin rule, 55 mm*] / M. DCC. LXXVII. /

12°. sig. π1 A-L^{12}; pag. [2] 262 [263]; $6 signed, arabic; direction line '*Tome II.*'; sheet catchwords.

[1] title; [2] blank; [1] A1r 'LA MORT / DE CÉSAR, / *TRAGÉDIE.* / *Tome II.* A'; [2] Avertissement; [3]-6 Préface de l'année 1723; [7]-13 Lettre de M. Algarotti, citoyen de Venise, à M. l'abbé Franquini, sur la tragédie de Jules-César, par monsieur de Voltaire; [14] Acteurs; [15]-64 La Mort de Cesar, tragédie; [65]-262 other texts; [263] Table des pièces contenues dans ce second volume.

Stockholm: Litt. Fr. Dram.

80P

LA MORT / DE CÉSAR, / *TRAGÉDIE.* / EN VERS ET EN TROIS ACTES. / Par Mr. DE VOLTAIRE. / [*ornamented rule, 82 mm*] / NOUVELLE ÉDITION. / [*ornamented rule, 84 mm*] / [*woodcut, flowers and fruit, 49 x 47 mm*] / *A PARIS*, / Chez RUAULT, Libraire, / rue de la Harpe. / [*ornamented rule, 66 mm*] / *M. DCC. LXXX.* /

8°. sig. A-D⁴; pag. 32; $2 signed, arabic (– A1); sheet catchwords.

[1] title; [2] Acteurs; [3]-32 La Mort de César, tragédie.

Arsenal: Rf 14264; Taylor: Vet Fr II B 1672 (2).

81T

LA MORT / *DE CÉSAR*, / *TRAGÉDIE* / Par Mr. de VOLTAIRE. / *Conforme à l'édition in-4°. donnée par l'Auteur.* / [*typographic ornament*] / A TOULOUSE, / Chez BROULHIET Libraire, rue Saint- / Rome, faisant coin de la rue du Mai. / [*thick-thin rule, 47 mm*] / M. DCC. LXXXI. / *Avec Permiſſion.* /

8°. sig. A-D⁴ E1; pag. 34; $2 signed, roman (– A1, B2); sheet catchwords.

[1] title; [2] Acteurs; [3]-34 La Mort de César. Tragédie.

BnC 1217.

Bn: Musique Th.981.

K84

OEUVRES / COMPLETES / DE / VOLTAIRE. / TOME SECOND. / [*swelled rule, 38 mm*] / DE L'IMPRIMERIE DE LA SOCIÉTÉ LITTÉRAIRE- / TYPOGRAPHIQUE. / 1784. /

8°. sig. π1 a² A-Dd⁸ Ee⁴ Ff1; pag. [2] iv 441 [442]; $4 signed, arabic (– a2, Ee3-4); direction line '*Théâtre. Tom. II.*' (sigs a, C-G, S, Z, Cc-Ff '*Théâtre.* Tome II.'); sheet catchwords.

[1] title; [2] blank; [i] a1*r* 'THEATRE. / *Théâtre.* Tome II. a'; [ii] blank; [iii]-iv Table des pieces contenues dans ce volume; [1]-290 other texts; [291] T2*r* 'LA MORT /DE CESAR, / TRAGEDIE. / Repréſentée, pour la première fois, le / 29 août 1732, & publiée en 1753. / T2'; [292] blank; [293]-295 Préface de l'édition de 1738; [296]-302 Lettre de M. Algarotti à M. l'abbé Franchini, envoyé de Florence, sur la tragédie de Jule-César,

par M. de Voltaire; [303]-309 Lettera del signor conte Algarotti al signore abbate Franchini, inviato del gran duca di Toscana a Parigi; [310] Personnages; [311]-358 La Mort de Cesar, tragédie; [359]-360 Notes et variantes sur la Mort de Cesar; [361]-[442] Alzire.

The Kehl text of *La Mort de César* includes variants at I.177-178, 185, 292, II.159, III.83 and 233, and errors at III.118 and 204.

Two more settings of this volume followed in 1785, one in octavo, the other in duodecimo. The errors at III.118 and 204 were corrected.

Taylor: VF.

89A

LA MORT / DE / CÉSAR, / *TRAGÉDIE* / DE M. DE VOLTAIRE, / *Repréfentée, pour la premiere fois, au College* / *d'Harcourt, le 11 Août 1735.* / NOUVELLE ÉDITION. / [*woodcut, classical temple, 44 x 44 mm*] / A AMSTERDAM. / [*thick-thin rule, 46 mm*] / M. DCC. LXXXIX. /

8°. sig. A-E⁴; pag. 39; $1 signed (– A1); sheet catchwords.

[1] title; [2] Acteurs; [3]-39 La Mort de César, tragédie.

Arsenal: Rf 14266 (with some manuscript notes and alterations for a performance).

89P1

LA MORT / DE CÉSAR, / TRAGÉDIE / EN TROIS ACTES ET EN VERS, / DE VOLTAIRE. / [*rule, 83 mm*] / NOUVELLE ÉDITION. / [*rule, 85 mm*] / [*woodcut, basket of fruit, 62 x 39 mm*] / *A PARIS,* / Chez DELALAIN, rue & à côté de la / comédie françaife. / [*rule, 30 mm*] / M. DCC. LXXXIX. /

8°. sig. A-D⁴; pag. 31 [32]; $2 signed, arabic (– A1); sheet catchwords.

[1] title; [2] Acteurs; [3]-31 La Mort de César, tragédie; [32] On trouve à Avignon, chez les frères Bonnet, imprimeurs, libraires, vis-à-vis le Puits des Bœufs, un assortiment de pièces de théatre, imprimées dans le même goût.

Arsenal: Rf 14265.

89P2

LA MORT / DE CÉSAR, / *TRAGÉDIE* / EN TROIS ACTES ET EN VERS. / *DE VOLTAIRE.* / [*thick-thin rule, 83 mm*] / NOUVELLE ÉDITION. / [*thin-thick rule, 83 mm*] / [*woodcut, satyr and goat, 54 x 41 mm*] / *A PARIS,* / Chez DIDOT, l'aîné, Imprimeur & Li- / braire, Rue Pavée. / [*swelled rule, 30 mm*] / M. DCC. LXXXIX. /

8°. sig. A-D⁴; pag. 31 [32] (p.9, 25 not numbered); $2 signed, arabic (– A1); sheet catchwords.

[1] title; [2] Acteurs; [3]-31 La Mort de César, tragédie; [32] On trouve à Avignon, chez les frères Bonnet, imprimeurs-libraires, vis-à-vis le Puits des Bœufs, un assortiment de pièces de théâtre, imprimées dans le même goût.

Wayne State University Library, Detroit.

92P

LA MORT DE CÉSAR, / *TRAGEDIE* / EN TROIS ACTES. / DE VOLTAIRE; / *Repréſentée pour la première fois par les Comédiens / Français ordinaires du Roi, le 29 Août 1743.* / [*rule, 50 mm*] / Prix 24 sols. / [*rule, 50 mm*] / [*woodcut, house and trees, 36 x 15 mm*] / *A PARIS.* / Chez CHAMBON, Libraire, rue de Bievre N° 34. / [*swelled rule, 50 mm*] / 1792. /

8°. sig. A-C⁸; pag. 47; $3 signed, arabic (– A1-2); sheet catchwords.

[1] title; [2] Acteurs; [3-4] Préface des éditeurs; [5]-47 La Mort de César, tragédie.

Also found with the imprint '*A PARIS.* / Chez P. Guelliot, Libraire, maison de M. Frazé, / rue de la ʙucherie, N°. 11 / [*swelled rule, 50 mm*] / 1792.', in which the 'B' of 'Bucherie' is a small capital. The remainder of the volume was produced from the same setting of type, probably during the one run of the press.

ImV: D Mort 2/1792/1 (Chambon); Yale University Library: Hf 753212 (Guelliot).

93G

LA MORT / DE CÉSAR, / *TRAGÉDIE* / EN TROIS ACTES, / Par M. DE VOLTAIRE, / *NOUVELLE ÉDITION.* / [*woodcut, flowers, 46 x 24 mm*] / A GENEVE, / Chez les Freres CRAMER, Imprimeurs - Libraire. / [*swelled rule, 69 mm*] / M. DCC. XCIII. /

8°. sig. A-D⁴; pag. 31; $2 signed, arabic (– A1); sheet catchwords.

[1] title; [2] Acteurs; [3]-31 Mort de César, tragédie.

Produced by the same printer as the 1797 edition.

Arsenal: Rf 14267.

94B

LA MORT / DE CÉSAR, / *TRAGÉDIE* / DE M. DE VOLTAIRE, / *Repréfentée, pour la premiere fois, au College* / *d'Harcourt, le 11 Août 1735.* / NOUVELLE ÉDITION. / [*woodcut, classical temple, 43 x 45 mm*] / *A BORDEAUX*, / Chez PIERRE PHILLIPPOT, Imprimeur- / Libraire, Foffés de la Commune, N°. 22. / [*thick-thin rule, 48 mm*] / L'an IIIᵉ. de la République. /

8°. A-E⁴; pag. 40; $1 signed (– A1); sheet catchwords.

[1] title; [2] Personnages; [3]-40 La Mort de César, tragédie.

Comédie-Française: 1 Mor Vol.

94L

LA MORT DE CÉSAR, / TRAGÉDIE / EN TROIS ACTES, / DE VOLTAIRE, / *AVEC les changemens fait par le Citoyen* GOHIER, / *Ministre de la Justice;* / Représentée au Théâtre de la République, à Paris. / [*woodcut, musical and theatrical emblems, 54 x 50 mm*] / *A COMMUNE-AFFRAN-CHIE*, / Chez L. CUTTY, Imprimeur, Place et Maison / de la Charité. / [*swelled rule, 35 mm*] / L'AN SECOND DE LA RÉPUBLIQUE. /

8°. sig. A-B⁸ C⁴ (– C4); pag. 37; $4 signed, arabic (– A1, A4, C2-3); sheet catchwords.

[1] title; [2] blank; [3]-37 La Mort de César, tragédie.

The Bn copy is followed by a manuscript of seven leaves, headed 'Nouveau denouement de la Mort de Cesar'. It ends 'Les changemens contenus dans ce denouement, dont j'ai ce jour donné copie à monsieur Beuchot, sont les seuls que je reconnaisse et qu'il ne faut pas confondre avec ceux qu'on a altérés et imprimés à mon insçu à *Commune affranchie*

(Lyon) l'an second de la republique chez L. Cutty imprimeur place et maison de la Charité. Paris 4 mai 1829. Gohier.'

Bn: Rés. Z Beuchot 582; Comédie-Française: 1 Mor Vol.

94P1

LA MORT / DE CESAR, / TRAGÉDIE / DE M. DE VOLTAIRE. / [*woodcut monogram, 35 x 26 mm*] / A PARIS, / Chez Jacob-Sion, Imprimeur, rue Saint-Jacques, / N°. 152, maison de M. Morin, libraire. / *Et se vend*, / Chez WEBERT, Libraire au Palais-Royal, gallerie de / N°. 218. / [*swelled rule, 26 mm*] / *L'an second de la Liberté.* /

8°. sig. π^2 A-F^4; pag. [4] 44; $2 signed, arabic (– D2, E2, F1); sheet catchwords (that for π on π2r).

Library of Congress, Washington DC.

94P2

LA MORT DE CÉSAR, / TRAGÉDIE, / EN TROIS ACTES ET EN VERS. / DE VOLTAIRE. / *Représentée pour la premiere fois par les comédiens* / *Français, le 29 août 1743.* / *NOUVELLE ÉDITION.* / Conforme a la représentation. / [*swelled rule, 55 mm*] / A PARIS, / Chez Chambon, Libraire Rue des Grands / Augustins, N° 25. / [*double rule, 43 mm*] / 1794. /

8°. sig. A-E^4; pag. 39 (p.39 not numbered; p.18 numbered '10', 35 '53'); $2 signed, arabic (– A1; E2 signed 'Eij'); sheet catchwords.

[1] title; [2] Acteurs; [3]-[39] La Mort de César, tragédie.

This is not from the same setting of type as the 1792 edition.

ImV: D Mort 2/1794/1; Bibliothèque nationale et universitaire, Strasbourg: Cd 168694/42 (3).

97G

LA MORT / DE CÉSAR, / *TRAGÉDIE* / EN TROIS ACTES, / Par M. de Voltaire, / [*rule, 92 mm*] / *NOUVELLE ÉDITION.* / [*rule, 92 mm*] / [*woodcut, as 1793 edition*] / *A GENEVE*, / Chez les Freres Cramer, Imprimeurs – Libraires. / [*thick-thin rule, 56 mm*] / M. DCC. XCVII. /

8°. sig. A-C^4 D^2 π1; pag. 29 (p.10 not numbered); $2 signed, arabic (– A1, C2, D2); sheet catchwords (– D2*v*).

[1] title; [2] Acteurs; [3]-29 La Mort de César, tragédie.
Produced by the same printer as the 1793 edition.
Arsenal: Rf 14268.

7. Translations and adaptations

This list of translations of *La Mort de César* does not claim to be
exhaustive and is largely based upon secondary sources, to which
the reader is referred for further information.[128]

English

To his adaptations of *Zaïre* (1733) and *Alzire* (1736), Aaron Hill added
in 1753 that of *La Mort de César*, under the title of *The Roman revenge*
(the first known edition is the 'second', of 1754).

This five-act tragedy had been preceded by considerably less free
translations of extracts from Voltaire's three-act play, including the
whole of II.v, which appeared in *The Prompter* 145 (26 March 1736),
edited by Hill (see D. J. Fletcher, 'Aaron Hill, translator of *La Mort de
César*', *Studies* 138 (1975), p.73-79). The critical reception of the first

---

[128] Sources include: Hans Fromm, *Bibliographie Deutscher Übersetzungen aus dem
Französischen 1700-1948* (Baden-Baden 1950-1953), vi.277; Paul Wallich and
Hans von Müller, *Die Deutsche Voltaire-Literatur des achtzehnten Jahrhunderts* (Berlin
1921); Theodore Besterman's three bibliographies, 'A provisional bibliography
of Italian editions and translations of Voltaire', *Studies* 18 (1961), p.263-310, 'A
provisional bibliography of Scandinavian and Finnish editions and translations
of Voltaire', *Studies* 47 (1966), p.53-92, 'Provisional bibliography of Portuguese
editions of Voltaire', *Studies* 76 (1970), p.15-35; Luigi Ferrari, *Le Traduzioni
italiane del teatro tragico francese nei secoli XVIIᵉ e XVIIIᵉ. Saggio bibliografico*
(Paris 1925); Jeroom Vercruysse, 'Bibliographie provisoire des traductions
néerlandaises et flamandes de Voltaire', *Studies* 116 (1973), p.19-46; Francisco
Lafarga, *Voltaire en España (1734-1835)* (Barcelona 1982); Christopher Todd,
'A provisional bibliography of published Spanish translations of Voltaire', *Studies*
161 (1976), p.43-136; Marek Ostaszewicz, 'La destinée d'une tragédie: la *Mort
de César* en Pologne', *Kwartalnik neofilologiczny* 27 (1980), p.405-12; *Bibliografia
Literatury Polski: Nowy Korbut*, vols. 4-6 Oświecenie (1966-1972); A.-M. Rousseau,
L'Angleterre et Voltaire, Studies 145-147 (1976), iii.977-1016.

performance of Hill's play at Bath in the summer of 1753 is dealt with in H. L. Bruce, 'English adaptations of Voltaire's plays', *Mln* 32 (1917), p.247-48.

The Roman revenge, a tragedy, by Aaron Hill. Second edition. London, W. Owen, 1754. pag. iv 105.

The Roman revenge, a tragedy. Acted at the theatre in Bath, in *The Dramatic works of Aaron Hill, Esq,* London 1760, ii.261-327.

The Death of Caesar, in *The Works of M. de Voltaire,* London 1761-1763, vol.xiii. Translated by T. Smollett and others.

The Death of Caesar, in *The Dramatic works of M. de Voltaire,* London 1781, vol.i. Translated by Hugh Downman.

Italian

La Morte de Cesare, tragedia, in *Le Tragedie del Signore di Voltaire adattate all'uso del Teatro Italiano,* Firenze 1752, i.[237]-90. Prose translation by Antonio Maria Ambrogi, with minor modifications including amalgamation of II.i-ii and III.ii-iii, v-vi.

Il Cesare, e il Maometto tragedie del signor di Voltaire. Venezia, Giambatista Pasquali, 1762. pag. 265 [*sic,* for 269]. Translated by Melchiorre Cesarotti.

La Morte di Cesare, in *Scelta di alcune eccellenti tragedie francesi tradotte in verso sciolto italiano,* Liegi [Modena] 1764-1768, ii.207-62 (1764). Translated by Agostini Paradisi. The false imprint of Liège may be accounted for by an expected Inquisitorial prohibition (see Ferrari, p.290, n.2). Paradisi sent Voltaire a manuscript (see D8418, 5 August 1759, and Voltaire's comments on the translation, D8573; for the manuscript, see BV, p.1023, no.54).

La Morte di Cesare. n.p.n.d. A separate edition of the Paradisi translation.

La Morte di Cesare, in *Teatro del Signor di Voltaire trasportato in lingua italiana,* Venezia 1771, i.[253]-323. The second edition of Cesarotti's translation, which includes Voltaire's letter to him (D13099; 10 January 1766), thanking him for sending the translation, and comparing his verse style to that of Terence. Cesarotti's translation was republished singly and in collected works on ten subsequent occasions during the eighteenth century in Italy (see Ferrari, p.174-78).

La Morte di Cesare, in *Poesie di Girolamo Gastaldi Genovese fra gli Arcadi sinopio Attéo*, s.l. 1779, i.[105]-76. Translated by Girolamo Gastaldi.

La Morte di Cesare. Parma, Filippo Carmignani, [1786]. pag. viii 52. Translated by Gianfrancesco Corradi, performed at the Collegio de' Nobili at Parma in 1786.

Spanish

La Muerte de Cesar. Manuscript of 67 leaves, 205 x 150 mm. Translated by Antonio Zacagnini. This translation accommodates a final scene of his own invention in which abundant scope for spectacle is indicated in the stage directions, which accompany Antony's incitement of the crowd to hatred of the assassins and wholesale murder and arson. (Biblioteca Menéndez Pelayo, Santander: ms 42).

La Muerte de Cesar. Madrid, Blas Román, 1791. pag. xii 87 v 150. Translated by Mariano Luis de Urquijo.

La Muerte de Cesar. Manuscript of 71 leaves, 195 x 140 mm. Translated by Francisco Altés. (Biblioteca de Catalunya, Barcelona: ms 840).

La Muerte de Cesar. Barcelona, Imprenta de la Viuda Roca, 1823. pag. 54. Translated by Francisco Altés. The liberal political stance of Altés leads him to make a radically different change in the ending of his *Muerte de Cesar*, by contrast with that of Zacagnini: the plebeians are shown supporting Caesar's assassins and rejoicing in the victory over despotism by the defenders of freedom. In the manuscript version of the play cited above, Altés makes light of this drastic departure from Voltaire's text. It is significant, however, that when his translation was later included in a collection of plays published in 1866-1868, it did not contain the 'liberal' dénouement.

La Muerte de Cesar, translated by Francisco Altés, in *Teatro selecto antiguo y moderno nacional y extranjero*, ed. Francisco José Orellana, Barcelona 1866-1868, v.[619]-635.

Portuguese

A Morte de Cesar, tragedia de Mr Voltaire. Coimbra, Imprensa da Universidade, 1821. pag. 63. Translated by Manoel Joaquim Borges de Paiva in decasyllabic blank verse.

Dutch

De Dood van Cesar; treurspel. Amsteldam, Izaak Duim, 1737. pag. vi 41 iii. (BL: C 44 d 21). Translated by Jacob Voordaagh. This appears to be the first published translation of *Mort de César*, and includes a dedication by the translator to Voltaire, dated 24 February 1737. Voltaire was aware of this translation: see D1286, 18 February 1737.

De Dood van Cesar, treurspel. Amsteldam, Izaak Duim, 1740. pag. 64. Translated by C. Sebille.

De Dood van Cesar, treurspel. Amsteldam, Izaak Duim, 1756. pag. viii 41 iii. The Voordaagh translation.

De Dood van Julius Cesar, eersten Keyser der Romeynen. Gend, J. F. Vander Schueren, 1785. pag. viii 3-34. Translated by Antheunis, in blank verse, with an introduction.

De Dood van Cezar, treurspel, in drie bedryven. Amsteldam, Pieter Johannes Uylenbroek, 1801. pag. 58. Translated by H. Tollens.

De Dood van Julius Cesar, eersten Keyser der Romeynen. Gend, P. A. Kimpe, 1803. pag. viii 42 ii. A new edition of the 1785 translation.

German

For the 1737 edition of the Scharffenstein translation, see above, p.124.

Cäsars Tod. Ein Trauerspiel. Braunschweig, Leipzig 1749. pag. 59. The Scharffenstein translation.

Cäsars Tod, in *Sämmtliche Schauspiele nebst den dazu gehörigen Schriften,* Nürnberg, Bauer & Raspe, 1766-1771, vol.ii.

Cäsars Tod, Ein Trauerspiel. n.p.n.d. [*c.* 1770]. pag. 59.

Der Tod Julius Cäsars. Ein Trauerspiel in 3 Aufz. Bayreuth, Lübeck 1792. pag. 93. Translated by Johann Friedrich Leonhard Menzel.

Zäsars Tod. Trauerspiel in 3 Aufz. Metrisch übers. Glogau, Günther, 1805.

Cäsar. Leipzig, Brockhaus, 1821 (Classisches Theater der Franzosen 3). Translated by Friedrich Peucer.

Swedish

La Mort de Cesar, tragédie de M. de Voltaire. Cæsars död, sorge-spel i tre öpningar. Stockholm, Lars Salvius, 1764. pag. 109. Translated by C. Manderström.

Cesars Död. Stockholm, J. Hörberg, 1829. pag. iv 49. Translated by J. Remmer.

Cæsars död, in *Öfversättningar fran främmande författare af Henrik Westin,* Göteborg 1885, p.103-50.

Russian

Tragediya Smert' Tsesarevicha v trekh deistviyakh. Sankt Peterburg, 1777. pag. 67. Translated by Vasily Ievlev.

Tragediya Smert' Tsesarevicha. Moskva 1787. pag. 63.

An anonymous undated manuscript translation of the play into Russian is held by the Herzog-August-Bibliothek, Wolfenbüttel, a facsimile edition of which can be found in *Slavische Propyläen, Texte in Neu- und Nachdrucken* 19 (München 1967).

Polish

Śmierć Cezara Tragedya. Wyprawiona, Roku Pańskiego, 1755. An abridged translation by Wojciech Mokronowski. The translator was at pains to produce a text which would be suitable for performance by a cast made up of pupils at the Jesuit college in Warsaw. Voltaire's tragedy was explicitly chosen in preference to those of Conti and Buckingham on the grounds of its author's superior workmanship, but the text of his play did not receive as much respect as his reputation did from the college's preceptor of poetry, Mokronowski: in the name of liberty and national identity, two of the most striking features of Voltaire's version of Caesar's death – the father-son relationship and Antony's funeral oration – are excluded and the emphasis on the portrayal of the freedom-fighters opposing despotism is consequently enhanced.

A translation was made for a performance at the Piarist college in 1756 by Stanislaw Hieronim Konarski, or Augustyn Józef Orłowski (who also translated *Mérope, Zaïre* and *Alzire*): no manuscript or edition is known.

Śmierć Cezara. Tragedia, extracts in *Wybór różnych gatunków poezji,* ed. Sz. Bielski (1806-1807), iii.117-20. A translation for performance at the Piarist college, 1786, by Ildefons Zubowski.

Śmierć Cezara. Tragedia, extracts in *Rozrywki dla Dzieci* 9 (1828), p.249-52. Translated by Mikołaj Adam Dzieduszycki (*c.* 1790).

Śmierć Cezara Trajedya w trzech aktach Z dziet Woltera tłumaczona przez Antoniego Wybranowskiego. Lublin 1815. pag. 52.

Śmierć Cezara. A manuscript translation, dated 29 November 1821, by Dominik Lisiecki, performed at Warsaw in 1818 and 1820 and at Vilno in 1821. (National Library, Warsaw: BN 1039/BOZ).

Parodies

Worthy of mention is a parody of *La Mort de César* which takes the contrast in Voltaire's play between the rigorous austerity of the conspirators and the hedonistic attitude of their victim into the realm of farce: *La Mort de Mardi-Gras, tragi-comédie, ou comédie faite pour pleurer, ou tragédie pour rire, en un acte et en vers, par des membres de l'Académie de Cocagne,* Paris 1809 (Bn: Rés. Z Bengesco 663). The gastronomic flavour of this text is evident in the *dramatis personae* – Mardi-Gras (César), Carême (Cassius), Dindonneau (Brutus), – and is at its strongest in the oration of Tranchelard, modelled with joyous irreverence, as the following extract shows, upon Voltaire's version of the speech of Shakespeare's Antony:

> Du plus grand des gourmands voilà donc ce qui reste!
> Ses souliers, son habit, sa culotte et sa veste.
> (*Il découvre la bedaine de Mardi-Gras.*)
> Voyez, là du revers d'un énorme merlan
> Le barbare Carême a déchiré son flanc:
> Là de hideux harengs lancés par des mains sûres
> A sa bedaine ont fait de profondes blessures.
> Plus loin de haricots un baril tout entier
> A porté dans son sang un poison meurtrier.

8. *Editorial principles*

The base text is w75G*, the corrected copy of the Leningrad *encadrée*. Variants are drawn from 35H, 36HA, 36P, 36A, 36L, w38, w48D, w51, w56, w68 and K (and from MF35, MF35A and MF43). Variations in punctuation are not retained and simple misprints are not recorded in the critical apparatus. The base text has been corrected at: III.118, 204, 376 and 393.

Modernisation of the base text

The spelling of the names of persons and places has been respected and the original punctuation retained.

The following aspects of orthography and grammar in the base text have been modified to conform to modern usage:

1. Consonants
    - the consonant *p* was not used in: tems, nor in its compound: longtems
    - the consonant *t* was not used in syllable endings *–ans* and *–ens*: enfans, garans, sermens, etc.
    - double consonants were used in: allarmer, allarmes, apperçois, fidelle, rappeller
    - a single consonant was used in: couroux, falait, scêlons
    - archaic forms were used, as in: domter, hazarder, indomté, promt

2. Vowels
    - *y* was used in place of *i* in: ayeux, enyvrement

3. Accents
The acute accent
    - was used in place of the grave in: siécle
The grave accent
    - was not used in: déja
The circumflex accent
    - was not used in: ame, bucher, grace, plait
    - was used in: chûte, diadême, scêlons, sû, toûjours, vû
The dieresis
    - was used in: jouïr, obeïr, ruïne

4. Capitalisation
    - initial capitals were attributed to: Consul, Dictateur, Empereur, Empire, Monarque, Monde, Préteur, Reine, Roi, Sénat, Sénateur
    - and to adjectives denoting nationality: Romain

5. Points of grammar
  – the cardinal number *cent* was invariable
  – the final *–s* was not used in the second person singular of the imperative: crain, poursui, pren, reconnai, ren, tien, etc
  – the plural in *–x* was used in: loix

6. Various
  – the ampersand was used
  – the hyphen was used in: c'est-là, grand-homme

LA MORT·
DE CESAR,
TRAGEDIE
DE M· DE VOLTAIRE·
NOUVELLE EDITION,
Revuë, corrigée & augmentée par l'Auteur.

Avec un Avertiſſement & une Lettre à ce ſujet.

Imprimée A LONDRES chez INNIS
Et ſe vend, A PARIS,
Chez JEAN-BAPTISTE-CLAUDE BAUCHE,
à la deſcente du Pont-neuf, près les Auguſtins, à S. Jean dans le Déſert.

M. DCC. XXXVI.

1. *La Mort de César*: title-page of the first authorised edition (36P),
published in Paris by Bauche (Taylor Institution, Oxford).

LA MORT
DE CÉSAR,
TRAGÉDIE

LETTERA DEL SIGNOR CONTE ALGAROTTI
AL SIGNORE ABATE FRANCHINI,
INVIATO DEL GRAN DUCA DI TOSCANA
A PARIGI

Io non so per che cagione cotesti signori si abbiano a maravigliar
tanto che io mi sia per alcune settimane ritirato alla campagna, e
in un angolo di una provincia como e' dicono. Ella nò che non
se ne maraviglia punto; la qual pur sa à che fine io mi vada
cercando varj paesi, e quali cose io m'abbia potuto trovare in   5
questa campagna. Qui lungi dal tumulto di Parigi vi si gode una
vita condita dà piaceri della mente; e ben si può dire che a queste
cene no manca nè Lambert nè Molière.[1] Io do l'ultima mano a'
miei *Dialoghi*, i quali han trovata molta grazia innanzi gli occhi
così della bella Emilia, come del dotto Voltaire; e quasi direi allo   10
specchio di essi io vò studiando i bei modi della culta conversazione che vorrei pur trasferire nella mia operetta. Ma che dira ella
se dal fondo di questa provincia io le manderò cosa che dovriano
pur tanto desiderare cotesti signori *inter beatae fumum et opes
strepitumque Romae*?[2] Questa si è il *Cesare* del nostro Voltaire non   15
alterato o manco, ma quale è uscito delle mani dell' autore suo.
Io non dubito che ella non sia per prendere, in leggendo questa
tragedia, un piacer grandissimo; e credo che anch'ella vi ravviserà
dentro un nuovo genere di perfezione a che si può recare il teatro
tragico francese. Benchè un gran paradosso parrà cotesto à coloro   20
che credono spenta la fortuna di quello insieme con Cornelio e
Racine, e nulla fanno immaginare sopra le costoro produzioni.
Ma certo niente pareva, non sono ancora molti anni passati, che
si avesse a desiderare nella musica vocale dopo Scarlatti, o nella

[1] Cf. Boileau, *Satires*, III.v.34: 'Nous n'avons, m'a-t-il dit, ni Lambert ni
Molière'.
[2] Horace, *Carmina*, III.xxix.11-12.

strumentale dopo Corelli. Pur nondimeno il Marcello ed il Tartini   25
ne han fatto sentire che vi avea così nell'altra alcun termine più
là. Intantochè egli pare non accorgersi l'uomo de' luoghi che
rimangono ancora vacui nelle arti se non dopo occupati. Così
interverrà nel teatro; e la morte di Giulio Cesare mostrerà *nescio
quid majus quanto* al genere delle tragedie francesi. Che se la   30
tragedia, a distinzione della commedia, è la imitazione di un'azione
che abbia in se del terribile e del compassionevole, è facile à
vedere, quanto questa che non è intorno à un matrimonio o à un
amoretto, ma che è intorno à un fatto atrocissimo e alla più gran
rivoluzione che sia avvenuta nel più grande imperio del mondo,   35
è facile dico à vedere quanto ella venga ad essere più distinta
dalle commedie delle altre tragedie francesi, e monti dirò così
sopra un coturno più alto di quelle. Ma non è già per tutto ciò
che io credo che i più non sieno per sentirla altrimenti. Non fa
mestieri aver veduto *mores hominum multorum et urbes per sapere*[3]   40
che i più bei ragionamenti del mondo se ne vanno quasi sempre
con la peggio quando egli hanno à combattere contra le opinioni
radicate dall' usanza e dall' autorità di quel sesso, il cui imperio
si stende sino alle provincie scientifiche. L'amore che è signor
dispotico delle scene francesi vorrà difficilmente comportare, che   45
altre passioni vogliano partire il regno con esso lui; e non sò
come una tragedia dove no entran donne, tutta sentimenti di
libertà e patriche di politica, potrà piacere là dove odono Mitridate
fare el galante sul punto di muovere il campo verso Roma,[4] e
dove odono Cesare medesimo che novello *Orlando* si vanta di   5c

26   w68, K: sentire che sentire che
     w56, w68, K: così nell'una come nell'altra

---

[3] Horace, *Ars poetica*, 142.
[4] Pietro Jacopo Martelli, in his *Dialoghi della tragedia antica e moderna* (Bologna
1735), criticises Racine's amorous Mithridate. See A. Salza, *L'Ab. Antonio Conti
e le sue tragedie* (Pisa 1898), p.48; cf. also Voltaire's own preface to the play on
this same point (see below, appendix II).

aver fatto giostra con Pompeo in Farsaglia per i belli occhi di
Cleopatra. E forse che il Cesare del *Voltaire* potrà correre la
medesima fortuna à Parigi che Temistocle, Alcibiade e quegli
altri grandi nomini della Grecia corsero in Atene; i quali erano
ammirati da tutta la terra e sbanditi à un tempo medesimo della
patria loro.

Come sia, il Voltaire ha preso in questa tragedia ad imitare la
severità del teatro inglese, e segnatamente Shakespeare uno de'
loro poëti, in cui dicesi, en non a torto, che vi sono errori
innumerabili e pensieri inimitabili, *faults innumerable and thoughts
inimitable*. Del che il suo *Cesare* medesimo ne fà pienissima fede.
E ben ella può credere che il nostro poëta ha fatto quell' uso di
Shakespeare che Virgilio faceva de Ennio. Egli ha espresso in
francese le due scene ultimi della tragedia inglese, le quali, toltono
alcune mende, sono come quelle due di Burro e di Narciso
con Nerone del *Britannico*, due specchi cioè de eloquenza nel
persuadere altrui le cose le più contrarie tra loro sullo stesso
argomento. Ma chi sa se anche da questo lato, voglio dire a cagion
della imitazione di Shakespeare, questa tragedia non sia per
piacere meno che no si vorrebbe? A niuno è nascosto come la
Francia e l'Inghilterra sono rivali nella politica, nel commercio,
nella gloria delle armi e delle lettere.

Littora littoribus contraria fluctibus undae.[5]

E si potrebbe dare il caso la poesia inglese fosse accolta a Parigi
allo stesso modo della filosofia che è stata loro recata dal medesimo
paese. Ma certo dovranno sapere i Francesi non picciolo grado à
chi è venuto ad arricchire in certa maniera il loro Parnasso di una
sorgente novella. Tanto più che grandissima è la discrezione con
che ad imitare gl'Inglesi s'è fatto il nostro poëta, come colui che

55

60

65

70

75

---

51   K: per li begli occhi
56   K: Come che sia
57   W56:   Sakespeare

[5] Virgil, *Aeneis*, v.628.

ha trasportato nel teatro di Francia la severità delle loro tragedie   80
senza la ferocità. Nella quale idea d'imitazione egli ha di gran
lunga superato Addissono, il quale ne suo *Catone* ha mostrato a'
suoi non tanto la regolarità del teatro francese quanto la importu-
nità degli amori de quello. E non ciò egli è venuto à corrompere
uno de' pochissimi drammi moderni, in cui lo stile sia veramente   85
tragico, e in cui i Romani parlino latino, à dir così, e non
spagnuolo.

Ma un romore senza dubbio grandissimo ella sentirà levarsi
contro à questa tragedia, perchè ella sia di tre atti solamente.
Aristotile, egli è il vero, parlando nella poetica della lunghezza   90
dell' azione teatrale, non si spiega così chiaramente sopra questa
tal divisione in cinque atti, ma ognuno sa quei versi della poetica
latina:

> *Neve minor neu sit quinto productior actu*
> *Fabula quae posci vult et spectata reponi.*[6]   95

Il qual precetto da Orazio per la commedia egualmente che per
la tragedia. Ma se pur vi ha delle commedie di Molière di trè atti
e non più, e che ciò non ostante son tenute buone, non so perchè
non vi possa ancora essere una buona tragedia che sia di tre atti,
e non di cinque.   100

> *Quid autem*
> *Caecilio Plautoque dabit Romanus ademptum*
> *Virgilio Varioque?*[7]

E forse che sarebbe per lo migliore se la maggior parte delle
tragedie di oggidì si riducessero a trè atti solamente; dacchè si   105
vede che per aggiungere i cinque, il più degli autori sono pur
stati costretti ad appiccarvi degli episodi, i quali allungano il
componimento e ne sceman l'efferto, snervando come fanno
l'azione principale. E il Racine medesimo per somiglianti ragioni
compose gia l'*Ester* di tre atti e non più. Che se i Greci nelle loro   110

---

[6] Horace, *Ars poetica*, 189-190.
[7] Horace, *Ars poetica*, 53-55.

172

tragedie benchè semplicissime furono religiosi osservatori della divisione in cinque atti, è da far considerazione, oltre che per lo più gli atti sono anzi brevi che nò, che il coro vi occupa una grandissima parte del dramma.

Io non so se quivi io bene m'apponga; questo so certo che mi giova parlar di poesia con esso lei che ne potrebbe esser maestro come ella ne è talora leggiadrissimo artefice. *Pollio et ipse facit nova carmina.*[8] Sicchè ella ben saprà scorgere la bellezza di questa tragedia, molti versi della quale hanno di già occupato un luogo nella mia memoria, e vi risuonan dentro in maniera che io non gli potrei far tacere. E pigliando principalmente ad esaminare la costituzione della favola, ella potrà meglio giudicare di chichesia se il Voltaire siccome ha aperto tra' suoi una nuova carriera così ancora ne sia giunto alla metà. Ma che non vien ella medesima a Cirey a communicarci le dotte sue riflessioni? ora massimamente che ne assicurano essere per la pace gia segnata composte le cose di Europa. Niente allora quì mancherebbe al desiderio mio, e a niuno potrebbe parer nuovo in Parigi che io mi rimanessi in una provincia.

Cirey 12 Octobre 1735

115
120
125
130

[8] Virgil, *Eclogae,* III.86.

ACTEURS

Jules-César, dictateur.

Marc-antoine, consul.

Junius brutus, préteur.

Cassius,
Cimber,
Decimus,   } sénateurs
Dolabella,
Casca,

Les Romains.

Licteurs.

La scène est à Rome au Capitole.

a   36p, k: PERSONNAGES
1   36p: César, dictateur.
2-3   36p: Dolabella, ami de César. / Junius brutus.//
3   35h: Junius brutus.//
4-8   35h: Cassius. / Cimber. / Dolabella.
        36p: Casca. / Cimber. / Cinna. / Decimus.
6   k: Décime
    36p: Conjurés
7-8   w51: Dolabella. / Cinna. / Casca.

ACTE PREMIER

SCÈNE PREMIÈRE

CÉSAR, ANTOINE

ANTOINE

César, tu vas régner; voici le jour auguste,
Où le peuple romain, pour toi toujours injuste,
Changé par tes vertus, va reconnaître en toi
Son vainqueur, son appui, son vengeur, et son roi.
Antoine, tu le sais, ne connaît point l'envie.   5
J'ai chéri plus que toi la gloire de ta vie;
J'ai préparé la chaîne où tu mets les Romains,
Content d'être sous toi le second des humains;
Plus fier de t'attacher ce nouveau diadème,
Plus grand de te servir que de régner moi-même.   10
Quoi! tu ne me réponds que par de longs soupirs!
Ta grandeur fait ma joie, et fait tes déplaisirs!
Roi de Rome et du monde, est-ce à toi de te plaindre?
César peut-il gémir, ou César peut-il craindre?
Qui peut à ta grande âme inspirer la terreur?   15

CÉSAR

L'amitié, cher Antoine; il faut t'ouvrir mon cœur.
Tu sais que je te quitte, et le destin m'ordonne
De porter nos drapeaux aux champs de Babilone.
Je pars, et vais venger sur le Parthe inhumain
La honte de Crassus et du peuple romain.   20

---

11   36P: Quoi! tu ne réponds [cancel: β]
14   36P, omitted [cancel: César doit-il gémir, ou César doit-il craindre?]
20   35H: et le peuple

L'aigle des légions, que je retiens encore,
Demande à s'envoler vers les mers du Bosphore;
Et mes braves soldats n'attendent pour signal,
Que de revoir mon front ceint du bandeau royal.
Peut-être avec raison César peut entreprendre   25
D'attaquer un pays qu'a soumis Alexandre:
Peut-être les Gaulois, Pompée et les Romains,
Valent bien les Persans subjugués par ses mains.
J'ose au moins le penser; et ton ami se flatte
Que le vainqueur du Rhin peut l'être de l'Euphrate.   30
Mais cet espoir m'anime, et ne m'aveugle pas.
Le sort peut se lasser de marcher sur mes pas:
La plus haute sagesse en est souvent trompée;
Il peut quitter César, ayant trahi Pompée;
Et dans les factions, comme dans les combats,   35
Du triomphe à la chute il n'est souvent qu'un pas.
J'ai servi, commandé, vaincu, quarante années;
Du monde entre mes mains j'ai vu les destinées;
Et j'ai toujours connu qu'en chaque événement,
Le destin des Etats dépendait d'un moment.[1]   40
Quoi qu'il puisse arriver, mon cœur n'a rien à craindre;
Je vaincrai sans orgueil, ou mourrai sans me plaindre.
Mais j'exige en partant, de ta tendre amitié,
Qu'Antoine à mes enfants soit pour jamais lié;
Que Rome par mes mains défendue et conquise,   45

21   35H: je tiens
28   35H: Valaient bien
     36A: bien ces Persans
34   36P: Il peut trahir César, après le grand Pompée.
35   35H, 36A: La valeur fait beaucoup... mais dans les grands combats,
     36P: Parmi les factions, le trouble et les combats,
42   35H: et mourrai
44   MF43: enfants à jamais soit lié

[1] Cf. Shakespeare, *Julius Caesar*, IV.iii.216-217, Brutus: 'There is a tide in the affairs of men / Which taken at the flood leads on to fortune'.

Que la terre à mes fils, comme à toi, soit soumise:
Et qu'emportant d'ici le grand titre de roi,
Mon sang et mon ami le prennent après moi.
Je te laisse aujourd'hui ma volonté dernière.
Antoine, à mes enfants il faut servir de père.   50
Je ne veux point de toi demander des serments,
De la foi des humains sacrés et vains garants;
Ta promesse suffit, et je la crois plus pure
Que les autels des dieux entourés du parjure.[2]

ANTOINE

C'est déjà pour Antoine une assez dure loi,   55
Que tu cherches la guerre et le trépas sans moi,
Et que ton intérêt m'attache à l'Italie,
Quand la gloire t'appelle aux bornes de l'Asie.
Je m'afflige encor plus de voir que ton grand cœur
Doute de sa fortune, et présage un malheur: 60
Mais je ne comprends point ta bonté qui m'outrage.
César, que me dis-tu de tes fils, de partage?
Tu n'as de fils qu'Octave, et nulle adoption
N'a d'un autre César appuyé ta maison.

CÉSAR

Il n'est plus temps, ami, de cacher l'amertume,   65
Dont mon cœur paternel en secret se consume.

---

51 35H: veux pas de
54 35H: de parjure.
    36A: des lieux entourés

[2] César's sentiments (lines 51-54) recall the long speech of Shakespeare's
Brutus in *Julius Caesar*, II.i.114-140, beginning: 'No not an oath' and provide a
glaring contrast with those of Voltaire's Brutus (see *Mort de César*, II.iv.191 ff).
The attitude of the historical Caesar would seem to have been different; an oath
of allegiance was taken in his name, by decree of the senate, at the beginning
of 44 B.C.

Octave n'est mon sang qu'à la faveur des lois:
Je l'ai nommé César, il est fils de mon choix.
Le destin, (dois-je dire, ou propice, ou sévère?)
D'un véritable fils en effet m'a fait père;   70
D'un fils que je chéris, mais qui pour mon malheur,
A ma tendre amitié répond avec horreur.

ANTOINE

Et quel est cet enfant? Quel ingrat peut-il être,
Si peu digne du sang dont les dieux l'ont fait naître?

CÉSAR

Ecoute: Tu connais ce malheureux Brutus,   75
Dont Caton cultiva les farouches vertus.
De nos antiques lois ce défenseur austère,
Ce rigide ennemi du pouvoir arbitraire,
Qui toujours contre moi, les armes à la main,
De tous mes ennemis a suivi le destin;   80
Qui fut mon prisonnier aux champs de Thessalie,
A qui j'ai malgré lui sauvé deux fois la vie,
Né, nourri loin de moi chez mes fiers ennemis.

ANTOINE

Brutus! il se pourrait...

CÉSAR

                    Ne m'en crois pas. Tiens, lis.

ANTOINE

Dieux! la sœur de Caton, la fière Servilie!   85

72   35H, 36A: A sucé pour son père une invincible horreur.
77   35H: lois le défenseur
78   35H, 36P: Ce fatal ennemi
82   35H, 36P: deux fois sauvé
85   36P: Quoi! la sœur

CÉSAR

Par un hymen secret elle me fut unie.
Ce farouche Caton, dans nos premiers débats,
La fit presque à mes yeux passer en d'autres bras:
Mais le jour qui forma ce second hyménée,
De son nouvel époux trancha la destinée.   90
Sous le nom de Brutus mon fils fut élevé.
Pour me haïr, ô ciel! était-il réservé?
Mais lis: tu sauras tout par cet écrit funeste.

ANTOINE (*Il lit.*)

César, je vais mourir. La colère céleste
Va finir à la fois ma vie et mon amour.   95
Souviens-toi qu'à Brutus César donna le jour:
Adieu. Puisse ce fils éprouver pour son père
L'amitié qu'en mourant te conservait sa mère.
                                        Servilie.
Quoi! faut-il que du sort la tyrannique loi,
César, te donne un fils si peu semblable à toi?   100

CÉSAR

Il a d'autres vertus; son superbe courage
Flatte en secret le mien, même alors qu'il l'outrage.
Il m'irrite, il me plaît. Son cœur indépendant
Sur mes sens étonnés prend un fier ascendant.
Sa fermeté m'impose, et je l'excuse même,   105
De condamner en moi l'autorité suprême.
Soit qu'étant homme et père, un charme séducteur,

89   35H: forma le second
     36P: son second
97   35H, 36P: fils retrouver dans son
99   35H: Dieux! faut-il
     36P: Ah! faut-il
102   MF35: qu'il m'outrage

L'excusant à mes yeux, me trompe en sa faveur;
Soit qu'étant né Romain, la voix de ma patrie
Me parle malgré moi contre ma tyrannie;   110
Et que la liberté que je viens d'opprimer,
Plus forte encor que moi, me condamne à l'aimer.
Te dirai-je encor plus? Si Brutus me doit l'être,
S'il est fils de César, il doit haïr un maître.
J'ai pensé comme lui, dès mes plus jeunes ans;   115
J'ai détesté Sylla, j'ai haï les tyrans.³
J'eusse été citoyen, si l'orgueilleux Pompée
N'eût voulu m'opprimer sous sa gloire usurpée.
Né fier, ambitieux, mais né pour les vertus,
Si je n'étais César, j'aurais été Brutus.   120
Tout homme à son état doit plier son courage.⁴
Brutus tiendra bientôt un différent langage,
Quand il aura connu de quel sang il est né.
Crois-moi, le diadème à son front destiné,
Adoucira dans lui sa rudesse importune;   12
Il changera de mœurs en changeant de fortune.

119   35H: Et né pour commander, mais
      36P: Né pour l'ambition, mais

³ The criticism of Sulla's violent methods of government forms part of the
clémence /rigueur debate which is continued by César and Antoine in the last
scene of this act. The debate finds a parallel in the work of Montesquieu, in his
short *Dialogue de Sylla et d'Eucrate*, where the latter opposes terrorism and
tyranny: 'Pour qu'un homme soit au-dessus de l'humanité, il en coûte trop cher
à tous les autres'. Sulla is condemned in the *Considérations sur les causes de la
grandeur des Romains et de leur décadence,* but so is Caesar, whose moderation and
clemency are exposed as means of consolidating tyranny. Brutus the tyrannicide
receives extravagant praise. See Laurence Echard, *The Mix'd state,* III.iii.355: 'He
[Caesar] first took care to pardon all such as had been in arms against him, and
greatly tax'd the cruelty of Sylla, and thereby obtain'd as great a name for
clemence as before he had for valour'.
  ⁴ Cf. *Eriphyle,* II.i: 'Pliez à votre état ce fougueux caractère'; *Alzire,* I.iv: 'Tu
dois à ton état plier ton caractère'; *Oreste,* I.iii: 'Pliez à votre état ce superbe
courage'.

La nature, le sang, mes bienfaits, tes avis,
Le devoir, l'intérêt, tout me rendra mon fils.

ANTOINE

J'en doute. Je connais sa fermeté farouche:[5]
La secte dont il est n'admet rien qui la touche.   130
Cette secte intraitable, et qui fait vanité
D'endurcir les esprits contre l'humanité,
Qui dompte et foule aux pieds la nature irritée,
Parle seule à Brutus, et seule est écoutée.
Ces préjugés affreux, qu'ils appellent devoir,   135
Ont sur ces cœurs de bronze un absolu pouvoir.
Caton même, Caton, ce malheureux stoïque,
Ce héros forcené, la victime d'Utique,
Qui fuyant un pardon qui l'eût humilié,[6]
Préféra la mort même à ta tendre amitié;   140
Caton fut moins altier, moins dur, et moins à craindre,

140   35H: Préfère la
        35H, 36P, 36A, W51: à la tendre

[5] Cf. Conti, *Il Cesare*, III.i, Antonio to Cesare:
          Bruto è sì pien delle sue stoiche idee,
          Che nè il paterno amor, nè i doni tuoi
          Han potuto ammollir l'anima schiva;
          Giunio Bruto, e Catone ha sempre in bocca.
[6] In a long and eulogistic note on Cato in *Le Triumvirat* (III.i), Voltaire quotes
the following lines from an ode by Houdar de La Motte:
          Caton d'une âme plus égale
          Sous l'heureux vainqueur de Pharsale
          Eût souffert que l'homme pliât,
          Mais, incapable de se rendre
          Il n'eut pas la force d'attendre
          Un pardon qui l'humiliât.
In contrast to Antoine's disapproval of Cato's suicide (a note of censure echoed
by Brutus, II.iv.127-132), Voltaire's attitude to the decision of Caesar's enemy
to escape by death from a tyranny which he could no longer prevent was one
of approbation and he is scathing in his criticism of La Motte.

Que l'ingrat qu'à t'aimer ta bonté veut contraindre.

CÉSAR

Cher ami, de quels coups tu viens de me frapper!
Que m'as-tu dit?

ANTOINE

Je t'aime, et ne te puis tromper.

CÉSAR

Le temps amollit tout.

ANTOINE

Mon cœur en désespère. 145

CÉSAR

Quoi, sa haine!…

ANTOINE

Crois-moi.

CÉSAR

N'importe, je suis père.
J'ai chéri, j'ai sauvé mes plus grands ennemis:
Je veux me faire aimer de Rome et de mon fils;
Et conquérant des cœurs vaincus par ma clémence,
Voir la terre et Brutus adorer ma puissance. 150
C'est à toi de m'aider dans de si grands desseins:
Tu m'as prêté ton bras, pour dompter les humains;
Dompte aujourd'hui Brutus, adoucis son courage,
Prépare par degrés cette vertu sauvage

143   36A: me percer!

Au secret important qu'il lui faut révéler,   155
Et dont mon cœur encore hésite à lui parler.

ANTOINE

Je ferai tout pour toi; mais j'ai peu d'espérance.

SCÈNE II

CÉSAR, ANTOINE, DOLABELLA

DOLABELLA

César, les sénateurs attendent audience;
A ton ordre suprême ils se rendent ici.

CÉSAR

Ils ont tardé longtemps… Qu'ils entrent.

ANTOINE

                                    Les voici.   160
Que je lis sur leur front de dépit et de haine!

158   35H: Seigneur, les sénateurs demandent audience,
        36P: Déjà les sénateurs attendent audience.
159   35H, 36P: Vous avez [36P: César a] commandé qu'ils se rendent ici.

SCÈNE III

CÉSAR, ANTOINE, BRUTUS, CASSIUS, CIMBER, DECIMUS, CINNA, CASCA, ETC. LICTEURS.

CÉSAR *assis.*

Venez, dignes soutiens de la grandeur romaine,
Compagnons de César. Approchez, Cassius,
Cimber, Cinna, Décime, et toi mon cher Brutus.
Enfin voici le temps, si le ciel me seconde,   165
Où je vais achever la conquête du monde,
Et voir dans l'Orient le trône de Cyrus
Satisfaire, en tombant, aux mânes de Crassus.
Il est temps d'ajouter, par le droit de la guerre,
Ce qui manque aux Romains des trois parts de la terre.   170
Tout est prêt, tout prévu pour ce vaste dessein:
L'Euphrate attend César; et je pars dès demain.
Brutus et Cassius me suivront en Asie;
Antoine retiendra la Gaule et l'Italie.
De la mer Atlantique, et des bords du Bétis,   175
Cimber gouvernera les rois assujettis.
Je donne à Decimus la Grèce et la Lycie,
A Marcellus le Pont, à Casca la Syrie.[7]
Ayant ainsi réglé le sort des nations,

161d   35H, no stage direction
169   35H, 36P: par les droits
177-178   K:
         Je donne à Marcellus la Grèce et la Lycie,
         A Décime le Pont, à Casca la Syrie.

[7] The ancient evidence about provinces and their governors in 44 B.C. is confused and inaccurate. As a corrective, R. Syme adopts the view of W. Sternkopf, *Hermes* 47 (1912), p.321 ff. On lines 165-171, see Syme, *The Roman revolution* (Oxford 1939), p.102, n.6.

Et laissant Rome heureuse et sans divisions,   180
Il ne reste au sénat, qu'à juger sous quel titre
De Rome et des humains je dois être l'arbitre.
Sylla fut honoré du nom de dictateur;
Marius fut consul, et Pompée empereur.
J'ai vaincu le dernier; et c'est assez vous dire,   185
Qu'il faut un nouveau nom pour un nouvel empire,
Un nom plus grand, plus saint, moins sujet aux revers,
Autrefois craint dans Rome, et cher à l'univers.
Un bruit trop confirmé se répand sur la terre,[8]
Qu'en vain Rome aux Persans ose faire la guerre;   190
Qu'un roi seul peut les vaincre et leur donner la loi:
César va l'entreprendre, et César n'est pas roi.
Il n'est qu'un citoyen connu par ses services,
Qui peut du peuple encore essuyer les caprices...
Romains, vous m'entendez, vous savez mon espoir;   195
Songez à mes bienfaits, songez à mon pouvoir.

CIMBER

César, il faut parler. Ces sceptres, ces couronnes,
Ce fruit de nos travaux, l'univers que tu donnes,
Seraient aux yeux du peuple, et du sénat jaloux,

185   K: vaincu ce dernier
188   35H, 36P: Trop longtemps craint
193   35H-W68: fameux par [W48D, W56: pour] ses services
          W75G, line omitted; added by Voltaire in W75G*
195   35H: Qui... mais vous m'entendez
199-200 36P:
        Ne sont point des bienfaits dont nos cœurs soient épris.
        Reprends tes dons, César, ils sont à trop haut prix.

[8] Cf. *Il Cesare*, III.i:

ANTONIO
Corre la voce, e ciò con Cotta io spargo,
Leggersi scritto in non oscure note
Entro de' sacri Sibillini libri,
Che solo un Re può soggiogare i Parti.

Un outrage à l'Etat, plus qu'un bienfait pour nous.   200
Marius, ni Sylla, ni Carbon, ni Pompée,
Dans leur autorité sur le peuple usurpée,
N'ont jamais prétendu disposer à leur choix
Des conquêtes de Rome, et nous parler en rois.
César, nous attendions de ta clémence auguste   205
Un don plus précieux, une faveur plus juste,
Au-dessus des Etats donnés par ta bonté...

CÉSAR

Qu'oses-tu demander, Cimber?

CIMBER

               La liberté.

CASSIUS

Tu nous l'avais promise; et tu juras toi-même
D'abolir pour jamais l'autorité suprême;   210
Et je croyais toucher à ce moment heureux,
Où le vainqueur du monde allait combler nos vœux.
Fumante de son sang, captive, désolée,
Rome dans cet espoir renaissait consolée.
Avant que d'être à toi nous sommes ses enfants;   215
Je songe à ton pouvoir; mais songe à tes serments.

BRUTUS

Oui, que César soit grand: mais que Rome soit libre.
Dieux! maîtresse de l'Inde, esclave au bord du Tibre!
Qu'importe que son nom commande à l'univers,

---

205   36P: Nous avons attendu de
209   35H: tu jurais
213   36P-W51: captive et désolée,
218   MF43: esclave aux bords du

Et qu'on l'appelle reine, alors qu'elle est aux fers?   220
Qu'importe à ma patrie, aux Romains que tu braves,
D'apprendre que César a de nouveaux esclaves?
Les Persans ne sont pas nos plus fiers ennemis;
Il en est de plus grands. Je n'ai point d'autre avis.

CÉSAR

Et toi, Brutus, aussi?[9]

ANTOINE *à César.*

Tu connais leur audace: 225
Vois si ces cœurs ingrats sont dignes de leur grâce.

CÉSAR

Ainsi vous voulez donc, dans vos témérités,
Tenter ma patience, et lasser mes bontés?
Vous qui m'appartenez par le droit de l'épée,
Rampants sous Marius, esclaves de Pompée;   230
Vous qui ne respirez qu'autant que mon courroux
Retenu trop longtemps s'est arrêté sur vous:
Républicains ingrats, qu'enhardit ma clémence,
Vous qui devant Sylla garderiez le silence;

220   35H: l'appelle Rome, alors
        36P: Et qu'on la traite en reine
223   35H: Ces Persans
        35H-W51:   sont point nos
224   35H-W48D: n'ai pas d'autre
227   35H-W48D: donc, par vos
232   35H, 36P: s'arrête encor sur

[9] Voltaire chooses to echo at this point the 'Et tu Brute?' of Shakespeare's *Julius Caesar*, III.i.77. The phrasing of the question probably originated in Suetonius (*Julius Caesar*, 82). Antoine's version of César's dying words (III.viii.391) stresses Suetonius's τεϰνον to underline the parricide (see above, p.38).

Vous que ma bonté seule invite à m'outrager,   235
Sans craindre que César s'abaisse à se venger.
Voilà ce qui vous donne une âme assez hardie,
Pour oser me parler de Rome et de patrie,
Pour affecter ici cette illustre hauteur,
Et ces grands sentiments devant votre vainqueur.   240
Il les fallait avoir aux plaines de Pharsale.
La fortune entre nous devient trop inégale.
Si vous n'avez su vaincre, apprenez à servir.

BRUTUS

César, aucun de nous n'apprendra qu'à mourir.
Nul ne m'en désavoue, et nul en Thessalie   245
N'abaissa son courage à demander la vie.
Tu nous laissas le jour, mais pour nous avilir:
Et nous le détestons, s'il te faut obéir.
César, qu'à ta colère aucun de nous n'échappe:
Commence ici par moi; si tu veux régner, frappe.[10]   250

CÉSAR

Ecoute... et vous sortez.

(Les sénateurs sortent.)

Brutus m'ose offenser?

237   35H: Qui vous donne à mes yeux une
240   36P: ces fiers sentiments
241   35H, 36P: Il la fallait
246   35H, 36P: N'avilit son courage
247   35H, 36P: pour nous asservir
251   35H, 36P: Demeure... et
251a 35H, no stage direction
      36A-W68, stage direction added by asterisk; reference at foot of page

[10] Cf. *Il Cesare*, III.iii, Bruto to Cesare: 'Se tu destini / O l'esilio, o la morte a i due Tribuni, / Eccoti il capo mio: sfoga in me l'ira'.

Mais sais-tu de quels traits tu viens de me percer?
Va, César est bien loin d'en vouloir à ta vie.
Laisse là du sénat l'indiscrète furie.
Demeure. C'est toi seul qui peux me désarmer.   255
Demeure. C'est toi seul que César veut aimer.

BRUTUS

Tout mon sang est à toi, si tu tiens ta promesse;
Si tu n'es qu'un tyran, j'abhorre ta tendresse;
Et je ne peux rester avec Antoine et toi,
Puisqu'il n'est plus Romain, et qu'il demande un roi.[11]   260

SCÈNE IV

CÉSAR, ANTOINE

ANTOINE

Eh bien, t'ai-je trompé? Crois-tu que la nature
Puisse amollir une âme, et si fière, et si dure?
Laisse, laisse à jamais dans son obscurité
Ce secret malheureux qui pèse à ta bonté.
Que de Rome, s'il veut, il déplore la chute;   265
Mais qu'il ignore au moins quel sang il persécute.
Il ne mérite pas de te devoir le jour.
Ingrat à tes bontés, ingrat à ton amour,

252   35H, 36P: me frapper
259   35H, 36P: Et ne peux demeurer avec
260   35H: Puisqu'il n'est pas Romain, et veut avoir un roi.

[11] Cf. *Il Cesare*, III.iii, Bruto to Cesare: 'Roma non nudre un cittadin sì vile, / Che d'esser Re degnasse'.

Renonce-le pour fils.

CÉSAR

Je ne le puis: je l'aime.[12]

ANTOINE

Ah! cesse donc d'aimer l'éclat du diadème:[13]　　　　　　　　　27c
Descends donc de ce rang, où je te vois monté;
La bonté convient mal à ton autorité;
De ta grandeur naissante elle détruit l'ouvrage.
Quoi! Rome est sous tes lois, et Cassius t'outrage!
Quoi Cimber! quoi Cinna! ces obscurs sénateurs,　　　　　　　27*
Aux yeux du roi du monde affectent ces hauteurs!
Ils bravent ta puissance, et ces vaincus respirent!

CÉSAR

Ils sont nés mes égaux; mes armes les vainquirent;
Et trop au-dessus d'eux, je leur puis pardonner
De frémir sous le joug que je veux leur donner.　　　　　　　28

ANTOINE

Marius de leur sang eût été moins avare.

269　36P: Abandonne ce fils.
270　35H-W75G: aimer l'orgueil du
　　　w75G*: ⟨l'orgueil⟩ V↑ l'éclat
274　35H: Cassius l'outrage
280　35H-W51: je leur veux donner

[12] Cf. *Il Cesare*, III.i, Cesare to Antonio (who has been urging him to condemn Bruto to death): 'Io troppo l'amo'.
[13] In Voltaire's *Brutus* (I.iv), Messala referring to the Roman senators, says: 'Leur orgueil foule aux pieds l'orgueil du diadème'. In *La Henriade*, there is the following reference to Henri (1.216-218): 'Souvent sous l'humble toit du laboureur charmé, / Fuyant le bruit des cours, et se cherchant lui-même, / Il avait déposé l'orgueil du diadème' (ed. O. Taylor, Voltaire 2, p.377).

Sylla les eût punis.

CÉSAR

Sylla fut un barbare,
Il n'a su qu'opprimer. Le meurtre et la fureur
Faisaient sa politique, ainsi que sa grandeur.
Il a gouverné Rome au milieu des supplices;   285
Il en était l'effroi, j'en serai les délices.
Je sais quel est le peuple, on le change en un jour:
Il prodigue aisément sa haine et son amour.[14]
Si ma grandeur l'aigrit, ma clémence l'attire.
Un pardon politique à qui ne peut me nuire,   290
Dans mes chaînes qu'il porte, un air de liberté
A ramené vers moi sa faible volonté.
Il faut couvrir de fleurs l'abîme où je l'entraîne,
Flatter encor ce tigre à l'instant qu'on l'enchaîne,
Lui plaire en l'accablant, l'asservir, le charmer,   295
Et punir mes rivaux en me faisant aimer.

ANTOINE

Il faudrait être craint: c'est ainsi que l'on règne.

CÉSAR

Va, ce n'est qu'aux combats que je veux qu'on me craigne.

292   K: Ont ramené
294   35H: encor le tigre

[14] César's low opinion of the populace (shared by Brutus who later refers to 'ce vil peuple', II.iii.66; and 'ce peuple mou, volage, et facile à fléchir', II.iv.177; and by Antoine who exploits 'ce peuple inconstant et facile', III.viii.406) echoes Voltaire's earlier *Brutus*, in which Arons (I.ii) shows his scorn of 'ce peuple indocile et barbare, / Que la fureur conduit, réunit et sépare, / Aveugle dans sa haine, aveugle en son amour, / Qui menace et qui craint, règne et sert en un jour' and Messala voices the same contempt for 'ce peuple volage' (I.iv), 'un vil peuple' (II.v). Tullie (III.v) too, has no respect for 'un vil peuple'. The same view is to be found in *La Henriade*, x.390-392.

ANTOINE

Le peuple abusera de ta facilité.

CÉSAR

Le peuple a jusqu'ici consacré ma bonté.   300
Vois ce temple que Rome élève à la clémence.

ANTOINE

Crains qu'elle n'en élève un autre à la vengeance:
Crains des cœurs ulcérés, nourris de désespoir,
Idolâtres de Rome, et cruels par devoir.
Cassius alarmé prévoit qu'en ce jour même   305
Ma main doit sur ton front mettre le diadème.
Déjà même à tes yeux on ose en murmurer.
Des plus impétueux tu devrais t'assurer.
A prévenir leurs coups daigne au moins te contraindre.

CÉSAR

Je les aurais punis, si je les pouvais craindre.   31
Ne me conseille point de me faire haïr.
Je sais combattre, vaincre, et ne sais point punir.
Allons, et n'écoutant ni soupçon ni vengeance,
Sur l'univers soumis régnons sans violence.

Fin du premier acte.

301   35H: Vois le temple
      35H-W75G: à ma clémence
      W75G*: ⟨ma⟩ ↑la
307   35H, 36P: on ose murmurer
313   35H, 36A: ni soupçons ni

192

ACTE II

SCÈNE PREMIÈRE

BRUTUS, ANTOINE, DOLABELLA

ANTOINE

Ce superbe refus, cette animosité,
Marquent moins de vertu que de férocité.
Les bontés de César, et surtout sa puissance,
Méritaient plus d'égards et plus de complaisance:
A lui parler du moins vous pourriez consentir.   5
Vous ne connaissez pas qui vous osez haïr;
Et vous en frémiriez, si vous pouviez apprendre...

BRUTUS

Ah! je frémis déjà, mais c'est de vous entendre.
Ennemi des Romains, que vous avez vendus,
Pensez-vous ou tromper, ou corrompre Brutus?[1]   10
Allez ramper sans moi sous la main qui vous brave;
Je sais tous vos desseins, vous brûlez d'être esclave.

---

8   35H-W48D: j'en frémis
9-10   35H:
      Malheureux courtisans qui vendez cet Etat
      A vos tyrans! Brutus ne parle qu'au sénat
   MF35:
      Malheureux courtisan, qui vendez cet Etat.
      Brutus à vos tyrans ne parle qu'au sénat
12   35H: vos désirs, vous

[1] In D937 Voltaire singles out the MF35 variant as a particularly atrocious
example of mutilation which should have dispelled any suspicion of his responsibility for the pirated edition of the play.

Vous voulez un monarque, et vous êtes Romain!

ANTOINE

Je suis ami, Brutus, et porte un cœur humain.
Je ne recherche point une vertu plus rare: 15
Tu veux être un héros, va, tu n'es qu'un barbare;
Et ton farouche orgueil, que rien ne peut fléchir,
Embrassa la vertu, pour la faire haïr.

SCÈNE II

BRUTUS *seul.*

Quelle bassesse, ô ciel! et quelle ignominie![2]
Voilà donc les soutiens de ma triste patrie!   20
Voilà vos successeurs, Horace, Décius,

13   MF35:   vous êtes Romains!
16   35H-W75G: héros, mais tu
     W75G*:   ⟨mais⟩ ᴠ↑va,
17-18   35H:
            Et si le grand César s'en remet à ma foi,
            Il deviendra tyran, pour se venger de toi.
18   36P: Embrasse la

[2] The general import of these lines is summed up in Cassius's: 'Age thou art shamed! / Rome, thou hast lost the breed of noble bloods!' (*Julius Caesar*, I.ii.149-150).

Et toi, vengeur des lois, toi mon sang, toi Brutus![3]
Quels restes, justes dieux! de la grandeur romaine!
Chacun baise en tremblant la main qui nous enchaîne.
César nous a ravi jusques à nos vertus,   25
Et je cherche ici Rome, et ne la trouve plus.[4]
Vous que j'ai vus périr, vous immortels courages,
Héros, dont en pleurant j'aperçois les images,
Famille de Pompée, et toi, divin Caton,
Toi dernier des héros du sang de Scipion,   30
Vous ranimez en moi ces vives étincelles
Des vertus dont brillaient vos âmes immortelles.
Vous vivez dans Brutus, vous mettez dans mon sein
Tout l'honneur qu'un tyran ravit au nom romain.
Que vois-je, grand Pompée, au pied de ta statue?   35
Quel billet, sous mon nom, se présente à ma vue?
Lisons: *Tu dors, Brutus, et Rome est dans les fers!*
Rome, mes yeux sur toi seront toujours ouverts;
Ne me reproche point des chaînes que j'abhorre.
Mais quel autre billet à mes yeux s'offre encore?   40
Non, tu n'es pas Brutus. Ah! reproche cruel!
César! tremble, tyran, voilà ton coup mortel.
Non, tu n'es pas Brutus! Je le suis, je veux l'être.

22   35H: vengeurs des
34   36P, with stage direction after 34: *Il s'approche de la statue de Pompée.*
37   36A-W51: Lisons* [the asterisk refers to a stage direction, given at the
end of this scene: *Il prend le billet.*]

[3] Cf. *Julius Caesar*, ii.i.53-54: 'My ancestors did from the streets of Rome / The
Tarquin drive, when he was called a king'. These lines are spoken by Brutus
after he has been goaded by reading the letter brought to him by his servant.
Brutus's speech has the same general shape in Voltaire's play – with the reading
of the letter preceded by soliloquising; the pattern is not similar in every detail
however. Earlier in Shakespeare's play (i.ii.159-161), Cassius reminds Brutus:
'There was a Brutus once that would have brooked / Th'eternal devil to keep
his state in Rome / As easily as a king'.
[4] Cf. *Julius Caesar*, ii.i.52: 'Shall Rome stand under one man's awe? What,
Rome?'.

Je périrai, Romains, ou vous serez sans maître.
Je vois que Rome encore a des cœurs vertueux.   45
On demande un vengeur, on a sur moi les yeux:
On excite cette âme, et cette main trop lente:
On demande du sang... Rome sera contente.[5]

SCÈNE III

BRUTUS, CASSIUS, CINNA, CASCA, DECIMUS, SUITE

CASSIUS

Je t'embrasse, Brutus, pour la dernière fois.
Amis, il faut tomber sous les débris des lois.   50
De César désormais je n'attends plus de grâce;
Il sait mes sentiments, il connaît notre audace.
Notre âme incorruptible étonne ses desseins;
Il va perdre dans nous les derniers des Romains.
C'en est fait, mes amis, il n'est plus de patrie,   55
Plus d'honneur, plus de lois, Rome est anéantie;
De l'univers et d'elle il triomphe aujourd'hui.
Nos imprudents aïeux n'ont vaincu que pour lui.
Ces dépouilles des rois, ce sceptre de la terre,
Six cents ans de vertus, de travaux et de guerre,   60
César jouit de tout, et dévore le fruit

50   35H, 36P: tomber dans la chute des lois
52   35H, 36P: connaît mon audace
57   35H: je triomphe

[5] Cf. *Julius Caesar*, II.i.55-58, where Brutus's reaction to the letter is similar.

Que six siècles de gloire à peine avaient produit.[6]
Ah Brutus! es-tu né pour servir sous un maître?
La liberté n'est plus.

BRUTUS

Elle est prête à renaître.

CASSIUS

Que dis-tu? mais quel bruit vient frapper mes esprits?   65

BRUTUS

Laisse-là ce vil peuple, et ses indignes cris.

CASSIUS

La liberté, dis-tu?... Mais quoi... le bruit redouble.[7]

---

63   35H: Justes dieux! se peut-il que Brutus ait un maître!
64   36A: Ta liberté

[6] Cf. *Julius Caesar*, I.ii.92, where Cassius begins to turn Brutus against Caesar
with the words: 'Well, honour is the subject of my story' and particularly
I.ii.134-135, and 150-157, where his anger with Caesar's autocratic style of
government reaches its pitch.

[7] In *Julius Caesar* Cassius and Brutus react with curiosity to the noise of the
crowd in the distance. When they question Casca, they ask him why the crowd
shouted 'thrice' (although the stage directions indicate only two outbursts, and
Voltaire follows this indication, lines 65, 67). The 'vil peuple, et ses indignes
cris' are represented in Casca's colourful account by the hissing and clapping
of 'the tag-rag people'.

SCÈNE IV

BRUTUS, CASSIUS, CIMBER, DECIMUS

CASSIUS

Ah! Cimber, est-ce toi? parle, quel est ce trouble?

DECIMUS

Trame-t-on contre Rome un nouvel attentat?
Qu'a-t-on fait? qu'as-tu vu?

CIMBER

                La honte de l'Etat.   70
César était au temple, et cette fière idole
Semblait être le dieu qui tonne au Capitole.[8]
C'est là qu'il annonçait son superbe dessein,
D'aller joindre la Perse à l'Empire romain.
On lui donnait les noms de foudre de la guerre,   75
De vengeur des Romains, de vainqueur de la terre:

67b 35H: BRUTUS, CASSIUS, CIMBER, CASCA
      36P: BRUTUS, CASSIUS, CIMBER, DECIMUS, CASCA, CINNA
68   36P: toi? Quel est ce nouveau trouble?
68-70 35H:

            CASSIUS
    Ah! Cimber, est-ce toi, quel est ce nouveau trouble?
    Tu parais interdit. Qu'a-t-on fait? Qu'as-tu vu?
            CIMBER
    Le secret des tyrans est enfin reconnu.

[8] Cf. Cassius's remarks in Shakespeare's *Julius Caesar*: 'Why, man, he doth bestride the narrow world / Like a Colossus' (i.ii.135 ff); 'and this man / Is now become a god' (i.ii.115-116). Conti's Cassio, in *Il Cesare* (iii.iv) echoes this last quotation: 'L'uom di sè si fa Dio'.

Mais parmi tant d'éclat, son orgueil imprudent
Voulait un autre titre, et n'était pas content.
Enfin parmi ces cris, et ces chants d'allégresse,
Du peuple qui l'entoure Antoine fend la presse: 80
Il entre: ô honte! ô crime indigne d'un Romain!
Il entre, la couronne, et le sceptre à la main.
On se tait: on frémit: lui, sans que rien l'étonne,
Sur le front de César attache la couronne;
Et soudain devant lui se mettant à genoux,   85
César, règne, dit-il, sur la terre et sur nous.
Des Romains à ces mots les visages pâlissent;
De leurs cris douloureux les voûtes retentissent.
J'ai vu des citoyens s'enfuir avec horreur,
D'autres rougir de honte et pleurer de douleur.   90
César, qui cependant lisait sur leur visage
De l'indignation l'éclatant témoignage,
Feignant des sentiments longtemps étudiés,
Jette et sceptre et couronne, et les foule à ses pieds.
Alors tout se croit libre, alors tout est en proie   95
Au fol enivrement d'une indiscrète joie.
Antoine est alarmé: César feint, et rougit;
Plus il cèle son trouble, et plus on l'applaudit.
La modération sert de voile à son crime:[9]
Il affecte à regret un refus magnanime.   100
Mais malgré ses efforts, il frémissait tout bas,
Qu'on applaudît en lui les vertus qu'il n'a pas.[10]

---

77   35H-W48D: orgueil impudent
90   36P: pleurer de fureur
91   35H: leurs visages

---

[9] Casca, in his account of Caesar's renunciation of the crown, says: 'but for all that, to my thinking, he would fain have had it' (*Julius Caesar*, I.ii.240).

[10] La Harpe, *Commentaire sur le théâtre de Voltaire*, p.143: 'On peut comparer ces deux beaux vers à ceux-ci de Corneille dans la *Mort de Pompée*: "Une maligne joie en son cœur s'élevait / Dont sa gloire indignée à peine le sauvait"'.

Enfin ne pouvant plus retenir sa colère,
Il sort du Capitole avec un front sévère.[11]
Il veut que dans une heure on s'assemble au sénat.   105
Dans une heure, Brutus, César change l'Etat.
De ce sénat sacré la moitié corrompue,
Ayant acheté Rome, à César l'a vendue;
Plus lâche que ce peuple, à qui dans son malheur,
Le nom de roi du moins fait toujours quelque horreur.   110
César déjà trop roi, veut encor la couronne:
Le peuple la refuse, et le sénat la donne;
Que faut-il faire enfin, héros qui m'écoutez?

CASSIUS

Mourir, finir des jours dans l'opprobre comptés.
J'ai traîné les liens de mon indigne vie,   115
Tant qu'un peu d'espérance a flatté ma patrie.
Voici son dernier jour, et du moins Cassius
Ne doit plus respirer, lorsque l'Etat n'est plus.
Pleure qui voudra Rome, et lui reste fidèle;
Je ne peux la venger, mais j'expire avec elle.[12]   120
Je vais où sont nos dieux... Pompée et Scipion,

en regardant leurs statues.

Il est temps de vous suivre, et d'imiter Caton.

110   35H, 36P, 36A: fait encor quelque
121   35H: où vont nos
121a   35H, 36A, no stage direction

[11] In Shakespeare's play, Brutus draws Cassius's attention to Caesar's manifest displeasure: 'but, look, Cassius, / The angry spot doth glow on Caesar's brow' (I.iii.182-183).
[12] Shakespeare's Cassius voices similar sentiments (I.ii.93-96):
                    I cannot tell what you and other men
                    Think of this life; but, for my single self,
                    I had as lief not be as live to be
                    In awe of such a thing as I myself.

BRUTUS

Non, n'imitons personne, et servons tous d'exemple:
C'est nous, braves amis, que l'univers contemple;
C'est à nous de répondre à l'admiration   125
Que Rome en expirant conserve à notre nom.[13]
Si Caton m'avait cru, plus juste en sa furie,
Sur César expirant il eût perdu la vie;
Mais il tourna sur soi ses innocentes mains;
Sa mort fut inutile au bonheur des humains.   130
Faisant tout pour la gloire, il ne fit rien pour Rome;
Et c'est la seule faute où tomba ce grand homme.

CASSIUS

Que veux-tu donc qu'on fasse en un tel désespoir?

BRUTUS, *montrant le billet*.

Voilà ce qu'on m'écrit, voilà notre devoir.

CASSIUS

On m'en écrit autant, j'ai reçu ce reproche.   135

BRUTUS

C'est trop le mériter.

CIMBER

L'heure fatale approche.

---

129   35H, 36P: sur lui ses
133   36P, this line given to DECIMUS
133-137a 35H: Mais César dans une heure est nommé souverain.
133a   36P, no stage direction

[13] It is Cassius, in Shakespeare's *Julius Caesar*, who remarks (prophetically) upon the attention which the tyrannicides will attract (III.i.112-114).

Dans une heure un tyran détruit le nom romain.

BRUTUS

Dans une heure à César il faut percer le sein.

CASSIUS

Ah! je te reconnais à cette noble audace.

DECIMUS

Ennemi des tyrans, et digne de ta race,   140
Voilà les sentiments que j'avais dans mon cœur.

CASSIUS

Tu me rends à moi-même, et je t'en dois l'honneur;
C'est là ce qu'attendaient ma haine et ma colère
De la mâle vertu qui fait ton caractère.
C'est Rome qui t'inspire en des desseins si grands: 145
Ton nom seul est l'arrêt de la mort des tyrans.
Lavons, mon cher Brutus, l'opprobre de la terre;
Vengeons ce Capitole, au défaut du tonnerre.
Toi Cimber, toi Cinna, vous Romains indomptés,
Avez-vous une autre âme et d'autres volontés?   150

CIMBER

Nous pensons comme toi, nous méprisons la vie.
Nous détestons César, nous aimons la patrie;
Nous la vengerons tous; Brutus et Cassius
De quiconque est Romain raniment les vertus.

137 36P: heure César détruit
140-141   35H, 36P, these lines given to CIMBER

DECIMUS

Nés juges de l'Etat, nés les vengeurs du crime,   155
C'est souffrir trop longtemps la main qui nous opprime;
Et quand sur un tyran nous suspendons nos coups,
Chaque instant qu'il respire est un crime pour nous.

CIMBER

Admettrons-nous quelque autre à ces honneurs
                                        suprêmes?

BRUTUS

Pour venger la patrie il suffit de nous-mêmes.   160
Dolabella, Lépide, Emile, Bibulus,
Ou tremblent sous César, ou bien lui sont vendus.
Cicéron, qui d'un traître a puni l'insolence,
Ne sert la liberté que par son éloquence,
Hardi dans le sénat, faible dans le danger,   165
Fait pour haranguer Rome, et non pour la venger.
Laissons à l'orateur, qui charme sa patrie,
Le soin de nous louer, quand nous l'aurons servie.
Non, ce n'est qu'avec vous que je veux partager
Cet immortel honneur, et ce pressant danger.   170
Dans une heure au sénat le tyran doit se rendre:
Là, je le punirai; là, je le veux surprendre;
Là, je veux que ce fer, enfoncé dans son sein,

154a-158   35H:
                    CASSIUS
        Jamais pour accomplir ses plus dignes ouvrages,
        Le ciel n'a rassemblé de si fermes courages.
        Dieux, pour perdre César, et venger les Romains,
        Vous deviez faire choix des plus grands des humains
154a-158a   36P, Decimus's speech omitted
159   K: Admettons-nous
167   36P: charme la patrie

Venge Caton, Pompée, et le peuple romain.[14]
C'est hasarder beaucoup. Ses ardents satellites   175
Partout du Capitole occupent les limites;
Ce peuple mou, volage, et facile à fléchir,[15]
Ne sait s'il doit encor l'aimer ou le haïr.
Notre mort, mes amis, paraît inévitable;[16]
Mais qu'une telle mort est noble et désirable!   180
Qu'il est beau de périr dans des desseins si grands,
De voir couler son sang dans le sang des tyrans!
Qu'avec plaisir alors on voit sa dernière heure!
Mourons, braves amis, pourvu que César meure,
Et que la liberté, qu'oppriment ses forfaits,   185
Renaisse de sa cendre, et revive à jamais.[17]

CASSIUS

Ne balançons donc plus, courons au Capitole:
C'est là qu'il nous opprime, et qu'il faut qu'on l'immole.
Ne craignons rien du peuple, il semble encor douter;
Mais si l'idole tombe, il va la détester.   19(

BRUTUS

Jurez donc avec moi, jurez sur cette épée,
Par le sang de Caton, par celui de Pompée,
Par les mânes sacrés de tous ces vrais Romains
Qui dans les champs d'Afrique ont fini leurs destins,

[14] Conti stresses Bruto's intention that the dictator should be slain in the Senate, by arguing against the precipitate murder being urged by Porzia (backed by Cassio): 'Del Dittator fu pubblico il delitto; / Sia pubblico il gastigo. Nel Senato / Perciò si uccida, o non s'uccida' (*Il Cesare*, III.v).

[15] Cf. *Julius Caesar*, III.i.98-99: 'Men, wives and children stare, cry out and run / As it were doomsday'.

[16] Cf. *Julius Caesar*, III.i.100: 'That we shall die, we know'.

[17] This passage finds a (palpably gorier) parallel in Shakespeare's play (III.i.106-111) where Brutus urges his fellow-assassins to bathe their hands in Caesar's blood, wave their dripping weapons aloft and cry 'Peace, freedom and liberty!'.

Jurez par tous les dieux, vengeurs de la patrie,   195
Que César sous vos coups va terminer sa vie.

CASSIUS

Faisons plus, mes amis, jurons d'exterminer
Quiconque ainsi que lui prétendra gouverner:
Fussent nos propres fils, nos frères, ou nos pères:
S'ils sont tyrans, Brutus, ils sont nos adversaires.   200
Un vrai républicain n'a pour père et pour fils,
Que la vertu, les dieux, les lois et son pays.[18]

BRUTUS

Oui, j'unis pour jamais mon sang avec le vôtre.
Tous dès ce moment même adoptés l'un par l'autre,
Le salut de l'Etat nous a rendus parents.   205
Scellons notre union du sang de nos tyrans.

Il s'avance vers la statue de Pompée.

Nous le jurons par vous, héros, dont les images
A ce pressant devoir excitent nos courages;
Nous promettons, Pompée, à tes sacrés genoux,
De faire tout pour Rome, et jamais rien pour nous;   210
D'être unis pour l'Etat, qui dans nous se rassemble,
De vivre, de combattre, et de mourir ensemble.
Allons, préparons-nous: c'est trop nous arrêter.

202   35H, 36P: les lois de son
204   35H, 36A: l'un pour l'autre
205   35H-W51:   le salut et l'Etat

[18] It is Bruto who utters such thoughts in Conti's *Il Cesare*, (II.vii): 'Stimol d'onore in generoso patto / Solo cura la Patria. A lei siam nati, / A lei tutto si doni'. Cf. Addison's *Cato*, IV.iv, Cato beholds his dead son and says: 'Portius, behold thy brother, and remember / Thy life is not thy own, when Rome demands it'.

SCÈNE V

CÉSAR, BRUTUS

CÉSAR

Demeure. C'est ici que tu dois m'écouter;
Où vas-tu, malheureux?

BRUTUS

Loin de la tyrannie.   215

CÉSAR

Licteurs, qu'on le retienne.

BRUTUS

Achève, et prends ma vie.[19]

CÉSAR

Brutus, si ma colère en voulait à tes jours,
Je n'aurais qu'à parler, j'aurais fini leur cours.
Tu l'as trop mérité. Ta fière ingratitude
Se fait de m'offenser une farouche étude.   220
Je te retrouve encore avec ceux des Romains,
Dont j'ai plus soupçonné les perfides desseins;
Avec ceux qui tantôt ont osé me déplaire,
Ont blâmé ma conduite, ont bravé ma colère.

216   35HA: Achève, prends

[19] In his edition of the play, Beuchot notes that this second hemistich occurs
in *Le Cid*, i.iv, in the editions for which Voltaire was responsible.

BRUTUS

Ils parlaient en Romains, César; et leurs avis,   225
Si les dieux t'inspiraient, seraient encor suivis.

CÉSAR

Je souffre ton audace, et consens à t'entendre:
De mon rang avec toi je me plais à descendre.
Que me reproches-tu?

BRUTUS

        Le monde ravagé,
Le sang des nations, ton pays saccagé:[20]   230
Ton pouvoir, tes vertus, qui font tes injustices,
Qui de tes attentats sont en toi les complices;
Ta funeste bonté, qui fait aimer tes fers,
Et qui n'est qu'un appât pour tromper l'univers.[21]

CÉSAR

Ah! c'est ce qu'il fallait reprocher à Pompée.   235
Par sa feinte vertu la tienne fut trompée.
Ce citoyen superbe, à Rome plus fatal,
N'a pas même voulu César pour son égal.
Crois-tu, s'il m'eût vaincu, que cette âme hautaine,
Eût laissé respirer la liberté romaine?   240

238   35H: Ne voulait point de maître, et César pour égal.

[20] Cf. Addison's *Cato*, i.i, Portius to Marcus: 'Already Caesar / Has ravaged more than half the globe, and sees / Mankind grown thin by his destructive sword'.

[21] Cf. Corneille's *Sertorius*, iii.ii:

      Et votre empire est d'autant plus dangereux
      Qu'il rend de vos vertus les peuples amoureux,
      Qu'en assujetissant vous avez l'art de plaire,
      Qu'on croit n'être en vos fers qu'esclave volontaire.

Sous un joug despotique il t'aurait accablé.
Qu'eût fait Brutus alors?

BRUTUS

Brutus l'eût immolé.

CÉSAR

Voilà donc ce qu'enfin ton grand cœur me destine?
Tu ne t'en défends point. Tu vis pour ma ruine,
Brutus!

BRUTUS

Si tu le crois, préviens donc ma fureur.   245
Qui peut te retenir?

CÉSAR (*Il lui présente la lettre de Servilie.*)

La nature, et mon cœur.
Lis, ingrat, lis, connais le sang que tu m'opposes;
Vois qui tu peux haïr, et poursuis si tu l'oses.

BRUTUS

Où suis-je? Qu'ai-je lu? me trompez-vous, mes yeux?[22]

CÉSAR

Eh bien! Brutus, mon fils!

---

241   35H-W51: Ah! sous un joug de fer il t'aurait [35H: l'aurait] accablé.
244-245   35H, 36P: ruine. / BRUTUS / Si tu le crois ainsi, préviens

---

[22] Alcméon's discovery that he is the son of Eriphyle prompts a similar
reaction: 'Je ne sais où je suis', and, of course, the inevitable tears (*Eriphyle*,
IV.v).

BRUTUS

Lui, mon père! grands dieux! 250

CÉSAR

Oui, je le suis, ingrat! Quel silence farouche!
Que dis-je? quels sanglots échappent de ta bouche?
Mon fils... Quoi, je te tiens muet entre mes bras!
La nature t'étonne, et ne t'attendrit pas!

BRUTUS

O sort épouvantable, et qui me désespère! 255
O serments! ô patrie! ô Rome toujours chère!
César!... Ah, malheureux! j'ai trop longtemps vécu.

CÉSAR

Parle. Quoi! d'un remords ton cœur est combattu!
Ne me déguise rien. Tu gardes le silence?
Tu crains d'être mon fils, ce nom sacré t'offense? 260
Tu crains de me chérir, de partager mon rang;
C'est un malheur pour toi d'être né de mon sang!
Ah! ce sceptre du monde, et ce pouvoir suprême,
Ce César, que tu hais, les voulait pour toi-même.
Je voulais partager, avec Octave et toi, 265
Le prix de cent combats, et le titre de roi.

BRUTUS

Ah! dieux!

CÉSAR

Tu veux parler, et te retiens à peine?
Ces transports sont-ils donc de tendresse ou de haine?
Quel est donc le secret qui semble t'accabler?

BRUTUS

César...

CÉSAR

Eh bien, mon fils?

BRUTUS

Je ne puis lui parler.   270

CÉSAR

Tu n'oses me nommer du tendre nom de père?

BRUTUS

Si tu l'es, je te fais une unique prière.

CÉSAR

Parle. En te l'accordant, je croirai tout gagner.

BRUTUS

Fais-moi mourir sur l'heure, ou cesse de régner.

CÉSAR

Ah! barbare ennemi, tigre que je caresse!   275
Ah! cœur dénaturé qu'endurcit ma tendresse!
Va, tu n'es plus mon fils. Va, cruel citoyen,
Mon cœur désespéré prend l'exemple du tien;
Ce cœur, à qui tu fais cette effroyable injure,
Saura bien comme toi vaincre enfin la nature.   280
Va, César n'est pas fait pour te prier en vain;
J'apprendrai de Brutus à cesser d'être humain.
Je ne te connais plus. Libre dans ma puissance,

283   35H, 36A: ne le connais
36L: ne le connais pas.

Je n'écouterai plus une injuste clémence.
Tranquille, à mon courroux je vais m'abandonner;   285
Mon cœur trop indulgent est las de pardonner.
J'imiterai Sylla, mais dans ses violences;
Vous tremblerez, ingrats, au bruit de mes vengeances.
Va, cruel, va trouver tes indignes amis.
Tous m'ont osé déplaire, ils seront tous punis.   290
On sait ce que je puis, on verra ce que j'ose:
Je deviendrai barbare, et toi seul en es cause.

BRUTUS

Ah! ne le quittons point dans ses cruels desseins,
Et sauvons, s'il se peut, César et les Romains.

Fin du second acte.

285   35H, 36P: à mes fureurs je
287   36L: dans ces violences
289   36HA: Va, cruel, trouver
290   MF43:   Ils m'ont osé

ACTE III

SCÈNE PREMIÈRE

CASSIUS, CIMBER, DECIMUS,
CINNA, CASCA, LES CONJURÉS

CASSIUS

Enfin donc l'heure approche, où Rome va renaître.
La maîtresse du monde est aujourd'hui sans maître.
L'honneur en est à vous, Cimber, Casca, Probus,
Décime. Encore une heure, et le tyran n'est plus.
Ce que n'ont pu Caton, et Pompée, et l'Asie,   5
Nous seuls l'exécutons, nous vengeons la patrie;
Et je veux qu'en ce jour on dise à l'univers,
Mortels, respectez Rome, elle n'est plus aux fers.

CIMBER

Tu vois tous nos amis, ils sont prêts à te suivre,
A frapper, à mourir, à vivre s'il faut vivre,   10
A servir le sénat dans l'un ou l'autre sort,
En donnant à César, ou recevant la mort.

DECIMUS

Mais d'où vient que Brutus ne paraît point encore;
Lui, ce fier ennemi du tyran qu'il abhorre?
Lui qui prit nos serments, qui nous rassembla tous,   1

c 35H: CASSIUS, CIMBER, LES CONJURÉS
   36P, CINNA omitted
   36A-W68, K: DÉCIME [also 12a]
12a-19 35H, these lines given to CIMBER

212

Lui qui doit sur César porter les premiers coups?
Le gendre de Caton tarde bien à paraître.
Serait-il arrêté? César peut-il connaître?...
Mais le voici. Grands dieux! qu'il paraît abattu!

SCÈNE II

CASSIUS, BRUTUS, CIMBER, CASCA, DECIMUS, LES CONJURÉS

CASSIUS

Brutus, quelle infortune accable ta vertu?   20
Le tyran sait-il tout? Rome est-elle trahie?

BRUTUS

Non, César ne sait point qu'on va trancher sa vie.
Il se confie à vous.

DECIMUS

    Qui peut donc te troubler?

BRUTUS

Un malheur, un secret, qui vous fera trembler.

CASSIUS

De nous ou du tyran c'est la mort qui s'apprête.   25

19b-c 35H: CASSIUS, BRUTUS, CIMBER, DÉCIME.
  36P adds: CINNA
  36P-w68, K: DÉCIME
23 35H, 36P, this question given to CIMBER

Nous pouvons tous périr; mais trembler, nous!

BRUTUS

                            Arrête;
Je vais t'épouvanter par ce secret affreux.
Je dois sa mort à Rome, à vous, à nos neveux,
Au bonheur des mortels; et j'avais choisi l'heure,
Le lieu, le bras, l'instant, où Rome veut qu'il meure: 30
L'honneur du premier coup à mes mains est remis;
Tout est prêt. Apprenez que Brutus est son fils.

CIMBER

Toi, son fils!

CASSIUS

De César!

DECIMUS

O Rome!

BRUTUS

                       Servilie
Par un hymen secret à César fut unie;
Je suis de cet hymen le fruit infortuné.   3⟨

CIMBER

Brutus, fils d'un tyran!

CASSIUS

                  Non, tu n'en es pas né;
Ton cœur est trop romain.

33   35H, 36P, Decimus's exclamation given to CIMBER

BRUTUS

　　　　　　Ma honte est véritable.
Vous, amis, qui voyez le destin qui m'accable,[1]
Soyez par mes serments les maîtres de mon sort.
Est-il quelqu'un de vous d'un esprit assez fort,　　　　　40
Assez stoïque, assez au-dessus du vulgaire,
Pour oser décider ce que Brutus doit faire?
Je m'en remets à vous. Quoi! vous baissez les yeux!
Toi, Cassius, aussi, tu te tais avec eux!
Aucun ne me soutient au bord de cet abîme!　　　　　45
Aucun ne m'encourage, ou ne m'arrache au crime!
Tu frémis, Cassius! et prompt à t'étonner...

CASSIUS

Je frémis du conseil que je vais te donner.

BRUTUS

Parle.

CASSIUS

　　　　Si tu n'étais qu'un citoyen vulgaire,
Je te dirais: Va, sers, sois tyran sous ton père;　　　　50
Ecrase cet Etat que tu dois soutenir;
Rome aura désormais deux traîtres à punir:
Mais je parle à Brutus, à ce puissant génie,
A ce héros armé contre la tyrannie,

39　36P: Vous, faits par mes serments

[1] Lines 38-45 are quoted by Thiriot as given here in his letter of October 1735 to the *Observations sur les écrits modernes* (D929), except for line 39 where the 36P reading: *Vous, faits* is given instead of *Soyez* (see the editorial commentary on this letter). In the same letter, Thiriot quotes almost all of Cassius's speech (lines 69-90) as it stands here except for differences of punctuation and the obvious misreading *sermons* for *serments* in line 89.

Dont le cœur inflexible, au bien déterminé,   55
Epura tout le sang que César t'a donné.
Ecoute, tu connais avec quelle furie
Jadis Catilina menaça sa patrie?

BRUTUS

Oui.

CASSIUS

Si le même jour, que ce grand criminel
Dut à la liberté porter le coup mortel;   6
Si lorsque le sénat eut condamné ce traître,
Catilina pour fils t'eût voulu reconnaître,
Entre ce monstre et nous forcé de décider,
Parle: qu'aurais-tu fait?

BRUTUS

Peux-tu le demander?
Penses-tu qu'un instant ma vertu démentie,   6
Eût mis dans la balance un homme et la patrie?

CASSIUS

Brutus, par ce seul mot ton devoir est dicté.
C'est l'arrêt du sénat, Rome est en sûreté.
Mais, dis, sens-tu ce trouble, et ce secret murmure,[2]

---

59   35H: que sa coupable main
60   35H: Devait anéantir l'éclat du nom romain
63   35H, 36P: nous tout prêt à décider
69-70   36P, omitted [cancel: β, with variant]

---

[2] Cf. Crébillon, *Sémiramis* (1717), v.iv. Ninias says to his father Sémiramis: 'Rendez-moi votre cœur, mais tel que la nature / Le demande pour moi par un secret murmure'.

Qu'un préjugé vulgaire impute à la nature?   70
Un seul mot de César a-t-il éteint dans toi
L'amour de ton pays, ton devoir et ta foi?
En disant ce secret, ou faux ou véritable,
Et t'avouant pour fils, en est-il moins coupable?
En es-tu moins Brutus? en es-tu moins Romain?   75
Nous dois-tu moins ta vie, et ton cœur, et ta main?
Toi, son fils! Rome enfin n'est-elle plus ta mère?
Chacun des conjurés n'est-il donc plus ton frère?
Né dans nos murs sacrés, nourri par Scipion,
Elève de Pompée, adopté par Caton,   80
Ami de Cassius, que veux-tu davantage?
Ces titres sont sacrés, tout autre les outrage.
Qu'importe qu'un tyran, vil esclave d'amour,[3]
Ait séduit Servilie, et t'ait donné le jour?
Laisse là les erreurs, et l'hymen de ta mère;   85
Caton forma tes mœurs, Caton seul est ton père;
Tu lui dois ta vertu, ton âme est toute à lui:
Brise l'indigne nœud que l'on t'offre aujourd'hui:
Qu'à nos serments communs ta fermeté réponde;
Et tu n'as de parents que les vengeurs du monde.   90

BRUTUS

Et vous, braves amis, parlez, que pensez-vous?

CIMBER

Jugez de nous par lui, jugez de lui par nous.

70   36P cancel: Qu'un sentiment secret arrache à la nature?
71   35H, 36P: éteint en toi
83   K: esclave de l'amour
92   36P: Juge de nous par lui, juge de

[3] La Harpe, in his *Commentaire sur le théâtre de Voltaire*, gives the Kehl reading and adds: 'Il y avait dans les premières éditions *vil esclave d'amour*; c'était une faute. L'article est absolument nécessaire. On ne peut pas plus dire *esclave d'amour* qu'*esclave de crainte, esclave d'ambition*'.

D'un autre sentiment si nous étions capables,
Rome n'aurait point eu des enfants plus coupables.
Mais à d'autres qu'à toi pourquoi t'en rapporter?   95
C'est ton cœur, c'est Brutus, qu'il te faut consulter.

BRUTUS

Eh bien, à vos regards mon âme est dévoilée;[4]
Lisez-y les horreurs dont elle est accablée.
Je ne vous cèle rien, ce cœur s'est ébranlé;
De mes stoïques yeux des larmes ont coulé.   100
Après l'affreux serment, que vous m'avez vu faire,
Prêt à servir l'Etat, mais à tuer mon père,
Pleurant d'être son fils, honteux de ses bienfaits,
Admirant ses vertus, condamnant ses forfaits,
Voyant en lui mon père, un coupable, un grand homme,   105
Entraîné par César, et retenu par Rome,
D'horreur et de pitié mes esprits déchirés,
Ont souhaité la mort que vous lui préparez.
Je vous dirai bien plus, sachez que je l'estime.
Son grand cœur me séduit, au sein même du crime;   110
Et si sur les Romains quelqu'un pouvait régner,
Il est le seul tyran que l'on dût épargner.
Ne vous alarmez point: ce nom que je déteste,
Ce nom seul de tyran l'emporte sur le reste.
Le sénat, Rome, et vous, vous avez tous ma foi:[5]   115
Le bien du monde entier me parle contre un roi.
J'embrasse avec horreur une vertu cruelle;

117-124   35H:
          J'en frémis à vos yeux, mais je vous suis fidèle.

[4] Brutus's speech to his fellow conspirators, especially lines 109-116, is parallelled by the soliloquy in *Julius Caesar*, II.i, where Brutus stifles less formidable qualms of conscience.
[5] Thiriot (D929) quotes a passage which begins with lines 115-116 and continues with the first ten lines of the 35H variant cited here; this more

J'en frissonne à vos yeux; mais je vous suis fidèle.
César me va parler; que ne puis-je aujourd'hui
L'attendrir, le changer, sauver l'Etat et lui!　　　　　120
Veuillent les immortels, s'expliquant par ma bouche,
Prêter à mon organe un pouvoir qui le touche!
Mais si je n'obtiens rien de cet ambitieux,
Levez le bras, frappez, je détourne les yeux.[6]
Je ne trahirai point mon pays pour mon père:　　　　125
Que l'on approuve, ou non, ma fermeté sévère,
Qu'à l'univers surpris cette grande action
Soit un objet d'horreur ou d'admiration:
Mon esprit peu jaloux de vivre en la mémoire,
Ne considère point le reproche ou la gloire;　　　　130
Toujours indépendant, et toujours citoyen,

> Vous n'exigerez pas que ma vertu cruelle
> Des sentiments humains me puisse dépouiller;
> Vous demandez son sang, je ne puis m'en souiller.
> Rome qui le condamne, et pour qui je décide,
> A besoin de vengeance, et non de parricide.
> César me va parler... en l'état où je suis,
> Tâcher de le sauver, est tout ce que je puis.
> Veuillent les justes dieux s'expliquant par ma bouche,
> Prêter à mon organe un pouvoir qui le touche!...
> Mais si je n'obtiens rien, s'il mérite la mort,
> Je détourne les yeux, laisse faire le sort.

118　w75G, κ84: à mes yeux [κ85: β]
119　36P: me doit parler
128　35H, 36P: un sujet d'horreur
129　35H: esprit plus jaloux

moderate version, where Brutus is more explicit in his rejection of the idea of personally shedding Caesar's blood, strengthens Thiriot's line of argument.

[6] Cf. Brutus's attitude in his interview with his father later, III.iv.203. In Voltaire's *Brutus* (I.ii), Arons refers to Brutus's attitude towards Tarquin: 'Un fils ne s'arme point contre un coupable père; / Il détourne les yeux, le plaint, et le révère'. The death of Coligny is described in *La Henriade*; the assassin, Besme, in this case averts his eyes as he strikes: 'Et bientôt dans le flanc ce monstre furieux, / Lui plonge son épée, en détournant les yeux' (II.231-232).

Mon devoir me suffit, tout le reste n'est rien.
Allez, ne songez plus qu'à sortir d'esclavage.[7]

CASSIUS

Du salut de l'Etat ta parole est le gage.
Nous comptons tous sur toi, comme si dans ces lieux   135
Nous entendions Caton, Rome même et nos dieux.

SCÈNE III

BRUTUS seul.

Voici donc le moment, où César va m'entendre;
Voici ce Capitole, où la mort va l'attendre.
Epargnez-moi, grands dieux, l'horreur de le haïr.
Dieux, arrêtez ces bras levés pour le punir!   140
Rendez, s'il se peut, Rome à son grand cœur plus chère,
Et faites qu'il soit juste, afin qu'il soit mon père.
Le voici. Je demeure immobile, éperdu.
O mânes de Caton, soutenez ma vertu!

132   35H, 36P: suffit, l'univers ne m'est rien
136b   35H, 36P: BRUTUS//
140   36P: arrêtez les bras

[7] Cf. Voltaire's *Brutus*, v.viii; Brutus's remark after his son has been led away to be executed: 'Rome seule a mes soins; mon cœur ne connaît qu'elle;' and his final exclamation (v.ix), 'Rome est libre; il suffit [...] Rendons grâces aux dieux!'

SCÈNE IV

CÉSAR, BRUTUS

CÉSAR

Eh bien, que veux-tu? Parle. As-tu le cœur d'un homme? 145
Es-tu fils de César?

BRUTUS

Oui, si tu l'es de Rome.

CÉSAR

Républicain farouche, où vas-tu t'emporter?
N'as-tu voulu me voir que pour mieux m'insulter?
Quoi! tandis que sur toi mes faveurs se répandent,
Que du monde soumis les hommages t'attendent, 150
L'Empire, mes bontés, rien ne fléchit ton cœur?
De quel œil vois-tu donc le sceptre?

BRUTUS

Avec horreur.

CÉSAR

Je plains tes préjugés, je les excuse même.
Mais peux-tu me haïr?

BRUTUS

Non, César, et je t'aime.[8]

151 35H: mes bontés viennent fléchir ton
154 35H: Non, non, César, je t'aime

[8] Lines 154-162 are quoted by Thiriot in D929. Apart from differences of
punctuation, there is only one variant: *sacrifirais* in line 161.

Mon cœur par tes exploits fut pour toi prévenu,   155
Avant que pour ton sang tu m'eusses reconnu.
Je me suis plaint aux dieux de voir qu'un si grand homme
Fût à la fois la gloire et le fléau de Rome.
Je déteste César avec le nom de roi:
Mais César citoyen serait un dieu pour moi;   160
Je lui sacrifierais ma fortune et ma vie.

CÉSAR

Que peux-tu donc haïr en moi?

BRUTUS

                      La tyrannie.
Daigne écouter les vœux, les larmes, les avis
De tous les vrais Romains, du sénat, de ton fils.
Veux-tu vivre en effet le premier de la terre,   165
Jouir d'un droit plus saint que celui de la guerre,
Être encor plus que roi, plus même que César?

CÉSAR

Eh bien?

BRUTUS

           Tu vois la terre enchaînée à ton char:
Romps nos fers, sois Romain, renonce au diadème.

CÉSAR

Ah! que proposes-tu?

BRUTUS

                 Ce qu'a fait Sylla même.   17
Longtemps dans notre sang Sylla s'était noyé;
Il rendit Rome libre, et tout fut oublié.
Cet assassin illustre, entouré de victimes,

En descendant du trône effaça tous ses crimes.
Tu n'eus point ses fureurs, ose avoir ses vertus.   175
Ton cœur sut pardonner; César, fais encor plus.
Que servent désormais les grâces que tu donnes?
C'est à Rome, à l'Etat qu'il faut que tu pardonnes:
Alors, plus qu'à ton rang nos cœurs te sont soumis;
Alors tu sais régner, alors je suis ton fils.   180
Quoi! je te parle en vain?

                          CÉSAR

                          Rome demande un maître;
Un jour à tes dépens tu l'apprendras peut-être.
Tu vois nos citoyens plus puissants que des rois.
Nos mœurs changent, Brutus; il faut changer nos lois.
La liberté n'est plus que le droit de se nuire: 185
Rome, qui détruit tout, semble enfin se détruire.
Ce colosse effrayant, dont le monde est foulé,
En pressant l'univers, est lui-même ébranlé.
Il penche vers sa chute, et contre la tempête
Il demande mon bras pour soutenir sa tête.[9]   190

181   35H, 36P: Rome a besoin d'un maître
183-192 35H:
              Tu verras qu'un Etat maître de tant de rois
              Se nuit par sa grandeur, et tombe par son poids.
190   36P: pour affermir sa

[9] The image of a colosse is used in Shakespeare's *Julius Caesar* (I.ii.134-135)
by Cassius to refer to Caesar: 'Why, man he doth bestride the narrow world /
Like a colossus'. Voltaire's use of the image in *Brutus* (II.v), where Messala
employs the expression 'Colosse qu'un vil peuple éleva sur nos têtes' to describe
Brutus, is nearer Shakespeare's than it is to its use here to suggest a top-
heavy state which needs the prop of Caesar's personal authority. Nearer to
Shakespeare's image, too, (apart from the idea of decrepitude) is that in
Voltaire's *Eriphyle* (III.i), where Hermogide says:
              Mon crédit, mon pouvoir adoré si longtemps,
              N'est-qu'un colosse énorme ébranlé par les ans,
              Qui penche vers sa chute, et dont le poids immense
              Veut, pour se soutenir, la suprême puissance.

Enfin depuis Sylla, nos antiques vertus,
Les lois, Rome, l'Etat, sont des noms superflus.[10]
Dans nos temps corrompus, pleins de guerres civiles,
Tu parles comme au temps des Dèces, des Emiles.
Caton t'a trop séduit, mon cher fils, je prévois   195
Que ta triste vertu perdra l'Etat et toi.
Fais céder, si tu peux, ta raison détrompée
Au vainqueur de Caton, au vainqueur de Pompée,
A ton père qui t'aime, et qui plaint ton erreur.
Sois mon fils en effet, Brutus, rends-moi ton cœur;   200
Prends d'autres sentiments, ma bonté t'en conjure;
Ne force point ton âme à vaincre la nature.
Tu ne me réponds rien: tu détournes les yeux?

BRUTUS

Je ne me connais plus. Tonnez sur moi, grands dieux!

193-194   36P, omitted [cancel: β, with variant]
193   36P: Dans ces temps malheureux de discordes civiles
204   w75G, k84:   Je ne te connais plus. [k85: β]

[10] In Buckingham's *Julius Caesar, altered*, Caesar voices similar views in the scene of the crowning ceremony (I.iii). In *Cinna* (II.i), Cinna is made the critic of a political liberty which has become mere licence, and the advocate of government by 'un bon chef à qui tout obéisse' (see lines 570-590, many of which are recalled by César's speech, and some echoed directly; see for example, line 576: 'Produit des citoyens plus puissants que des rois' and César's reference, line 183, to 'les citoyens plus puissants que des rois!'). Earlier in *Brutus* (I.iv), Voltaire had put into the mouth of Messala similar sentiments: 'Le plus vil citoyen, dans sa bassesse extrême / Ayant chassé les rois, pense être roi lui-même'. See in *Eriphyle*, Polémon's advice to his queen (I.iv):

> Je ne le puis céler: l'Etat demande un maître;
> Déjà les factions commencent à renaître;
> Tous ces chefs dangereux, l'un de l'autre ennemis,
> Divisés d'intérêt et pour le crime unis,
> Par leurs prétentions, leurs brigues et leurs haines,
> De l'Etat qui chancelle embarrassent les rênes.

Line 190 recalls Corneille's Ptolomée, who pictures Pompey expressing the hope (*La Mort de Pompée*, I.i.28) that Egypt 'Pourra prêter l'épaule au monde chancelant'.

César...

CÉSAR

Quoi! tu t'émeus? ton âme est amollie?   205
Ah! mon fils...

BRUTUS

Sais-tu bien qu'il y va de ta vie?
Sais-tu que le sénat n'a point de vrai Romain,
Qui n'aspire en secret à te percer le sein?
Que le salut de Rome, et que le tien te touche.
Ton génie alarmé te parle par ma bouche: 210
Il me pousse, il me presse, il me jette à tes pieds.

(Il se jette à ses genoux.)

César, au nom des dieux dans ton cœur oubliés,
Au nom de tes vertus, de Rome, et de toi-même,
Dirai-je, au nom d'un fils qui frémit et qui t'aime,
Qui te préfère au monde, et Rome seule à toi,   215
Ne me rebute pas.

CÉSAR

Malheureux, laisse-moi.
Que me veux-tu?

BRUTUS

Crois-moi, ne sois point insensible.

206   35H, 36P: Sais-tu qu'il
211a   35H-W56, stage direction follows 208: *Il se jette à genoux.*

CÉSAR

L'univers peut changer; mon âme est inflexible.[11]

BRUTUS

Voilà donc ta réponse?

CÉSAR

Oui, tout est résolu.
Rome doit obéir, quand César a voulu.[12]   22c

BRUTUS *d'un air consterné.*

Adieu, César.

CÉSAR

Eh, quoi! d'où viennent tes alarmes?
Demeure encor, mon fils. Quoi! tu verses des larmes!
Quoi! Brutus peut pleurer! Est-ce d'avoir un roi?
Pleures-tu les Romains?

BRUTUS

Je ne pleure que toi.
Adieu, te dis-je.

---

218   35H: César est indulgent, mais il est inflexible
219-220   35H:
Oui. César doit régner.
Tout le sénat m'attend, et va me couronner.

---

[11] Cf. *Julius Caesar*, III.i.60-62 ff, Caesar: 'But I am constant as the northern star, / Of whose true-fixed and resting quality / There is no fellow in the firmament'. Brutus's vain pleading with Caesar, offering him the last chance to avoid death is paralleled in Shakespeare's play by the same suppliant postures of the conspirators who form a ring round their victim.
[12] Antony in Shakespeare's *Julius Caesar* says: 'When Caesar says 'do this,' it is performed.' (I.ii.10).

226

CÉSAR

O Rome! ô rigueur héroïque![13]   225
Que ne puis-je à ce point aimer ma république!

SCÈNE V

CÉSAR, DOLABELLA, ROMAINS

DOLABELLA

Le sénat par ton ordre au temple est arrivé:
On n'attend plus que toi, le trône est élevé.
Tous ceux qui t'ont vendu leur vie et leurs suffrages,
Vont prodiguer l'encens au pied de tes images.   230
J'amène devant toi la foule des Romains;
Le sénat va fixer leurs esprits incertains.
Mais si César croyait un vieux soldat qui l'aime,[14]
Nos présages affreux, nos devins, nos dieux même,
César différerait ce grand événement.   235

CÉSAR

Quoi! lorsqu'il faut régner, différer d'un moment!

230   35H, 36P: Vont, l'encens à la main, adorer tes images
233   35H: qui t'aime
      K: un citoyen qui l'aime
234   35H, 36P: Ces présages

[13] Cf. *Discours sur la tragédie*, prefacing Voltaire's *Brutus*, where Antony's audience in Shakespeare's *Julius Caesar* is described as 'ces mêmes Romains à qui Brutus avaient inspiré sa rigueur et sa barbarie'.
[14] The Kehl editions defend their reading on the grounds of its greater historical accuracy; Dolabella was only twenty-seven when he committed suicide to avoid capture by Cassius's forces in the war which followed Caesar's death.

Qui pourrait m'arrêter, moi?

DOLABELLA

               Toute la nature
Conspire à t'avertir par un sinistre augure.
Le ciel qui fait les rois, redoute ton trépas.

CÉSAR

Va, César n'est qu'un homme, et je ne pense pas   240
Que le ciel de mon sort à ce point s'inquiète,
Qu'il anime pour moi la nature muette,
Et que les éléments paraissent confondus,
Pour qu'un mortel ici respire un jour de plus.
Les dieux du haut du ciel ont compté nos années;   245
Suivons sans reculer nos hautes destinées.[15]
César n'a rien à craindre.[16]

DOLABELLA

               Il a des ennemis
Qui sous un joug nouveau sont à peine asservis.
Qui sait s'ils n'auraient point conspiré leur vengeance?

CÉSAR

Ils n'oseraient.

248   35H: sous un jour nouveau

---

[15] César's response to Dolabella's apprehensions recalls the words of Caesar to Calpurnia in Shakespeare's play (II.ii.26-30, 32-35).

[16] Cf. Voltaire's remark in the *Commentaires sur Corneille*, on *Nicomède*, IV.iii.46 ('Mais un monarque enfin comme un autre homme expire'): 'Quoique ce vers soit un peu prosaïque, il est si vrai, si ferme, si naturel, si convenable au caractère de Nicomède, qu'il doit plaire beaucoup, ainsi que le reste de la tirade. On aime ces vérités dures et fières, surtout quand elles sont dans la bouche d'un personnage que les relève encore par sa situation' (Voltaire 55, p.775).

DOLABELLA

Ton cœur a trop de confiance.[17]   250

CÉSAR

Tant de précautions contre mon jour fatal
Me rendraient méprisable, et me défendraient mal.

DOLABELLA

Pour le salut de Rome il faut que César vive;
Dans le sénat au moins permets que je te suive.

CÉSAR

Non, pourquoi changer l'ordre entre nous concerté?   255
N'avançons point, ami, le moment arrêté;
Qui change ses desseins découvre sa faiblesse.

DOLABELLA

Je te quitte à regret. Je crains, je le confesse.
Ce nouveau mouvement dans mon cœur est trop fort.

CÉSAR

Va, j'aime mieux mourir que de craindre la mort.   260
Allons.

---

260   35H: J'aime mieux mourir

[17] Dolabella echoes Shakespeare's Calpurnia (II.ii.49): 'Your wisdom is consumed in confidence'.

SCÈNE VI

DOLABELLA, ROMAINS

DOLABELLA

Chers citoyens, quel héros, quel courage,
De la terre et de vous méritait mieux l'hommage?
Joignez vos vœux aux miens, peuples, qui l'admirez,
Confirmez les honneurs qui lui sont préparés.
Vivez pour le servir, mourez pour le défendre…   265
Quelles clameurs, ô ciel! quels cris se font entendre!

LES CONJURÉS *derrière le théâtre.*

Meurs, expire, tyran. Courage, Cassius.

DOLABELLA

Ah! courons le sauver.

SCÈNE VII

CASSIUS *un poignard à la main,*[18]
DOLABELLA, ROMAINS

CASSIUS

C'en est fait, il n'est plus.

268a   35H, scene misnumbered: VIII
268c   36A adds: LES CONJURÉS

---

[18] Cf. Voltaire's reference to *Julius Caesar*, III.ii, in his *Discours sur la tragédie*: 'avec quel ravissement je voyais Brutus, tenant encore un poignard, teint du sang de César, assembler le peuple romain'.

DOLABELLA

Peuples, secondez-moi, frappons, perçons ce traître.

CASSIUS

Peuples, imitez-moi, vous n'avez plus de maître.   270
Nation de héros, vainqueurs de l'univers,
Vive la liberté; ma main brise vos fers.

DOLABELLA

Vous trahissez, Romains, le sang de ce grand homme?

CASSIUS

J'ai tué mon ami, pour le salut de Rome.[19]
Il vous asservit tous, son sang est répandu.   275
Est-il quelqu'un de vous de si peu de vertu,
D'un esprit si rampant, d'un si faible courage,
Qu'il puisse regretter César et l'esclavage?[20]
Quel est ce vil Romain, qui veut avoir un roi?
S'il en est un, qu'il parle, et qu'il se plaigne à moi.[21]   280

---

271   35H, 36P: Nations de
273   35H, 36P: Vous oubliez, Romains

---

[19] In Shakespeare's *Julius Caesar*, III.ii, Brutus says (his speech is in prose): 'I slew my best lover for the good of Rome'. Cf. *Discours sur la tragédie*, Voltaire's translation of Brutus's speech: 'J'ai tué de cette main mon meilleur ami pour le salut de Rome'.

[20] Cf. *Julius Caesar*: 'Who is here so base that would be a bondman?'; *Discours sur la tragédie*: 'Y a-t-il quelqu'un parmi vous assez lâche pour regretter la servitude?'; also *Julius Caesar*: 'Had you rather Caesar were living, and die all slaves, than that Caesar were dead, to live all free men?'; *Discours sur la tragédie*: 'Voudriez-vous César vivant, et mourir ses esclaves, plutôt que d'acheter votre liberté par sa mort?'.

[21] Cf. *Julius Caesar*: 'If any, speak; for him have I offended'; *Discours sur la tragédie*: 'S'il en est un seul, / Qu'il parle, qu'il se montre; c'est lui que j'ai offensé'.

Mais vous m'applaudissez, vous aimez tous la gloire.

ROMAINS

César fut un tyran, périsse sa mémoire.

CASSIUS

Maîtres du monde entier, de Rome heureux enfants,
Conservez à jamais ces nobles sentiments.
Je sais que devant vous Antoine va paraître;   285
Amis, souvenez-vous que César fut son maître;
Qu'il a servi sous lui dès ses plus jeunes ans,
Dans l'école du crime et dans l'art des tyrans.
Il vient justifier son maître et son empire;
Il vous méprise assez pour penser vous séduire.   29c
Sans doute il peut ici faire entendre sa voix:
Telle est la loi de Rome; et j'obéis aux lois.
Le peuple est désormais leur organe suprême,
Le juge de César, d'Antoine, de moi-même.
Vous rentrez dans vos droits indignement perdus;   29
César vous les ravit, je vous les ai rendus:
Je les veux affermir. Je rentre au Capitole;

281a   35H:
          ROMAIN
       Nous avons en horreur César et sa mémoire
292-301   35H:
       Telle est la loi de Rome, et nous cédons aux lois.
       Qu'il vous parle, il le faut; mais gardez qu'il ne loue
       Ce public ennemi que Rome désavoue.
       Tandis que nous allons dans vos murs délivrés,
       Renverser d'un tyran les marbres adorés;
       Prévenir des méchants les fureurs intestines;
294   36P: Le juge des tyrans, d'Antoine, de nous-même.
297-300   36P:
       Je les vais affermir, je cours au Capitole.
       Brutus vous a vengés. Il m'attend, et j'y vole.
       Je vais avec Brutus dans vos murs désolés,
       Rappeler la justice, et les dieux exilés,

Brutus est au sénat, il m'attend, et j'y vole.
Je vais avec Brutus, en ces murs désolés,
Rappeler la justice, et nos dieux exilés;   300
Etouffer des méchants les fureurs intestines,
Et de la liberté réparer les ruines.
Vous, Romains, seulement consentez d'être heureux,
Ne vous trahissez pas, c'est tout ce que je veux;
Redoutez tout d'Antoine, et surtout l'artifice.²²   305

ROMAINS

S'il vous ose accuser, que lui-même il périsse.

CASSIUS

Souvenez-vous, Romains, de ces serments sacrés.

ROMAINS

Aux vengeurs de l'Etat nos cœurs sont assurés.

306   35H: S'il nous ose accuser, que lui-même périsse.
       36A: S'il vous accuse: que lui-même il périsse
307   36P: vos serments
307a-309   35H:
ROMAIN
       O vengeur de l'Etat, nos cœurs sont assurés;
       Tout prêts pour ta défense à recourir aux armes;
       Mais Antoine paraît.
308   36P: Au vengeur

²² Cf. *Discours sur la tragédie*, where Voltaire describes Antony's funeral-oration in *Julius Caesar*: 'Antoine, par un discours *artificieux*, ramène insensiblement ces esprits superbes'.

SCÈNE DERNIÈRE

ANTOINE, ROMAINS, DOLABELLA

UN ROMAIN

Mais Antoine paraît.

AUTRE ROMAIN

Qu'osera-t-il nous dire?

UN ROMAIN

Ses yeux versent des pleurs, il se trouble, il soupire.[23]   31

UN AUTRE

Il aimait trop César.

ANTOINE, *montant à la tribune aux harangues.*

Oui, je l'aimais, Romains;[24]

308b   36P: ROMAIN
309a-311   35H, 36A:
               ANTOINE, ROMAINS
                    ROMAIN
               Ses yeux versent des larmes.
                 AUTRE ROMAIN
          Il aimait trop César.
309   MF35A: Antoine vient à vous
311a   35H, no stage direction

[23] Cf. *Julius Caesar*, III.ii, Second plebeian: 'Poor soul! His eyes are red as fire with weeping'.
[24] Cf. *Julius Caesar*, III.194: 'That I did love thee, Caesar, O, 'tis true!' In his translation of Brutus's funeral-oration, in the *Discours sur la tragédie*, Voltaire uses these same words ('Oui, je l'aimais, Romains!') although they do not (unlike the greater part of the translation) correspond closely to anything in the original. Cf. *Mort de César*, I.ii.144, Antoine's remark to César: 'Je t'aime et ne te puis tromper'.

234

Oui, j'aurais de mes jours prolongé ses destins.
Hélas! vous avez tous pensé comme moi-même;
Et lorsque de son front ôtant le diadème,
Ce héros à vos lois s'immolait aujourd'hui,   315
Qui de vous en effet n'eût expiré pour lui?
Hélas! je ne viens point célébrer sa mémoire;²⁵
La voix du monde entier parle assez de sa gloire;
Mais de mon désespoir ayez quelque pitié,
Et pardonnez du moins des pleurs à l'amitié.²⁶   320

UN ROMAIN

Il les fallait verser quand Rome avait un maître.
César fut un héros; mais César fut un traître.

AUTRE ROMAIN

Puisqu'il était tyran, il n'eut point de vertus.

316   36P: Qui de nous
317   35H: ne veux point
      MF35A: Je ne viens point ici célébrer
320a-324   35H:
                        ROMAIN
            Ne viens point nous vanter les vertus de ton maître.
            César fut un héros, mais César fut un traître;
            Nous avons en horreur ses funestes vertus,
            Et nous approuvons tous Cassius et Brutus.
321   MF35A: Il en fallait
322a-324   MF35A, 36P-W56:
                        AUTRE ROMAIN
            Puisqu'il était tyran, il n'eut point de vertus,
            Et nous approuvons [MF35A, 36P: avouons] tous Cassius et Brutus

²⁵ Cf. *Julius Caesar*, III.ii.75: 'I come to bury Caesar not to praise him'.
²⁶ Cf. *Julius Caesar*, III.ii.86: 'He was my friend, faithful and just to me', and
III.ii.106-108: 'Bear with me; / My heart is in the coffin there with Caesar, / And
I must pause till it come back to me'.

UN TROISIÈME

Oui, nous approuvons tous Cassius et Brutus.

ANTOINE

Contre ses meurtriers je n'ai rien à vous dire;²⁷   32ᴄ
C'est à servir l'Etat que leur grand cœur aspire.
De votre dictateur ils ont percé le flanc;
Comblés de ses bienfaits, ils sont teints de son sang.
Pour forcer des Romains à ce coup détestable,
Sans doute il fallait bien que César fût coupable;²⁸   33ᴄ
Je le crois. Mais enfin César a-t-il jamais
De son pouvoir sur vous appesanti le faix?
A-t-il gardé pour lui le fruit de ses conquêtes?
Des dépouilles du monde il couronnait vos têtes.
Tout l'or des nations, qui tombaient sous ses coups,   33ᴣ
Tout le prix de son sang fut prodigué pour vous.²⁹
De son char de triomphe il voyait vos alarmes:
César en descendait pour essuyer vos larmes.³⁰

---

328   35ʜ: Comblés de ses bontés, ils
329   35ʜ: Pour se déterminer à
338   36ᴘ: Lui-même en descendait

---

²⁷ Cf. *Julius Caesar*, ɪɪɪ.ii.101: 'I speak not to disprove what Brutus spoke', and ɪɪɪ.ii.126-128: 'I will not do them wrong; I rather choose / To wrong the dead, to wrong myself and you, / Then I will wrong such honourable men'. Shakespeare, who is not followed by Voltaire in this respect, makes great play with the ironic use of 'honourable' (see lines 83-84, 213, 215-216).

²⁸ Cf. *Julius Caesar*, ɪɪɪ.ii.78-81: 'The noble Brutus / Hath told you Caesar was ambitious. / If it were so, it was a grievous fault, / And grievously hath Caesar answered it'.

²⁹ Cf. *Julius Caesar*, ɪɪɪ.ii.89-91: 'He hath brought many captives home to Rome, / Whose ransoms did the general coffers fill: / Did this in Caesar seem ambitious?'

³⁰ Cf. *Julius Caesar*, ɪɪɪ.ii.92: 'When that the poor have cried, Caesar hath wept'.

236

Du monde qu'il soumit vous triomphez en paix,
Puissants par son courage, heureux par ses bienfaits.   340
Il payait le service: il pardonnait l'outrage.
Vous le savez, grands dieux! vous dont il fut l'image;
Vous, dieux, qui lui laissiez le monde à gouverner,
Vous savez si son cœur aimait à pardonner.

ROMAINS

Il est vrai que César fit aimer sa clémence.   345

ANTOINE

Hélas! si sa grande âme eût connu la vengeance,
Il vivrait, et sa vie eût rempli nos souhaits.
Sur tous ses meurtriers il versa ses bienfaits.
Deux fois à Cassius il conserva la vie.
Brutus... où suis-je? ô ciel! ô crime! ô barbarie!   350

339   36P: vous triomphiez
339-344   35H:
            Dieux! quels amis jamais a-t-il abandonnés?
            Dieux! à quels ennemis n'a-t-il pas pardonné?
345   35H, this line given to ROMAIN
346   35H: si son grand cœur eût
347   35H: rempli vos souhaits
350-367   35H:
            Brutus (ô crime horrible! ô comble de furie!)
            Brutus était son fils: ce monstre forcené
            A versé sous vos yeux le sang dont il est né.
            Hélas! je vois frémir vos généreux courages;
            Je vois déjà les pleurs qui mouillent vos visages.
            Oui, Brutus fut son fils: mais vous qui m'écoutez,
            Vous étiez ses enfants, dans son cœur adoptés.
            Savez-vous, citoyens, sa volonté dernière?
                  ROMAIN
            Que dis-tu! Parle.
                  ANTOINE
                        Rome est son héritière.
            Sa famille est l'Etat, ses trésors sont à vous.
            Sa vie et son trépas étaient utiles à tous.

Chers amis, je succombe; et mes sens interdits...
Brutus son assassin!... ce monstre était son fils.

ROMAINS

Ah dieux!

ANTOINE

Je vois frémir vos généreux courages;
Amis, je vois les pleurs qui mouillent vos visages.[31]
Oui, Brutus est son fils; mais vous qui m'écoutez,   35?
Vous étiez ses enfants dans son cœur adoptés.
Hélas! si vous saviez sa volonté dernière![32]

ROMAINS

Quelle est-elle? parlez.

ANTOINE

Rome est son héritière.
Ses trésors sont vos biens; vous en allez jouir;
Au-delà du tombeau César veut vous servir.   36?
C'est vous seuls qu'il aimait: c'est pour vous qu'en Asie
Il allait prodiguer sa fortune et sa vie.
O Romains, disait-il, peuple-roi que je sers,

Cassius et Brutus eût-il fait davantage?
            ROMAIN
Voilà donc des vertus le prix et le partage!
César fut en effet le père du sénat.
360   MF35A: Au-delà de la tombe il voulait vous servir;

---

[31] Cf. *Julius Caesar*, III.ii.194-195: 'O, now you weep, and I perceive you feel /
The dint of pity. These are gracious drops'.
[32] Cf. *Julius Caesar*, III.ii.146-147: ''Tis good you know not that you are his
heirs; / For if you should, O, what would come of it?'

Commandez à César, César à l'univers.[33]
Brutus ou Cassius eût-il fait davantage? 365

ROMAINS

Ah! nous les détestons. Ce doute nous outrage.

UN ROMAIN

César fut en effet le père de l'Etat.

ANTOINE

Votre père n'est plus: un lâche assassinat
Vient de trancher ici les jours de ce grand homme,
L'honneur de la nature et la gloire de Rome. 370
Romains, priverez-vous des honneurs du bûcher
Ce père, cet ami, qui vous était si cher?
On l'apporte à vos yeux.

(*Le fond du théâtre s'ouvre; des licteurs apportent le corps de César,
couvert d'une robe sanglante; Antoine descend de la tribune,
et se jette à genoux auprès du corps.*)

ROMAINS

O spectacle funeste!

366-367 36P, these lines given to ROMAINS
372   35H: Ce père, ce héros qui
373   35H: On l'amène à vos yeux.
373a-c   35H, no stage direction
373d   35H, this line given to ROMAIN

[33] Cf. *Julius Caesar*, III.ii.119-120: 'But yesterday the word of Caesar might /
Have stood against the world; now lies he there'.

ANTOINE

Du plus grand des Romains voilà ce qui vous reste;[34]
Voilà ce dieu vengeur, idolâtré par vous,   375
Que ses assassins même adoraient à genoux;
Qui toujours votre appui, dans la paix, dans la guerre,
Une heure auparavant faisait trembler la terre;
Qui devait enchaîner Babilone à son char;
Amis, en cet état connaissez-vous César?   380
Vous les voyez, Romains, vous touchez ces blessures,
Ce sang qu'ont sous vos yeux versé des mains parjures.
Là, Cimber l'a frappé; là, sur le grand César
Cassius et Décime enfonçaient leur poignard.
Là, Brutus éperdu, Brutus l'âme égarée,   385
A souillé dans ses flancs sa main dénaturée.[35]
César le regardant d'un œil tranquille et doux,
Lui pardonnait encore en tombant sous ses coups.
Il l'appelait son fils, et ce nom cher et tendre
Est le seul qu'en mourant César ait fait entendre: 39(
O mon fils! disait-il.[36]

374   35H, MF35A, 36P: plus grand des humains voilà
      MF35: qui nous reste
376   W75G: ces assassins
381   MF35A, W48D, W51: Vous le voyez
      MF35A: ses blessures
381-392   35H, absent

[34] A faint echo of the poignant, spontaneous reaction, expressed by Antony in *Julius Caesar* (III.ii.148-150), when he first sees the dead body of Caesar: 'O mighty Caesar! Dost thou lie so low? / Are all thy conquests, glories, triumphs, spoils / Shrunk to this little measure?'.

[35] Cf. *Julius Caesar*, III.ii.175-177: 'Look, in this place ran Cassius's dagger through; / See what a rent the envious Casca made; / Through this, the well-beloved Brutus stabbed'.

[36] Superficially, these lines could be regarded as a conflation of Antony's account of Caesar's death (*Julius Caesar*, III.i.185-190) and the actual presentation of the assassination and Caesar's dying words (III.i.77): '*Et tu Brute?* – Then fall Caesar!' The revelatory and significant divergence between Voltaire and Shakespeare at this point is discussed above, p.33-34.

240

ACTE III, SCÈNE VIII

UN ROMAIN

O monstre, que les dieux
Devaient exterminer avant ce coup affreux![37]

AUTRES ROMAINS, *en regardant le corps
dont ils sont proches.*

Dieux! son sang coule encor.

ANTOINE

           Il demande vengeance,
Il l'attend de vos mains et de votre vaillance.
Entendez-vous sa voix? Réveillez-vous, Romains;   395
Marchez, suivez-moi tous contre ses assassins;
Ce sont là les honneurs qu'à César on doit rendre.
Des brandons du bûcher qui va le mettre en cendre,
Embrasons les palais de ces fiers conjurés:
Enfonçons dans leur sein nos bras désespérés.   400
Venez, dignes amis; venez, vengeurs des crimes,
Au dieu de la patrie immoler ces victimes.

392a-393   35H:
             ROMAIN
   Dieux! son sang coule encore.
     MF35A, 36P:
  AUTRE ROMAIN, *en regardant le corps dont il est proche.*
   Dieux! son sang
393   W75G: Dieu!
394   35H: de mes mains
396   35H: contre ces assassins
400   35H, absent

[37] Voltaire reproaches La Marre (D1034): 'Vous paraissez surtout avoir d'autant plus de tort, de dire que les Romains approuvaient le parricide de Brutus, qu'à la fin de la pièce, les Romains se soulèvent contre les conjurés, que, lorsqu'ils apprennent que Brutus a tué son père; ils s'écrient: O monstre! que les dieux devaient exterminer'.

ROMAINS

Oui, nous les punirons; oui, nous suivrons vos pas.
Nous jurons par son sang de venger son trépas.
Courons.

ANTOINE *à Dolabella.*

Ne laissons pas leur fureur inutile;   405
Précipitons ce peuple inconstant et facile;
Entraînons-le à la guerre, et sans rien ménager,
Succédons à César, en courant le venger.[38]

Fin du troisième et dernier acte.

402a-405   35H:

ROMAIN
Punissons les auteurs de cet assassinat,
Sous les drapeaux d'Antoine courons tous au combat.
405   35H: Ami, ne laissons pas
407   35H: Que la guerre commence,
408a   35H, this indication omitted
36A: Fin

[38] Antoine's final words, and his indifference to the prospect of the horrors of civil war, recall Shakespeare's Antony, both in his callous satisfaction (*Julius Caesar*, III.ii.265-266: 'Now let it work. Mischief, thou art afoot, / Take thou what course thou wilt') and in his earlier evocation (III.i.262, 273) of 'domestic fury, and fierce civil strife' and of the way in which Caesar's spirit raging for revenge 'shall let slip the dogs of war'.

APPENDIX I

'Avertissement'

The 'Avertissement' which precedes 36P and 36L was composed by La Marre, and it was he who bore the brunt of Voltaire's dissatisfaction with it. From the outset, however, there had been so many fingers in this particular pie, that it becomes difficult to distinguish the sources of its various ingredients. The author of *La Mort de César* had himself provided the model which was to form the basis of the 'petite préface' (to Thiriot, 13 October 1735; D928). A rough draft which La Marre sent to Cirey was scrutinised and corrected by Voltaire and Mme Du Châtelet towards the end of December 1735 and sent back to Paris. In a letter to Berger of 22 December (D969), Voltaire says he has cut out all the praise which La Marre had thought fit to heap upon his benefactor, but favours the idea of including a blunt but unprovocative refutation of the calumnies to which he had been subjected. It would seem that at this stage of its preparation the 'Avertissement' did in fact include (with the approval of Voltaire who found it 'très sage, et même intéressant') 'une réponse simple, naïve, et pleine de vérité à des calomnies atroces et personnelles imprimées dans vingt libelles' (to Thiriot, 26 December; D972). By the New Year, however, Voltaire had changed his mind about the form and content of the 'Avertissement' and in a letter to Thiriot of 13 January (D987) he instructed him to ask La Marre to compose 'une préface historique touchant la pièce de Jules Cesar'. His directive is short but explicit: 'Il n'y a qu'à mettre ensemble le commencement et la fin de sa préface en retranchant tout ce qui est personel'. Voltaire's change of tactics did not involve a change of heart: he had probably decided by this time that the rebuttal of defamatory charges was a personal responsibility. He took appropriate action to which the final paragraphs of the preface he composed for 36A, as well as the

243

Epître sur la calomnie included in the same edition, bear witness. The revised (and presumably the final) form of the 'Avertissement' may owe something to d'Argental, who had been asked to keep a watchful eye on it and see it safely through the press with the Algarotti letter which made up the rest of the prefatory material.

Despite the successive revisions of the original version and Voltaire's unfavourable reaction to the text which finally emerged from them, enough of his own suggestions were implemented by La Marre to give the 'Avertissement' an interest and value which it would not otherwise have had. The abbé doubtless distorted some of Voltaire's views, but on the whole there is no reason to reject his claim that he is merely echoing his master's voice: 'Je ne fais que répéter ici ce que j'ai souvent ouï dire à celui dont je donne l'ouvrage au public'. The claim is supported by comparison with the preface which Voltaire wrote to replace the 'Avertissement': elements common to both include closely similar accounts of the genesis of Voltaire's play; references to plays about Caesar's assassination by Buckingham, Conti and Mlle Barbier; scathing treatment of the French habit of incongruously introducing *galanterie* into tragedy coupled with pride at the reversal of this practice in a play totally devoid of conventional romantic interest, and a flattering reference to Algarotti and the translation (or rather, adaptation) of his letter which accompanied both the 'Avertissement' and Voltaire's own preface.

The mixture of admiration and repulsion which, with shifts only of emphasis, characterised Voltaire's attitude to Shakespeare from his first contact with him until his final reaction against the excesses of adulatory *anglomanes* is already apparent in the antithetical 'Ses pièces sont des monstres dans lesquelles il y a des parties qui sont des chefs d'œuvre de la nature'. The 'monstrosity' of English tragedy had been remarked upon in the earlier preface to *Brutus*, and Voltaire was to refer tersely to 'l'ouvrage monstrueux de Shakespeare' which provided the creative impulse for the composition of *La Mort de César* in the preface which he wrote for it later. La Marre's more ample illustrations of the 'monstrosity' of Julius Caesar in the third paragraph of his

'Avertissement' are in accord with the critical remarks which Voltaire often made about Shakespeare, and English tragedy in general, in his correspondence at this time and which reflect the orthodox literary judgements of such cultured and cosmopolitan spirits as Bolingbroke. In a letter to Formont of 15 November 1735 (D942), referring to Dryden's *All for love*, Voltaire says: 'Sa Cléopâtre est un monstre, comme la plupart des pièces anglaises, ou plutôt toutes les pièces de ce pays là, j'entends les pièces tragiques; il y a seulement une scène de Ventidius et d'Antoine qui est digne de Corneille. C'est là le sentiment de milord Bolingbroke et de tous les bons auteurs; c'est ainsi que pensait Addison'. The same sentiment is expressed more trenchantly in a letter of 3 November 1735 (D934) which refers specifically to '*Shakespear*, le Corneille de Londre, grand fou, d'ailleurs et ressemblant plus souvent à Gilles qu'à Corneille'. The following sentence of the letter, however, redresses the balance: 'Mais il a des morceaux admirables'. La Marre sounds the same note in his 'Avertissement' and faithfully reflects Voltaire's attitude: critical reservations but, what was more important, a recognition of Shakespeare's strokes of genius and their power to inspire creative effort in other writers.

* * *

AVERTISSEMENT

Il y a près de huit années que plusieurs personnes prièrent l'auteur de *la Henriade* de leur faire connaître le génie et le goût du théâtre anglais. Il traduisit en vers une scène de Jules César de Shakespear, dans laquelle Antoine expose aux yeux du peuple romain le corps sanglant de César. Cette scène anglaise passe pour un des morceaux les plus frappants et les plus pathétiques qu'on ait jamais mis sur aucun théâtre. Le peuple romain conduit de la haine à la pitié et à la vengeance par la harangue d'Antoine, est

5

245

un spectacle digne de tous ceux qui aiment véritablement la
tragédie.   10

Les amis de M. de V... le prièrent de donner une traduction
du reste de la pièce: mais c'était une entreprise impossible.
Shakespear père de la tragédie anglaise, est aussi le père de la
barbarie qui y règne. Son génie sublime sans culture et sans goût,
a fait un chaos du théâtre qu'il a créé.   15

Ses pièces sont des monstres dans lesquelles il y a des parties
qui sont des chefs-d'œuvre de la nature. Sa tragédie intitulée *La
Mort de César*, commence par son triomphe au Capitole, et finit
par la mort de Brutus et Cassius à la bataille de Philippes. On
assassine César sur le théâtre. On voit des sénateurs bouffonner   20
avec la lie du peuple. C'est un mélange de ce que le tragique a
de plus terrible, et de ce que la farce a de plus bas. Je ne fais que
répéter ici ce que j'ai souvent ouï dire à celui dont je donne
l'ouvrage au public. Il se détermina pour satisfaire ses amis à faire
un Jules César, qui sans ressembler à celui de Shakespear fût   25
pourtant tout entier dans le goût anglais. On dit que c'est la
première parmi celles qui méritent d'être connues où l'on n'ait
point introduit de femmes. A peu près dans ce temps-là, le noble
Vénitien monsieur l'abbé Conti, qui joint le talent de la poésie à
la philosophie la plus sublime, avait fait imprimer sa tragédie   30
italienne de la mort de Jules César. Le feu duc de Bukinham, père
de celui qui vient de mourir à Rome, en fit aussi une sur le même
sujet. Ces quatre tragédies entièrement différentes les unes des
autres, se ressemblent en un seul point, c'est qu'elles sont toutes
sans amour.   35

On joua il y a environ trente ans une tragédie de la mort de
César sur le théâtre des Comédiens français, et on ne manqua pas
de rendre César et Brutus amoureux.

C'est aux gens de lettres, étrangers et français, à qui nous
présentons ce petit ouvrage de M. de V... à juger s'il a mieux fait   40
de peindre ces deux grands hommes tels qu'ils étaient, que de
donner sous leurs noms des Français galants.

Cette tragédie qui n'a jamais été destinée au théâtre de Paris
fut représentée il y a quatre ans à l'hôtel de Sassenage, et très

bien exécutée: mais la scène de Shakespear, dans laquelle Antoine   45
monte à la tribune aux harangues, pour faire voir au peuple la
robe sanglante de César, ne put être représentée à cause du petit
espace du théâtre, qui suffisait à peine au petit nombre d'acteurs
qui jouent dans cette pièce.

Elle fut jouée depuis au collège d'Harcourt par les pensionnaires   50
de ce collège avec une intelligence et une dignité peu ordinaire à
l'âge des acteurs. L'auteur aurait sans doute été très satisfait, s'il
avait pu voir cette représentation.

La tragédie transcrite à la hâte au collège d'Harcourt a été
imprimée furtivement. On croirait presque que l'éditeur et l'impri-   55
meur ont disputé à qui ferait le plus de fautes. C'est ce qui a
déterminé l'auteur à faire une édition de cet ouvrage, qu'il était
résolu de ne point faire paraîtttre, parce qu'il lui manque pour le
soutenir l'illusion du théâtre: secours si nécessaire à ce genre de
poésie. C'est au public à l'apprécier ce qu'il vaut; les louanges   60
des amis et les critiques des ennemis sont également inutiles
devant ce tribunal. Je sais que bien des gens se récrient sur
l'atrocité de Brutus qui tue César, quoiqu'il le connaisse pour son
père. Mais on les prie de se souvenir que chez les Romains l'amour
de la liberté était poussé jusqu'à la fureur, et qu'un parricide dans   65
certaines circonstances était regardé comme une action de courage
et même de vertu. Nous avons parmi les Lettres de Cicéron une
lettre de ce même Brutus, dans laquelle il dit qu'il tuerait son père
pour le salut de la république; et d'ailleurs la tragédie, et surtout
la tragédie anglaise, n'est pas faite pour les choses à demi terribles.   70

Nous ajoutons à cet *Avertissement* une lettre de monsieur le
marquis Algaroti, qui à l'âge de vingt-quatre ans est déjà regardé
comme un bon poète, un bon philosophe, et un savant. Son estime
et son amitié pour monsieur de V... leur fait honneur à tous deux.

APPENDIX II

'Préface des éditeurs'

This preface was written by Voltaire himself to replace La Marre's 'Avertissement' with which it has often been confused by editors, including those responsible for the Kehl edition. It was first published in the form in which it appears here in 36A. The last two paragraphs, which are taken up almost exclusively with an attack upon Jean-Baptiste Rousseau (or with self-defence, as Voltaire saw it) were omitted from the four-volume *Œuvres de M. de Voltaire* (Amsterdam, Ledet or Desbordes, 1738-1750; siglum w38). Subsequently, this revised version of the preface was used by other editors who introduced it as the 'Préface des éditeurs de l'édition de 1738' (w48D, w50, w51 and T64P).

Voltaire's attempt to invalidate the rival claim of Saint-Evremond to primacy in the propagation of knowledge of English literature in France receives support from the information provided by an illuminating reference to Saint-Evremond's *Sir Politick Would-be* in an impartial biographical sketch by Desmaizeaux which precedes an edition of the French *émigré*'s works:

Le Duc de Buckingham, M. d'Aubigny et lui se voyoient souvent, et s'entretenoient sur toutes sortes de matieres; mais particulierement sur les Pieces de Théatre des differentes Nations. Comme M. de Saint-Evremond n'entendoit pas l'Anglois, ces Messieurs lui expliquoient ce que les Poëtes Dramatiques de cette Nation avoient composé de meilleur; et il s'en formoit une idée si nette et si exacte, que quarante ans après, il s'en souvenoit encore fort distinctement. Cette lecture lui fournit les Reflexions qu'il a faites sur les Tragedies et sur les Comedies Angloises, dans quelques-uns de ses Ouvrages. Ce fut aussi cette espece d'étude, qui donna occasion à ces Messieurs de travailler ensemble à la Comedie de *Sir Politick Would-be*. Chacun fournissoit une partie des Caracteres, et M. de Saint-Evremond leur donnoit la forme. Ceux qui trouveront cette Comédie un peu trop longue, doivent se souvenir qu'elle a été faite *à la maniere des Anglois*, qui dans ce tems-là faisoient

248

leurs Pieces de Théatre extrêmement longues; et d'ailleurs il faut remarquer que cette Piece n'ayant pas été faite pour être joüée, on s'est plus appliqué à bien marquer les Caracteres, qu'à animer l'Action par des intrigues attachantes, et par un dénouëment peu attendu.[1]

The disparaging treatment of Saint-Evremond represents an addition to the material presented in La Marre's 'Avertissement'. Another fresh element of the same sort is the oblique introduction of Fontenelle ('un des plus beaux génies de France'), who had not been referred to, even covertly, by La Marre, but who is here put in the dock with Mlle Barbier for the crime of presenting Caesar and Brutus as *galants*.

Voltaire objected to La Marre's lack of finesse, particularly to the blatant way in which the 'Avertissement' presented parricide as, in the eyes of the ancient Romans, excusable and even admirable in certain circumstances. Yet he himself abandons the discretion he urges upon his *protégé* (see D1034) and summarily dismisses the possible charge that he had allowed Brutus to condone parricide with the dogmatic and unacceptable: 'On sait que César était son père; il n'en faut pas davantage pour justifier cette hardiesse'. The objection to such a cavalier attitude towards historical fact is made by Voltaire himself in his *Commentaires sur Corneille* ('Remarques sur le *Comte d'Essex*', I.i.123; Voltaire 55, p.1006): 'On demande jusqu'à quel point il est permis de falsifier l'histoire dans un poème? Je ne crois pas qu'on puisse changer sans déplaire les faits ni même les caractères connus du public. Un auteur qui représenterait César battu à Pharsale serait aussi ridicule que celui qui dans un opéra introduisait César sur la scène chantant *alla fuga, allo scampo, signori*!'

* * *

---

[1] Pierre Desmaizeaux, *Vie de M. de Saint-Evremond* (1705); quoted by René Ternois, *Œuvres en prose de Saint-Evremond*, iii.32.

249

PRÉFACE DES ÉDITEURS

Nous donnons cette édition de la tragédie de la Mort de César de monsieur de Voltaire: nous pouvons dire qu'il est le premier qui ait fait connaître les muses anglaises en France. Il traduisit en vers il y a quelques années plusieurs morceaux des meilleurs poètes d'Angleterre, pour l'instruction de ses amis, et par là il engagea beaucoup de personnes à apprendre l'anglais; en sorte qu'aujourd'hui cette langue est devenue familière aux gens de lettres. C'est rendre service à l'esprit humain de l'orner ainsi des richesses des pays étrangers.

Parmi les morceaux les plus singuliers des poètes anglais que notre ami nous traduisit, il nous donna la scène d'Antoine et du peuple romain prise de la tragédie de Jules-César, écrite il y a cent cinquante ans par le fameux Shakespear, et jouée encore aujourd'hui avec un très grand concours, sur le théâtre de Londres. Nous le priâmes de nous donner le reste de la pièce; mais il était impossible de la traduire.

Shakespear était un grand génie, mais qui vivait dans un siècle grossier, et l'on retrouve dans ses pièces la grossièreté de ce temps beaucoup plus que le génie de l'auteur. M. de Voltaire au lieu de traduire l'ouvrage monstrueux de Shakespear, composa dans le goût anglais, ce Jules-César que nous donnons au public. Ce n'est pas ici une pièce telle que le *Sir Politick* de M. de St Evremond, qui n'ayant aucune connaissance du théâtre anglais, et n'en sachant pas même la langue, donna son *Sir Politick*, pour faire connaître la comédie de Londres aux Français. On peut dire que cette comédie du *Sir Politick* n'était ni dans le goût des Anglais, ni dans celui d'aucune autre nation.

Il est aisé d'apercevoir dans la tragédie de la Mort de César le génie et le caractère des écrivains anglais, aussi bien que celui du peuple romain. On y voit cet amour dominant de la liberté, et ces hardiesses que les auteurs français ont rarement.

Il y a encore en Angleterre une autre tragédie de la Mort de César composée par le duc de Buckingham. Il y en a une en italien de M. l'abbé Conti noble vénitien. Ces pièces ne se ressemblent qu'en un seul point, c'est qu'on n'y trouve point 35 d'amour. Aucun de ces auteurs n'a avili ce grand sujet par une intrigue de galanterie; mais il y a environ trente-cinq ans que l'un des plus beaux génies de France s'étant associé avec mademoiselle Barbier, pour composer Jules-César, il ne manqua pas de représenter César et Brutus amoureux et jaloux. Cette petitesse ridicule 40 est un des plus grands exemples de la force de l'habitude, personne n'ose guérir le théâtre français de cette contagion. Il a fallu que dans Racine, Mithridate, Alexandre, Porus aient été galants. Corneille n'a jamais évité cette faiblesse. Il n'a fait aucune pièce sans amour, et il faut avouer que dans ses tragédies (si vous 45 exceptez le Cid et Polyeucte) cette passion est aussi mal peinte, qu'elle y est étrangère. Notre auteur a donné peut-être ici dans un autre excès. Bien des gens trouvent dans sa pièce trop de férocité; ils voient avec horreur que Brutus sacrifie à l'amour de sa patrie non seulement son bienfaiteur, mais son père. On n'a à 50 répondre autre chose, sinon que tel était le caractère de Brutus, et qu'il faut peindre les hommes tels qu'ils étaient. On a encore une lettre de ce fier Romain dans laquelle il dit qu'il immolerait son propre père à la république. On sait que César était son père; il n'en faut pas davantage pour justifier cette hardiesse. 55

On imprime au-devant de cette édition, la lettre du marquis Algaroti, jeune homme déjà connu pour un bon poète, et pour un bon philosophe, et ami de M. de Voltaire.

On met à la suite de la tragédie de César, l'Epître de notre auteur sur la calomnie, ouvrage déjà connu: il y a un trait de 60 satire violent. Il ne s'est jamais permis la satire personnelle que contre Rousseau, comme Despreaux ne se l'est permise que contre Rollet, voici les vers qui regardent cet homme:

L'affreux Rousseau loin de cacher en paix
Des jours tissus d'opprobre et de forfaits, 65
Vient rallumer aux marais de Bruxelles

58-91   w38 onwards: Voltaire.//

D'un feu mourant les pâles étincelles,
Et contre moi croit rejeter l'affront
De l'infamie écrite sur son front.
Eh! que pourront tous les traits satiriques,   70
Que d'un bras faible il décoche aujourd'hui,
Et ce ramas de larcins marotiques
Moitié français et moitié germaniques? etc.

La conduite de Rousseau, et les mauvais vers qu'il fait depuis
quinze ans justifient assez ce trait. Notre auteur n'est pas le seul   75
que Rousseau ait déchiré dans les vers durs qu'il compose tous
les jours. Il en a fait aussi contre l'illustre M. de Fontenelle, contre
M. l'abbé du Bos, homme très sage, très savant et très estimé;
contre M. l'abbé Bignon, le protecteur des sciences, contre M. le
maréchal de Noailles, à qui on ne peut rien reprocher, que d'avoir   80
autrefois protégé Rousseau. Enfin il vomit les injures les plus
méprisables contre ce qu'il y a de plus respectable dans le monde,
et contre tous ses bienfaiteurs. Il faut avouer qu'il est bien permis
à M. de Voltaire de témoigner, en passant, dans un de ses
ouvrages, ce dédain et cette exécration avec lesquels tous les   85
honnêtes gens regardent et Rousseau, et tout ce que Rousseau
imprime depuis quelques années. C'est trop longtemps nous
arrêter sur un sujet si désagréable; nous finissons en informant le
public que nous allons donner une très belle et très correcte
édition de la Henriade et des autres ouvrages de notre auteur,   90
tous revus, corrigés, et beaucoup augmentés.

APPENDIX III

'Lettre de M. N... à M. N...'

This is the French version of the Algarotti letter, on which see above p.114-17 and 169-73.

* * *

LETTRE DE M. N... À M. N... SUR LA TRAGÉDIE DE JULES-CÉSAR, PAR M. DE VOLTAIRE

J'ai différé jusqu'à présent, Monsieur, de vous envoyer le Jules-César que vous me demandez, pour vous faire part de celui de M. de Voltaire.

L'édition qu'on en a faite à Paris il y a quelques mois, est très informe. On y reconnaît assez la main de quelqu'un du genre de ceux que Pétrone appelle *doctores umbratici*.[1] Elle est défectueuse au point qu'on y trouve des vers qui n'ont pas le nombre de syllabes nécessaire.[2] Cependant la critique a jugé cette pièce avec la même sévérité, que si M. de Voltaire l'eût donnée lui-même au public. Ne serait-il pas injuste d'imputer au Titien le mauvais coloris d'un de ses tableaux barbouillés par un peintre moderne? J'ai été assez heureux pour qu'il m'en soit tombé entre les mains un manuscrit digne de vous être envoyé; et voilà enfin le tableau tel qu'il est sorti des mains du maître. J'ose même l'accompagner des réflexions que vous m'avez demandées.

[1] Petronius, *Satyricon*, II: 'Nondum umbraticus doctor ingenia deleverat'. This is the only point in this letter which is specifically taken up by Voltaire in the censorious letter (D1034) he sent to La Marre after the appearance of 36P.

[2] Cf. Voltaire's letter to Thiriot of 4 October 1735: 'Peut-on m'imputer des vers sans rime, sans mesure et sans raison dont cette édition misérable est parsemée' (D924).

253

Il faudrait ignorer qu'il y a une langue française et un théâtre pour ne pas savoir à quel degré de perfection Corneille et Racine ont porté le dramatique. Il semblait qu'après ces grands hommes, il ne restait plus rien à souhaiter, et que tâcher de les imiter, était tout ce qu'on pouvait faire de mieux. Désira-t-on quelque chose dans la peinture après la Galathée de Raphaël? Cependant la célèbre tête de Michel Ange dans le petit Farnèse donna l'idée d'un genre plus terrible et plus fier auquel cet art pouvait être élevé. Il semble que dans les beaux-arts on ne s'aperçoit qu'il y avait des vides qu'après qu'ils sont remplis. La plupart des tragédies de ces maîtres, soit que l'action se passe à Rome, à Athène, ou à Constantinople, ne contient qu'un mariage concerté, traversé, ou rompu. On ne peut s'attendre à rien de mieux dans ce genre, où l'amour donne avec un souris ou la paix ou la guerre. Il me paraît qu'on pourrait donner au dramatique un ton supérieur à celui-ci. Le Jules-César m'en est une preuve; l'auteur de la tendre Zaïre ne respirant ici que des sentiments d'ambition, de vengeance, et de liberté.

La tragédie doit être l'imitation des grands hommes. C'est ce qui la distingue de la comédie; mais si les actions qu'elle représente, sont aussi des plus grandes, cette distinction n'en sera que plus marquée, et l'on peut atteindre par ce moyen à un genre supérieur. N'admire-t-on pas davantage Marc Antoine à Phillipes qu'à Actium. Je ne doute pourtant pas que ces raisons ne puissent essuyer de fortes contradictions. Il faudrait avoir bien peu de connaissance de l'homme pour ne pas savoir que les préjugés l'emportent presque toujours sur la raison, et surtout les préjugés autorisés par un sexe qui impose une loi qu'on suit toujours avec plaisir.

L'amour est depuis trop longtemps en possession du théâtre français, pour souffrir que d'autres passions y prennent sa place. C'est ce qui me fait croire que le Jules-César pourrait bien avoir le même sort que les Thémistocles, les Alcibiades, et les autres grands hommes d'Athène admirés de toute la terre, pendant que l'ostracisme les bannissait de leur patrie.

M. de Voltaire a imité en quelques endroits Shakespear poète anglais qui a réuni dans la même pièce les puérilités les plus ridicules et les morceaux les plus sublimes. Il en a fait le même usage que Virgile faisait des ouvrages d'Ennius; il a imité de l'auteur anglais les deux dernières scènes qui sont deux des plus beaux modèles d'éloquence qu'il y ait au théâtre.

Quum flueret lutulentus, erat quod tollere velles.[3]

N'est-ce point un reste de barbarie en Europe de vouloir que les bornes que la politique et la fantaisie des hommes ont prescrites pour la séparation des Etats, servent aussi de limites aux sciences et aux beaux-arts, dont les progrès pourraient s'étendre par un commerce mutuel des lumières de ses voisins. Cette réflexion convient même mieux à la nation française qu'à toute autre. Elle est dans le cas de ces auteurs dont le public exige plus à mesure qu'il en a plus reçu; elle est si généralement polie et cultivée, que cela met en droit d'exiger d'elle que non seulement elle approuve, mais qu'elle cherche même à s'enrichir de ce qu'elle trouve de bon chez ses voisins.

Tros Rutulusve fuat, nullo discrimine habebo.[4]

Une objection dont je ne vous parlerais pas, si je ne l'eusse entendu faire, est sur ce que cette tragédie n'est qu'en trois actes. C'est dit-on pécher contre le théâtre, qui veut que le nombre des actes soit fixé à cinq. Il est vrai qu'une des règles, est qu'à toute rigueur la représentation ne dure pas plus de temps que n'aurait duré l'action, si véritablement elle fût arrivée. On a borné avec raison le temps à trois heures, parce qu'une plus longue durée lasserait l'attention, et empêcherait qu'on ne pût réunir aisément dans le même point de vue les différentes circonstances de l'action qui se passe. Sur ce principe on a divisé les actes en cinq pour la commodité des spectateurs et de l'auteur, qui peut faire arriver dans ces intervalles quelque événement nécessaire au nœud ou au dénouement de la pièce. Toute l'objection se réduit donc à

[3] Horace, *Satirae*, I.iv.11.
[4] Virgil, *Aeneis*, x.108.

n'avoir fait durer l'action du César que deux heures au lieu de trois. Si ce n'est pas un défaut, le nombre des actes n'en doit pas être un non plus, puisque la même raison qui veut qu'une action de trois heures soit partagée en cinq actes, demande aussi qu'une action de deux heures ne le soit qu'en trois. Il ne s'ensuit pas de ce que la plus grande étendue qui a été prescrite est de trois heures, qu'on ne puisse pas la rendre moindre; et je ne vois point pourquoi une tragédie assujettie aux trois unités, d'ailleurs pleine d'intérêts, excitant la terreur et la compassion; enfin faisant en deux heures ce que les autres font en trois, ne serait pas une excellente tragédie. Une statue dans laquelle les belles proportions et les autres règles de l'art sont observées, ne laisse pas d'être une belle statue, quoiqu'elle soit plus petite qu'une autre, faite sur les mêmes règles. Je ne crois pas que personne trouve la Vénus de Médicis moins belle dans son genre, que le Gladiateur, parce qu'elle n'a que quatre pieds de hauteur, et que le Gladiateur en a six. M. de Voltaire a peut-être voulu donner à son César moins d'étendue que l'on en donne communément aux pièces dramatiques, pour sonder le goût du public par un essai, si l'on peut appeler de ce nom une pièce aussi achevée. Il s'agit pour cela d'une révolution dans le théâtre français, et c'eût été peut-être trop hasarder, que de commencer par parler de liberté et de politique trois heures de suite à une nation accoutumée à voir soupirer Mitridate, sur le point de marcher vers le Capitole. On doit tenir compte à M. de Voltaire de ce ménagement, et ne lui point faire d'ailleurs un crime de n'avoir mis ni amour, ni femmes dans sa pièce: nées pour inspirer la mollesse et les sentiments, elles ne pourraient jouer qu'un rôle ridicule entre Brutus et Cassius, *atroces animae*.[5] Elles en jouent de si brillants partout ailleurs qu'elles ne doivent pas se plaindre de n'en avoir aucun dans le César. Je ne vous parlerai point des beautés de détail qui sont sans nombre dans cette pièce, ni de la force de la poésie, pleine d'images et de sentiments. Que ne doit-on pas attendre de

[5] Cf. Horace, *Carmina*, II.i.24: 'Atrocem animum Catonis'.

256

l'auteur de Brutus et de la Henriade? La scène de la conspiration me paraît des plus belles et des plus fortes qu'on ait encore vues sur le théâtre; elle fait voir en action ce qui jusqu'à présent ne s'était presque toujours passé qu'en récit.

> *Segnius irritant animos demissa per aures*
> *Quamquae sunt oculis subjecta fidelibus,*[6]

120

La mort même de César se passe presque à la vue des spectateurs, ce qui nous épargne un récit qui, quelque beau qu'il fût, ne pourrait qu'être froid: les événements et les circonstances qui l'accompagnent étant trop connus de tout le monde.

125

Je ne puis assez admirer combien cette tragédie est pleine de choses, et combien les caractères sont grands et soutenus. Quel prodigieux contraste entre César et Brutus! Ce qui d'ailleurs rend ce sujet extrêmement difficile à traiter, c'est l'art qu'il faut pour peindre d'un côté Brutus avec une vertu féroce à la vérité, et presque ingrat, mais ayant en main la bonne cause; au moins selon les apparences, et par rapport au temps où l'auteur nous transporte; et de l'autre côté César rempli de clémence, et des vertus les plus aimables, comblant de bienfaits ses ennemis, mais voulant opprimer la liberté de sa patrie. Il faut s'intéresser également pour tous les deux pendant le cours de la pièce, quoiqu'il semble que les passions doivent s'entrenuire et se détruire réciproquement à la fin, comme feraient deux forces égales et opposées, et par conséquent ne produire aucun effet, et renvoyer les spectateurs sans agitation.[7] Ce sont ces réflexions qui ont fait dire à un homme du métier[a] qu'il regardait ce sujet comme l'écueil des poètes tragiques, et qu'il l'aurait proposé

130

135

140

---

[a] M. Martelli qui a écrit beaucoup de tragédies en italien. Il s'est servi d'une nouvelle espèce de vers rimés qu'il avait imaginée d'après les vers alexandrins. Cette nouveauté n'a pas été favorable à ses pièces.

---

[6] Horace, *Ars poetica*, 180-181.
[7] The whole of this paragraph could be said to remedy the lacuna which Voltaire criticises in La Marre's 'Avertissement' (see D1034).

volontiers à quelqu'un de ses rivaux. Il semble que M. de Voltaire non content de ses difficultés, en ait voulu faire naître de nouvelles, en faisant Brutus fils de César, ce qui d'ailleurs est fondé sur 145 l'histoire. Il a aussi trouvé par-là le moyen de se ménager de très belles situations, et de jeter dans sa pièce un nouvel intérêt, qui se réunit tout entier à la fin pour César. La harangue d'Antoine produit cet effet; et elle est à mon avis le modèle de l'éloquence la plus séduisante. Enfin, je crois que l'on peut dire avec vérité, 150 que M. de Voltaire a ouvert une nouvelle carrière, et qu'il atteint le but en même temps.

APPENDIX IV

The original Algarotti letter

This is the text of the letter actually sent by Algarotti; see above, p.114-17. Variants are given from the *Opera del conte Algarotti* (Cremona 1778-1784), siglum 83.

* * *

[Letter from Algarotti to Giulio Franchini-Taviani]

Adunque cotesti signori prendonsi gran maraviglia, che io me ne resti tuttavia alla campagna, e in un angolo, per dir come loro, di una provincia. Non così ella, che sa quel che mi muova a cercare varii paesi. Per non entrare nelle descrizioni poetiche della felicità della vita campestre, le dirò in semplici parole, come lungi dal   5
tumulto di Parigi qui si fa una vita condita da' piaceri della mente: e ben si può dire con quel poeta, che a queste cene non manca nè Lambert nè Moliere. Io do l'ultima mano a' miei dialoghi, che pur han trovata molta grazia innanzi gli occhi così della bella Emilia, como del dotto Voltaire: e da essi sto raccogliendo i bei   10
modi della conversazione, che vorrei poter trasfondere nella mia operetta. Ma ecco che da questa provincia io le mando cosa, che dovrebbono aver pur cara cotesti signori *inter beatae fumum et opes strepitumque Romae*. Le mando il Giulio Cesare del nostro Voltaire, non alterato o guasto, ma tal quale egli uscì dalla penna dell'autor   15
suo.[1] E mi pare esser certo, che a lei dovrà sommamente piacere di scorgere in questa tragedia un nuovo genere di bellezza, a che

4-5   83:   paesi. Qui lungi dal

[1] Cf. *Lettre de M. N...*, lines 12-13.

può essere innalzato il teatro francese. Sebbene troppo la nuova cosa parrà cotesta a quelli, che credono dopo la morte di Cornelio e Racine spenta la fortuna di esso, e nulla sanno vedere al di là delle costoro produzioni. A chi un tempo fa sarebbe caduto nel pensiero, che restasse da aggiungere nulla alla musica vocale dopo lo Scarlatti, ovvero alla strumentale dopo il Corelli? Pur nondimeno il Marcello e il Tartini ci hanno mostrato, che ci avea così nell'una, come nell'altra alcun segno più là. E' pare che l'uomo non s'accorga de' luoghi che rimangono ancora vacui nelle arti, se non dopo occupati.[2] Così il Giulio Cesare mostrerà *nescio quid majus*, quanto al genere delle tragedie francesi. Che se la tragedia, a distinzion della commedia, è la imitazion di un'azione che abbia in sè del terribile e del compassionevole; è facile a vedere quanto questa, che non è intorno a un matrimonio o a un amoretto, ma intorno a un fatto atrocissimo, e alla più gran rivoluzione che sia avvenuta nel più grande imperio del mondo; è facile, dico, a vedere, quanto ella venga ad essere più distinta dalla commedia, che non sono le altre tragedie francesi, e salga sopra un coturno più alto di assai. Ma io temerei non per questo appunto dovesse avere dal pubblico meno grata accoglienza il nuovo Giulio Cesare. Non fa mestieri aver veduto *mores hominum multorum et urbes*, per sapere che i più bei ragionamenti del mondo se ne vanno quasi sempre con la peggio, quando eglino hanno a combattere opinioni avvalorate dall'usanza e dall'autorità di quel sesso, il cui imperio si stende sino alle provincie scientifiche. L'amore è signor despotico delle scene francesi; e una tragedia, dove non han che far donne, tutta sentimenti di libertà e pratiche di politica, non darà naturalmente nella cruna di gente avvezza ad udire Mitridate fare il galante sul punto di muovere il campo verso Roma,[3] e a vedere Sertorio e Regolo damerini. Nè sarebbe

20

25

3c

3·

4·

4

38   83: Cesare. Ma tutto questo è niente al più delle persona: non fa

[2] Cf. *Lettre de M. N...*, lines 16-25.
[3] Cf. *Lettre de M. N...*, lines 103-106.

da farsi maraviglia, che il Cesare del Voltaire corresse la medesima
fortuna a Parigi, che Temistocle, Alcibiade e quegli altri grandi
uomini della Grecia corsero in Atene, ammirati da tutto il mondo,   50
e sbanditi dalla loro patria.[4]

In questa tragedia il Voltaire ha preso ad imitare la severità del
teatro inglese, e singolarmente Shakespeare, in cui dicesi, e con
ragione, che ci sono errori innumerabili e pensieri inimitabili;
faults innumerable, and thoughts inimitable: del che è una riprova la   55
medesima sua *Morte di Giulio Cesare*. E ben ella può credere, che
il nostro poeta ha tolto di Shakespeare quello che di Ennio
toglieva Virgilio. Egli ha espresso in francese le due ultime scene
di quella tragedia, le quali, toltone alcune mende, sono un vero
specchio di eloquenza:[5] come le due di Burro et de Narciso con   60
Nerone, nel trarre gli animi delle medesime persone in sentenze
contrarie.[6] Pur chi sa, se anche per tale imitazione non venga dai
più fatto il processo al nostro poeta? A niuno è nascosto, come
la Francia e l'Inghilterra sono rivali nelle cose politiche, nel
commercio, nella gloria delle armi, e delle lettere;   65

Litora litoribus contraria, fluctibus undae:

e potrebbe darsi, che la poesia degl'Inglesi fosse accolta a Parigi
allo stesso modo che la loro filosofia. Quanti clamori non sonosi
levati all'accademia contro il Maupertuis. Non par egli che po-
nendo in luogo della materia sottile e de'vortici l'attrazione abbia   70
egli tentato di sovvertire in Francia lo stato? Ma finalmente
dovranno sapere i Francesi non picciolo grado ad uno, che in

61-63   83: contrarie. Ma chi sa, se per tale imitazione appunto non venga
fatto a questa tragedia meno applauso. A niuno
64   83: politiche, di stato nel commercio
68-71   83: filosofia. Ma finalmente

[4] Cf. *Lettre de M. N...*, lines 34-50.
[5] Cf. *Lettre de M. N...*, lines 52-56.
[6] In his *Risposta al Sig. Martelli* (p.72), Conti praises Racine's treatment of the
clemency/cruelty debate in *Britannicus*.

certo modo arricchisce il loro Parnaso di una sorgente novella:[7] tanto più che grandissima è la discrezione, con che il nostro poeta fecesi ad imitare il teatro inglese, trasportando nel suo la severità di quello, e non la ferocità. Nel che egli ha di gran lunga superato Addissono, il quale nel Catone ha mostrato agl'Inglesi non tanto la regolarità del teatro francese, quanto la sconvenevolezza di que' suoi amori: e con ciò è venuto a guastare uno dei pochissimi drammi moderni, in cui lo stile è veramente tragico, e i Romani parlano romano e non spagnuolo.[8]

Ma quando non si storcessero contro a questa tragedia per altro motivo, lo farebbono almeno perch'è di tre soli atti.[9] Aristotele in vero parlando nella Poetica della lunghezza dell'azion teatrale, non si spiega così chiaramente sopra il numero degli atti in che vuolsi dividerla. Ognuno però sa a mente quei versi della Poetica latina, *Neve minor, neu sit quinto productior actu Fabula, quae posci vult, et spectata reponi*; precetto che viene da Orazio prescritto non meno per la commedia che per la tragedia. Ora se pur vi ha delle commedie di Moliere di tre atti e non più, e che ciò non ostante son tenute buone; non se perchè non vi possa ancora essere una buona tragedia che sia di tre atti, e non de cinque.

> *Quid autem*
> *Caecilio Plautoque dabit Romanus ademptum*
> *Virgilio Varioque?*

E forse non sarebbe del tutto fuor di ragione, che una gran parte delle moderne tragedie si riducessero a tre atti solamente; troppo spesso incontra, che per arrivare ai cinque i più degli

87   83:   neu sit
97   83:   solamente; mentre si vede, che per

[7] Cf. *Lettre de M. N...*, lines 58-68, with omission.
[8] Voltaire's view of Addison's *Cato* as the first English tragedy satisfying neo-classical canons of taste, but vitiated by *galanterie*, is given in the eighteenth *Lettre philosophique*. The same view had been put forward by Conti in his *Risposta al Sig. Martelli* (p.55).
[9] Cf. *Lettre de M. N...*, lines 70-71.

autori vi appiccano episodii, che allungano il componimento e ne
tolgon l'unità. E già il savio Racine non volle distendere la sua   100
Ester più là di tre atti. Che se i Greci nelle loro tragedie, benchè
semplicissime, ritennero costantemente la divisione in cinque atti;
bisogna far considerazione, che assai più brevi che i nostri sogliono
essere gli atti dei loro drammi, tenendone il coro una parte non
picciola. E non so se io ben mi ricordi; ma il Ciclope di Euripide   105
non contiene che soli ottocento versi. Tanto poco e' scrupuleggia-
vano sulla lunghezza degli atti che da noi si vogliono assai più
pieni.

Ma che mi distendo io in parole sopra tali cose con lei? *Pollio
et ipse facit nova carmina.* A lei sta il diffinire, se il Voltaire, siccome   110
egli ha aperto tra' suoi una nuova via, così ancora ne sia giunto
al termine.[10] E che non vien ella a Cirey a comunicarci in persona
le dotte sue riflessioni;[11] ora massimamente che siamo assicurati,
essere per la pace già segnata composte le cose di Europa? Niente
allora qui mancherebbe al desiderio mio, e a niuno in Parigi   115
potrebbe parer nuovo, che io mi rimanessi in una provincia.

100   83:   E però l'istesso Racine
103   83:   che ciò non sempre torna così bene al nostro teatro; non tanto
perchè nostro costume è il fare gli atti più lunghi, quanto perchè tra noi non
ha luogo il coro, che appresso di loro occupava una grandissima parte del
dramma.//

[10] Cf. *Lettre de M. N...*, lines 150-153.
[11] The same invitation was made by Voltaire (D938).

APPENDIX V

'Lettre de M. L... à M. D...'

This short letter was a late addition to the material prefacing 36P and is not present in all copies. It is also found in the second issue of 36L and in 36R.

One can only speculate upon the date of the letter, the identity of the author and that of the addressee. The initials L and D obviously provide no clue; the Algarotti-Franchini letter was headed 'Lettre de *M. N... à M. N...*'. From internal evidence it appears that the writer of the letter had been sent a manuscript copy of *La Mort de César* upon which he had been asked to comment, particularly with a view to the possible repercussions of the play upon public opinion and the consequent effects upon the stability of the country's political regime. The sender of this letter to M. L... was, it can be assumed, in an official position which involved him in assessing the extent to which Voltaire's play could be regarded as subversive in character, and did not feel debarred from soliciting the judgement of trusted friends on this question. Chauvelin, the *garde des sceaux*, had already received a note (D909), after the appearance of 35H, from a pious gentleman, Claude Le Pelletier, full of alarm at the prospect of the sedition and even attempts at assassination which would be encouraged by Voltaire's play. Chauvelin sent this letter to Hérault, the *lieutenant de police*, and it may be conjectured that it was the latter, a school-friend of Voltaire, who is designated as M. D... and that M. L... was another member of the circle of friends and acquaintances of Voltaire. There is a plausible case for believing that M. L... was the duc de Richelieu, who besides being a friend of the author of *La Mort de César* was linked to him by the fact that Mme Du Châtelet had been his mistress before becoming Voltaire's. This supposition is supported by the first paragraph of the letter. M. L... is an ardent supporter of Corneille,

264

and what he says about the effect of that dramatist's work upon him echoes what Mme Du Châtelet wrote to Richelieu in June 1735 (D876), after having seen a perfomance of *Héraclius*: 'je n'ai jamais trouvé Corneille si sublime, il a étonné mon âme. Le sentiment d'admiration est si rarement excité qu'il me semble que c'est un de ceux qui fait le plus grand plaisir'. The way in which M. L... addresses M. D... as 'Monsieur le Raciniste' recalls Mme Du Châtelet's tone of amicable opposition to Voltaire's advocacy of Racine, which stemmed from the admiration engendered in him (and in Hérault, one may presume) at Louis-le-Grand. It may be added that the Cornelian aspect of *La Mort de César* (see D869) would have made its appeal to both Mme Du Châtelet and Richelieu.

As for the date of this letter, it may be assumed that the manuscript copy which formed the basis of 36P was perused by Hérault some time after 12 October 1735, when Voltaire was despatching an amended copy of his work to Franchini (D927). The result of Hérault's assessment of the play was that it received a *permission tacite*, mentioned by Voltaire in a letter to Thiriot of 2 February 1736 (D999), so that the letter reproduced below, which probably constituted a response to Hérault's soundings, must have been written between these two dates.

The arguments in favour of publication put forward by the writer of the letter are based on the supposition that Voltaire had written a work of high literary merit merely for the delectation of an educated reading-public. Such enlightened readers would be aware of the irrelevance of the political situation presented in the play to that of contemporary France, it is implied; they were not likely to make the mistake of equating the public-spirited citizens of a republic struggling to safeguard threatened institutions with the disloyal subjects of a monarchy seeking to overthrow the existing regime for personal ends. The idea of 'ce poème' making its primary appeal to the reader, rather than the spectator, is supported by the admiration which M. L... shows for the skill which Voltaire has shown in the versification. He was as conscious as M. L... of the extent to which a play was dependent for its success on the performers, and often professed to aim at winning the appreciation of a limited public of connoisseurs. Yet, one element which found favour with M. L... points to a different aspect of Voltaire's work: 'Dans la tragédie de M. de Voltaire les personnages s'y peignent par les actions'. The emphasis upon action serves to remind us that this was one of the more revolutionary features of English drama which Voltaire wished to introduce into the still fairly staid French theatre. This note, out of harmony with the dominant conservatism of the letter, recalls the bolder ideal of innovation by imitation which is invoked in the letter of Algarotti. However muted it is, it suggests Voltaire's ambition of ultimately being able to so mould the taste of French theatre-goers that they would accept some of the '*hardiesses*' which had so beguiled him during his stay in England.

* * *

LETTRE DE M. L... À M. D...

Je ne puis assez vous remercier, Monsieur, de m'avoir confié *la Mort de César*, tragédie de M. de Voltaire. J'ai lu ce poème avec toute l'attention dont je suis capable. J'ai admiré une prodigieuse quantité de beaux vers; vers que j'appelle cornéliens, car ne vous en déplaise, Monsieur le Raciniste, il faut que je vous écrive ce que je vous ai dit et redit plusieurs fois. Corneille flatte mon amour-propre, il me persuade de l'excellence de mon être; il élève mon âme, et je lui en sais gré. Racine, quoique admirable, m'attriste quelquefois en m'attendrissant, il développe trop mes faiblesses, il me dégrade, et j'en suis un peu fâché.

Je reviens à M. de Voltaire. Je crois qu'on verra avec grand plaisir sa Mort de César imprimée. On sent bien par la constitution de ce poème que l'auteur ne l'a pas composé pour le donner au Théâtre Français. Les personnages récitants, peuvent, par le fonds des choses, et surtout par la véhémence de la déclamation, faire des impressions sur le plus grand nombre des spectateurs, contraires au repos de l'Etat monarchique, dans lequel nous sommes assez heureux de vivre. Mais ce plus grand nombre de spectateurs, ne sera plus affecté à la lecture de cet ouvrage saillant, comme il le serait à la représentation. Et cette lecture satisfera infiniment les gens éclairés, pour lesquels l'auteur a travaillé. 20

L'époque historique que M. de Voltaire a choisie lui a fourni les caractères de ses personnages, tous ennemis de César qui veut opprimer la liberté.

Le poète donne à chacun des conjurés quelque coup de pinceau 25 qui les différencie entre eux, quoique allant au même but. Ce ne sont pas des portraits vagues, souvent fourrés dans une scène par le poète dramatique, pour y donner, à ce qu'il croit, de l'éclat, mais qui malgré la beauté des vers, refroidit la scène. Toute beauté étrangère à la chose, cesse d'être beauté. Dans la tragédie de 30 M. de Voltaire les personnages s'y peignent par les actions. Voilà la bonne, et peut-être l'unique manière de peindre, soit dans la tragédie, soit dans la comédie.

Tout ce que l'on dit contre la puissance arbitraire ne peut choquer. Qui est-ce qui parle? des Romains, dans l'éclat le plus 35 florissant de la république.

S'il s'agissait de renverser un Etat monarchique, et que des esprits chauds, amateurs de la nouveauté, et cherchant dans une autre forme de gouvernement, des avantages que leur peu de vertu n'a pu leur procurer; que ces esprits, dis-je, tinssent les 40 mêmes propos que tiennnent Brutus et Cassius pour maintenir la république, on ne pourrait les supporter.

Je fais une grande différence du Brutus de Tarquin au Brutus de César. Le premier est un rebelle, le second est un citoyen.

Que M. de Voltaire n'amolisse jamais ni ses caractères, ni sa 45 versification, qu'il néglige toujours les petits ornements pour frapper le grand. Il peut s'attirer des envieux, mais les gens sensés l'admireront. Voilà mon avis.

Je suis, etc.

2. 'Prologue' for *La Mort de César*: a copy, in an unknown hand, sent by Voltaire to Mme Truchis de La Grange with D3660 (Bibliothèque municipale, Besançon).

APPENDIX VI

Prologue

The *vers d'occasion* by Voltaire which the *Almanach littéraire* (AL) published in 1783 (p.230-32) were conveniently set in context:

La tragédie de *La Mort de César*, que les Comédiens ont reprise cette année a été, comme on sait, souvent jouée dans les collèges, mais il est singulier qu'elle l'ait été quelquefois dans les maisons religieuses. Les pensionnaires du Couvent de Beaune, la donnèrent en 1747, pour la fête de la Prieure; et elles écrivirent en corps à Voltaire, pour le prier de leur envoyer un prologue en l'honneur de la bonne Mère. Il dicta sur-le-champ les vers suivants.

The lines which followed are not identical in all particulars with those of the prologue which Voltaire sent to Mme Truchis de La Grange on 7 June 1748. Voltaire's accompanying letter (D3660) shows his eagerness to please the pious Visitandines of Beaune:

Je voudrois que ce prologue fût plus digne de vous, et répondît mieux à l'honneur que vous me faites; mais que dire sur Jules Cesar dans un couvent? J'ay tâché au moins de rappeller autant que j'ay pu les idées de cette catastrophe aux idées de relligion, et de soumission a dieu, qui sont les principes de votre vie et de votre retraitte.

His unwonted attempt to express his respect for the Christian religion is most evident in the Trinitarian sentiment of the final line. The text that follows is a modernised version of the manuscript copy sent with D3660, at the Bibliothèque municipale, Besançon, ms 1442, f.437r (see fig.2).

* * *

PROLOGUE

Osons-nous retracer des féroces vertus
Devant des vertus si paisibles?
Osons-nous présenter ces spectacles terribles
A ces regards si doux, à nous plaire assidus?
Cesar ce roi de Rome, et si digne de l'être,   5
Tout héros qu'il était fut un injuste maître;
Et vous régnez sur nous par le plus saint des droits.
On détestait son joug, nous adorons vos lois;
Pour vous et pour ces lieux quelle scène étrangère
Que ces troubles, ces cris, ce sénat sanguinaire,   10
Ce vainqueur de Pharsale au temple assassiné,
Ces meurtriers sanglants, ce peuple forcené?
Toutefois des Romains on aime encore l'histoire,
Leurs grandeurs, leurs forfaits vivent, dans la mémoire,
La jeunesse s'instruit dans ces faits éclatants,   1
Dieu lui-même a conduit ces grands événements.
Adorons de sa main ces coups épouvantables
Et jouissons en paix de ces jours favorables,
Qu'il fait luire aujourd'hui sur des peuples soumis
Eclairés par sa grâce, et sauvés par son fils.   2

1   AL: de feroces
9   AL: Pour nous
16   AL: les grands

Zaïre

critical edition

by

Eva Jacobs

ACKNOWLEDGEMENTS

In preparing this edition, I received valuable help on particular points from Mlle Chastang, of the Bibliothèque nationale, Mme Sylvie Chevalley, lately of the Archives de la Comédie-Française, and the late Professor O. R. Taylor, and I wish to record my gratitude for their kindness. I should also like to thank the French government, whose award of a one-month bursary helped me to complete the research for this edition in France.

Ulla Kölving and Andrew Brown, of the Voltaire Foundation, undertook the final stages of the preparation of the text for publication, and the completeness of the bibliographical material is, to an important degree, due to their contribution. They have been generous with their time and expertise, and I am very conscious of the great debt that I owe them.

INTRODUCTION

1. *Composition*

On 29 May 1732, Voltaire was so excited at the progress of his new tragedy that he wrote separate letters about it to his two great friends living in Rouen, Cideville and Formont. This is the first we hear of his latest play, apparently as yet unnamed, but the description of it he gives to Cideville shows that the subject has already crystallised in his mind:

La scène sera dans un lieu bien singulier, l'action se passera entre des Turcs et des crétiens. Je peindray leurs mœurs autant qu'il me sera possible, et je tâcheray de jetter dans cet ouvrage tout ce que la religion crétienne semble avoir de plus patétique, et de plus intéressant, et tout ce que l'amour a de plus tendre et de plus cruel. (D493)

To Formont he is even more explicit:

Tout le monde me reproche ici que je ne mets point d'amour dans mes pièces. Ils en auront cette fois-ci, je vous jure, et ce ne sera pas de la galanterie. Je veux qu'il n'y ait rien de si turc, de si chrétien, de si amoureux, de si tendre, de si furieux que ce que je versifie à présent pour leur plaire. J'ai déjà l'honneur d'en avoir fait un acte. Ou je suis fort trompé, ou ce sera la pièce la plus singulière que nous ayons au théâtre. Les noms de Montmorency, de s^t Louis, de Saladin, de Jésus et de Mahomet s'y trouveront. On y parlera de la Seine et du Jourdain, de Paris et de Jérusalem. On aimera, on baptisera, on tuera, et je vous enverrai l'esquisse dès quelle sera brochée. (D494)

Voltaire had embarked upon this new venture partly to take his mind off his own dissatisfaction with his latest tragedy. *Eriphyle* had not pleased the public, and he himself had serious doubts about the text. The success of *Œdipe* in 1718 was beginning to be distant history and Voltaire needed desperately to repeat the triumph at the Comédie-Française that had since eluded him for so long. Each new tragedy he worked upon so intensely bore all

277

his hopes. With *Zaïre*, at last, he was not disappointed: it was a huge dramatic success.

One can scarcely speak of stages in the composition of *Zaïre*, for to the act that was finished on 29 May were so rapidly added four more that on 25 June Voltaire was able to announce to Formont, who had sent him a few words of advice about his new tragedy, that they had come too late:

La tragédie était faite. Elle ne m'a coûté que vingt-deux jours.[1]

This almost incredible speed of composition is a measure of Voltaire's enthusiasm for his subject. He felt he had a theme which would inspire the public as it was inspiring him. In the many letters that he wrote about this time mentioning his new tragedy, he continues to stress the same elements of the work: love, the contrast between Turkish and Christian manners, and the role of religion.

The emphasis on love is certainly surprising. Voltaire had begun his career as a tragic poet with the conviction that French tragedy needed renewal and that this could be achieved through going back to its origins in Greek tragedy. He felt strongly that the French had diminished tragedy by making love the obligatory centre of interest in their plays, and as he first wrote it, his own *Œdipe* had no love element at all. Contact with the English stage during his exile served to convince him that French tragedy had degenerated into being merely a series of conversations between lovers. A famous passage, among many similar ones written at about the time he was composing *Zaïre*, sets down his views on tragedy and admits to the influence upon him of English drama:

La France n'est pas le seul pays où l'on fasse des tragédies; et notre goût, ou plutôt notre habitude de ne mettre sur le théâtre, que de longues conversations d'amour, ne plaît pas chez les autres nations. Notre théâtre

---

[1] D497. Voltaire was occasionally to alter this figure slightly in speaking of the composition of *Zaïre*, notably in the 'Avertissement' which appeared in w38 and most subsequent editions, but we may suppose that the first figure he gives is the most accurate (see below, 'Lettre à monsieur de La Roque', p.420, l.38).

est vide d'action et de grands intérêts, pour l'ordinaire [...] Si vous aviez vu jouer la scène entière de Shakespeare, telle que je l'ai vue et telle que je l'ai à peu près traduite, nos déclarations d'amour et nos confidentes vous paraîtraient de pauvres choses auprès.[2]

Both before[3] and after the composition of *Zaïre*, Voltaire attacked the importance accorded to love in French tragedy. Does he temporarily forget these attacks in the claims he makes for the role of love in *Zaïre?* Not entirely, for he is careful when describing his new play to reintroduce the distinction between *amour* and *galanterie*,[4] a distinction which allows him to pander to the public taste for love stories while apparently remaining true to his principles: 'Ils en auront cette fois-ci [...] et ce ne sera pas de la galanterie' (D494). That such a distinction is perfectly legitimate is obvious. Whether Voltaire himself managed to observe it in *Zaïre* is another matter. At all events, Voltaire, determined this time to conquer the public, unashamedly includes love as a major ingredient in his new play.

The second major ingredient that Voltaire stresses in his letters is 'les mœurs turques opposées aux mœurs chrétiennes' (D497). *Zaïre* was written at the time when Voltaire was at the height of his admiration for English drama and was ready to experiment with various ways of incorporating the things he had learnt in England into his own plays. On one point he is explicit, for in the first 'Epître dédicatoire' to *Zaïre* he declares:

C'est au théâtre anglais que je dois la hardiesse que j'ai eue de mettre sur la scène les noms de nos rois et de nos anciennes familles du royaume. Il me paraît, que cette nouveauté pourrait être la source d'un genre de tragédie qui nous est inconnu jusqu'ici, et dont nous avons besoin.[5]

---

[2] D940. This letter, of 14 November 1735, was written to Desfontaines after he had criticised *La Mort de César*, which had appeared in an unauthorised version.

[3] See a long discussion entitled 'De l'amour' in Voltaire's *Discours sur la tragédie* which acts as a dedication of *Brutus* to Bolingbroke (1731; M.ii.322-24).

[4] See 'De l'amour', where the distinction is already made.

[5] See below, p.399.

This specific and narrow claim is, however, related to a more general realisation he also owed to England: that it is possible to write tragedy without achieving the degree of abstraction and universality that had been characteristic of seventeenth-century classical drama. With the expansion of travel and a new awareness of the variety of customs, religions and conditions throughout the world, it became increasingly difficult for the eighteenth century to envisage human nature as an abstract concept, divorced from time and place, universally and eternally the same. Montesquieu, among others, was forcing his contemporaries to accept that aspects of life such as social organisation and religion not only influence, but perhaps also create the individual; that a woman brought up in the strictness of an oriental harem, for instance, does react very differently from one living in the free atmosphere of the salons, and that the differences between them are not merely superficial.

In saying that he has attempted to contrast *mœurs turques* with *mœurs chrétiennes*, Voltaire is certainly reflecting his generation's growing awareness of the variety of mankind. The idea that it is possible to incorporate this awareness into art, that it is possible to reproduce a much more concrete reality in drama, came to him from his experience of the English theatre. But there was a further reason why Voltaire was interested in portraying Turkish manners in his play. If, as he said, contemporary tragedy was dying a slow death through consisting only of interminable conversations between lovers, one of the ways of bringing it to life again, he believed, was to introduce more colour and movement upon the stage: what he calls *spectacle*. The introduction of *mœurs turques* into his play allowed for such elements of visual enjoyment as vaguely oriental scenery[6] and costumes. Orosmane

---

[6] It is likely, although I have not been able to obtain direct evidence of this, that the scenery in the production of *Zaïre* at the Comédie-Française, consisting of a backcloth painted in perspective and painted flats, would have suggested an oriental setting, possibly with minarets and other Eastern decorative motifs. But there would have been nothing new in this. Earlier 'oriental' plays produced at the Comédie-Française certainly had this kind of scenery. Racine's *Bajazet* is

was certainly dressed in furs,[7] and the actors of the Comédie-Française had to provide five *habits à la turque*.[8] Voltaire felt that the public was eager for the information on the East and the visual pleasure afforded by an 'oriental' play, and, like the emphasis on love, the introduction of *mœurs turques* shows his determination to woo and win the audience.

The third element of the play Voltaire stresses in his letters is the role of religion. Opposed to *mœurs turques* are *mœurs chrétiennes*. It is possible to argue that Voltaire could have written a play very similar to *Zaïre* without the introduction of Christianity. If the story is seen primarily as one of love, misunderstanding, jealousy and murder in an exotic setting, it is very easy to conceive a plot that would offer the same ingredients with a purely Turkish theme. Seen in this way, the Christian element becomes a sort of additional embellishment to the play, or a pleasantly familiar foil to *mœurs turques*. Zaïre is then a young girl separated from her lover by an obstacle that happens to be religion. She would, however, be an equally touching figure if she were faced, for instance, with a conflict between her love for a man and her parents' disapproval of him, for personal or social reasons, perhaps. But Voltaire wanted to do much more than present his public with yet another girl in love, or even with another girl in

---

an obvious example. But Voltaire's emphasis on *mœurs turques*, as opposed to a merely conventional oriental setting, is new.

[7] H. C. Lancaster suggests that these furs are meant to denote Orosmane's Scythian ancestry. But it seems more probable that they serve as a symbol of wealth and status. In any case, the wearing of furs is not unknown in the East; see H. C. Lancaster, *French tragedy in the time of Louis XV and Voltaire, 1715-1774* (Baltimore 1950), i.144.

[8] In spite of some evidence of 'Turkish' costumes in the first production of *Zaïre*, Voltaire's efforts at introducing more realism, and hence more variety, upon the stage met with little success until he was supported by Lekain in the middle years of the century, see J.-J. Olivier, *Henri-Louis Le Kain* (Paris 1907), ch.7 *passim*. Even Lekain was far from wholly successful in his attempts to reform costume at the Comédie-Française. He himself played Orosmane in full oriental costume, but Nérestan, played beside him by Molé, was still dressed as a gentleman of the court of Louis xv.

love in a strange and romantic setting. He wanted to enlarge the scope of tragedy to include *grands intérêts* (see above, p.279), which we may take to mean themes of more than merely personal importance. He wanted to write tragedy with a serious purport and moral purpose. This is a major reason why, in *Zaïre*, the conflict for the heroine is not that of having to choose between two people, or two emotions, or simply love and duty, for it is not at all certain that Zaïre's duty is clearly to her family and to Christianity. The conflict is between love and Christianity in a particular situation. Voltaire expressly introduced Christianity into his play because its importance in Western civilisation could confer upon his work the epic grandeur that he was seeking. Only in this way, he believed, could a tragedy of lasting greatness be written, a tragedy which would achieve more than the ephemeral applause of fashion and carry his name into posterity. But the immediate test was with his contemporaries, and this he was soon ready to face.

2. *Performance and reception*

Voltaire sent his new play to some friends to read, and read it himself to others, and many, in typical eighteenth-century fashion, were moved to tears. In spite of this favourable advance publicity, however, the first performance of *Zaïre*, given at the Comédie-Française on 13 August 1732, was not an unqualified success, for, as Voltaire himself later recounted:

Les acteurs jouaient mal, le parterre était tumultueux, et j'avais laissé dans la pièce quelques endroits négligés qui furent relevés avec un tel acharnement que tout l'intérêt était détruit. (D526)

But the play soon recovered from this near set-back and was given ten times to full houses in August and September, and twenty-one more times between 12 November and 11 January of the following year.[9] An excited Voltaire wrote to his Norman friends on 25 August:

Soufrez mon cher Cideville que je me livre avec vous en liberté au plaisir de voir réussir ce que vous avez aprouvé. Ma satisfaction s'augmente en vous la communiquant. Jamais pièce ne fut si bien jouée que Zaire à la quatrième représentation. Je vous souhaittois bien là. Vous auriez vu que le public ne hait pas votre amy. Je parus dans une loge et tout le parterre me batit des mains. Je rougissois, je me cachois, mais je serois un fripon si je ne vous avouois pas que j'étois sensiblement touché. (D515)

Mathieu Marais, who was not specially sympathetic to Voltaire, was forced to admit that the crowds at each performance were such that 'on s'y étouffe'[10] and a little later he added tartly, 'Il y a eu un combat à Paris pour la pièce de Voltaire, qui par là est devenue tragique.'[11]

Voltaire modestly attributed his success to the actors, and notably to Mlle Gaussin, who played the role of Zaïre:

J'ai bien peur de devoir aux grands yeux noirs de m^{lle} Gaussin, au jeu des acteurs et au mélange nouveau des plumets et des turbans ce qu'un autre croirait devoir à son mérite. (D526)

Other parts were played by the following actors: Dufresne (Orosmane), Sarrazin (Lusignan), Grandval (Nérestan), Legrand de Belleville (Châtillon), Mlle Jouvenot (Fatime).

For Voltaire himself, the triumph of *Zaïre* was somewhat marred by the performance at the rival Comédie-Italienne of two parodies of his play. The first of these, entitled *Arlequin au Parnasse, ou la folie de Melpomène*, was written by the abbé Nadal and played on 2 December 1732.[12] It is not strictly speaking a parody although

[9] A note to D515 has 10 November instead of 12 November (see *Registres*, p.708-709).

[10] Letter to Bouhier, 28 August 1732 (*Journal et mémoires*, iv.406).

[11] Letter to Bouhier, 4 September 1732 (iv.410).

[12] The *Mercure de France* for December 1732, p.2667, gives the date of the first performance as 4 December, but the 'Registres' of the Comédie-Italienne show that the first performance was in fact on 2 December. See Clarence D. Brenner, *The Théâtre italien, its repertory, 1716-1793* (Berkeley 1961), p.104.

it is printed in the first volume of a famous collection of parodies,[13] but rather, as it correctly calls itself, a *comédie critique*. It portrays the Muse of Tragedy, Melpomene, as mad, for only madness, suggests the author, could have produced the five acts of *Zaïre*. The five acts themselves are personified in the play and come forward to catalogue their own faults and to quarrel among themselves. The author's hatred of Voltaire is manifest in the preface to the play, where the success of *Zaïre* is compared to that of a painted coquette, but hatred has not clouded his judgment, and many of the criticisms of *Zaïre* in *Arlequin au Parnasse* are very much to the mark. A few days later, on 9 December, a second parody of *Zaïre* appeared at the Comédie-Italienne, entitled *Les Enfants trouvés, ou le sultan poli par l'amour*, whose three authors were all actors in the company.[14] This is a true parody, obtaining its effects by lowering the whole tone of the play, so as to deflate its more absurdly dramatic aspects. It is comic and often pungent, but without being spiteful. *Les Enfants trouvés* is less original than Nadal's *comédie critique*, but much more amusing. Voltaire, in a letter written about 15 December (D545), told Formont that both plays had failed at the Comédie-Italienne but the *Mercure de France* in its first mention of *Les Enfants trouvés* in the same month states that the parody 'est fort applaudie' (p.2673). In the second volume for December 1732 (p.2868-83), the *Mercure* gives more details: the first performance was not a success, but later ones have confirmed its popularity with the public.[15] The *Mercure* then goes on to give a long summary of the parody, as it had already done for *Arlequin au Parnasse* (p.2667-73).

Publicity on this scale given to two plays which mocked the

---

[13] *Les Parodies du nouveau théâtre italien, ou recueil des parodies représentées sur le théâtre de l'Hôtel de Bourgogne, par les comédiens italiens ordinaires du roy* (Paris 1738).

[14] Dominique, Romagnesi and Francesco Riccoboni, *Les Enfans trouvez, ou le sultan poli par l'amour: parodie de la tragédie de Zaïre, de monsieur de Voltaire* (Paris 1733).

[15] *Les Enfants trouvés* was given ten times in December 1732 and three times in January 1733, and it was revived from time to time until as late as 1756.

success of *Zaïre* infuriated Voltaire, but other attacks came which were potentially more serious. Two of these, in particular, were made by known enemies of Voltaire, but that does not prevent them from containing criticism of substance. The first of these was by the abbé Nadal. He had not waited for the performance of *Arlequin au Parnasse* to make public his opinion of *Zaïre*. On the very day after the performance of Voltaire's tragedy, he wrote a *Lettre à madame la comtesse de F*** sur la tragédie de Zaïre*.[16] Inspired, no doubt, by personal jealousy, for he was a rival tragedian, the abbé lists with perspicacity a number of technical faults in *Zaïre*: inconsistency of characterisation, incredibility in certain aspects of the plot, reliance upon accident in working out the story, superfluity of some of the characters. But the main attack is directed against what Nadal claims is the total effect of the play upon the audience: to demonstrate that the power of love is stronger than that of religion.[17]

A more extreme opinion along the same lines was advanced by Jean-Baptiste Rousseau, who saw in *Zaïre* an opportunity to gain a telling point in his long and bitter quarrel with Voltaire:[18]

Ceux qui m'avoient mandé, il y a quatre mois, que la fine morale de cet ouvrage étoit de prouver que les Sarrazins, êtoient plus honnêtes gens que les chrétiens, m'en avoient donnée une fausse idée. Il ne paroît point que l'autheur ait eû ce dessein en vuë. Le sentiment qui y Règne d'un boût à l'autre, tend seulement à faire voir que tous les efforts de la grâce, n'ont aucun pouvoir sur nos passions. Ce dogme Impie, et

---

[16] Augustin Nadal, *Œuvres mêlées* (Paris 1738), i.316-23. Nadal's *Lettre* was not, of course, a private comment from one friend to another, but was intended to be circulated among a large circle of acquaintances.

[17] It is interesting to compare Voltaire's own dissatisfaction with the first performance of *Zaïre* (see above, p.282) with Nadal's statement deploring that 'le succès en est si brillant'. Nadal's opinion of the success of the first night is borne out by Formont, who had been present (D521). But Voltaire repeats several times in his letters that the first performance of *Zaïre* had been a failure. Perhaps he was disappointed in the public's reaction, which may, nevertheless, have been generally favourable.

[18] A detailed account of their protracted battle is to be found in H. Grubbs, *Jean-Baptiste Rousseau* (Princeton 1941).

aussi injurieux au bon sens qu'à la Religion, fait l'unique fondement de sa fable.[19]

While it is difficult for us to know whether Rousseau honestly thought that Voltaire was setting out to destroy belief in the efficacy of Divine Grace, it is certain that he had aimed at one of his enemy's most vulnerable points. He knew that Voltaire was already suspect to the Church, and he was prepared to stop at nothing to get him into as much trouble as possible. An anonymous well-wisher leapt to Voltaire's defence on 8 March 1733, in a letter printed in the *Mercure de France* of April 1733,[20] and exonerated him from impiety, but admitted that there were a number of weaknesses in the play. But whatever enlightenment or confusion might emerge from such writings, the public remained indifferent to the many petty squabbles of authors and continued to enjoy *Zaïre*. Throughout the eighteenth century, it was considered one of the great tragedies of the French classical theatre, and if hostile criticism was not entirely stilled, the chorus of praise from public and critics alike drowned the dull murmurs of dissenters on the side.

Zaïre was quickly translated into several foreign languages. In Italy, at least[21] eight different translations of the play were published during Voltaire's lifetime, and some of these were reprinted more than once before the turn of the century. New Italian

---

[19] D561. This letter from Rousseau to Launay is dated 13 January 1733, and was first printed in *Le Glaneur historique, critique, moral, littéraire, galant et calotin* (La Haye 6 April 1733), iii, no.xxviii.

[20] *Lettre de M. L... à M. l'abbé S... en lui renvoyant la lettre de M. Rousseau, sur la Zaïre de M. de Voltaire*, p.651-56 (see D572).

[21] The bibliography of translations of *Zaïre* in Italy is extremely complicated and much of the work on this subject still remains to be done. The fullest information is to be found in L. Ferrari, *Le Traduzioni italiane del teatro tragico francese nei secoli XVII° e XVIII°* (Paris 1925). An earlier article by E. Bouvy, 'Zaïre en Italie' (*Annales de la Faculté des lettres de Bordeaux*, 4ᵉ série, 23ᵉ année, 1901, i.22-28), also gives useful information, not always entirely compatible with that found in Ferrari. Th. Besterman, 'A provisional bibliography of Italian editions and translations of Voltaire', *Studies* 18 (1961), p.263-310, is a 'preliminary bibliography' and is less complete on *Zaïre* than Ferrari or Bouvy.

translations continued moreover to appear after Voltaire's death and throughout the nineteenth century. *Zaïre* was acted in several different Italian towns, and the play was also the basis of opera libretti.[22] Holland had a translation as early as 1734,[23] and a second one in 1745,[24] after which *Zaïre* travelled north to Scandinavia, appearing in three separate Danish translations in 1756, 1757 and 1766, and in Swedish in 1773 and 1774.[25] A German translation in alexandrines by J. J. Schwabe was first published in Gottsched's *Deutsche Schaubühne* (ii) in 1741 and was popular in the German repertory.[26] This translation was reprinted several times both singly and in collections of plays, but its popularity did not prevent another translator, Johannes Joachim Eschenburg, from offering the public another version, in blank verse this time, in 1776. Various other translations appeared after Voltaire's death and throughout the nineteenth century, and *Zaïre* was almost certainly the most popular of Voltaire's tragedies in Germany.[27]

---

[22] See Bouvy, p.22.

[23] *Zaïre, of de Koningklyke Slavin, Treurspel* (Amsterdam 1734), translated by G. Klinkhamer. The British Library has some curious manuscript poems about *Zaïre* also by Govert Klinkhamer (mss. 24, 338).

[24] *Zaïre, bekeerde Turkinne, Treurspel* (Amsterdam 1745), translated by Frederik Duim. This is an adaptation rather than a translation, for at the end of the play Orosmane, impressed by Zaïre's conversion, sends her back to France laden with rich gifts, and Lusignan dies of joy (see Lessing, *Hamburgische Dramaturgie*, ed. Otto Mann, Stuttgart 1958, p.67-68). Two further Dutch translations of *Zaïre*, one in verse and one in prose, were published in Amsterdam in 1777; see J. Vercruysse, 'Bibliographie provisoire des traductions néerlandaises et flamandes de Voltaire', *Studies* 116 (1973), p.19-64, which gives more information on *Zaïre* in Dutch.

[25] See Th. Besterman, 'A provisional bibliography of Scandinavian and Finnish editions of Voltaire', *Studies* 47 (1966), p.53-92.

[26] See J. G. Robertson, *Lessing's dramatic theory* (Cambridge 1939), p.70. A gala performance of Schwabe's translation was given in Bonn on 8 April 1760 in honour of Clement Augustus, elector and archbishop of Cologne. As so often, Voltaire's known hostility to the Church does not seem to have perturbed anyone concerned. A copy of the text, listing the actors and specially printed for this performance, is in the Bibliothèque nationale.

[27] See H. Fromm, *Bibliographie Deutscher Übersetzungen aus dem Französischen 1700-1948* (Baden-Baden 1950-1953), vi.284-85.

The earliest known Spanish translation of *Zaïre* which can be dated with certainty was published in Cadiz in 1765 with the title *Combates de amor y ley*, and with the rather curious feature that all the characters have been renamed by the translator. The nearest in name to his original is Otoman, who is Orosmane, but Zaïre has become Arlaja, and Fatime is Celinda. Otherwise, the translator, Fernando Jugaccis Pilotos, whose real name may have been Francisco Del Postigo,[28] follows Voltaire's text very closely, without, however, acknowledging his debt to Voltaire at all. A better-known translation of Voltaire's play was that produced by the famous Pablo de Olavide, a Peruvian by birth, who was to become a public figure of importance in Spain and France.[29] His version, entitled *La Zayda*, had several separate editions, published without the name of the author or translator, in various Spanish cities, including Salamanca, Barcelona and Madrid, in the years from 1770 until the end of the century.[30] It was performed in Seville in 1772,[31] at intervals in Barcelona from 1775 to 1789,[32] and sixteen times in Madrid between 1790 and 1794.[33] Pablo de Olavide had visited Les Délices in 1762 or 1763, but it is not certain whether his translation of *Zaïre* was made before or after his visit.[34] In 1783, another Spanish translator, Vicente García de

---

[28] See I. L. McClelland, *Spanish drama of pathos, 1750-1808* (Liverpool 1970), i.135. McClelland has some interesting comments on the importance of *Zaïre* for the development of Spanish tragedy in the 1760s and 1770s. On Spanish translations of *Zaïre* generally, see Christopher Todd, 'A provisional bibliography of published Spanish translations of Voltaire', *Studies* 161 (1976), p.121-25.

[29] See M. Defourneaux, *Pablo de Olavide ou l'Afrancesado (1725-1803)* (Paris 1959).

[30] See Pablo de Olavide, *Obras dramáticas desconocidas*, ed. E. Núñez (Lima 1971), p.xvii. Olavide's translation of *Zaïre* is on p.178-236.

[31] See Defourneaux, p.284. Defourneaux also gives interesting information on changes in the text made by the censorship at the time of the performances in Seville.

[32] A. Par, 'Representaciones teatrales en Barcelona durante el siglo xviii', *Boletín de la Real academia española* 16 (1929), p.326-46, 492-513, 594-614.

[33] See F. Lafarga, *Voltaire en España, 1734-1835* (Barcelona 1982), p.170.

[34] A. Par, p.78.

La Huerta, avowedly basing himself on Pablo de Olavide's modest effort, offered a new *Zaïre* to his compatriots, this time transformed by the glorious title *La Fe triunfante del amor y cetro* – Faith triumphant over love and the sceptre! This translation, too, ran to several editions,[35] and it had several performances in Seville and Madrid during the first half of the nineteenth century.[36] Like Voltaire's original play, these translations inspired a successful parody, *Zara*, by Ramón de La Cruz.[37] Spain's neighbour, Portugal, lagged behind, but in 1783 there appeared a rather literal Portuguese translation of *Zaïre* by Pedro António.[38]

This list of translations and adaptations of *Zaïre*, while bearing impressive witness to the popularity of the play in Europe in the eighteenth century, is almost certainly incomplete.[39]

In addition to being translated into so many European languages, *Zaïre* was also performed in several European cities, either in the original French, or, more usually, in translation, during Voltaire's lifetime. But nowhere was the success of the play greater than in England. As early as February 1733 John Nourse offered the Paris edition for sale in London. The abbé Prévost claims that the English were not impressed with it.[40] But this did

---

[35] See A. M. Coe, *Catálogo bibliográfico y crítico de las comedias anunciadas en los periódicos de Madrid desde 1661 hasta 1819* (Baltimore 1935), p.99.

[36] F. Lafarga, p.173.

[37] See McClelland, i.314 ff.

[38] See Th. Besterman, 'Provisional bibliography of Portuguese editions of Voltaire', *Studies* 76 (1970), p.32. According to Theodore Besterman, the translator's full name is Pedro António Pereira, known as Pedrinhó.

[39] I have done research on eighteenth-century translations of *Zaïre* at the British Library and the Bibliothèque nationale, and I have given full bibliographical references to secondary sources where these are available. But to trace and identify all eighteenth-century translations of *Zaïre* would entail lengthy and complicated investigations in the libraries of Europe, and would be a major piece of research in its own right. This survey lays no claim to such completeness.

[40] *Le Pour et contre* (Paris 1733), i.ii. Prévost's assertion is perhaps borne out by the fact that a French company of actors resident at the Haymarket Theatre from October 1734 until June 1735 played *Zaïre* only once, on Thursday, 9 January 1735. But an amateur performance in French given at Chelsea by the 'young Gentlemen at Mr Dorney's Boarding School' as early as May 1733 had

not prevent two English men of letters from trying to gain fame and fortune by producing their own translations of Voltaire's play. In 1735, the first, by a certain Johnson, was being sold at 1s. a copy, but nothing further is known of it.[41] The second, however, by Aaron Hill, was exceedingly successful when first produced at Drury Lane on 12 January 1736.[42] It ran for fourteen performances and thereafter became the most frequently acted adaptation of all Voltaire's plays upon the English stage. Perhaps Hill's *Zara* owed its initial success, in part at least, to the performance in the title role of Mrs Cibber, a beautiful and talented new actress. After a revival at Covent Garden in 1751 with Mrs Cibber again in her original part, it seems to have been played in London at either Drury Lane or Covent Garden practically every season for about the next thirty-five years, and most famous eighteenth-

apparently been well received, for it was repeated twice further. See *The London stage 1660-1800* (Carbondale 1960-1968), iii, *1729-1747*, ed. Arthur H. Scouten.

[41] Its existence is vouched for by *The Gentleman's magazine* (v.279), but I have been unable to trace a copy. Is the translator possibly Charles Johnson (1679-1748), who was a fairly successful playwright and renowned plagiarist, and who adapted other plays from the French? But I can find no reference to an adaptation of *Zaïre* by him.

[42] Aaron Hill must have begun his translation of *Zaïre* soon after copies became available in England, for *The Gentleman's magazine* of May 1733 (p.261-62) printed his version of Lusignan's great scene in act 2, without, however, giving the translator's name. Before its professional production at Drury Lane, Hill's *Zara* had been given at the end of May and beginning of June 1735 by an amateur group at Sir Richard Steele's great music room in York Buildings, Villars (now Villiers) Street, with Hill's nephew acting Osman (Orosmane) and an elderly friend of Hill's, William Bond, playing the part of Lusignan. Hill intended to give the proceeds of the performance to William Bond, but Bond collapsed while on the stage on the first night and died soon after. Six subsequent performances were given, including the last on 9 July at the Haymarket Theatre. The incident of Bond's collapse and death is referred to in the cancelled 'Avertissement' to w42 (see below, p.391). See *The Prompter* (10 June 1735), no.60; T. Davies, *Memoirs of the life of David Garrick* (London 1780), i.136-37; H. L. Bruce, *Voltaire on the English stage* (Berkeley 1918), p.24 ff., and *The London stage 1660-1680*. Bruce says that three performances in all of Hill's *Zara* were given by the *ad hoc* company, but *The London stage* lists eight, the first of which was a public rehearsal on 29 May (see also D679 and commentary).

century English actors probably played in *Zara* at some time or other in their career.[43] Hill's *Zara* is not a literal translation of *Zaïre*, for its author has openly tried to make the play as attractive as possible to an English audience. This, he seems to think, means more heroism, more sentiment, more ranting,[44] and, to judge by his success, he was right. *Zara* ran to several editions.[45] It was acted not only in London, but also in Edinburgh, Dublin, Bath and Bristol, as well as crossing the Atlantic to delight the ladies and gentlemen of Boston, New York, Philadelphia and Baltimore.[46]

Voltaire's correspondence records a number of private performances of *Zaïre* in which Voltaire himself took part. He played Lusignan as early as January 1733, at the house of Mme de Fontaine-Martel, a few days before that lady's death (D564). In a performance at Cirey, however, in February 1739, he took the role of Orosmane.[47] Berlin, in January 1751, saw him as Lusignan again, and in April 1755 at Les Délices, he acted Lusignan to Lekain's Orosmane (D6229 and D6231). Henceforth, he seems to have limited himself to the part of Lusignan, partly no doubt because he considered his age and appearance unsuitable for Orosmane, but perhaps also because he enjoyed declaiming what is certainly the best poetry in the play. It is generally thought that Lusignan was Voltaire's favourite acting part. At any rate, the number of known private performances of *Zaïre* he gave

[43] H. L. Bruce, p.24 ff.

[44] For Voltaire's opinion of Hill's version of his play, see his second dedication to Fawkener, p.411-14 below. An interesting analysis of Garrick's own prompt-copy of *Zara* shows that on the stage Garrick excised many of Hill's more excessive embellishments after 1766. See F. L. Bergmann, 'Garrick's *Zara*', *PMla* 74 (1959), p.225-32.

[45] H. L. Bruce, p.26. For further information on *Zara*, see A.-M. Rousseau, *L'Angleterre et Voltaire*, Studies 145-147 (1976), p.386-96 and 1028-30.

[46] See L. P. Waldo, *The French drama in America in the eighteenth century and its influence on the American drama of that period, 1701-1800* (Baltimore 1942). Waldo states (p.124) that '*Zara* became almost as popular in America as it had once been in England [...] All the larger American cities witnessed it.'

[47] D1876 gives an amusing account of this performance, written by Desmarest and Mme de Graffigny; cf. Graffigny, i.317-18.

suggests that, even if he was not blind to the failings of his tragedy, he shared the public's fondness for this particular play.

The correspondence also records a number of other performances, private, semi-private[48] and public, all over Europe, from Dublin[49] as far as St Petersburg, and corroborates the general impression of the enormous popularity that Zaïre enjoyed with eighteenth-century audiences.

The popularity of the play lasted well into the nineteenth century. It continued to be performed in France, Europe and North America, and was re-published in French and in translation many times.[50] Zaïre became the most frequently acted tragedy of Voltaire's at the Comédie-Française and received 488 performances between 1732 and 1936, thus oustripping Racine's own 'Turkish' play in popularity.[51] But it has not been performed there, or anywhere else, since 1936, and tastes have changed so much that it is doubtful whether a successful revival would be possible.

3. Publication

The first editions of Zaïre were printed in Rouen by or for Claude-François Jore, through the good offices of Cideville and Formont, and were co-published by Jore and Jean-Baptiste Bauche of Paris.

Voltaire sent a manuscript of the play to Cideville in Rouen on 3 August 1732 (D507), but the earliest dated mention of

---

[48] School performances, for instance.

[49] See D6956 in which an aspiring translator of *Alzire* writes to Voltaire: 'Two years ago I saw one of the theatres in Dublin torn to pieces in an instant by the furious spectators, because an imprudent actor had refused to repeat for the third time a scene of *Zaïre*.'

[50] There are Rumanian translations for 1854 and 1896, a Hungarian one for 1895, and a Greek one is listed for as early as 1836. An English translation in 'rhyme verse' was privately printed by its author in Worthing in 1854. *Zaïre* was also adapted in operatic or musical versions in several languages in the nineteenth century.

[51] See H. C. Lancaster, *French tragedy*, i.147.

publication occurs on 12 December, when Cideville gives advice to Voltaire on the epistles to Fawkener and Mlle Gaussin, 'deux pièces que vous souhaités qui soient à la teste de l'édition de vostre Zaire' (D543). It is possible that the first printing of the play was already well advanced by this time, although most of the relevant letters[52] cannot be dated with certainty and are published in the correspondence in a sequence open to doubt. In D545 and D548 (which should be placed early in December) Voltaire announces to Formont and to Cideville the despatch of the epistles to Jore, for their comments; as we have seen, Cideville responded on 12 December (further remarks appear in D551); Voltaire's reply to Cideville's letter of the 12th mentions the sending of a revised version of the Fawkener text, 'telle que je souhaitte qu'elle soit imprimée' (D549, plausibly dated 20 December); a letter to Formont, probably written the next day, contains the same information along with Voltaire's account of discussions with Antoine Louis de Rouillé, the official responsible for the booktrade (D552). Rouillé had considered that the passage concerning Adrienne Lecouvreur in the epistle to Fawkener (l.226-234 and variant) was too strong to be officially passed for publication and had proposed the publication of two 'editions', one without the epistle and with *privilège*, the other with the epistle and without *privilège*, to be published by *permission tacite*. Voltaire had written to Jore to confirm this arrangement: 'Je lui ai recommandé d'imprimer l'épître à part avec un nouveau titre et de me l'envoyer à Versailles, tandis que l'édition entière de la tragédie viendra à la chambre syndicale avec toutes les formalités ridicules dont la librairie est enchevêtrée'. By 30 December (D555) this solution was in doubt, having been inadvertently made public by Cideville, and on 4 January (D559) Voltaire announced that he had had to revise the epistle to make it fit for publication in the changed circumstances.

As a result of these tractations the first Jore printings of *Zaïre*

---

[52] D544, D545, D548, D549, D552.

are found in a variety of states. The earliest, the title-page of which carries the names of both Jore and Bauche (see figure 1), consisted of the play alone, with the 'Privilège', the 'Approbation' and an errata (33R, state 1). Jore was also responsible for a second setting of the play (33RP) and may have produced a third, of which only one sheet is known (see the Taylor Institution copy of 33RP). The title leaf of some copies of 33R was then replaced with (or joined by) a gathering of eight leaves containing a new title-page without Jore's name (figure 2), the revised version of the 'Epître dédicatoire' and the 'Epître à Mlle Gaussin' (33R, state 2). The one copy of 33RP containing this additional gathering also includes a previously unrecorded printing of the original version of the 'Epître dédicatoire', accompanied by yet another title-page (figure 3). We may identify this printing of the epistle as the one referred to by Voltaire in D552.

Since both 33R and 33RP required a cancel at A5 and an errata leaf, it is probable that they were printed in quick succession, perhaps prior to publication and at all events before the arrival in Rouen of the text of the cancel, sent by Voltaire on 4 January (D559). The two printings are found with or without the epistles and may well have been regarded as interchangeable by the publishers. We do not know if the two together made up the edition of 2500 copies stipulated by Voltaire (D548), an instruction which Jore may not have felt obliged to follow. The one surviving sheet of what could have been a third complete printing incorporates the text of the cancel, but its presence in a copy consisting mainly of sheets of 33RP again suggests that the various Jore settings of the play constituted but one edition, in the publishing sense of that term.

Be this as it may, it seems likely that the play first appeared without the prefatory matter; the original version of the epistles was suppressed, probably before publication; and then during the first weeks of 1733 copies were available both with and without the second version of the epistles, depending upon the attitude of the authorities at different times and in different places. Further details may be found in Voltaire's correspondence and in the papers of the président Bouhier.[53]

Another French edition, the printer of which is unknown, is also found both with and without the epistles (33x, states 1 and 2); an English edition (33L) follows state 2 of 33R, as does the Amsterdam edition (33A). The latter includes, however, several modifications to the epistle.

Voltaire revised the text of the play in 1736, for the Bauche edition published in or around June of that year (36A; see D1035, D1036, D1054) and replaced the dedicatory epistle with an entirely new version, later to be known as the 'Seconde lettre à monsieur Fawkener'.[54] This text is less polemical than the first and is largely concerned with reflections on the differences between French and English drama, arising out of Hill's version of Zaïre. Further changes to the play were made two years later, for the Amsterdam Œuvres (w38), after which few alterations of any substance occurred.

[53] See D561, D563, D565n; Hélène Monod-Cassidy, Un voyageur-philosophe au XVIIIe siècle: l'abbé Jean-Bernard Le Blanc (Cambridge, Mass. 1941), p.165; Journal de la cour et de Paris, ed. Henri Duranton (Saint-Etienne 1981), p.29, 45-46, 52-54; Correspondance littéraire du président Bouhier, ed. Henri Duranton (Saint-Etienne 1974-1988), xii.198, 204, 206, 208-209.The Journal, p.52-54, gives details of some of the cuts made to the epistle to Fawkener, corresponding to the readings of MS3 for the variants to l.44, 133-162 and 234-235.

[54] The French found matter for laughter in the original dedication of Zaïre to a merchant. In a short comedy satirising Voltaire's Temple du Goût and intended for the Comédie-Italienne, the abbé d'Allainval took the opportunity of mocking Voltaire's introduction of a common English merchant into the aristrocratic world of literary patronage. D'Allainval's comedy, also entitled Le Temple du Goût (La Haye 1733), was rejected by the Italians, who instead stole the general idea for a comedy of their own, to which they again gave the same title (D631, D642 and D647). In d'Allainval's play, Fawkener, transparently renamed Kafener, appears in several scenes, claiming a place in the Temple of Taste simply because he is a friend of Voltaire's. He is shown as a boor, inelegantly dressed, smoking a pipe, and using seafaring jargon in a most inappropriate way. The 'Seconde lettre' afforded Voltaire some revenge, for in 1735 Fawkener had been appointed ambassador to Turkey and is duly addressed as such in the revised epistle.

4. Historical background

Voltaire chose the history of the Crusades as the background to the *grands intérêts* of his play. In the popular imagination, the Crusades were still seen as a glorious epic of religious fervour and noble deeds, in which brave men sacrificed themselves to liberate Jerusalem from the infidel. The very word Crusades would conjure up the heroes of the past – saint Louis, Guy de Lusignan, Richard Cœur-de-Lion. But if the legends satisfied the people, those who desired more serious information about the Crusades could find it. Voltaire himself probably owned the two most important histories of the Crusades which were available at the time he was writing *Zaïre*. The first, by the Jesuit Louis Maimbourg, had originally appeared in 1675, and Voltaire had in his library the third edition of this popular work.[55] The second was the abbé Claude Fleury's much admired *Histoire ecclésiastique* which appeared over the years 1691-1738, and of which Voltaire had one of the many virtually simultaneous editions.[56] The abbé Fleury's erudite tomes included a great deal of information about the Crusades, all conveyed in an unexpectedly objective manner. Voltaire's obsessive concern with the deeds and misdeeds of men in the name of Christianity meant, of course, that he was particularly interested in the history of the Crusades. In 1750-1751 he published in the *Mercure de France*[57] an *Histoire des croisades*,

[55] *Histoire des croisades pour la délivrance de la Terre Sainte* (Paris 1684-1685; BV, no.2262).

[56] *Histoire ecclésiastique* (Paris 1720-1738; BV, no.1350). Voltaire seems to have owned volumes 2-36. Volumes 21-36 were in fact a continuation of the work by J.-C. Fabre and C.-P. Goujet. Claude Fleury died in 1723. We cannot be certain, of course, that Voltaire already owned in 1732 the books which appear in the catalogue of his library at Ferney, but in the case of works as famous as those of Maimbourg and Fleury, it is a not unreasonable assumption that he already knew them even if he did not actually possess them at that time.

[57] *MF*, septembre, octobre, décembre 1750, février 1751.

which was later to become part of his *Essai sur les mœurs*[58] and which owed a great deal to Fleury's erudition.

Voltaire's known interest in the history of the Crusades might lead one to expect that in *Zaïre* the historical material relating to the Crusades would be reasonably exact. Certainly the play contains what is apparently a wealth of authentic historical material. It is possible, for instance, to establish the time at which the events supposedly take place: May 1249, during the period of the seventh Crusade. On 25 August 1248, Louis IX, after three years of preparation for a great Crusade, set sail from Aigues-Mortes for Cyprus. The ruler of Cyprus, Henri de Lusignan, who was also recognised by Christians as king of Jerusalem,[59] welcomed the Crusaders warmly and they decided to winter on the island. The Muslims expected them to make for Syria first, but when king Louis left Limassol on 30 May 1249, he turned instead towards Egypt and attacked Damietta, on the Nile Delta. This is the episode referred to by Orosmane in act 3, scene 1, when he tells Corasmin that the Crusaders are heading not for Palestine, but for Egypt. Starting from the fixed point of 1249, it is possible to discover how closely the historical material of the play corresponds to reality.

Orosmane, in *Zaïre*, is the ruler of Jerusalem. In 1249, the city was indeed under Muslim rule, having been finally lost to Christianity in 1244, when the Chorasmian hordes had sacked the city and expelled all its Christian inhabitants. The Chorasmians, a large Turkish tribe of landless mercenaries, were always ready to help one or other of the Muslim rulers against the Christians, and this may well be why Voltaire gave the name Corasmin to Orosmane's adviser, who is clearly hostile to the Christians in the play.[60] But the ruler of Jerusalem in 1249 was not called

---

[58] The first edition of the *Essai sur les mœurs* that Voltaire himself recognised was that of 1756.

[59] In 1248, Jerusalem was once again in Muslim hands, as it is in the play, but this did not prevent the Pope from nominating a Christian king (see Fleury, xvii.430).

[60] Voltaire spells the name of the tribe as 'Corasmins' in his *Essai sur les mœurs*.

Orosmane, nor in fact did Orosmane really exist.[61] Orosmane's father, however, recalled in the play, is an important historical figure. Noradin, or Nur ed-Din[62] to be more exact, who became king of Syria, led the Muslim world in its counter-attack against the Christian invaders. He was the first Muslim ruler to be animated primarily by a sense of religious duty in his fight against the alien settlers. Since he died in 1174, Orosmane, his supposed son, would have to be at least seventy-five years old in 1249, an age which hardly befits the handsome lover of the play. In fact Nur ed-Din left only one son, as-Saleh Ismael, who died when he was eighteen.

The potted history of the Crusades which Orosmane relates to Zaïre in act 1 (ii.177-180) suggests that the famous Muslim ruler, Saladin (Salah ed-Din), certainly the most legendary of all the Muslim leaders in the fight against the Crusaders, was succeeded in his role as liberator of Muslim lands by Nur ed-Din. In reality, Saladin was the son and nephew of two of Nur ed-Din's generals and continued the Holy War that Nur ed-Din had begun. He died in 1193, but not before he had united Islam against the Christians and expelled them from Jerusalem (1187). While Voltaire is accurate in allowing Zaïre to remind Fatime of Saladin's clemency, for his treatment of his captives was of a kindness and humanity that astonished his very enemies,[63] there is no evidence that Saladin's mother was a Christian, and this seems to be pure invention on Voltaire's part.[64]

After Saladin's death, the precarious unity of Islam once again dissolved, and the area broke up as before into separate states

[61] His name is already found in Scudéry's tragi-comedy, *L'Amour tyrannique* (1639), where the character concerned is king of Cappadocia in Asia Minor, and in Scarron's *Le Prince corsaire* (published posthumously in 1663), also a tragi-comedy, where Orosmane is the pirate prince of the title.

[62] For the spelling of oriental names, I have mostly adopted the forms used by Steven Runciman in his *A history of the crusades* (Cambridge 1951-1954).

[63] See *Essai sur les mœurs*, ch.56, 'De Saladin' (*Essai*, i.575-81).

[64] See IV.i.59-62. Voltaire makes no mention of Saladin's mother in the *Essai sur les mœurs*.

under separate rulers, as often at war with each other as against the Christians. After a few years of confused family warfare, a nephew of Saladin's, al-Malik al-Kamil, often called Meledin by Latin chroniclers,[65] became sultan of Egypt. Voltaire is historically plausible in suggesting that he would be Orosmane's 'secret ennemi' (III.i.15), for Syria and Egypt were frequently at war after Saladin's death. But Meledin died in 1238, and in 1249 the ruler of Egypt was as-Saleh Ayub, who was also ruler of Syria, having at last managed to re-unite the Muslims again by capturing Damascus in 1245. It was from as-Saleh Ayub that king Louis IX took Damietta, before losing at Mansourah to his successor, Turanshah, soon after. But neither ruler was ever called Meledin.

As far as the Christian side of the Crusades is concerned, 1249 is an important date in the seventh Crusade, the Crusade of saint Louis. But the names recalled by Voltaire are representative rather of the third Crusade, which seems to have inspired him more. Not that the references are by any means specific; Voltaire seems to have chosen deliberately to be vague. For who is Lusignan? Or Châtillon for that matter? Lusignan and Châtillon are certainly famous French crusading names. Members of both families settled in the East and held major fiefs there. But individual members of a family were naturally identified by a Christian name, and Voltaire has studiously avoided giving his two characters any particular identity of this kind. In fact, the only important Châtillon historically was Renaud.[66] Lusignan is supposed in the play to be a 'prince du sang des rois de Jérusalem'. For twenty years he has languished in the dungeons of Jerusalem, having been captured by Noradin at Caesarea. There were members of the Lusignan family still surviving in 1249, nephews and great-nephews of Guy de Lusignan, who had been king of Jerusalem

---

[65] Fleury, xvi.488.

[66] But Maimbourg, *Histoire des croisades*, 2nd ed. (Paris 1682), ii.195 ff., mentions several other members of the family, adding 'qu'il se trouvera peu de familles en France qui aient contribué tant de grands hommes pour la Guerre Sainte.'

from 1186 to 1192. They were fairly firmly entrenched as the royal dynasty of Cyprus, and at times were also recognised as rulers of Jerusalem, though there were other claimants to Jerusalem when it was in Christian hands. But no single Lusignan alive in 1249 or captured in 1229, if we take the other fixed point, the time in the play of Lusignan's capture, corresponds to the character Voltaire portrays. He seems rather to have built up a composite picture, taking elements from various members of the family, and adding plausible attendant circumstances.

The most famous Lusignan was undoubtedly Guy. He became king of Jerusalem through his marriage with king Baudouin IV's sister, Sibylle. He owed his throne in large part to the support of Renaud de Châtillon, for the legality of his succession was fiercely contested for a while. It was while Guy was king that Jerusalem was captured by Saladin in October 1187, though Guy at that time was already Saladin's prisoner, having been taken at the battle of Hattin, near Tiberias, a few weeks earlier. Châtillon was to an important extent responsible for the vigour of Saladin's campaigns against the Christians, for he broke a truce of four years' standing with the Muslims by attacking their caravans along the trade routes. Whatever the moral value of the Christian knights, they fought bravely against Saladin, and accounts of their heroic battles have certainly inspired some of Voltaire's lines in *Zaïre*. Châtillon, incidentally, was captured at Hattin with Guy de Lusignan, and although the king was courteously treated, Saladin himself struck off Châtillon's head with his sword, as a punishment for brigandage. Guy de Lusignan was released by Saladin in July 1188 against an oath that he would never again take up arms against the Muslims, an oath which he promptly broke, on the pretext that it had been made under duress. He took part in the third Crusade, lost the throne of Jerusalem through a vote of the Council of Knights and Barons of Palestine, and was compensated by Richard Cœur-de-Lion with the throne of Cyprus. He died in Cyprus in 1194.

But although the main exploits of Renaud de Châtillon and Guy de Lusignan relate to the time of Saladin, Châtillon had previously been captured in 1160 by Nur ed-Din and held by him imprisoned for sixteen years. Another Lusignan, Hugues, had also been captured by Nur ed-Din in 1164 at Artah. So Voltaire is really confusing names and episodes at will, intent on suggestion and association, rather than on accuracy of fact. Other Lusignans may have suggested further details. For instance, Lusignan's supposed descent from the Bouillons (II.i.57), who were the first Christian rulers of Jerusalem, is not true of Guy, but may be said to be true of his great-nephew, Henry I, king of Cyprus, who was descended from the Bouillons through his mother Alix, and whose descendants remained kings of Cyprus and Jerusalem until the final loss of Palestine in 1291.

The Lusignan of *Zaïre* believes he has lost all his children at the siege of Caesarea, though in fact two of them, Nérestan and Zaïre, he discovers to have survived. Guy de Lusignan was the father of young children by his wife, Sibylle, but there is some disagreement among historians as to the number of children they had. He lost his children and his wife during the siege of Acre, which the Crusaders were trying to capture from Saladin in 1189. But they died of disease, not in a massacre. None of Guy's children survived him, so Nérestan and Zaïre are inventions in so far as Lusignan suggests Guy rather than anyone else.

It is obvious, therefore, that while the historical material used in *Zaïre* is not without some basis in fact, its relationship to truth is far from rigorous. Voltaire is trying to conjure up an atmosphere in his play, to suggest an epoch. In order to do this, he does not need historical exactitude, but apparent plausibility. He knows that he will achieve this better with the vague use of well-known names and events than with obscure factual details. There is in fact a surprising amount of detail in the play, which Voltaire seems to have introduced in order to evoke history and give the illusion of truth, but the historical material cannot be fitted into one coherent picture corresponding to reality.

Voltaire, in any case, did not lay claim to historical exactitude. On the contrary, he said in his letter to the editor of the *Mercure de France*, published in that journal in August 1732, 'Je n'ai pris dans l'histoire que l'époque de la guerre de St Louis; tout le reste est entièrement d'invention' (see below, p.420). But this is an exaggeration. The play is full of names and events that Voltaire did not invent. They do not all fit into the 'époque de la guerre de St Louis'. History is present, and it is as important to the play as invention; but it remains subservient to the poet's imagination. The audience of a play must be moved rather than informed. The statement of fact yields to the arousing of emotion.[67]

5. *Literary sources*

Any examination of the literary sources of *Zaïre* must centre on the question of Voltaire's debt to *Othello*, a question which has been debated almost since the play appeared. Voltaire acknowledged no such debt, for while in the 'Epître dédicatoire' published in 1733 he claims to have imitated English models when introducing national historical characters into his play (see below, p.399), he makes mention neither of *Othello*, nor, directly, of Shakespeare. But the prologue to Aaron Hill's 'Englished' *Zaïre*[68] takes it for granted that Voltaire's inspiration for his play was *Othello*. After bemoaning the fact that Nature has never previously allied in one author 'A *Racine*'s Judgement, with a *Shakespeare*'s Fire!', the writer announces that at last such a combination has arisen:

> From *English* Plays, *Zara*'s *French* Author fir'd,
> Confess'd his Muse, beyond herself, inspir'd;

[67] Further points of detail relating to the historical material are dealt with in the notes. The only serious study of the historical sources of *Zaïre* is that by Robert Pike, 'Fact and fiction in *Zaïre*', *PMla* 51 (June 1936), p.436-39. While this article contains some useful factual material, it is at the same time frequently inaccurate. I am greatly indebted for my information on the Crusades to Maimbourg, Fleury and Runciman.

[68] This prologue, designed to introduce the play to the audience in the theatre, was written and 'spoke by' Colley Cibber, whose daughter-in-law played Zara.

From rack'd *Othello*'s Rage, he rais'd his Style,
And snatch'd the Brand, that lights his Tragick Pile:[69]

By the time Voltaire was writing the second 'Epître dédicatoire', he was already acquainted with Hill's *Zara* and must have read Cibber's prologue (D1035). But although the second 'Epître' treats extensively of the differences between French and English drama, there is still no mention of Shakespeare, let alone of *Othello*. It can only be assumed that Voltaire chose to ignore the suggestion that his play owed something to *Othello*. But why? Was it because he simply accepted Cibber's analysis as being a matter of fact? Was it because he did not want to draw his own countrymen's attention to his 'borrowings' from *Othello*? Was it because Cibber's words were so outrageously untrue that in his opinion they did not merit discussion? We cannot tell, and good and bad interpretations have continued to be put on Voltaire's silence on this matter. But whether Cibber's words merited discussion or not, they heralded a long debate on *Zaïre*'s debt to *Othello*, a debate which has at times been extraordinarily acrimonious.

The abbé Le Blanc, writing from England to the président Bouhier in 1738, set the tone for those intent on showing that Voltaire was a plagiarist:

Cette Piece pour le fonds n'est autre que celle de Shakespear dont je vous parle. *Orosmane* est *Othello* la vertueuse *Zaïre* est la sage *Desdemona*. On trouve dans la Piece de M^r De Voltaire, une partie des beautés de détail de celle de Shakespear, le nœud de l'une & l'autre Piece ne vaut pas grand chose & le dénoument est précisément le meme. l'unique difference consiste en ce que le furieux *Othello* étrangle *Desdemona* aux yeux des spectateurs. Orosmane plus poli, mais non moins cruel se contente de poignarder *Zaïre*. Le Discours d'*Orosmane* après qu'il s'est tué lui même est presque tout imité de celui d'*Othello* qui est dans le même cas.[70]

---

[69] A. Hill, *The Tragedy of Zara, as it is acted at the Theatre-Royal in Drury-Lane* (London, J. Watts, 1736).

[70] H. Monod-Cassidy, *Un voyageur-philosophe au XVIIIe siècle* (Cambridge 1941), p.289.

Others followed him. Lessing, in 1767, took up Cibber's image of the snatched brand to turn it into a savagely ironic denigration of *Zaïre*:

doch ist Othello offenbar das Vorbild des Orosman gewesen. Cibber sagt, Voltaire habe sich des Brandes bemächtiget, der den tragischen Scheiterhaufen des Shakespeare in Glut gesetzt. Ich hätte gesagt: eines Brandes aus diesem flammenden Scheiterhaufen; und noch dazu eines, der mehr dampft, als leuchtet und wärmet.[71]

The influential French critic, Villemain, in his *Cours de littérature française*, published in 1838, introduced his discussion of *Zaïre* with the words, 'J'imagine Voltaire lisant l'*Othello* de Shakespeare', and presents Voltaire consciously adopting and adapting the characters one by one. Villemain's intention is not to devalue *Zaïre*, for he has considerable admiration for the play.[72] But the assumption that *Zaïre* is an imitation of *Othello* could only harm Voltaire's tragedy, for in making such a comparison all, except the most bigoted admirers of French classicism,[73] had to concede the overwhelming superiority of Shakespeare's genius. None the less, this assumption became a commonplace of criticism, so that such respected critics as Emile Faguet and Gustave Lanson accepted the reality of Voltaire's debt.[74] In the same period, however, other French scholars, who concentrated rather more thoroughly on the question, were reaching the conclusion that *Zaïre* owed little or nothing to *Othello*. Fontaine, in his critical

---

[71] Lessing, *Hamburgische Dramaturgie*, ed. Mann, p.62.

[72] A.-F. Villemain, *Cours de littérature française: tableau du dix-huitième siècle, première partie* (Paris 1838), i.275 ff.

[73] It is amusing to find that in July 1776 the comte d'Argental wrote to Voltaire to support him in his campaign against the growing influence of Shakespeare on French drama in these terms: 'L'Otello tant vanté et qu'on avoit osé comparer à Zaïre est le tombeau du sens commun' (D20224).

[74] E. Faguet, *Le Dix-huitième siècle* (Paris 1890), p.253, says: '*Zaïre*, c'est *Othello* avec beaucoup de *Mithridate*'. G. Lanson, *Voltaire* (Paris 1906), p.97, corroborates: 'le jaloux Orosmane tuant la tendre Zaïre, transposition gracieuse d'*Othello*, du Shakespeare en biscuit'.

edition of *Zaïre*,[75] is at pains to show the differences between *Othello* and *Zaïre*, notably in the portrayal of Othello and Orosmane, but he ignores the question of whether these differences may be due only to Voltaire's lack of success in imitating *Othello*. Henri Lion[76] similarly stresses the tradition of French classical tragedy which makes *Zaïre* so different from *Othello*, but again avoids the issue of whether Voltaire attempted to imitate Shakespeare's tragedy, even though he does accept that some elements of *Zaïre* are taken from *Othello*. An obscure dissertation by Richard Arndt[77] exonerating Voltaire from the charge of plagiarism was, however, completely overshadowed by the influential Thomas Lounsbury's *Shakespeare and Voltaire* (New York 1902). Giving a list of parallels between *Othello* and *Zaïre*, Lounsbury claimed that Voltaire's imitation of Shakespeare was 'distinctly perceptible', and he proceeded to wax indignant over Voltaire's lack of acknowledgment of his debt (p.78-79). Lounsbury's attack provoked a reasoned reply from E. J. Dubedout,[78] making many of the same points as Fontaine and Lion. Many years later, in his well-known *Minuet*, F. C. Green came back to the attack on Lounsbury's thesis. His discussion of *Zaïre* offers an extended and penetrating comparison of the play with *Othello*, beginning with the words, '*Zaïre*, far from revealing Shakespearean influence on Voltaire, is convincing proof of the impossibility of any real *rapprochement*, let alone a fusion of the two types of tragedy, English and French',[79] and concluding with the concession that Shakespeare may have suggested to Voltaire the idea of a tragedy based on male jealousy. Moreover, in his determination to combat and destroy for ever Lounsbury's commonly accepted view,

[75] (Paris 1889), p.xxxii ff.
[76] H. Lion, *Les Tragédies et les théories dramatiques de Voltaire* (Paris 1895), p.73 ff.
[77] R. Arndt, *Zur Entstehung von Voltaires Zaïre* (Marburg 1906).
[78] E. J. Dubedout, 'Shakespeare and Voltaire; *Othello* and *Zaïre*', *Modern philology* 3 (1905-1906), p.305-12.
[79] *Minuet: a critical survey of French and English literary ideas in the eighteenth century* (London 1935), p.62.

Green comes back to the subject of *Othello* and *Zaïre* in a special appendix to his book, entitled 'Some comments on T. Lounsbury's 'Shakespeare and Voltaire' (p.467 ff.), and attempts once more to show that Lounsbury's analysis is entirely false.[80] But for all his efforts, Green did not succeed in settling the debate in the direction he wanted, for the most recent developed discussion of Voltaire as a dramatist[81] comes back again to the question of the influence of *Othello*, introducing the topic with the categorical statement that 'any reader acquainted with *Othello* [...] cannot fail to see the obvious similarities between the two plays' (p.87). Surprisingly, however, J. R. Vrooman does not really concentrate on the similarities, but gives instead an extended description of *Zaïre* which is indeed intended to 'examine some of the principal divergencies' (p.91) between the plays, but which in fact quickly discards any comparative element.

The ground has thus been gone over many times. If in general terms one may divide the two sides in the confrontation as, on the one hand, those who claim that *Zaïre* owes a great deal to *Othello*, and, on the other, those who concentrate upon the differences between the two plays, the antagonists appear to be irreconcilable. But close attention to the arguments put forward by each side reveals that the positions are not really so far apart. Setting aside such irrelevancies as Lounsbury's moral indignation or the occasional chauvinism of some of the French critics, it seems to be generally agreed, because undeniable, that there are similarities in the basic plot of the two plays. In both, a powerful master of men is in love with an innocent young girl and kills her through jealousy; in both, there is an adviser to the lover, whose counsels exacerbate the situation; in both, the beloved is brutally questioned, brutally treated by her adoring and suffering lover; in both, the murder is followed by a sudden revelation of

[80] Lounsbury had also insisted that Voltaire copies parts of *King Lear* in *Zaïre*. F. C. Green is equally scathing about this assertion.

[81] J. R. Vrooman, *Voltaire's theatre: the cycle from Œdipe to Mérope*, Studies 75 (1970).

the truth and the lover's suicide. But even on this simple level, while the similarities may not be just coincidental, the differences are surely more important. The roles of Corasmin and Iago are not really comparable: Iago instigates the plot, Corasmin is as unaware of the truth as his master. Desdemona, on the other hand, has no responsibility for the events and is completely bewildered, but Zaïre is to some extent responsible for and aware of what is happening: she puts off her wedding and knows that this alone is enough to cause Orosmane's suffering. What she does not suspect is the added jealousy that will lead to Orosmane's murderous rage. In the absence of any word on the subject from Voltaire himself, there seems to be no reason for supposing or denying that he consciously borrowed elements of his plot from *Othello*. We simply do not know. Only one scene in *Zaïre* appears to offer similarities with *Othello* that it is difficult to dismiss as at least possibly coincidental. Orosmane's last speech, in which he tells Nérestan how to report the events of the play to his compatriots (v.x.215-26) cannot fail to recall Othello's suicide speech, in which he tells Ludovico to relate the events to the Venetian senate. Both Othello and Orosmane insist that the truth be told, both suggest that in spite of their guilt they deserve some pity, both speak of their love, and in both speeches the climax is the speaker's suicide. There are important differences in language and imagery, but the similarity in content cannot be denied.

But if these speeches appear to offer strong evidence for the imitation of *Othello* by Voltaire, those who wish to minimise or discount Shakespeare's influence on Voltaire can point to innumerable differences in the plays, differences that are fully recognised by their antagonists, even such determined ones as Lounsbury. For it is equally undeniable that the whole emphasis of the plays is different, as has been frequently pointed out by those who insist that *Zaïre* owes nothing, or at any rate nothing significant, to *Othello*. While *Othello* is centrally the story of Othello, *Zaïre* is centrally the story of Zaïre. It is not primarily a story of jealousy, but, as Voltaire himself pointed out, a love story. Jealousy provides the dénouement, but there is no portrayal of jealousy as in *Othello*, of its ravages, of its destruction of the personality. Orosmane's sudden jealousy, which is based on a misunderstanding, leads him to the same tragic murder as Othello, but with far less justification, and, let it be said, plausibility. The conflict of the play is Zaïre's. She is a young girl who, at the moment of happiness, is faced with an insoluble problem, with the incompatible demands of love and her newly-discovered family and religion. Her moral and emotional dilemma is of universal interest and multiple application, and it is a dilemma of which she is perfectly conscious. That this situation provides a totally different focus of interest from *Othello* and that the play is essentially in the French classical tradition in every way is again accepted by both sides in the long drawn-out debate. It becomes increasingly obvious that the quarrel lacks substance and is a matter of tone and emphasis rather than a dispute about facts. It is also obvious that those who continue to underline the imitation of *Othello* make little contribution to any understanding of the play, while those who deny all imitation or influence of *Othello* on *Zaïre* are perhaps trying to protect Voltaire quite unnecessarily.

The agreed 'French-ness' of *Zaïre* has, of course, led to a search for Voltaire's French sources. Among the various suggestions offered with an astonishing lack of scholarly rigour by the commentators are to be found Tristan l'Hermite's *Marianne*,[82] Corneille's *Horace*,[83] and *Polyeucte*.[84] More obscure is Chateaubrun's *Mahomet Second*.[85] But the favourite ground for hunting the literary sources of *Zaïre* remains the plays of Racine. In view of Voltaire's known and frequently-expressed admiration for Racine, as well as his constant effort to emulate and surpass his master in the same genre, it is hardly surprising that parallels and echoes

[82] N.-M. Bernardin, 'Le théâtre de Voltaire: *Zaïre*', *Revue des cours et conférence* 22 (20 juin 1914), p.664.

[83] Bernardin, p.671, where he suggests that the evocation of the topography of Jerusalem is borrowed from a similar passage in *Horace*, act 5, scene 3.

[84] *Polyeucte* is frequently mentioned as a source of the Christian elements in *Zaïre*.

[85] Suggested by H. C. Lancaster, *French tragedy*, i.143.

between the works of the two writers have not been difficult to find. There is hardly a play of Racine's that has not at one time or another been suggested as an important source of *Zaïre*. *Mithridate*,[86] *Andromaque*, *Britannicus*,[87] *Bérénice*[88] and, above all, *Bajazet*[89] are presumed to have been drawn upon by Voltaire for *Zaïre*. But critics rarely make the distinction between a vague similarity and a conscious imitation, between coincidence and copying, or even between an earlier text known to the author and one so obscure as to be almost certainly unknown to him, possibly because such a distinction is often very difficult to make. Of the various French plays suggested as sources of *Zaïre*, only *Bajazet*, it seems, needs to be taken at all seriously as making a direct contribution to the genesis of Voltaire's tragedy. In writing his own Turkish play, Voltaire could not fail to remember Racine's famous Turkish play, a play which also has love and jealousy as its principal theme. But even here the resemblances remain superficial: the setting, the intercepted letter, the murder and suicide. The tone of the two plays is entirely different, as indeed is the plot. It is doubtful that prolonged study of *Bajazet* leads to greater understanding of *Zaïre*, so that its importance as a literary source of Voltaire's tragedy must not be exaggerated.

The argument that Voltaire owed more to Dryden than to Shakespeare has been put forward by T. W. Russell,[90] but this scholar has made his thesis difficult to take seriously because of a number of major inaccuracies in its application to *Zaïre*. It is not true, for instance, that Zaïre's 'soliloquy' (it is not a soliloquy!) about religion (i.i.101-127) comes when she is 'torn between her love for the Sultan, who has offered to make her his wife, and

---

[86] See above, p.304, note 74.

[87] Both suggested by H. C. Lancaster, i.142-43. He also mentions a number of earlier Turkish plays in France, as well as plays with plots and characters taken from medieval French history, p.143.

[88] See J. R. Vrooman (p.87), who adds other previously suggested sources and influences.

[89] The comparison of *Zaïre* with *Bajazet* is a commonplace of criticism.

[90] T. W. Russell, *Voltaire, Dryden and heroic tragedy* (New York 1946).

her loyalty to her father and brother, who insist that she be baptised and return to France' (p.94: she does not know that she has a father and brother at this point – and she has never been to France), although it is true that Voltaire copied and translated passages from Dryden in his notebooks (Voltaire 81, p.52, 63, 239-40, 405-406) that these lines paraphrase. More important is the total inaccuracy of the assertion that it is certain that Voltaire had Dryden in mind when writing *Zaïre* because there is a long discussion about Dryden's indecent portrayal of love in *All for love* in Voltaire's preface to his play (p.92-93). Russell is here referring to the 'Epître dédicatoire' to Fawkener, but omits to mention that the passage he describes is in the second 'Epître', written only in 1736! But apart from such glaring mistakes, Russell's general thesis that *Zaïre* is 'heroic romance tragedy' after the manner of Dryden's *The Indian Emperor* rather than classical tragedy after the manner of Voltaire's illustrious French predecessors does not appear to stand up to examination. The various modifications that Voltaire brought to French classical tragedy, which Russell ascribes to the influence of Dryden's example, can be better accounted for in other ways, for Voltaire's efforts to renew tragedy began with his very first play and never ceased throughout his life.

Dismissing earlier dramatists as offering the 'true source' of *Zaïre*, Alexander Krappe in 1925[91] proposed instead a short story by Giambattista Giraldi taken from the *Hecatommithi* and first published in 1565. It is the sixth tale of the eighth day. Interestingly enough, another tale from the *Hecatommithi* furnished Shakespeare with the story of *Othello*.[92] But whereas the connection between Giraldi's tale and *Othello* is very close and can therefore be used to reveal a great deal about Shakespeare's treatment of his material, that between the story Krappe suggests and *Zaïre* is extremely distant, and indeed Krappe makes almost no attempt to analyse how Voltaire used the material. His 'discovery', if a

[91] A. Krappe, 'The source of Voltaire's *Zaïre*', *Mln* 22 (1925), p.305-309.
[92] The seventh story of the third day.

discovery it is, thus remains entirely arid and self-condemned as a rather pointless hypothesis.[93]

It is undeniable that the search for the literary sources of *Zaïre* has not led in the past to any great enlightenment and that the expenditure of time, paper and ink on this subject has been largely unjustified. The quarrels about Voltaire's imitation of *Othello* could have been entirely avoided with less prejudice on both sides and more clear-thinking. Other suggestions may have some marginal scholarly interest, but nothing significant has been discovered that can be used in any way to add to a greater understanding or appreciation of the play. It is surely more fruitful to consider the work as a product of inspiration – what other source could there be for a whole tragedy written in twenty-two days? - an inspiration made up indeed of a cultural heritage and literary reminiscences on the one hand, and of a conscious effort to do something new and successful on the other. Voltaire himself told his friends what he was aiming at, and his view of the play is best expressed in his own words:

J'ai enfin tâché de peindre ce que j'avais depuis si longtemps dans la tête, les mœurs turques opposées aux mœurs chrétiennes, et de joindre dans un même tableau ce que notre religion peut avoir de plus imposant et même de plus tendre avec ce que l'amour a de plus touchant et de plus furieux.[94]

Since the study of Voltaire's literary sources turns out to be at best rather peripheral to the play, it may perhaps be more fruitful to concentrate on those aspects of *Zaïre* of which he was fully conscious, and which interested him as a creative artist.

---

[93] See H. C. Lancaster, i.143, note 59.
[94] w9 D497. See above, p.277-82.

6. 'Les mœurs turques opposées aux mœurs chrétiennes': Turkish manners

Excited as it was by the exotic, Voltaire's public could not fail to be attracted by the promise contained in the words 'les mœurs turques opposées aux mœurs chrétiennes' – 'mœurs chrétiennes' standing both for the behaviour and beliefs of the Crusaders in the play, and for the particular civilisation of Voltaire's public. As far as the crusading spirit is concerned, it may be said that Voltaire gives a reasonably accurate, if over-simple picture of its important elements: religious fanaticism, loyalty, courage, intransigence, and scorn for the infidel. This may indeed not seem much, but it is disappointing to find that the portrayal of 'les mœurs turques' in *Zaïre* amounts to even less, in spite of the author's brave pronouncements. The action takes place in the Sultan's seraglio, and here and there Voltaire throws in a few linguistic props of an oriental nature: *sérail, esclave, calife, soudan*. But there is no real description of life in the seraglio, nothing comparable to Montesquieu's horrifying portrayal of the enclosed claustrophobic world of the harem in his *Lettres persanes*. There is one subject, particularly, on which Voltaire had the opportunity of giving his audience serious information about Turkish customs: that is the subject of marriage. Zaïre is about to marry Orosmane. But instead of real information on the nature of a Muslim marriage in the context of a harem, we get the edifying spectacle of Orosmane protesting loudly that he is not like other Muslim princes: he intends to abolish the harem and savour the joys of monogamy. So that in his behaviour towards Zaïre, he acts not at all like a Muslim prince, but like a French nobleman. A comparison suggests itself with Pyrrhus, who, in Racine's *Andromaque*, does not act like a Greek princeling with his concubine, but like a seventeenth-century French suitor courting his mistress. But Racine did not claim that he was going to paint 'les mœurs grecques'. Voltaire's principal aim, in spite of the stress on 'les mœurs turques', is to keep the hero sympathetic to an audience brought up on Western romantic notions of exclusive and ever-lasting love. Where he has had to choose between *bienséance* and *vraisemblance*, he has chosen *bienséance*, as French classical tragedians always tended to do. But his choice is more obvious, because less subtly managed, than Racine's, where one always has a sense of the reality behind the façade of propriety. Voltaire's contemporaries, while demanding the observance of *bienséance*, did not hesitate to applaud also the mockery made of Voltaire's rather clumsy solutions in a parody of *Zaïre* given at the Comédie-Italienne (see above, p.284). In this highly amusing short play, Diaphane (who is Orosmane – transparently so!) disclaims fervently, thus echoing his serious counterpart, any resemblance to other sultans:

> Je suis peu leur example, & loin de me gêner,
> A mes seuls sentimens je me laisse entraîner.
> Au sein des voluptés bien loin que je m'endorme,
> Si je tiens un Serrail, ce n'est que pour la forme; [...]
> Tout usage ancien cede à ma politique,
> Et je suis un Sultan de nouvelle fabrique.[95]

This quotation makes the point nicely that 'les mœurs turques' in *Zaïre* remain somewhat theoretical. Voltaire might argue that Orosmane does describe those facets of Muslim life that he says he is going to reject (I.ii.161 ff.), but that is certainly not what would normally be thought of as a portrayal of Turkish manners and customs.

There are frequent mentions of the Muslim hatred of Christians in *Zaïre*, but again the action hardly bears out the description. Orosmane, once more to keep the audience's sympathy, behaves with exemplary courtesy and generosity towards his enemies, and the carnage between Muslim and Christian tends to be forgotten in the elaborate civilities that he and Nérestan exchange.[96] The

---

[95] Dominique, Romagnesi and Francesco Riccoboni, *Les Enfants trouvés*, p.6.
[96] Voltaire could, however, claim that Saladin's reputation for humanity and clemency even towards his enemies justified the character of Orosmane.

relationship between them is characterised by a delightful passage in the parody where Temire (Zaïre) explains to Alcidor (Lusignan) that he owes his release from captivity to Carabin (Nérestan):

> C'est à ce Cavalier, dont l'entreprise heureuse
> Excite du Sultan la pitié génereuse;
> Pour votre délivrance il offroit un grand prix,
> Mais le Roi n'en veut point, & vous partez *gratis*.

And Carabin chips in:

> Entre gens du métier c'est ainsi qu'on en use,
> On s'oblige l'un l'autre, & l'argent se refuse.[97]

It is clear, therefore, that Voltaire's enthusiasm for realism and local colour, of which he made so much in his various letters to his friends, was strictly tempered by his awareness of what his public would be prepared to accept on stage, by the demands of the plot, and possibly also by his own feelings and prejudices. What remains after all this is little enough: a superficial oriental flavour just sufficiently strong to attract the ordinary eighteenth-century theatre-goer without in any way distressing or disorientating him.

7. 'Ce que notre religion peut avoir de plus imposant et même de plus tendre': Zaïre as Christian tragedy

In August 1732, Voltaire's contemporaries were treated to the rather alarmingly edifying spectacle of an apparently Christian play written by an arch-enemy of the established Catholic Church. Some of his more perspicacious countrymen refused to take the Christianity of the play at face value and accused the author of tortuous anti-religious propaganda: of showing that love is a stronger force than religion, for instance; or that Muslims are

---

[97] *Les Enfants trouvés*, p.10.

more humane than Christians; or that Divine Grace is powerless in the face of the passions (see above, p.285-86). But the anonymous reply to some of these attacks, printed in the *Mercure de France* of April 1733 (see above, p.286) apparently convinced most people, for the 'Avertissement' to the 1738 edition states of *Zaïre*: 'On l'appelle à Paris, *tragédie chrétienne*, et on l'a jouée fort souvent à la place de *Polyeucte*'. *Polyeucte* was traditionally given as the last play before the Comédie-Française shut down for the Easter recess, since it was presumed to leave theatre-goers in a suitable frame of mind for the religious festivities to follow.[98] *Zaïre* must thus have been accepted by Voltaire's contemporaries in general as offering similarly elevating fare. Among other indications[99] that *Zaïre* was interpreted by many of Voltaire's contemporaries as a Christian play is a letter from Voltaire himself to his friend Formont in which he answers the charge that a frivolous dedication is inappropriate before a Christian play: 'On me reprochera, dit on, de mettre une lettre badine, à la tête d'une

---

[98] The custom of giving *Polyeucte* as the last play before the Easter recess was still quite rigorously observed during the first third of the eighteenth century. But after 1734 and 1735 when *Zaïre* was substituted for *Polyeucte*, various other plays were also gradually introduced. *Zaïre* was given on the last day in 1734, 1735, 1744 and 1751. In 1748, it was given on the previous day. 'Fort souvent' in the 1738 'Avertissement' seems something of an exaggeration for two such occasions! (see *Registres*, p.595).

[99] The Bibliothèque nationale has preserved a curious printed programme of a performance that was given on 29 August 1736: *Zaïre, tragédie, sera représentée au Collège des Barnabites de Montargis, pour la distribution des prix donnés par son Altesse Sérénissime Monseigneur le Duc d'Orléans, le 29 août 1736, à une heure précise. A Paris chez C. L. et C. C. Thiboust, père et fils, MDCCXXXVI.* The eight-page programme contains a short prologue and a resumé of the acts. Bound with it is the programme of an accompanying ballet: *Les Combats de la Vertu, ballet pour la tragédie de Zaïre.* This gives, in its introduction to the allegorical themes of the ballet, a wholly educative interpretation of *Zaïre*: 'La victoire que remporte l'amour de la vertu dans le cœur de Zaïre, après un long combat contre l'inclination qu'elle a pour Orosmane, étant une vive image de ce qui se passe tous les jours dans le cœur des hommes, et le trait le plus frappant de cette tragédie, on a cru pour se conformer aux règles du ballet devoir représenter dans les entractes *Les Combats de la Vertu* (1) Contre l'ignorance; (2) Contre la timidité; (3) Contre l'inconstance; (4) Contre l'amour propre'.

tragédie chrétienne. Ma pièce n'est pas, dieu merci, plus chrétienne que turque. J'ai prétendu faire une tragédie tendre et intéressante et non pas un sermon'.[100] But although Voltaire is here denying the validity of the label *tragédie chrétienne*, he himself had previously, in a series of letters to various friends, stressed the Christian element in the play. Along with confusion caused by Voltaire's contradictory statements and the conflicting views of his contemporaries, there remains the essential paradox implicit in the suggestion that Voltaire could have written a 'Christian play' at all. The question of religion in *Zaïre* has since exercised many minds and has rightly been seen as central to the interpretation of the play.

It is clear that Voltaire's main motivation for introducing the Christian theme into his play was his desire to enlarge the scope of tragedy to include *grands intérêts* (see above, p.282). *Zaïre* is played out against an epic backcloth: the history of the Crusades, the loss of Jerusalem to the Muslims and, to go back to an even more awe-inspiring theme, the very death of Christ. Zaïre's decision to become a Christian is not seen as a private matter, between her and her conscience, so to speak. She is the daughter of royal princes, a descendant of the kings of Jerusalem who lived, fought and died to keep Jerusalem a Christian city. Her father, the last defender of Jerusalem, has spent twenty years in a deep dungeon because of his faith. Her mother was killed in front of his very eyes, and her two brothers were killed as Christians, for their Christianity. Once she knows this, once she can no longer, as at the beginning of the play, claim comforting ignorance of her birth and religion, can Zaïre betray the faith for which her family has suffered so much? This is not an artificial problem, nor one unknown to modern times. Furthermore, in the case of Zaïre, this act of betrayal would be taking place in the very city where Christ suffered and died on the Cross in order to save all Christians. Zaïre's rejection of Christ would be the more direct,

---

[100] D552. In connection with this, it is amusing to read D525, in which Cideville describes how a reading of *Zaïre* made the archbishop of Rouen and 'une assemblée de grands vicaires' weep copious tears.

the more poignant in this city, where God himself lived among men.

The history of Christianity, then, from the death of Christ, through the glorious Crusades, to the loss of Jerusalem, is the background of the play, against which is played out the fate of individuals. There is no doubt that Voltaire was inspired by this background as a poetic theme. In *Zaïre* there is an epic quality that raises the play above an ordinary love story concerned with the fate of individuals in a private predicament. This aspect of the play can stand comparison with Racine's *Andromaque*, where the events of the war of Troy provide a similar epic backcloth, and where the characters' feelings about the events integrate the epic and tragic qualities of the drama. Lusignan's great speech in act 2, scene 3 has that quality of sublimity that French classical tragedy sought to achieve. It was, and rightly so, much admired. Lusignan recalls the fall of Jerusalem, the murder of his family and, in the climax of this speech, evokes images that to all Christians conjure up memories and associations and facts that are part of their feelings for their religion (II.iii.355-374). In this context, with emotions at their highest pitch both within the play and among the audience, Zaïre's simple profession of faith seems right, appropriate and, again, sublime.

Lusignan's is certainly the finest of the speeches where Voltaire seems to have been genuinely inspired by the poetic possibilities of the Christian theme, but there are others: Châtillon's description of the fall of Jerusalem in act 2, scene 1 (l.59-110), and, though to a lesser extent, some of Nérestan's lines. At the beginning of the nineteenth century, Chateaubriand, who felt an intense admiration for the Christian poetry of *Zaïre*, argued that a religion which could inspire its declared enemy to such heights of poetic religious fervour deserved to be taken seriously.[101] While his argument is ingenious, it is difficult to believe he offered it in

---

[101] *Génie du christianisme* (Paris 1802), II.ii, ch.5, 'Suite du Père. Lusignan'; cf. ch.8, where Chateaubriand describes the religious theme as essential to the structure of the play.

entire good faith. Its plausibility depends on the 'Christian' passages in *Zaïre* being taken in isolation, regardless of the total effect of the play. The total effect of the play was in fact seen quite differently by another famous nineteenth-century Frenchman, the historian Michelet, who said of *Zaïre*: 'Bref, le drame avec ses sermons, ce verbiage qui ne trompait personne, pour l'effet est anti-chrétien'.[102] Michelet was factually wrong in stating that the Christianity of the play 'ne trompait personne', and he was wrong, too, in dismissing the long, moving, speeches as sermons and verbiage. But was he perhaps right in saying that in total effect the play is anti-Christian, even if many of Voltaire's contemporaries were unable to see this, or chose to ignore it?

The contradictions leading to conflicting interpretations are at the heart of the play itself. It seems clear that while Voltaire was writing, he was carried away by Christianity and its history as a poetic theme and genuinely inspired by his own historical visions. Nor did he ever become coldly critical of his own poetic imagination, for later in his life he several times played the part of Lusignan on his private stage, and he acted with a depth of feeling and pathos that frequently made his audience weep with him (see above, p.291). Yet at the same time he was anti-catholic, bitterly anti-catholic: his intellect rebelled at the illogicality of so many aspects of the Christian faith; his heart rebelled at the harshness of a theology that offered men salvation so often in exchange for their present happiness. Could Voltaire disguise these fundamental feelings in *Zaïre*? Did he try to? Or was he perhaps deviously trying to influence his audience by showing them some of the objections to Christianity in an ostensibly Christian play? But for once it seems unlikely that Voltaire is being so consciously aggressive: the Christian poetry of the play is too spontaneous, too convincing for that. A possible attitude to the anomalies of the play is to accept them for what they are and recognise that Voltaire himself has not attempted to reconcile its contradictory

---

[102] *Histoire de France*, nouv. éd. (Paris 1876-1878), xviii.122.

aspects, reflecting the two sides of his personality: the poetic, sensitive side, responding to the grandeur and pathos of Christian history; the intellectual, critical side, rejecting Christianity with his mind – and with his heart, for Voltaire could never overcome his horror at all the evils that had been perpetrated by and upon mankind in the name of religion. It is because Voltaire makes no attempt to resolve the contradictions in *Zaïre* that totally different interpretations have been put upon the play and that, in the end, it is unsatisfactory as tragedy. It lacks the fulfilling sense of logic and inexorability that is found in the best tragedy of the preceding century. It makes too many demands upon the reader. It appeals to our hearts, and then provides an incompatible appeal to our minds, so that where we should be sympathetic and involved, we are perhaps only angry and frustrated.

The appeal of the Christian poetry is clear enough, and Michelet's bigotry in denying it does him no credit. But Michelet does provide a starting-point for seeing why this *tragédie chrétienne* may be interpreted as anti-Christian in its total effect. 'Le vif intérêt', he says, 'est pour un musulman, le noble et touchant Orosmane [...] Les chrétiens discoureurs, Nérestan, Châtillon, déplaisent furieusement au public; ils viennent à contre-temps' (xviii.121-22). Orosmane is the hero of this touching love-story, involving two entirely blameless characters, who deserve happiness. Even when he kills Zaïre, we feel that this is an unfortunate accident, and we are angry with the situation rather than with him, and perhaps even more with Nérestan, whose intransigent fanaticism has brought about the situation. But if Orosmane is more likeable than Nérestan, it is not a necessary or logical conclusion that Christianity is at fault, and, in spite of Michelet's argument, this alone would not make the play anti-Christian.[103] Nérestan's fanaticism is, of course, attributable to his interpretation of Christianity. He shows no understanding of his sister's predicament

---

[103] It might be similarly argued, and frequently was, especially in the seventeenth century, that in *Polyeucte* Sévère is more attractive than Polyeucte. But it would be foolish to suggest on these grounds that the play is anti-Christian.

and no pity for her suffering. He is concerned only with ensuring that she becomes a baptised Christian and is thus saved. The logic of this attitude is contained within the theology of Catholicism, which states that salvation through faith is the goal, and that present happiness in this world should be gladly sacrificed to achieve this goal. Nérestan's acceptance of this theology is absolute, uncritical and rigorous. To this extent, his rôle may be seen as an indirect attack on Catholicism. It remains true, however, that sincere Catholics have envisaged their religion in other ways, so that there is a personal element in Nérestan's faith that must prevent us from generalising about the interpretation of the play on the basis of his role alone.

If the play is anti-Christian in its total effect, it is for another, more fundamental reason. There is an important character in *Zaïre* who does not appear in the *dramatis personae*. He is constantly invoked by the other characters, he is often the cause of their acting in a certain way, and, above all, the other characters expect him to intervene at any moment. This unseen and unheard participant is God: the God of the Christians. The Christians in the play attribute Zaïre's conversion to him, and Zaïre puts her trust in God's love and mercy. But her prayer that God may show clemency and pardon her is not granted. A series of unfortunate coincidences and misunderstandings leads eventually to her murder at the hands of her lover. Once again we find that Voltaire is suggesting the classic case against the notion of a God involved in human affairs proposed by those who cannot reconcile the doctrine of the omniscience and omnipotence of God with the presence of evil in the universe. If God can prevent happenings such as those of the play, why does He not do so? In some ways, the total effect of *Zaïre* is not as dissimilar to the message of *Candide* as one might at first imagine. *Zaïre*, too, shows that everything is not for the best in the best of all possible worlds. Of course, almost any tragedy does that; but *Zaïre* does so in a characteristically Voltairean way. Voltaire raises philosophical doubts in his audiences – or readers – just as he does in so many of his other works. Does God exist? Does He intervene in human affairs? If He can prevent it, why does He allow suffering? In this play, the well-intentioned suffer horrible deaths. They may in any tragedy. But here they suffer for God and because of God. They expect, and are right to expect, His help. He offers none. Rather than believe that God could be so cruel, is it not preferable to believe that He does not exist? After all, if Zaïre had not accepted belief in the Christians' God, she would have married Orosmane and, we are led to think, have lived happily ever after. For her, life without the Christians' God would have meant happiness. It is noteworthy that Voltaire kills her off deliberately before she has actually been baptised, so that technically she has not been saved: she is not baptised, she has not repented of wanting to marry a Muslim – on the contrary, she hopes to the end that they will be able to marry. Do we assume, as an eighteenth-century Christian reader should, that she will face everlasting punishment? Is religious complacency possible here, even for a believer?

Of course, for Nérestan, the fanatic of the play, there is no problem. God has punished Zaïre for loving an infidel (v.x.171-172). Fatime adds to the reader's disquiet by emphasising that Zaïre hoped that God would take pity on her. Her lines (v.x.177-179) are the last important words on the subject of God in the play, and we may well conclude that it ends with God's absence or indifference – or non-existence – established. How different from the ending of *Polyeucte*, where the action of Divine Grace transforms tragedy into triumph!

All this is not to suggest that there is anything systematic about what can be seen as Voltaire's attack on the Christian notion of God in this play. What emerges rather are his own doubts, his own awareness of the logical flaws in the Christian position. And he seems to have made no attempt to reconcile the conflicting claims of Christian poetry and of his rigorously logical and sceptical mind.

One important passage in *Zaïre*, however, is more obviously sceptical, in the familiar Voltairean vein. This is Zaïre's speech in act 1, scene 1 (l.101-127), during the course of which Zaïre herself analyses the process by which an individual decides upon one or other of the many religions of the world. Zaïre is here acting simply as Voltaire's mouthpiece, and he himself seems quite unperturbed by the unlikeliness of a situation where an innocent young girl, brought up in the utterly enclosed world of the oriental harem, suddenly comes out with a rational, perhaps even cynical description of the origins of religious choice in the individual. More subtle is the end of this speech, where Zaïre's words on Christian love towards all men can only be interpreted as heavy sarcasm – not on Zaïre's part, obviously, but on Voltaire's. While allowing Zaïre to take literally Christianity's view of itself that it makes the world a better and happier place, Voltaire offers a play whose action pointedly belies this assumption. As a historian, he looked back and was appalled at all the horrors that had been committed in the name of religion. In some ways, the action of Zaïre may be said to add to this catalogue of horrors. The story is fictitious, but the historical background is not, and the story arises directly out of historical circumstance.

It seems clear, then, that only a prejudiced or naïve reading of the play could lead to the conclusion that it is in any sense a Christian play, if by that it is meant a play calculated to inspire respect for or adhesion to Christianity in the audience. The fact that such a conclusion has from time to time been reached remains simply a curious fact of literary history.

8. 'Ce que l'amour a de plus touchant et de plus furieux'

It was largely to its appeal as a touching love story that Zaïre owed its overwhelming and long-lasting success with the theatre-going public. Voltaire, obliged to confess defeat in his attempts to attract the public by more dignified means, rather self-consciously set the bait: 'Il a donc fallu me plier aux mœurs du temps, et commencer tard à parler d'amour' (see below, p.420). The public was captivated. But Voltaire continued to insist that in writing a love story, he was not merely deferring to public taste, because he did not intend to limit himself to the public's desire for conventional *galanterie* in drama (see above, p.279). Hence the emphasis not only on the 'touching' aspect of love, but also on the 'furious'. Implicit in Voltaire's many pronouncements on this subject is the criticism that his fellow tragedians' concern in portraying love is not with the truth, but with satisfying the public's prejudices and fantasies. As for his own hero, he claims that, far from behaving like every other hero of tragedy, whatever his supposed situation in life, as 'un jeune abbé à la toilette d'une bégueule', Orosmane is 'le plus passionné, le plus fier, le plus cruel et le plus malheureux de tous les hommes' (D497). On the whole, however, Voltaire's self-styled revolutionary treatment of love did not startle or shock his contemporaries as much as he may have hoped – or perhaps feared – for in reality the portrayal of Orosmane hardly bears out this description (see above, p.312-13). Critical opinion has tended to concentrate rather upon the portrayal of Zaïre, upon the 'touching' heroine rather than the 'furious' hero. The reason is not only that she is the natural focus of the play (see above, p.307), but also that her role rings much more true. In portraying Zaïre, Voltaire did not need to compromise with the public's taste, as he did in the case of Orosmane, in spite of his protestations to the contrary. In so far as Orosmane has received his share of the praise, it is for lines such as his simple 'Zaïre, vous pleurez' (IV.ii.116), upon which many a commentator has waxed lyrical, rather than as a 'furious' and barbaric lover.

Contemporary opinion tended to interpret the play simply as an unhappy love story, telling the tale of two wholly attractive and civilised people caught in a disastrous web of circumstances. Jean-Jacques Rousseau chose Zaïre, *pièce enchanteresse*, as he called it, to illustrate his contention that tragedy, far from helping to moderate human passions, could only serve to exacerbate them:

Je serois curieux de trouver quelqu'un, homme ou femme qui s'osât vanter d'être sorti d'une représentation de Zaïre bien prémuni contre l'amour [...] de toutes les Tragédies qui sont au Théâtre, nulle autre ne montre avec plus de charmes le pouvoir de l'amour et l'empire de la beauté.[104]

La Harpe's lengthy analysis of *Zaïre*, made in the late 1780s, concentrates likewise on the power of the play as a touching love story. La Harpe puts the play above all others he knows:

tout me fait voir dans *Zaïre* l'ouvrage le plus éminemment tragique que l'on ait jamais conçu. Elle fait pleurer le peuple comme les gens instruits; et quand les ressorts et l'exécution sont admirés des connaisseurs, si l'effet peut aller jusqu'à devenir pour ainsi dire populaire, c'est sans contredit le plus grand triomphe d'un art qui a pour but principal d'émouvoir les hommes rassemblés.[105]

The uncritical admiration he manifests towards *Zaïre* cannot fail to astonish the modern reader. It is particularly Voltaire's success in provoking the audience to tears that La Harpe stresses. Like all his contemporaries, he exonerates Orosmane from all blame, thinking of him as an ill-fated, not as a cruel or violent lover. The eighteenth-century public was not concerned with realism in the portrayal of love, but with a certain range of familiar emotions. Voltaire, in spite of his more daring promises, in *Zaïre* at any rate, gave them what they wanted. They shed copious tears, and were well satisfied. 'Ce que l'amour a... de plus furieux' does not find expression in *Zaïre*. The portrayal of love in both hero and heroine is wholly gracious and civilised, and Racine's heroes have much to learn in comportment from these two noble characters. The murder, which is almost an accident, and certainly the result of chance, appears not as the inevitable climax of Orosmane's ferocity, but as the pathetic culmination of a series of misunderstandings, in which Orosmane is as blameless as Zaïre. In *Zaïre*, in so far as it is a story concerned with individuals, pathos replaces tragedy. If there is tragedy, it is in the larger context – the context

---

[104] *Lettre à Mr d'Alembert sur les spectacles*, ed. M. Fuchs (Lille, Genève 1948), p.73-74.
[105] *Lycée, ou cours de littérature* (Paris 1840-1847), ii.246.

324

of the futility of religious wars, of the peculiar human disposition which claims knowledge of absolute truth in the realm of the unknowable. But such considerations, though real and important, and suggested by the play, are not truly within the play, which remains above all, as Voltaire's public rightly felt, a touching love story.

9. Conclusion

It is sad that a play which is probably the best, which was certainly the most popular of Voltaire's tragedies, and which still has so much to offer in interest to the historian of literature, must be deemed a failure when judged according to the highest criteria of art. These were the criteria by which Voltaire himself wanted to be judged,[106] but he would no doubt still be surprised to discover that posterity's verdict on his tragedies is so unfavourable. He might be tempted to ascribe this lack of appreciation to the barbarity of an age blind to the beauties of a severe and difficult art form, but he would be quite wrong. It is possibly an awareness of the necessity for something approaching perfection that has led to the modern neglect of *Zaïre*, after so many decades of popularity with the public. Earlier periods, while certainly fully aware of the many failings of the play as regards plot, characterisation and diction, were perhaps more tolerant. Voltaire himself readily admitted the fundamental weakness of one aspect of his play, the plot, depending as it does on a number of incredible circumstances. In a passage of *Le Temple du Goût*, Voltaire gave the Goddess of Criticism the following words, addressed to him:

> Donnez plus d'intrigue à *Brutus*,
> Plus de vraisemblance à *Zaïre*;[107]

---

[106] *Parallèle d'Horace, de Boileau, et de Pope* (M.xxiv.226-27).
[107] *Le Temple du Goût*, ed. E. Carcassonne (Genève 1953), p.156.

It would be idle to rehearse after so many others[108] the long list
of obvious improbabilities which detract from the plot. But among
a number of lesser points, one essential criticism of the plot stands
out: that it hinges upon an accident of language. The inevitable,
so essential a part of what is felt to be the tragic mode, is replaced
by the contingent. In Dominique's parody, the point is wittily
made. The 'catastrophe' is averted precisely by a change of
language, which underlines how artificial is Voltaire's avoidance
of the same result in his tragedy. Temire (Zaïre) is waiting for
Carabin (Nérestan) and Diaphane (Orosmane) is hiding:

DIAPHANE

J'entens encor du bruit, & j'aperçois le traître,
La lanterne qu'il tient me le fait reconnoître;
Je vais les immoler à ma juste fureur.

TEMIRE

Est-ce vous, Carabin?

Scene XVII. & derniere
CARABIN, & les susdits Acteurs.

CARABIN

Estes-vous là, ma sœur?

DIAPHANE

Sa sœur! Ah, j'allois faire une belle sottise!
Cet éclaircissement m'épargne une méprise.[109]

Weakness in characterisation has received less attention than
faults in the plot from earlier critics of *Zaïre*, possibly because
while it is easy to discern, it is difficult to analyse. Most critics seem
to be content with vague formulae, suggesting some mysterious
deficiency in Voltaire's ability to *peindre les âmes*. The fact that in
Voltaire's characters we feel the author's presence may be a clue
to this deficiency. The best example in this play is Zaïre's famous

---

[108] For example, Nadal, H. Lion, H. C. Lancaster.
[109] *Les Enfants trouvés*, p.26-27.

speech about religion at the beginning of the tragedy (i.i.101-127), a speech which it is impossible to justify in terms of her character (see above, p.321-22). But only a little less blatantly inappropriate is Orosmane's first speech, when, meeting his beloved again after two days' absence, he launches headlong into a historical, political and social survey, to which on the stage the hapless actress playing the part of Zaïre merely has to listen![110] These glaring anomalies are perhaps not entirely typical of Voltaire's weakness in characterisation, but they point to the conclusion that he was unable to give his characters enough autonomy to make them wholly coherent.

In contrast to the relative silence on this matter, critics and scholars have readily dissected Voltaire's poetic diction. Voltaire, believing passionately that great tragedy had to be not only drama, but literature also, invites critical examination of his language. Perhaps unwisely, for it simply does not stand up to detailed analysis. It is, of course, astonishing that Voltaire, who required the tragedian to aim at the highest possible achievement in poetry, should have considered it feasible to write a complete tragedy in twenty-two days. He was inspired, no doubt, but inspiration, while allowing the poet to write some perfect lines, some perfect passages, is unlikely to enable him to sustain a high level of craftsmanship through the five long acts of a tragedy. In *Zaïre*, the writing is often slipshod, if judged by exacting standards. Voltaire knew well that haste in writing had led to carelessness, and he made several alterations to his verse, both before and after the first performance of the play. A charming story is told that the actors of the Comédie-Française became so weary of having to learn, unlearn and re-learn lines, that they refused to accept

---

[110] I.ii.157-214. There is an interesting analysis of these lines in the *Mémoires* of Mlle Clairon, who astonishingly castigates her great fellow actor and rival, Lekain, in the part of Orosmane, for obliging her to 'entendre parler d'affaires où je voulais qu'on me parlât d'amour'. An editor's note to this remark rather timidly suggests that Voltaire is *as much* to blame as Lekain! See *Mémoires* (Paris 1822), p.313 ff.

any further amendments. Voltaire, in despair, one day sent the leading actor, who was holding a dinner party for his colleagues, a huge pie. When opened, the pie was found to contain a vast number of partridges, each one holding little pieces of folded paper in its beak. Unfolded, the papers revealed corrected lines of *Zaïre*. In the circumstances, the actors could hardly refuse to learn them.[111] True or not, this story epitomises Voltaire's concern for his craft; but at the same time the versification of *Zaïre* is perhaps its principal weakness. Signs of haste are everywhere apparent. A compensating aspect of haste may be an impression of naturalness, but this is not enough to offset repetitions, padding, redundant adjectives mechanically applied, long-winded circumlocutions, over-abstraction and even grammatical error.[112]

Voltaire's sentimental contemporaries were ready to overlook all the faults in the play, for *Zaïre* satisfied them as a moving and pathetic love story. To succeed as a tragic love story for a modern audience, *Zaïre* would have to be more convincing dramatically, more profound psychologically, and altogether denser and more forceful in its poetic language. Racine provides the model – at once the pinnacle and the norm – for classical tragedy. Voltaire cannot match up to his great master. But to obvious shortcomings in plot, characterisation and style must be added a less obvious, but more important failing in the play. In *Zaïre*, Voltaire is trying to do too many things at the same time, and they are not all compatible. He wants to write great tragedy; he wants movement and action in his play; he wants to evoke the spirit of the Crusades; he wants to preach religious tolerance; he wants to paint Turkish customs; he wants to please a French audience; he wants to write poetry of a high order; he wants to fulfil a clear moral purpose. The result is a play which tends to pull the reader in different emotional and intellectual directions. It is only by discounting the

[111] Desnoiresterres, i.448. Cf. P. M. Conlon, *Voltaire's literary career from 1728 to 1750*, Studies 14 (1961), p.128-29.

[112] There is an excellent study of the language of *Zaïre* in the edition of the play produced by M. Fontaine (Paris 1889), p.xxxvi-li and *passim* in the notes.

role of religion in the play that one can see it simply as a pathetic love story. It is only by giving a very naïve interpretation to the role of Christianity in the play that one can accept it as a 'Christian tragedy'. It is only by ignoring the splendid Christian poetry that one can see the play as offering merely anti-religious propaganda. There is no doubt that these various contradictions and anomalies contribute to the relative weakness of *Zaïre* as drama and literature. But there is equally no doubt that they make for the fascination of the play for the careful modern reader. As a tragedy, *Zaïre* leaves much to be desired. As a characteristic product of Voltaire's complex mind and soul, the play cannot fail to provide continuing stimulus and enjoyment.

10. *Manuscripts*

No original manuscript of the play is known, but a fragment with holograph corrections passed at auction on three occasions between 1855 and 1891 (see below, MS6). The prompt-copy of *Zaïre* (MS1) offers an early version of the text, the readings of which are given in the variants to the present edition. Also taken into account are MS2 and MS3, which record suppressed versions of the epistle to Fawkener.

MS 1

Zaïre / Tragedie /

Contemporary copy, with corrections and alterations for performances at the Comédie-Française; 232 x 357 mm; 44 leaves, folded and gathered to form 4 sections of 14, 10, 14 and 6 leaves, paginated 1-87 (the first leaf transposed); recently recased in the original limp vellum cover, stamped on the spine 'ZAÏRE (SOUFFLEUR) 1732'.

1 Acteurs; 2 title, as above; 3-18 act 1 (p.13 blank); 19-36 act 2; 37-52 act 3; 53-70 act 4; 71-83 act 5; 84 blank; 85 list of actors; 86-87 pencilled list of some of the actors appearing in some of the scenes; [88] blank.

Comédie-Française, MS 112.

This is probably the original prompt-copy of *Zaïre*, written in the legible hand of the company's official *escrivain* and *souffleur*, Jean Baptiste Minet.[113] It was presumably made by Minet from a manuscript copy by Voltaire himself. On 9 July 1732, Voltaire wrote to Thiriot that his play was 'now in the hands of the players' (D502). Around this time Minet must have been copying out both the prompt-copy and the individual actors' roles. On 21 August, during the very successful first run of the play (see above, p.283), Voltaire dashed off a quick note to Cideville including the phrase, 'je n'ay qu'un instant pour corriger des vers de Zaire' (D514). The prompt-copy retains considerable evidence of the corrections Voltaire made on this, and presumably other, occasions – perhaps including, if the story is not apocryphal, the corrections offered by the little partridges (see above, p.327-28)! The original text copied by Minet has many alterations to wording written in above the lines also by Minet, no doubt on Voltaire's instructions. Where the new material has proved too extensive to incorporate by crossing out and insertion. Minet has taken fresh paper, written the changes out in full, and pasted the new paper over the old text with glue or sealing wax (on p.41, 47, 50, 51, 55, 61, 66, 75 and 80). In places, the original text is still readable under the loosely pasted corrections. In others, where the new piece has adhered closely, the original text cannot be read. In addition to Minet's corrections, there are others of a relatively minor nature in a later hand, mostly written above Minet's lines. In the same hand, in the margin besides Zaïre's speech at 1.101-127, is a note which reads 'change p[our] Mlle Clairon'. It may be safely assumed, therefore, that these additions to the prompt copy were made when Mlle Clairon took over the role of Zaïre.[114] In every case, the new additions corres-

[113] See Sylvie Chevalley, 'Le "sieur Minet"', *Studies* 62 (1968), p.273-83. I am grateful to Mme Chevalley for the information that the writing is Minet's. Her article mentions (p.276) a bill for expenses presented by Minet to the Comédie-Française on 26 March 1733, in which he explains that he has not been paid by Voltaire for copying either *Eriphyle* or *Zaïre*.

[114] In spite of all efforts, I have been unable to discover exactly when Mlle Clairon took over the rôle of Zaïre from Mlle Gaussin at the Comédie-Française. The first dated reference I have found is to the year 1756, when 'Mme de Guys, une Grecque, femme d'un riche négociant, fit présent à Mlle Clairon, durant son séjour à Marseille, d'une robe orientale pour jouer *Zaïre*, afin de remplacer la robe traditionnelle à paniers' (voir H. Lyonnet, *Dictionnaire des comédiens français*, i.346). But Collé recounts (i.333-34) that Mlle Hus fit son début at

pond to the printed text of the editions and are therefore of no independent textual interest.

MS1*

Minet's manuscript copy is treated in this edition as offering variants to the base text. Only Minet's own text has been reproduced, the later corrections providing no readings different from those of the *édition encadrée*. But Minet's own text falls into two categories: the first is the original copy, made from a manuscript provided by Voltaire; the second is constituted by the corrections written above the line or pasted over the original text, corrections which Minet presumably received from Voltaire himself. Such interventions are recorded in the critical apparatus under the siglum MS1*.

MS2

La / Zaÿre / De M. de Voltaire / auec / Une Epître Dédicatoire. / Nouvelle Edition. / Hic frango calamos, Vigila- / taque carmina linquo. / à Paris / 1732: /

A manuscript of an early version of the 'Epître dédicatoire', bound at the head of a copy of the first edition of *Zaïre*.

[i] manuscript title, as above; [ii] blank; 1-28 Epître dedicatoire à Monsieur Fakener marchand anglois; [29-32] blank.

Arsenal: 8° BL 13641.

The text offered by this manuscript is similar to, but not identical with, that of the earliest known printed text of the epistle (33RV). The date of 1732, given on the title of the manuscript, may simply reflect the premature circulation of copies of the edition dated 1733 – but it is not impossible that a 1732 printing of the play or the epistle remains to be discovered.

The edition bound after the manuscript is described below, under 33R (state 2). It includes the printed text of the 'Epître' from that edition,

---

the Comédie-Française in *Zaïre* in July 1751. She was Mlle Clairon's pupil, and this may suggest that Mlle Clairon had played the rôle. But it may mean that she was trying to introduce a rival in the part to Mlle Gaussin.

possibly a proof copy, which has been annotated with some of the readings from the manuscript.

MS3

Retranchemens que M^r. de Voltaire a faits a l'Épître qu'il avoit remise a l'examen, pour être imprimée a la tête de sa tragedie de Zäire.

A copy of the passages removed by Voltaire from the 'Epître', bound in a volume from the collection of François-Louis Jamet (1710-1778).

Bn: Rés. p Z 150 (1).

Variants provided by this text are recorded in the critical apparatus, at l.44, 133-162, 162-171, 222, 224-225, 228-229, 234-235, 242-256.

MS4

Année 1764. / Quatrième Rosle. Chatillon. / Dans Zaïre, Tragédie de M^r De Voltaire. /

A copy by Lekain of the role of Châtillon, in a volume of similar copies of other roles from the period 1760 to 1767.

[1] title, as above; [2] Personnages; 1-4 Rosle de Chatillon (p.4, 'Fin du rosle de Chatillon de 123 vers').

Comédie-Française.

MS5

An old copy of the role of Fatime, probably transcribed from an edition and offering no variant readings.

Bn: N3018, f.78-81.

MS6

A copy of part of act 2 and all of act 3, in 23 folio pages, supposedly with holograph corrections, passed at three sales in the nineteenth century: *Catalogue d'une très belle collection de lettres autographes et manuscrits* [the Gratet-Duplessis collection] (Charavay, 10 décembre 1855), p.110, no.999, 'avec cartons, variantes et corrections de la main de Voltaire'; *Catalogue de lettres autographes, documents historiques, curiosités révolutionnaires, livres, sceaux, etc. composant le cabinet de M. le baron de Girardot ancien secrétaire-général de la préfecture de la Loire-Inférieure* (Charavay, Paris 13-14 juin 1879), p.30, no.259, 'avec des corrections autographes'; *Catalogue de l'importante collection de lettres autographes composant le cabinet de feu M. le marquis de Queux de Saint-Hilaire* (Charavay, Paris 5-6 janvier 1891), p.44, no.259, which reprints the 1879 description. The manuscript, the history of which was kindly brought to our attention by Jean de Booy, has not been reported since.

MS7

A calligraphic copy, 'dédiée à mesdames de France, par Louis-Ant. Callet', in 98 quarto leaves, passed at a sale by Silvestre (Paris 27-31 mars 1893), p.28, no.391.

11. *Editions*

The 1733 editions of *Zaïre* present several bibliographical difficulties, not all of which are resolved in the following pages. The basic pattern is similar to that which applied to many of Voltaire's earlier dramatic works. The first edition (33R) was printed in France (in this case at Rouen, by or for Jore), without the preliminary texts. An early version of the 'Epître dédicatoire' and the 'Epître à Mlle Gaussin' were then printed together as a separate gathering of eight leaves, the first page of which provided a new title (see 33RV). This gathering (of which a revised version soon appeared) was intended to replace the original title leaf, but copies of the play survive with two titles (and 33RV has all three). Jore also produced another edition (33RP) from a different setting of type, and may have been reponsible for a third, of which only one sheet is known.

Copies of the Amsterdam edition (33A) vary one from another only in the imprint, either Ledet or Desbordes; the English edition (33L) is known in only one state; but 33X, a French edition, is again found both with and without the preliminary texts and with two different titles.

Thirty more separate editions were published during Voltaire's lifetime, but only 36A appears to have been produced with the participation of the author. Of the collected editions recorded below, several benefited from Voltaire's collaboration, notably W38, W48D, W51P, W56 (and new editions thereof), W68, W70L and W75G – but few changes of substance to the text of *Zaïre* were made after 1738.

33R

[State 1] ZAYRE, / *TRAGEDIE*. / REPRESENTÉE A PARIS / Aux mois d'Aouſt, Novem- / bre & Décembre 1732. / [*woodcut, 42 x 29 mm*] / *Imprimée à Rouen* / Chez JORE Pere & Fils, / *Et ſe vend* / A PARIS, / Chez JEAN-BAPTISTE BAUCHE, à la deſcente du / Pont-neuf, proche les Auguſtïns, à Saint Jean- / Baptiſte dans le deſert. / [*rule, 49 mm*] / MDCCXXXIII. / *AVEC PRIVILEGE DU ROY.* /

8°. sig. π^4 (π1 blank) A-F⁸ ¹π1 ($\pm$ A5); pag. [*8*] 95 [96-97]; \$4 signed, arabic (– A1); sheet catchwords.

[*1-2*] blank; [*3*] title; [*4*] blank; [*5-7*] Privilège du roi; [*8*] blank, but for catchword 'ZAYRE,'; [1] A1*r* 'ZAYRE, / *TRAGEDIE*.'; 2 Personnages; 3-95 Zayre, tragédie; [96] Approbation; [97] Fautes à corriger dans la tragédie de Zayre.

The description given above corresponds to what we believe to be the earliest issue of the first edition of *Zaïre*, printed in Rouen by or for Jore.

The first two leaves (a blank and the title), were then removed and replaced by a gathering of eight leaves (¹A⁸) containing a new title (without Jore's name) and the two epistles; the original leaves containing the 'Privilège' (π3-4) remained, with the following result:

[State 2] LA / ZAYRE, / DE M. DE VOLTAIRE, / Repreſentée à Paris aux mois / d'Aouſt, Novembre & Dé- / cembre 1732. / Augmentée de l'Epitre Dédicatoire. / *Eſt etiam crudelis amor.* / Broché trente ſols. / [*wood-cut, vase of flowers with foliage, 30 x 20 mm*] / *A Rouen,* / A PARIS, / Chez JEAN-BAPTISTE BAUCHE, à la deſcente du / Pont-neuf, proche les Auguſtins, à Saint Jean- / Baptiſte dans le Déſert. / [*rule, 61 mm*] / M. DCC. XXXIII. / *AVEC PRIVILEGE DU ROY.* /

334

8°. sig. ¹A⁸ π3-4 A-F⁸ ¹π1 (± A5); pag. [20] 95 [96-97]; \$4 signed, arabic (– ¹A1, ¹A4, A1; ¹A2 signed 'A', ¹A3 'Aij'); sheet catchwords.

[1] title; [2] blank; [3-14] Epître dédicatoire à monsieur Fakener marchand anglais; [15-16] Epître à mademoiselle Gossin, jeune actrice qui a représenté le rôle de Zaïre avec beaucoup de succès; [17-19] Privilège du roy; [20] blank, but for catchword 'ZAYRE,'; [1]-[97] as state 1.

Both states of this edition were cancelled, at A5 (1.133-136), and the cancel exists in at least four different settings, all of which give essentially the same text. These cancels were also used to correct 33RP, the second Jore printing.

Sheets of 33R may be distinguished from those of 33RP by a number of misprints, found only in 33R: on p.21, l.18, 'Répandfur'; p.28, the 'L' at the start of the penultimate line has slipped upwards; p.47, l.11, 'L'honncur'; p.75, last line, 'gravédans'; p.91, last line, 'Regatde'. On p.3, the height of the characters used for 'ZAYRE' is 6.5 mm.

State 1. Bn: Rés. Z Beuchot 889 (1) (¹π1 present); Arsenal: Rf 14176 (uncut copy; ¹π1 absent); Comédie-Française (mounted copy, with the date of the title altered by hand to 'MDCCXXXII.': see the note on MS2, above).

State 2. Bn: Rés. Z Bengesco 26 (π3-4 bound after ¹A7); – Rés. p Yf 475 (not cancelled; the original title, π2, preserved after ¹A8; ¹π1 absent); Arsenal: 8° BL 13641 (original title preserved; on this copy, see above, MS2); – Rf 14177.

Hybrid states. See below, 33RP and 33RV.

33R*

A copy of one of the 1733 editions with holograph corrections to the 'Epître', was described by Jeroom Vercruysse, 'Notes inédites de Voltaire', *Studi francesi* 20 (1963), p.[258]-59. The corrections and alterations transcribed by M. Vercruysse are reproduced in the critical apparatus to the present edition (l.154-155, 158, 242-272).

Académie royale de Belgique, Brussels: 9026 Stassart 5111 (missing).

33RP

ZAYRE, / *TRAGEDIE.* / REPRESENTÉE A PARIS / Aux mois d'Aouſt, Novem- / bre & Décembre 1732. / [*woodcut, as* 33A] / *Imprimée à Rouen* / Chez Jore Pere & Fils, / *Et se vend* / A PARIS, / Chez JEAN-BAPTISTE BAUCHE, à la defcente du / Pont-neuf, proche les Auguftins, à Saint Jean- / Baptifte dans le defert. / [*rule, 52 mm*] / MDCCXXXIII. / *AVEC PRIVILEGE DU ROY.* /

8°. sig. π1 $^1\pi^2$ A-F^8 ($\pm$ A5); pag. [*6*] 95 [96]; $4 signed, arabic (– A1); sheet catchwords (– π1*v*, $^1\pi$2*v*; – A8*v* in Taylor copy).

[*1*] title; [*2*] blank; [*3-5*] Privilège du roi; [*6*] blank; [1] A1*r* 'ZAYRE, / *TRAGEDIE.*'; 2 Personnages; 3-95 Zaire, tragédie; [96] Aprobation.

Produced by the same printer as 33R (the woodcut headpiece on p.3 is identically damaged), 33RP may be identified by the 'Jore' of the title (not small capitals), by the length of the rule on the title, by the absence of a catchword on p.[*6*], by the height of 'ZAYRE' on p.3 (8.5 mm) and by the absence of the misprints and other irregularities listed under 33R above. It corrects the last of the errors listed in the errata of 33R (to give 'd'un ami' on p.94), but A5 is still a cancel. It is likely that the 'Privilège' was printed for this edition from the standing type of 33R: the last line of p.[*3*] begins 'ramxation', probably as a result of the manipulation of the page during reimposition.

In the Taylor copy of 33RP, sheet A of the text belongs neither to 33R nor to 33RP. It could be that this sheet alone was set up in type three times, as a result of some accident or miscalculation; or that this copy of sheet A is the sole survivor of a complete third printing by Jore. It may be identified by the misprint 'confirmée' on the first line of p.9 and by the absence of a catchword on A8*v*. It reproduces the cancelled text of 33R and 33RP and corrects the first item in the errata, on p.13 (I.213); the error on p.14 (I.228) subsists.

Bn: Rés. Z Bengesco 25; ImV: D Zaïre 1733/1 (uncancelled); Taylor: V3 Z3 1733 (1) (hybrid copy, see above); Bodley: Vet M4 f 3 (2).

33RV

LA ZAYRE / DE MONSIEUR / DE VOLTAIRE. / AVEC UNE EPI-TRE / DEDICATOIRE. / NOUVELLE EDITION. / *Hic frango calamos, vigilataque car-* / *mina linquo.* / [*woodcut, foliage and birds, 49 x 34 mm*] / A PARIS. / [*rule, 53 mm*] / MDCCXXXIII. /

A combination of elements from 33R and 33RP with an additional title and an early and previously unrecorded version of the 'Epître dédicatoire': ^{1}A^8 from 33R state 2; π2-4 from 33R state 1; §^{8} unique to this edition; A-F^8 from 33RP.

Sig. §^{8} consists of: [*1*] title, as above; [*2*] blank; [*3-14*] Epître dédicatoire, à monsieur Fakener marchand anglais; [*15-16*] Epître à mademoiselle Gossin, jeune actrice qui a représenté le rôle de Zaïre avec beaucoup de succès.

This printing of the 'Epître' offers a text related to those of MS2 and MS3: variants are recorded in the critical apparatus.

Österreichische Nationalbibliothek, Vienna: BE 10 W 5 (3) (from the library of Prince Eugene of Savoie-Carignan).

33A

ZAYRE, / TRAGEDIE / DE / M. DE VOLTAIRE, / Reprefentée à Paris aux mois / d'Août, Novembre & Dé- / cembre 1732. / Augmentée de l'Epitre Dédicatoire. / *Eft etiam crudelis amor.* / *NOUVELLE EDITION* / revuë & corrigée par l'Auteur. / [*intaglio engraving*] / A AMSTERDAM, / Chez *JAQUES DESBORDES.* [*or* Chez *ETIENNE LEDET.*] / M. DCC. XXXIII. / [*lines 1, 4, 10 and 13 in red*]

8°. sig. *^{8} **^{2} A-F^8 G^6 (G6 blank); pag. XVII [xviii-xx] 106; $5 signed, arabic (– *1, **2); page catchwords.

[i] title; [ii] blank; [iii]-XV Epître dédicatoire à monsieur Fakener marchand anglais; [xvi]-XVII Epître à mademoiselle Gossin, jeune actrice qui a représenté le rôle de Zaïre avec beaucoup de succès; [xviii] blank; [xix] **2r 'ZAYRE, / *TRAGEDIE.*'; [xx] Personnages; [1]-106 Zayre, tragédie.

This Dutch edition, based on 33R, is typical of those produced for Ledet and Desbordes. Voltaire made changes to the epistle to Fawkener, at l.167 and 222-244; see also the variant to l.242.

On p.[xx], the catchword reads 'ZARYE'.

Bn: Rés. Z Beuchot 890 (Ledet); – 16° Yf 332 (1) (Desbordes; an uncut copy); Arsenal: Rf 14179 (Desbordes); ImV: A 1732/1 (3) (Desbordes; a large paper copy, bound at the end of volume 2 of a copy of w32); – BE 15 (3) (Ledet); Taylor: V3 Z3 1733 (3) (Ledet); – V3 Z3 1733 (4) (Ledet; half-title bound before title); – V3 Z3 1733 (5) (Desbordes).

337

33L

LA / ZAYRE, / DE M. DE VOLTAIRE, / Reprefentée à Paris aux mois / d'Aouſt, Novembre & Dé- / cembre 1732. / Augmentée de l'Epitre Dédicatoire, / *Eſt etiam crudelis amor.* / Broché trente ſols. / [*woodcut, vase of flowers above small head, 26 x 19 mm*] / A PARIS, / Chez JEAN-BAPTISTE BAUCHE, à la deſcente du / Pont-neuf, proche les Auguſtins, à Saint Jean- / Baptiſte dans le Déſert. / [*rule, 70 mm*] / M. DCC. XXXIII. / *AVEC PRIVILEGE DU ROY.* /

8°. sig. π^8 A-F^8 $^1\pi$1; pag. [*16*] 95 [96-97]; $4 signed, arabic (– A1; π2 signed 'A', π3 'A2'); sheet catchwords.

[*1*] title; [*2*] blank; [*3-14*] Epître dédicatoire à monsieur Fakener marchand anglais; [*15-16*] Epître à mademoiselle Gossin, jeune actrice qui a représenté le rôle de Zaïre avec beaucoup de succès; [1] A1*r* 'ZAYRE, / *TRAGEDIE.*'; 2 Personages; 3-95 Zayre, tragédie; [96] Approbation; [97] Fautes à corriger dans la tragédie de Zayre.

The typography and ornaments of this edition indicate that it was printed in England. The text follows 33R, but line I.134 is omitted.

André-Michel Rousseau (*Studies* 147, p.1028, no.399) lists a 1733 London edition by J. Nourse, from a 'source indirecte'. This could be it.

ImV: D Zaïre 1733/2; Taylor: V3 Z3 1733 (2); – V3 M7 1736 (2)/5 (lacks $^1\pi$1); BL: 640 e 19 (2) (lacks $^1\pi$1).

33X

[State 1] ZAYRE. / *TRAGEDIE / DE MONSIEUR / DE VOL-TAIRE,* / REPRESENTE'E / A PARIS / AUX MOIS D'AOUST, / Novembre & Décembre / 1732. / *Se vend ving-quatre* [*sic*] *ſols.* / [*typographic ornament*] / Imprimé à Roüen, / Chez JORE Pére & Fils. / [*rule, 48 mm*] / MDCCXXXIII. / *AVEC APPROBATION.* /

12°. sig. A-H^6 (A1 blank); pag. [*4*] 91; $3 signed, roman (– A1-3; A4 signed 'Aij'); sheet catchwords.

[*1-2*] blank; [*3*] title; [*4*] blank; [1] A3*r* 'ZAYRE. / *TRAGEDIE.* / [*rule, 68 mm*] / *APPROBATION.* / J'ai lû [...] trente-deux. / DEMONGRIF.'; 2 Personnages; 3-91 Zayre, tragédie.

This edition was revised in a similar fashion to 33R, with the replacement of A1-2 by two new gatherings, ã^4 and ẽ^4:

338

[State 2] LA / ZAYRE / DE MONSIEUR / DE VOLTAIRE, / REPRE-SENTE'E / A PARIS / AUX MOIS D'AOUST, / Novembre & Décembre / 1732. / *Augmentée de l'Epître Dédicatoire.* / Eft etiam crudelis amor. / *Broché trente fols.* / [*typographic ornament*] / *Imprimé à Roüen,* / Chez Jore Pére & Fils. / [*rule, 49 mm*] / MDCCXXXIII. / *AVEC APPROBATION.* /

12°. sig. ã⁴ ẽ⁴ A3-6 B-H⁶; pag. [*16*] 91; $3 signed, roman (– ã1, A3; ã2 signed 'ã', ã3 'ãij', ã4 'ãiij', A4 'Aij'); sheet catchwords.

[*1*] title; [*2*] blank; [*3-14*] Epître dédicatoire à monsieur Fakener marchand anglais; [*15-16*] Epître à mademoiselle Gossin, jeune actrice, qui a représenté le rôle de Zaïre avec beaucoup de succès; [1]-91 as state 1.

This French edition follows the text of 33R, as corrected by the errata.

Bn: Rés. Z Beuchot 888 (state 1); Arsenal: Rf 14178 (state 2); Bpu: Ariana 1069 (1) (with both titles).

36A

ZAÏRE, / *TRAGEDIE* / DE M. DE VOLTAIRE, / *NOUVELLE EDI-TION*, / Revûë, corrigée & augmentée par l'Au- / teur, avec une nouvelle Epitre / dédicatoire. / *Eft etiam crudelis amor.* / Le prix eft de trente fols. / [*woodcut, 60 x 37 mm*] / A PARIS, / Chez Jean-Baptiste-Claude Bauche, / près les Auguftins, à la defcente du Pont-Neuf, / à S. Jean dans le Defert. / [*rule, 66 mm*] / M. DCC. XXXVI. / *AVEC PRIVILEGE DU ROY.* /

8°. sig. ã⁸ A-F⁸; pag. xiv [xv-xvi] 95 [96]; $4 signed, roman (– ã1, A1, E4; D4 signed 'Diij'); sheet catchwords.

[i] title; [ii] blank; iij-xiv A monsieur le chevalier Fakener, ambassadeur d'Angleterre à la Porte ottomane; [xv-xvi] Avertissement; [1] A1r 'ZAÏRE, / *TRAGEDIE.*'; 2 Personages; 3-95 Zaïre, tragédie; [96] Approbation.

Voltaire revised the text of *Zaïre* for this edition, which was published by Bauche in or around June 1736 (see D1035, D1036, D1054). The original epistles to Fawkener and to Mlle Gaussin were dropped in favour of the second letter to Fawkener, and the 'Avertissement' was added (see below, appendix I, p.525). Variants occur at I.268, 269, II.217, 293, 294, 387, III.130, 198, 224, 239-240, 272, 327-332, 334, IV.63, 64, 176, 177, 347, V.106-107, 127 and 174. When Voltaire revised *Zaïre* for the 1738 collected edition of his works, all but two of these readings were abandoned, probably by accident rather than design.

Bn: Rés. Z Beuchot 77 (2); – Rés. Z Bengesco 29.

36B

ZAÏRE, / *TRAGEDIE* / DE M. DE VOLTAIRE. / *NOUVELLE EDITION.* / Revûë, corrigée & augmentée par l'Au- / teur, avec une nouvelle Epitre / dédicatoire. / *Eſt etiam crudelis amor.* / Le prix eſt de trente ſols. / [*woodcut, 60 x 37 mm*] / A PARIS, / Chez JEAN-BAPTISTE-CLAUDE BAUCHE / près les Auguſtins, à la deſcente du Pont-Neuf, / à S. Jean dans le Deſert. / [*rule, 75 mm*] / M. DCC. XXXVI. / *AVEC PRIVILEGE DU ROY.* /

8°. sig. a⁸ A-F⁸; pag. xiv [xv-xvi] 95 [96]; $4 signed, roman (– a1, A1, E4); sheet catchwords.

[i] title; [ii] blank; iij-xiv A monsieur le chevalier Fakener, ambassadeur d'Angleterre à la Porte ottomane; [xv-xvi] Avertissement; [1] A1*r* 'ZAÏRE, / *TRAGEDIE*.'; 2 Personnages; 3-95 Zaïre, tragédie; [96] Approbation.

May be distinguished from 36A by the length of the rules on the title and by the variants on p.55 (III.276, 279-280). Unless otherwise stated in the critical apparatus, the text is that of 36A.

Bn: 8°. Yth 19441; Arsenal: 8° BL 13642; Taylor: V3 Z3 1736.

36C

ZAYRE / TRAGEDIE. / REPRESENTE'E A PARIS / aux Mois d'Août, Novembre & / Décembre 1732. / *Par Monſieur DE VOLTAIRE.* / [*woodcut, urn with foliage, 53 x 34 mm*] / *Imprimée à Roüen* / Chez JORE Pere & Fils, / *Et ſe vend* / A PARIS, / Chez JEAN-BAPTISTE BAUCHE, à la deſcente du Pont / neuf, proche les Auguſtins, à Saint Jean-Baptiſte / dans le deſert. / [*rule, 44 mm*] / M. DCC. XXXVI. / *AVEC PRIVILEGE DU ROI.* /

8°. sig. A-G⁴; pag. '54'[=55]; $1 signed (– A1; + C2, signed 'Cij'); sheet catchwords.

[1] title; [2] blank; [3] A2*r* 'ZAYRE / *TRAGEDIE*.'; [4] Personnages; 5-'54'[=55] Zayre, tragédie; '54'[=55] Approbation.

Arsenal: Rf 14180.

340

36D

ZAYRE, / TRAGEDIE / DE / M. DE VOLTAIRE. / Reprefentée à Paris aux mois d'Août, / Novembre & Décembre 1732. / Augmentée de l'Epitre Dédicatoire. / *Eft etiam crudelis amor.* / *NOUVELLE EDITION.* / Revuë & corrigée par l'Auteur. / [*woodcut, 59 x 44 mm*] / A AMSTERDAM, / *AUX DE'PENS DE LA COMPAGNIE.* / M. DCC. XXXVI. / [*lines 1, 4, 7, 9, 11 and 13 in red*]

12°. sig. π1 ã⁸ A⁴ B-E¹² (E12 blank); pag. [2] XV [xvi-xviii] 100; $6 signed, arabic (– ã5-6, A3-4); page catchwords.

[*1*] title; [2] blank; I-XIII Epître dédicatoire à monsieur Fakener marchand anglais; XIV-XV Epître à mademoiselle Gossin, jeune actrice, qui a représenté le rôle de Zaïre avec beaucoup de succès; [xvi] blank; [xvii] A1r 'ZAYRE, / *TRAGEDIE.*'; [xviii] Personnages; [1]-100 Zayre, tragédie.

Bound with separate editions of *Œdipe, Mariamne, Brutus* and *L'Indiscret* under a title on a single octavo leaf:

OEUVRES / DE / M. VOLTAIRE, / *CONTENANT* / L'ŒDIPE, MA-RIAMNE, BRUTUS, / L'INDISCRET & ZAÏRE. / [*intaglio engraving of Minerva and Mercury with printing presses, motto* 'TRINIS STIMULIS PRESSA', *plate size 65 x 52 mm*] / A AMSTERDAM, / *AUX DE'PENS DE LA COMPAGNIE.* / [*rule, 65 mm*] / M. DCC. XXXVI. / [*lines 1, 3, 5, 6, 7 and 9 in red*]

See Charles Wirz, 'L'Institut et musée Voltaire en 1981', *Genava* n.s.30 (1982), p.187-89, who plausibly suggests that this edition was produced in Rouen. There is no evidence that Voltaire was involved in its publication, but it may be the edition referred to by him in D1160.

ImV: A 1736/1 (2-5).

W37

OEUVRES / DE MONSIEUR / DE / VOLTAIRE. / SUIVANT LA / NOUVELLE EDITION / D'AMSTERDAM de 1733. / *Revuë, corrigée & augmentée par l'Auteur.* / TOME TROISIEME. / [*woodcut* / A BASLE. / [*rule*] / Chez JEAN BRANDMULLER & FILS. / M. DCC. XXXVII. / [*lines 1, 4, 9 and 11 in red*]

8°. sig. π1 A-Y⁸ Z⁶; pag. [2] 364; $5 signed, arabic (– A1, O1, V5; E4 signed 'B4'); direction line '*Tome III.*' (– A, O); page catchwords.

[*1*] title; [2] blank; [1] A1*r* 'ZAYRE, / *TRAGEDIE* / DE MONSIEUR / DE / VOLTAIRE, / Repréſentée à Paris aux mois d'Août, / Novembre & Décembre 1732. / Augmentée de l'Epitre Dédicatoire. / *Eſt etiam crudelis amor.* / Revuë & corrigée par l'Auteur. / [*woodcut, 38 x 28 mm*] / A BASLE. / [*rule, 86 mm*] / M. DCC. XXXVII.'; [2] blank; [3]-14 Epître dédicatoire à monsieur Fakener marchand anglais; 14-15 Epître à mademoiselle Gossin, jeune actrice qui a représenté le rôle de Zaïre avec beaucoup de succès; [16] Personnages; 17-122 Zayre, tragédie; [123]-364 other texts.

There is no evidence that Voltaire was involved in the publication of this edition.

Stockholm: Litt. fransk.

w38

OEUVRES / DE / M. DE VOLTAIRE. / Nouvelle Edition, / *Revue, corrigée & conſidérablement augmentée,* / *avec des Figures en Taille-douce.* / *TOME TROISIÈME.* / [*intaglio engraving*] / A AMSTERDAM, / Chez JAQUES DESBORDES. [*or* Chez ETIENNE LEDET & Compagnie.] / M. DCC. XXXVIII. / [*lines 1, 3, 7 and 9 in red*]

8°. sig. *² A-Aa⁸ Bb⁸ (– Bb2.7 = D3, D2 of volume 2; – Bb3.6 = F1, F2); pag. [*4*] XIX [xx] 372 (p.335 numbered '333' in some copies); $5 signed, arabic (– *1, Bb4); no volume indication in direction line; page catchwords (p.[*4*] 'AVER-').

[*1*] title; [2] blank; [*3-4*] Pièces contenues dans le tome III; [i] A1*r* 'LA / ZAYRE, / *TRAGÉDIE.* / A'; [ii] blank; [iii] Avertissement; [iv] blank; V-XVII Epître dédicatoire, à monsieur Fakener marchand anglais, depuis, ambassadeur à Constantinople; [xviii]-XIX Epître à mademoisel le [*sic*] Gossin, jeune actrice qui a représenté le rôle de Zaïre avec beaucoup de succès; [xx] Acteurs; [1]-114 Zayre, tragédie; [115]-372 other texts.

This edition, produced in part under Voltaire's supervision, is the last to include revisions of any substance to the text of *Zaïre*: see I.103, 134, II.387-388, III.130, 225, 279-281 (effected by the cancel at F2; that for F1 corrects a misprint), 327-333, IV.63, 64, 131, V.127.

There is a new 'Avertissement' (printed below, p.391); the 1733 epistles to Fawkener and Mlle Gaussin are restored, the former based upon 33A, with the addition of note *a*.

342

Copies of this edition are also found with title-pages dated 1739 (transcription as above, except 'M^R. DE VOLTAIRE.' and 'M. DCC. XXXIX.'); the text of volume 1 exists in two settings, but all the copies of volume 3 so far examined are from but the one setting and printing. The edition was reissued in 1743: see below, w43 (of which the copy cited contains both cancels and cancellans).

Several copies of w38 were corrected by hand, by or for Voltaire; on p.96 of the Br copy, the word 'fidélité' at v.15 has been amended in an obscure fashion; on p.7 of the Hénault copy, 'loi' is altered to 'foi' (I.102) and 'en ces lieux' replaced by 'la loy'.

Bn: Rés. Z Beuchot 4 (Ledet; Hénault's copy, corrected by hand); Ye 9213 (Ledet); Arsenal: Rés. 8° B 34042 (Desbordes; corrected by hand); Br: FS 277 A (3) (Ledet; corrected by Voltaire).

w39

OEUVRES / DE / M. VOLTAIRE, / *CONTENANT* / L'OEDIPE, MA-RIAMNE, BRUTUS, / L'INDISCRET & ZAÏRE. / *Nouvelle Edition, revûë, corrigée, & enrichie de / Figures en Taille-douce.* / [intaglio engraving, motto 'ERUDIT ET DITAT'] / A AMSTERDAM, / *AUX DE'PENS DE LA COM-PAGNIE.* / M. DCC. XXXIX. / [lines 1, 3, 5, 9 and 11 in red]

8°. sig. π1 A-Dd⁸; pag. [2] 431 (p.17 numbered '71'); $4 signed, arabic (– B3, H4, M2, Y4); sheet catchwords.

[1] title; [2] blank; 1-332 other texts; [333] X7r 'ZAYRE, / *TRAGEDIE.*'; [334] blank; 335-346 Epître dédicatoire à monsieur Fakener, marchand anglais; [347] Epître à mademoiselle Gossin jeune actrice, qui a représenté le rôle de Zaïre avec beaucoup de succès; 348 Personnages; 349-431 Zayre, tragédie.

Voltaire mentioned this edition in D1907 and D1985, but was not involved in its production. It is based on w38.

Bn: Rés. Z Bengesco 470 (1); – Rés. Z Beuchot 5.

w40

OEUVRES / DE / M^R. DE VOLTAIRE. / NOUVELLE EDITION, / *Revûë, corrigée & confidérablement augmentée* / *avec des Figures en Taille-douce.* / TOME TROISIE'ME. / [intaglio engraving] / A AMSTERDAM, / Aux Dépens de la Compagnie. / M. DCC. XL. / [lines 1, 3, 7 and 9 in red]

12°. sig. πι A-P¹² Q²; pag. 'XVIII'[=xix] [xx] 343 (p.88 numbered 86, 237 '137'); $6 signed, arabic (− I5, Q2; O3 signed 'N3', O5 'N5'); direction line '*Tome III.*' (sig. C '*Tome II.*'); sheet catchwords.

[*1*] title; [*2*] blank; [i-ii] Pièces contenues dans le tome III; [iii-iv] Avertissement; V-XVII Epître dédicatoire, à monsieur Fakener marchand angalis, depuis, ambassadeur à Constantinople; [xviii]-'XVIII'[=xix] Epître à mademoiselle Gossin, jeune actrice qui a représenté le rôle de Zaïre avec beaucoup de succès; [xx] Acteurs; [1]-114 Zayre, tragédie; [115]-343 other texts.

This may be the edition attributed by Voltaire to Paupie (at The Hague) in D2412, but it was probably printed at Rouen.

Arsenal: 8° BL 34045 (3); Rés. Z Bengesco 5*bis* (3).

W41R

OEUVRES / DE / Mᴿ. DE VOLTAIRE. / Nᴏᴜᴠᴇʟʟᴇ Eᴅɪᴛɪᴏɴ, / *Revuë, corrigée & confidérablement augmentée,* / *avec des Figures en Taille-douce.* / *TOME TROISIE'ME.* / [*intaglio engraving*] / A AMSTERDAM, / Aux Dépens de la Compagnie. / M. DCC. XLI. / [*lines 1, 3, 7 and 9 in red*]

12°. sig. πι A-P¹² Q²; pag. [*2*] XX 344 (p.54 numbered '4', 265 '165', 297 '197'); $6 signed, arabic (− Q2); direction line '*Tome III.*'; page catchwords.

[*1*] title; [*2*] blank; I-II Pièces contenues dans le tome III; III-IV Avertissement; V-XVII Epître dédicatoire à monsieur Fakener marchand anglais, depuis, ambassadeur à Constantinople; XVIII-XIX Epître à mademoiselle Gossin, jeune actrice, qui a représenté le rôle de Zaïre avec beaucoup de succès; XX Acteurs; 1-114 Zayre, tragédie; [115]-344 other texts.

Another edition based on w38.

Bn: Rés. Z Beuchot 6 (2,1).

W41C (1742)

ŒUVRES / DE / M. DE VOLTAIRE. / NOUVELLE EDITION, / *Revûe, corrigée & confidérablement / augmentée, avec des Figures en / Taille-douce.* / TOME TROISIEME. / [*typographic ornament*] / A AMSTERDAM, / Aux dépens de la Compagnie. / MDCCXLII. /

[half-title] ŒUVRES / DE / M. DE VOLTAIRE. / TOME TROIS-
IE'ME. /

12°. sig. π^2 A-O^{12}; pag. [4] 314 22; $6 signed, arabic (O2 signed '*',
O3 '*2', O4 '*3', O5 '*4', O6 '*5'); direction line '*Tome III.*' (sig. E '*ome
III.*'); sheet catchwords.

[1] half-title; [2] blank; [3] title; [4] blank; 1 Pièces contenues dans le
tome III; 2 Avertissement; 3-15 Epître dédicatoire à monsieur Fakener
marchand anglais, depuis, ambassadeur à Constantinople; 16-17 Epître
à mademoiselle Le Gossin, jeune actrice qui a représentée le rôle de
Zaïre avec beaucoup de succès; 18 Acteurs; 19-106 Zayre, tragédie;
[107]-314, [1]-22 other texts.

This edition of the *Œuvres* was suppressed at Voltaire's request, but see
the entry next below.

Bn: Rés. Z Bengesco 471 (3).

w42

[engraved title] ŒUVRES / *MÉLÉES DE M*^{R}. / DE VOLTAIRE / *NOUVELLE
EDITION* / *Revûe* / *sur toutes les précedentes* / *et Confidérablement* / *Augmentée.* /
TOME III. / *A GENEVE* / *Chez Bousquet* / 1742. /

12°. sig. π1 A-N^{12} O^2 (± A1, F9, H6); pag. [2] 314 [315-316] (p.295
numbered '195'); $6 signed, arabic (– O2; A1 signed 'A*', F9 '*Tome III.*
*', H6 '*Tome III.* M6*'); direction line '*Tome III.*'; sheet catchwords.

[1] title; [2] blank; 1 Pièces contenues dans le tome III; 2 Avertissement;
3-15 Epître dédicatoire à monsieur Fakener marchand anglais, depuis,
ambassadeur à Constantinople; 16-17 Epître à mademoiselle Le [*sic*]
Gossin, jeune actrice qui a représenté le rôle de Zayre avec beaucoup
de succès; 18 Acteurs; 19-106 Zayre, tragédie; [107]-314 other texts;
[315-316] Errata du troisième volume.

This edition is in general a reissue of the sheets of w41c, with cancels
and other amendments introduced at Voltaire's instigation. The text of
Zaïre is unchanged but the leaf containing the 'Avertissement' was
cancelled and a paragraph added: see below, p.391.

The Stockholm copy carries corrections by Voltaire, at I.133-136, II.87
(of a misprint), II.222 and III.333.

Bn: Rés. Z Beuchot 51; – Z 24569; Stockholm: Litt. fr.

w43

OEUVRES / DE / M^R. DE VOLTAIRE. / Nouvelle Edition, / *Revue, corrigée & confidérablement augmentée,* / *avec des Figures en Tailles-douces.* / *TOME TROISIEME.* / [*woodcut*] / A AMSTERDAM et A LEIPZIG, / *Chez ARKSTÉE et MERKUS.* / MDCCXLIII. / [*in red and black*]

8°. sig. *² A-Aa⁸ Bb⁸ (– Bb2.7 = D3, D2 of volume 2; – Bb3.6 = F1, F2); pag. [*4*] XIX [*xx*] 372; $5 signed, arabic (– *1); page catchwords.

[*1*] title; [*2*] blank; [*3-4*] Pièces contenues dans le tome III.

A reissue of the sheets of w38.

Universitäts- und Stadt-Bibliothek, Köln: 1955 G 1260.

w46

OEUVRES / DIVERSES / DE MONSIEUR / DE VOLTAIRE. / *NOU-VELLE EDITION,* / Recueillie avec foin, enrichie de Piéces / Curieufes, & la feule qui contienne / fes véritables Ouvrages. / *Avec Figures en Taille-Douce.* / TOME TROISIÉME. / [*woodcut, armillary sphere, 28 x 34 mm*] / A LONDRES, / Chez JEAN NOURSE. / M. DCC. XLVI. / [*lines 1, 4, 10 and* 'JEAN NOURSE.' *in red*]

[*half-title*] OEUVRES / DIVERSES / DE MONSIEUR / DE VOL-TAIRE. / [*treble rule, 70 mm*] / *TOME TROISIEME.* /

12°. sig. π² *¹² **⁶ B-X¹² Y⁶ (Y6 blank); pag. [*4*] XXXI [*xxxii*] 492 [*493-494*] (p.334 numbered '335', 363 '263'); $6 signed, arabic (– **4; **3 signed '**5', **5 'Tome III. A', **6 'A2'); direction line '*Tome III.*' (+ M6; sig. F 'Tome III.'); page catchwords.

[*1*] half-title; [*2*] blank; [*3*] title; [*4*] blank; [i] *1r 'ZAYRE. / *TRAGE-DIE*, / Repréfentée pour la premiere fois / le 13. Août 1732. / *Tome III.* *'; [ii] blank; [iii]-IV Avertissement; [v]-XVII Epître dédicatoire à monsieur Fakener marchand anglais, depuis, ambassadeur à Constantinople; [xviii]-XIX Epître à mademoiselle Gossin, jeune actrice qui a représenté le rôle de Zaïre avec beaucoup de succès; XX-XXXI Seconde lettre à monsieur Fakener, tirée d'une seconde édition de Zayre; [xxxii] Acteurs; [1]-94 Zayre, tragédie; [95]-492 other texts; [493-494] Fautes à corriger.

Voltaire may have had some hand in this edition (see *Lettres philosophiques*, ed. G. Lanson and A. M. Rousseau, Paris 1964, i.XVIII). The text of *Zaïre*

346

follows the tradition set by w38, with new readings at l.79-80 of the epistle to Fawkener, l.24 of that to Mlle Gaussin and at i.100, ii.368, v.88 and 117.

Bn: Rés. Z Beuchot 8 (3); Staatsbibliothek, Bamberg.

47N

ZAYRE, / TRAGÉDIE FRANCAISE, / Qui fera reprefentée devant / LEURS MAJESTÉS / Sur le Theatre Royal de Portici / *Dans le courrant des mois d'Avril,* / *& de May*, 1747. / [*woodcut*] / [*rule*] / *Imprimée A Naples & fe vend chés Jacques Brun* / *Libraire français rüe Tolede vis a vis le* / *Palais de S.E. le Prince de Stilliano.* / [*rule*] / Avec permiffion de Sa Majefté. /

8°. sig. π1 a⁴ A-F⁸; pag. 96 (p.86 numbered '68'); $4 signed, arabic (– a2-4, E4, F4); page catchwords.

[*1*] title; [*2*] blank; [*3-7*] A sa majesté la reyne (signed, p.[*7*], Valentin Delahaye); [*8-9*] Noms des personnages, et des acteurs; [*10*] blank; 1-96 Zayre, tragédie.

Biblioteca universitaria, Messina: 155 A 23.

48P1

ZAYRE, / TRAGEDIE / REPRE'SENTE'E A PARIS, / pour la premére [*sic*] fois, aux Mois d'Août, / Novembre & Décembre 1732. / *Par Monfieur DE VOLTAIRE.* / NOUVELLE E'DITION, / *Revuë & corrigée fur toutes celles qui ont paru jusqu'à* / *ce jour.* / [*woodcut, martial emblems, 77 x 58 mm*] / A PARIS, / Chez Jean-Baptiste Bauche, à la defcente du / Pont neuf, proche les Auguftins, à Saint Jean- / Baptifte dans le défert. / [*rule, 88 mm*] / M. DCC. XLVIII. / *AVEC PRIVILEGE DU ROY.* /

8°. sig. A-H⁴; pag. xj 12-64; $2 signed, arabic (– A1, G2); sheet catchwords.

[i] title; [ii] Avertissement; iij-x Epître dédicatoire à monsieur Faukener, marchand anglais, depuis ambassadeur d'Angleterre à Constantinople; xj Epître à mademoiselle Gossin, jeune actrice, qui a représenté le rôle de Zayre avec beaucoup de succès; 12 Personnages; 13-64 Zayre, tragédie; 64 Approbation.

Arsenal: GD 19341; ImV.

48P2

ZAYRE, / *TRAGEDIE*, / REPRÉSENTÉE A PARIS, / pour la premiere fois, aux mois d'Août, / Novembre & Décembre 1732. / *Par Monſieur de VOLTAIRE*. / NOUVELLE ÉDITION, / *Revuë & corrigée ſur toutes celles qui ont paru / juſqu'à ce jour*. / [*woodcut, 53 x 33 mm*] / *A PARIS*, / Chez JEAN-BAPTISTE BAUCHE, à la deſcente / du Pont neuf, proche les Auguſtins, à Saint / Jean-Baptiſte dans le Déſert. / [*thin-thick-thin rule, 63 mm*] / M. DCC. XLVIII. / *AVEC PRIVILEGE DU ROY*. /

8°. pag. 72.

Bibliothèque publique et universitaire, Neuchâtel: D3558.

w48D

OEUVRES / DE / Mr. DE VOLTAIRE / *NOUVELLE EDITION* / REVUE, CORRIGÉE / ET CONSIDERABLEMENT AUGMENTÉE / PAR L'AUTEUR / ENRICHIE DE FIGURES EN TAILLE-DOUCE. / *TOME CINQUIEME*. / [*engraving, plate size 81 x 72 mm*] / *A DRESDE 1748*. / CHEZ GEORGE CONRAD WALTHER / LIBRAIRE DU ROI. / *AVEC PRIVILEGE*. / [*lines 1, 3, 5, 7, 9, 11 and 13 in red*]

8°. sig. π² A-Gg⁸ Hh⁴ (± V5); pag. [4] 488 (p.289 numbered '189'); $5 signed, arabic (– Hh4); direction line 'VOLT. Tom. V.'; page catchwords.

[*1*] title; [*2*] blank; [*3*] Table des pièces contenues dans le tome V; [*4*] blank; [1] A1r 'ZAYRE. / *TRAGEDIE*. / *Repréſentée pour la premiere fois le 13. Août / 1732*. / VOLT. Tom. V.   A   AVER-'; [2] Avertissement; 3-12 Epître dédicatoire à monsieur Fakener, marchand anglais, depuis ambassadeur à Constantinople; 13-14 Epître à mademoiselle Gossin, jeune actrice qui a représenté le rôle de Zayre avec beaucoup de succès; 15-23 Seconde lettre au même monsieur Fakener, alors ambassadeur à Constantinople, tirée d'une seconde édition de Zayre; [24] Acteurs; [25]-112 Zayre, tragédie; [113]-488 other texts; 488 Fautes à corriger.

An edition produced with Voltaire's participation. *Zaïre* follows w38, with new readings at I.100, 268, III.95-96, 281, 333, IV.124, V.88 and 117. The epistle to Fawkener has new readings at l.35, 79-80, 252-253.

Bn: Rés. Z Beuchot 12 (5); Taylor: V1 1748 (5).

348

W48R

[COLLECTION / *COMPLETE* / DES ŒUVRES / *de Monsieur* / DE VOLTAIRE, / NOUVELLE ÉDITION, / *Augmentée de ſes dernieres Pieces de Théâtre,* / *& enrichie de 61 Figures en taille-douce.* / TOME TROISIEME. / *PREMIERE PARTIE.* / [*typographic ornament*] / *A AMSTERDAM,* / AUX DÉPENS DE LA COMPAGNIE. / [*thick-thin rule, 48 mm*] / M. DCC. LXIV. /]

12°. sig. π1 A-T¹² V² (– A10; A9 + *A⁶; O11 + *O²); pag. [2] XXX 312 [313-314] *315 315* *315 315* 315-440 (p.110 numbered '101'); $6 signed, arabic (– V2; *A1 signed '*Tome III.*   *A7', *A2 '*A8', *A3 '*A9', *O1 '*Tome III.*   *O7'); direction line '*Tome III.*'; page catchwords.

[1] title; [2] blank; [i] A1*r* 'LA / ZAYRE, / *TRAGÉDIE.* / *Tome III.*   A   AVER-'; [ii] blank; III-IV Avertissement; V-XVII Epître dédicatoire à monsieur Fakener, marchand anglais, depuis ambassadeur à Constantinople; XVIII-XIX Epître à mademoiselle Gossin, jeune actrice, qui a représenté le rôle de Zaïre avec beaucoup de succès; XX-XXIX II épître à monsieur Fakener, tirée d'une seconde édition de Zayre (text added by sig. *A⁶); XXX Acteurs; [1]-114 Zaïre, tragédie; [115]-440 other texts.

No copy of the original (1748) issue of this edition is known. It was suppressed at Voltaire's request (see D3667, D3677, D3669, D3884), but the sheets reappeared in 1764, under new titles, and with corrections, additions and supplementary volumes. The description given above is that of the 1764 version.

With one exception, the sheets of *Zaïre* date from 1748: leaf A10, which must have contained the last page of the epistle to Mlle Gaussin and (presumably) a list of characters, was removed and replaced by a gathering of six leaves (*A⁶). This gathering inserts the second epistle to Fawkener.

Gesamthochschul-bibliothek, Kassel: 1948 C 266 (4).

W50

LA / HENRIADE / ET AUTRES / OUVRAGES / *DU MÊME AU-TEUR.* / NOUVELLE EDITION, / Revuë, corrigée, avec des augmentations conſiderables, / particuliéres & incorporées dans tout ce Recueil, / *Enrichi de 56. Figures.* / TOME CINQUIE'ME. / [*woodcut, face in framed sun-burst, 43 x 30 mm*] / A LONDRES, / *AUX DE'PENS DE LA SOCIETE'*. / M. DCC. LI. / [*lines 2, 4, 6, 10, 11 and 13 in red*]

[*half-title*] OEUVRES / DE / MONSIEUR / DE VOLTAIRE. / *TOME CINQUIE'ME*. /

12°. sig. π^2 *^{2} A-L^{12} $^1\pi^2$ M-V^{12} X^4 $^2\pi$1; pag. [*8*] XXXIV 230 [*4*] [231-232] 233-453 [454-455] (p.134 numbered '234', 152 '252', 293 '193', 351 '451'); \$6 signed, arabic (– *2, X3-4; K3 signed 'K'); direction line 'VOLT. *Tome V.*'; page catchwords.

[*1*] half-title; [*2*] blank; [*3*] title; [*4*] blank; [*5-8*] Table des pièces et titres contenus au tome cinquième; [i] A1r 'ZAYRE, / *TRAGÉDIE*. / *Représentée pour la premiére fois / le* 13. *Août* 1732. / VOLT. *Tome V*. A AVER-'; [ii] blank; III-IV Avertissement; V-XVIII I. Epître dédicatoire à monsieur Fakener, marchand anglais, depuis ambassadeur à Constantinople; XIX-XX Epître à mademoiselle Gossin, jeune actrice, qui a représenté le rôle de Zaïre avec beaucoup de succès; XXI-XXXIII II. Epître au même monsieur Fakener, alors ambassadeur à Constantinople, tirée d'une seconde édition de Zayre; XXXIV Acteurs; [1]-114 Zayre, tragédie; [115]-453 other texts; [454] blank; [455] Errata du tome V.

There is no evidence that Voltaire was involved in the preparation of this edition.

ImV: A 1751/1 (5); Bibliothèque municipale, Grenoble.

W51

ŒUVRES / DE / M. DE VOLTAIRE. / NOUVELLE EDITION, / Confidérablement augmentée, / *Enrichie de Figures en taille-douce*. / TOME V. / [*typographic ornament*] / [*thick-thin rule, 57 mm*] / M. DCC. LI. / [*thin-thick rule, 57 mm*] / [*lines 1, 3, 5, 7 and 8 in red*]

[*half-title*] ŒUVRES / DE / M. DE VOLTAIRE. /

12°. sig. π^2 A-Ll^{8,4}; pag. [*4*] 408 (p.232 numbered '32'); \$4,2 signed, roman; direction line '*Tome V.*' (sig. V '*Tome V*'); sheet catchwords.

[1] A1r 'ZAYRE, / *TRAGÉDIE*, / Repréfentée pour la premiére fois / le Mardi 13. août 1732. / *Tome V*. A'; [2] blank; [3]-4 Avertissement; 5-18 I. Epître dédicatoire à monsieur Fakener, marchand anglais, depuis ambassadeur à Constantinople; 19-20 Epître à mademoiselle Gossin, jeune actrice, qui a représenté le rôle de Zayre avec beaucoup de succès;

21-35 II. Epître au même monsieur Fakener, alors ambassadeur à Constantinople, tirée d'une seconde édition de Zayre; [36] Acteurs; [37]-124 Zayre, tragédie; [125]-408 other texts.

An edition produced in Paris by Michel Lambert, with the collaboration of Voltaire. New readings (some of them unique) are found at I.102, 103, II.6, III.95, 333, IV.32, 77, 186 and V.30, and at l.61 and 197 of the epistle to Fawkener.

Taylor: V1 1751 (5).

52B

ZAYRE, / *TRAGÉDIE.* / Par M. DE VOLTAIRE. / *Repréfentée pour la prémiere fois le 13 / Août 1732.* / [*typographic ornament*] / A BERLIN, / Aux dépens de la Compagnie. / [*thick-thin rule, 60 mm*] / *M. DCC. LII.* /

12°. sig. A-D¹² E⁸; pag. 112; $5 signed, roman (– A1, E5); sheet catchwords.

[1] title; [2] Avertissement; 3-14 I. épître dédicatoire à monsieur Fakener, marchand anglais, depuis ambassadeur à Constantinople; 15 Epître à Melle Gossin, jeune actrice, qui a représenté le rôle de Zayre avec beaucoup de succès; 16-25 II. épître au même monsieur Fakener, alors ambassadeur à Constantinople. Tirée d'une seconde édition de Zayre; [26] Acteurs; 27-112 Zayre, tragédie.

Taylor: V3 O3 1752.

52P

ZAYRE, / TRAGEDIE / REPRÉSENTÉE A PARIS, / pour la premiere fois, aux mois d'Août, / Novembre & Décembre 1732. / *Par Monfieur DE VOLTAIRE.* / NOUVELLE E'DITION. / *Revuë & corrigée fur toutes celles qui ont paru jufqu'à / ce jour.* / [*woodcut, martial emblems, 75 x 56 mm*] / A PARIS, / Chez JEAN-BAPTISTE BAUCHE, à la defcente du / Pont neuf, proche les Auguftins, à Saint Jean- / Baptifte dans le défert. / [*rule, 85 mm*] / M. DCC. LII. / *AVEC PRIVILE'GE DU ROI.* /

8°. sig. A-H⁴; pag. 64; $2 signed, arabic (– A1, G2); sheet catchwords.

[i] title; [ii] Avertissement; iij-x Epître dédicatoire à monsieur Faukener, marchand anglais, depuis ambassadeur d'Angleterre à Constantinople; xj Epître à mademoiselle Gossin, jeune actrice, qui a représenté le rôle

351

de Zayre avec beaucoup de succès; 12 Personnages; 13-64 Zayre, tragédie; 64 Approbation.

Universitätsbibliothek, Marburg: XVIC 911 q.

52V

ZAYRE. / *TRAGEDIE.* / EN CINQ ACTES. / [*woodcut, 70 x 54 mm*] / *VIENNE EN AUTRICHE,* / Chez Jean Pierre van Ghelen, Imprimeur / de la Cour de sa Majesté Imperiale / & Royale. / [*thick-thin rule, 65 mm*] / M D CC LII. /

8°. sig. A-E⁸ F²; pag. 84; $5 signed, arabic (– A1); page catchwords.

[1] title; [2] Acteurs; [3]-84 Zayre, tragédie.

Österreichische Nationalbibliothek: 214760.

W52

OEUVRES / DE / Mʳ· DE VOLTAIRE / *NOUVELLE EDITION* / REVUE, CORRIGE'E / ET CONSIDERABLEMENT AUGMENTE'E / PAR L'AUTEUR / ENRICHIE DE FIGURES EN TAILLE-DOUCE. / *TOME SEPTIEME.* / [*intaglio engraving*] / *A DRESDE 1752.* / CHEZ GEORGE CONRAD WALTHER / LIBRAIRE DU ROI. / *AVEC PRIVILEGE.* / [*lines 1, 3, 5, 7, 9, 11 and 13 in red*]

12°. sig. π² A-Nn⁸,⁴ Oo⁴ (± A4); pag. [4] 440 (p.350 numbered '450', 351 '451', 352 '452'; p.158 not numbered); $5,3 signed, arabic (E5 signed 'Ee5'); direction line 'VOLT. Tom. VII.' (+ A4 cancel; M1 '. Tom. VII.'); page catchwords.

[1] title; [2] blank; [3] Table des pieces contenues dans le tome VII; [4] blank; [1] A1r 'ZAYRE, / TRAGEDIE. / *Représentée pour la premiere fois le* / *13. Août 1732.* / VOLT. Tom. VII. A   AVER-'; Zayre, tragédie; [2] Avertissement; 3-12 Epître dédicatoire à monsieur Fakener, marchand anglais, depuis ambassadeur à Constantinople; 13-14 Epître à mademoiselle Gossin, jeune actrice qui a représenté le rôle de Zayre avec beaucoup de succès; 15-23 Seconde lettre au même monsieur Fakener, alors ambassadeur à Constantinople, tirée d'une seconde édition de Zayre; [24] Acteurs; [25]-96 Zayre, tragédie; [97]-440 other texts; 440 Fautes à corriger.

At the foot of p.440, 'Imprimé à Leipsic chez Jean Gottlob Immanuel Breitkopf, 1752.'

A new edition by the publisher of w48D, in a smaller format.

Vienna: *38.L.1.

T53

Le Théâtre de M. de Voltaire. Nouvelle édition qui contient un recueil complet de toutes les pièces de théâtre que l'auteur a données jusqu'ici. Amsterdam, chez François-Canut Richoff, près le comptoir de Cologne, 1753.

Only volume 4 of this edition is known, containing *Samson, Pandore, La Prude, Rome sauvée* and *Le Duc de Foix.*

Bn: Yf 12337.

55B

ZAYRE, / *TRAGÉDIE* / *Par Monſieur* DE VOLTAIRE. / Repréſentée pour la premiére fois le 13. / Août 1732. / [*woodcut, indians and cargo, 58 x 34 mm*] / A PARIS, / Et ſe vend à BRUXELLES; / Chez PHILIPPE-JOSEPH LEMMENS, Imprimeur / & Libraire ruë de l'Evêque. M.D.CC.LV. / [*thick-thin rule, 40 mm*] / *Avec Approbation.* /

8°. sig. A-I⁴; pag. 72; $2 signed, arabic (– A1); sheet catchwords.

[1] title; [2] Acteurs; [3]-72 Zayre, tragédie; 72 Approbation.

Bound with other works under a collective title: 'NOUVEAU / RE-CUEIL / CHOISI ET MÊLÉ / DES MEILLEURES PIECES / DU / NOUVEAU THEATRE / FRANCOIS / ET / ITALIEN, / Aussi de pluſieurs Auteurs Modernes. / TOME III. / [*woodcut, 47 x 31 mm*] / A PARIS, / [*rule, 71 mm*] / Et ſe vend à BRUXELLES, / Chez PHILIPPE JOSEPH LEMMENS, Imprimeur / & Libraire, ruë de l'Evêque. 1747.'

Br: VI 59141 A.

55M

ZAYRE, / *TRAGÉDIE.* / PAR DE VOLTAIRE. / Repréſentée à Munich / en 1755. / [*woodcut, head in cartouche, 69 x 54 mm*] / [*rule, 78 mm*] / [*rule, 51 mm*] / Chez JEAN JAQUES VÖTTER, Imprimeur de la Cour, / & des Etats de Baviére. /

8°. sig. A-G⁸ H⁴; pag. 119; $5 signed, arabic (– A1, H4); page catchwords.

[1] title; [2] Acteurs; [3]-119 Zayre, tragédie.

Bayerische Staatsbibliothek, München: Bav. 4010 XI (3).

56P

ZAYRE, / TRAGEDIE / *DE M. DE VOLTAIRE*, / NOUVELLE ÉDI-TION, / Revuë, corrigée & augmentée par l'Auteur. / *Repréfentée pour la premiere fois par* / *les Comédiens Ordinaires du Roi,* / *le 13. Août 1732.* / *Eft etiam crudelis amor.* / [*thick-thin rule, 59 mm*] / Le Prix eft de 30 f. / [*thin-thick rule, 59 mm*] / [*typographic ornament*] / A PARIS, / Chez DUCHESNE, Libraire, rue S. Jacques, / au-deffous de la Fontaine S. Benoît, / au Temple du Goût. / [*thick-thin rule, 57 mm*] / M. DCC. LVI. / *Avec Approbation & Privilége du Roi.* /

[*half-title*] ZAIRE, / TRAGEDIE / *DE M. DE VOLTAIRE.* /

12°. sig. π^2 A-D^{12} (vertical chain-lines in π^2); pag. [*4*] 96; $6 signed, arabic (– C3; B5 signed 'C5', D6 'D5'); direction line '*Tome III.*'; page catchwords.

[*1*] half-title; [*2*] On trouve chez le même libraire [...]; [*3*] title; [*4*] blank; [1] A1r 'ZAYRE, / *TRAGEDIE*; / Repréfentée pour la premiere fois / le 13. Août 1732. / *Tome III.*   A'; [2] Acteurs; [3]-96 Zayre, tragédie.

Apparently a fragment of an unknown collection, perhaps of Voltaire's works: the errors in the signatures suggest that this separate edition was reimposed from the formes of the collection; on p. 96 there is a catchword for 'ALZIRE,'. The sheets of this edition were reissued in 1760: see 60P.

Arsenal: Rf 14182.

W56

OUVRAGES / DRAMATIQUES / AVEC / *LES PIECES RELATI-VES A CHACUN.* / TOME SECOND. / [*woodcut, lyre and trumpets, 75 x 62 mm*] / [*thick-thin rule, 57 mm*] / *MDCCLVI.* / [*lines 2, 4 and rule in red*]

[*half-title*] COLLECTION / COMPLETTE / DES / ŒUVRES / *de Mr. de VOLTAIRE,* / PREMIERE EDITION. / *TOME HUITIEME.* /

8°. sig. π^2 A-Cc^8 Dd^6; pag. [*4*] 428 (p.7 not numbered; p.267 numbered '67'); $4 signed, arabic; direction line '*Théatre* Tom. II.' (sigs R, Y, Bb '*Theatre* Tom. II.'); page catchwords.

354

[*1*] half-title; [*2*] blank; [*3*] title; [*4*] blank; [1] A1*r* 'ZAYRE, / TRAGE-
DIE, / *Repréfentée pour la premiére fois le* 13. / *Août* 1732. / *Théatre* Tom.
II. A AVER-'; [2] Avertissement; 3-14 Epître dédicatoire à monsieur
Fakener, marchand anglais, depuis ambassadeur à Constantinople; 15-
16 Epître à mademoiselle Gossin, jeune actrice qui a représenté le rôle
de Zayre avec beaucoup de succès; 17-27 Seconde lettre au même
monsieur Fakener, alors ambassadeur à Constantinople, tirée d'une
seconde édition de Zayre; [28] Acteurs; [29]-118 Zayre, tragédie; [119]-
426 other texts; 427-428 Ouvrages dramatiques contenus dans ce volume: avec les pièces qui sont rélatives à chacun.

The first printing of the Cramer *Collection complette*, produced under
Voltaire's supervision.

Changes to the text were made at I.102, II.11, III.149 and V.14.

Bn: Z 24583.

W57G1

OUVRAGES / DRAMATIQUES / AVEC / *LES PIECES RELATI-*
VES A CHACUN. / TOME SECOND. / [*woodcut, globe in cartouche, 86*
x 76 mm] / [*thick-thin rule, 58 mm*] / *MDCCLVII.* / [*lines 2, 4 and rule in*
red]

[*half-title*] COLLECTION / COMPLETTE / DES / ŒUVRES / *de Mr.*
de VOLTAIRE, / PREMIERE EDITION. / *TOME HUITIEME.* /

8°. sig. π^2 A-Cc^8 Dd^6; pag. [*4*] 428 (p.17 numbered '255'); $4 signed,
arabic; direction line '*Théatre* Tom. II.' (sigs A, E, M, S, Z, Dd '*Théâtre*
Tom. II.'); page catchwords.

[*1*] half-title; [*2*] blank; [*3*] title; [*4*] blank; [1] A1*r* 'ZAYRE, / TRAGÈ-
DIE, / *Repréfentée pour la premiére fois le* 13. / *Août* 1732. / *Théatre* Tom.
II. A AVER-'; [2] Avertissement; 3-14 Epître dédicatoire à monsieur
Fakener, marchand anglais, depuis ambassadeur à Constantinople; 15-
16 Epître à mademoiselle Gossin, jeune actrice qui a représenté le rôle
de Zayre avec beaucoup de succès; '255'[=17]-27 Seconde lettre au
même monsieur Fakener, alors ambassadeur à Constantinople: tirée
d'une seconde édition de Zayre; [28] Acteurs; [29]-118 Zayre, tragédie;
[119]-426 other texts; 427-428 Ouvrages dramatiques contenus en ce
volume: avec les pièces qui sont rélatives à chacun.

This new edition of w56 may be distinguished from the other 1757

Cramer setting of this volume by the woodcuts: p.16 'a'; p.64 'g'; p.82 'j' (for reproductions, see Voltaire 48, p.105-106).

Leningrad: 11-74; Taylor: V1 1757 8A (lacks π1); Bodleian: 27524 e 81.

W57G2

OUVRAGES / DRAMATIQUES / AVEC / *LES PIECES RELATI-VES A CHACUN.* / TOME SECOND. / [*woodcut, globe in cartouche, 86 x 76 mm*] / [*thick-thin rule, 58 mm*] / *MDCCLVII.* / [*lines 2, 4 and rule in red*]

[*half-title*] COLLECTION / COMPLETTE / DES / ŒUVRES / *de Mr. de VOLTAIRE,* / PREMIERE EDITION. / *TOME HUITIEME.* /

8°. sig. π² A-Cc⁸ Dd⁶; pag. [*4*] 428 (p.322 numbered '332'); $4 signed, arabic; direction line '*Théatre* Tom. II.' (sig. G '*Thèatre* Tom. II.'; sig. Dd '*Théâtre* Tom. II.'); page catchwords.

[*1*] half-title; [*2*] blank; [*3*] title; [*4*] blank; [1] A1r 'ZAYRE, / *TRAGÉ-DIE,* / *Repréſentée pour la première fois* / *le* 13. *Août* 1732. / *Théatre* Tom. II.   A   AVER-'; [2] Avertissement; 3-14 Epître dédicatoire à monsieur Fakener, marchand anglais, depuis ambassadeur à Constantinople; 15-16 Epître à mademoiselle Gossin, jeune actrice qui a représenté le rôle de Zayre avec beaucoup de succès; 17-27 Seconde lettre au même monsieur Fakener, alors ambassadeur à Constantinople, tirée d'une seconde édition de Zayre; [28] Acteurs; [29]-118 Zayre, tragédie; [119]-426 other texts; 427-428 Ouvrages dramatiques contenus en ce volume: avec les pièces qui sont rélatives à chacun.

See the entry next above. Woodcuts in this setting include: p.16 'i'; p.64 'j'; p.82 'g'.

Taylor: V1 1757 8A.

W57P

ŒUVRES / DE / M. DE VOLTAIRE, / SECONDE EDITION / Conſidérablement augmentée, / *Enrichie de Figures en taille-douce.* / TOME II. / Contenant ſes Piéces de Théâtre. / [*typographic ornament*] / [*thick-thin rule, 58 mm*] / M. DCC. LVII. / [*thin-thick rule, 57 mm*] / [*lines 1, 3, 5, 7 and 9 in red*]

[*half-title*] ŒUVRES / DE / M. DE VOLTAIRE. /

12°. sig. π^2 A-Nn^{8,4}; pag. [*4*] 431 (p.61 numbered '6', 66 '6', 108 '106' 109 '107', 139 '13', 291 '192'); $4,2 signed, roman (Z2 signed 'Zji'); direction line '*Tome II.*'; sheet catchwords.

[*1*] half-title; [*2*] blank; [*3*] title; [*4*] Pièces contenues dans ce volume; [1]-319 other texts; [320] blank; [321] Dd5*r* 'ZAYRE, / *TRAGEDIE*, / Représentée pour la première fois le 13 / Août 1732.'; [322] Avertissement; 323-333 Epître dédicatoire à monsieur Fakener, marchand anglais, depuis ambassadeur à Constantinople; 334-335 Epître à mademoiselle Gossin, jeune actrice, qui a représenté le rôle de Zayre avec beaucoup de succès; 336-347 Seconde lettre au même M. Fakener, alors ambassadeur à Constantinople, tirée d'une seconde édition de Zayre; 348 Acteurs; [349]-431 Zayre, tragédie.

An edition produced in Paris by or for Michel Lambert.

Bn: Z 24643.

58P

ZAYRE, / *TRAGÉDIE* / REPRÉSENTÉE A PARIS, / Pour la premiere fois, aux mois d'Août, / Novembre & Décembre 1732. / *Par Monsieur DE VOLTAIRE*. / NOUVELLE ÉDITION. / *Revue & corrigée sur toutes celles qui ont paru jusqu'à / ce jour.* / [*woodcut, shining sun, motto 'Indesinenter', 55 x 45 mm*] / A PARIS, / Chez JEAN-BAPTISTE BAUCHE, à la descente du / Pont neuf, proche les Augustins, à Saint Jean- / Baptiste dans le désert. / [*treble rule, 58 mm*] / M. DCC. LVIII. / *AVEC PRIVILEGE DU ROI.* /

8°. sig. A-H^4; pag. xj 12-64; $1 signed (– A1); sheet catchwords.

[i] title; [ii] Avertissement; iij-x Epître dédicatoire à monsieur Faukener, marchand anglais, depuis ambassadeur d'Angleterre à Constantinople; xj Epître à mademoiselle Gossin, jeune actrice, qui a représenté le rôle de Zayre avec beaucoup de succès; 12 Personnages; 13-64 Zayre, tragédie.

Collection of Jean-Daniel Candaux, Geneva.

60A

G. L. van Roosbroeck, 'Notes on Voltaire', *Mln* 39 (1924), p.9, lists a 1760 edition in 50 pages by Chambeau of Avignon, from a copy in the University of Minnesota. We have been unable to trace this or any other copy of the edition.

60P

ZAYRE, / TRAGÉDIE / *DE M. DE VOLTAIRE*; / *Repréfentée pour la première fois par les* / *Comédiens Ordinaires du Roi,* / *le* 13. *Août* 1732. / Nouvelle Edition, revue, corrigée & / augmentée par l'Auteur. / *Eft etiam crudelis amor.* / [*thick-thin rule, 61 mm*] / Le Prix eft de 30 fols. / [*thin-thick rule, 61 mm*] / [*typographic ornament*] / A PARIS, / Chez DUCHESNE, Libraire, rue Saint Jacques, / au-deffous de la Fontaine S. Benoît, / au Temple du Goût. / [*thick-thin rule, 61 mm*] / M. DCC. LX. / *Avec Approbation & Privilége du Roi.* /

12°. sig. a¹² A-D¹²; pag. 24 96; $6 signed, arabic (– a1, C3; B5 signed 'C5', D6 'D5'); direction line '*Tome III.*'; page catchwords.

[1] title; [2] On trouve chez le même libraire [...]; [3]-12 Epître dédicatoire à monsieur Fakener; marchand angalis, depuis ambassadeur à Constantinople; 13-14 Epître à Melle Gaussin, jeune actrice, qui a représenté le rôle de Zayre avec beaucoup de succes; 15-24 Second lettre au même M. Fakener, alors ambassadeur à Constantinople, tirée d'une seconde édition de Zayre; [1]-96 as 56P.

A reissue of the sheets of 56P, with the addition of the preliminary texts.

Bibliothèque municipale Amiens: BL 2062A.

T62

[*within ornamented border*] LE / THÉATRE / DE / M. DE VOLTAIRE. / *NOUVELLE ÉDITION.* / Qui contient un Recuëil complet de toutes / les Pièces de Théâtre que l'Auteur a / données jufqu'ici. / TOME SE-COND. / [*woodcut, basket of fruit, 37 x 33 mm*] / *A AMSTERDAM*, / Chez FRANÇOIS-CANUT RICHOFF, / près le Comptoir de Cologne. / [*thick-thin rule, 53 mm*] / M. DCC. LXII. /

12°. sig. ã² A-Z⁸ Aa² (Aa2 blank); pag. [4] 370; $4 signed, arabic (– ã1, A3-4; ã2 signed 'aij', D2 'C2', R2 'E2'); direction line '*Théâtre. Tome II.*' (sigs N, T '*Théâtre. Tom. II.*'); sheet catchwords.

[1] title; [2] blank; [3-4] Table des ouvrages dramatiques contenus en ce volume: avec les pièces qui sont rélatives à chacun; [1] A1r '*ZAYRE,* / *TRAGEDIE.* / *Représentée pour la premiére fois le* 13. / *Août* 1732. / *Théâtre. Tome II.* A'; [2] Avertissement; 3-13 Epître dédicatoire à monsieur Fakener, marchand anglais, depuis ambassadeur à Constantinople; 14-15 Epître à mademoiselle Gossin, jeune actrice qui a représenté le rôle

de Zayre avec beaucoup de succès; 16-27 Seconde lettre au même Mr Fakener, alors ambassadeur à Constantinople, tirée d'une seconde édition de Zayre; [28] Acteurs; 29-102 Zayre, tragédie; [103]-370 other texts.

Another 'Richoff' collection of the theatre, possibly printed in Rouen.

Bn: Rés. Z Bengesco 123 (2).

63A

ZAYRE, / *TRAGÉDIE* / PAR M. DE VOLTAIRE, / *Repréfentée pour la première fois sur le Théâtre / des Comédiens Français ordinaires du Roi, aux / Mois d'Août & Décembre 1742.* / [*type ornament*] / A AVIGNON, / Chez LOUIS CHAMBEAU, Imprimeur-Libraire / prés les RR. PP. Jéfuites. / [*treble rule, 50 mm*] / M. DCC. LXIII. /

8°. sig. A-F⁴ G1; pag. 50 (p.45 numbered '27'); $2 signed, arabic (F2 signed 'E2'); sheet catchwords.

[1] title; [2] Acteurs; 3-50 Zayre, tragédie.

Biblioteca nazionale centrale, Firenze (G1 defective with loss of text).

64P

ZAYRE, / *TRAGÈDIE,* / EN VERS / ET / EN CINQ ACTES. / Par M. DE VOLTAIRE. / [*typographic ornament*] / A PARIS, / CHEZ LES LIBRAI-RES ASSOCIÉS. / [*thick-thin rule, 47 mm*] / M. DCC. LXIV. /

12°. sig. A-C¹² (C11-12 blank); pag. 68; $5 signed, roman (– A1); sheet catchwords.

[1] title; [2] Acteurs; 3-68 Zayre, tragédie.

ImV: BE 19 (7); Taylor: V3 A2 1764 (32).

T64A

[*within ornamented border*] / LE / THEATRE / DE / M. DE VOLTAIRE. / *NOUVELLE EDITION.* / Qui contient un Recuëil complet de toutes / les Piéces de Théâtre que l'Auteur a / données jufqu'ici. / TOME SE-COND. / [*woodcut, two cherubs embracing, 32 x 23 mm*] / A AMSTER-DAM, / Chez FRANÇOIS-CANUT RICHOFF, / près le comptoir de Cologne. / [*thick-thin rule, 44 mm*] / M. DCC. LXIV. /

12°. sig. a² A-Gg⁸,⁴ Hh⁶; pag. [*4*] 370 (p.138 numbered '318', 208 '108', 209 '109', 244 '44', 291 '29'); $4,2 signed, arabic (– a1, K2, Hh4; a2 signed 'Aij'); direction line '*Théâtre. Tome II.*'; sheet catchwords.

[*1*] title; [2] blank; [*3-4*] Table des ouvrages dramatiques contenus en ce volume: avec les pièces qui sont rélatives à chacun; [1] A1*r* 'ZAYRE, / TRAGEDIE. / *Repréfentée pour la premiére fois le* / 13. *Août* 1732. / *Théâtre. Tome II.* A'; [2] Avertissement; 3-12 Epître dédicatoire à monsieur Fakener, marchand anglais, depuis ambassadeur à Constantinople; 13-14 Epître à mademoiselle Gossin, jeune actrice qui a représenté le rôle de Zayre avec beaucoup de succès; 15-24 Seconde lettre au même Mr Fakener, alors ambassadeur à Constantinople, tiré d'une seconde édition de Zayre; [25] blank, but for signature '*Théâtre. Tome II.* C'; [26] Acteurs; 27-102 Zayre, tragédie; [103]-371 other texts.

ImV: BC 1764/1 (2); BL: 11735 aa 1 (2).

T64G

LE / THÉATRE / DE MONSIEUR / *DE VOLTAIRE.* / NOUVELLE ÉDITION, / *Qui contient un Récueil complet de tou-* / *tes les Pièces que l'Auteur a données* / *jufqu'à ce jour.* / TOME SECOND. / [*woodcut, two cherubs and suspended globe, 28 x 22 mm, as in volume 6*] / *A GÉNÉVE,* / Chez les Freres Cramer, Libraires. / [*thick-thin rule, composed of 3 elements, 46 mm*] / M. DCC. LXIV. /

12°. sig. π1 A-Aa⁶ Bb²; pag. [2] 291 [292] (p.14 numbered '41'); $3 signed, roman (– Bb2; O2 signed Niij', P2 'Piij'); direction line '*Tome II.*' (sigs E, L, Bb '*Tome II*'; sig. Y '*Tome I.*'); sheet catchwords.

[*1*] title; [2] blank; 1-100 other texts; [101] I3*r* 'ZAYRE, / *TRAGEDIE.* / *Repréfentée pour la premiere fois le* 13. / *Août* 1732. / I iij'; [102] Avertissement; 103-114 Epître dédicatoire à monsieur Fakener, marchand anglais, depuis ambassadeur à Constantinople; 115 Epître à Mlle Gossin, jeune actrice, qui joua le rôle de Zaïre avec beaucoup de succès; [116] Acteurs; 117-194 Zayre, tragédie; 195-205 Seconde lettre à monsieur Fakener, ambassadeur à Constantinople; [206] blank; [207]-291 other texts; [292] Table des pièces contenues dans le II. volume.

The imprint is spurious.

Arsenal: Rf 14092 (2).

T64P

ŒUVRES / *DE* / THÉATRE / *DE* / M. DE VOLTAIRE, / *De l'Académie Française, de celle de Berlin,* / *& de la Société Royale de Londres, &c.* / TOME PREMIER. / [*woodcut, the 'Temple du goût', 47 x 28 mm*] / A PARIS, / Chez Duchesne, Libraire, rue Saint Jacques, / au-deſſous de la Fontaine Saint Benoît, / au Temple du Goût. / [*thick-thin rule, 47 mm*] / M. DCC. LXIV. / *Avec Approbation & Privilége du Roi.* / [*lines 1, 3, 5, 8, 9 and 13 in red*]

12°. sig. a⁴ A-R¹² S⁶; pag. [*8*] 420; signed $6 arabic (– a1, a3-4, D4, O5, S4-6; a2 signed 'aij'); direction line '*Tome I.*'; sheet catchwords.

[*1*] title; [*2*] blank; [*3*] Avis du libraire sur cette edition; [*4*] Approbation (24 novembre 1764, Marin); [*4-6*] Privilège du roi; [*7*] Table des pieces qui composent le théatre de M. de Voltaire; [*8*] Catalogue des ouvrages de M. de Voltaire, qui se trouvent chez Duchesne, libraire; [1]-312 other texts; [313] O1r '*ZAYRE,* / *TRAGÉDIE,* / *Repréſentée pour la première fois, par* / *les Comédiens ordinaires du Roi,* / le 13 *Août* 1732. / *Tome I.* O'; [314] Avertiſſement; [315] Epître dédicatoire à monsieur Fakener, marchand anglais, depuis ambassadeur à Constantinople; 326 Epître à mademoiselle Gaussin, jeune actrice, qui a représenté le rôle de Zayre avec beaucoup de succès; 327-337 Seconde lettre au même M. Fakener, alors ambassadeur à Constantinople, tirée d'une seconde édition de Zayre; 338 Acteurs; [339]-420 Zayre, tragédie.

This Duchesne edition of the theatre was much decried by Voltaire. It was reissued in 1767 (see T67).

Leningrad: 11-100 (a4 bound after a1); Zentralbibliothek, Luzern: B 2172 (1).

w64G

OUVRAGES / DRAMATIQUES, / *AVEC* / LES PIÉCES RELATIVES / A CHACUN. / *TOME SECOND.* / [*woodcut, lute and lyre within cartouche, 60 x 37 mm*] / [*thick-thin rule, 69 mm*] / M. DCC. LXIV. /

[*half-title*] COLLECTION / COMPLETTE / DES / ŒUVRES / *de Mr. de VOLTAIRE,* / DERNIERE EDITION. / *TOME HUITIEME.* /

8°. sig. A-Gg⁸ Hh²; pag. 483 (p.401 numbered '201'; p.422 numbered '22' in Merton copy); $4 signed, arabic (– A1-2, Hh2); direction line

'*Théâtre*. Tom. II.' (sigs C, Q, Dd '*Théatre*. Tom. II.'; sig. Hh 'Théâtre. *Tom. II.*'); page catchwords.

[1] half-title; [2] blank; [3] title; [4] blank; [5] A3*r* 'ZAYRE, / *TRAGÉ-DIE*, / *Repréſentée pour la première fois* / *le* 13 *Août* 1732. / A3   AVER-'; [6] Avertissement; 7-18 Epître dédicatoire à monsieur Fakener, marchand anglais, depuis ambassadeur à Constantinople; 19-20 Epître à mademoiselle Gossin, jeune actrice, qui a représenté le rôle de Zayre avec beaucoup de succès; 21-31 Seconde lettre au même monsieur Fakener, alors ambassadeur à Constantinople, tirée d'une seconde édition de Zayre; 32-44 Lettre à monsieur de La Roque, sur la tragédie de Zayre, 1732; 44 Acteurs; [45]-122 Zayre, tragédie; [123]-480 other texts; 481-483 Table des pièces contenues dans ce volume.

The 'Lettre à monsieur de La Roque' appears for the first time in this edition, which is in general a new setting of w57G.

Leningrad: 11-6; Merton College, Oxford: 36 f 10.

65

ZAYRE, / *TRAGÉDIE* / EN CINQ ACTES, / *Par M.* DE *VOLTAIRE.* / Repréſentée pour la premiere fois, le 13 / Août 1732. / [*typographic ornament*] / *A BESANÇON*, / Chez FANTET, Libraire, plus haut que / la Place Saint Pierre. / [*rule, composed of three elements, 49 mm*] / M. DCC. LXV. / *AVEC PERMISSION.* /

8°. sig. A-G⁴ H²; pag. 59; $2 signed, arabic (– A1, H2); sheet catchwords.

[1] title; [2] Acteurs; [3]-59 Zayre, tragédie.

Bibliothèque municipale, Amiens: BL 2058 A 6.

66

ZAYRE, / *TRAGÉDIE* / PAR M. DE VOLTAIRE: / *Repréſentée pour la premiere fois par les Comédiens* / *Français, ordinaires du Roi, aux Mois d'Août* & / *Décembre* 1742. / [*typographic ornament*] / A AVIGNON, / Chez *LOUIS CHAMBEAU*, Imprimeur-Libraire; / près les RR. PP. Jéſuites. / [*thin-thick-thin rule, 49 mm*] / M. DCC. LXVI. /

8°. sig. A-F⁴ G²; pag. 51; $2 signed, arabic (– A1, G2); sheet catchwords.

[1] title; [2] Acteurs; [3]-51 Zayre, tragédie.

Princeton University Library: Ex 32391.999 (3).

T66

[*within ornamented border*] LE / THEATRE / DE / M. DE VOLTAIRE. / *NOUVELLE ÉDITION*. / Qui contient un Recueil complet de toutes / les Piéces de Théâtre que l'Auteur a / données juſqu'ici. / TOME SE-COND. / [*woodcut, basket of fruit and foliage suspended from bracket, 30 x 25 mm*] / *A AMSTERDAM*, / Chez FRANÇOIS-CANUT RICHOFF, / près le Comptoir de Cologne. / [*thick-thin rule, 42 mm*] / M. DCC. LXVI. /

12°. sig. π^2 A-Q^{12} (Q10-12 blank; π1 presumed blank); pag. [4] 378 (p.215 numbered '21', 219 '129', 302 '203'); \$6 signed, arabic; direction line '*Théâtre. Tome II.*' (sigs C, E, H, I, P '*Théâtre. Tome II.*'; sigs D, L '*Theatre. Tome II.*'; sig. A '*Thèatre. Tome II.*'; sig. B '*Thatre. Tome II.*'; sig. G '*Theatre Tome II.*'); sheet catchwords.

[*1-2*] presumed blank; [*3*] title; [*4*] blank; [1] A1r '*ZAYRE, / TRAGÉ-DIE, / Repréſentée pour la premiere fois / le 13 Août 1732. / Thèatre. Tome II.* A'; [2] Avertissement; 3-13 Epître dédicatoire à monsieur Fakener, marchand anglais, depuis ambassadeur à Constantinople; 14-15 Epître à mademoiselle Gossin, jeune actrice qui a représenté le rôle de Zayre avec beaucoup de succès; 16-27 Seconde lettre au même monsieur Fakener, alors ambassadeur à Constantinople: tirée d'une seconde édition de Zayre; [28] Acteurs; 29-102 Zayre, tragédie; [103]-376 other texts; 377-378 Table des pièces contenues dans ce second volume.

University of Aberdeen Library: MH 84256 T (2) (lacks π1).

67P1

ZAYRE, / *TRAGÉDIE* / PAR M. DE VOLTAIRE, / *Repréſentée pour la premiere fois ſur le Théâ-* / *tre des Comédiens Français ordinaires du* / *Roi, au Mois d'Août, Novembre & Dé-* / *cembre 1742.* / [*woodcut, spray of flowers, 49 x 32 mm*] / A PARIS, / Chez LA VEUVE DUCHESNE, Ruë St. / Jacques au Temple du Goût. / [*thick-thin rule, 56 mm*] / M. DCC. LXVII. /

8°. sig. π^4 B-F^4 G^2; pag. 51 (p.19 numbered '16'); \$2 signed, roman (–G2; B2 signed arabic 'B2', F2 'F2'); sheet catchwords.

[1] title; [2] Acteurs; [3]-51 Zayre, tragédie.

Taylor: M3 M2 1806 (7).

67P2

ZAYRE, / *TRAGÉDIE* / DE M. DE VOLTAIRE; / *Repréſentée pour la premère fois, par* / *les Comédiens ordinaires du Roi,* / *le* 13 *Août* 1732. / Nouvelle Édition, revûe, corrigée & / augmentée par l'Auteur. / *Eſt etiam crudelis amor.* / [*rule, 41 mm*] / Le prix eſt de 30 ſols. / [*rule, 41 mm*] / [*typographic ornament*] / *A PARIS,* / Chez la Veuve DUCHESNE, Libraire, rue Saint / Jacques, au-deſſous de la Fontaine Saint- / Benoît, au Temple du Goût. / [*thick-thin rule, 45 mm*] / M. DCC. LXVII. / *AVEC APPROBA-TION ET PRIVILÉGE.* /

12°. sig. A-D¹² E⁶; pag. 108; $6 signed, arabic (– A1, E4-6); sheet catchwords.

[1] title; [2] On trouve chez le même libraire [...]; 3-13 Epître dédicatoire à monsieur Fakener, marchand anglais, depuis ambassadeur à Constantinople; 14 Epître à mademoiselle Gaussin, jeune actrice, qui a représenté le rôle de Zayre avec beaucoup de succès; 15-25 Seconde lettre au même M. Fakener, alors ambassadeur à Constantinople, tirée d'une seconde édition de Zayre; 26 Acteurs; [27]-108 Zayre, tragédie.

Bn: Rés. Z Beuchot 891.

T67

ŒUVRES / *DE THEATRE* / DE / M. DE VOLTAIRE, / Gentilhomme Ordinaire du Roi, de / l'Académie Françaiſe, / &c. &c. / *NOUVELLE ÉDITION,* / *Revûe & corrigée exactement ſur l'Edition* / *de Genève in-4°.* / TOME PREMIER. / [*woodcut, bagpipes, 45 x 14 mm*] / *A PARIS,* / Chez la Veuve DUCHESNE, Libraire, rue Saint- / Jacques, au-deſſous de la Fon-taine Saint- / Benoît, au Temple du Goût. / [*thick-thin rule, 57 mm*] / M. DCC. LXVII. /

12°. sig. π² A-R¹² S⁶ (± M9); pag. [4] 420; signed $6 arabic (– D4, O5, S4-6; M9 cancel signed '*Tome I.* ✳'); direction line '*Tome I.*'; sheet catchwords.

[*1*] title; [*2*] blank; [*3*] Avertissement; [*4*] Table des pièces contenues dans ce premier volume; [*4*] Errata de ce premier volume [affects p.28, 29, 31, 71, 258, 259]; [1]-420 see T64P.

Only the prelims and M9 are different from T64P, of which this is a reissue.

Bn: Rés. Yf 3387; BL: C 69 b 10 (1).

т68

LE / THÉATRE / *DE* / M. DE VOLTAIRE. / *NOUVELLE ÉDI-TION*. / Qui contient un Recueil complet de toutes / les Pieces de Théâtre que l'Auteur a / données juſqu'ici. / *TOME SECOND*. / [*woodcut, similar to volume 1, transposed left to right, 30 x 24 mm*] / *A AMSTERDAM*, / Chez FRANÇOIS CANUT RICHOFF, / près le Comptoir de Cologne. / [*ornamented rule, 38 mm*] / M. DCC. LXVIII. /

A reissue of т66, using the same sheets under a new title page.

Bn: Yf 4258.

w68

THEATRE / Complet / DE / *M^R. DE VOLTAIRE.* / [*rule, 128 mm*] / TOME PREMIER. / [*rule, 127 mm*] / *CONTENANT* / OEDIPE, MARIAMNE, BRUTUS, LA MORT / DE CESAR, ZAYRE, ALZIRE, avec toutes / les piéces rélatives à ces Drames. / [*rule, 119 mm*] / *GENEVE*. / [*thin-thick rule, 119 mm*] / M. DCC. LXVIII. /

[*half-title*] COLLECTION / Complette / DES / *ŒUVRES* / DE / M^R. DE VOLTAIRE. / [*thick-thin rule, 119 mm*] / *TOME SECOND*. / [*thin-thick rule, 119 mm*] /

4°. sig. π² A-Yyy⁴ Zzz1; pag. 546 (p.219 numbered '223', 314 '14'); $3 signed, roman; direction line '*Tom*. III. *& du Théâtre le premier.*' (sigs Cc-Ee, Zzz '*Tom*. *III*. & du Théâtre le premier.'); sheet catchwords.

[*1*] half-title; [*2*] blank; [*3*] title; [*4*] blank; [1]-5 Avertissement; [6]-360 other texts; [361] Zz1r '*ZAYRE*, / *TRAGÉDIE*. / [*rule, 119 mm*] / *Repréſentée pour la première fois le 13. Août 1732.* / [*rule, 120 mm*] / *Tom.* III. *& du Théâtre le premier.* Zz'; [362] Avertissement; 363-371 Epître dédicatoire à Mr Fakener, marchand anglais, depuis ambassadeur à Constantinople; 372-373 Epître à mademoiselle Gossin, jeune actrice, qui a représenté le rôle de Zayre avec beaucoup de succès; 374-381 Seconde lettre au même monsieur Fakener, alors ambassadeur à Constantinople, tirée d'une seconde édition de Zayre; 382-390 Lettre à monsieur de La Roque, sur la tragédie de Zayre, 1732; 390 Acteurs; 391-466 Zayre, tragédie; [467]-544 other texts; 545-546 Table des pièces contenues dans ce troisième volume.

The Cramer quarto edition, supervised by Voltaire. The text of *Zaïre* follows w56.

Taylor: VF.

69C

ZAYRE, / *TRAGÉDIE*, / Par Mr. DE VOLTAIRE. / Suivant la nouvelle édition in 4°· 1768. / *Repréſentée ſur le Théâtre de la Cour, par* / *les Comédiens François ordinaires du Roi,* / *le* 18 *Decembre* 1769. / [*woodcut, 50 x 32 mm*] / [*thick-thin rule, 83 mm*] / *A COPENHAGUE,* / Chez CL. PHILIBERT, / Imprimeur-Libraire. / [*rule, 80 mm*] / MDCCLXIX. / *Avec Permiſſion du Roi.* /

8°. sig. A-E⁸; pag. 79 [80]; $5 signed, arabic (– A1); page catchwords.

[1] title; [2] Acteurs; [3]-79 Zayre, tragédie; [80] Avertissement.

Uppsala: Fransk teater XVII (5).

70P

ZAYRE, / *TRAGÉDIE* / EN CINQ ACTES ET EN VERS. / PAR MONSIEUR DE VOLTAIRE. / / *Repréſentée pour la premiere fois, ſur le* / *Théatre des Comédiens Français ordinaires* / *du Roi, aux mois d'Août, Novembre* & / *Décembre* 1742. / [*woodcut, cupid with torch, 31 x 24 mm*] / *A PARIS,* / Chez la Veuve Duchesne, Rue / St. Jacques. / [*thick-thin rule, 62 mm*] / M. DCC. LXX.

8°. sig. A-F⁴; pag. 48; $2 signed, arabic (– A1); sheet catchwords.

[1] title; [2] Acteurs; 3-48 Zayre, tragédie.

Bibliothèque municipale et universitaire, Clermont-Ferrand: 70329.

T70

LE / THEATRE / *DE* / M. DE VOLTAIRE, / *NOUVELLE EDITION.* / Qui contient un recueil complet de toutes / les Pieces de Théâtre que l'Auteur a don- / nées juſqu'ici. / *TOME SECOND.* / [*woodcut, shell in scroll frame, 49 x 30 mm*] / *A AMSTERDAM,* / Chez François Canut Richoef, / près le Comptoir de Cologne. / [*thick-thin rule, 55 mm*] / M. DCC. LXX. /

12°. sig. π1 A-Q¹² (Q10-12 blank); pag. [2] 378 (219 numbered '119');

$6 signed, arabic; direction line '*Théatre. Tome II.*' (sig. N '*Théâtre Tome II.*'); sheet catchwords.

[*1*] title; [2] blank; [1] A1*r* 'ZAYRE, | *TRAGÉDIE*, | *Repréſentée pour la premiere fois | le 13 Août 1732.* | *Théatre. Tome II.* A'; [2] Avertissement; 3-13 Epître dédicatoire à monsieur Fakener, marchand anglais, depuis ambassadeur à Constantinople; 14-15 Epître à mademoiselle Gossin, jeune actrice qui a représenté le rôle de Zayre avec beaucoup de succès; 16-27 Seconde lettre au même monsieur Fakener, alors ambassadeur à Constantinople: tirée d'une seconde édition de Zayre; [28] Acteurs; 29-102 Zayre, tragédie; [103]-376 other texts; 377-378 Table des pièces contenues dans ce second volume.

Bn: Yf 4264.

W70G

OUVRAGES / DRAMATIQUES, / *AVEC* / LES PIÉCES RELATI-VES / A CHACUN. / *TOME SECOND.* | [*woodcut, lute and lyre within cartouche, 60 x 37 mm*] | [*thick-thin rule, 70 mm*] | M. DCC. LXX. |

[*half-title*] COLLECTION / COMPLETTE / DES / ŒUVRES / DE / M*R*. *de VOLTAIRE.* / DERNIERE EDITION. / *TOME HUITIEME.* |

8°. sig. A-Gg⁸ Hh²; pag. 483; $4 signed, arabic (– A1-2, Hh2); direction line '*Théatre.* Tom. II.' (– A; sigs B, F, G, O, P, X, Z, Bb, Cc, Ff, Gg '*Théatre.* Tom. II.'; sigs I, V '*Théâtre* Tom. II.'; sig. Hh 'Théâtre. *Tom. II.*'); page catchwords.

[1] half-title; [2] blank; [3] title; [4] blank; [5] A3*r* 'ZAYRE, | *TRAGÉ-DIE.* | *Repréſentée pour la première fois | le* 13. *Août* 1732. | A3 AVER-'; [6] Avertissement; 7-18 Epître dédicatoire à monsieur Fakener, marchand anglais, depuis ambassadeur à Constantinople; 19-20 Epître à mademoiselle Gossin, jeune actrice, qui a représenté le rôle de Zayre avec beaucoup de succès; 21-31 Seconde lettre au même monsieur Fakener, alors ambassadeur à Constantinople, tirée d'une seconde édition de Zayre; 32-44 Lettre à monsieur de La Roque, sur la tragédie de Zayre, 1732; 44 Acteurs; [45]-122 Zayre, tragédie; [123]-480 other texts; 481-483 Table des pièces contenues dans ce volume.

Another Cramer edition in the w56 tradition.

Taylor: V1 1770G/1 (8).

71P

ZAYRE, / *TRAGÉDIE.* / Par Monfieur DE VOLTAIRE. / *Repréfentée pour la premiere fois par les Comédiens* / *François ordinaires du Roi, au Mois d'Août &* / *Decembre* 1742. / [*thick-thin rule, 54 mm*] / *NOUVELLE ÉDITION.* / [*thin-thick rule, 54 mm*] / [*woodcut, flowers within cartouche, 56 x 50 mm*] / A PARIS, / Chez la Veuve Allouel, Quay des Gévres, à la / Croix Blanche. / [*ornamented rule, 53 mm*] / M. DCC. LXXI. / *Avec Approbation & Privilège du Roi* /

8°. sig. A-F⁴ G²; pag. 51; $2 signed, arabic (– A1, E2; D2 signed 'D'); sheet catchwords.

[1] title; [2] Acteurs; [3]-51 Zayre, tragédie.

Bn: Yth 19444.

W71

THEATRE / *COMPLET* / DE / *Mᴿ. DE VOLTAIRE*, / [*rule, 73 mm*] / TOME PREMIER. / [*rule, 73 mm*] / *CONTENANT* / ŒDIPE, MARIAMNE, BRUTUS, LA MORT / de CESAR, ZAYRE, ALZIRE, avec toutes / les piéces rélatives à ces Drames. / [*woodcut, beached ship, 36 x 27 mm*] / *GENEVE*, / [*ornamented rule, 36 mm*] / M. DCC. LXXI. /

[*half-title*] COLLECTION / *COMPLETTE* / DES / *ŒUVRES* / DE / Mᴿ. DE VOLTAIRE. / [*ornamented rule, 74 mm*] / *TOME SECOND.* / [*ornamented rule, 74 mm*] /

12°. sig. π² A-T¹² V⁴; pag. [4] 464; $6 signed, arabic (– L2, V3-4); direction line '*Tome III. & du Théâtre le premier.*' (sigs A, E, F '*Tome* III. *& du Théâtre le premier.*'); sheet catchwords.

[*1*] half-title; [*2*] blank; [*3*] title; [*4*] blank; [1]-308 other texts; [309] N11*r* 'ZAYRE, / *TRAGÉDIE.* / [*ornamented rule, 69 mm*] / *Repréfentée pour la première fois le 13 Août 1732.* / [*ornamented rule, 69 mm*]'; [310] Avertissement; 311-319 Epître dédicatoire à Mr Fakener, marchand anglais, depuis ambassadeur à Constantinople; 320 Epître à mademoiselle Gossin, jeune actrice, qui a représenté le rôle de Zayre avec beaucoup de succès; 321-328 Seconde lettre au même monsieur Fakener, alors ambassadeur à Constantinople, tirée d'une seconde édition de Zayre; 329-337 Lettre à monsieur de La Roque, sur la tragédie de Zayre, 1732; 338 Acteurs; 339-398 Zayre, tragédie; [399]-462 other texts; 463-464 Table des pièces contenues dans ce troisième [*sic*] volume.

An edition by Plomteux of Liège, based on w68.

Taylor: VF; Uppsala: Litt. fr.

72P

ZAYRE, / *TRAGÉDIE*, / REPRÉSENTÉE A PARIS, / pour la premiere fois, aux mois d'Août, / Novembre & Décembre 1732. / *PAR Monfieur DE VOLTAIRE*. / NOUVELLE ÉDITION. / *Revue & corrigée fur toutes celles qui ont paru jusqu'à / ce jour*. / [*woodcut, figures holding pierced hearts, 39 x 40 mm*] / A PARIS, / Chez JEAN-BAPTISTE BAUCHE, à la defcente / du Pont-neuf, proche les Auguftins, à Saint / Jean-Baptifte dans le défert. / [*thick-thin rule, 48 mm*] / M. DCC. LXXII. / *Avec Approbation & Privilège du Roi*. /

8°. sig. A-I⁴; pag. xj [xii] [13]-72; $2 signed, roman (– A1); sheet catchwords.

[i] title; [ii] Avertissement; iij-x Epître dédicatoire à monsieur Faukener, marchand anglais, depuis ambassadeur d'Angleterre à Constantinople; xj Epître à mademoiselle Gossin, jeune actrice, qui a représenté le rôle de Zaïre avec beaucoup de succès; [xii] Personnages; [13]-72 Zayre, tragédie.

Taylor: V3 Z3 1772.

W70L (1772)

THÉATRE / COMPLET / *DE* / Mᴿ. DE VOLTAIRE. / LE TOUT REVU ET CORRIGÉ / PAR L'AUTEUR MEME. / TOME SECOND, / *CONTENANT* / ZAYRE, ALZIRE, MÉROPE, / ET LE FANATISME. / [*woodcut, Corsini 106 bis*] / *A LAUSANNE*, / CHEZ FRANÇ. GRASSET ET COMP. / [*ornamented rule, 80 mm*] / M. DCC. LXXII. /

[*half-title*] *COLLECTION* / COMPLETTE / *DES* / ŒUVRES / *DE* / Mᴿ. DE VOLTAIRE. / [*ornamented rule, 82 mm*] / *TOME QUINZIEME*. / [*ornamented rule, 82 mm*] /

8°. sig. a-b⁸ c² A-Z⁸; pag. XXXV [xxxvi] 368 (p.227 not numbered); $5 signed, arabic (– a1-2, c2); direction line '*Théatre*. Tom. II.' (sigs c, F, K, M, N, Q, T '*Théâtre*. Tome II.'; sigs A, C, I, L, S '*Théâtre* Tom. II.'); sheet catchwords.

[1] half-title; [2] blank; [3] title; [4] blank; [5] a3r 'ZAYRE, / *TRAGÉ-DIE*, / Repréfentée pour la première fois le / 13 Août 1732. / a3'; [6]

Avertissement; VII-XVIII Epître dédicatoire, à monsieur Fakener, marchand anglais, depuis ambassadeur à Constantinople; XIX-XX Epître à mademoiselle Gossin, jeune actrice, qui a représenté le rôle de Zayre avec beaucoup de succès; XXI-XXXI Seconde lettre au même monsieur Fakener, alors ambassadeur à Constantinople, tirée d'une seconde édition de Zayre; XXXII Avertissement de l'auteur; XXXII Avertissement des éditeurs; XXXIII-XXXV Table des pièces contenues dans ce volume; [xxxvi] Acteurs; [1]-80 Zayre, tragédie; [81]-368 other texts.

Also issued with a cancel half-title: 'THÉATRE / COMPLET / DE / M^R. DE VOLTAIRE. / [*ornamented rule, 79 mm*] / *TOME SECOND.* / [*ornamented rule, 79 mm*]'.

The theatre volumes of the Grasset edition were revised by Voltaire. The only change affecting *Zaïre* was the addition of a new preliminary text: see below, appendix II, p.526.

Taylor: V1 1770L (15).

W72P

ŒUVRES / *DE M. DE VOLTAIRE.* / [*thick-thin rule, 75 mm*] / THÉA-TRE. / TOME SECOND, / *Contenant* / *ZAÏRE, ALZIRE, ou LES AMÉRICAINS;* / *MÉROPE, LE FANATISME, ou* / *MAHOMET.* / [*woodcut, cupid with torch, 30 x 24 mm*] / *A NEUFCHATEL.* / [*ornamented rule, 61 mm*] / M. DCC. LXXIII. /

[*half-title*] ŒUVRES / DE THÉATRE / *DE M. DE VOLTAIRE.* / TOME SECOND. /

12°. sig. A-T¹² V⁶ (V5-6 blank); pag. [4] 464; $6 signed, roman (– P5, V4-6); direction line 'Th. *Tome II.*'; sheet catchwords.

[*1*] half-title; [*2*] blank; [*3*] title; [*4*] blank; [1] A1r 'ZAYRE, / *TRAGÉ-DIE;* / Repréſentée, pour la première fois, / le 13 Août 1732. / Th. *Tome II.* A'; [2] Avertissement; 3-16 Epître dédicatoire à monsieur Fakener, marchand anglais, depuis ambassadeur à Constantinople; 17-18 Epître à mademoiselle Gossin, jeune actrice, qui a représenté le rôle de Zayre avec beaucoup de succès; 19-33 Seconde lettre au même M. Fakener, alors ambassadeur à Constantinople, tirée d'une seconde édition de Zayre; 34-49 Lettre à monsieur de La Roque, sur la tragédie de Zayre, 1732; [50] Personnages; [51]-136 Zayre, tragédie; [137]-464 other texts.

An edition based on w68, attributed to Panckoucke.

Arsenal: Rf 14095 (2).

W72X

OUVRAGES / DRAMATIQUES, / *AVEC* / LES PIECES RELATI-
VES / A CHACUN. / *TOME SECOND.* / [*typographic ornament*] / [*ornamented rule, 63 mm*] / M. DCC. LXXII. /

[*half-title*] COLLECTION / COMPLETTE / DES / ŒUVRES / DE /
M^R. DE VOLTAIRE, / DERNIERE ÉDITION. / *TOME HUITIE-
ME.* /

8°. sig. A-Ff⁸; pag. 463 (p.201 numbered '200', 205 '204'); $4 signed,
arabic (– A1-2, C4; T3 signed 'S3', T4 'T', V3 'V4', Bb4 'Bb2', Ee3
'E03'); direction line '*Théâtre.* Tom. II.' (sigs A, Y, Aa, Cc '*Théâtre.*
Tome II.'; sigs K, N, Q '*Théatre.* Tom. II.'); page catchwords.

[1] half-title; [2] blank; [3] title; [4] blank; [5] A3r 'ZAYRE, / *TRAGÉ-
DIE,* / *Repréſentée pour la premiere fois* / *le 13 Août 1732.* / A3'; [6] Avertissement; 7-16 Epître dédicatoire à monsieur Fakener, marchand anglais,
depuis ambassadeur à Constantinople; 17-18 Epître à mademoiselle
Gossin, jeune actrice, qui a représenté le rôle de Zayre avec beaucoup
de succès; 19-28 Seconde lettre au même monsieur Fakener, alors
ambassadeur à Constantinople, tiré d'une seconde édition de Zayre; 29-
38 Lettre à monsieur de La Roque, sur la tragédie de Zayre, 1732; [39]
blank; 40 Acteurs; [41]-113 Zayre, tragédie; [114] blank; [115]-460 other
texts; 461-463 Table des pièces contenues dans ce volume.

The last edition of the w56-style *Collection complette.*

Stockholm: Litt. fr.

73A

ZAYRE, / *TRAGÉDIE.* / EN VERS ET EN CINQ ACTES. / Par Mr.
DE VOLTAIRE. / [*ornamented rule, 68 mm*] / *NOUVELLE ÉDITION.* /
[*ornamented rule, 68 mm*] / [*woodcut, flowers in cartouche, 45 x 32 mm*] / A
AVIGNON, / Chez *LOUIS CHAMBEAU,* Imprimeur-Libraire / près le
Collège. / [*ornamented rule, 57 mm*] / M. DCC. LXXIII. /

8°. sig. A-F⁴ G²; pag. 51; $2 signed, arabic (– A1, G2); sheet catchwords.

[1] title; [2] Acteurs; [3]-51 Zayre, tragédie.

ImV: D Zaïre 1773/1; Arsenal: Rf 14184.

73P

ZAYRE, / *TRAGÉDIE* / EN CINQ ACTES ET EN VERS, / Par M. DE VOLTAIRE, / *Repréſentée pour la premiere fois ſur le* / *Théatre des Comédiens Français ordinaires* / *du Roi, le 13 Août 1742.* / [*rule, 84 mm*] / NOUVELLE ÉDITION, / *Revue ſur celle* in-4°. *de Geneve.* / [*rule, 84 mm*] / [*ornamented rule, 59 mm*] / Le prix eſt de 12 ſols. / [*ornamented rule, 59 mm*] / [*woodcut, theatrical emblems, 30 x 28 mm*] / A PARIS, / Chez la Veuve DUCHESNE, Libraire rue S. Jacques au deſſous / de la Fontaine S. Benoît, au Temple du Goût. / [*ornamented rule, 59 mm*] / M. DCC. LXXIII. /

8°. sig. A-H⁴ I²; pag. 68; $2 signed, roman (– A1, I2); sheet catchwords.

[1] title; [2] Acteurs; [3]-68 Zayre, tragédie.

Arsenal: Rf 14183.

T73

THÉATRE / COMPLET / *DE* / Mᴿ. DE VOLTAIRE. / LE TOUT REVU ET CORRIGÉ / PAR L'AUTEUR MÊME. / TOME SECOND. / *CONTENANT* / LA MORT DE CÉSAR, ZAYRE, / ET ALZIRE. / [*typographical ornament*] / *A AMSTERDAM,* / Chez les LIBRAIRES ASSOCIÉS. / [*ornamented rule, 66 mm*] / M. DCC. LXXIII. /

12°. sig. π1 A-L¹² M⁴; pag. [2] 271 (the '1' of p.137 misplaced); $6 signed, arabic (– M3-4); direction line '*Tome II.*' (sig. B '*Tome I.*'); sheet catchwords.

[1] title; [2] blank; [1]-65 other texts; [66] blank; [67] C1or 'ZAYRE, / *TRAGÉDIE.* / Repréſentée pour la première fois / le 13 Août 1732.'; [68] Avertissement; 69-80 Epître dédicatoire, à monsieur Fakener, marchand anglais, depuis ambassadeur à Constantinople; 81-82 Epître à mademoiselle Gossin, jeune actrice, qui a représenté le rôle de Zayre avec beaucoup de succès; 83-93 Seconde lettre au même monsieur Fakener, alors ambassadeur à Constantinople, tirée d'une seconde édition de Zayre; 94 Avertissement de l'auteur; 94-95 Avertissement des éditeurs; [96] Acteurs; 97-180 Zayre, tragédie; [181]-270 other texts; 271 Table des pièces contenues dans ce second volume.

Zentralbibliothek, Solothurn: Qb 2566 (2).

74P1

ZAÏRE, / *TRAGÉDIE* / DE M. DE VOLTAIRE. / *Édition revue & corrigée fur toutes celles qui ont / paru jufqu'à ce jour.* / [*woodcut, flowers and foliage, 57 x 41 mm*] / *A PARIS,* / Par la Compagnie des Libraires. / [*thick-thin rule, 58 mm*] / M. DCC. LXXIV. /

8°. A-H⁴; pag. 63; $1 signed (– A1); direction line '*Zaïre.*' (– A); sheet catchwords.

[1] title; [2] Acteurs; [3]-63 Zaïre, tragédie.

Bibliothèque municipale, Nantes: 28763.

74P2

ZAYRE, / *TRAGÉDIE,* / REPRÉSENTÉE A PARIS, / pour la premiere fois, aux mois / d'Août, Novembre & Décembre / 1732. / *Par Monfieur* DE *VOLTAIRE.* / NOUVELLE ÉDITION, / *Revue & corrigée fur toutes celles qui ont paru / jusqu'à ce jour.* / [*woodcut, spray of flowers, 62 x 52 mm*] / A PARIS, / Par la Compagnie des Libraires. / [*thick-thin rule, 67 mm*] / M. DCC. LXXIV. /

8°. pag. 66.

Private collection.

T74

COLLECTION / *DE* / TRAGÉDIES, COMÉDIES, / ET DRAMES / *CHOISIS* / DES PLUS CÉLÈBRES AUTEURS MODERNES. / [*orna-mented rule, 59 mm*] / *TOME DIXIEME.* / [*ornamented rule, 58 mm*] / [*woodcut, including vase of flowers, 47 x 43 mm*] / *A LIVOURNE* 1775. / [*ornamented rule, 81 mm*] / Chez Thomas Masi et Compagnie, / Editeurs & Imprimeurs-Libraires. / *Avec Approbation.* /

8°. sig. A-Aa⁸ Bb⁶; pag. 394 [395]; $4 signed, arabic (– A1, F2, F4, P2, P4, R3, T3, V3, X4, Aa3, Bb4); direction line '*Tom. X.*' (– A); sheet catchwords.

[1] title; [2] blank; [3] A2r 'ZAYRE / *TRAGÉDIE* / Par Monfieur DE VOLTAIRE. / A2'; [4] Acteurs; [5]-86 Zayre tragédie; [87]-394 texts by other authors; [395] Table des pièces contenues dans ce dixième volume.

Arsenal: Rondel Rec. 45 X.

75P

ZAYRE, / TRAGÉDIE / *EN CINQ ACTES* / ET EN VERS, / *Par M.
de Voltaire.* / *Repréfentée pour la premiere fois par les Comé-* / *diens Français
ordinaires du Roi, aux mois* / *d'Août, Novembre & Décembre* 1742. / [*ornamented
rule*] / NOUVELLE EDITION. / [*ornamented rule*] / [*typographic ornament*] /
A PARIS, / Chez DELALAIN, rue & à côté de la Comédie / Françoife. /
[*ornamented rule*] / M. DCC. LXXV. / *Avec Approbation & Privilege du Roi.* /

8°. sig. A-F⁴; pag. 48; $2 signed, roman (– A1; A2 signed 'A'); sheet
catchwords.

[1] title; [2] Acteurs; [3]-48 Zayre, tragédie.

At the foot of p.48: 'On trouve à Avignon, chez Jacques Garrigan,
imprimeur-libraire place Saint-Didier, un assortiment de pièces de théâtre, imprimés dans le même goût.'

Bibliothèque municipale, Toulouse: Fa D 1303 (1).

75X

[*within ornamented border*] ZAYRE, / *TRAGÉDIE.* / Par M. DE VOL-
TAIRE. / [*woodcut, shell and floral motif, 36 x 26 mm*] / [*ornamented rule, 46
mm*] / M. DCC. LXXV. /

8°. sig. A-E⁸ F1; pag. 82; $4 signed, roman (– A1; D4 signed 'Biv');
sheet catchwords.

[1] title; [2] Acteurs; 3-82 Zayre, tragédie.

BL: 11736 d 5 (3).

W75G

[*within ornamented border*] OUVRAGES / *DRAMATIQUES,* / PRÉCÉ-
DÉS ET SUIVIS / DE TOUTES LES PIÉCES QUI LEUR / SONT
RELATIFS. [*sic*] / [*rule, 75 mm*] / TOME SECOND. / [*rule, 75 mm*] / *M.
DCC. LXXV.* /

[*half-title, within ornamented border*] TOME TROISIÉME. /

8°. sig. π² A-Bb⁸ Cc² (Cc2 blank); pag. [4] 402; $4 signed, roman (–
Cc2); direction line '*Théatre.* Tom. II.'; sheet catchwords.

[*1*] half-title; [*2*] blank; [*3*] title; [*4*] blank; [1] A1r 'ZAYRE, / *TRAGÉ-
DIE.* / [*rule, 75 mm*] / *Repréfentée pour la première fois le 13 Août 1732.* /

374

[*rule, 74 mm*] / *Théatre*. Tom. II.   A'; [2] Avertissement; 3-13 Epître dédicatoire à Mr Fakener, marchand anglais, depuis ambassadeur à Constantinople; 14-15 Epître à mademoiselle Gossin, jeune actrice, qui a représenté le rôle de Zayre avec beaucoup de succès; 16-26 Seconde lettre au même monsieur Fakener, alors ambassadeur à Constantinople, tirée d'une seconde édition de Zayre; 27-38 Lettre à monsieur de La Roque, sur la tragédie de Zayre, 1732; 38 Acteurs; 39-116 Zayre, tragédie; [117]-400 other texts; 401-402 Table des pièces contenues dans ce volume.

The Cramer *encadrée* edition, the last to be revised by Voltaire and which provides the base text for the present edition. Voltaire corrected certain volumes by hand in preparation for a further edition, but *Zaïre* was not amended.

Taylor: VF; – V1 1775 (3).

w75x

[*within ornamented border*] OUVRAGES / *DRAMATIQUES*, / Précédés et suivis / *DE TOUTES LES PIÉCES QUI LEUR* / *SONT RELATI-VES*. / [*rule, 74 mm*] / TOME SECOND. / [*rule, 72 mm*] / [*typographic ornament*] / [*ornamented rule, 78 mm*] / *M. DCC. LXXV*. /

[*half-title, within ornamented border*] ŒUVRES / DE / M^R. *DE VOL-TAIRE*. / [*rule, 71 mm*] / TOME TROISIÈME. / [*rule, 70 mm*] /

8°. sig. π^2 A-Bb^8 Cc^2 (Cc2 blank); pag. [4] 402 (p.52 numbered '5fl', 302 '202', 325 '324', 351 '251', 391 '291'); \$4 signed, roman (– Cc2); direction line '*Théatre*. Tom. II.' (sigs A, Z, Bb '*Théatre*. Tome II.'; sigs D, E, G-I '*Théatre* Tom. II.'; sig. Cc '*Théatre*, Tom. II.'); sheet catchwords.

[*1*] half-title; [*2*] blank but for border; [*3*] title; [*4*] blank but for border; [1] A1r 'ZAYRE, / *TRAGÉDIE*. / [*rule, 78 mm*] / *Repréſentée pour la première fois le* 13 *Août* 1732. / [*rule, 78 mm*] / *Théatre*. Tome II.   A'; [2] Avertissement; 3-13 Epître dédicatoire à M. Fakener, marchand anglais, depuis ambassadeur à Constantinople; 14-15 Epître à mademoiselle Gossin, jeune actrice, qui a représenté le rôle de Zayre avec beaucoup de succès; 16-26 Seconde lettre au même monsieur Fakener, alors ambassadeur à Constantinople, tirée d'une seconde édition de Zayre; 27-38 Lettre à monsieur de La Roque, sur la tragédie de Zayre, 1732; 38 Acteurs; 39-116 Zayre, tragédie; [117]-400 other texts; 401-402 Table des pièces contenues dans ce volume.

An imitation of w75G, possibly produced for Panckoucke. The theatre volumes follow the text of w75G.

Bn: Z 24832; Taylor: VF (lacks Cc2; has half-title of volume 2).

T76G

[*within ornamented border*] THÉÂTRE / COMPLET / *DE* / *M. DE VOL-TAIRE*. / Divisé en 9 Volumes. / [*rule, 78 mm*] / *TOME SECOND.* / [*rule, 77 mm*] / [*typographical ornament*] / *A GENEVE.* / [*thick-thin rule, 74 mm*] / 1776. /

A reissue of the sheets of w75G under a title apparently produced by the printer of w75X.

Westfield College, London: 8599.

T76X

THÉÂTRE / COMPLET / DE MONSIEUR / DE VOLTAIRE. / TOME PREMIER. / *Contenant* Œdipe, Mariamne, / Brutus, la Mort de César, / Zayre, *avec toutes les Pièces* / *relatives à ces Drames.* / [*woodcut, cock with two books and hour-glass, signed* 'Caron', *55 x 38 mm*] / [*ornamented rule, 51 mm*] / M. DCC. LXXVI. / [*lines 1, 3, 5 and date in red*]

[*half-title*] THÉÂTRE / *COMPLET* / DE MONSIEUR / *DE VOL-TAIRE,* / TOME PREMIER, / *Contenant* Œdipe, Mariamne, / Brutus, la Mort de César, / Zayre, *avec toutes les Pièces relatives* / *à ces Drames.* /

8°. sig. π^2 A-Kk^8 Ll^6; pag. [*4*] 540; $4 signed, roman (– Y2, Ll4); direction line '*Théatre. Tom. I.*' (sigs H, K '*Théatre. Tome I.*'); sheet catchwords.

[*1*] half-title; [*2*] blank; [*3*] title; [*4*] blank; [*1*]-416 other texts; [417] Dd1r '*ZAYRE,* / TRAGÉDIE. / [*rule, 74 mm*] / *Représentée pour la première fois le 13* / *Août 1732.* / [*rule, 72 mm*] / *Théatre.* Tom. I.   Dd'; [418] Avertissement; [419]-430 Epître dédicatoire à M. Fakener, marchand anglais, depuis ambassadeur à Constantinople; [431]-432 Epître à mademoiselle Gossin, jeune actrice, qui a représenté le rôle de Zayre avec beaucoup de succès; [433]-444 Seconde lettre au même monsieur Fakener, alors ambassadeur à Constantinople, tirée d'une seconde édition de Zayre; [445]-458 Lettre à monsieur de La Roque, sur la tragédie de Zayre, 1732; 458 Acteurs; [459]-538 Zayre, tragédie; [539]-540 Table des pièces contenues dans ce premier volume.

376

Arsenal: Rf 14096 (1).

77N

ZAYRE, / *TRAGÉDIE*, / EN CINQ ACTES ET EN VERS. / Par Mr.
De VOLTAIRE. / [*thick-thin rule, 63 mm*] / LE PRIX EST DE 20.
GRAINS. / [*thin-thick rule, 63 mm*] / [*typographic ornament*] / NAPLES / DE
L'IMPRIMERIE DE JEAN GRAVIER. / MDCCLXXVII. / [*rule, 26 mm*] / *AVEC
APPROBATION ET PRIVILEGE.* /

8°. sig. π^2 (π1 blank) A-E^8; pag. [*4*] 79 (p.44 not numbered); $4 signed,
arabic; page catchwords.

[*1-2*] blank; [*3*] title; [*4*] Acteurs; 1-79 Zayre, tragédie.

Bn: Yth 19443.

77P

ZAYRE, / *TRAGÉDIE.* / EN CINQ ACTES, / *ET EN VERS.* / Par M.
De VOLTAIRE. / [*ornamented rule, 83 mm*] / *NOUVELLE ÉDITION.* /
Corrigée fur l'édition de Genève. / [*ornamented rule, 83 mm*] / [*woodcut, doves
and foliage, 42 x 33 mm*] / *A PARIS*, / Chez RUAULT, Libraire, / rue de la
Harpe. / [*ornamented rule, 65 mm*] / *M. DCC. LXXVII.* /

8°. sig. A-F^4 G1; pag. 50 (p.19 numbered '29', 23 '2'); $2 signed, arabic
(– A1); sheet catchwords.

[1] title; [2] Acteurs; 3-50 Zayre, tragédie.

ImV: D Zaïre 1777/1.

T77

THÉATRE / *COMPLET* / DE M. DE VOLTAIRE; / *NOUVELLE
ÉDITION*, / *Revue & corrigée par l'AUTEUR.* / TOME SECOND. /
CONTENANT / LA MORT DE CÉSAR, ZAÏRE, ALZIRE / *ou* LES AME-
RICAINS. / [*woodcut, as volume 1, but inverted*] / *A AMSTERDAM*, / Chez
les LIBRAIRES ASSOCIÉS. / [*thick-thin rule, 55 mm*] / M. DCC. LXXVII. /

12°. sig. π^1 A-L^{12}; pag. [2] 262 [263]; $6 signed, arabic; direction line
'*Tome II.*'; sheet catchwords.

[*1*] title; [*2*] blank; [1]-64 other texts; [65] C9r 'ZAYRE, / *TRAGÉDIE.* /
Repréfentée pour la première fois / le 13 Août 1732.'; 66 Avertissement;

377

67-77 Epître dédicatoire à monsieur Fakener, marchand anglais, depuis ambassadeur à Constantinople; 77-78 Epître à mademoiselle Gossin, jeune actrice qui a représenté le rôle de Zaïre avec beaucoup de succès; 78-88 Seconde lettre au même monsieur Fakener, alors ambassadeur à Constantinople, tirée d'une seconde édition de Zayre; [89] Avertissement de l'auteur; Avertissement des éditeurs; [90] Acteurs; [91]-171 Zayre, tragédie; [172] blank; [173]-262 other texts; [263] Table des pièces contenues dans ce second volume.

Stockholm: Litt. Fr. Dram.

78P

ZAYRE, / *TRAGEDIE.* / EN CINQ ACTES / *ET EN VERS.* / Par Monſieur DE VOLTAIRE. / [*ornamented rule, 84 mm*] / *NOUVELLE ÉDITION.* / *Corrigée fur l'édition de Genève.* / [*ornamented rule, 84 mm*] / [*woodcut, emblems of the arts, 43 x 32 mm*] / *A PARIS,* / Chez DIDOT, l'aîné, Imprimeur / & Libraire, Rue Pavée. / [*ornamented rule, 63 mm*] / *M. DCC LXXVIII.* /

8°. pag. 50.

Description based upon a photocopy of the title; this edition may well be an issue of 77P.

Private collection.

K84

OEUVRES / COMPLETES / DE / VOLTAIRE. / TOME SECOND. / [*swelled rule, 38 mm*] / DE L'IMPRIMERIE DE LA SOCIÉTÉ LITTÉ-RAIRE- / TYPOGRAPHIQUE. / 1784.

8°. sig. π1 a² A-Dd⁸ Ee⁴ Ff¹; pag. [2] iv 441 [442]; $4 signed, arabic (– a2, Ee3-4); direction line '*Théâtre. Tom. II.*'; sheet catchwords.

[*1*] title; [2] blank; [i] a1*r* 'THEATRE. / *Théâtre.* Tome II.   a'; [ii] blank; [iii]-iv Table des pieces contenues dans ce volume; [1] A1*r* 'ZAIRE, / *TRAGEDIE* / Repréſentée, pour la première fois, / le 13 août 1732. / *Théâtre. Tom. II.*   A'; [2] Avertissement; [3]-13 Epître dedicatoire a M. Falkener, négociant anglais, depuis ambassadeur à Constantinople; 13-14 Epître a mademoiselle Gaussin, jeune actrice, qui a représenté le rôle de Zaïre avec beaucoup de succès; [15]-24 Seconde lettre au même M.

Falkener, alors ambassadeur à Constantinople. Tirée d'une seconde édition de Zaïre; [25]-35 Lettre à monsieur de La Roque, sur la tragédie de Zaïre, 1732; [36] Personnages; [37]-110 Zaïre, tragedie; [111] Variantes de Zaire; [112] Notes; [113]-[442] other texts.

This first setting of the Kehl edition follows w75G, except at l.160 of the first epistle to Fawkener, l.38-39 and 46 of the second and at l.106, 156, II.314, III.75, 201, 218, 224, v.14 and 71.

Taylor: VF.

к85

OEUVRES / COMPLETES / DE / VOLTAIRE. / TOME SECOND. / [*swelled rule, 38 mm*] / DE L'IMPRIMERIE DE LA SOCIÉTÉ LITTÉ-RAIRE- / TYPOGRAPHIQUE. / 1785.

[*half-title*] OEUVRES / COMPLETES / DE / VOLTAIRE. /

8°. sig. π^2 a² A-Dd⁸ Ee⁴ Ff² (Ff2 blank); pag. [2] iv 441 [442] (p.215 numbered '213', 223 '225'); \$4 signed, arabic (– a2, Ee3-4); direction line '*Théâtre*. Tome II.'); sheet catchwords.

[*1*] half-title; [2] blank; [*3*] title; [*4*] blank; [i] a1r 'THEATRE. / *Théâtre*. Tome II. a'; [ii] blank; [iii]-iv Table des pieces contenues dans ce volume; [1] A1r 'ZAÏRE, / *TRAGEDIE*. / Repréſentée, pour la première fois, le / 13 auguſte 1732. / *Théâtre. Tome II.* A'; [2] Avertissement; [3]-13 Epître dedicatoire a M. Falkener, négociant anglais, depuis ambassadeur à Constantinople; 13-14 Epître a mademoiselle Gaussin, jeune actrice, qui a représenté le rôle de Zaïre avec beaucoup de succès; [15]-24 Seconde lettre au même M. Falkener, alors ambassadeur à Constantinople. Tirée d'une seconde édition de Zaïre; [25]-35 Lettre à monsieur de La Roque, sur la tragédie de Zaïre, 1732; [36] Personnages; [37]-110 Zaïre, tragedie; [111] Variantes de Zaire; [112] Notes; [113]-[442] other texts.

In this second setting of the Kehl edition, 'auguste' replaces 'août' and 'et' is substituted for '&'. It differs textually from к84 at l.224 of the 'Seconde lettre'.

Taylor: VF.

Parodies

Augustin Nadal, *Arlequin au Parnasse, ou la folie de Melpomène* (Paris 1733). First performed at the Comédie-Italienne on 2 December 1732.

Dominique, Romagnesi and Francesco Riccoboni, *Les Enfans trouvez, ou le sultan poli par l'amour: parodie de la tragédie de Zaire, de monsieur de Voltaire* (Paris 1733). First performed at the Comédie-Italienne on 9 December 1732.

Bibliothèque nationale, F 9248, f.59-82. An anonymous parody, somewhat more indecent than *Les Enfants trouvés*. Many of its lines are taken directly from Voltaire's own text. The line 'Quel caprice étonnant que je ne conçois pas' (IV.124), which first appeared in w48D, shows that this parody must have been written after 1748.

Jean-Florent-Joseph de Neufville de Brunaubois-Montador, *Lettre au sujet de la rentrée de la demoiselle Le Maure à l'Opéra* (Bruxelles 1740). This is a parody of act 3, scene 4 of *Zaïre* which is directed not at mocking the play, but at satirising Mlle Le Maure. It was not intended to be acted.

M. de Vessaire, *Caquire* (Chio s.d.). A pseudonymous five-act verse parody of *Zaïre* which went through several editions. It is attributed variously to a number of gentlemen of Lyons, and Brenner (4976) states that it was performed 'en société' in that town. But J.-M. Quérard, *Les Supercheries littéraires dévoilées*, says nothing of performances, and the work itself is so childishly obscene that it is difficult to imagine that it was performed, even in private. See D545 and commentary and 'Une parodie de *Zaïre*', *L'Intermédiaire des chercheurs et curieux* 36 (1897), p.721; 37 (1898), p.298-99, 357-58, 830; 38 (1899), p.878.

12. *Editorial principles*

The base text is w75G, and variants are drawn from MS1, MS1*, 33R, 36A, w38, w46, w48D, w51, w52, w56, w57P, w68, w70L, K84 and K85. Variants for the epistle to Fawkener are also taken from 33RV, MS2, MS3, 33R* and 33A and from the *Mercure de France* (MF) for the epistle to Mlle Gaussin and the La Roque letter. Except in the epistle to Fawkener, and where otherwise stated, the siglum 33R indicates all the 1733 editions, 36A stands also for 36B and K stands for both K84 and K85.

Simple misprints are not recorded in the critical apparatus, nor are variations in punctuation having no effect upon the sense of the text.

The notes are mainly concerned with the elucidation of references which cannot be easily explained by the use of standard general works of reference. Resemblances between Voltaire's lines and those of Corneille or Racine have not been pointed out. These resemblances are frequent, but Voltaire is not guilty of plagiarism. He read and re-read the French tragedians of the previous century, and their influence upon his writing was as unconscious on his part as it was pervasive.

Modernisation of the base text

The spelling of the names of persons and places has been respected and the original punctuation retained.

The following aspects of orthography and grammar in the base text have been modified to conform to modern usage:

1. Consonants
   - the consonant *p* was not used in: tems, nor in its compound: longtems
   - the consonant *t* was not used in syllable endings *-ans* and *-ens*: monumens, négocians, etc.
   - double consonants were used in: allarmes, annoblir, fidelle (but also: fidèle), infidelle (and: infidèle), jetter, rappeller, serrail
   - a single consonant was used in: courier, falait, falu
   - archaic forms were used, as in: batême, batiser, bienfaicteur, hazarder, Mamelus, promt

2. Vowels
   - *y* was used in place of *i* in: asyle, aye, ayeux, enyvré, essuye, payen,
   - *ai* was used in place of *é* in: paitri

3. Accents
The acute accent
   - was used in place of the grave in: entiérement, grossiéreté, piéce
   - was not used in: desespéré, desespoir, deshonneur, repliquer
The grave accent
   - was not used in: déja
The circumflex accent
   - was not used in: ame, épitre, grace, idolatrie, théatre

- was used in: aîle, anathême, avoûrai, blasphême, Chrêtien, chûte, diadême, éperdûment, mêlange, plûpart, prophête, toûjours

The dieresis

- was used in: éblouïr, ingénuë, jouïr, jouïssance, obéïs, perduë, poëte, poëtiquement, vuë

4. Capitalisation
   - initial capitals were attributed to: Ambassade, Ambassadeur, Calife, Cardinal, Chevalier, Chrêtien, Christianisme, Conseil, Dames, Diable, Dieux, Docteur, Empire, Législateur, Madame, Magistrat, Maître, Messieurs, Ministère, Ministre, Monarque, Monsieur, Officier, Parlement, Payen, Pontife, Primatie, Prince, Reine, Religion, République, Roi, Royaume, Saint, Seigneur, Soudan, Sultan, Sultane, Univers
   - and to adjectives denoting nationality and creed

5. Points of grammar
   - the final –s was not used in the second person singular of the imperative: appren, croi, di, fai, plain, pren, reçoi, tien, voi
   - the plural in –x was used in: loix

6. Various
   - the ampersand was used
   - the hyphen was used in: à-peu-près, au-lieu, aussi-bien, genre-humain, grands-hommes, jusques-là, mot-à-mot, non-plus, tout-d'un-coup, très-persuadé, très-peu, très-grand
   - mademoiselle, monsieur, saint were abbreviated: Mlle., Mr., St.

ŹAYRE,

TRAGEDIE.

REPRESENTE'E A PARIS.

Aux mois d'Aouſt, Novembre & Décembre 1732.

Imprimée à Rouen
Chez J O R E Pere & Fils,

Et ſe vend
A P A R I S,
Chez JEAN-BAPTISTE BAUCHE, à la deſcente du
Pont-neuf, proche les Auguſtins, à Saint Jean-
Baptiſte dans le deſert.

M D C C X X X I I I.

AVEC PRIVILEGE DU ROY.

3. *Zaïre*: title-page of the first issue of the first edition, printed in Rouen by Jore (Taylor Institution, Oxford).

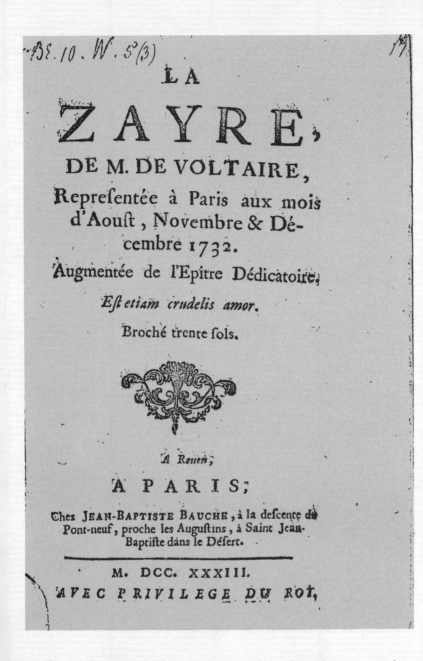

LA
ZAYRE,
DE M. DE VOLTAIRE,

Repreſentée à Paris aux mois
d'Aouſt , Novembre & Dé-
cembre 1732.

Augmentée de l'Epitre Dédicatoire.

Eſt etiam crudelis amor.

Broché trente ſols.

A Rouen;

A PARIS;

Chez JEAN-BAPTISTE BAUCHE , à la deſcente du
Pont-neuf, proche les Auguſtins , à Saint Jean-
Baptiſte dans le Déſert.

M. DCC. XXXIII.
AVEC PRIVILEGE DU ROI,

4. *Zaïre*: title-page of the second issue of the first edition, printed in
Rouen by Jore (Österreichische Nationalbibliothek, Wien).

LA ZAYRE

DE MONSIEUR

DE VOLTAIRE.

AVEC UNE EPITRE
DEDICATOIRE.

NOUVELLE EDITION.

Hic frango calamos, vigilataque car-
mina linquo.

A PARIS.

MDCCXXXIII.

5. *Zaïre*: title-page of the issue of the first edition containing the first version of the epistle to Fawkener (Österreichische Nationalbibliothek, Wien).

ZAYRE,

TRAGÉDIE.

*Représentée pour la première fois
le 13 août 1732.*

AVERTISSEMENT

Ceux qui aiment l'histoire littéraire seront bien aises de savoir comment cette pièce fut faite. Plusieurs dames avaient reproché à l'auteur, qu'il n'y avait pas assez d'amour dans ses tragédies. Il leur répondit, qu'il ne croyait pas que ce fût la véritable place de l'amour, mais que puisqu'il leur fallait absolument des héros amoureux, il en ferait tout comme un autre. La pièce fut achevée en dix-huit jours: elle eut un grand succès. On l'appelle à Paris, *tragédie chrétienne*, et on l'a jouée fort souvent à la place de *Polyeucte.*[1]

5

a-9 33R, 36A, absent (added in w38)
5-6 w42: héros bien amoureux
7 K: en vingt-deux jours
9 w42 cancel: de *Polieucte. Zayre* a fourni depuis peu un événement singulier à Londres; un gentilhomme anglais nommé M. Bond[2] passionné pour les spectacles, avait fait traduire cette pièce, et avant de la donner au théâtre public, il la fit jouer dans la grande salle des bâtiments d'York par ses amis; il y représentait le rôle de Lusignan; il mourut sur le théâtre au moment de la reconnaissance: les comédiens l'ont jouée depuis avec succès.

[1] See above, p.315 and note.
[2] See above, p.290, note 42. William Bond was apparently a 'gentleman', but he seems to have made a living chiefly by pursuing a rather undistinguished literary career.

EPÎTRE DÉDICATOIRE A M. FAKENER, MARCHAND ANGLAIS, DEPUIS AMBASSADEUR À CONSTANTINOPLE.[1]

Vous êtes Anglais,[2] mon cher ami, et je suis né en France; mais ceux qui aiment les arts sont tous concitoyens. Les honnêtes gens qui pensent ont à peu près les mêmes principes, et ne composent qu'une république; ainsi il n'est pas plus étrange de voir aujourd'hui une tragédie française dédiée à un Anglais, ou à un Italien, que si un citoyen d'Ephèse, ou d'Athènes, avait autrefois adressé son ouvrage à un Grec d'une autre ville. Je vous offre donc cette tragédie comme à mon compatriote dans la littérature, et comme à mon ami intime.

Je jouis en même temps du plaisir de pouvoir dire à ma nation,

5

1(

a-272 33R, absent from some copies
       36A, omitted
a-c   33RV, MS2, 33R, 33A: Epître dédicatoire, à monsieur Fakener, marchand anglais.//
       W51: I. épître dédicatoire

[1] Owing to his difficulties with censorship, Voltaire had to alter his first 'Epître dédicatoire' to Fawkener. The earliest known printed version is 33RV; that amended to meet the objections of the authorities is found in 33R; differences between these two versions, along with other variants, are recorded in MS2 and MS3. Some of the variants were published in the 1820 Lequien edition of Voltaire's *Œuvres complètes*, drawn perhaps from MS2.

[2] Voltaire's purpose in dedicating his play to an English merchant was, apart from giving Fawkener a mark of his respect and affection, to jolt his countrymen's prejudices. A number of the subjects examined at greater length in the *Lettres philosophiques* are touched upon in this 'Epître', which is written in very much the same spirit as Voltaire's first major polemical work. Voltaire's friends warned him that some of his remarks were liable to get him into trouble, but he defended his 'Epître', claiming that it contained only 'des vérités utiles adoucies par un badinage innocent', which could not possibly offend anybody (see D551 and D552).

de quel œil les négociants sont regardés chez vous,[3] quelle estime
on sait avoir en Angleterre pour une profession qui fait la grandeur
de l'Etat; et avec quelle supériorité quelques-uns d'entre vous
représentent leur patrie dans leur parlement, et sont au rang des
législateurs.   15

Je sais bien que cette profession est méprisée de nos petits-
maîtres; mais vous savez aussi, que nos petits-maîtres et les vôtres
sont l'espèce la plus ridicule, qui rampe avec orgueil sur la surface
de la terre.

Une raison encore, qui m'engage à m'entretenir de belles-   20
lettres avec un Anglais plutôt qu'avec un autre, c'est votre heureuse liberté de penser; elle en communique à mon esprit; mes
idées se trouvent plus hardies avec vous.

> Quiconque avec moi s'entretient,
> Semble disposer de mon âme: 25
> S'il sent vivement, il m'enflamme;
> Et s'il est fort, il me soutient.
> Un courtisan pétri de feinte,
> Fait dans moi tristement passer
> Sa défiance et sa contrainte;   30
> Mais un esprit libre, et sans crainte,
> M'enhardit, et me fait penser.
> Mon feu s'échauffe à sa lumière,
> Ainsi qu'un jeune peintre instruit
> Sous le Moine et sous l'Argilière   35
> De ces maîtres qui l'ont conduit
> Se rend la touche familière;

11   MS2:   regardés en Angleterre, quelle
12   MS2:   avoir chez vous pour
14   33RV, MS2, 33R, 33A: dans le parlement
22   33RV, MS2:   à mon âme, mes
23-34   33RV, MS2:   avec vous. ¶Ainsi le jeune
35   33RV, MS2, 33R, 33A, W38-W51:   Sous Coypel et [33RV: ou] sous

[3] See *Lettres philosophiques*, ed. Lanson and Rousseau (Paris 1964), i.121-22.

Il prend malgré lui leur manière,
Et compose avec leur esprit.
C'est pourquoi Virgile se fit   40
Un devoir d'admirer Homère.
Il le suivit dans sa carrière,
Et son émule il se rendit,
Sans se rendre son plagiaire.

Ne craignez pas qu'en vous envoyant ma pièce, je vous en   45
fasse une longue apologie; je pourrais vous dire, pourquoi je n'ai
pas donné à Zayre une vocation plus déterminée au christianisme,
avant qu'elle reconnût son père, et pourquoi elle cache son secret
à son amant, etc.[4] Mais les esprits sages, qui aiment à rendre
justice, verront bien mes raisons, sans que je les indique; pour les   5
critiques déterminés, qui sont disposés à ne me pas croire, ce
serait peine perdue que de les leur dire.

38-39   33RV, MS2:
                S'illumine de leur lumière
                Imagine avec leur esprit;
43   MS2:   Et son émule se rendit
44   33RV, MS2, MS3 add after line 44:
                Ainsi dans les bras d'un mari,
                Une femme lui faisant fête
                De son amant tendre et chéri
                Se remplit vivement la tête,
                Elle voit là son cher objet,
                Elle en a l'âme possédée,
                Et fait un fils qui, trait pour trait,
                Est bientôt le vivant portrait
                De celui dont elle eut l'idée.
45   MS2:   Ne croyez pas
        33RV: envoyant Zaïre, je
46-54   33RV: apologie, ni que je donne une belle dissertation métaphysique
pour prouver régulièrement la bonté de ma pièce au public qui ne m'en croirait
pas sur ma parole; je vous dirai seulement que Zaïre est une pièce assez simple,
50   MS2:   indique et pour
52   MS2, 33R, 33A, W38-W57P, W70L: que de leur dire mes raisons.

---

[4] These two points were among the major criticisms of the play made by
those who saw the early performances.

Je me vanterai avec vous d'avoir fait seulement une pièce assez
simple, qualité dont on doit faire cas de toutes façons.

Cette heureuse simplicité   55
Fut un des plus dignes partages
De la savante antiquité.
Anglais, que cette nouveauté
S'introduise dans vos usages.
Sur votre théâtre infecté   60
D'horreurs, de gibets, de carnages,
Mettez donc plus de vérité,
Avec de plus nobles images:
Addisson l'a déjà tenté;
C'était le poète des sages.   65
Mais il était trop concerté;
Et dans son *Caton* si vanté,
Ses deux filles, en vérité,
Sont d'insipides personnages.
Imitez du grand Addisson   70
Seulement ce qu'il a de bon:
Polissez la rude action
De vos Melpomènes sauvages;
Travaillez pour les connaisseurs
De tous les temps, de tous les âges,   75
Et répandez dans vos ouvrages
La simplicité de vos mœurs.[5]

Que messieurs les poètes anglais ne s'imaginent pas que je
veuille leur donner *Zayre* pour modèle: je leur prêche la simplicité

---

55   33RV, MS2: Cette noble simplicité
56   MS2: plus heureux partages
61   W51: De gibets et de batelages,
66   MS2, absent
79-80   33RV, MS2, 33R, 33A, W38: la simplicité, le naturel, et

---

[5] The whole of this development is echoed in the *Lettres philosophiques* (ii.84-85).

naturelle, et la douceur des vers; mais je ne me fais point du tout 80
le saint de mon sermon. Si *Zayre* a eu quelque succès, je le dois
beaucoup moins à la bonté de mon ouvrage, qu'à la prudence que
j'ai eue de parler d'amour le plus tendrement qu'il m'a été possible.
J'ai flatté en cela le goût de mon auditoire: on est assez sûr de
réussir, quand on parle aux passions des gens plus qu'à leur 85
raison. On veut de l'amour, quelque bon chrétien que l'on soit;
et je suis très persuadé que bien en prit au grand Corneille de ne
s'être pas borné dans son *Polyeucte* à faire casser les statues de
Jupiter par les néophytes; car telle est la corruption du genre
humain, que peut-être 90

> De Polyeucte la belle âme
> Aurait faiblement attendri,
> Et les vers chrétiens qu'il déclame
> Seraient tombés dans le décri,
> N'eût été l'amour de sa femme 95
> Pour ce païen son favori,
> Qui méritait bien mieux sa flamme
> Que son bon dévot de mari.

Même aventure à peu près est arrivée à Zayre. Tous ceux qui
vont aux spectacles, m'ont assuré, que si elle n'avait été que 100
convertie, elle aurait peu intéressé; mais elle est amoureuse de la
meilleure foi du monde, et voilà ce qui a fait sa fortune. Cependant
il s'en faut bien, que j'aie échappé à la censure.

> Plus d'un éplucheur intraitable

80   MS2: vers, je
80-81   MS2: point le saint
88   MS2: borné à faire
90-91   33RV: que / De Polyeucte
96   33RV: Pour un païen
97-98   MS2, 33R:
>   Qui régnait bien plus dans son âme
>   Que son indifférent mari.
100   33RV: au spectacle
101   33RV: elle aurait été sifflée; mais
102-103   33RV: fortune; au reste, mon ami, cette pièce a eu bien des censeurs.

M'a vétillé, m'a critiqué: 105
Plus d'un railleur impitoyable
Prétendait que j'avais croqué,
Et peu clairement expliqué
Un roman très peu vraisemblable,
Dans ma cervelle fabriqué; 110
Que le sujet en est tronqué,
Que la fin n'est pas raisonnable;
Même on m'avait pronostiqué
Ce sifflet tant épouvantable,
Avec quoi le public choqué 115
Régale un auteur misérable.
Cher ami, je me suis moqué
De leur censure insupportable.
J'ai mon drame en public risqué,
Et le parterre favorable 120
Au lieu du sifflet m'a claqué.
Des larmes même ont offusqué
Plus d'un œil, que j'ai remarqué
Pleurer de l'air le plus aimable.
Mais je ne suis point requinqué 125
Par un succès si désirable:
Car j'ai comme un autre marqué
Tous les *déficits* de ma fable.
Je sais qu'il est indubitable,
Que pour former œuvre parfait, 130
Il faudrait se donner au diable,
Et c'est ce que je n'ai pas fait.

Je n'ose me flatter que les Anglais fassent à *Zayre* le même

132 MS2: n'ai point fait.
133-162 33RV, MS2, MS3: Si on peut répondre de quelque chose, je m'imagine [MS2-3: j'imagine] que cette pièce de théâtre sera la dernière que je risquerai,
j'aime les lettres, mais plus je les aime, plus je souhaiterais de les voir dignement
accueillies [MS2: accueillir] [MS3: plus je suis fâché de les voir peu accueillir], on
jouit ici peut-être avec trop [MS3: avec un peu trop] d'indifférence des plaisirs 5
qu'un homme procure avec beaucoup de peines [MS3: peine]. Voyez [MS3: Voici],

397

honneur qu'ils ont fait à *Brutus*,[a] dont on a joué la traduction sur

[a] M. de Voltaire s'est trompé; on a traduit et joué *Zaïre* en Angleterre avec beaucoup de succès.

par exemple, un spectacle représenté à la cour, on y va par étiquette comme à une cérémonie ordinaire, sans daigner s'y intéresser, sans s'informer souvent du nom de l'auteur, que pour l'accabler en passant d'un mot de critique méprisant, et quelquefois absurde, on le tourne en ridicule bien ou mal au Théâtre Italien et à la Foire [MS3: critique médisante, et souvent absurde, enfin ce même public qui l'a applaudi va le voir tourner en ridicule au Théâtre italien et à la Foire et jouit de son humiliation avec plus de joie qu'il n'a joui de ses veilles,] ce n'est pas [MS2: le] tout: la calomnie le poursuit avec fureur, on cherche à le perdre, quand on ne peut l'avilir. Si l'homme de lettres est médiocre, il tombe dans le mépris le plus humiliant; s'il réussit il se fait les ennemis les plus cruels. Je sais et il faut le dire aux étrangers pour l'honneur de ma nation, qu'il [MS3: il] n'y a point de pays dans l'Europe où il y ait tant de belles fondations pour les arts, nous avons des académies de toute espèce, mais le frelon y prend trop souvent la place de l'abeille. Ce n'est pas assez de ces places qu'on est en possession de donner à la brigue, il faudrait des prix pour le mérite, car si ceux qui se distinguent un peu n'étaient soutenus par quelque récompense honorable, et par l'attrait le plus flatteur de la considération, tous les beaux-arts pourraient bien dépérir un jour au milieu des abris [MS2: arbres] élevés pour eux, et ces arbres plantés par Louis Quatorze dégénéreraient faute de [MS3 replaces lines 20v-25v by: l'abeille, ce n'est pas assez de ces honneurs frivoles, souvent avilis par ceux qu'on en veut orner, on trouve dans ces lieux avec étonnement le faiseur de madrigaux, souvent encore des gens plus obscurs, que rien ne sauve du mépris public que leur peu de renommée, le mérite que quelquefois on y admet, ou s'y refuse ou s'y voit avec indignation, il semble même que pour remplir cette place, il faille être plus accablé de la risée publique qu'honoré des applaudissements qu'on donne aux auteurs révérés, les têtes qu'on y couronne de laurier n'en sont pas à tel point couvertes qu'on n'y découvre encore les restes du chardon qui ceignait leur front sacré, mais quand il serait vrai que ces places fondées pour le mérite ne fussent remplies que par lui, que sont-elles sans les récompenses? et que deviennent les arts, s'ils ne sont soutenus par les regards du maître et par l'attrait le plus flatteur de la considération? ils peuvent dépérir au milieu des abris élevés pour eux, abris que le temps détruit tous les jours, bâtiments dont la mémoire subsiste et dont à peine on reconnaît la trace, les arbres plantés par Louis XIV dégénèrent faute de]

n.*a* 33RV, MS2, MS3, 33R, 33A, absent (added in W38)
134 33R, 33A, W38-W51: on va jouer la

le théâtre de Londres.[6] Vous avez ici la réputation de n'être ni   135
assez dévots pour vous soucier beaucoup du vieux Lusignan, ni
assez tendres pour être touchés de Zayre. Vous passez pour aimer
mieux une intrigue de conjurés, qu'une intrigue d'amants. On
croit qu'à votre théâtre on bat des mains au mot de *patrie*, et chez
nous à celui d'*amour*; cependant la vérité est que vous mettez de   140
l'amour tout comme nous dans vos tragédies. Si vous n'avez pas
la réputation d'être tendres, ce n'est pas que vos héros de théâtre
ne soient amoureux; mais c'est qu'ils expriment rarement leur
passion d'une manière naturelle. Nos amants parlent en amants,
et les vôtres ne parlent encore qu'en poètes.   145

Si vous permettez que les Français soient vos maîtres en
galanterie, il y a bien des choses en récompense que nous pour-
rions prendre de vous. C'est au théâtre anglais que je dois la
hardiesse que j'ai eue de mettre sur la scène les noms de nos rois
et des anciennes familles du royaume. Il me paraît, que cette   150
nouveauté pourrait être la source d'un genre de tragédie qui nous
est inconnu jusqu'ici, et dont nous avons besoin. Il se trouvera
sans doute des génies heureux, qui perfectionneront cette idée,
dont *Zayre* n'est qu'une faible ébauche. Tant que l'on continuera
en France de protéger les lettres, nous aurons assez d'écrivains.   155
La nature forme presque toujours des hommes en tout genre de
talent; il ne s'agit que de les encourager et de les employer. Mais
si ceux qui se distinguent un peu n'étaient soutenus par quelque
récompense honorable, et par l'attrait plus flatteur de la considéra-

---

154-155   33R*: ébauche. ⟨β⟩ $^{V\uparrow}$ Si L'on veut en France proteger
158   33R*: peu ⟨β⟩ $^{V\uparrow}$ ne sont soutenus

[6] Voltaire's *Brutus*, first played in Paris at the end of 1730, was translated by
William Duncombe in 1732. It was accepted for production by the managers
of Drury Lane, but not actually played until November 1734. Voltaire had heard
of the translation, for Cideville mentions it in a letter to him dated 11 August
1733 (D644). This is why the 1733 editions have 'dont on va jouer'. This
reading should have been corrected in w38 but was overlooked until w56, which
introduces 'dont on a joué'. Duncombe's translation was published in 1745 and
a second edition appeared in 1747.

tion,[7] tous les beaux-arts pourraient bien dépérir un jour au milieu   16c
des abris élevés pour eux: et ces arbres plantés par Louis XIV
dégénéreraient faute de culture: le public aurait toujours du goût,
mais les grands maîtres manqueraient. Un sculpteur dans son
académie verrait des hommes médiocres à côté de lui, et n'élèverait
pas sa pensée jusqu'à Girardon et au Pujet; un peintre se contente-   16
rait de se croire supérieur à son confrère, et ne songerait pas à
égaler le Poussin. Puissent les successeurs de Louis XIV suivre
toujours l'exemple de ce grand roi, qui donnait d'un coup d'œil
une noble émulation à tous les artistes! Il encourageait à la fois
un Racine et un van Robais[8]... Il portait notre commerce et notre   17
gloire par-delà les Indes; il étendait ses grâces sur des étrangers
étonnés d'être connus et récompensés par notre cour. Partout où
était le mérite, il avait un protecteur dans Louis XIV.

> Car de son astre bienfaisant
> Les influences libérales,   17
> Du Caire au bord de l'Occident
> Et sous les glaces boréales,
> Cherchaient le mérite indigent.
> Avec plaisir ses mains royales

160   K: dépérir au milieu
162-171   33RV, MS2, MS3: le public aura toujours du goût, mais les grands
maîtres manqueront, un sculpteur dans son académie verra des hommes médiocres à côté de lui et n'élèvera pas sa pensée jusqu'à Girardon et au Pujet [MS2-
3: à Puget], un peintre se contentera de se croire [MS2-3: d'être] supérieur à son
confrère, et ne songera pas à égaler Le Poussin, Louis XIV donnait d'un coup
d'œil une noble émulation à tous les artistes, M. Colbert le père des arts sous
Louis Quatorze [MS3: sous ce grand roi] encourageait à la fois un Racine et un
Van-robès, il portait notre commerce et notre gloire par-delà les [MS2: au-delà
des] Indes, il étendait les libéralités de son maître sur des étrangers
167   33R: Les successeurs de Louis XIV suivront toujours sans doute l'exemple

[7] The wording here recalls the heading of chapter 23 of the *Lettres philosophiques*, 'Sur la considération qu'on doit aux gens de lettres'.
[8] Josse Van Robais (1630-1685). Colbert invited this Dutch cloth manufacturer
to settle in France, where he established a flourishing business.

Répandaient la gloire et l'argent,   180
Le tout sans brigue et sans cabales.
Guillelmini, Viviani,
Et le céleste Cassini,
Auprès des lis venaient se rendre;
Et quelque forte pension   185
Vous aurait pris le grand Newton,
Si Newton avait pu se prendre.
Ce sont là les heureux succès
Qui faisaient la gloire immortelle
De Louis et du nom français.   190
Ce Louis était le modèle
De l'Europe et de vos Anglais.
On craignait que par ses progrès
Il n'envahît à tout jamais
La monarchie universelle;   195
Mais il l'obtint par ses bienfaits.[9]

Vous n'avez pas chez vous des fondations pareilles aux monu-
ments de la munificence de nos rois; mais votre nation y supplée.
Vous n'avez pas besoin des regards du maître pour honorer et
récompenser les grands talents en tout genre. Le chevalier Steele   200
et le chevalier van Brouk,[10] étaient en même temps auteurs
comiques et membres du parlement. La primatie du docteur

193   33RV, MS2, 33R, 33A, W38-W57P: On craignit
197   W51: Vous n'avez pas besoin chez vous des
      33RV, MS2, 33R, 33A: de fondations
198   33RV: munificence de notre Louis Quatorze, mais
      MS2: munificence de Louis Quatorze, mais

[9] This extended panegyric upon Louis xiv heralds Voltaire's praise in *Le Siècle
de Louis XIV*, on which he was already working in 1732.
[10] Voltaire is letting his enthusiasm run away with him. While Sir Richard
Steele was indeed a member of Parliament, Sir John Vanbrugh was never elected
to the House of Commons. In the *Lettres philosophiques*, when speaking of
Vanbrugh, Voltaire makes no mention of his membership of the Commons
(ii.107-108).

Tillotson, l'ambassade de M. Prior, la charge de M. Newton, le
ministère de M. Addisson, ne sont que les suites ordinaires de la
considération qu'ont chez vous les grands hommes. Vous les   205
comblez de biens pendant leur vie, vous leur élevez des mausolées
et des statues après leur mort; il n'y a jusqu'aux actrices célèbres
qui n'aient chez vous leur place dans les temples à côté des grands
poètes.[11]

> Votre Ofilds[b] et sa devancière   210
> Bracegirdle la minaudière,
> Pour avoir su dans leurs beaux jours
> Réussir au grand art de plaire,
> Ayant achevé leur carrière,
> S'en furent, avec le concours   215
> De votre république entière,
> Sous un grand poêle de velours,
> Dans votre église pour toujours,
> Loger de superbe manière.
> Leur ombre en paraît encor fière,   220
> Et s'en vante avec les Amours:

[b] Fameuse actrice mariée à un seigneur d'Angleterre.

207   33RV, MS2: il n'y a pas jusqu'aux
n.*b* 33RV, MS2, MS3, 33R, 33A, W38, absent (added in W48D)
215   W46, W51: avec leur concours
217   33RV: Sous un beau poêle

[11] Cf. *Lettres philosophiques*, ii.159.

Tandis que le divin Molière,
Bien plus digne d'un tel honneur,
A peine obtint le froid bonheur
De dormir dans un cimetière;   225
Et que l'aimable le Couvreur,
A qui j'ai fermé la paupière,
N'a pas eu même la faveur
De deux cierges et d'une bière;
Et que monsieur de Laubinière   230
Porta la nuit par charité,
Ce corps autrefois si vanté,
Dans un vieux fiacre empaqueté,
Vers le bord de notre rivière.

222-244   33R:

> Que chez vous à jamais respire
> Cet heureux goût pour les beaux-arts;
> Qu'il soit l'âme de notre empire;
> Qu'avec Londres Paris conspire
> A s'unir sous les étendards
> Du docte dieu qui nous inspire,
> Du dieu dont la charmante lyre
> Doit à jamais nous interdire
> Le bruit des trompettes de Mars

Puissent l'Angleterre et la France jouir longtemps de cette paix si nécessaire aux lettres, comme au commerce; puissions-nous conserver cette supériorité que les beaux-arts nous ont donnée sur tant d'autres peuples. La terre

222   33RV, MS2, MS3: le sage Molière
224-225   33RV, MS2, MS3:

> Obtint [MS2-3: Obtient] à peine la faveur
> D'un misérable cimetière,

226   33RV, MS2: Que notre aimable
228-229   33RV, MS2, MS3: Ne put avoir [MS3: trouver] un enterreur,
234   33RV: Vers les bords
234-235   MS2, MS3:

> Vers les bords de notre rivière
> Que mon cœur en a palpité!
> Cher ami, que j'ai détesté
> La rigueur inhospitalière
> Dont ce cher objet fut traité!
> Cette gothique indignité

Voyez-vous pas à ce récit   235
L'amour irrité qui gémit,
Qui s'envole en brisant ses armes,
Et Melpomène tout en larmes,
Qui m'abandonne, et se bannit
Des lieux ingrats qu'elle embellit   240
Si longtemps de ses nobles charmes?

Tout semble ramener les Français à la barbarie dont Louis xiv
et le cardinal de Richelieu les ont tirés. Malheur aux politiques
qui ne connaissent pas le prix des beaux-arts! La terre est couverte
de nations aussi puissantes que nous. D'où vient cependant que   245
nous les regardons presque toutes avec peu d'estime? C'est par
la raison qu'on méprise dans la société un homme riche, dont
l'esprit est sans goût et sans culture. Surtout ne croyez pas, que
cet empire de l'esprit, et cet honneur d'être le modèle des autres
peuples, soit une gloire frivole. Elle est la marque infaillible de   25c

N'a-t-elle donc pas révolté
Les Muses et l'Europe entière?
Voyez-vous

242-256 33RV, MS2, MS3: Voilà en partie, mon cher Fakener, les raisons
pour lesquelles je prends congé pour jamais, comme [MS3: congé, comme] je le
crois et comme je ne l'assure pourtant pas de notre théâtre français, permettez-
moi d'ajouter à cette épître dédicatoire dictée par mon cœur et par ma liberté
une petite pièce de vers assez connue dans ce pays-ci, et qui trouve naturellement

242-272 33R*: Voila en partie pour quoy bien des autheurs prendroient
Congé Du Theatre francais, si La passion D'ecrire n'étoit pas une de celles que
Les rigueurs ne font qu'augmenter. Voyez par exemple une piece representée
à La Cour. On y va par etiquette Comme a une Ceremonie ordinaire Sans
Daigner s'y interesser ou sans s'informer Du nom de L'autheur que pour
L'accabler en passant d'un mot de critique meprisant, et quelquefois absurde.
C'est ainsi qu'on traite presque tous les arts, on en est environné, et on dedaigne
de Les regarder, a force de nous etre accoutumés au bon nous pourions
insensiblement retomber dans La barbarie.

242 33A: Voilà comme les beaux-arts sont aujourd'hui traités en France.
C'est dans la patrie de Corneille qu'on jette des acteurs à la voirie, et qu'on
méprise les auteurs qui réussissent. Le courtisan aussi insolent que bas nous
dédaigne; la superstition nous persécute; la jalousie nous calomnie; l'ignorance
nous tourne en ridicule, et tout semble ramener

250 K: Ce sont les marques infaillibles de

la grandeur d'un empire: c'est toujours sous les plus grands princes que les arts ont fleuri, et leur décadence est quelquefois l'époque de celle d'un Etat. L'histoire est pleine de ces exemples; mais ce sujet me mènerait trop loin. Il faut que je finisse cette lettre déjà trop longue, en vous envoyant un petit ouvrage, qui   255
trouve naturellement sa place à la tête de cette tragédie. C'est une épître en vers à celle qui a joué le rôle de Zayre: je lui devais au moins un compliment pour la façon dont elle s'en est acquittée:

> Car le prophète de la Mecque
> Dans son sérail n'a jamais eu   260
> Si gentille Arabesque ou Grecque;
> Son œil noir, tendre et bien fendu,
> Sa voix, et sa grâce intrinsèque,
> Ont mon ouvrage défendu
> Contre l'auditeur qui rebèque: 265
> Mais quand le lecteur morfondu
> L'aura dans sa bibliothèque,
> Tout mon honneur sera perdu.

Adieu, mon ami; cultivez toujours les lettres et la philosophie, sans oublier d'envoyer des vaisseaux dans les échelles du Levant.   270
Je vous embrasse de tout mon cœur.

V.

252-253   33R, 33A, W38, W46:   décadence est l'époque
263   33RV, 33R, 33A, W38-W57P: extrinsèque

EPÎTRE À MADEMOISELLE GOSSIN,
JEUNE ACTRICE,

Qui a représenté le rôle de Zayre
avec beaucoup de succès.[1]

Jeune Gossin, reçois mon tendre hommage,
Reçois mes vers au théâtre applaudis,
Protège-les, *Zayre* est ton ouvrage,
Il est à toi, puisque tu l'embellis.
Ce sont tes yeux, ces yeux si pleins de charmes,   5
Ta voix touchante, et tes sons enchanteurs,
Qui du critique ont fait tomber les armes.
Ta seule vue adoucit les censeurs.
L'illusion, cette reine des cœurs,
Marche à ta suite, inspire les alarmes,   10
Le sentiment, les regrets, les douleurs,
Et le plaisir de répandre des larmes.
    Le dieu des vers, qu'on allait dédaigner,
Est par ta voix aujourd'hui sûr de plaire;
Le dieu d'amour, à qui tu fus plus chère,   15
Est par tes yeux bien plus sûr de régner.
Entre ces dieux désormais tu vas vivre:

a-27   33R, absent from some copies
          33A, absent
  1   MF: reçois pour tendre
  6   MF, omitted
  8   MF: Ton seul aspect adoucit
 12   MF: Le doux plaisir

[1] This poem first appeared in the *Mercure de France* for November 1732. This explains Voltaire's reference to it in the variant reading of MS2 and MS3 as 'une petite pièce de vers assez connue dans ce pays-ci' (see above, p.404, lines 242-256v).

Hélas! longtemps je les servis tous deux;
Il en est un que je n'ose plus suivre.
Heureux cent fois le mortel amoureux,   20
Qui tous les jours peut te voir et t'entendre,
Que tu reçois avec un souris tendre,
Qui voit son sort écrit dans tes beaux yeux,
Qui pénétré de leurs feux qu'il adore,
A tes genoux oubliant l'univers,   25
Parle d'amour, et t'en reparle encore!
Et malheureux qui n'en parle qu'en vers!

18   MF: les suivis tous
19   MF: que je ne puis plus
24   W46, W51:   Qui consumé de ces feux
     MF, K: leur feu
24-25   33R, W38:
         Qui meurt d'amour, qui te plaît, qui t'adore,
         Qui pénétré de cent plaisirs divers,
27   MF: Mais malheureux

SECONDE LETTRE
AU MÊME MONSIEUR FAKENER,
ALORS AMBASSADEUR
À CONSTANTINOPLE,
tirée d'une seconde édition de Zayre

Mon cher ami; (car votre nouvelle dignité d'ambassadeur rend seulement notre amitié plus respectable, et ne m'empêche pas de me servir ici d'un titre plus sacré que le titre de ministre: le nom d'ami est bien au-dessus de celui d'Excellence.)

Je dédie à l'ambassadeur d'un grand roi et d'une nation libre, le même ouvrage que j'ai dédié au simple citoyen, au négociant anglais.[a]

Ceux qui savent combien le commerce est honoré dans votre patrie, n'ignorent pas aussi qu'un négociant y est quelquefois un législateur, un bon officier, un ministre public.

Quelques personnes, corrompues par l'indigne usage de ne rendre hommage qu'à la grandeur, ont essayé de jeter un ridicule sur la nouveauté d'une dédicace faite à un homme qui n'avait alors que du mérite. On a osé, sur un théâtre[1] consacré au mauvais

---

[a] Ce que M. de Voltaire avait prévu dans sa dédicace de *Zaïre* est arrivé; M. Fakener a été un des meilleurs ministres, et est devenu un des hommes des plus considérables de l'Angleterre. C'est ainsi que les auteurs devraient dédier leurs ouvrages, au lieu d'écrire des lettres d'esclave à des gens dignes de l'être.

a-234 33R, w38, absent (added in 36A)
a-e 36A: A monsieur le chevalier Fakener, ambassadeur d'Angleterre à la Porte ottomane.
n.*a* 36A, w51, absent (added in w52)

---

[1] See above, p.295, note 54. In spite of Voltaire's assertions here, d'Allainval's play does not appear to have ever been performed (see D642).

goût et à la médisance, insulter à l'auteur de cette dédicace; et à   15
celui qui l'avait reçue, on a osé lui reprocher d'être^b un négociant.
Il ne faut point imputer à notre nation une grossièreté si honteuse,
dont les peuples les moins civilisés rougiraient. Les magistrats,
qui veillent parmi nous sur les mœurs, et qui sont continuellement
occupés à réprimer le scandale, furent surpris alors. Mais le mépris   20
et l'horreur du public pour l'auteur connu de cette indignité, sont
une nouvelle preuve de la politesse des Français.

Les vertus qui forment le caractère d'un peuple, sont souvent
démenties par les vices d'un particulier. Il y a eu quelques hommes
voluptueux à Lacédémone. Il y a eu des esprits légers et bas en   25
Angleterre. Il y a eu dans Athènes des hommes sans goût, impolis
et grossiers; et on en trouve dans Paris.

Oublions-les, comme ils sont oubliés du public, et recevez ce
second hommage. Je le dois d'autant plus à un Anglais, que cette
tragédie vient d'être embellie à Londres. Elle y a été traduite et   30
jouée avec tant de succès,[2] on a parlé de moi sur votre théâtre
avec tant de politesse et de bonté, que j'en dois ici un remerciement
public à votre nation.

Je ne peux mieux faire, je crois, pour l'honneur des lettres, que
d'apprendre ici à mes compatriotes les singularités de la traduction   35
et de la représentation de *Zayre* sur le théâtre de Londres.

^b   On joua une mauvaise farce à la Comédie italienne de Paris, dans
laquelle on insultait grossièrement plusieurs personnes de mérite, et
entre autres, M. Fakener. Le sieur Hérault, lieutenant de police, permit
cette indignité, et le public la siffla.

n.*b*   36A, w38, absent (added in w48D)
n.*b*, 4   K: la siffla. C'est ce même Hérault à qui M. de Voltaire disait un
jour: Monsieur, que fait-on à ceux qui fabriquent de fausses lettres de cachet?
– On les pend – C'est toujours bien fait, en attendant qu'on traite de même ceux
qui en signent de vraies.
25   36A, w48D, w51: Il y a des

[2] See above, p.289-91.

Monsieur Hille, homme de lettres, qui paraît connaître le théâtre mieux qu'aucun auteur anglais, me fit l'honneur de traduire la pièce, dans le dessein d'introduire sur votre scène quelques nouveautés, et pour la manière d'écrire les tragédies, et pour celle de les réciter. Je parlerai d'abord de la représentation. 40

L'art de déclamer était chez vous un peu hors de la nature; la plupart de vos acteurs tragiques s'exprimaient souvent plus en poètes saisis d'enthousiasme, qu'en hommes que la passion inspire. Beaucoup de comédiens avaient encore outré ce défaut; 45 ils déclamaient des vers ampoulés, avec une fureur et une impétuosité, qui est au beau naturel, ce que des convulsions sont à l'égard d'une démarche noble et aisée.

Cet air d'empressement semblait étranger à votre nation; car elle est naturellement sage, et cette sagesse est quelquefois prise 50 pour de la froideur par les étrangers. Vos prédicateurs ne se permettent jamais un ton de déclamateur. On rirait chez vous d'un avocat qui s'échaufferait dans son plaidoyer. Les seuls comédiens étaient outrés. Nos acteurs, et surtout nos actrices de Paris, avaient ce défaut, il y a quelques années: ce fut Mlle le 5 Couvreur qui les en corrigea. Voyez ce qu'en dit un auteur italien de beaucoup d'esprit et de sens.

> La legiadra Couvreur sola non trotta
> Per quella strada dove i suoi compagni
> Van di galoppo tutti quanti in frotta, 6
> Se avvien ch'ella pianga, o che si lagni
> Senza quegli urli spaventosi loro,
> Tu muove si che in pianger l'accompagni.

Ce même changement que Mlle le Couvreur avait fait sur notre scène, Mlle Cibber vient de l'introduire sur le théâtre anglais, ε dans le rôle de Zayre. Chose étrange, que dans tous les arts ce ne soit qu'après bien du temps qu'on vienne enfin au naturel et au simple!

38-39 K: traduire ma pièce
47 K: que les convulsions

Une nouveauté qui va paraître plus singulière aux Français, c'est qu'un gentilhomme de votre pays, qui a de la fortune et de la considération, n'a pas dédaigné de jouer sur votre théâtre le rôle d'Orosmane.[3] C'était un spectacle assez intéressant de voir les deux principaux personnages remplis, l'un par un homme de condition, et l'autre par une jeune actrice de dix-huit ans, qui n'avait pas encore récité un vers en sa vie.

Cet exemple d'un citoyen, qui a fait usage de son talent pour la déclamation, n'est pas le premier parmi vous. Tout ce qu'il y a de surprenant en cela, c'est que nous nous en étonnions.

Nous devrions faire réflexion, que toutes les choses de ce monde dépendent de l'usage et de l'opinion. La cour de France a dansé sur le théâtre avec les acteurs de l'Opéra, et on n'a rien trouvé en cela d'étrange, sinon que la mode de ces divertissements ait fini. Pourquoi sera-t-il plus étonnant de réciter que de danser en public? Y a-t-il d'autre différence entre ces deux arts, sinon que l'un est autant au-dessus de l'autre, que les talents où l'esprit a quelque part sont au-dessus de ceux du corps? Je le répète encore, et je le dirai toujours, aucun des beaux-arts n'est méprisable, et il n'est véritablement honteux que d'attacher de la honte aux talents.

Venons à présent à la traduction de *Zayre*, et au changement qui vient de se faire chez vous dans l'art dramatique.[4]

[3] As in the early performances at Villars Street (see above, p.290, note 42), the part of Orosmane at Drury Lane was first taken by Aaron Hill's nephew, who was not a professional actor. He was, however, slated by the critics and abandoned his part to a member of the Drury Lane company, who, being unprepared, had to read it on stage until he had learnt it. See Thomas Davies, *Memoirs of the life of David Garrick* (London 1780), i.137.

[4] The following two paragraphs, in which Voltaire claims on Hill's behalf that he abolished the practice of English playwrights of ending each act with a rhyming couplet comprising a simile, gave rise to some controversy. Lessing, in his *Hamburgische Dramaturgie*, stated firstly, that it was untrue that the rhyming couplets at the end of acts always or even normally comprised a simile; secondly, that all Hill's acts, contrary to what Voltaire says here, do end with a rhyming couplet; and thirdly, that the practice continued as before, even though Voltaire said that Hill's example had killed the fashion. See Lessing, *Hamburgische Dramaturgie*, ed Mann, p.63-65.

Vous aviez une coutume à laquelle M. Addisson, le plus sage
de vos écrivains, s'est asservi lui-même; tant l'usage tient lieu de
raison et de loi. Cette coutume peu raisonnable était de finir
chaque acte par des vers d'un goût différent du reste de la pièce,   95
et ces vers devaient nécessairement renfermer une comparaison.
Phèdre en sortant du théâtre se comparait poétiquement à une
biche,[5] Caton à un rocher,[6] Cléopatre à des enfants qui pleurent
jusqu'à ce qu'ils soient endormis.[7]

[5] The only English play of the period that I have been able to discover with
'Phèdre' as a character is Edmund Smith's *Phaedra and Hippolitus*, which is a free
adaptation of Racine's *Phèdre*. It was first performed in 1707 and ran to several
editions. But no act ends with a simile in which Phaedra compares herself to a
doe. Is Voltaire perhaps thinking of the passage in act 1, scene 1, where Phaedra,
raving, confesses her love for Hippolitus to her minister, Lycon?

> I'll think no more,
> I'll to the Woods among the happier Brutes:
> Come, let's away, hark the shrill Horn resounds,
> The jolly Huntsmens Cries rend the wide Heav'ns:
> Come, o'er the Hills pursue the bounding Stagg,
> Come chase the Lion and the foamy Boar,
> Come rouse up all the Monsters of the Wood,
> For there, e'vn there, *Hippolitus* will guard me.

(*Phaedra and Hippolitus*, 3rd ed., London 1720, p.8). But Voltaire's memory is
usually more reliable than this, and it seems likely that I have not traced the
passage he is thinking of.

[6] Voltaire is almost certainly thinking of the eponymous hero of Addison's
Cato, but no such image is expressed as a simile at the end of any act by Cato
himself. But Voltaire may be recalling Sempronius' speech in act 2 where he
compares Cato to Mount Atlas:

> Thou has seen Mount Atlas:
> While Storms and Tempests thunder on its Brows,
> And Oceans break their Billows at its Feet,
> It stands unmoved, and glorie's in its Height.
> Such is that haughty Man...

(*Cato, a tragedy*, London 1713, p.30). It is far less likely that Voltaire had in
mind an obscure play entitled *Cato of Utica*, translated in 1716 from the French
original of Deschamps by John Ozell. Voltaire may well have seen this play on
3 or 31 December 1726, when it was given at the Drury Lane Theatre. In any
case, this play does not have a simile in which Cato compares himself to a rock.

[7] In Dryden's *All for Love*, Cleopatra ends act 3 with the couplet:

412

Le traducteur de *Zayre* est le premier qui ait osé maintenir les   100
droits de la nature contre un goût si éloigné d'elle. Il a proscrit
cet usage; il a senti que la passion doit parler un langage vrai, et
que le poète doit se cacher toujours pour ne laisser paraître que
le héros.

C'est sur ce principe qu'il a traduit avec naïveté, et sans aucune   105
enflure, tous les vers simples de la pièce, que l'on gâterait, si on
voulait les rendre beaux.

> On ne peut désirer ce qu'on ne connaît pas.[8]

> * *

> J'eusse été près du Gange esclave des faux dieux,
> Chrétienne dans Paris, musulmane en ces lieux.[9]   110

> * *

> Mais Orosmane m'aime, et j'ai tout oublié.[10]

> * *

> Non, la reconnaissance est un faible retour,
> Un tribut offensant, trop peu fait pour l'amour.[11]

> * *

> Je me croirais haï d'être aimé faiblement.[12]

> * *

> Je veux avec excès vous aimer et vous plaire.[13]   115

> * *

> L'art n'est pas fait pour toi, tu n'en as pas besoin.[14]

There I till Death will his unkindness weep:
As harmless infants moan themselves to sleep.

[8] I.i.19.
[9] I.i.107-108.
[10] I.i.136.
[11] I.i.143-144.
[12] I.ii.208.
[13] I.ii.210.
[14] IV.ii.144.

* *

L'art le plus innocent tient de la perfidie.[15]

Tous les vers qui sont dans ce goût simple et vrai, sont rendus mot à mot dans l'anglais. Il eût été aisé de les orner; mais le traducteur a jugé autrement que quelques-uns de mes compatriotes; il a aimé, et il a rendu toute la naïveté de ces vers. En effet, le style doit être conforme au sujet. *Alzire*, *Brutus* et *Zayre* demandaient, par exemple, trois sortes de versifications différentes.

Si Bérénice se plaignait de Titus, et Ariane de Thésée,[16] dans le style de *Cinna*, Bérénice et Ariane ne toucheraient point.

Jamais on ne parlera bien d'amour, si on cherche d'autres ornements que la simplicité et la vérité.

Il n'est pas question ici d'examiner s'il est bien de mettre tant d'amour dans les pièces de théâtre. Je veux que ce soit une faute, elle est et sera universelle; et je ne sais quel nom donner aux fautes qui font le charme du genre humain.

Ce qui est certain, c'est que dans ce défaut les Français ont réussi plus que toutes les autres nations anciennes et modernes mises ensemble. L'amour paraît sur nos théâtres avec des bienséances, une délicatesse, une vérité, qu'on ne trouve point ailleurs. C'est que de toutes les nations la française est celle qui a le plus connu la société.

Le commerce continuel si vif et si poli des deux sexes, a introduit en France une politesse assez ignorée ailleurs.

La société dépend des femmes. Tous les peuples qui ont le malheur de les enfermer sont insociables. Et des mœurs encore austères parmi vous, des querelles politiques, des guerres de religion, qui vous avaient rendus farouches, vous ôtèrent, jusqu'au temps de Charles II, la douceur de la société, au milieu même de la liberté. Les poètes ne devaient donc savoir ni dans aucun pays,

125   36A, w46: style de Cornélie

[15] IV.ii.146
[16] Ariane in Thomas Corneille's tragedy of that name.

ni même chez les Anglais, la manière dont les honnêtes gens traitent l'amour.

La bonne comédie fut ignorée jusqu'à Molière, comme l'art d'exprimer sur le théâtre des sentiments vrais et délicats fut ignoré jusqu'à Racine, parce que la société ne fut, pour ainsi dire, dans sa perfection que de leur temps. Un poète, du fond de son cabinet, ne peut peindre des mœurs qu'il n'a point vues; il aura plutôt fait cent odes et cent épîtres, qu'une scène où il faut faire parler la nature. 150

Votre Dryden, qui d'ailleurs était un très grand génie, mettait dans la bouche de ses héros amoureux, ou des hyperboles de rhétorique, ou des indécences, deux choses également opposées à la tendresse. 155

Si M. Racine fait dire à Titus:

> Depuis cinq ans entiers chaque jour je la vois, 160
> Et crois toujours la voir pour la première fois,[17]

votre Dryden fait dire à Antoine:

'Ciel! comme j'aimai! Témoin les jours et les nuits qui suivaient en dansant sous vos pieds. Ma seule affaire était de vous parler de ma passion; un jour venait, et ne voyait rien qu'amour; un autre venait, et c'était de l'amour encore. Les soleils étaient las de nous regarder, et moi je n'étais point las d'aimer.'[18] 165

Il est bien difficile d'imaginer qu'Antoine ait en effet tenu de pareils discours à Cléopatre.

Dans la même pièce, Cléopatre parle ainsi à Antoine: 170

'Venez à moi, venez dans mes bras, mon cher soldat; j'ai été trop longtemps privée de vos caresses. Mais quand je vous embrasserai, quand vous serez tout à moi, je vous punirai de vos cruautés, en laissant sur vos lèvres l'impression de mes ardents baisers.'[19] 175

---

[17] *Bérénice*, ii.545-546.
[18] *All for love*, ii.i.
[19] *All for love*, iii.i. Cf. *Lettres philosophiques*, ii.83, where Voltaire speaks of Dryden as an 'auteur plus fécond que judicieux'.

Il est très vraisemblable que Cléopatre parlait souvent dans ce goût: mais ce n'est point cette indécence qu'il faut représenter devant une audience respectable.

Quelques-uns de vos compatriotes ont beau dire, C'est là la pure nature; on doit leur répondre que c'est précisément cette nature qu'il faut voiler avec soin.

Ce n'est pas même connaître le cœur humain, de penser qu'on doit plaire davantage en présentant ces images licencieuses. Au contraire, c'est fermer l'entrée de l'âme aux vrais plaisirs. Si tout est d'abord à découvert, on est rassasié. Il ne reste plus rien à chercher, rien à désirer, et on arrive tout d'un coup à la langueur en croyant courir à la volupté. Voilà pourquoi la bonne compagnie a des plaisirs que les gens grossiers ne connaissent pas.

Les spectateurs en ce cas font comme les amants, qu'une jouissance trop prompte dégoûte: ce n'est qu'à travers cent nuages qu'on doit entrevoir ces idées, qui feraient rougir, présentées de trop près. C'est ce voile qui fait le charme des honnêtes gens; il n'y a point pour eux de plaisir sans bienséance.

Les Français ont connu cette règle plus tôt que les autres peuples, non pas parce qu'*ils sont sans génie et sans hardiesse*,[20] comme le dit ridiculement l'inégal et impétueux Dryden, mais parce que depuis la régence d'Anne d'Autriche, ils ont été le peuple le plus sociable et le plus poli de la terre; et cette politesse n'est point une chose arbitraire, comme ce qu'on appelle civilité; c'est une loi de la nature qu'ils ont heureusement cultivée plus que les autres peuples.

Le traducteur de *Zayre* a respecté presque partout ces bienséan-

---

196 36A, w46: comme le dit Dryden

[20] I have not found this exact formulation used by Dryden, but Voltaire is almost certainly thinking of the passage in the preface to *All for love*, where Dryden, speaking of French drama, says: 'All their Wit is in their Ceremony; they want the Genius which animates our Stage: and therefore 'tis but necessary, when they cannot please, that they should take care not to offend' (*The Dramatick works*, London 1735, iv, sig. H10v).

416

ces théâtrales, qui vous doivent être communes comme à nous; mais il y a quelques endroits où il s'est livré encore à d'anciens usages.

Par exemple, lorsque dans la pièce anglaise Orosmane vient annoncer à Zayre qu'il croit ne la plus aimer, Zayre lui répond en se roulant par terre. Le sultan n'est point ému de la voir dans cette posture de ridicule et de désespoir, et le moment d'après il est tout étonné que Zayre pleure.

Il lui dit cet hémistiche:

> Zayre, vous pleurez.

Il aurait dû lui dire auparavant:

> Zayre, vous vous roulez par terre.[21]

Aussi ces trois mots: *Zayre, vous pleurez*, qui font un grand effet sur notre théâtre, n'en ont fait aucun sur le vôtre, parce qu'ils étaient déplacés. Ces expressions familières et naïves tirent toute leur force de la seule manière dont elles sont amenées. *Seigneur, vous changez de visage*,[22] n'est rien par soi-même; mais le moment où ces paroles si simples sont prononcées dans *Mithridate*, fait frémir.

Ne dire que ce qu'il faut, et de la manière dont il le faut, est, ce me semble, un mérite, dont les Français, si vous m'en exceptez, ont plus approché que les écrivains des autres pays. C'est, je crois, sur cet art que notre nation doit en être crue. Vous nous apprenez des choses plus grandes et plus utiles: il serait honteux à nous de ne le pas avouer. Les Français qui ont écrit contre les découvertes du chevalier Newton sur la lumière, en rougissent; ceux qui combattent la gravitation en rougiront bientôt.[23]

205

210

215

220

225

---

215   36A: un très grand effet
222-223   36A: est me semble
224   K85: les écrivains dans les autres

[21] *Zara*, IV.i. Voltaire perhaps overstates his case, although his point remains valid. The stage direction has 'throws herself on the ground'.
[22] *Mithridate*, I.1112.
[23] Cf. *Lettres philosophiques*, chapters 15-16.

Vous devez vous soumettre aux règles de notre théâtre, comme 230
nous devons embrasser votre philosophie. Nous avons fait d'aussi
bonnes expériences sur le cœur humain, que vous sur la physique.
L'art de plaire semble l'art des Français, et l'art de penser paraît
le vôtre. Heureux, monsieur, qui comme vous les réunit! etc.

234 36A: Heureux qui

LETTRE
À MONSIEUR DE LA ROQUE,
sur la tragédie de Zayre, 1732[1]

Quoique pour l'ordinaire vous vouliez bien prendre la peine,
Monsieur, de faire les extraits des pièces nouvelles, cependant
vous me privez de cet avantage, et vous voulez que ce soit moi
qui parle de *Zayre*. Il me semble que je vois M. le Normand,
ou M. Cochin,[2] réduire un de leurs clients à plaider sa cause.   5
L'entreprise est dangereuse, mais je vais mériter au moins la
confiance que vous avez en moi par la sincérité avec laquelle je
m'expliquerai.

Zayre est la première pièce de théâtre, dans laquelle j'aie osé
m'abandonner à toute la sensibilité de mon cœur. C'est la seule   10
tragédie tendre que j'aie faite. Je croyais dans l'âge même des
passions les plus vives, que l'amour n'était point fait pour le
théâtre tragique. Je ne regardais cette faiblesse que comme un
défaut charmant qui avilissait l'art des Sophocles. Les connaisseurs
qui se plaisent plus à la douceur élégante de Racine qu'à la force   15
de Corneille, me paraissent ressembler aux curieux qui préfèrent
les nudités du Corrège au chaste et noble pinceau de Raphaël.

Le public qui fréquente les spectacles, est aujourd'hui plus que

---

a-277   33R-W57G2, W7OL, absent (added in W64G)
a-c   MF: Lettre de M. de Voltaire à M. D. L. R. sur la Tragédie de Zaïre
5   MF adds footnote to 'Cochin': *Deux fameux avocats*
   MF: plaider lui-même sa cause
16   MF: me paraissaient ressembler

---

[1] Antoine de La Roque was editor of the *Mercure de France*. Voltaire's letter
first appeared in the *Mercure* of August 1732, p.1828-43. In 1770 he disavowed
it: see below, appendix II, p.526.
[2] Alexis Normant (1697-1745) and Henri Cochin (1687-1747) were the most
famous lawyers of their time.

jamais dans le goût du Corrège. Il faut de la tendresse et du sentiment; c'est même ce que les acteurs jouent le mieux. Vous trouverez vingt comédiens qui plairont dans Andronic[3] et dans Hippolite, et à peine un seul qui réussisse dans Cinna et dans Horace. Il a donc fallu me plier aux mœurs du temps, et commencer tard à parler d'amour.

J'ai cherché du moins à couvrir cette passion de toute la bienséance possible; et pour l'annoblir, j'ai voulu la mettre à côté de ce que les hommes ont de plus respectable. L'idée me vint de faire contraster dans un même tableau, d'un côté, l'honneur, la naissance, la patrie, la religion; et de l'autre, l'amour le plus tendre et le plus malheureux; les mœurs des mahométans et celles des chrétiens; la cour d'un soudan et celle d'un roi de France; et de faire paraître, pour la première fois, des Français sur la scène tragique. Je n'ai pris dans l'histoire que l'époque de la guerre de St Louis; tout le reste est entièrement d'invention. L'idée de cette pièce étant si neuve et si fertile, s'arrangea d'elle-même; et au lieu que le plan d'*Eriphile* m'avait beaucoup coûté, celui de *Zayre* fut fait en un seul jour; et l'imagination échauffée par l'intérêt qui régnait dans ce plan, acheva la pièce en vingt-deux jours.

Il entre peut-être un peu de vanité dans cet aveu, (car où est l'artiste sans amour propre?) mais je devais cette excuse au public, des fautes et des négligences qu'on a trouvées dans ma tragédie. Il aurait été mieux sans doute d'attendre à la faire représenter que j'en eusse châtié le style; mais des raisons, dont il est inutile de fatiguer le public, n'ont pas permis qu'on différât. Voici, Monsieur, le sujet de cette pièce.

La Palestine avait été enlevée aux princes chrétiens par le conquérant Saladin. Noradin, Tartare d'origine, s'en était ensuite rendu maître. Orosmane, fils de Noradin, jeune homme plein de grandeur, de vertus et de passions, commençait à régner avec gloire dans Jérusalem. Il avait porté sur le trône de la Syrie la

---

[3] Jean de Campistron's *Andronic* had been a great success in 1685 and remained in the repertory of the Comédie-Française throughout most of the eighteenth century.

franchise et l'esprit de liberté de ses ancêtres. Il méprisait les règles austères du sérail, et n'affectait point de se rendre invisible aux étrangers et à ses sujets, pour devenir plus respectable. Il traitait avec douceur les esclaves chrétiens, dont son sérail et ses Etats étaient remplis. Parmi ces esclaves il s'était trouvé un enfant, 55 pris autrefois au sac de Césarée, sous le règne de Noradin. Cet enfant ayant été racheté par des chrétiens à l'âge de neuf ans, avait été amené en France au roi St Louis, qui avait daigné prendre soin de son éducation et de sa fortune. Il avait pris en France le nom de Nérestan; et étant retourné en Syrie, il avait été fait 60 prisonnier encore une fois, et avait été enfermé parmi les esclaves d'Orosmane. Il retrouva dans la captivité une jeune personne avec qui il avait été prisonnier dans son enfance, lorsque les chrétiens avaient perdu Césarée. Cette jeune personne, à qui on avait donné le nom de Zayre, ignorait sa naissance, aussi bien 65 que Nérestan et que tous ces enfants de tribut qui sont enlevés de bonne heure des mains de leurs parents, et qui ne connaissent de famille et de patrie que le sérail. Zayre savait seulement qu'elle était née chrétienne. Nérestan et quelques autres esclaves un peu plus âgés qu'elle, l'en assuraient. Elle avait toujours conservé un 70 ornement qui renfermait une croix, seule preuve qu'elle eût de sa religion. Une autre esclave nommée Fatime, née chrétienne, et mise au sérail à l'âge de dix ans, tâchait d'instruire Zayre du peu qu'elle savait de la religion de ses pères. Le jeune Nérestan, qui avait la liberté de voir Zayre et Fatime, animé du zèle qu'avaient 75 alors les chevaliers français, touché d'ailleurs pour Zayre de la plus tendre amitié, la disposait au christianisme. Il se proposa de racheter Zayre, Fatime et dix chevaliers chrétiens, du bien qu'il avait acquis en France, et de les amener à la cour de St Louis. Il eut la hardiesse de demander au soudan Orosmane la permission 80 de retourner en France sur sa seule parole, et le sultan eut la générosité de le permettre. Nérestan partit, et fut deux ans hors de Jérusalem.

Cependant la beauté de Zayre croissait avec son âge, et la naïveté touchante de son caractère la rendait encore plus aimable 85 que sa beauté. Orosmane la vit et lui parla. Un cœur comme le sien ne pouvait l'aimer qu'éperdument. Il résolut de bannir la mollesse qui avait efféminé tant de rois de l'Asie et d'avoir dans Zayre une amie, une maîtresse, une femme, qui lui tiendrait lieu de tous les plaisirs, et qui partagerait son cœur avec les devoirs 90 d'un prince et d'un guerrier. Les faibles idées du christianisme, tracées à peine dans le cœur de Zayre, s'évanouirent bientôt à la vue du soudan; elle l'aima autant qu'elle en était aimée, sans que l'ambition se mêlât en rien à la pureté de sa tendresse.

Nérestan ne revenait point de France. Zayre ne voyait qu'Oros- 95 mane et son amour. Elle était prête d'épouser le sultan, lorsque le jeune Français arriva. Orosmane le fait entrer en présence même de Zayre. Nérestan apportait avec la rançon de Zayre et de Fatime, celle de dix chevaliers qu'il devait choisir. J'ai satisfait à mes serments, dit-il au soudan: c'est à toi de tenir ta promesse, 100 de me remettre Zayre, Fatime et les dix chevaliers; mais apprends que j'ai épuisé ma fortune à payer leur rançon: *Une pauvreté noble est tout ce qui me reste*; je viens me remettre dans tes fers. Le soudan satisfait du grand courage de ce chrétien, et né pour être plus généreux encore, lui rendit toutes les rançons qu'il apportait, et 105 lui donna cent chevaliers au lieu de dix, et le combla de présents; mais il lui fit entendre que Zayre n'était pas faite pour être rachetée, et qu'elle était d'un prix au-dessus de toutes rançons. Il refusa aussi de lui rendre, parmi les chevaliers qu'il délivrait, un prince de Lusignan, fait esclave depuis longtemps dans Césarée. 110

Ce Lusignan, le dernier de la branche des rois de Jérusalem, était un vieillard respecté dans l'Orient, l'amour de tous les chrétiens, et dont le nom seul pouvait être dangereux aux Sarra-sins. C'était lui principalement que Nérestan avait voulu racheter. Il parut devant Orosmane accablé du refus qu'on lui faisait de 11 Lusignan et de Zayre. Le soudan remarqua ce trouble; il sentit

---

89   MF: un ami
97   MF: Français arrive. Orosmane
103   MF: *reste*: je ne puis me racheter moi-même; je viens
105-106   MF: apportait, lui donna
108   MF: toutes les rançons

dès ce moment un commencement de jalousie que la générosité de son caractère lui fit étouffer. Cependant il ordonna que les cent chevaliers fussent prêts à partir le lendemain avec Nérestan.

Zayre, sur le point d'être sultane, voulut donner au moins à Nérestan une preuve de sa reconnaissance. Elle se jette aux pieds d'Orosmane pour obtenir la liberté du vieux Lusignan. Orosmane ne pouvait rien refuser à Zayre. On alla tirer Lusignan des fers. Les chrétiens délivrés étaient avec Nérestan dans les appartements extérieurs du sérail; ils pleuraient la destinée de Lusignan: surtout le chevalier de Châtillon, ami tendre de ce malheureux prince, ne pouvait se résoudre à accepter une liberté qu'on refusait à son ami et à son maître, lorsque Zayre arrive et leur amène celui qu'ils n'espéraient plus.

Lusignan, ébloui de la lumière qu'il revoyait après vingt années de prison, pouvant se soutenir à peine, ne sachant où il est et où on le conduit, voyant enfin qu'il était avec des Français et reconnaissant Châtillon, s'abandonna à cette joie mêlée d'amertume que les malheureux éprouvent dans leur consolation. Il demande à qui il doit sa déliverance. Zayre prend la parole en lui présentant Nérestan: C'est à ce jeune Français, dit-elle, que vous, et tous les chrétiens, devez votre liberté. Alors le vieillard apprend que Nérestan a été élevé dans le sérail avec Zayre; et se tournant vers eux, Hélas! dit-il, puisque vous avez pitié de mes malheurs, achevez votre ouvrage, instruisez-moi du sort de mes enfants. Deux me furent enlevés au berceau, lorsque je fus pris dans Césarée; deux autres furent massacrés devant moi avec leur mère. O mes fils! ô martyrs! veillez du haut du ciel sur mes autres enfants, s'ils sont vivants encore. Hélas! j'ai su que mon dernier fils et ma fille, furent conduits dans ce sérail. Vous qui m'écoutez, Nérestan, Zayre, Châtillon, n'avez-vous nulle connaissance de ces tristes restes du sang de Godefroi et de Lusignan?

Au milieu de ces questions, qui déjà remuaient le cœur de Nérestan et de Zayre, Lusignan aperçut au bras de Zayre un

---

134   MF: dans leurs consolations.

ornement qui renfermait une croix: il se ressouvint que l'on avait 150
mis cette parure à sa fille lorsqu'on la portait au baptême; Châtillon
l'en avait ornée lui-même, et Zayre avait été arrachée de ses bras
avant que d'être baptisée. La ressemblance des traits, l'âge, toutes
les circonstances, une cicatrice de la blessure que son jeune fils
avait reçue, tout confirme à Lusignan qu'il est père encore; et la 155
nature parlant à la fois au cœur de tous les trois, et s'expliquant par
des larmes: Embrassez-moi, mes chers enfants, s'écria Lusignan, et
revoyez votre père. Zayre et Nérestan ne pouvaient s'arracher de
ses bras. Mais, hélas! dit ce vieillard infortuné, goûterai-je une
joie pure? Grand Dieu qui me rends ma fille, me la rends-tu 160
chrétienne? Zayre rougit et frémit à ces paroles. Lusignan vit sa
honte et son malheur, et Zayre avoua qu'elle était musulmane.
La douleur, la religion et la nature, donnèrent en ce moment des
forces à Lusignan; il embrassa sa fille, et lui montrant d'une main
le tombeau de Jésus-Christ, et le ciel de l'autre, animé de son 165
désespoir, de son zèle, aidé de tant de chrétiens, de son fils et du
Dieu qui l'inspire, il touche sa fille, il l'ébranle; elle se jette à ses
pieds et lui promet d'être chrétienne.

Au moment arrive un officier du sérail qui sépare Zayre de son
père et de son frère, et qui arrête tous les chevaliers français. 170
Cette rigueur inopinée était le fruit d'un conseil qu'on venait de
tenir en présence d'Orosmane. La flotte de St Louis était partie
de Chypre, et on craignait pour les côtes de Syrie; mais un second
courrier ayant apporté la nouvelle du départ de St Louis pour
l'Egypte, Orosmane fut rassuré; il était lui-même ennemi du 175
soudan d'Egypte. Ainsi n'ayant rien à craindre ni du roi ni des
Français qui étaient à Jérusalem, il commanda qu'on les renvoyât
à leur roi, et ne songea plus qu'à réparer, par la pompe et la
magnificence de son mariage, la rigueur dont il avait usé envers
Zayre. 180

Pendant que le mariage se préparait, Zayre désolée demanda

---

150   MF: il se souvint que
152   MF: Zaïre lui avait
153   MF: avant d'être

au soudan la permission de revoir Nérestan encore une fois. Orosmane, trop heureux de trouver une occasion de plaire à Zayre, eut l'indulgence de permettre cette entrevue. Nérestan revit donc Zayre; mais ce fut pour lui apprendre que son père 185 était prêt d'expirer, qu'il mourait entre la joie d'avoir retrouvé ses enfants, et l'amertume d'ignorer si Zayre serait chrétienne, et qu'il lui ordonnait en mourant d'être baptisée ce jour-là même de la main du pontife de Jérusalem.[4] Zayre attendrie et vaincue, promit tout et jura à son frère qu'elle ne trahirait point le sang dont elle 190 était née, qu'elle serait chrétienne, qu'elle n'épouserait point Orosmane, qu'elle ne prendrait aucun parti avant que d'avoir été baptisée.

A peine avait-elle prononcé ce serment qu'Orosmane, plus amoureux et plus aimé que jamais, vient la prendre pour la 195 conduire à la mosquée. Jamais on n'eut le cœur plus déchiré que Zayre; elle était partagée entre son Dieu, sa famille et son nom qui la retenaient, et le plus aimable de tous les hommes qui l'adorait. Elle ne se connut plus; elle céda à la douleur, et s'échappa des mains de son amant, le quittant avec désespoir et le laissant 200 dans l'accablement de la surprise, de la douleur et de la colère.

Les impressions de jalousie se réveillèrent dans le cœur d'Orosmane. L'orgueil les empêcha de paraître, et l'amour les adoucit. Il prit la fuite de Zayre pour un caprice, pour un artifice innocent, pour la crainte naturelle à une jeune fille, pour toute autre chose 205 enfin que pour une trahison. Il vit encore Zayre, lui pardonna et l'aima plus que jamais. L'amour de Zayre augmentait par la tendresse indulgente de son amant. Elle se jette en larmes à ses

---

197   MF: sa famille, son nom

---

[4] Tolerance of the Christians varied considerably during the periods when Jerusalem was under Muslim rule at the time of the Crusades. There were certainly times when open Christian worship in the churches of the city was allowed upon payment by the Christians of special taxes, and the idea of a priest being available in Jerusalem under Orosmane's rule – though hardly able to enter the seraglio, one would think – is not fanciful.

425

genoux, le supplie de différer le mariage jusqu'au lendemain. Elle comptait que son frère serait alors parti, qu'elle aurait reçu le baptême, que Dieu lui donnerait la force de résister. Elle se flattait même quelquefois que la religion chrétienne lui permettrait d'aimer un homme si tendre, si généreux, si vertueux, à qui il ne manquait que d'être chrétien. Frappée de toutes ces idées, elle parlait à Orosmane avec une tendresse si naïve et une douleur si vraie, qu'Orosmane céda encore, et lui accorda le sacrifice de vivre sans elle ce jour-là. Il était sûr d'être aimé; il était heureux dans cette idée, et fermait les yeux sur le reste.

Cependant dans les premiers mouvements de jalousie, il avait ordonné que le sérail fût fermé à tous les chrétiens. Nérestan trouvant le sérail fermé, et n'en soupçonnant pas la cause, écrivit une lettre pressante à Zayre; il lui mandait d'ouvrir une porte secrète qui conduisait vers la mosquée, et lui recommandait d'être fidèle.

La lettre tomba entre les mains d'un garde qui la porta à Orosmane. Le soudan en crut à peine ses yeux. Il se vit trahi; il ne douta pas de son malheur et du crime de Zayre. Avoir comblé un étranger, un captif de bienfaits; avoir donné son cœur, sa couronne à une fille esclave, lui avoir tout sacrifié; ne vivre que pour elle, et en être trahi pour ce captif même; être trompé par les apparences du plus tendre amour; éprouver en un moment ce que l'amour a de plus violent, ce que l'ingratitude a de plus noir, ce que la perfidie a de plus traître; c'était sans doute un état horrible. Mais Orosmane aimait, et il souhaitait de trouver Zayre innocente. Il lui fait rendre ce billet par un esclave inconnu. Il se flatte que Zayre pouvait ne point écouter Nérestan; Nérestan seul lui paraissait coupable. Il ordonne qu'on l'arrête et qu'on l'enchaîne; et il va, à l'heure et à la place du rendez-vous, attendre l'effet de la lettre.

La lettre est rendue à Zayre, elle la lit en tremblant; et après avoir longtemps hésité, elle dit enfin à l'esclave, qu'elle attendra

222 MF: de lui ouvrir
235-236 MF: Il se flattait que

426

Nérestan, et donne ordre qu'on l'introduise. L'esclave rend compte de tout à Orosmane.

Le malheureux soudan tombe dans l'excès d'une douleur mêlée de fureur et de larmes. Il tire son poignard, et il pleure. Zayre   245
vient au rendez-vous dans l'obscurité de la nuit. Orosmane entend sa voix et son poignard lui échappe. Elle approche, elle appelle Nérestan; et à ce nom Orosmane la poignarde.

Dans l'instant on lui amène Nérestan enchaîné, avec Fatime complice de Zayre. Orosmane hors de lui s'adresse à Nérestan,   250
en le nommant son rival: C'est toi qui m'arraches Zayre, dit-il, regarde-la avant que de mourir; que ton supplice commence avec le sien; regarde-la, te dis-je. Nérestan approche de ce corps expirant. Ah, que vois-je! ah! ma sœur! barbare, qu'as-tu fait?...
A ce mot de sœur, Orosmane est comme un homme qui revient   255
d'un songe funeste; il connaît son erreur; il voit ce qu'il a perdu; il s'est trop abîmé dans l'horreur de son état pour se plaindre. Nérestan et Fatime lui parlent; mais de tout ce qu'ils disent il n'entend autre chose, sinon qu'il était aimé. Il prononce le nom de Zayre, il court à elle; on l'arrête, il retombe dans l'engourdisse-   260
ment de son désespoir. Qu'ordonnes-tu de moi? lui dit Nérestan. Le soudan, après un long silence, fait ôter les fers à Nérestan, le comble de largesses, lui et tous les chrétiens, et se tue auprès de Zayre.

Voilà, monsieur, le plan exact de la conduite de cette tragédie   265
que j'expose avec toutes ses fautes. Je suis bien loin de m'enorgueillir du succès passager de quelques représentations. Qui ne connaît l'illusion du théâtre? Qui ne sait qu'une situation intéressante, mais triviale, une nouveauté brillante et hasardée, la seule voix d'une actrice, suffisent pour tromper quelque temps le   270
public? Quelle distance immense entre un ouvrage souffert au théâtre et un bon ouvrage! J'en sens malheureusement toute la différence. Je vois combien il est difficile de réussir au gré des connaisseurs. Je ne suis pas plus indulgent qu'eux pour moi-

252   MF: commence par
257   MF: il est trop

même; et si j'ose travailler, c'est que mon goût extrême pour cet 275
art l'emporte encore sur la connaissance que j'ai de mon peu de
talent.[5]

277 MF ends: talent. Je suis &c.

[5] This letter, which in spite of the suggestions of the first paragraph provides
a summary of the plot rather than a discussion of the play, nevertheless throws
some light upon Voltaire's dramatic technique. The summary he gives resembles
a short story, and it might well be thought that *Zaïre* is more satisfactory as a
short story than as a tragedy. The plot depends on incident and accident, so
that all the essential elements of the action are present in the summary. In
contrast, the summary of a tragedy by Racine gives far less idea of its essential
elements, which reside in the subtle interplay of characters and a more mysterious poetic quality that defies analysis. Part of the reason for Voltaire's ultimate
failure as a tragic dramatist may well be that he thought of the play as a
dramatised fiction.

ACTEURS

OROSMANE, soudan de Jérusalem.

LUSIGNAN, prince du sang des rois de Jérusalem.

ZAYRE, FATIME, esclaves du soudan.

NÉRESTAN, CHÂTILLON, chevaliers français.

CORASMIN, MÉLÉDOR, officiers du soudan.

Un esclave.

Suite.

La scène est au sérail de Jérusalem.

a   33R, 36A, K: Personnages
5-7   36A: CORASMIN, chef du sérail. / MÉLÉDOR, esclave / Suite.

430

ACTE PREMIER

SCÈNE PREMIÈRE

ZAYRE, FATIME

FATIME

Je ne m'attendais pas, jeune et belle Zayre,
Aux nouveaux sentiments que ce lieu vous inspire.
Quel espoir si flatteur, ou quels heureux destins,
De vos jours ténébreux ont fait des jours sereins?
La paix de votre cœur augmente avec vos charmes;   5
Cet éclat de vos yeux n'est plus terni de larmes;
Vous ne les tournez plus vers ces heureux climats,
Où ce brave Français devait guider nos pas;
Vous ne me parlez plus de ces belles contrées,
Où d'un peuple poli les femmes adorées   10
Reçoivent cet encens que l'on doit à vos yeux;
Compagnes d'un époux, et reines en tous lieux,
Libres sans déshonneur, et sages sans contrainte,
Et ne devant jamais leurs vertus à la crainte.
Ne soupirez-vous plus pour cette liberté?   15
Le sérail d'un soudan, sa triste austérité,
Ce nom d'esclave enfin, n'ont-ils rien qui vous gêne?
Préférez-vous Solyme aux rives de la Seine?

ZAYRE

On ne peut désirer ce qu'on ne connaît pas.
Sur les bords du Jourdain le ciel fixa nos pas.   20
Au sérail des soudans dès l'enfance enfermée,

14 MS1: ne doivent jamais

Chaque jour ma raison s'y voit accoutumée.
Le reste de la terre anéanti pour moi,
M'abandonne au soudan, qui nous tient sous sa loi:
Je ne connais que lui, sa gloire, sa puissance: 25
Vivre sous Orosmane est ma seule espérance,
Le reste est un vain songe.

FATIME

              Avez-vous oublié
Ce généreux Français, dont la tendre amitié
Nous promit si souvent de rompre notre chaîne?
Combien nous admirions son audace hautaine!   30
Quelle gloire il acquit dans ces tristes combats
Perdus par les chrétiens sous les murs de Damas![1]
Orosmane vainqueur, admirant son courage,
Le laissa sur sa foi partir de ce rivage.
Nous l'attendons encor; sa générosité   35
Devait payer le prix de notre liberté.
N'en aurions-nous conçu qu'une vaine espérance?

ZAYRE

Peut-être sa promesse a passé sa puissance.
Depuis plus de deux ans il n'est point revenu.
Un étranger, Fatime, un captif inconnu,   40
Promet beaucoup, tient peu, permet à son courage
Des serments indiscrets pour sortir d'esclavage.
Il devait délivrer dix chevaliers chrétiens,
Venir rompre leurs fers, ou reprendre les siens.
J'admirai trop en lui cet inutile zèle.   4
Il n'y faut plus penser.

---

[1] Christian armies besieged Damascus in 1148, but had to abandon the siege after suffering terrible losses, thus bringing to an end the Second Crusade. Damascus in fact never fell into Christian hands throughout the period of the Crusades.

FATIME

Mais s'il était fidèle,
S'il revenait enfin dégager ses serments,
Ne voudriez-vous pas?...

ZAYRE

Fatime, il n'est plus temps.
Tout est changé...

FATIME

Comment? que prétendez-vous dire?

ZAYRE

Va, c'est trop te celer le destin de Zayre;   50
Le secret du soudan doit encor se cacher;
Mais mon cœur dans le tien se plaît à s'épancher.
Depuis près de trois mois qu'avec d'autres captives
On te fit du Jourdain abandonner les rives,
Le ciel, pour terminer les malheurs de nos jours,   55
D'une main plus puissante a choisi le secours.
Ce superbe Orosmane...

FATIME

Eh bien!

ZAYRE

Ce soudan même,
Ce vainqueur des chrétiens... chère Fatime... il m'aime...
Tu rougis... je t'entends... garde-toi de penser
Qu'à briguer ses soupirs je puisse m'abaisser,   60
Que d'un maître absolu la superbe tendresse
M'offre l'honneur honteux du rang de sa maîtresse,
Et que j'essuie enfin l'outrage et le danger
Du malheureux éclat d'un amour passager.

Cette fierté qu'en nous soutient la modestie,   65
Dans mon cœur à ce point ne s'est pas démentie.
Plutôt que jusque-là j'abaisse mon orgueil,
Je verrais sans pâlir les fers et le cercueil.
Je m'en vais t'étonner; son superbe courage
A mes faibles appas présente un pur hommage;   70
Parmi tous ces objets à lui plaire empressés,
J'ai fixé ses regards, à moi seule adressés;
Et l'hymen confondant leurs intrigues fatales,
Me soumettra bientôt son cœur et mes rivales.

FATIME

Vos appas, vos vertus, sont dignes de ce prix;   75
Mon cœur en est flatté, plus qu'il n'en est surpris:
Que vos félicités, s'il se peut, soient parfaites!
Je me vois avec joie au rang de vos sujettes.

ZAYRE

Sois toujours mon égale, et goûte mon bonheur;
Avec toi partagé je sens mieux sa douceur.   80

FATIME

Hélas! puisse le ciel souffrir cet hyménée!
Puisse cette grandeur, qui vous est destinée,
Qu'on nomme si souvent du faux nom de bonheur,
Ne point laisser de trouble au fond de votre cœur!
N'est-il point en secret de frein qui vous retienne?   85
Ne vous souvient-il plus que vous fûtes chrétienne?

ZAYRE

Ah! que dis-tu! Pourquoi rappeler mes ennuis?
Chère Fatime, hélas! sais-je ce que je suis?
Le ciel m'a-t-il jamais permis de me connaître?

Ne m'a-t-il pas caché le sang qui m'a fait naître? 90

FATIME

Nérestan qui naquit non loin de ce séjour,
Vous dit que d'un chrétien vous reçûtes le jour;
Que dis-je? Cette croix qui sur vous fut trouvée,
Parure de l'enfance, avec soin conservée,
Ce signe des chrétiens que l'art dérobe aux yeux, 95
Sous ce brillant éclat d'un travail précieux,
Cette croix, dont cent fois mes soins vous ont parée,
Peut-être entre vos mains est-elle demeurée,
Comme un gage secret de la fidélité
Que vous deviez au Dieu que vous aviez quitté. 100

ZAYRE

Je n'ai point d'autre preuve; et mon cœur qui s'ignore,
Peut-il admettre un Dieu que mon amant abhorre?
La coutume, la loi plia mes premiers ans
A la religion des heureux musulmans.
Je le vois trop: les soins qu'on prend de notre enfance, 105
Forment nos sentiments, nos mœurs, notre créance.
J'eusse été près du Gange esclave des faux dieux,
Chrétienne dans Paris, musulmane en ces lieux.
L'instruction fait tout; et la main de nos pères

90 MS1: qui me fit naître?
91 MS1: qui lui-même est né dans ce séjour
95 MS1: Ce monument sacré que l'art
100 MS1, 33R-W38: vous avez quitté.
102 MS1, 33R-W48D: Peut-il suivre une foi [w38-w48D: loi] que ['loi' altered
by hand to 'foi' in some copies of w38]
    w51: Pourrait-il suivre un Dieu
    w52: Peut-il admettre ce que
103 w38-w48D: La coutume en ces lieux plia ['en ces lieux' altered by hand
to 'la loy' in some copies of w38]
105 MS1: Tu le sais trop: les
106 K: notre croyance

Grave en nos faibles cœurs ces premiers caractères,   110
Que l'exemple et le temps nous viennent retracer,
Et que peut-être en nous Dieu seul peut effacer.²
Prisonnière, en ces lieux, tu n'y fus renfermée
Que lorsque ta raison, par l'âge confirmée,
Pour éclairer ta foi te prêtait son flambeau: 115
Pour moi des Sarrasins esclave en mon berceau,
La foi de nos chrétiens me fut trop tard connue.
Contre elle cependant, loin d'être prévenue,
Cette croix, je l'avoue, a souvent malgré moi
Saisi mon cœur surpris de respect et d'effroi: 120
J'osais l'invoquer même avant qu'en ma pensée,
D'Orosmane en secret l'image fût tracée.
J'honore, je chéris ces charitables lois,
Dont ici Nérestan me parla tant de fois;
Ces lois, qui de la terre écartant les misères,   125

117   MS1:   La foi de tes chrétiens à peine m'est connue
119-122   MS1, added at the foot of f.1r
120   MS1:   Saisi mon faible cœur de respect
123   MS1:   J'estime, je chéris vos honorables [MS1*: β]
124   MS1:   me parlait quelquefois [MS1: β]

² It is possible that Voltaire owes this development to a reminiscence of
Dryden, for he quotes in his notebooks two passages that together suggest
similar ideas:

            Dryden about Relligion
        The common cry is ever relligion's test
        The Turk's at Constantinople best
        Idols in India, Popery at Rome
        And our own worship only true at home...
                    to prove religion true
        If either wit, or sufferings could suffice
        All faiths afford the constant, and the wise.
        And yet ev'n they by education sway'd
        In age deffend what infancy obey'd.

See Voltaire 81, p.52; cf. p.63, 239-40, 405-406; cf. also, *Lettres philosophiques*,
ii.83, l.122, variant.

436

Des humains attendris font un peuple de frères;
Obligés de s'aimer, sans doute, ils sont heureux.

FATIME

Pourquoi donc aujourd'hui vous déclarer contre eux?
A la loi musulmane à jamais asservie,
Vous allez des chrétiens devenir l'ennemie;   130
Vous allez épouser leur superbe vainqueur.

ZAYRE

Eh! qui refuserait le présent de son cœur?
De toute ma faiblesse il faut que je convienne;
Peut-être sans l'amour j'aurais été chrétienne;
Peut-être qu'à ta loi j'aurais sacrifié: 135
Mais Orosmane m'aime, et j'ai tout oublié.
Je ne vois qu'Orosmane, et mon âme enivrée
Se remplit du bonheur de s'en voir adorée.
Mets-toi devant les yeux sa grâce, ses exploits;
Songe à ce bras puissant, vainqueur de tant de rois,   140
A cet aimable front que la gloire environne:
Je ne te parle point du sceptre qu'il me donne:
Non, la reconnaissance est un faible retour,

129   MS1: musulmane en esclave asservie
133-136   MS1, 33R uncancelled:
        Je servais, il m'élève à la grandeur suprême;
        Mon cœur est né sensible, il me chérit, et j'aime;
        Quand les yeux du soudan s'attachent sur les miens,
        Puis-je me souvenir des chaînes des chrétiens?
        [33R cancel: β with variant, l.134][3]
134   33R, 36A: Peut-être que sans lui j'aurais
        33L, omitted

[3] The text of the cancel was sent by Voltaire to Rouen on 4 January 1733
(see D559). The original reading was reinstated by Voltaire in the Stockholm
copy of w42.

Un tribut offensant, trop peu fait pour l'amour.
Mon cœur aime Orosmane, et non son diadème;   145
Chère Fatime, en lui je n'aime que lui-même.
Peut-être j'en crois trop un penchant si flatteur;
Mais si le ciel sur lui déployant sa rigueur,
Aux fers que j'ai portés eût condamné sa vie,
Si le ciel sous mes lois eût rangé la Syrie,   150
Ou mon amour me trompe, ou Zayre aujourd'hui
Pour l'élever à soi descendrait jusqu'à lui.

FATIME

On marche vers ces lieux; sans doute, c'est lui-même.

ZAYRE

Mon cœur, qui le prévient, m'annonce ce que j'aime.
Depuis deux jours, Fatime, absent de ce palais,   155
Enfin mon tendre amour le rend à mes souhaits.

SCÈNE II

OROSMANE, ZAYRE, FATIME

OROSMANE

Vertueuse Zayre, avant que l'hyménée[4]
Joigne à jamais nos cœurs et notre destinée,

150 MS1: Si Solyme à mes lois se voyait asservie
156 K: Enfin son tendre
156b MS1 adds: ESCLAVES

---

[4] See above, p.327 and note.

J'ai cru, sur mes projets, sur vous, sur mon amour,
Devoir en musulman vous parler sans détour.   160
Les soudans qu'à genoux cet univers contemple,
Leurs usages, leurs droits, ne sont point mon exemple;
Je sais que notre loi, favorable aux plaisirs,
Ouvre un champ sans limite à nos vastes désirs;
Que je puis à mon gré, prodiguant mes tendresses,   165
Recevoir à mes pieds l'encens de mes maîtresses;
Et tranquille au sérail, dictant mes volontés,
Gouverner mon pays du sein des voluptés;
Mais la mollesse est douce, et sa suite est cruelle.
Je vois autour de moi cent rois vaincus par elle;   170
Je vois de Mahomet ces lâches successeurs,
Ces califes tremblants dans leurs tristes grandeurs,
Couchés sur les débris de l'autel et du trône,
Sous un nom sans pouvoir languir dans Babilone:[5]
Eux, qui seraient encore, ainsi que leurs aïeux,   175
Maîtres du monde entier, s'ils l'avaient été d'eux.
Bouillon leur arracha Solyme et la Syrie;[6]
Mais bientôt pour punir une secte ennemie,
Dieu suscita le bras du puissant Saladin;[7]
Mon père, après sa mort, asservit le Jourdain;[8]   180

161   MS1:   Les sultans [throughout]

[5] After the death of Mohammed, the title of Caliph was borne for many centuries by the head of the Muslim community. In 1249, the Caliphate was based on Baghdad, designated here poetically as *Babylone*, although in fact Baghdad is some sixty miles north of what was Babylon. The name Babylon has always, of course, carried suggestions of depravity in Judæo-Christian civilisations. The Caliphate of Baghdad, founded in 762, came to a virtual end with the sack of the city by the Mongols in 1258.

[6] Godefroi de Bouillon, the leader and hero of the First Crusade, took Jerusalem in 1099.

[7] Saladin won Jerusalem back from the Christians in 1187.

[8] Voltaire gives as Orosmane's supposed father Noradin, first mentioned by name in II.i.33. For a discussion of the historical Saladin and Noradin see above, p.298.

Et moi, faible héritier de sa grandeur nouvelle,
Maître encore incertain d'un Etat qui chancelle,
Je vois ces fiers chrétiens, de rapine altérés,
Des bords de l'Occident vers nos bords attirés;
Et lorsque la trompette, et la voix de la guerre,   185
Du Nil au Pont-Euxin font retentir la terre,
Je n'irai point en proie à de lâches amours,
Aux langueurs d'un sérail abandonner mes jours.
J'atteste ici la gloire, et Zayre, et ma flamme,
De ne choisir que vous pour maîtresse et pour femme,   190
De vivre votre ami, votre amant, votre époux,
De partager mon cœur entre la guerre et vous.[9]
Ne croyez pas non plus, que mon honneur confie
La vertu d'une épouse à ces monstres d'Asie,
Du sérail des soudans gardes injurieux,   195
Et des plaisirs d'un maître esclaves odieux.
Je sais vous estimer autant que je vous aime,
Et sur votre vertu me fier à vous-même.
Après un tel aveu, vous connaissez mon cœur.
Vous sentez qu'en vous seule il a mis son bonheur.   200
Vous comprenez assez quelle amertume affreuse
Corromprait de mes jours la durée odieuse,
Si vous ne receviez les dons que je vous fais,
Qu'avec ces sentiments que l'on doit aux bienfaits.
Je vous aime, Zayre; et j'attends de votre âme   205
Un amour qui réponde à ma brûlante flamme.
Je l'avouerai, mon cœur ne veut rien qu'ardemment;
Je me croirais haï d'être aimé faiblement.
De tous mes sentiments tel est le caractère.
Je veux avec excès vous aimer et vous plaire.   2

---

192   MS1:   Et partager

[9] For this declaration of intended monogamy on Orosmane's part, see above, p.312-13.

Si d'une égale amour votre cœur est épris,
Je viens vous épouser, mais c'est à ce seul prix;
Et du nœud de l'hymen l'étreinte dangereuse
Me rend infortuné, s'il ne vous rend heureuse.

ZAYRE

Vous, seigneur, malheureux! Ah! si votre grand cœur   215
A sur mes sentiments pu fonder son bonheur,
S'il dépend en effet des mes flammes secrètes,
Quel mortel fut jamais plus heureux que vous l'êtes!
Ces noms chers et sacrés, et d'amant et d'époux,
Ces noms nous sont communs: et j'ai par-dessus vous   220
Ce plaisir si flatteur à ma tendresse extrême,
De tenir tout, seigneur, du bienfaiteur que j'aime;
De voir que ses bontés font seules mes destins,
D'être l'ouvrage heureux de ses augustes mains,
De révérer, d'aimer un héros que j'admire.   225
Oui, si parmi les cœurs soumis à votre empire,
Vos yeux ont discerné les hommages du mien,
Si votre auguste choix…

SCÈNE III

OROSMANE, ZAYRE, FATIME, CORASMIN

CORASMIN
Cet esclave chrétien,

211   w51, w57p: Si d'un égal amour
213   33r: Et des nœuds de [33r errata, 33rp Taylor copy: β]
214   ms1*: si vous n'êtes heureuse
226   ms1: Et, si parmi
228   ms1, 33r: Un esclave [33r errata: β]
228b ms1 adds: ESCLAVES

Qui sur sa foi, seigneur, a passé dans la France,
Revient au moment même, et demande audience.   230

FATIME

O ciel!

OROSMANE

Il peut entrer. Pourquoi ne vient-il pas?

CORASMIN

Dans la première enceinte il arrête ses pas.
Seigneur, je n'ai pas cru qu'aux regards de son maître
Dans ces augustes lieux un chrétien pût paraître.

OROSMANE

Qu'il paraisse. En tous lieux, sans manquer de respect,   23
Chacun peut désormais jouir de mon aspect.
Je vois avec mépris ces maximes terribles,
Qui font de tant de rois des tyrans invisibles.

230a   MS1, with stage direction: *à part*
234a-235   MS1:
                    OROSMANE
Qu'il paraisse.
                SCÈNE IV
OROSMANE, ZAÏRE, FATIME, ESCLAVES
                OROSMANE
        En tous lieux, sans manquer de respect,
[with subsequent renumbering of scenes]

SCÈNE IV

OROSMANE, ZAYRE, FATIME, CORASMIN, NÉRESTAN

NÉRESTAN

Respectable ennemi qu'estiment les chrétiens,
Je reviens dégager mes serments et les tiens;   240
J'ai satisfait à tout, c'est à toi d'y souscrire;
Je te fais apporter la rançon de Zayre,
Et celle de Fatime, et de dix chevaliers,
Dans les murs de Solyme illustres prisonniers.
Leur liberté par moi trop longtemps retardée,   245
Quand je reparaîtrais leur dut être accordée:
Sultan, tiens ta parole, ils ne sont plus à toi,
Et dès ce moment même ils sont libres par moi.
Mais grâces à mes soins, quand leur chaîne est brisée,
A t'en payer le prix ma fortune épuisée,   250
Je ne le cèle pas, m'ôte l'espoir heureux
De faire ici pour moi ce que je fais pour eux.
Une pauvreté noble est tout ce qui me reste.
J'arrache des chrétiens à leur prison funeste;
Je remplis mes serments, mon honneur, mon devoir,   255
Il me suffit: je viens me mettre en ton pouvoir;
Je me rends prisonnier, et demeure en otage.

OROSMANE

Chrétien, je suis content de ton noble courage;
Mais ton orgueil ici se serait-il flatté
D'effacer Orosmane en générosité?   260
Reprends ta liberté, remporte tes richesses,

246   MS1: Lorsque je paraîtrais leur
251   MS1: le cèle point

A l'or de ces rançons joins mes justes largesses:
Au lieu de dix chrétiens que je dus t'accorder,
Je t'en veux donner cent; tu les peux demander.
Qu'ils aillent sur tes pas apprendre à ta patrie,   265
Qu'il est quelques vertus au fond de la Syrie;
Qu'ils jugent en partant, qui méritait le mieux,
Des Français, ou de moi, l'empire de ces lieux.[10]
Mais parmi ces chrétiens que ma bonté délivre,
Lusignan ne fut point réservé pour te suivre: 270
De ceux qu'on peut te rendre il est seul excepté;
Son nom serait suspect à mon autorité:
Il est du sang français qui régnait à Solyme;
On sait son droit au trône, et ce droit est un crime:
Du destin qui fait tout, tel est l'arrêt cruel: 275
Si j'eusse été vaincu, je serais criminel.
Lusignan dans les fers finira sa carrière,
Et jamais du soleil ne verra la lumière.
Je le plains, mais pardonne à la nécessité
Ce reste de vengeance et de sévérité.   280
Pour Zayre, crois-moi, sans que ton cœur s'offense,
Elle n'est pas d'un prix qui soit en ta puissance;
Tes chevaliers français, et tous leurs souverains,
S'uniraient vainement pour l'ôter de mes mains.
Tu peux partir.

---

268   MS1, 33R, W38-W46: Des Lusignans, ou moi [MS1*: β]
      36A: Des chrétiens ou
269   36A: ces captifs que
275   MS1: tel est l'ordre cruel [MS1*: β]

[10] In actual fact, Crusading families settled in the East did not really regard themselves as French. An old-established family like the Lusignans would have adopted ways of life and customs quite foreign to western Europe whence their ancestors came. The Franks, as the earlier Crusaders settled in the East came to be called, often resented interference in their lives from later waves of fanatical Western Christians.

NÉRESTAN

Qu'entends-je? Elle naquit chrétienne.   285
J'ai pour la délivrer ta parole et la sienne;
Et quant à Lusignan, ce vieillard malheureux,
Pourrait-il?...

OROSMANE

Je t'ai dit, chrétien, que je le veux.
J'honore ta vertu; mais cette humeur altière,
Se faisant estimer, commence à me déplaire: 290
Sors, et que le soleil levé sur mes Etats,
Demain près du Jourdain ne te retrouve pas.

Nérestan sort.

FATIME

O Dieu, secourez-nous.

OROSMANE

Et vous, allez, Zayre,
Prenez dans le sérail un souverain empire,
Commandez en sultane, et je vais ordonner   295
La pompe d'un hymen qui vous doit couronner.

286   MS1:   Sultan, j'eus en partant ta parole
292a   MS1, no stage direction
       33R, W38-W46:   *il sort*
293   MS1:
                    SCÈNE VI
OROSMANE, ZAÏRE, FATIME, CORASMIN, ESCLAVES
                    OROSMANE
            Et vous, allez, Zaïre

445

SCÈNE V

OROSMANE, CORASMIN

OROSMANE

Corasmin, que veut donc cet esclave infidèle?
Il soupirait... ses yeux se sont tournés vers elle.
Les as-tu remarqués?

CORASMIN

Que dites-vous, seigneur?
De ce soupçon jaloux écoutez-vous l'erreur?   30•

OROSMANE

Moi jaloux! qu'à ce point ma fierté s'avilisse!
Que j'éprouve l'horreur de ce honteux supplice!
Moi, que je puisse aimer comme l'on sait haïr!
Quiconque est soupçonneux invite à le trahir.
Je vois à l'amour seul ma maîtresse asservie;   30•
Cher Corasmin, je l'aime avec idolâtrie.
Mon amour est plus fort, plus grand que mes bienfaits.
Je ne suis point jaloux... si je l'étais jamais...
Si mon cœur!... Ah! chassons cette importune idée.
D'un plaisir pur et doux mon âme est possédée.   3•
Va, fais tout préparer pour ces moments heureux,
Qui vont joindre ma vie à l'objet de mes vœux.
Je vais donner une heure aux soins de mon empire,
Et le reste du jour sera tout à Zayre.

Fin du premier acte.

296b MSI adds: ESCLAVES
300 MSI: Quoi, d'un soupçon

ACTE II

SCÈNE PREMIÈRE

NÉRESTAN, CHÂTILLON

CHÂTILLON

O brave Nérestan, chevalier généreux,
Vous qui brisez les fers de tant de malheureux,
Vous, sauveur des chrétiens qu'un Dieu sauveur envoie,
Paraissez, montrez-vous, goûtez la douce joie,
De voir nos compagnons pleurant à vos genoux,   5
Baiser l'heureuse main qui nous délivre tous.
Aux portes du sérail en foule ils vous demandent;
Ne privez point leurs yeux du héros qu'ils attendent,
Et qu'unis à jamais sous notre bienfaiteur...

NÉRESTAN

Illustre Châtillon, modérez cet honneur;   10
J'ai rempli d'un Français le devoir ordinaire;[1]
J'ai fait ce qu'à ma place on vous aurait vu faire.

CHÂTILLON

Sans doute; et tout chrétien, tout digne chevalier,

---

6 w51: qui les délivre
11 ms1, 33r-w51, w57p: d'un chrétien le

---

[1] See note on I.iv.268. Nérestan, although a Frank by birth, has spent many years in France and may well be supposed to have adopted the spirit of a French knight. It is certainly as a French knight that he appears in the play. The change from *chrétien* in the earlier versions of this line to *Français* may be due to Voltaire's desire to court popularity by flattering his compatriots.

Pour sa religion se doit sacrifier;
Et la félicité des cœurs tels que les nôtres,   15
Consiste à tout quitter pour le bonheur des autres.
Heureux à qui le ciel a donné le pouvoir
De remplir comme vous un si noble devoir!
Pour nous, tristes jouets du sort qui nous opprime,
Nous malheureux Français, esclaves dans Solyme,   20
Oubliés dans les fers, où longtemps sans secours
Le père d'Orosmane abandonna nos jours:
Jamais nos yeux sans vous ne reverraient la France.

NÉRESTAN

Dieu s'est servi de moi, seigneur. Sa providence
De ce jeune Orosmane a fléchi la rigueur.   25
Mais quel triste mélange altère ce bonheur!
Que de ce fier soudan la clémence odieuse
Répand sur ses bienfaits une amertume affreuse!
Dieu me voit et m'entend; il sait si dans mon cœur
J'avais d'autres projets que ceux de sa grandeur.   30
Je faisais tout pour lui: j'espérais de lui rendre
Une jeune beauté, qu'à l'âge le plus tendre
Le cruel Noradin fit esclave avec moi,
Lorsque les ennemis de notre auguste foi,
Baignant de notre sang la Syrie enivrée,   3
Surprirent Lusignan vaincu dans Césarée:[2]

14   MS1:   doit se sacrifier
35   33R: Couvrant de notre [33R errata: β]

[2] It is not clear whether Voltaire intends Caesarea in Palestine or Caesarea Philippi in Syria (modern Baniyas). Caesarea Palestinae is a more famous town and a far more important one in the history of the Crusades. But it remained Christian from the time it was captured in 1101 until Baibars took it back for the Muslims in 1265. Caesarea Philippi was a fortress town, greatly fought over in the 1120s and '30s. In 1140 it had been won by the Christians, but Nur ed-Din did in fact recapture it in 1165. So there may be a connection in Voltaire's mind between Noradin and Caesarea Philippi. But Guy de Lusignan was

Du sérail des sultans sauvé par des chrétiens,
Remis depuis trois ans dans mes premiers liens,
Renvoyé dans Paris sur ma seule parole,
Seigneur, je me flattais, espérance frivole!   40
De ramener Zayre à cette heureuse cour,
Où Louis des vertus a fixé le séjour.[3]
Déjà même la reine à mon zèle propice,
Lui tendait de son trône une main protectrice.
Enfin lorsqu'elle touche au moment souhaité,   45
Qui la tirait du sein de sa captivité,
On la retient... Que dis-je... Ah! Zayre elle-même,
Oubliant les chrétiens, pour ce soudan qui l'aime...
N'y pensons plus... Seigneur, un refus plus cruel
Vient m'accabler encor d'un déplaisir mortel;   50
Des chrétiens malheureux l'espérance est trahie.

CHÂTILLON

Je vous offre pour eux ma liberté, ma vie;
Disposez-en, seigneur, elle vous appartient.

NÉRESTAN

Seigneur, ce Lusignan, qu'à Solyme on retient,
Ce dernier d'une race en héros si féconde,   55
Ce guerrier dont la gloire avait rempli le monde,
Ce héros malheureux de Bouillon descendu,
Aux soupirs des chrétiens ne sera point rendu.

CHÂTILLON

Seigneur, s'il est ainsi, votre faveur est vaine:

55   MS1: Ce chef d'une maison en [MS1*: β]
57   MS1*: Ce prince malheureux

captured at Hattin not Caesarea. Robert Pike ('Fact and fiction in *Zaïre*') suggests
that *Césarée* is merely a convenient rhyming word.
[3] Louis IX (1215-1270), canonised in 1297.

Quel indigne soldat voudrait briser sa chaîne,   60
Alors que dans les fers son chef est retenu?
Lusignan, comme à moi, ne vous est pas connu.
Seigneur, remerciez ce ciel, dont la clémence
A pour votre bonheur placé votre naissance,
Longtemps après ces jours à jamais détestés,   65
Après ces jours de sang et de calamités,
Où je vis sous le joug de nos barbares maîtres,
Tomber ces murs sacrés conquis par nos ancêtres.
Ciel! si vous aviez vu ce temple abandonné,
Du Dieu que nous servons le tombeau profané,   70
Nos pères, nos enfants, nos filles et nos femmes,
Aux pieds de nos autels expirant dans les flammes,
Et notre dernier roi courbé du faix des ans,
Massacré sans pitié sur ses fils expirants![4]
Lusignan,[5] le dernier de cette auguste race,   75
Dans ces moments affreux ranimant notre audace,
Au milieu des débris des temples renversés,
Des vainqueurs, des vaincus, et des morts entassés,[6]

62   MS1: comme à nous, ne

[4] Guy de Lusignan was king of Jerusalem when it was taken by Saladin in 1187, but he was not killed during the battle as he was already Saladin's prisoner at the time. Nor did his children die on that occasion. See above, p.298-300.

[5] The identity of the Lusignan who is described as bravely defending the Holy City is left purposely vague by Voltaire: it is not the king himself, but a member of his *race* who rallies the remnants of the Crusaders and takes them to Caesarea, where he is chosen as their leader. It is in fact unlikely that any Lusignan was among the defenders of Jerusalem. But Guy's brother, Geoffroy, took part with him in the siege of Acre in 1189.

[6] This description of the carnage in Jerusalem is poetic rather than historically exact. Saladin's entry into Jerusalem was in strange contrast to that of the Christians in 1099, which had been accompanied by a terrible massacre of Jews and Muslims living in the city. Saladin entered the city and allowed the Christians to leave with much of their wealth. There was no murder and no looting. The account given of this event by Voltaire in his *Essai sur les mœurs* (*Essai*, i.576) stresses Saladin's unexpected mercy towards the Christians. But in *Zaïre* poetic necessity takes precedence over historical fact.

Terrible, et d'une main reprenant cette épée,
Dans le sang infidèle à tout moment trempée;   80
Et de l'autre à nos yeux montrant avec fierté
De notre sainte foi le signe redouté,
Criant à haute voix, Français, soyez fidèles...
Sans doute en ce moment, le couvrant de ses ailes,
La vertu du Très-Haut, qui nous sauve aujourd'hui,   85
Aplanissait sa route, et marchait devant lui;
Et des tristes chrétiens la foule délivrée
Vint porter avec nous ses pas dans Césarée.
Là, par nos chevaliers, d'une commune voix,
Lusignan fut choisi pour nous donner des lois.   90
O mon cher Nérestan! Dieu qui nous humilie,
N'a pas voulu sans doute, en cette courte vie,
Nous accorder le prix qu'il doit à la vertu;
Vainement pour son nom nous avons combattu.
Ressouvenir affreux, dont l'horreur me dévore!   95
Jérusalem en cendre, hélas! fumait encore,
Lorsque dans notre asile attaqués et trahis,
Et livrés par un Grec à nos fiers ennemis,[7]
La flamme, dont brûla Sion[8] désespérée,
S'étendit en fureur aux murs de Césarée: 100
Ce fut là le dernier de trente ans de revers;
Là je vis Lusignan chargé d'indignes fers:
Insensible à sa chute, et grand dans ses misères,
Il n'était attendri que des maux de ses frères.
Seigneur, depuis ce temps, ce père des chrétiens,   105
Resserré loin de nous, blanchi dans ses liens,
Gémit dans un cachot, privé de la lumière,
Oublié de l'Asie, et de l'Europe entière.

---

[7] The hostility between the Latin Christians and the Orthodox Christians often led to treachery and betrayals by both sides during this period, to the great advantage of the Muslim enemy.

[8] *Sion.* The name of a hill in Jerusalem, but here used to denote the town itself.

Tel est son sort affreux; et qui peut aujourd'hui,
Quand il souffre pour nous, se voir heureux sans lui?   110

NÉRESTAN

Ce bonheur, il est vrai, serait d'un cœur barbare.
Que je hais le destin qui de lui nous sépare!
Que vers lui vos discours m'ont sans peine entraîné!
Je connais ses malheurs, avec eux je suis né.
Sans un trouble nouveau je n'ai pu les entendre;   115
Votre prison, la sienne, et Césarée en cendre,
Sont les premiers objets, sont les premiers revers,
Qui frappèrent mes yeux à peine encore ouverts.
Je sortais du berceau; ces images sanglantes
Dans vos tristes récits me sont encor présentes.   120
Au milieu des chrétiens dans un temple immolés,
Quelques enfants, seigneur, avec moi rassemblés,
Arrachés par des mains de carnage fumantes,
Aux bras ensanglantés de nos mères tremblantes,
Nous fûmes transportés dans ce palais des rois,   125
Dans ce même sérail, seigneur, où je vous vois.
Noradin m'éleva près de cette Zayre,
Qui depuis... pardonnez si mon cœur en soupire,
Qui depuis égarée en ce funeste lieu,
Pour un maître barbare abandonna son Dieu.   130

CHÂTILLON

Telle est des musulmans la funeste prudence.
De leurs chrétiens captifs ils séduisent l'enfance;
Et je bénis le ciel propice à nos desseins,
Qui dans vos premiers ans vous sauva de leurs mains.
Mais, seigneur, après tout, cette Zayre même,   135
Qui renonce aux chrétiens pour le soudan qui l'aime,

---

133   MS1*:   bénis le sort propice
         MS1:   à mes desseins

De son crédit au moins nous pourrait secourir:
Qu'importe de quel bras Dieu daigne se servir?
M'en croirez-vous? Le juste, aussi bien que le sage,
Du crime et du malheur sait tirer avantage.   140
Vous pourriez de Zayre employer la faveur
A fléchir Orosmane, à toucher son grand cœur,
A nous rendre un héros, que lui-même a dû plaindre,
Que sans doute il admire, et qui n'est plus à craindre.

NÉRESTAN

Mais ce même héros, pour briser ses liens,   145
Voudra-t-il qu'on s'abaisse à ces honteux moyens?
Et quand il le voudrait, est-il en ma puissance
D'obtenir de Zayre un moment d'audience?
Croyez-vous qu'Orosmane y daigne consentir?
Le sérail à ma voix pourra-t-il se rouvrir?   150
Quand je pourrais enfin paraître devant elle,
Que faut-il espérer d'une femme infidèle,
A qui mon seul aspect doit tenir lieu d'affront,
Et qui lira sa honte écrite sur mon front?
Seigneur, il est bien dur, pour un cœur magnanime,   155
D'attendre des secours de ceux qu'on mésestime.
Leurs refus sont affreux, leurs bienfaits font rougir.

CHÂTILLON

Songez à Lusignan, songez à le servir.

NÉRESTAN

Eh bien... Mais quels chemins jusqu'à cette infidèle
Pourront... On vient à nous. Que vois-je? ô ciel! c'est
                                                    elle.   160

---

142   MS1*: à gagner son
151   MS1: Enfin quand je pourrais paraître

SCÈNE II

ZAYRE, CHÂTILLON, NÉRESTAN

ZAYRE à *Nérestan.*

C'est vous, digne Français, à qui je viens parler.
Le soudan le permet, cessez de vous troubler;
Et rassurant mon cœur, qui tremble à votre approche,
Chassez de vos regards la plainte et le reproche.
Seigneur, nous nous craignons, nous rougissons tous
deux;   165
Je souhaite et je crains de rencontrer vos yeux.
L'un à l'autre attachés depuis notre naissance,
Une affreuse prison renferma notre enfance;
Le sort nous accabla du poids des mêmes fers,
Que la tendre amitié nous rendait plus légers.   17c
Il me fallut depuis gémir de votre absence;
Le ciel porta vos pas aux rives de la France:
Prisonnier dans Solyme, enfin je vous revis;
Un entretien plus libre alors m'était permis.
Esclave dans la foule, où j'étais confondue,   17
Aux regards du soudan je vivais inconnue:
Vous daignâtes bientôt, soit grandeur, soit pitié,
Soit plutôt digne effet d'une pure amitié,
Revoyant des Français le glorieux empire,
Y chercher la rançon de la triste Zayre: 18
Vous l'apportez: le ciel a trompé vos bienfaits;
Loin de vous dans Solyme il m'arrête à jamais.
Mais quoi que ma fortune ait d'éclat et de charmes,
Je ne puis vous quitter sans répandre des larmes.
Toujours de vos bontés je vais m'entretenir,   18
Chérir de vos vertus le tendre souvenir,
Comme vous des humains soulager la misère,
Protéger les chrétiens, leur tenir lieu de mère:

Vous me les rendez chers, et ces infortunés...

NÉRESTAN

Vous, les protéger! vous, qui les abandonnez!   190
Vous, qui des Lusignans foulant aux pieds la cendre...

ZAYRE

Je la viens honorer, seigneur, je viens vous rendre
Le dernier de ce sang, votre amour, votre espoir:
Oui, Lusignan est libre, et vous l'allez revoir.

CHÂTILLON

O ciel! Nous reverrions notre appui, notre père!   195

NÉRESTAN

Les chrétiens vous devraient une tête si chère!

ZAYRE

J'avais sans espérance osé la demander:
Le généreux soudan veut bien nous l'accorder:
On l'amène en ces lieux.

NÉRESTAN

          Que mon âme est émue!

ZAYRE

Mes larmes malgré moi me dérobent sa vue.   200
Ainsi que ce vieillard j'ai langui dans les fers:
Qui ne sait compatir aux maux qu'on a soufferts?

NÉRESTAN

Grand Dieu! que de vertu dans une âme infidèle!

198 MS1: bien vous l'accorder

455

SCÈNE III

ZAYRE, LUSIGNAN, CHÂTILLON, NÉRESTAN, PLUSIEURS ESCLAVES CHRÉTIENS

LUSIGNAN

Du séjour du trépas quelle voix me rappelle?
Suis-je avec des chrétiens?... Guidez mes pas tremblants.   205
Mes maux m'ont affaibli plus encor que mes ans.

En s'asseyant.

Suis-je libre en effet?

ZAYRE

            Oui, seigneur; oui, vous l'êtes.

CHÂTILLON

Vous vivez, vous calmez nos douleurs inquiètes.
Tous nos tristes chrétiens...

LUSIGNAN

            O jour! ô douce voix!
Châtillon, c'est donc vous? c'est vous que je revois!   21
Martyr, ainsi que moi, de la foi de nos pères,
Le Dieu que nous servons finit-il nos misères?
En quels lieux sommes-nous? Aidez mes faibles yeux.

CHÂTILLON

C'est ici le palais qu'ont bâti vos aïeux;

203c   MS1 adds: DEUX CHEVALIERS FRANÇAIS
203d   MS1, with stage direction: *soutenu par les deux chevaliers français*
206a   MS1: (*Il s'assied*)

456

Du fils de Noradin c'est le séjour profane. 215

ZAYRE

Le maître de ces lieux, le puissant Orosmane,
Sait connaître, seigneur, et chérir la vertu.

En montrant Nérestan.

Ce généreux Français, qui vous est inconnu,
Par la gloire amené des rives de la France
Venait de dix chrétiens payer la délivrance: 220
Le soudan, comme lui, gouverné par l'honneur,
Croit, en vous délivrant, égaler son grand cœur.

LUSIGNAN

Des chevaliers français tel est le caractère;
Leur noblesse en tout temps me fut utile et chère.
Trop digne chevalier, quoi! vous passez les mers, 225
Pour soulager nos maux, et pour briser nos fers?
Ah! parlez, à qui dois-je un service si rare?

NÉRESTAN

Mon nom est Nérestan; le sort longtemps barbare,
Qui dans les fers ici me mit presque en naissant,
Me fit quitter bientôt l'empire du Croissant. 230
A la cour de Louis, guidé par mon courage,
De la guerre sous lui j'ai fait l'apprentissage;
Ma fortune et mon rang sont un don de ce roi,
Si grand par sa valeur, et plus grand par sa foi.
Je le suivis, seigneur, aux bords de la Charente,[9] 235

217 36A: Sait respecter, seigneur
222 'délivrant' altered by Voltaire to 'rendant libre' in the Stockholm copy
of w42

[9] Louis IX defeated the English, led by Henry III, at Taillebourg-sur-Charente
in 1242. Delacroix evoked the battle in a famous picture painted in 1837 and
now in the Musée de Versailles.

457

Lorsque du fier Anglais la valeur menaçante,
Cédant à nos efforts trop longtemps captivés,
Satisfit en tombant aux lis qu'ils ont bravés.
Venez, prince, et montrez au plus grand des monarques,
De vos fers glorieux les vénérables marques.   240
Paris va révérer le martyr de la croix,
Et la cour de Louis est l'asile des rois.

LUSIGNAN

Hélas! de cette cour j'ai vu jadis la gloire.
Quand Philippe à Bovine enchaînait la victoire,[10]
Je combattais, seigneur, avec Montmorenci,[11]   24?
Melun, Destaing, de Nesle, et ce fameux Couci.[12]
Mais à revoir Paris je ne dois plus prétendre:
Vous voyez qu'au tombeau je suis prêt à descendre:
Je vais au roi des rois demander aujourd'hui
Le prix de tous les maux que j'ai soufferts pour lui.   25
Vous, généreux témoins de mon heure dernière,
Tandis qu'il en est temps, écoutez ma prière:
Nérestan, Châtillon, et vous... de qui les pleurs

245   MS I: Je combattis, seigneur

[10] Lusignan claims to have fought with the French at the Battle of Bouvines. While it is unlikely that any of the Frankish Lusignans were present at that battle, it is probable that at least one member of the French branch of that family, who were the powerful Counts of La Marche, helped Philippe Auguste, king of France, in this famous battle against the emperor Otto IV in 1214.

[11] Matthieu II de Montmorency (1174-1230) commanded the right wing of the French army at Bouvines.

[12] Adam II, vicomte de Melun, commanded the vanguard of the French army at Bouvines. Dieudonné d'Estaing is reputed to have saved Philippe Auguste's life during the battle. There is no mention of any member of the de Nesle family in any account of the Battle of Bouvines, but Simon de Nesle was one of Louis IX's most trusted knights, and Voltaire may simply have his name in mind as belonging roughly to the period he is talking about in Zaïre. Enguerrand III de Coucy was one of the knights chosen to remain with the king at the head of the French army.

Dans ces moments si chers honorent mes malheurs.
Madame, ayez pitié du plus malheureux père,   255
Qui jamais ait du ciel éprouvé la colère,
Qui répand devant vous des larmes que le temps
Ne peut encor tarir dans mes yeux expirants.
Une fille, trois fils, ma superbe espérance,
Me furent arrachés dès leur plus tendre enfance: 260
O mon cher Châtillon, tu dois t'en souvenir.

CHÂTILLON

De vos malheurs encor vous me voyez frémir.

LUSIGNAN

Prisonnier avec moi dans Césarée en flamme,
Tes yeux virent périr mes deux fils et ma femme.

CHÂTILLON

Mon bras chargé de fers ne les put secourir.   265

LUSIGNAN

Hélas! et j'étais père, et je ne pus mourir!
Veillez du haut des cieux, chers enfants que j'implore,
Sur mes autres enfants, s'ils sont vivants encore.
Mon dernier fils, ma fille, aux chaînes réservés,
Par de barbares mains pour servir conservés,   270
Loin d'un père accablé, furent portés ensemble
Dans ce même sérail où le ciel nous rassemble.

CHÂTILLON

Il est vrai, dans l'horreur de ce péril nouveau,
Je tenais votre fille à peine en son berceau:
Ne pouvant la sauver, seigneur, j'allais moi-même   275

264 MS1: virent percer mes

Répandre sur son front l'eau sainte du baptême,
Lorsque les Sarrasins de carnage fumants,
Revinrent l'arracher à mes bras tout sanglants.
Votre plus jeune fils, à qui les destinées
Avaient à peine encore accordé quatre années,   28c
Trop capable déjà de sentir son malheur,
Fut dans Jérusalem conduit avec sa sœur.

NÉRESTAN

De quel ressouvenir mon âme est déchirée!
A cet âge fatal j'étais dans Césarée:
Et tout couvert de sang, et chargé de liens,   28
Je suivis en ces lieux la foule des chrétiens.

LUSIGNAN

Vous... seigneur!... Ce sérail éleva votre enfance?...

En les regardant.

Hélas! de mes enfants auriez-vous connaissance?
Ils seraient de votre âge, et peut-être mes yeux...
Quel ornement, madame, étranger en ces lieux?   2ç
Depuis quand l'avez-vous?

ZAYRE

                         Depuis que je respire,
Seigneur... Eh quoi! d'où vient que votre âme soupire?

LUSIGNAN

Ah! daignez confier à mes tremblantes mains...

286   MS I: ces lieux Zaïre et les chrétiens
287   MS I: Ce sérail de tous deux vit élever l'enfance! [MS I*: β]
287a   MS I, no stage direction

460

ZAYRE

De quel trouble nouveau tous mes sens sont atteints!
Seigneur, que faites-vous?

LUSIGNAN

        O ciel! ô Providence!   295
Mes yeux, ne trompez point ma timide espérance;
Serait-il bien possible? Oui, c'est elle... Je vois
Ce présent qu'une épouse avait reçu de moi,
Et qui de mes enfants ornait toujours la tête,
Lorsque de leur naissance on célébrait la fête: 300
Je revois... Je succombe à mon saisissement.

ZAYRE

Qu'entends-je? et quel soupçon m'agite en ce moment?
Ah, seigneur!...

LUSIGNAN

        Dans l'espoir dont j'entrevois les charmes,
Ne m'abandonnez pas, Dieu qui voyez mes larmes,
Dieu mort sur cette croix, et qui revis pour nous,   305
Parle, achève, ô mon Dieu! ce sont là de tes coups.
Quoi! madame, en vos mains elle était demeurée?
Quoi! tous les deux captifs, et pris dans Césarée?

ZAYRE

Oui, seigneur.

NÉRESTAN

Se peut-il?

293 36A, with stage direction: *Elle lui donne la croix*
294 MSI, with stage direction: *Lusignan baise le bracelet*
     36A, with stage direction: *Il l'approche de sa bouche en pleurant*
300 MSI: on préparait la fête.

LUSIGNAN

            Leur parole, leurs traits,
De leur mère en effet sont les vivants portraits.   31c
Oui, grand Dieu, tu le veux, tu permets que je voie.
Dieu, ranime mes sens trop faibles pour ma joie.
Madame... Nérestan... Soutiens-moi, Châtillon...
Nérestan, si je dois nommer encor ce nom,
Avez-vous dans le sein la cicatrice heureuse   31
Du fer dont à mes yeux une main furieuse...

NÉRESTAN

Oui, seigneur, il est vrai.

LUSIGNAN

              Dieu juste! heureux moments!

NÉRESTAN *se jetant à genoux.*

Ah, seigneur! ah, Zayre!

LUSIGNAN

              Approchez, mes enfants.

NÉRESTAN

Moi, votre fils!

ZAYRE

        Seigneur.

LUSIGNAN

              Heureux jour qui m'éclaire!

314 K: si je dois vous nommer de ce nom
318a MS1: *aux genoux de Lusignan.*

Ma fille! mon cher fils! embrassez votre père. 320

CHÂTILLON

Que d'un bonheur si grand mon cœur se sent toucher!

LUSIGNAN

De vos bras, mes enfants, je ne puis m'arracher.
Je vous revois enfin, chère et triste famille,
Mon fils, digne héritier... Vous... hélas! vous? ma fille!
Dissipez mes soupçons, ôtez-moi cette horreur, 325
Ce trouble qui m'accable au comble du bonheur.
Toi qui seul as conduit sa fortune et la mienne,
Mon Dieu qui me la rends, me la rends-tu chrétienne?
Tu pleures, malheureuse, et tu baisses les yeux!
Tu te tais! je t'entends! ô crime! ô justes cieux! 330

ZAYRE

Je ne puis vous tromper: sous les lois d'Orosmane...
Punissez votre fille... Elle était musulmane.

LUSIGNAN

Que la foudre en éclats ne tombe que sur moi!
Ah, mon fils! A ces mots j'eusse expiré sans toi.
Mon Dieu, j'ai combattu soixante ans pour ta gloire; 335
J'ai vu tomber ton temple, et périr ta mémoire;
Dans un cachot affreux abandonné vingt ans,
Mes larmes t'imploraient pour mes tristes enfants:
Et lorsque ma famille est par toi réunie,
Quand je trouve une fille, elle est ton ennemie! 340
Je suis bien malheureux... c'est ton père, c'est moi,

328   MSI: Grand Dieu
329   MSI, with stage direction: *à Zaïre.*
335   MSI: Grand Dieu

463

C'est ma seule prison qui t'a ravi ta foi.
Ma fille, tendre objet de mes dernières peines,
Songe au moins, songe au sang qui coule dans tes veines:
C'est le sang de vingt rois, tous chrétiens comme moi;   345
C'est le sang des héros, défenseurs de ma loi;
C'est le sang des martyrs... O fille encor trop chère!
Connais-tu ton destin? sais-tu quelle est ta mère?
Sais-tu bien qu'à l'instant que son flanc mit au jour
Ce triste et dernier fruit d'un malheureux amour,   350
Je la vis massacrer par la main forcenée,
Par la main des brigands à qui tu t'es donnée?
Tes frères, ces martyrs égorgés à mes yeux,
T'ouvrent leurs bras sanglants tendus du haut des cieux.
Ton Dieu que tu trahis, ton Dieu que tu blasphèmes,   355
Pour toi, pour l'univers, est mort en ces lieux mêmes,
En ces lieux où mon bras le servit tant de fois,
En ces lieux où son sang te parle par ma voix.
Vois ces murs, vois ce temple envahi par tes maîtres:
Tout annonce le Dieu qu'ont vengé tes ancêtres.   360
Tourne les yeux, sa tombe est près de ce palais;
C'est ici la montagne où lavant nos forfaits,
Il voulut expirer sous les coups de l'impie;
C'est là que de sa tombe il rappela sa vie.
Tu ne saurais marcher dans cet auguste lieu,   365
Tu n'y peux faire un pas, sans y trouver ton Dieu;
Et tu n'y peux rester sans renier ton père,
Ton honneur qui te parle, et ton Dieu qui t'éclaire.
Je te vois dans mes bras, et pleurer et frémir;
Sur ton front pâlissant Dieu met le repentir: 370
Je vois la vérité dans ton cœur descendue;
Je retrouve ma fille après l'avoir perdue;
Et je reprends ma gloire et ma félicité,
En dérobant mon sang à l'infidélité.

367   MS1: sans outrager ton
368   w46: C'est ton père qui te parle

464

NÉRESTAN

Je revois donc ma sœur?... Et son âme...

ZAYRE

Ah, mon père!   375
Cher auteur de mes jours, parlez, que dois-je faire?

LUSIGNAN

M'ôter, par un seul mot, ma honte et mes ennuis,
Dire, Je suis chrétienne.

ZAYRE

Oui... seigneur... Je le suis.

LUSIGNAN

Dieu, reçois son aveu du sein de ton empire.

SCÈNE IV

ZAYRE, LUSIGNAN, CHÂTILLON, NÉRESTAN, CORASMIN

CORASMIN

Madame, le soudan m'ordonne de vous dire,   380
Qu'à l'instant de ces lieux il faut vous retirer,

---

378   MS I: Je la suis
379c   MS I adds: DEUX CHEVALIERS FRANÇAIS, ESCLAVES

Et de ces vils chrétiens[13] surtout vous séparer.
Vous, Français, suivez-moi: de vous je dois répondre.

CHÂTILLON

Où sommes-nous, grand Dieu! Quel coup vient nous
confondre?

LUSIGNAN

Notre courage, amis, doit ici s'animer.   385

ZAYRE

Hélas, seigneur!

LUSIGNAN

O vous que je n'ose nommer,
Jurez-moi de garder un secret si funeste.

ZAYRE

Je vous le jure.

LUSIGNAN

Allez, le ciel fera le reste.

Fin du second acte.

382   MSI: Et de ces étrangers surtout
385   MSI: courage, ami, doit
387   36A: Adieu!... gardez surtout un secret
387-388 MSI, 33R:
        Adieu!... gardez surtout un secret si funeste;
        Soyez fidèle, allez, le ciel fera le reste. [MSI*: β]

[13] Although all the printed editions have *Et de ces vils chrétiens*, it appears that as late as 1792 the actors went on using the version given by the prompt copy. Palissot comments on this line in the 1792 edition of Voltaire's *Œuvres*: 'Les comédiens, au lieu de dire *& de ces vils chrétiens*, y substituent *& de ces étrangers*, & j'ose dire qu'ils ont raison'.

466

ACTE III

SCÈNE PREMIÈRE

OROSMANE, CORASMIN

OROSMANE

Vous étiez, Corasmin, trompé par vos alarmes;
Non, Louis contre moi ne tourne point ses armes;
Les Français sont lassés de chercher désormais
Des climats que pour eux le destin n'a point faits;
Ils n'abandonnent point leur fertile patrie,   5
Pour languir aux déserts de l'aride Arabie,[1]
Et venir arroser de leur sang odieux,
Ces palmes que pour nous Dieu fait croître en ces lieux.
Ils couvrent de vaisseaux la mer de la Syrie.
Louis, des bords de Chypre, épouvante l'Asie;   10
Mais j'apprends que ce roi s'éloigne de nos ports;
De la féconde Egypte il menace les bords;[2]
J'en reçois à l'instant la première nouvelle.
Contre les mameluks[3] son courage l'appelle;
Il cherche Mélédin, mon secret ennemi;   15

---

c MS1 adds: ESCLAVES
d MS1: OROSMANE, *un billet à la main*
15 MS1: mon cruel ennemi [MS1*: β]

---

[1] *Arabie* is here used for Syria.
[2] See above, p.296-97.
[3] The Mamelukes were originally white male slaves, mainly Turks and Circassians, who formed the élite of the Egyptian army. In May 1250, while saint Louis was the sultan's prisoner, the Mamelukes killed the legitimate sultan, Turanshah, and took over the government themselves, under their general, Baibars.

Sur leurs divisions mon trône est affermi.
Je ne crains plus enfin l'Egypte, ni la France.[4]
Nos communs ennemis cimentent ma puissance;
Et prodigues d'un sang qu'ils devraient ménager,
Prennent, en s'immolant, le soin de me venger.   20
Relâche ces chrétiens; ami, je les délivre;
Je veux plaire à leur maître, et leur permets de vivre:
Je veux que sur la mer on les mène à leur roi,
Que Louis me connaisse, et respecte ma foi.
Mène-lui Lusignan; dis-lui que je lui donne   25
Celui que la naissance allie à sa couronne,
Celui que par deux fois mon père avait vaincu,
Et qu'il tint enchaîné tandis qu'il a vécu.

CORASMIN

Son nom cher aux chrétiens...

OROSMANE

                Son nom n'est point à craindre.

CORASMIN

Mais, seigneur, si Louis...

OROSMANE

                Il n'est plus temps de feindre.   3
Zayre l'a voulu; c'est assez: et mon cœur,
En donnant Lusignan, le donne à mon vainqueur.
Louis est peu pour moi; je fais tout pour Zayre;
Nul autre sur mon cœur n'aurait pris cet empire.
Je viens de l'affliger, c'est à moi d'adoucir   3
Le déplaisir mortel qu'elle a dû ressentir,
Quand, sur les faux avis des desseins de la France,

[4] See above, p.299.

468

J'ai fait à ces chrétiens un peu de violence.
Que dis-je? Ces moments perdus dans mon conseil,
Ont de ce grand hymen suspendu l'appareil: 40
D'une heure encore, ami, mon bonheur se diffère;
Mais j'emploierai du moins ce temps à lui complaire.
Zayre ici demande un secret entretien
Avec ce Nérestan, ce généreux chrétien...

CORASMIN

Et vous avez, seigneur, encor cette indulgence?   45

OROSMANE

Ils ont été tous deux esclaves dans l'enfance;
Ils ont porté mes fers, ils ne se verront plus;
Zayre enfin de moi n'aura point un refus.
Je ne m'en défends point; je foule aux pieds pour elle
Des rigueurs du sérail la contrainte cruelle.   50
J'ai méprisé ces lois, dont l'âpre austérité
Fait d'une vertu triste une nécessité.
Je ne suis point formé du sang asiatique;
Né parmi les rochers au sein de la Taurique,
Des Scythes[5] mes aïeux je garde la fierté,   55

---

[5] In his *Essai sur les mœurs*, Voltaire interprets very widely the name *Scythe*: 'Les Scythes sont ces mêmes barbares que nous avons depuis appelés Tartares; ce sont ceux-là mêmes qui, longtemps avant Alexandre, avaient ravagé plusieurs fois l'Asie, et qui ont été les dépradateurs d'une grande partie du continent. Tantôt sous le nom de Monguls ou de Huns, ils ont asservi la Chine et les Indes; tantôt sous le nom de Turcs, ils ont chassé les Arabes qui avaient conquis une partie de l'Asie' (*Essai*, i.51). According to Herodotus, with whose account Voltaire was certainly familiar, the Scythians, famous in antiquity for their warlike qualities, inhabited the area north of the Black Sea bounded by the Danube to the west and the Don to the east. But there were no Scythians as such left in the thirteenth century. The tribe had been wiped out or absorbed by the Sarmatians in the second century A.D. It is not clear why Voltaire has chosen to give Orosmane Scythian forebears. Is it because he wants to explain his hero's rejection of Muslim customs, or his impetuous character, or both? It may be that he identifies the Scythian with virtue and courage, as in his *conte*, *La Princesse de Babylone*.

Leurs mœurs, leurs passions, leur générosité:
Je consens qu'en partant Nérestan la revoie;
Je veux que tous les cœurs soient heureux de ma joie.
Après ce peu d'instants volés à mon amour,
Tous ses moments, ami, sont à moi sans retour.   60
Va, ce chrétien attend, et tu peux l'introduire.
Presse son entretien, obéis à Zayre.

SCÈNE II

CORASMIN, NÉRESTAN

CORASMIN

En ces lieux, un moment, tu peux encor rester.
Zayre à tes regards viendra se présenter.

SCÈNE III

NÉRESTAN *seul.*

En quel état, ô ciel! en quels lieux je la laisse!   65
O ma religion! ô mon père! ô tendresse!
Mais je la vois.

59   MS1: Passé ce peu [MS1*: β]

SCÈNE IV

ZAYRE, NÉRESTAN

NÉRESTAN

Ma sœur, je puis donc vous parler?
Ah! dans quel temps le ciel nous voulut rassembler!
Vous ne reverrez plus un trop malheureux père.

ZAYRE

Dieu, Lusignan!

NÉRESTAN

Il touche à son heure dernière.   70
Sa joie en nous voyant, par de trop grands efforts,
De ses sens affaiblis a rompu les ressorts;
Et cette émotion, dont son âme est remplie,
A bientôt épuisé les sources de sa vie.
Mais pour comble d'horreurs, à ces derniers moments,   75
Il doute de sa fille, et de ses sentiments;
Il meurt dans l'amertume, et son âme incertaine
Demande en soupirant si vous êtes chrétienne.

ZAYRE

Quoi, je suis votre sœur, et vous pouvez penser
Qu'à mon sang, à ma loi, j'aille ici renoncer?   80

NÉRESTAN

Ah, ma sœur! cette loi n'est pas la vôtre encore;

70 MSI: Hélas, seigneur!
74 MSI: Va bientôt épuiser les restes de sa vie
75 MSI: d'horreur, à ces derniers
    K: d'horreur

471

Le jour qui vous éclaire est pour vous à l'aurore;
Vous n'avez point reçu ce gage précieux,
Qui nous lave du crime, et nous ouvre les cieux.
Jurez par nos malheurs, et par votre famille,   85
Par ces martyrs sacrés, de qui vous êtes fille,
Que vous voulez ici recevoir aujourd'hui
Le sceau du Dieu vivant qui nous attache à lui.

ZAYRE

Oui, je jure en vos mains, par ce Dieu que j'adore,
Par sa loi que je cherche, et que mon cœur ignore,   90
De vivre désormais sous cette sainte loi...
Mais, mon cher frère... Hélas! que veut-elle de moi?
Que faut-il?

NÉRESTAN

Détester l'empire de vos maîtres,
Servir, aimer ce Dieu qu'ont aimé nos ancêtres,
Qui né près de ces murs est mort ici pour nous,   9
Qui nous a rassemblés, qui m'a conduit vers vous.
Est-ce à moi d'en parler? Moins instruit que fidèle,
Je ne suis qu'un soldat, et je n'ai que du zèle.
Un pontife sacré viendra jusqu'en ces lieux,
Vous apporter la vie, et dessiller vos yeux.   10
Songez à vos serments, et que l'eau du baptême

82   MS1: qui nous éclaire
85   MS1: par notre famille
93-98 MS1:
    ⟨Que dois-je faire enfin?
        NÉRESTAN
                Moins instruit que fidèle,
    Je ne suis qu'un soldat⟩
95   W51: Qui né dans ces remparts est
95-96 MS1*, 33R-W46:
    Qui naquit, qui souffrit, qui mourut en ces lieux,
    Qui nous a rassemblés, qui m'amène à vos yeux.

Ne vous apporte point la mort et l'anathème.
Obtenez qu'avec lui je puisse revenir.
Mais à quel titre, ô ciel! faut-il donc l'obtenir?
A qui le demander dans ce sérail profane?... 105
Vous, le sang de vingt rois, esclave d'Orosmane!
Parente de Louis! fille de Lusignan!
Vous chrétienne, et ma sœur, esclave d'un soudan!
Vous m'entendez... je n'ose en dire davantage:
Dieu, nous réserviez-vous à ce dernier outrage? 110

ZAYRE

Ah, cruel! poursuivez, vous ne connaissez pas
Mon secret, mes tourments, mes vœux, mes attentats.
Mon frère, ayez pitié d'une sœur égarée,
Qui brûle, qui gémit, qui meurt désespérée.
Je suis chrétienne, hélas!... j'attends avec ardeur 115
Cette eau sainte, cette eau, qui peut guérir mon cœur.
Non, je ne serai point indigne de mon frère,
De mes aïeux, de moi, de mon malheureux père.
Mais parlez à Zayre, et ne lui cachez rien,
Dites... quelle est la loi de l'empire chrétien?... 120
Quel est le châtiment pour une infortunée,
Qui loin de ses parents aux fers abandonnée,
Trouvant chez un barbare un généreux appui,
Aurait touché son âme, et s'unirait à lui?

NÉRESTAN

O ciel! que dites-vous? Ah! la mort la plus prompte 125
Devrait...

ZAYRE

C'en est assez, frappe, et préviens ta honte.

NÉRESTAN

Qui vous, ma sœur?

473

ZAYRE

C'est moi que je viens d'accuser.
Orosmane m'adore... et j'allais l'épouser.

NÉRESTAN

L'épouser! est-il vrai, ma sœur? Est-ce vous-même?
Vous, la fille des rois?

ZAYRE

Frappe, dis-je; je l'aime.   13

NÉRESTAN

Opprobre malheureux du sang dont vous sortez,
Vous demandez la mort, et vous la méritez:
Et si je n'écoutais que ta honte et ma gloire,
L'honneur de ma maison, mon père, sa mémoire,
Si la loi de ton Dieu, que tu ne connais pas,   13
Si ma religion ne retenait mon bras,
J'irais dans ce palais, j'irais au moment même,
Immoler de ce fer un barbare qui t'aime,
De son indigne flanc le plonger dans le tien,
Et ne l'en retirer que pour percer le mien.   14
Ciel! tandis que Louis, l'exemple de la terre,
Au Nil épouvanté ne va porter la guerre,
Que pour venir bientôt, frappant des coups plus sûrs,
Délivrer ton Dieu même, et lui rendre ces murs:
Zayre, cependant, ma sœur, son alliée,   14
Au tyran d'un sérail par l'hymen est liée?
Et je vais donc apprendre à Lusignan trahi,

130   MS1, 33R: Reprenez vos esprits.
      36A: M'osez-vous avouer? / ZAÏRE / Frappe,
143   MS1: portant des coups [MS1*: β]

Qu'un Tartare[6] est le dieu que sa fille a choisi?
Dans un moment affreux, hélas! ton père expire,
En demandant à Dieu le salut de Zaïre.   150

ZAYRE

Arrête, mon cher frère... arrête, connais-moi;
Peut-être que Zaïre est digne encor de toi.
Mon frère, épargne-moi cet horrible langage;
Ton courroux, ton reproche, est un plus grand outrage,
Plus sensible pour moi, plus dur que ce trépas,   155
Que je te demandais, et que je n'obtiens pas.
L'état où tu me vois accable ton courage;
Tu souffres, je le vois; je souffre davantage.
Je voudrais que du ciel le barbare secours,
De mon sang, dans mon cœur, eût arrêté le cours;   160
Le jour qu'empoisonné d'une flamme profane,
Ce pur sang des chrétiens brûla pour Orosmane,
Le jour que de ta sœur Orosmane charmé...
Pardonnez-moi, chrétiens; qui ne l'aurait aimé?
Il faisait tout pour moi; son cœur m'avait choisie;   165
Je voyais sa fierté pour moi seule adoucie.
C'est lui qui des chrétiens a ranimé l'espoir:
C'est à lui que je dois le bonheur de te voir:
Pardonne; ton courroux, mon père, ma tendresse,
Mes serments, mon devoir, mes remords, ma faiblesse,   170
Me servent de supplice, et ta sœur en ce jour
Meurt de son repentir plus que de son amour.

149   MS1, 33R-W52, W57P: En ce moment
      W56, W68, K: Dans ce moment

[6] While confusion between Scythians and Tartars is not uncommon (see note above), Nérestan here seems to be using the word *Tartare* vaguely, as a term of abuse.

NÉRESTAN

Je te blâme, et te plains; crois-moi, la Providence
Ne te laissera point périr sans innocence:
Je te pardonne, hélas! ces combats odieux;   175
Dieu ne t'a point prêté son bras victorieux:
Ce bras, qui rend la force aux plus faibles courages,
Soutiendra ce roseau plié par les orages.
Il ne souffrira pas qu'à son culte engagé,
Entre un barbare et lui ton cœur soit partagé.   180
Le baptême éteindra ces feux dont il soupire,
Et tu vivras fidèle, ou périras martyre.
Achève donc ici ton serment commencé;
Achève, et dans l'horreur dont ton cœur est pressé,
Promets au roi Louis, à l'Europe, à ton père,   185
Au Dieu qui déjà parle à ce cœur si sincère,
De ne point accomplir cet hymen odieux,
Avant que le pontife ait éclairé tes yeux,
Avant qu'en ma présence il te fasse chrétienne,
Et que Dieu par ses mains t'adopte et te soutienne.   190
Le promets-tu, Zayre?...

ZAYRE

                          Oui, je te le promets:
Rends-moi chrétienne et libre; à tout je me soumets.
Va, d'un père expirant, va fermer la paupière;
Va, je voudrais te suivre, et mourir la première.

NÉRESTAN

Je pars, adieu, ma sœur, adieu: puisque mes vœux   195
Ne peuvent t'arracher à ce palais honteux,
Je reviendrai bientôt, par un heureux baptême,

174 33R: périr dans l'innocence [33R errata: β]
179 MS1: à ses lois engagé [MS1*: β]
187 MS1: cet hyménée affreux [MS1*: β]

T'arracher aux enfers, et te rendre à toi-même.

SCÈNE V

ZAYRE *seule.*

Me voilà seule, ô Dieu! que vais-je devenir?
Dieu, commande à mon cœur de ne te point trahir.   200
Hélas! suis-je en effet, ou Française, ou sultane?
Fille de Lusignan, ou femme d'Orosmane?
Suis-je amante, ou chrétienne? O serments que j'ai faits!
Mon père, mon pays, vous serez satisfaits.
Fatime ne vient point. Quoi! dans ce trouble extrême,   205
L'univers m'abandonne! on me laisse à moi-même!
Mon cœur peut-il porter seul, et privé d'appui,
Le fardeau des devoirs qu'on m'impose aujourd'hui?
A ta loi, Dieu puissant, oui, mon âme est rendue;
Mais fais que mon amant s'éloigne de ma vue.   210
Cher amant! ce matin l'aurais-je pu prévoir,
Que je dusse aujourd'hui redouter de te voir?
Moi, qui de tant de feux justement possédée,
N'avais d'autre bonheur, d'autre soin, d'autre idée,
Que de t'entretenir, d'écouter ton amour,   215
Te voir, te souhaiter, attendre ton retour?
Hélas! et je t'adore; et t'aimer est un crime.

198   36A: T'arracher à tes fers, et
201   K: effet, française, ou musulmane?
215   MSI, 33R-W68: t'entretenir, écouter

SCÈNE VI

ZAYRE, OROSMANE

OROSMANE

Paraissez, tout est prêt; le beau feu qui m'anime,
Ne souffre plus, madame, aucun retardement;
Les flambeaux de l'hymen brillent pour votre amant;   220
Les parfums de l'encens remplissent la mosquée;
Du dieu de Mahomet la puissance invoquée
Confirme mes serments, et préside à mes feux.
Mon peuple prosterné pour vous offre ses vœux.
Tout tombe à vos genoux; vos superbes rivales,   225
Qui disputaient mon cœur, et marchaient vos égales,
Heureuses de vous suivre, et de vous obéir,
Devant vos volontés vont apprendre à fléchir.
Le trône, les festins, et la cérémonie,
Tout est prêt; commencez le bonheur de ma vie.   230

ZAYRE

Où suis-je, malheureuse, ô tendresse! ô douleur!

OROSMANE

Venez.

217b MS1: OROSMANE, ZAÏRE, CORASMIN
218 K: prêt, et l'ardeur qui m'anime
221 MS1: l'encens fument dans la [MS1*: β]
224 36A: Mes sujets prosternés offrent pour vous leurs vœux
     MS1: pour vous forme ses
     K: peuple consterné
225 MS1, 36A: Venez. En ce moment vos superbes [MS1*: β]
     33R: Venez en ce moment, vos superbes

ZAYRE

Où me cacher?

OROSMANE

Que dites-vous?

ZAYRE

Seigneur.

OROSMANE

Donnez-moi votre main, daignez, belle Zayre...

ZAYRE

Dieu de mon père! hélas! que pourrai-je lui dire?

OROSMANE

Que j'aime à triompher de ce tendre embarras!   235
Qu'il redouble ma flamme, et mon bonheur!...

ZAYRE

Hélas!

OROSMANE

Ce trouble à mes désirs vous rend encor plus chère;

235-240 MS I:
 ⟨Que j'aime à triompher de ce tendre embarras!
 [MS I*: Je vois avec transport un si tendre embarras]
 Il redouble ma flamme et mon bonheur⟩
 [MS I*, pasted over and replaced by:]
 Cher et charmant objet de ma constante foi,
 Venez, ne tardez plus...
   ZAÏRE
    Ah, grand dieu, soutiens-moi.

479

D'une vertu modeste il est le caractère.
Digne et charmant objet de ma constante foi,
Venez, ne tardez plus.

ZAYRE

                    Fatime, soutiens-moi...   240
Seigneur.

OROSMANE

    O ciel! eh quoi!

ZAYRE

                    Seigneur, cet hyménée
Etait un bien suprême à mon âme étonnée.
Je n'ai point recherché le trône et la grandeur.
Qu'un sentiment plus juste occupait tout mon cœur!
Hélas! j'aurais voulu qu'à vos vertus unie,   24⁴
En méprisant pour vous les trônes de l'Asie,
Seule, et dans un désert auprès de mon époux,
J'eusse pu sous mes pieds les fouler avec vous.
Mais... seigneur... ces chrétiens...

OROSMANE

                    Ces chrétiens... Quoi! madame?
Qu'auraient donc de commun cette secte et ma flamme?   25

ZAYRE

Lusignan, ce vieillard accablé de douleurs,
Termine en ces moments sa vie et ses malheurs.

239-240   36A:
          Digne et charmant objet de mes feux, de ma foi.
          Idole de mon cœur!

 OROSMANE

Eh bien! quel intérêt si pressant et si tendre,
A ce vieillard chrétien votre cœur peut-il prendre?
Vous n'êtes point chrétienne; élevée en ces lieux,   255
Vous suivez dès longtemps la foi de mes aïeux.
Un vieillard qui succombe au poids de ses années,
Peut-il troubler ici vos belles destinées?
Cette aimable pitié, qu'il s'attire de vous,
Doit se perdre avec moi dans des moments si doux.   260

ZAYRE

Seigneur, si vous m'aimez, si je vous étais chère…

OROSMANE

Si vous l'êtes, ah Dieu!

ZAYRE

                    Souffrez que l'on diffère…
Permettez que ces nœuds par vos mains assemblés…

OROSMANE

Que dites-vous? ô ciel! est-ce vous qui parlez,
Zayre?

ZAYRE

Je ne puis soutenir sa colère.   265

OROSMANE

Zayre!

ZAYRE

Il m'est affreux, seigneur, de vous déplaire;
Excusez ma douleur… Non, j'oublie à la fois,

481

Et tout ce que je suis, et tout ce que je dois.
Je ne puis soutenir cet aspect qui me tue.
Je ne puis... Ah! souffrez que loin de votre vue,   270
Seigneur, j'aille cacher mes larmes, mes ennuis,
Mes vœux, mon désespoir, et l'horreur où je suis.

Elle sort.

SCÈNE VII

OROSMANE, CORASMIN

OROSMANE

Je demeure immobile, et ma langue glacée
Se refuse aux transports de mon âme offensée.
Est-ce à moi que l'on parle? ai-je bien entendu?   275
Est-ce moi qu'elle fuit? ô ciel! et qu'ai-je vu?
Corasmin, quel est donc ce changement extrême?
Je la laisse échapper! je m'ignore moi-même.

CORASMIN

Vous seul causez son trouble, et vous vous en plaignez.
Vous accusez, seigneur, un cœur où vous régnez!   280

---

272   36A: Mes vœux, mon amour même et l'horreur
276   36B, omitted
279-280   MS1, 33R, 36A, W38 uncancelled:
      Peut-être accusez-vous ce trouble trop charmant,
      Que l'innocence inspire à l'aspect d'un amant.
      [MS1*: β, with inverted lines]
      36B: Vous accusez peut-être un cœur où vous régnez
      Vous causez ses soupirs, et vous vous en plaignez.

OROSMANE

Mais pourquoi donc ces pleurs, ces regrets, cette fuite,
Cette douleur si sombre en ses regards écrite?
Si c'était ce Français!... quel soupçon! quelle horreur!
Quelle lumière affreuse a passé dans mon cœur!
Hélas! je repoussais ma juste défiance: 285
Un barbare, un esclave, aurait cette insolence?
Cher ami, je verrais un cœur comme le mien,
Réduit à redouter un esclave chrétien?
Mais parle, tu pouvais observer son visage,
Tu pouvais de ses yeux entendre le langage: 290
Ne me déguise rien, mes feux sont-ils trahis?
Apprends-moi mon malheur... tu trembles... tu frémis...
C'en est assez.

CORASMIN

              Je crains d'irriter vos alarmes.
Il est vrai que ses yeux ont versé quelques larmes;
Mais, seigneur, après tout, je n'ai rien observé   295
Qui doive...

OROSMANE

              A cet affront, je serais réservé?
Non, si Zayre, ami, m'avait fait cette offense,
Elle eût avec plus d'art trompé ma confiance.
Le déplaisir secret de son cœur agité,
Si ce cœur est perfide, aurait-il éclaté?   300

281 MS1: Mais pourquoi ces horreurs, ce trouble, cette fuite
     MS1*: donc ces pleurs? mais pourquoi cette fuite.
     33R, 36A: pleurs, ce trouble, cette
     W38-W46: pleurs, cette horreur, cette ['horreur' altered by Voltaire to
'trouble' in the Stockholm copy of W42]
285-288 MS1, absent [MS1*: β pasted in]
291 MS1: Réponds; est-il aimé? Mes [MS1*: β]
297 MS1: Si Zaïre, après tout, m'avait fait [MS1*: β]

Ecoute, garde-toi de soupçonner Zayre.
Mais, dis-tu, ce Français gémit, pleure, soupire:
Que m'importe après tout le sujet de ses pleurs?
Qui sait si l'amour même entre dans ses douleurs?
Et qu'ai-je à redouter d'un esclave infidèle,   305
Qui demain pour jamais se va séparer d'elle?

CORASMIN

N'avez-vous pas, seigneur, permis, malgré nos lois,
Qu'il jouît de sa vue une seconde fois?
Qu'il revînt en ces lieux?

OROSMANE

                              Qu'il revînt? lui ce traître,
Qu'aux yeux de ma maîtresse il osât reparaître?   31c
Oui, je le lui rendrais, mais mourant, mais puni,
Mais versant à ses yeux le sang qui m'a trahi:
Déchiré devant elle, et ma main dégouttante
Confondrait dans son sang le sang de son amante...
Excuse les transports de ce cœur offensé;   31
Il est né violent, il aime, il est blessé.
Je connais mes fureurs, et je crains ma faiblesse;

303-306 MS1:
         Quoi, malheureux, c'est moi dont la facilité
         L'invitait à trahir ma générosité!
         Mais qu'ai-je à craindre, ami? Cet esclave infidèle
         Dès demain pour jamais se va séparer d'elle.
         [MS1*, pasted over and replaced by β]
312   MS1:   ce sang
313   MS1:   Expirant à mes pieds; et ma [MS1*: β]
317-319   MS1:
         Mais il sait de ses feux arrêter l'imprudence.
         Je retiendrai mon bras trop prompt dans sa vengeance:
         La honte serait jointe encore à mon tourment.
         Je ne veux point qu'on dise aux peuples d'Occident
         Qu'un chrétien trop heureux dans son indigne flamme
         Osa me disputer ma maîtresse et ma femme.

A des troubles honteux je sens que je m'abaisse.
Non, c'est trop sur Zayre arrêter un soupçon;
Non, son cœur n'est point fait pour une trahison: 320
Mais ne crois pas non plus que le mien s'avilisse
A souffrir des rigueurs, à gémir d'un caprice,
A me plaindre, à reprendre, à redonner ma foi;
Les éclaircissements sont indignes de moi.
Il vaut mieux sur mes sens reprendre un juste empire; 325
Il vaut mieux oublier jusqu'au nom de Zayre.
Allons, que le sérail soit fermé pour jamais;
Que la terreur habite aux portes du palais;
Que tout ressente ici le frein de l'esclavage.
Des rois de l'Orient suivons l'antique usage. 330
On peut pour son esclave, oubliant sa fierté,
Laisser tomber sur elle un regard de bonté;
Mais il est trop honteux de craindre une maîtresse;

Je ne puis sur Zaïre arrêter mon soupçon
[MSI*, pasted over and replaced by β]
320   MSI: pour tant de trahison [MSI*: β]
325-336 MSI:
J'oublierai pour jamais qu'un jour dans mon empire,
Mes regards au hasard ont tombé sur Zaïre.
Qu'aux chrétiens cependant le sérail soit fermé.
O ciel! Pourquoi faut-il qu'Orosmane ait aimé?
[MSI*, pasted over; β added on the verso]
327-336 33R:
Allons... mais qu'aux chrétiens le sérail soit fermé.
O ciel! Pourquoi faut-il qu'Orosmane ait aimé.
327-332 36A:
Corasmin, que ces murs soient fermés pour jamais,
Fais veiller la terreur aux portes du palais;
Que tout subisse ici le frein de l'esclavage,
Des lois de l'Orient suivons l'austère usage,
On peut sans s'avilir, abaissant sa fierté,
Jeter sur son esclave un regard de bonté.
333 w38-w46: Mais il est trop honteux d'avoir une faiblesse ['d'avoir une
faiblesse' altered by Voltaire to 'de craindre sa maîtresse' in the Stockholm copy
of w42]

Aux mœurs de l'Occident laissons cette bassesse.
Ce sexe dangereux, qui veut tout asservir,   335
S'il règne dans l'Europe, ici doit obéir.

Fin du troisième acte.

334   36A: cette faiblesse
336   MS1*: S'il commande en

486

ACTE IV

SCÈNE PREMIÈRE

ZAYRE, FATIME

FATIME

Que je vous plains, madame, et que je vous admire!
C'est le dieu des chrétiens, c'est Dieu qui vous inspire;
Il donnera la force à vos bras languissants,
De briser des liens si chers et si puissants.

ZAYRE

Eh! pourrai-je achever ce fatal sacrifice?   5

FATIME

Vous demandez sa grâce, il vous doit sa justice:
De votre cœur docile il doit prendre le soin.

ZAYRE

Jamais de son appui je n'eus tant de besoin.

FATIME

Si vous ne voyez plus votre auguste famille,
Le Dieu que vous servez vous adopte pour fille: 10
Vous êtes dans ses bras, il parle à votre cœur;
Et quand ce saint pontife, organe du Seigneur,
Ne pourrait aborder dans ce palais profane…

ZAYRE

Ah! j'ai porté la mort dans le sein d'Orosmane.

J'ai pu désespérer le cœur de mon amant! 15
Quel outrage, Fatime, et quel affreux moment!
Mon Dieu, vous l'ordonnez, j'eusse été trop heureuse.

FATIME

Quoi, vous regretteriez cette chaîne honteuse,
Hasarder la victoire, ayant tant combattu?

ZAYRE

Victoire infortunée! inhumaine vertu! 20
Non, tu ne connais pas ce que je sacrifie.
Cet amour si puissant, ce charme de ma vie,
Dont j'espérais, hélas! tant de félicité,
Dans toute son ardeur n'avait point éclaté.
Fatime, j'offre à Dieu mes blessures cruelles; 25
Je mouille devant lui de larmes criminelles
Ces lieux, où tu m'as dit qu'il choisit son séjour;
Je lui crie en pleurant, Ote-moi mon amour,
Arrache-moi mes vœux, remplis-moi de toi-même;
Mais, Fatime, à l'instant les traits de ce que j'aime, 30
Ces traits chers et charmants, que toujours je revois,
Se montrent dans mon âme entre le ciel et moi.
Eh bien, race des rois, dont le ciel me fit naître,
Père, mère, chrétiens, vous, mon Dieu, vous, mon maître,
Vous qui de mon amant me privez aujourd'hui, 35
Terminez donc mes jours, qui ne sont plus pour lui.
Que j'expire innocente, et qu'une main si chère
De ces yeux qu'il aimait ferme au moins la paupière.
Ah! que fait Orosmane? Il ne s'informe pas,
Si j'attends loin de lui la vie ou le trépas; 40
Il me fuit, il me laisse, et je n'y peux survivre.

32   w51:   entre Dieu même et moi
38   ms1:   qu'il aima ferme

FATIME

Quoi vous! fille des rois, que vous prétendez suivre,
Vous dans les bras d'un Dieu, votre éternel appui?...

ZAYRE

Eh! pourquoi mon amant n'est-il pas né pour lui?
Orosmane est-il fait pour être sa victime?   45
Dieu pourrait-il haïr un cœur si magnanime?
Généreux, bienfaisant, juste, plein de vertus,
S'il était né chrétien, que serait-il de plus?
Et plût à Dieu du moins que ce saint interprète,
Ce ministre sacré, que mon âme souhaite,   50
Du trouble où tu me vois vînt bientôt me tirer!
Je ne sais; mais enfin, j'ose encor espérer,
Que ce Dieu, dont cent fois on m'a peint la clémence,
Ne réprouverait point une telle alliance;
Peut-être de Zayre en secret adoré,   55
Il pardonne aux combats de ce cœur déchiré;
Peut-être en me laissant au trône de Syrie,
Il soutiendrait par moi les chrétiens de l'Asie.
Fatime, tu le sais, ce puissant Saladin,
Qui ravit à mon sang l'empire du Jourdain,   60
Qui fit comme Orosmane admirer sa clémence,
Au sein d'une chrétienne il avait pris naissance.[1]

FATIME

Ah! ne voyez-vous pas que pour vous consoler...

42   MS1: rois, des héros qu'il faut suivre
44   MS1: Mais pourquoi
56   MS1: Il recevrait les vœux de ce cœur
59   MS1: L'exemple en est récent. Ce fameux Saladin
63   MS1, 33R: Que faites-vous, madame? Eh! ne voyez-vous pas... [MS1*:
β]

      36A: Eh! ne voyez-vous pas que pour vous excuser.

[1] See above, p.298.

ZAYRE

Laisse-moi; je vois tout; je meurs sans m'aveugler:
Je vois que mon pays, mon sang, tout me condamne: 6
Que je suis Lusignan, que j'adore Orosmane;
Que mes vœux, que mes jours à ses jours sont liés.
Je voudrais quelquefois me jeter à ses pieds,
De tout ce que je suis faire un aveu sincère.

FATIME

Songez que cet aveu peut perdre votre frère,   7
Expose les chrétiens, qui n'ont que vous d'appui,
Et va trahir le Dieu, qui vous rappelle à lui.

ZAYRE

Ah! si tu connaissais le grand cœur d'Orosmane!

FATIME

Il est le protecteur de la loi musulmane;
Et plus il vous adore, et moins il peut souffrir   7
Qu'on vous ose annoncer un Dieu qu'il doit haïr.
Le pontife à vos yeux en secret va se rendre,
Et vous avez promis…

---

64 MS1, 33R: Oui, je vois tout; je meurs, et ne m'aveugle pas [MS1*: β]
    36A: Oui je vois tout hélas! je meurs sans m'abuser;
65 MS1: Je vois, malgré mes soins, que l'honneur me condamne [MS1*: β]
71 MS1: chrétiens dont vous êtes l'appui,
72 MS1: trahir un Dieu
73-76 MS1, absent
75 33R: il doit souffrir [33R errata: β]
77 MS1: Songez que votre frère en ce lieu doit se rendre
    33R: yeux cette nuit doit se rendre [33R errata: β]
    W51: vos vœux en
78 MS1: Que vous avez promis

ZAYRE

Eh bien, il faut l'attendre.
J'ai promis, j'ai juré de garder ce secret:
Hélas! qu'à mon amant je le tais à regret! 80
Et pour comble d'horreur je ne suis plus aimée.

SCÈNE II

OROSMANE, ZAYRE

OROSMANE

Madame, il fut un temps où mon âme charmée,
Ecoutant sans rougir des sentiments trop chers,
Se fit une vertu de languir dans vos fers.
Je croyais être aimé, madame, et votre maître, 85
Soupirant à vos pieds, devait s'attendre à l'être:
Vous ne m'entendrez point, amant faible et jaloux,
En reproches honteux éclater contre vous;
Cruellement blessé, mais trop fier pour me plaindre,
Trop généreux, trop grand, pour m'abaisser à feindre, 90
Je viens vous déclarer, que le plus froid mépris
De vos caprices vains sera le digne prix.
Ne vous préparez point à tromper ma tendresse,
A chercher des raisons, dont la flatteuse adresse,
A mes yeux éblouis colorant vos refus, 95
Vous ramène un amant qui ne vous connaît plus;
Et qui craignant surtout qu'à rougir on l'expose,
D'un refus outrageant veut ignorer la cause.

81b MS1: OROSMANE, ZAÏRE, ⟨FATIME⟩, CORASMIN, ESCLAVES
87 MS1: Je ne viens point, madame, amant
[MS1*: β with variant: m'entendrez pas]

Madame, c'en est fait, une autre va monter
Au rang que mon amour vous daignait présenter;   100
Une autre aura des yeux, et va du moins connaître
De quel prix mon amour et ma main devaient être.
Il pourra m'en coûter, mais mon cœur s'y résout.
Apprenez qu'Orosmane est capable de tout,
Que j'aime mieux vous perdre, et loin de votre vue   105
Mourir désespéré de vous avoir perdue,
Que de vous posséder, s'il faut qu'à votre foi
Il en coûte un soupir qui ne soit pas pour moi.
Allez, mes yeux jamais ne reverront vos charmes.

ZAYRE

Tu m'as donc tout ravi, Dieu, témoin de mes larmes!   11(
Tu veux commander seul à mes sens éperdus...
Eh bien, puisqu'il est vrai que vous ne m'aimez plus,
Seigneur...

OROSMANE

Il est trop vrai que l'honneur me l'ordonne,
Que je vous adorai, que je vous abandonne,
Que je renonce à vous, que vous le désirez,   11
Que sous une autre loi... Zayre, vous pleurez?

ZAYRE

Ah! seigneur! ah! du moins gardez de jamais croire,
Que du rang d'un soudan je regrette la gloire:
Je sais qu'il faut vous perdre, et mon sort l'a voulu:
Mais, seigneur, mais mon cœur ne vous est pas connu.   1:
Me punisse à jamais ce ciel qui me condamne,
Si je regrette rien que le cœur d'Orosmane!

102   MS1: prix mes bienfaits et mon cœur devaient
111   MS1, with stage direction after 111:   *à Orosmane.*

OROSMANE

Zayre, vous m'aimez!

ZAYRE

Dieu! si je l'aime, hélas!

OROSMANE

Quel caprice étonnant que je ne conçois pas!
Vous m'aimez? Eh, pourquoi vous forcez-vous, cruelle,　125
A déchirer le cœur d'un amant si fidèle?
Je me connaissais mal; oui, dans mon désespoir,
J'avais cru sur moi-même avoir plus de pouvoir.
Va, mon cœur est bien loin d'un pouvoir si funeste.
Zayre, que jamais la vengeance céleste　130
Ne donne à ton amant enchaîné sous ta loi,
La force d'oublier l'amour qu'il a pour toi!
Qui, moi? que sur mon trône une autre fût placée?
Non, je n'en eus jamais la fatale pensée:
Pardonne à mon courroux, à mes sens interdits,　135
Ces dédains affectés, et si bien démentis;
C'est le seul déplaisir que jamais dans ta vie,
Le ciel aura voulu que ta tendresse essuie.
Je t'aimerai toujours... Mais d'où vient que ton cœur,
En partageant mes feux, différait mon bonheur?　140
Parle. Etait-ce un caprice? Est-ce crainte d'un maître,
D'un soudan, qui pour toi veut renoncer à l'être?
Serait-ce un artifice? Epargne-toi ce soin;
L'art n'est pas fait pour toi, tu n'en as pas besoin:
Qu'il ne souille jamais le saint nœud qui nous lie!　145
L'art le plus innocent tient de la perfidie.
Je n'en connus jamais, et mes sens déchirés,

124　MS1, 33R-W46:　Quel caprice odieux que
　　33R:　ne connais pas! [33R errata: β]
131　W38-W46:　Me donne

Pleins d'un amour si vrai…

ZAYRE

Vous me désespérez.
Vous m'êtes cher, sans doute, et ma tendresse extrême
Est le comble des maux pour ce cœur qui vous aime.   15c

OROSMANE

O ciel! expliquez-vous. Quoi! toujours me troubler?
Se peut-il?…

ZAYRE

Dieu puissant, que ne puis-je parler?

OROSMANE

Quel étrange secret me cachez-vous, Zayre?
Est-il quelque chrétien qui contre moi conspire?
Me trahit-on? parlez.

ZAYRE

Eh! peut-on vous trahir?   15
Seigneur, entre eux et vous vous me verriez courir:
On ne vous trahit point, pour vous rien n'est à craindre;
Mon malheur est pour moi, je suis la seule à plaindre.

OROSMANE

Vous, à plaindre, grand Dieu!

ZAYRE

Souffrez qu'à vos genoux
Je demande en tremblant une grâce de vous.   1

OROSMANE

Une grâce! ordonnez, et demandez ma vie.

ZAYRE

Plût au ciel qu'à vos jours la mienne fût unie!
Orosmane... Seigneur... permettez qu'aujourd'hui,
Seule, loin de vous-même, et toute à mon ennui,
D'un œil plus recueilli contemplant ma fortune,   165
Je cache à votre oreille une plainte importune...
Demain tous mes secrets vous seront révélés.

OROSMANE

De quelle inquiétude, ô ciel, vous m'accablez!
Pouvez-vous?...

ZAYRE

       Si pour moi l'amour vous parle encore,
Ne me refusez pas la grâce que j'implore.   170

OROSMANE

Eh bien, il faut vouloir tout ce que vous voulez;
J'y consens; il en coûte à mes sens désolés.
Allez, souvenez-vous que je vous sacrifie
Les moments les plus beaux, les plus chers de ma vie.

ZAYRE

En me parlant ainsi, vous me percez le cœur.   175

OROSMANE

Eh bien, vous me quittez, Zayre?

ZAYRE

       Hélas, seigneur!

163   MS1: Seigneur, si vous m'aimez, permettez
176   36A: Et quoi, vous

SCÈNE III

OROSMANE, CORASMIN

OROSMANE

Ah! c'est trop tôt chercher ce solitaire asile,
C'est trop tôt abuser de ma bonté facile;
Et plus j'y pense, ami, moins je puis concevoir
Le sujet si caché de tant de désespoir.   18

Quoi donc! par ma tendresse élevée à l'empire,
Dans le sein du bonheur, que son âme désire,
Près d'un amant qu'elle aime, et qui brûle à ses pieds,
Ses yeux remplis d'amour, de larmes sont noyés.
Je suis bien indigné de voir tant de caprices.   18
Mais moi-même après tout eus-je moins d'injustices?
Ai-je été moins coupable à ses yeux offensés?
Est-ce à moi de me plaindre? On m'aime, c'est assez.
Il me faut expier, par un peu d'indulgence,
De mes transports jaloux l'injurieuse offense.   1ς
Je me rends, je le vois, son cœur est sans détours;
La nature naïve anime ses discours.
Elle est dans l'âge heureux où règne l'innocence;
A sa sincérité je dois ma confiance.
Elle m'aime sans doute; oui, j'ai lu devant toi,   1·
Dans ses yeux attendris, l'amour qu'elle a pour moi;
Et son âme éprouvant cette ardeur qui me touche,
Vingt fois pour me le dire a volé sur sa bouche.
Qui peut avoir un cœur assez traître, assez bas,
Pour montrer tant d'amour, et ne le sentir pas?   2·

176b   MSI adds: ESCLAVES
177   36A: Zaïre! ah c'est trop tôt me fuir dans cet asile
186   W51: tout, ai-je eu moins
188-196 MSI, omitted [MSI*, pasted addition: β]
197   MSI: Et son cœur enflammé de l'ardeur [MSI*: β]

496

SCÈNE IV

OROSMANE, CORASMIN, MÉLÉDOR

MÉLÉDOR

Cette lettre, seigneur, à Zayre adressée,
Par vos gardes saisie, et dans mes mains laissée...

OROSMANE

Donne... qui la portait?... Donne.

MÉLÉDOR

              Un de ces chrétiens,
Dont vos bontés, seigneur, ont brisé les liens:
Au sérail, en secret, il allait s'introduire;   205
On l'a mis dans les fers.

OROSMANE

          Hélas! que vais-je lire?
Laisse-nous... Je frémis.

200b MS1 adds: ESCLAVES
207-208 MS1:
    Laisse-nous.
             SCÈNE V
   OROSMANE, CORASMIN, ESCLAVES
         OROSMANE
     Je frémis.
         CORASMIN
        Cette lettre, seigneur.
De vos soupçons peut-être éclaircira l'erreur.

497

SCÈNE V

OROSMANE, CORASMIN

CORASMIN

Cette lettre, seigneur,
Pourra vous éclaircir, et calmer votre cœur.

OROSMANE

Ah! lisons; ma main tremble, et mon âme étonnée
Prévoit que ce billet contient ma destinée.   210
Lisons... 'Chère Zayre, il est temps de nous voir:
Il est vers la mosquée une secrète issue,
Où vous pouvez sans bruit, et sans être aperçue,
Tromper vos surveillants, et remplir notre espoir:
Il faut tout hasarder; vous connaissez mon zèle: 215
Je vous attends; je meurs, si vous n'êtes fidèle.'
Eh bien, cher Corasmin, que dis-tu?

CORASMIN

Moi, seigneur?
Je suis épouvanté de ce comble d'horreur.

OROSMANE

Tu vois comme on me traite.

CORASMIN

O trahison horrible!
Seigneur, à cet affront vous êtes insensible?   220
Vous, dont le cœur tantôt, sur un simple soupçon,

215 33R, W51: Il faut vous hasarder

498

D'une douleur si vive a reçu le poison?
Ah! sans doute l'horreur d'une action si noire
Vous guérit d'un amour qui blessait votre gloire.

OROSMANE

Cours chez elle à l'instant, va, vole, Corasmin: 225
Montre-lui cet écrit... Qu'elle tremble... et soudain
De cent coups de poignard que l'infidèle meure.
Mais avant de frapper... Ah! cher ami, demeure,
Demeure, il n'est pas temps. Je veux que ce chrétien
Devant elle amené... non... je ne veux plus rien...   230
Je me meurs... Je succombe à l'excès de ma rage.

CORASMIN

On ne reçut jamais un si sanglant outrage.

OROSMANE

Le voilà donc connu, ce secret plein d'horreur!
Ce secret qui pesait à son infâme cœur!
Sous le voile emprunté d'une crainte ingénue,   235
Elle veut quelque temps se soustraire à ma vue.
Je me fais cet effort, je la laisse sortir;
Elle part en pleurant... et c'est pour me trahir.
Quoi, Zayre!

CORASMIN

            Tout sert à redoubler son crime.
Seigneur, n'en soyez pas l'innocente victime,   240
Et de vos sentiments rappelant la grandeur...

OROSMANE

C'est là ce Nérestan, ce héros plein d'honneur,

239 MS1: Ah, perfide!

Ce chrétien si vanté, qui remplissait Solyme
De ce faste imposant de sa vertu sublime!
Je l'admirais moi-même, et mon cœur combattu   245
S'indignait qu'un chrétien m'égalât en vertu.
Ah! qu'il va me payer sa fourbe abominable!
Mais Zayre, Zayre est cent fois plus coupable.
Une esclave chrétienne, et que j'ai pu laisser
Dans les plus vils emplois languir sans l'abaisser!   250
Une esclave! Elle sait ce que j'ai fait pour elle.
Ah malheureux!

CORASMIN

                    Seigneur, si vous souffrez mon zèle,
Si parmi les horreurs qui doivent vous troubler,
Vous vouliez...

OROSMANE

                    Oui, je veux la voir et lui parler.
Allez, volez, esclave, et m'amenez Zayre.   25-

CORASMIN

Hélas! en cet état que pourrez-vous lui dire?

OROSMANE

Je ne sais, cher ami, mais je prétends la voir.

CORASMIN

Ah! seigneur, vous allez, dans votre désespoir,
Vous plaindre, menacer, faire couler ses larmes.

---

243   MS1: Ce Français si vanté, ce
254   MS1, with stage direction after 254: *aux esclaves.*
255a   MS1: SCÈNE VI [with subsequent renumbering] / OROSMANE,
CORASMIN / CORASMIN

Vos bontés contre vous lui donneront des armes;   260
Et votre cœur séduit, malgré tous vos soupçons,
Pour la justifier cherchera des raisons.
M'en croirez-vous? cachez cette lettre à sa vue.
Prenez pour la lui rendre une main inconnue.
Par là, malgré la fraude et les déguisements,   265
Vos yeux démêleront ses secrets sentiments,
Et des plis de son cœur verront tout l'artifice.

OROSMANE

Penses-tu qu'en effet Zayre me trahisse?...
Allons, quoi qu'il en soit, je vais tenter mon sort,
Et pousser la vertu jusqu'au dernier effort.   270
Je veux voir à quel point une femme hardie
Saura de son côté pousser la perfidie.

CORASMIN

Seigneur, je crains pour vous ce funeste entretien;
Un cœur tel que le vôtre...

OROSMANE

                              Ah! n'en redoute rien.
A son exemple, hélas! ce cœur ne saurait feindre.   275
Mais j'ai la fermeté de savoir me contraindre:
Oui, puisqu'elle m'abaisse à connaître un rival...

---

264   MS1: Par d'étrangères mains qu'elle lui soit rendue
268   MS1: Mais crois-tu qu'à ce point Zaïre [MS1*: β]
277-281   MS1:
        Tiens, puisqu'elle m'abaisse à connaître un rival,
        Ami, prends ce billet à tous trois si fatal:
        Va choisir de ce pas quelque esclave fidèle,
        Qui mette entre ses mains cette lettre cruelle.
        Va... je voulais la voir; j'éviterai ses yeux;
        [MS1*, β on pasted slip; l.279 gives β and alternative reading:
        Choisis pour le remettre un esclave]

Tiens, reçois ce billet à tous trois si fatal:
Va, choisis pour le rendre un esclave fidèle,
Mets en de sûres mains cette lettre cruelle;   280
Va, cours... Je ferai plus, j'éviterai ses yeux;
Qu'elle n'approche pas... C'est elle, justes cieux!

SCÈNE VI

OROSMANE, ZAYRE, CORASMIN

ZAYRE

Seigneur, vous m'étonnez; quelle raison soudaine,
Quel ordre si pressant près de vous me ramène?

OROSMANE

Eh bien, madame, il faut que vous m'éclaircissiez: 285
Cet ordre est important plus que vous ne croyez;
Je me suis consulté... Malheureux l'un par l'autre,
Il faut régler d'un mot et mon sort et le vôtre.
Peut-être qu'en effet ce que j'ai fait pour vous,
Mon orgueil oublié, mon sceptre à vos genoux,   290
Mes bienfaits, mon respect, mes soins, ma confiance,
Ont arraché de vous quelque reconnaissance.
Votre cœur par un maître attaqué chaque jour,
Vaincu par mes bienfaits, crut l'être par l'amour.
Dans votre âme, avec vous, il est temps que je lise;   295
Il faut que ses replis s'ouvrent à ma franchise.
Jugez-vous: répondez avec la vérité

282b   MSI adds: ESCLAVES
285   MSI: Eh bien, il faut ici que vous
295   MSI: Dans ce cœur, avec vous

Que vous devez au moins à ma sincérité.
Si de quelque autre amour l'invincible puissance
L'emporte sur mes soins, ou même les balance,   300
Il faut me l'avouer, et dans ce même instant,
Ta grâce est dans mon cœur; prononce, elle t'attend.
Sacrifie à ma foi l'insolent qui t'adore:
Songe que je te vois, que je te parle encore,
Que ma foudre à ta voix pourra se détourner,   305
Que c'est le seul moment où je peux pardonner.

ZAYRE

Vous, seigneur! vous osez me tenir ce langage?
Vous, cruel! Apprenez que ce cœur qu'on outrage,
Et que par tant d'horreurs le ciel veut éprouver,
S'il ne vous aimait pas, est né pour vous braver.   310
Je ne crains rien ici que ma funeste flamme;
N'imputez qu'à ce feu qui brûle encor mon âme,
N'imputez qu'à l'amour, que je dois oublier,
La honte où je descends de me justifier.
J'ignore si le ciel, qui m'a toujours trahie,   315
A destiné pour vous ma malheureuse vie.
Quoi qui'il puisse arriver, je jure par l'honneur,
Qui non moins que l'amour est gravé dans mon cœur,
Je jure que Zayre à soi-même rendue,
Des rois les plus puissants détesterait la vue,   320
Que tout autre, après vous, me serait odieux.
Voulez-vous plus savoir, et me connaître mieux?
Voulez-vous que ce cœur à l'amertume en proie,
Ce cœur désespéré devant vous se déploie?
Sachez donc qu'en secret il pensait malgré lui   325
Tout ce que devant vous il déclare aujourd'hui;
Qu'il soupirait pour vous avant que vos tendresses
Vinssent justifier mes naissantes faiblesses;
Qu'il prévint vos bienfaits, qu'il brûlait à vos pieds,

329 MS 1: qu'il tremblait à vos pieds

503

Qu'il vous aimait enfin, lorsque vous m'ignoriez; 330
Qu'il n'eut jamais que vous, n'aura que vous pour maître.
J'en atteste le ciel, que j'offense peut-être;
Et si j'ai mérité son éternel courroux,
Si mon cœur fut coupable, ingrat, c'était pour vous.

OROSMANE

Quoi! des plus tendres feux sa bouche encor m'assure! 335
Quel excès de noirceur! Zayre!… ah la parjure!
Quand de sa trahison j'ai la preuve en ma main!

ZAYRE

Que dites-vous? Quel trouble agite votre sein?

OROSMANE

Je ne suis point troublé. Vous m'aimez?

ZAYRE

                                   Votre bouche
Peut-elle me parler avec ce ton farouche, 340
D'un feu si tendrement déclaré chaque jour?
Vous me glacez de crainte, en me parlant d'amour.

OROSMANE

Vous m'aimez?

ZAYRE

          Vous pouvez douter de ma tendresse!
Mais encore une fois quelle fureur vous presse?
Quels regards effrayants vous me lancez! hélas! 34·
Vous doutez de mon cœur?

344 MS1: quelle douleur [MS1*: β]

 OROSMANE

Non, je n'en doute pas.
Allez, rentrez, madame.

SCÈNE VII

OROSMANE, CORASMIN

OROSMANE

Ami, sa perfidie
Au comble de l'horreur ne s'est pas démentie;
Tranquille dans le crime, et fausse avec douceur,
Elle a jusques au bout soutenu sa noirceur.   350
As-tu trouvé l'esclave? as-tu servi ma rage?
Connaîtrai-je à la fois son crime et mon outrage?

CORASMIN

Oui, je viens d'obéir; mais vous ne pouvez pas
Soupirer désormais pour ses traîtres appas:
Vous la verrez sans doute avec indifférence,   355
Sans que le repentir succède à la vengeance,
Sans que l'amour sur vous en repousse les traits.

OROSMANE

Corasmin, je l'adore encor plus que jamais.

347   MS1 gives β and alternative reading: (à Zaïre) Allez. (Aux esclaves)
Qu'on la remène
      36A: qu'on la remène. / ZAÏRE / O ciel! / SCÈNE VII
351   MS1:   As-tu choisi l'esclave?
352   MS1:   le crime
355   MS1:   Vous la verrez, seigneur, avec

CORASMIN

Vous? ô ciel! vous?

OROSMANE

    Je vois un rayon d'espérance.
Cet odieux chrétien, l'élève de la France,   360
Est jeune, impatient, léger, présomptueux,
Il peut croire aisément ses téméraires vœux:
Son amour indiscret, et plein de confiance,
Aura de ses soupirs hasardé l'insolence:
Un regard de Zayre aura pu l'aveugler: 365
Sans doute il est aisé de s'en laisser troubler:
Il croit qu'il est aimé; c'est lui seul qui m'offense;
Peut-être ils ne sont point tous deux d'intelligence:
Zayre n'a point vu ce billet criminel,
Et j'en croyais trop tôt mon déplaisir mortel.   370
Corasmin, écoutez... Dès que la nuit plus sombre
Aux crimes des mortels viendra prêter son ombre,
Sitôt que ce chrétien, chargé de mes bienfaits,
Nérestan, paraîtra sous les murs du palais,
Ayez soin qu'à l'instant la garde le saisisse,   375
Qu'on prépare pour lui le plus honteux supplice,
Et que chargé de fers il me soit présenté.
Laissez, surtout, laissez Zayre en liberté.
Tu vois mon cœur, tu vois à quel excès je l'aime.
Ma fureur est plus grande, et j'en tremble moi-même.   380
J'ai honte des douleurs où je me suis plongé;
Mais malheur aux ingrats qui m'auront outragé!

Fin du quatrième acte.

359 MS1, 36A: Vous, seigneur! vous!
366 MS1: ⟨charmer⟩ troubler
381 MS1: Je rougis des douleurs où je me sens plongé [MS1*: β]

ACTE V

SCÈNE PREMIÈRE

OROSMANE, CORASMIN, UN ESCLAVE

OROSMANE

On l'a fait avertir, l'ingrate va paraître.
Songe que dans tes mains est le sort de ton maître;
Donne-lui le billet de ce traître chrétien;
Rends-moi compte de tout, examine-la bien.
Porte-moi sa réponse. On approche... c'est elle.   5

> *A Corasmin.*

Viens, d'un malheureux prince ami tendre et fidèle,
Viens m'aider à cacher ma rage et mes ennuis.

SCÈNE II

ZAYRE, FATIME, L'ESCLAVE

ZAYRE

Eh qui peut me parler dans l'état où je suis?
A tant d'horreurs, hélas! qui pourra me soustraire?

c   MS1, 36A replace ESCLAVE with MÉLÉDOR throughout this act [MS1
adds: ESCLAVES]
d   MS1, 36A: OROSMANE *à Mélédor*
    33R-W52, W57P: OROSMANE, *à l'esclave.*
8   MS1: Ah, qui peut

507

Le sérail est fermé! Dieu! si c'était mon frère!　　　　　10
Si la main de ce Dieu, pour soutenir ma foi,
Par des chemins cachés, le conduisait vers moi!
Quel esclave inconnu se présente à ma vue?

L'ESCLAVE

Cette lettre en secret à mes mains parvenue,
Pourra vous assurer de ma fidélité.　　　　　15

ZAYRE

Donne.

(*Elle lit.*)

FATIME *à part pendant que Zayre lit.*

Dieu tout-puissant, éclate en ta bonté,
Fais descendre ta grâce en ce séjour profane,
Arrache ma princesse au barbare Orosmane.

ZAYRE *à Fatime.*

Je voudrais te parler.

FATIME *à l'esclave.*

Allez, retirez-vous;
On vous rappellera, soyez prêt, laissez-nous.　　　　　2

14　MSI, 33R-W52, W57P:　en mes mains
　　　K:　dans mes mains
16a　MSI:　*Elle lit bas.*

SCÈNE III

ZAYRE, FATIME

ZAYRE

Lis ce billet: hélas! dis-moi ce qu'il faut faire;
Je voudrais obéir aux ordres de mon frère.

FATIME

Dites plutôt, madame, aux ordres éternels
D'un Dieu qui vous demande aux pieds de ses autels.
Ce n'est point Nérestan, c'est Dieu qui vous appelle.   25

ZAYRE

Je le sais, à sa voix je ne suis point rebelle,
J'en ai fait le serment: mais puis-je m'engager,
Moi, les chrétiens, mon frère, en un si grand danger?

FATIME

Ce n'est point leur danger dont vous êtes troublée,
Votre amour parle seul à votre âme ébranlée.   30
Je connais votre cœur; il penserait comme eux,
Il hasarderait tout, s'il n'était amoureux.
Ah! connaissez du moins l'erreur qui vous engage.
Vous tremblez d'offenser l'amant qui vous outrage.
Quoi! ne voyez-vous pas toutes ses cruautés,   35
Et l'âme d'un Tartare, à travers ses bontés?[1]

21   MS1, with stage direction after 21:   *Fatime lit le billet, bas.*
25   MS1:   point Lusignan, c'est
30   W51:   à cette âme

---

[1] See Voltaire 33, p.279. Voltaire himself quotes this line as an example of
the use of 'Tartare' in the sense of 'barbare'.

Ce tigre encor farouche au sein de sa tendresse,
Même en vous adorant, menaçait sa maîtresse...
Et votre cœur encor ne s'en peut détacher?
Vous soupirez pour lui?

ZAYRE

Qu'ai-je à lui reprocher? 40
C'est moi qui l'offensais, moi qu'en cette journée
Il a vu souhaiter ce fatal hyménée;
Le trône était tout prêt, le temple était paré,
Mon amant m'adorait, et j'ai tout différé.
Moi, qui devais ici trembler sous sa puissance, 45
J'ai de ses sentiments bravé la violence;
J'ai soumis son amour, il fait ce que je veux,
Il m'a sacrifié ses transports amoureux.

FATIME

Ce malheureux amour, dont votre âme est blessée,
Peut-il en ce moment remplir votre pensée? 50

ZAYRE

Ah! Fatime, tout sert à me désespérer;
Je sais que du sérail rien ne peut me tirer:
Je voudrais des chrétiens voir l'heureuse contrée,
Quitter ce lieu funeste à mon âme égarée;
Et je sens qu'à l'instant, prompte à me démentir, 5
Je fais des vœux secrets pour n'en jamais sortir.
Quel état! quel tourment! Non, mon âme inquiète

51   MS1:   Tout m'accable; tout sert
53-56   MS1:
        Je vois qu'une barrière éternelle et barbare
        De l'univers entier pour jamais me sépare:
        Et peut-être mon cœur prompt à se démentir
        Fait des vœux en secret pour n'en jamais sortir.

Ne sait ce qu'elle doit, ni ce qu'elle souhaite;
Une terreur affreuse est tout ce que je sens.
Dieu, détourne de moi ces noirs pressentiments;   60
Prends soin de nos chrétienns, et veille sur mon frère;
Prends soin, du haut des cieux, d'une tête si chère.
Oui, je le vais trouver, je lui vais obéir:
Mais dès que de Solyme il aura pu partir,
Par son absence alors à parler enhardie,   65
J'apprends à mon amant le secret de ma vie:
Je lui dirai le culte où mon cœur est lié;
Il lira dans ce cœur, il en aura pitié.
Mais dussé-je au supplice être ici condamnée,
Je ne trahirai point le sang dont je suis née.   70
Va, tu peux amener mon cher frère en ces lieux.
Rappelle cet esclave.

SCÈNE IV

ZAYRE *seule.*

O Dieu de mes aïeux,
Dieu de tous mes parents, de mon malheureux père,
Que ta main me conduise, et que ton œil m'éclaire!

69 MS I: au trépas être
71 MS I: Oui, tu peux amener Nérestan en
    K: Va, tu peux amener mon frère dans ces
74 MS I, with stage direction after 74: *La nuit commence à paraître.*

SCÈNE V

ZAYRE, L'ESCLAVE

ZAYRE

Allez dire au chrétien, qui marche sur vos pas,   75
Que mon cœur aujourd'hui ne le trahira pas.
Que Fatime en ces lieux va bientôt l'introduire.

A part.

Allons, rassure-toi, malheureuse Zayre!

SCÈNE VI

OROSMANE, CORASMIN, L'ESCLAVE

OROSMANE

Que ces moments, grand Dieu, sont lents pour ma fureur!

A l'esclave.

Eh bien, que t'a-t-on dit? Réponds. Parle.

L'ESCLAVE

         Seigneur, 8

On n'a jamais senti de si vives alarmes.
Elle a pâli, tremblé, ses yeux versaient des larmes;
Elle m'a fait sortir, elle m'a rappelé,

74b MS1: ZAÏRE, MÉLÉDOR, FATIME
75 MS1: Allez dire au Français qui

512

Et d'une voix tremblante, et d'un cœur tout troublé,
Près de ces lieux, seigneur, elle a promis d'attendre   85
Celui qui cette nuit à ses yeux doit se rendre.

OROSMANE

A l'esclave.   *A Corasmin.*

Allez, il me suffit. Ote-toi de mes yeux,
Laissez-moi: tout mortel me devient odieux,
Laisse-moi seul, te dis-je, à ma fureur extrême.
Je hais le monde entier, je m'abhorre moi-même.   90

SCÈNE VII

OROSMANE *seul.*

Où suis-je? ô ciel! où suis-je? où porté-je mes vœux?
Zayre, Nérestan... couple ingrat, couple affreux,
Traîtres, arrachez-moi ce jour que je respire,
Ce jour souillé par vous... Misérable Zayre,
Tu ne jouiras pas... Corasmin, revenez.   95

---

84   33R: voix tombante
     MSI gives alternative readings: tremblante / tombante
87   MSI:
            Allez, il me suffit.
     SCÈNE VII [with subsequent renumbering]
            OROSMANE, CORASMIN
            OROSMANE (*à Corasmin.*)
                     Ote-toi de mes yeux,
88   MSI, 33R-W38, K: Laisse-moi
90   MSI, with stage direction after 90: *Corasmin se retire doucement; mais il est rappelé par Orosmane* [no new scene].
95   MSI: pas... *à Corasmin.* Corasmin

SCÈNE VIII

OROSMANE, CORASMIN

OROSMANE

Ah! trop cruel ami, quoi vous m'abandonnez?
Venez; a-t-il paru, ce rival, ce coupable?

CORASMIN

Rien ne paraît encore.

OROSMANE

O nuit! nuit effroyable!
Peux-tu prêter ton voile à de pareils forfaits?
Zayre... l'infidèle... après tant de bienfaits!   100
J'aurais d'un œil serein, d'un front inaltérable,
Contemplé de mon rang la chute épouvantable:
J'aurais su, dans l'horreur de la captivité,
Conserver mon courage et ma tranquillité;
Mais me voir à ce point trompé par ce que j'aime!...   105

CORASMIN

Eh! que prétendez-vous dans cette horreur extrême?
Quel est votre dessein?

OROSMANE

N'entends-tu pas des cris?

97   MS1: Eh bien, a-t-il paru
100   MS1, 33R, 36A: Corasmin!... Ciel! Amour!... après [MS1*: β]
106-107 36A:
             Eh seigneur, voulez-vous vous en punir vous-même?
                  à part
             Hélas, que je vous plains!

514

CORASMIN

Seigneur...

OROSMANE

Un bruit affreux a frappé mes esprits.
On vient.

CORASMIN

Non, jusqu'ici nul mortel ne s'avance;
Le sérail est plongé dans un profond silence;   110
Tout dort; tout est tranquille, et l'ombre de la nuit...

OROSMANE

Hélas! le crime veille, et son horreur me suit.
A ce coupable excès porter sa hardiesse!
Tu ne connaissais pas mon cœur et ma tendresse,
Combien je t'adorais! quels feux! Ah, Corasmin!   115
Un seul de ses regards aurait fait mon destin.
Je ne puis être heureux, ni souffrir que par elle.
Prends pitié de ma rage. Oui, cours... Ah, la cruelle!

CORASMIN

Est-ce vous qui pleurez? vous, Orosmane? ô cieux!

OROSMANE

Voilà les premiers pleurs qui coulent de mes yeux.   120
Tu vois mon sort, tu vois la honte où je me livre:
Mais ces pleurs sont cruels, et la mort va les suivre:
Plains Zayre, plains-moi; l'heure approche, ces pleurs

112   MS1:   horreur le suit
113   MS1:   A cet horrible excès
117   MS1, 33R-W38:   Je ne pus être
122   MS1:   sont affreux et [MS1*: β]

Du sang qui va couler sont les avant-coureurs.

CORASMIN

Ah! je tremble pour vous.

OROSMANE

Frémis de mes souffrances,   125
Frémis de mon amour, frémis de mes vengeances.
Approche, viens, j'entends... Je ne me trompe pas.

CORASMIN

Sous les murs du palais quelqu'un porte ses pas.

OROSMANE

Va saisir Nérestan, va, dis-je, qu'on l'enchaîne;
Que tout chargé de fers à mes yeux on l'entraîne!   130

SCÈNE IX

OROSMANE, ZAYRE et FATIME, *marchant pendant
la nuit dans l'enfoncement du théâtre.*

ZAYRE

Viens, Fatime.

---

127   MS1, 33R: J'entends quelqu'un, sans doute, et ne
         36A: On vient, il est trop vrai. Je ne
128   MS1: On marche. En ce palais
130d   MS1: ZAÏRE, *derrière la scène.*

OROSMANE

Qu'entends-je? est-ce là cette voix,
Dont les sons enchanteurs m'ont séduit tant de fois?
Cette voix qui trahit un feu si légitime?
Cette voix infidèle, et l'organe du crime?
Perfide!... vengeons-nous... quoi! c'est elle? ô destin!   135

Il tire son poignard.

Zayre! ah Dieu!... ce fer échappe de ma main.

ZAYRE *à Fatime.*

C'est ici le chemin, viens, soutiens mon courage.

FATIME

Il va venir.

OROSMANE

Ce mot me rend toute ma rage.

ZAYRE

Je marche en frissonnant, mon cœur est éperdu...
Est-ce vous, Nérestan, que j'ai tant attendu?   140

OROSMANE *courant à Zayre.*

C'est moi que tu trahis: tombe à mes pieds, parjure.

ZAYRE *tombant dans la coulisse.*

Je me meurs, ô mon Dieu!

131   MSI: Ah, qu'entends-je?
136a MSI: *à Fatime, et traversant le théâtre.*
139   MSI, with stage direction after 139:   *à Orosmane.*
140a MSI: *allant à Zaïre... et la poignardant dans la coulisse.*
141a MSI, no stage direction

OROSMANE

J'ai vengé mon injure.
Otons-nous de ces lieux. Je ne puis… Qu'ai-je fait?…
Rien que de juste… Allons, j'ai puni son forfait.
Ah! voici son amant que mon destin m'envoie,   145
Pour remplir ma vengeance et ma cruelle joie.

SCÈNE DERNIÈRE

OROSMANE, ZAYRE, NÉRESTAN, CORASMIN,
FATIME, ESCLAVES

OROSMANE

Approche, malheureux, qui viens de m'arracher,
De m'ôter pour jamais ce qui me fut si cher;
Méprisable ennemi, qui fais encor paraître
L'audace d'un héros avec l'âme d'un traître;   150
Tu m'imposais ici pour me déshonorer.
Va, le prix en est prêt; tu peux t'y préparer.
Tes maux vont égaler les maux où tu m'exposes,
Et ton ingratitude, et l'horreur que tu causes.
Avez-vous ordonné son supplice?

CORASMIN

Oui, seigneur.   155

OROSMANE

Il commence déjà dans le fond de ton cœur.

142a MS1: SCÈNE IX / OROSMANE, *seul.*
146b MS1: ZAÏRE, *morte dans la coulisse*

Tes yeux cherchent partout, et demandent encore
La perfide qui t'aime, et qui me déshonore.
Regarde, elle est ici.

NÉRESTAN

Que dis-tu? Quelle erreur...

OROSMANE

Regarde-la, te dis-je.

NÉRESTAN

Ah! que vois-je? Ah, ma sœur!   160
Zayre!... Elle n'est plus! Ah, monstre! Ah, jour horrible!

OROSMANE

Sa sœur! Qu'ai-je entendu? Dieu, serait-il possible?

NÉRESTAN

Barbare, il est trop vrai: viens épuiser mon flanc
Du reste infortuné de cet auguste sang.
Lusignan, ce vieillard, fut son malheureux père,   165
Il venait dans mes bras d'achever sa misère,
Et d'un père expiré j'apportais en ces lieux
La volonté dernière, et les derniers adieux;

---

158   MS1, with stage direction after 158: *Il montre à Nérestan Zaïre, morte dans la coulisse.*

160-163   MS1 is a confused jumble of crossing out, over-writing and repetition, which is pasted over and replaced by the text below:

    Ah! que vois-je? Ah! ma sœur...
       OROSMANE
Sa sœur! Qu'ai-je entendu? Dieu! Serait-il possible?
   NERESTAN, *le jour recommence à paraître.*
Zaïre!... Elle n'est plus! Ah, monstre! Ah, jour horrible!
Barbare, qu'as-tu fait? Viens épuiser mon flanc

Je venais, dans un cœur trop faible et trop sensible,
Rappeler des chrétiens le culte incorruptible.   170
Hélas! elle offensait notre Dieu, notre loi;
Et ce Dieu la punit d'avoir brûlé pour toi.

OROSMANE

Zayre!... Elle m'aimait? Est-il bien vrai, Fatime?
Sa sœur?... J'étais aimé?

FATIME

                              Cruel! voilà son crime.
Tigre altéré de sang, tu viens de massacrer   175
Celle qui malgré soi constante à t'adorer,
Se flattait, espérait que le Dieu de ses pères
Recevrait le tribut de ses larmes sincères;
Qu'il verrait en pitié cet amour malheureux,
Que peut-être il voudrait vous réunir tous deux.   180
Hélas! à cet excès son cœur l'avait trompée;
De cet espoir trop tendre elle était occupée;
Tu balançais son Dieu dans son cœur alarmé.

OROSMANE

Tu m'en as dit assez. O ciel! j'étais aimé!
Va, je n'ai pas besoin d'en savoir davantage...   185

NÉRESTAN

Cruel! qu'attends-tu donc pour assouvir ta rage?
Il ne reste que moi de ce sang glorieux,
Dont ton père et ton bras ont inondé ces lieux;

---

174   36A, with stage direction: aimé? *il tombe dans un fauteuil*
       36A: voilà ton crime
179-182   MS1, omitted
183a   36A, with stage direction: *se relevant*
185   MS1, with stage direction after 185: *Fatime s'en va.*

Rejoins un malheureux à sa triste famille,
Au héros dont tu viens d'assassiner la fille.   190
Tes tourments sont-ils prêts? Je puis braver tes coups;
Tu m'as fait éprouver le plus cruel de tous.
Mais la soif de mon sang, qui toujours te dévore,
Permet-elle à l'honneur de te parler encore?
En m'arrachant le jour, souviens-toi des chrétiens,   195
Dont tu m'avais juré de briser les liens;
Dans sa férocité ton cœur impitoyable,
De ce trait généreux serait-il bien capable?
Parle; à ce prix encor je bénis mon trépas.

OROSMANE *allant vers le corps de Zayre.*

Zayre!

CORASMIN

Hélas! seigneur, où portez-vous vos pas?   200
Rentrez, trop de douleur de votre âme s'empare.
Souffrez que Nérestan...

NÉRESTAN

Qu'ordonnes-tu, barbare?

OROSMANE *après une longue pause.*

Qu'on détache ses fers. Ecoutez, Corasmin,
Que tous ses compagnons soient délivrés soudain.
Aux malheureux chrétiens prodiguez mes largesses;   205
Comblés de mes bienfaits, chargés de mes richesses,
Jusqu'au port de Joppé[2] vous conduirez leurs pas.

---

189   MS1:   malheureux à l'auguste famille
199a   MS1:   CORASMIN, *arrêtant Orosmane.*

[2] *Joppé*: modern Jaffa.

CORASMIN

Mais, seigneur...

OROSMANE

Obéis, et ne réplique pas;
Vole, et ne trahis point la volonté suprême
D'un soudan qui commande, et d'un ami qui t'aime;   210
Va, ne perds point de temps, sors, obéis...[3]

A Nérestan.

Et toi,
Guerrier infortuné, mais moins encor que moi,
Quitte ces lieux sanglants, remporte en ta patrie
Cet objet que ma rage a privé de la vie.
Ton roi, tous tes chrétiens, apprenant tes malheurs,   215
N'en parleront jamais sans répandre des pleurs.
Mais si la vérité par toi se fait connaître,
En détestant mon crime, on me plaindra peut-être.
Porte aux tiens ce poignard, que mon bras égaré
A plongé dans un sein qui dut m'être sacré;   220
Dis-leur que j'ai donné la mort la plus affreuse
A la plus digne femme, à la plus vertueuse,
Dont le ciel ait formé les innocents appas;
Dis-leur qu'à ses genoux j'avais mis mes Etats;
Dis-leur que dans son sang cette main s'est plongée;   225
Dis que je l'adorais, et que je l'ai vengée.   *Il se tue.*

208   MSI: Les chrétiens...
210   33R: d'une ami [33R errata: β]
211a   MSI: SCÈNE XI / OROSMANE, NÉRESTAN, ESCLAVES / OROS-
MANE, *à Nérestan.*
214   MSI, 33R: Ce trésor que ma
218   MSI: En détestant ma rage, on
225   MSI: ⟨ce⟩ ↑son

[3] For this speech, see above, p.307.

Aux siens.

Respectez ce héros, et conduisez ses pas.

NÉRESTAN

Guide-moi, Dieu puissant, je ne me connais pas.
Faut-il qu'à t'admirer ta fureur me contraigne,
Et que dans mon malheur ce soit moi qui te plaigne? 230

Fin du cinquième et dernier acte.

227a MS I: SCÈNE XII et dernière / NÉRESTAN, *seul.*

APPENDIX I

The 1736 'Avertissement'

This notice was added by Voltaire to the Paris 1736 edition published by Bauche (36A). In w38 and subsequent authorised editions it was replaced by a completely different text under the same title, printed above at p.391.

* * *

AVERTISSEMENT

On a imprimé Français par un *a*, et on en usera ainsi dans la nouvelle édition de la Henriade. Il faut en tout se conformer à l'usage, et écrire autant qu'on peut comme on prononce; il serait ridicule de dire en vers, les *François* et les *Anglois*; puisqu'en prose tout le monde prononce *Français*. Il n'est pas même à croire que   5
jamais cette dure prononciation, *François*, revienne à la mode. Tous les peuples adoucissent insensiblement la prononciation de leur langue. Nous ne disons plus la Roine, mais la Reine. *Août*, se prononce *Oût*, etc. On dira toujours *Gaulois*, et *Français*, parce que l'idée d'une nation grossière inspire naturellement un son   10
plus dur, et que l'idée d'une nation plus polie, communique à la voix un son plus doux. Les Italiens en sont venus jusqu'à retrancher l'*h* absolument. Chez les Anglais la moitié des consonnes qui remplissaient leurs mots, et qui les rendaient trop durs, ne se prononcent plus. En un mot, tout ce qui contribue à rendre une   15
langue plus douce sans affectation, doit être admis.

APPENDIX II

'Avertissement de l'auteur' from the Grasset edition

The Grasset edition (w70L) appears to have been based, in part, upon a corrected copy of an edition of Voltaire's works supplied by himself: this is certainly the case with the theatre, which provides a number of unique readings and contains some strange notes by Voltaire probably not intended for public consumption. *Zaïre* includes (p.XXXII) an 'Avertissement de l'auteur' concerning the 'Lettre à M. de La Roque'. It is followed by an 'Avertissement des éditeurs' reading:

On avait placé mal à propos dans l'édition in 4° des Œuvres de monsieur de Voltaire, à la suite de sa seconde lettre à monsieur Fakener, une *lettre à monsieur de la Roque, sur la tragédie de Zayre 1732*, qu'il n'a jamais écrite et qui n'est point de lui: on l'a tirée du Mercure galant; par conséquent monsieur de Voltaire la désavoue. Nous avons constamment désiré de donner au public une collection complète des ses ouvrages, mais nous ne voulons pas, ainsi que l'ont fait bien d'autres avant nous, mêler le bon grain avec l'ivraie.

* * *

AVERTISSEMENT DE L'AUTEUR

Cette prétendue lettre n'est point de moi. Monsieur la Roque la mit sous mon nom, croyant mal à propos vendre son journal. Je prie l'éditeur de la supprimer non seulement comme très inutile, mais comme supposée; je le prie de mettre à la place un petit avertissement, par lequel il dira qu'il n'imprime point cette pièce qui n'est pas de moi, qui est tirée du Mercure galant et que je désavoue.

Voltaire.

Poésies

édition critique

par

Nicole Masson

A M. de Formont, en lui renvoyant les œuvres
de Descartes et de Malebranche

On trouve la première version de ce poème dans une lettre en vers et prose qu'adresse Voltaire en mai 1731 à Jean Baptiste Nicolas Formont et Pierre Robert Le Cornier de Cideville (D411). Mais très vite Voltaire a considéré que ces vers pouvaient être dissociés de la lettre. Dès 1735, il joint cette épître en vers lorsqu'il envoie à Cideville un recueil manuscrit de ses poésies fugitives. Le poème prend place dans les œuvres de l'auteur à partir de 1741, dans une édition non-autorisée dont les feuilles seront reprises sous l'égide de Voltaire en 1742 (w42). Nous avons choisi comme texte de base la forme la plus éloignée de la version épistolaire, celle de l'édition encadrée donnée en 1775 à Genève. Les vers y prennent un tour moins concret, ils ne sont plus adressés qu'à un seul correspondant et l'allusion au destinataire est des plus brèves.

Ce correspondant est Formont; c'est par l'intermédiaire de Cideville que Voltaire avait fait la connaissance de l'homme du monde, riche et oisif, qu'il était. Il était né à Rouen en 1694. La rencontre des deux hommes date de l'année 1731, lorsque Voltaire, alors en pourparlers avec l'éditeur Jore, séjourna quelque temps chez Cideville.

Il existe de ce poème deux versions manuscrites intéressantes: la première est celle de Leningrad qui contient quelques corrections de la main de Voltaire; la seconde, dont le texte est près de celui de D411 (que nous n'avons pas collationné), appartient au recueil envoyé à Cideville en 1735 et conservé à Rouen.

Notre texte de base (w75G) reprend, en corrigeant quelques coquilles, le texte des éditions w51, w56 et w68. La version reproduite dans w42 et w38 semble fautive, avec en particulier un vers faux au vers 30. Il est à noter que oc61 donne une version écourtée de l'épître en terminant sur le vers 24.

Manuscrits: MS1: copie avec corrections autographes (Leningrad, Aut.288, f.12). MS2: copie envoyée à Cideville par Voltaire (Cideville, Poésies de Voltaire, f.49-51*r*).

Editions: *Recueil de pièces fugitives en prose et en vers* (Paris, Prault fils, 1740 [1739]), p.213-214 (RP40); W42, V.151-152; W38 (1745), vi.170-171; W48D, iii.87-88; W51, iii.94-95; W56, ii.267-268; OC61, p.164-165; W68 (1771), xviii.361-362; W70L (1772), xxiii.181-182; W75G, xii.363-364; K, xiii.73-74.

Texte de base: W75G.

A M. de Formont, en lui renvoyant les œuvres de Descartes et de Mallebranche

Rimeur charmant, plein de raison,
Philosophe entouré de Grâces,
Epicure, avec Apollon,
S'empresse à marcher sur vos traces.
Je renonce au fatras obscur   5
Du grand rêveur de l'Oratoire,[a]
Qui croit parler de l'esprit pur,
Ou qui veut nous le faire accroire;
Nous disant qu'on peut, à coup sûr,
Entretenir Dieu dans sa gloire.   10

[a] Mallebranche.[1]

a   W38: en lui envoyant
a-b MS2: A M. de Formont à Rouen en lui envoyant les livres de Mallebranche et de Descartes
6   MS2: De ce rêveur
n.*a* RP40-W38, sans note (ajout de W48D)

[1] Dans les *Lettres philosophiques*, XIII, Voltaire parle des 'illusions sublimes' de Malebranche (éd. Lanson et Rousseau, i.168).

Ma raison n'a pas plus de foi
Pour René, le visionnaire.[b]
Songeur de la nouvelle loi;
Il éblouit plus qu'il n'éclaire;
Dans une épaisse obscurité   15
Il fait briller des étincelles.
Il a gravement débité
Un tas brillant d'erreurs nouvelles,
Pour mettre à la place de celles
De la bavarde antiquité.[2]   20
Dans sa cervelle trop féconde
Il prend, d'un air fort important,
Des dés pour arranger le monde;
Bridoye[3] en aurait fait autant,

[b] Descartes.

n.*b* RP40-W48D, sans note (ajout de W51)
14   MS2: Qui plus éblouit qu'il
15-17 MS2:
          Cet homme entouré d'étincelles
          Enfants de son cerveau gâté
          Avec méthode a débité
24   OC61: autant.//

[2] On peut lire à ce sujet dans les *Lettres philosophiques*, XIV: 'Descartes donna la vue aux aveugles, ils virent les fautes de l'Antiquité et les siennes' (éd. Lanson et Rousseau, ii.7).

[3] Bridoye est le juge qui dans le *Pantagruel* de Rabelais, au livre III, décidait des sentences sur des coups de dés. Dans les *Eléments de la philosophie de Newton*, II.i, Voltaire évoque pour les ridiculiser les 'cubes de matière' que Descartes imagine être les particules fondamentales. On en trouve ici l'écho avec les 'dés', mais Voltaire travestit le texte de Descartes qui ne parle pas de 'cubes' mais de 'parties' (cf. BV, no.999).

> Adieu. Je vais chez ma Sylvie;　　　　　　　　25
> Un esprit fait comme le mien,
> Goûte bien mieux son entretien,
> Qu'un roman de philosophie.[4]
> De ses attraits toujours frappé,
> Je ne la crois pas trop fidèle;　　　　　　　　30
> Mais puisqu'il faut être trompé,
> Je ne veux l'être que par elle.[5]

25-32　MS2:
> O qu'entre Cideville et vous,
> J'aurais voulu passer ma vie,
> C'est dans ce commerce si doux,
> Qu'est la bonne philosophie,
> Que n'ont point ces mystiques fous,
> Ni ces dévôts de loups garous,
> Gens députés, de l'autre vie,
> Nicole et Quenel, enfin tous,
> Tous ces auteurs de rapsodie,
> Dont le nom me met en courroux,
> Autant que leur livre m'ennuie.

29　MS1: ⟨je suis⟩^V↑ toujours

30　MS1: ⟨Sans pourtant la croire⟩ ^V↑β
　　w38: Je ne la crois pas fidèle.

32　MS1: ⟨Il est doux de⟩ ^V↑β

[4] Selon le *Grand vocabulaire français* (Paris 1767-1774), 'roman' se disait alors de toute fiction quelque peu invraisemblable. Voltaire a employé le terme à propos de la philosophie antérieure à Locke et Newton en d'autres occasions. Dans les *Lettres philosophiques*, il écrit notamment: 'Tant de raisonneurs ayant fait le roman de l'âme, un sage [Locke] est venu qui en a fait modestement l'histoire.' Et plus loin il dit de Descartes: '[Il] se livra à l'esprit de système; alors sa philosophie ne fut plus qu'un roman ingénieux, et tout au plus vraisemblable pour les ignorants' (éd. Lanson et Rousseau, i.168; ii.6). On voit que dès 1731, Voltaire a dans l'esprit toute la matière des futures *Lettres philosophiques*.

[5] Les vers 25 à 32 ne figurent pas dans la lettre de mai 1731 (D411). Voltaire a recours ici au prénom de théâtre Sylvie, qui renvoie à l'idée de l'amante, sans évoquer une femme réelle.

Les Poètes épiques. Stances

Lorsque *Le Nouvelliste du Parnasse* imprime pendant l'été 1731 les cinq premières strophes de ces stances, il croit bon de les introduire en ces termes: 'Je crois que vous me saurez gré de vous envoyer la Pièce suivante de M. de Voltaire; bien que le jugement qu'il porte sur les Poètes Epiques soit plus badin que solide' (p.310-12).

En effet, Voltaire, fort de ses récents succès dans le genre épique, n'hésite pas à mêler son nom à ceux si prestigieux d'Homère et de Virgile. Ainsi fait-il quelque peu rebondir la querelle sur Homère et même peut-être celle des Anciens et des Modernes. Ses formules à l'emporte-pièce sont fortement critiquées par le *Nouvelliste*, mais défendues avec non moins de véhémence par le rédacteur du *Mercure de France*, environ un mois plus tard, en août 1731 (p.1977-78).

Entre 1731 et 1735, sans qu'on puisse établir une date précise, Voltaire ajoute une sixième strophe à ses stances, d'un ton très différent, qui tend à accentuer l'impression de badinage. Il s'agit d'un compliment galant destiné à une jeune femme qu'on identifie généralement depuis Kehl comme étant la marquise Du Châtelet. C'est vers 1730, si l'on en croit la correspondance de Voltaire (D4046), qu'il l'avait rencontrée; l'ajout de ce compliment pourrait dater, comme le croyait Beuchot (M.viii.505, note), des débuts de leur liaison, vers 1733.

Les opinions exprimées dans ces stances sont à mettre en rapport avec l'*Essai sur la poésie épique*, paru d'abord en anglais, puis en français, en 1727.

Nous avons choisi comme texte de base la première version imprimée où figurent les six strophes. Il s'agit de w38.

On distingue plusieurs leçons du texte: *Le Nouvelliste du Parnasse* (NP), lettre XXIX, juillet-août 1731, p.310-12, *Le Mercure de France* (MF), août 1731, p.1977-78, et le *Journal* de Marais (Paris 1863-

1868), iv.266-67, lettre datée du 6 août 1731, ne présentent que les cinq premières strophes, avec quelques variantes importantes.

A partir du recueil manuscrit envoyé par Voltaire à Cideville en 1735, toutes les éditions offrent les six strophes: w38 et w42 sont similaires. w46, repris par w48D, w56, w75G et w68, comporte une faute au vers 3 dans la lecture d'un f long, et une variante au vers 15 qui affadit le jugement de Voltaire. w51 a la même variante au vers 15, mais ne présente pas la faute du vers 3.

Manuscrits: MS1: copie envoyée à Cideville par Voltaire (Cideville, Poésies de Voltaire, f.65). Deux copies secondaires: 1) Arsenal, MS 6810, f.65v; 2) Br, FS 321 A, p.51-52 (cinq strophes; voir J. Vercruysse, *Inventaire raisonné*, no.431).

Editions: NP (voir ci-dessus); MF (voir ci-dessus); w38, iv.139-140; w42, iv.113-114; w46, v.171-72; w48D, iii.163-164; w51, iii.165-166; w56, ii.127-128; w68, xviii.285-286; w70L (1772), xxii.380-381; w75G, xii.283-284; K, xii.295-296; MARAIS (vois ci-dessus).

Texte de base: w38.

Les Poètes épiques. Stances

Plein de beautés et de défauts,
Le vieil Homère a mon estime;
Il est, comme tous ses héros,

---

a   MF, w75G: Stances sur les poètes épiques
     K, avec sous-titre: A madame la marquise du Châtelet
1   w42: de beauté et
3   NP: est, ainsi que ses
     w46, w70L, w75G: tous les héros

Babillard outré, mais sublime.[1]

Virgile orne mieux la raison,   5
A plus d'art, autant d'harmonie;
Mais il s'épuise avec Didon,
Et rate à la fin Lavinie.[2]

De faux brillants, trop de magie,
Mettent le Tasse un cran plus bas;   10
Mais que ne tolère-t-on pas
Pour Armide et pour Herminie?[3]

Milton, plus sublime qu'eux tous,

4   w48D, w68: Babillard, outré
5   MARAIS: mieux, sa raison
6   NP: Est plus juste, a plus d'harmonie
     MS1: ⟨Est plus tendre, a plus d'harmonie⟩ $^{V\uparrow}\beta$
9   MARAIS: Des faux brillants
10 MARAIS: Ont mis le Tasse
13 MF: plus élevé qu'eux

[1] Premier point de divergence entre le *Nouvelliste* et le *Mercure*: pour le rédacteur du *Mercure*, 'Jamais peut-être n'a-t-on rendu plus de justice à Homère que dans le petit Quatrain qui renferme ce Portrait'. On peut déceler aussi, dans l'emploi de l'adjectif 'babillard', une réminiscence du *Parallèle burlesque sur Homère et Rabelais* de Charles Rivière Dufresny (*Œuvres*, 1731, v.298) où Rabelais dit: 'Homère et moi pouvons être à bon droit parallélisés, en ce que nous sommes par nature tant soit peu beaucoup digressionneurs et babillards.' Voltaire fait donc bien une implicite référence à la fameuse querelle.

[2] Le *Nouvelliste* fait un long commentaire sur l'origine du verbe 'rater', venant 'd'une arme à feu dont la poudre ne prend point'. Il critique le jugement de Voltaire: 'l'expression n'est donc pas juste; mais elle est plaisante et cela suffit peut-être dans une pièce badine'. Le *Mercure* s'inscrit en faux, tant en ce qui concerne Virgile, qu'en ce qui touche à la légèreté de la pièce: 'on n'en a pas jugé ainsi dans le public; il est vrai que ces Vers ont l'air badin, mais le jugement que M. de Voltaire porte sur les autres Poëtes Epiques, a parû judicieux'. A noter le sous-entendu scabreux, escamoté par la polémique, mais néanmoins présent dans les vers 7 et 8.

[3] Deux héroïnes de la *Jérusalem délivrée* du Tasse. Armide et Herminie ont beaucoup inspiré les peintres du dix-septième et du dix-huitième siècle dont Poussin, très apprécié par Voltaire.

A des beautés moins agréables;
Il n'a chanté que pour les fous,
Pour les anges, et pour les diables.[4]

Après Milton, après le Tasse,
Parler de moi serait trop fort;
Et j'attendrai que je sois mort,
Pour apprendre quelle est ma place.

Vous en qui tant d'esprit abonde,
Tant de grâce et de douceur,
Si ma place est dans votre cœur,
Elle est la première du monde.

15

20

15 NP: Mais il n'écrit que
    MARAIS: Il ne chante que
    W46, W51, W70L, W75G: Il semble chanter pour
17-18 NP, interversion des deux vers
20 NP: *apprendre*
21-24 NP, MF, MARAIS: ma place.//
24 W70L, W75G: Elle est dans la première

[4] Cette allusion aux anges et aux diables est due au thème de la grande épopée chrétienne de Milton, *Paradise lost* (1667). Cette œuvre comporte un passage que décrit un 'paradise of fools'.

Sur M. de La Faye

En 1716, Voltaire connaissait déjà Jean-François Leriget de La Faye. Une lettre de Voltaire, consacrée à quelques débats littéraires (D39), est dès cette époque adressée au chevalier. *Le Mercure de France* (MF) de juillet 1731 (p.1769-77) annonce la mort de La Faye; l'article nécrologique nous apprend qu'il était secrétaire du cabinet du roi, membre de l'Académie française. Grand collectionneur de livres et de tableaux, il se piquait lui-même de composer musique et poésie.

Aussitôt, la mort de ce personnage suscite quelques épitaphes en vers. Voltaire fait paraître la sienne dans le *Mercure* d'août 1731. Il semble avoir apprécié le caractère plutôt enjoué du chevalier. Dans une lettre de 1736 (10 février; D1009), il parle encore de lui en ces termes: '[le] charmant M. de La Faye qu'on ne peut trop regretter'.

Plus tard, le poème porte le titre de *Portrait de M. de La Faye*. Il est possible que ces huit vers aient trouvé place au bas d'un portrait le représentant.

Le texte a d'abord paru dans le *Mercure de France* d'août 1731, p.1921. Il est, dans ce périodique, signé M. de Voltaire. C'est cette version que nous avons choisi comme texte de base, puisqu'il s'agit d'une pièce de circonstance. Elle est adoptée dans l'ensemble des éditions, si on excepte OC61 qui contient une variante.

Manuscrits: Deux copies secondaires: 1) Pierpont Morgan Library, New York, MA 634, non folioté; 2) Bh, Rés.2025, f.123*r*

Editions: MF (août 1731), p.1921; OC61, p.196; TS61, p.385; W70L (1772), xxiii.304. Il figure aussi dans *Le Portefeuille trouvé* (Genève 1757), i.18; *Elite des poésies fugitives* (1770), v.116; *Epîtres* (Londres 1771), p.404-405 (titre: *Portrait de M. de La Fare*).

Texte de base: *Mercure de France*, août 1731, p.1921.

Sur M. de La Faye

Il a réuni le mérite,
Et d'Horace et de Pollion,
Tantôt protégeant Apollon,
Et tantôt chantant à sa suite.
Il reçut deux présents des dieux,   5
Les plus charmants qu'ils puissent faire.
L'un était le talent de plaire;
L'autre le secret d'être heureux.

a oc61, ts61, w70l: Portrait de M. de La Faye
4 oc61: marchant à sa suite

Épigramme sur l'abbé Terrasson

La victime de cette épigramme cruelle est l'objet d'un mépris constant de la part de Voltaire: l'abbé Jean Terrasson ne trouve jamais grâce à ses yeux. Dans le *Siècle de Louis XIV* (M.xiv.139), la mention qui est faite de son nom est sèche et brève; Voltaire n'aime pas ses 'méchants livres' (octobre 1731; D435) et répugne à les lire (8 août 1731; D422).

Si on se réfère à la correspondance, et en particulier aux deux lettres déjà citées, on devine que Voltaire a lu le roman de *Sethos, histoire ou vie tirée des monumens anecdotes de l'ancienne Egypte, traduite d'un manuscrit grec* (Paris 1731; BV, no.3263) entre août et octobre 1731 après bien des réticences. On peut supposer que l'épigramme date de cette période.

On y lit des insinuations scandaleuses sur le compte de l'abbé: Voltaire se fait sans doute l'écho de bruits qui courent, comme le laisse entendre une lettre de Mlle de Seine rapportée par Barbier (ii.91). On n'en trouvera bien entendu pas trace dans les panégyriques de Moncrif et de d'Alembert, composés à la mort de l'ecclésiastique en 1750, qui le représentent 'exempt des passions qui tourmentent l'âme'.[1] On est bien loin du personnage quelque peu grotesque que caricature Voltaire.

Texte de base: cette épigramme ne figure dans aucune édition du dix-huitième siècle. Elle a été publiée pour la première fois dans *Œuvres complètes*, éd. Lequien (Paris 1820-1826), xiv.305, qui fournit notre texte de base.

---

[1] Fr. Paradis de Moncrif, 'Lettre sur M. l'abbé Terrasson' (*MF*, janvier 1751, p.29-44) et J. Le Rond d'Alembert, *Eloge de M. l'abbé Terrasson* (Paris s.d.).

Épigramme sur l'abbé Terrasson

On dit que l'abbé Terrasson,
De Law et de La Motte apôtre,[2]
Va du b..... à l'Hélicon,
N'étant fait pour l'un ni pour l'autre.
Pour avoir un léger prurit,   5
Il se fait chatouiller la fesse.[3]
Manon le fouette, il la caresse;
Mais il b.... comme il écrit.
Un jour, dans la cérémonie,
On l'étrillait, il frétillait;   10
Notre p..... se travaillait
Dessus sa fesse racornie.
Entre monsieur l'abbé Du Bos,[4]
Qui, voyant fesser son confrère,
Dit tout haut, approuvant l'affaire: 15
'Frappez fort, il a fait *Sethos*'.

[2] Terrasson s'était fait connaître par une *Dissertation critique sur l'Iliade d'Homère, où à l'occasion de ce poème on cherche les règles d'une poétique fondée sur la raison et sur les exemples des anciens et des modernes* (Paris 1715) où il rejoignait le camp de La Motte dans la querelle des Anciens et des Modernes. Plus tard, en 1720, il publia trois *Lettres sur le nouveau système des finances* de Law. C'est grâce à ce fameux système qu'il s'enrichit... puis se ruina. Voltaire trouvait là de bonnes raisons d'attaquer l'abbé, au moins aussi fortes que son aversion pour *Sethos*.

[3] Barbier cite une lettre de Mlle de Seine, de mars 1735, où elle parle de Terrasson en ces termes: 'l'apologiste du système, qui doit vous donner incessamment les anecdotes secrètes et anciennes des flagellants'. Une note précise l'allusion: 'l'Abbé Jean Terrasson [...] avait été l'un des plus ardents admirateurs du système de Law. On l'accusait d'aller se faire fouetter dans les mauvais lieux' (ii.91).

[4] L'abbé Jean-Baptiste Du Bos passait pour le type même du critique littéraire et esthétique depuis la parution en 1719 de ses *Réflexions critiques sur la poésie et la peinture*, d'ailleurs rééditées en 1733.

Sur l'estampe du R. P. Girard et de la Cadière

Voltaire avait sans doute inscrit ce distique au bas d'une estampe populaire, introuvable aujourd'hui. Elle représentait vraisemblablement une femme en prière, sujette à des visions, et un jésuite la contemplant avec concupiscence. Cette scène illustrait une affaire qui fit beaucoup de bruit (cf. Barbier, i.357): le procès du père Jean-Baptiste Girard, recteur de la maison des jésuites de Toulon, et de Marie Marguerite Cadière, à Aix, à l'automne 1731. Selon le recueil des pièces du dossier, *Recueil général des pièces concernant le procès entre la demoiselle Cadière et le P. Girard* (La Haye 1731; cf. BV, no.2907), la jeune fille s'était plainte d'avoir été ensorcelée par le père Girard, qui, par ce subterfuge, avait abusé d'elle. Elle insinuait également, qu'usant toujours de magie, il l'avait fait avorter pour dissimuler son forfait. Le père Girard niait tout en bloc.

Un siècle plus tôt, dans la même région et pour des faits semblables, le père Louis Gaufridy avait été torturé et brûlé par l'Inquisition. En 1731, même si l'affaire prend un certain relief en raison de la polémique menée par les jansénistes contre la 'morale relâchée' des jésuites, même si l'avocat général réclame le bûcher, le public ne croit plus vraiment à la sorcellerie: il voit surtout dans ce procès une plaisante affaire de séduction.

Voltaire plus qu'un autre s'y intéresse: une lettre qu'il adresse à René Hérault, datée du 20 septembre 1731 (D431), nous apprend qu'il a failli être inquiété à ce propos. On avait fait paraître à Aix le recueil des factums du père Girard. Voltaire confie quelques craintes à son correspondant: 'j'aprends que les libraires croyant fort mal à propos que mon nom serviroit à faire débiter l'ouvrage, l'ont vendu publiquement comme de moy; je sçay de plus que cette indigne calomnie a pénétré jusqu'à m^r le garde des sceaux, et à m^r le Cardinal'. Il faut dire que la préface contenait des attaques contre le parlement et le gouvernement. On voit donc la réputation que s'était faite Voltaire dès 1731.

Le distique date de cet automne 1731, en pleine affaire, sans doute même après l'acquittement des deux parties le 19 octobre.

Ce distique ne fut publié que dans l'édition de Kehl. Il avait d'abord été inséré par Meister dans la livraison d'avril 1783 de la *Correspondance littéraire* (CL).

Manuscrits: CL: G1 O, f.340r; Bh 3867, f.63r; G2 1277, f.63r; Zu 8, f.71r (voir U. Kölving et J. Carriat, *Inventaire de la Correspondance littéraire de Grimm et Meister*, Studies 225-227 (1984), no.83:067).

Edition: K, xiv.296.

Texte de base: K.

Sur l'estampe du R. P. Girard et de la Cadière

Cette belle voit Dieu; Girard voit cette belle:
  Ah! Girard est plus heureux qu'elle!

1   CL: voit sa belle

A monsieur le maréchal de Richelieu, en lui envoyant plusieurs pièces détachées

Louis François Armand Du Plessis, duc de Richelieu, était connu pour avoir une vie amoureuse agitée. Il n'hésitait jamais à user de son charme, allant jusqu'à l'exercer sur les propres maîtresses du régent. Voltaire, dans une lettre à Thiriot de mai 1733 (D616), dit de lui: 'Il entend à merveilles l'art de plaire. C'est de tous les arts celui qu'en général les Anglais cultivent le moins et que Monsieur de Richelieu connaît le plus'.

Voltaire a longtemps fréquenté le duc. Il est donc difficile de dater ces vers qui devaient accompagner un envoi de livres ou de manuscrits. Cideville, cité par Clogenson (M.x.491), donne 1731 comme date de composition.

Les différentes éditions du poème ne présentent pas de variantes entre elles.

Editions: W72P, xiv.346; K, xiv.327. Il figure aussi dans l'*Almanach des muses* (Paris 1773), p.136.

Texte de base: W72P.

A monsieur le maréchal de Richelieu, en lui envoyant plusieurs pièces détachées

Que de ces vains écrits, enfants de mes beaux jours,
    La lecture au moins vous amuse:
Mais, charmant Richelieu, ne traitez point ma muse
    Ainsi que vos autres amours;
Ne l'abandonnez point, elle en sera plus belle: 5
Votre aimable suffrage animera ma voix.
    Richelieu, soyez-lui fidèle,
    Vous le serez pour la première fois.

A l'hôtel de Mantes

L'abbé Michel Linant est un des protégés de Voltaire. Originaire de la région rouennaise, et comme tel, connu de Formont et de Cideville, il a occupé diverses places de précepteur, chez Mme Du Châtelet notamment. On apprend, dans une lettre adressée à Cideville, du 29 mai 1733 (D615), que la mère de Linant tenait l'hôtel de La Ville de Mantes à Rouen.[1] C'est sans doute elle 'l'hôtesse au nez retroussé'...

Nous avons adopté comme texte de base celui du manuscrit olographe. Il présente quelques fautes d'orthographe que nous avons cru devoir rectifier. Il est à noter que Besterman citait ces vers en note de la lettre D615, avec quelques erreurs.

Ces vers figurent dans une lettre adressée à Cideville, datant de 1731. L'olographe de Voltaire est conservé à Rouen, dans les archives de l'Académie de Rouen. Il s'agit d'un document de quatre pages, 220 x 169 mm, dont le premier feuillet à été amputé de sa partie supérieure et le deuxième feuillet des deux tiers de sa partie inférieure. Clogenson, dans l'édition Moland de la correspondance, en cite des fragments en note. E. Meyer, dans un article intitulé 'Billets inédits de Voltaire' dans *La Grande revue* 25 (Paris 1931), p.451-52, a publié ces vers, mais des divergences de texte prouvent qu'il n'a pas dû voir le manuscrit olographe.

Manuscrits: MS1: manuscrit olographe (Cideville, Lettres de Voltaire à Cideville, liasse 1, lettre 7). MS2: copie par Cideville (Cideville, Poésies de Voltaire, f.109v-10r). Copie secondaire: Bn F12944, f.418v-19r.

Texte de base: MS1.

---

[1] 'J'avois adressé mon citadin de Hambourg chez la mère de notre abbé [Linant]. Ce n'est pas que je regarde le bordel de la ville de Mantes comme une bonne hôtelerie. Il y a longtemps que j'ay dit peu chrétiennement ce que j'en pensois' (D615).

À L'HÔTEL DE MANTES

[*A l'hôtel de Mantes*]

. . . .
. . . .

A l'hôtel de Mantes je gite
Soi disant de Mantes l'hôtel,
Mais horride[2] et damné bordel   5
Dont je veux sortir au plus vite,
Et franc bordel le trouvera
Qui comme nous s'y connaîtra.
Sans doute il est du nombre, car
Il a l'odeur du lupanar,   10
Arachné tapisse mes murs,
Draps y sont courts, lits y sont durs,
Boiteuses sont les escabelles;[3]
Et la bouteille au cou cassé
Y soutient de jaunes chandelles   15
Dont le bout y fut enfoncé
Par les deux mains simpiternelles[4]
De l'hôtesse au nez retroussé

---

a MS2: Impromptu envoyé à Rouen à M. de Cideville en 1731 à la fin du
carême.
14 MS2: Et bouteilles au
15 MS2: Soutiennent que

---

[2] Aucun dictionnaire ne mentionne cet adjectif formé sans doute sur le latin
'horridus'. Seul le *Dictionnaire de l'ancienne langue française* de Godefroy (Paris
1885) mentionne un nom 'horridité' avec pour sens 'horreur, frayeur' (iv.498).

[3] Dans son *Dictionnaire*, Richelet ne fait pas de distinction entre escabelle et
escabeau, 'siège de bois assez haut élevé sur quatre pieds', et il indique qu'on
ne se sert plus guère ni d'escabelle ni d'escabeau qui ne sont présentement que
des meubles de pauvres provinciaux ou de cabaretiers'.

[4] Dans ce même dictionnaire, il est précisé que 'sempiternel' est un mot
burlesque et satirique. L'orthographe 'simpiternelle' n'est pas attestée par les
dictionnaires.

. . . .
. . . .   20

Qui fut fait jadis avec soin
Par le cabaretier du coin.

    Mais allons sur ce bride en main,
Car mon cher dans votre paroisse,
Vous saurez vendredi prochain   25
Que de Manon[5] le fils divin,
Pour le salut du genre humain
Etant à sa dernière angoisse,
Voulut boire un verre de vin
Mais que d'un procédé fort aigre   30
Un damné de pharisien
Fit boire au bon Nazaréen
Un large bord[6] de vieux vinaigre
L'autre, sur son arbre arrangé
But le tout d'un air fort tranquille,   35
Mais il eut sans doute enragé
S'il eut resté sans Cideville
Au bordel où je suis logé.

19-20   MS2:
        Mon verre toujours encrassé
        Contient un vinaigre passé

    [5] Le prénom Manon, diminutif familier de Marie, évoque ici assez irrespec-
tueusement la Vierge.
    [6] L'exemple que donne Richelet de cette acception du mot 'bord' est: 'Un
rouge bord: verre tout plein de vin'.

LIST OF WORKS CITED

Adams, Percy G., 'Poe, critic of Voltaire', *Mln* 57 (1942), p.273-75.

Addison, Joseph, *Cato, a tragedy* (London 1713).

Alembert, Jean Le Rond d', *Eloge de M. l'abbé Terrasson* (Paris s.d.).

Algarotti, Francesco, *Opere* (Cremona 1778-1784).

– – (Venezia 1791-1794).

Allainval, Léonor Jean Christine Soulas d', *Le Temple du Goust* (La Haye 1733).

Almanach littéraire (1777-1793).

Arndt, Richard, *Zur Entstehung von Voltaires Zaïre* (Marburg 1906).

Ayres, Harry Morgan, 'Shakespeare's *Julius Caesar* in the light of some other versions', *PMla* 18 (1910), ii.183-227.

Barbier, Edmond Jean François, *Chronique de la régence et du règne de Louis XV (1718-1763)* (Paris 1867).

Barbier, Marie-Anne, *La Mort de César* (Paris 1710)

Baudin, Maurice, 'L'art de régner in seventeenth-century French tragedy', *Mln* 50 (1935), p.417-26.

Bengesco, Georges, *Voltaire: bibliographie de ses œuvres* (Paris 1882-1890).

Bergmann, Fred L., 'Garrick's *Zara*', *PMla* 74 (1959), p.225-32.

Bernardin, N.-M., 'Le théâtre de Voltaire: *Zaïre*', *Revue des cours et conférences* 22 (1914), p.659-72.

Bérubé, G.-L., 'Voltaire et *La Mort de César*', *L'Homme et la nature: actes de la Société canadienne d'étude du dix-huitième siècle* 1 (1982), p.15-20.

Besterman, Theodore, 'A provisional bibliography of Italian editions and translations of Voltaire', *Studies* 18 (1961), p.263-310.

– 'A provisional bibliography of Scandinavian and Finnish editions and translations of Voltaire', *Studies* 47 (1966), p.53-92.

– 'Provisional bibliography of Portuguese editions of Voltaire', *Studies* 76 (1970), p.13-35.

– *Voltaire* (Oxford 1976).

Bibliothèque de Voltaire: catalogue des livres (Moscou, Leningrad 1961).

Bibliothèque dramatique de monsieur de Soleinne (Paris 1843-1845).

Bibliothèque nationale, *Catalogue général des livres imprimés de la Bibliothèque nationale: auteurs, tome 214, Voltaire* (Paris 1978).

Bolingbroke, Henry St John, *Works* (London 1809).

Bouhier, Jean, *Correspondance littéraire du président Bouhier*, ed. Henri Duranton (Saint-Etienne 1974-1988).

Bouvy, Eugène, '*Zaïre* en Italie', *Bulletin italien, Annales de la Faculté de lettres de Bordeaux* 4ᵉ série (1901), i.22-28.

Boysse, Ernest, *Le Théâtre des jésuites* (Paris 1880).

Brenner, Clarence D., *The Théâtre italien, its repertory, 1716-1793* (Berkeley 1961).

Bruce, Harold Lawton, *Voltaire on the English stage* (Berkeley 1918).

Buckingham, John Sheffield, duke of, *Works* (London 1723).

Buffardin, Sextius, *Brutus et Cassius* (Paris An IV).

Carcopino, Jérôme, *Jules César*, 5th ed. (Paris 1968).

Catrou, François, and Rouillé, Pierre Julien, *Histoire romaine* (1725-1737).

Centlivre, Susanna, *The Wonder* (London 1714).

Chateaubriand, François René de, *Génie du christianisme* (Paris 1802).

Chetwood, William Rufus, *General history of the stage* (London 1749).

Chevalley, Sylvie, 'Le "Sieur Minet"', *Studies* 62 (1968), p.273-83.

Clairon, Claire Josèphe Léris de La Tude, known as Mlle, *Mémoires* (Paris 1822).

Clément, Jean Marie Bernard, *De la tragédie, pour servir de suite aux Lettres à Voltaire* (Amsterdam 1784).

Coe, Ada M., *Catálogo bibliográfico y crítico de las comedias anunciadas en los periódicos de Madrid desde 1661 hasta 1819* (Baltimore 1935).

Collé, Charles, *Journal et mémoires*, ed. H. Bonhomme (Paris 1868).

Collischonn, G. A. O., *Jacques Grévins Tragödie 'César' in ihrem Verhältnis zu Muret, Voltaire und Shakespeare*, Ausgaben und Abhandlungen aus dem Gebiete der Romanischen Philologie 52 (Marburg 1886).

Conlon, Pierre Marie, *Voltaire's literary career from 1728 to 1750*, Studies 14 (1961).

Conti, Antonio, *Il Cesare* (Faenza 1726).

Cottrell, Robert D., 'Ulcerated hearts: love in Voltaire's *La Mort de César*', *Literature and history in the age of ideas*, ed. C. Williams (Columbus 1975).

The Craftsman, ed. N. Amherst, Henry St John, Viscount Bolingbroke and W. Pulteney, new edition (London 1731-1737).

Cranston, Maurice, 'Voltaire: man of feeling', *The Listener* 83, 23 April 1970, p.541-42.

Davies, Thomas, *Memoirs of the life of David Garrick* (London 1780).

De Beer, Gavin, and Rousseau, André-Michel, *Voltaire's British visitors*, Studies 49 (1967).

Defaux, G., 'L'idéal politique de Voltaire dans *La Mort de César*', *Revue de l'Université d'Ottawa* 40 (1970), p.418-40.

Defourneaux, Marcelin, *Pablo de Olavide, ou l'Alfrancesado (1725-1803)* (Paris 1959).

Dennis, John, *The Critical works*, ed. Edward N. Hooker (Baltimore 1939-1943).

Deschanel, Emile, *Le Théâtre de Voltaire* (Paris 1883).

Desfontaines, Pierre François Guyot, *Observations sur les écrits modernes* (Paris 1735-1743).

Desnoiresterres, Gustave, *Voltaire et la société française au XVIIIe siècle* (Paris 1867-1876).

Dominique, Pierre F. Biancolelli, Romagnesi, Jean A, and Riccoboni, Francesco, *Les Enfans trouvez, ou le sultan poli par l'amour. Parodie de la tragédie de Zaïre* (Paris 1733).

Dryden, John, *The Dramatick works* (London 1735).

Dubedout, E. J., 'Shakespeare and Voltaire. *Othello* and *Zaïre*', *Modern philology* 3 (1906), p.305-12.

Dubos, Jean-Baptiste, *Réflexions critiques sur la poésie et la peinture* [1733].

Dufresny, Charles Rivière, *Œuvres* (Paris 1731).

Dupont-Ferrier, G., *Du collège de Clermont au lycée Louis-le-Grand* (Paris 1921).

Echard, Laurence, *The Roman history* (London 1695).

– *Histoire romaine*, tr. D. de Larroque and Desfontaines (Paris 1728).

Elledge, Scott B., ed., *Eighteenth-century critical essays* (Ithaca 1961).

Etienne, Charles Guillaume, and Martainville, Alphonse, *Histoire du théâtre français* (Paris 1802).

Faguet, Emile, *Le Dix-huitième siècle* (Paris 1890).

Fenger, Henning, *Voltaire et le théâtre anglais*, Orbis litterarum 7 (Copenhague 1949).

Ferrari, Luigi, *Le Traduzioni italiane del teatro tragico francese nei secoli XVIIe e XVIIIe* (Paris 1925).

Fletcher, Dennis J., 'Bolingbroke and the diffusion of Newtonianism in France', *Studies* 53 (1967), p.29-46.

– 'The fortunes of Bolingbroke in France in the eighteenth century', *Studies* 47 (1966), p.207-32.

– 'Three authors in search of a character: Julius Caesar as seen by Buckingham, Conti and Voltaire', *Mélanges à la mémoire de Franco Simone: France et Italie dans la culture européenne* (Genève 1981), ii.440-53.

Fleury, Claude, *Histoire ecclésiastique* (Paris 1720-1738).

Fromm, Hans, *Bibliographie Deutscher Übersetzungen aus dem Französischen 1700-1948* (Baden-Baden 1950-1953).

Garnier, Robert, *Œuvres complètes*, ed. Lucien Pinvert (Paris 1923).

The Gentleman's magazine (1733-1736).

Le Glaneur historique, critique, moral, littéraire, galant et calotin (La Haye 1731-1733).

Graffigny, Françoise d'Issembourg d'Happoncourt, Mme de, *Correspondance*, ed. J. A. Dainard *et al.* (Oxford 1985-).

Grand vocabulaire français (Paris 1767-1774).

Green, Frederick C., *Minuet: a critical survey of French and English literary ideas in the eighteenth century* (London 1935).

Grimm, Friedrich Melchior, *Correspondance littéraire*, ed. M. Tourneux (Paris 1877-1882).

Grubbs, Henry, *Jean-Baptiste Rousseau* (Princeton 1941).

Guérin de Bouscal, Guion, *La Mort de Brute et de Porcie* (Paris 1637).

Hampson, Norman, *The Enlightenment* (London 1968).

Hill, Aaron, *The Tragedy of Zara, as it is acted at the Theatre-Royal in Drury-Lane* (London 1736).

Joannidès, A., *La Comédie-Française de 1680 à 1900* (Paris 1901).

Jondorf, Gillian, *Robert Garnier and the themes of political tragedy in the sixteenth century* (Cambridge 1969).

Journal de la cour et de Paris, ed. Henri Duranton (Saint-Etienne 1981).

Knight, Wilson, *The Wheel of fire*, revised edition (London 1954).

Kölving, U., and Carriat, J., *Inventaire de la Correspondance littéraire de Grimm et Meister*, Studies 225-227 (1984).

Krappe, Alexander Haggerty, 'The sources of Voltaire's *Zaïre*', *Mln* 22 (1925), p.305-309.

Lafarga, Francisco, *Voltaire en España, 1734-1835* (Barcelona 1982).

La Harpe, Jean-François de, *Commentaire sur le théâtre de Voltaire* (Paris 1814).

– *Lycée, ou cours de littérature ancienne et moderne* (Paris 1799-1805).

Lancaster, H. Carrington, 'The Comédie-Française, 1701-1774: plays, actors, spectators, finances', *Transactions of the American philosophical society* 41, new series (1951), p.593-849.

– *French tragedy in the time of Louis XV*

and Voltaire, 1715-1774 (Baltimore 1950).

Lanson, Gustave, *Voltaire* (Paris 1906).

Lekain, Henri Louis, *Mémoires*, ed. F. Talma (Paris 1825).

Lessing, Gotthold Ephraim, *Hamburgische Dramaturgie*, ed. Otto Mann (Stuttgart 1958).

Lion, Henri, *Les Tragédies et les théories dramatiques de Voltaire* (Paris 1895).

The Literary magazine (London 1735-1736).

The London Stage 1660-1800 (Carbondale 1960-1968), part ii, *1700-1729*, ed. Emmet L. Avery; part iii, *1730-1747*, ed. Arthur H. Scouten.

Longchamp, Sébastien G., et Wagnière, Jean-Louis, *Mémoires sur Voltaire et sur ses ouvrages* (Paris 1826).

Lounsbury, Thomas R., *Shakespeare and Voltaire* (London 1902).

Lowenstein, Robert, *Voltaire as an historian of seventeenth-century French drama* (Baltimore, London 1935).

Lyonnet, H., *Dictionnaire des comédiens français* (Paris [1908]).

McClelland, I. L., *Spanish drama of pathos, 1750-1808* (Liverpool 1970).

Maimbourg, Louis, *Histoire des croisades pour la délivrance de la Terre Sainte* (Paris 1682).

– – (Paris 1684-1685).

Marais, Mathieu, *Journal et mémoires [...] sur la régence et le règne de Louis XV, 1715-1737*, ed. Lescure (Paris 1863-1868).

Mason, Haydn T., *Pierre Bayle and Voltaire* (Oxford 1963).

Mazouer, Charles, 'Les tragédies romaines de Voltaire', *Dix-huitième siècle* 18 (1986), p.359-71.

Le Mercure de France (1724-1794).

Meyer, E., 'Billets inédits de Voltaire',

La Grande revue 25 (Paris 1931), p.451-52.

Michelet, Jules, *Histoire de France* (Paris 1876-1878).

Mielck, Otto, 'John Sheffield Duke of Buckinghams Zweitheilung und Bearbeitung des Shakespeare'schen *Julius Caesar*', *Shakespeare Jahrbuch* 25 (1889), p.29-70.

Moncrif, François Paradis de, 'Lettre sur M. l'abbé Terrasson', *Mercure de France* (janvier 1751), p.29-44.

Monod-Cassidy, Hélène, *Un voyageur-philosophe au XVIIIe siècle: l'abbé Jean-Bernard Le Blanc* (Cambridge 1941).

Moureaux, José-Michel, *L'Œdipe de Voltaire: introduction à une psycho-lecture*, Archives des lettres modernes 146 (Paris 1973).

Murray, Gilbert, *Five stages of Greek religion* (London 1946).

Nadal, Augustin, *Arlequin au Parnasse, ou la folie de Melpomène. Comédie critique de Zaïre* (Paris 1733).

– *Œuvres mêlées* (Paris 1738).

Nicoll, Allardyce, *A history of English drama*, 3rd ed. (Cambridge 1955).

Le Nouvelliste du Parnasse (Paris 1731).

Olavide, Pablo de, *Obras dramáticas desconocidas*, ed. Estuardo Núñez (Lima 1971).

Olivier, Jean-Jacques, *Henri-Louis Le Kain de la Comédie-Française (1729-1778)* (Paris 1907).

– *Voltaire et les comédiens interprètes de son théâtre* (Paris 1900).

Ostaszewicz, Marek, 'La destinée d'une tragédie: la *Mort de César* en Pologne', *Kwartalnik neofilologiczny* 27 (1980), p.405-12.

Par, Alfonso, 'Representaciones teatrales en Barcelona durante el siglo XVIII', *Boletín de la Real academia española* 16 (1929), p.326-46, 492-513, 594-614.

Les Parodies du nouveau Théâtre italien, ou recueil des parodies représentées sur le théâtre de l'Hôtel de Bourgogne, par les comédiens italiens ordinaires du roy (Paris 1738).

Petkovic, Johann, *Voltaires Tragödie 'La Mort de César' verglichen mit Shakespeares 'Julius Cäsar'* (Wien 1909).

Phillips, James Emerson, *The State in Shakespeare's Greek and Roman plays* (New York 1940).

Pike, Robert, 'Fact and fiction in *Zaïre*', *PMla* 51 (1936), p.436-39.

Plutarch, *Parallel lives of the Greeks and Romans*, tr. Bernadotte Perrin, Loeb Classical Library (London, New York 1918-1920).

– *Lives*, tr. R. Steele (London 1713).

– *Les Vies des hommes illustres*, tr. Jacques Amyot (Genève 1535).

– – tr. A. Dacier (Amsterdam 1734).

Pomeau, René, 'Voltaire au collège', *Rhl* 52 (1952), p.1-10.

– 'Voltaire et le héros', *Revue des sciences humaines* 16 (1951), p.345-51.

– 'Voltaire et Shakespeare: du père justicier au père assassiné', *Littératures* 9-10 (1984), p.99-106.

Prévost, André François, *Le Pour et contre* (Paris 1733).

The Prompter (London 1734-1736).

Quérard, Joseph Marie, *La France littéraire* (Paris 1827-1864).

Recueil général des pièces concernant le procès entre la demoiselle Cadière et le P. Girard (La Haye 1731).

Richelet, Pierre, *Dictionnaire de la langue françoise* (Lyon 1769).

Riddle, Lawrence M., *The Genesis and sources of Pierre Corneille's tragedies from 'Médée' to 'Pertharite'* (Baltimore, Paris 1926).

Ridgway, Ronald S., *La Propagande philosophique dans les tragédies de Voltaire*, Studies 15 (1961).

– *Voltaire and sensibility* (Montreal, London 1973).

Rivoire, J. A., *Le Patriotisme dans le théâtre sérieux de la Révolution* (Paris 1950).

Robertson, John George, *Lessing's dramatic theory* (Cambridge 1939).

Robinove, Phyllis S., 'Voltaire's theater on the Parisian stage, 1789-1799', *French review* 32 (1959), p.534-38.

Roosbroeck, G. L. van, 'Notes on Voltaire', *Mln* 39 (1924), p.1-10.

Rousseau, André-Michel, *L'Angleterre et Voltaire*, Studies 145-147 (1976).

Rousseau, Jean-Jacques, *Lettre à Mr. d'Alembert sur les spectacles*, ed. M. Fuchs (Lille, Genève 1948).

Runciman, Steven, *A history of the crusades* (Cambridge 1951-1954).

Russell, Trusten Wheeler, *Voltaire, Dryden and heroic tragedy* (New York 1946).

Saint-Evremond, Charles de Marguetel de Saint-Denis, *Œuvres meslées*, 2nd ed. (London 1709).

– *Œuvres en prose*, ed. R. Ternois (Paris 1962-1969).

Salza, Abd-el-kader, *L'Ab. Antonio Conti e le sue tragedie* (Pisa 1898).

Scarron, Paul, *Le Prince corsaire* (Paris 1663).

Schimberg, André, *L'Education morale dans les collèges de la compagnie de Jésus en France sous l'Ancien Régime* (Paris 1913).

Scudéry, Georges de, *L'Amour tyrannique* (Paris 1639).

– *La Mort de César*, 2nd ed. (Paris 1637).

– – ed. H. L. Cook (New York 1930).

Seneca, *Four tragedies and Octavia*, ed. E. F. Watling (London 1966).

Shakespeare, William, *Julius Caesar*, ed. J. Dover Wilson (Cambridge 1949).

Smith, Edmund, *Phaedra and Hippolitus*, 3rd ed. (London 1720).

Suetonius, *Lives of the Caesars*, Loeb Classical Library (Cambridge, Mass., London 1913).

Syme, Ronald, *The Roman revolution* (Oxford 1939).

Taylor, Owen R., 'Voltaire's apprenticeship as a historian: *La Henriade*', *The Age of Enlightenment: studies presented to Theodore Besterman* (Edinburgh, London 1967).

Taylor, S. S. B., 'The definitive text of Voltaire's works: the Leningrad encadrée', *Studies* 124 (1974), p.7-132.

Terrasson, Jean, *Sethos, histoire ou vie tirée des monumens anecdotes de l'ancienne Egypte, traduite d'un manuscrit grec* (Paris 1731).

Todd, Christopher, 'A provisional bibliography of published Spanish translations of Voltaire', *Studies* 161 (1976), p.43-136

Ure, P., ed., *Julius Caesar: a casebook* (London 1968).

Velleius Paterculus, *Compendium of Roman history*, tr. F. W. Shipley, Loeb Classical Library (London, Cambridge 1955).

Vercruysse, Jeroom, 'Bibliographie provisoire des traductions néerlandaises et flamandes de Voltaire', *Studies* 116 (1973), p.19-64.

– *Inventaire raisonné des manuscrits voltairiens de la Bibliothèque royale Albert 1er*, Bibliologia 2 (Turnhout 1983).

– 'Notes inédites de Voltaire', *Studi francesi* 20 (1963), p.258-64.

– 'Voltaire et Marc Michel Rey', *Studies* 58 (1967), p.1707-63.

Villemain, Abel François, *Cours de littérature française: tableau du dix-huitième siècle* (Paris 1838).

– *Tableau de la littérature française au 18e siècle* (Paris 1873).

Voltaire, *Commentaires sur Corneille*, ed. David Williams, Voltaire 53-55 (1974-1975).

– *Corpus des notes marginales de Voltaire* (Berlin, Oxford 1979-).

– *Correspondence and related documents*, ed. Th. Besterman, Voltaire 85-135 (1968-1977).

– *Dictionnaire philosophique*, ed. J. Benda et R. Naves (Paris 1967).

– *Essai sur les mœurs*, ed. R. Pomeau (Paris 1963).

– *Letters concerning the English nation* (1733).

– *Lettres philosophiques*, ed. G. Lanson and A.-M. Rousseau (Paris 1964).

– *La Mort de César*, ed. A.-M. Rousseau (Paris 1964).

– *La Mort de César, tragédie en trois actes, de Voltaire, avec les changements faits par le citoyen Gohier, ministre de la justice* (Commune-Affranchie An II).

– *Notebooks*, ed. Th. Besterman, Voltaire 81-82 (1968).

– *Œuvres complètes* (Kehl 1784-1789).

– *Œuvres*, ed. Ch. Palissot (Paris 1792-1797).

– *Œuvres complètes*, ed. L. Moland (Paris 1877-1885).

– *Œuvres complètes / Complete works* (Genève, Banbury, Oxford 1968-).

– *Le Temple du Goût*, ed. E. Carcassonne (Genève 1953).

– *Zaïre*, ed. Fontaine (Paris 1889).

Vrooman, J. R., *Voltaire's theatre: the cycle from Œdipe to Mérope*, Studies 75 (1970).

Waldo, Lewis P., *The French drama in America in the eighteenth century and its influence on the American drama of that period, 1701-1800* (Baltimore 1942).

Wallich, Paul, and von Müller, Hans,

LIST OF WORKS CITED

Die Deutsche Voltaire-Literatur des achtzehnten Jahrhunderts (Berlin 1921).

Walpole, Robert, *Works* (London 1809).

Welschinger, Henri, *Le Théâtre de la Révolution, 1789-1799* (Paris 1880).

Werner, Stephen, 'Voltaire and Seneca', *Studies* 67 (1969), p.29-44.

White, Florence D., *Voltaire's Essay on epic poetry, a study and an edition* (New York 1915).

Williams, David, *Voltaire: literary critic*, *Studies* 48 (1966).

INDEX

Aubigny, Louis Stuart d', 248
Augustus, C. Octavius, 9*n*, 57, 59; (*Cinna*), 9*n*, 37, 57-60
Avery, Emmet L., 6*n*
Avrigni, Charles-Joseph Lœuillard d', 108
Ayres, Harry Morgan, 49*n*

Babylon, 175, 240, 439
Bacon, Francis, 72
Baculard d'Arnaud, François Thomas Marie, 96, 111, 112
Baghdad, 439*n*
Baibars, general, 468*n*
Balzac, Jean Louis Guez, seigneur de, 58
Baniyas, 449*n*
Barbier, Edmond Jean François, 541
Barbier, Marie-Anne, *La Mort de César*, 61-63, 244, 246, 249, 251
Bauche, Jean Baptiste Claude, 120, 123, 292, 294, 295, 334, 336, 338-340, 347, 348, 351, 357, 369, 525
Baudin, Maurice, 54*n*
Baudouin IV, king of Jerusalem, 300
Bayle, Pierre, 67, 68
Beaune, 269
Bengesco, Georges, 109, 119, 343
Bérénice (*Bérénice*), 414
Berger, protégé of Voltaire, 243
Bergmann, Fred L., 291*n*
Berlin, xxi
Bernard, Mlle, 62
Bernardin, N.-M., 308*n*
Bérubé, G.-L., 83*n*
Besterman, Theodore, 5*n*, 19, 38, 47, 93, 115, 156*n*, 286*n*, 287*n*, 289*n*, 544
Betis, river, 184
Beuchot, Adrien Jean Quentin, 62, 106, 154, 206*n*, 533
Bibliothèque française, 96
Biancolelli, Pierre F. (known as Dominique), 284, 313*n*, 326, 380
Bibulus (*Mort de César*), 203
Bielski, Sz., 160

Bignon, Jean Paul, 252
Black Sea, 440, 470*n*
Boileau-Despréaux, Nicolas, 169*n*, 251
Bolingbroke, Henry St John, 7, 12, 35, 40*n*, 245, 279*n*; *A letter on the spirit of patriotism*, 13
Bond, William, 290*n*, 391
Bonnel, frères, printers, 152
Booy, Jean de, 333
Borges de Paiva, Manoel Joaquim, 158
Bosporus, the, 176
Bouhier, Jean, 283, 295, 303
Bouillon, family, 301
Bouillon, Godefroi de, 423, 439, 450
Bousquet, Marc-Michel, 127
Bouvines, battle of, 459
Bouvy, Eugène, 286*n*, 287*n*
Boysse, Ernest, 16, 17*n*, 18*n*, 20*n*
Bracegirdle, Anne, 402
Brandmüller, Jean, 124, 341
Breitkopf, Jean Gottlob Immanuel, 352
Brenner, Clarence D., 283, 381
Bridoye (*Pantagruel*), 531
Brizard, Jean Baptiste Britard, known as, 103
Broulhiet, bookseller, 151
Bruce, Harold Lawton, 157, 290*n*, 291*n*
Brumoy, Pierre, 14
Brun, Jacques, 347
Brussels, 251
Brutus, Decimus (*Julius Caesar*), 25; (*Mort de César*), 174
Brutus, Lucius Junius, 23, 39, 62, 65, 71, 85
Brutus, Marcus Junius, 21, 23, 24, 28-31, 34, 38, 39, 62, 65, 67, 68, 70, 111, 180*n*, 247, 249; (*Cinna*), 58, 60; (*Il Cesare*), 39, 188*n*, 189*n*, 204*n*, 205*n*; (*Julius Caesar*), 7, 8, 22, 25, 28-31, 34, 40, 46, 49, 59, 69, 177*n*, 195*n*, 196*n*, 197*n*, 200*n*, 204*n*, 218*n*, 223*n*, 226*n*, 231*n*, 234*n*, 236*n*, 240*n*; (*Mort de Cé-*

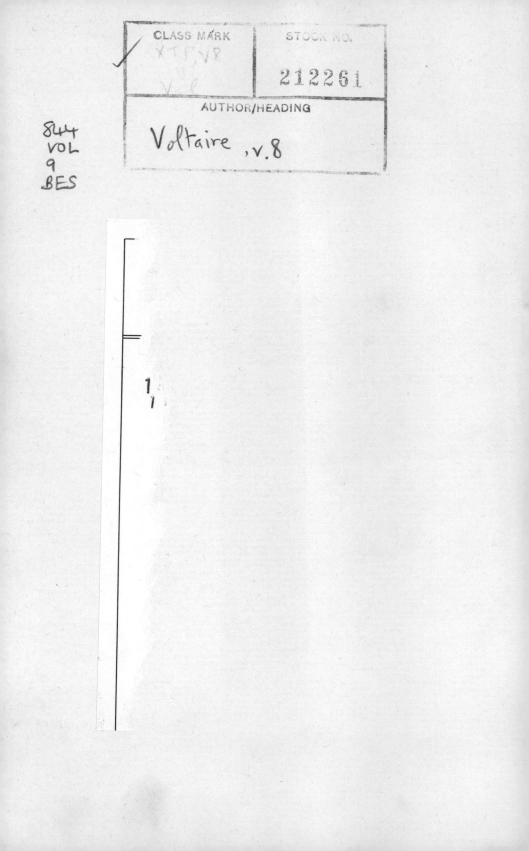